Julian's Gospel

Julian's Gospel

Illuminating the Life & Revelations of Julian of Norwich

Veronica Mary Rolf

Maryknoll, New York 10545

Founded in 1970, Orbis Books endeavors to publish works that enlighten the mind, nourish the spirit, and challenge the conscience. The publishing arm of the Maryknoll Fathers and Brothers, Orbis seeks to explore the global dimensions of the Christian faith and mission, to invite dialogue with diverse cultures and religious traditions, and to serve the cause of reconciliation and peace. The books published reflect the views of their authors and do not represent the official position of the Maryknoll Society. To learn more about Maryknoll and Orbis Books, please visit our website at www.maryknollsociety.org.

Published by Orbis Books, Box 302, Maryknoll, NY 10545-0302.

Manufactured in the United States of America

Library of Congress Cataloging-in-Publication Data

Rolf, Veronica Mary.
Julian's gospel : illuminating the life & revelations of Julian of Norwich / Veronica Mary Rolf.
pages cm
Includes bibliographical references and index.
ISBN 978-1-62698-036-5 (cloth)
1. Julian, of Norwich, 1343- 2. Julian, of Norwich, 1343- Revelations of divine love. I. Title.
BV5095.J84R65 2013
282.092—dc23
[B]

2013001271

For my beloved husband, Frederick,
Our son, David, and his wife, Leigh,
Our grandchildren, Adam and Matthew,
And our daughter, Eva Natanya:
The inspiration for everything.

Contents

Acknowledgments ... ix

A Note on Citations ... xi

Introduction ... 1

PART ONE
Julian's Life

1 *Norwich* ... 15

2 *Ancestry* ... 39

3 *Childhood* ... 59

4 *The Great Pestilence* ... 67

5 *Education* ... 85

6 *Marriage and Sexuality* ... 104

7 *War and Childbirth* ... 125

8 *Schism, Heresy, and Revolt* ... 143

9 *Preaching and Poetry* ... 168

10 *Corpus Christi Plays* ... 194

PART TWO
Julian's Revelations

11 *Three Gifts* ... 225

12 *The Vision* ... 258

13 *The Passion* ... 296

14 *The Dying* 334

15 *Transformation* 357

16 *Making All Things Well* 382

17 *The Great Deed* 403

18 *On Prayer* 431

19 *The Lord and the Servant* 462

20 *The Godly Will* 494

21 *The Motherhood of God* 512

22 *Close of the Day* 538

23 *Betrayal and Affirmation* 548

24 *At Her Window* 569

25 *A Gospel of Love* 589

Notes 597

Appendix 631

Bibliography 633

Index 645

Acknowledgments

I am immensely grateful to Larry Bouchard, PhD, Associate Professor of Religious Studies at the University of Virginia, who read the manuscript with a keen eye, making insightful suggestions and giving much-needed support. I also wish to thank Fr. John Bosman, MSC, Doctor of Sacred Theology, and Trent Pomplun, PhD, Professor of Theology at Loyola University, Maryland, who brought their great scholarship and devotion to close readings of the work, providing excellent comments. I owe heartfelt thanks to Sr. Beatrice Brennan, RSCJ, who first spoke Julian's words to me when I was her theology student in high school, setting me on a lifelong path of religious studies, and who, at the age of ninety-four, continues to give wise advice. Thanks also to Sr. Benedicta Ward, SLG, Reader in History of Christian Spirituality, Oxford University, whose groundbreaking work supported me thoroughly in this "new interpretation" of Julian's life story. And I am continually grateful for the Camaldolese monks of Incarnation Monastery in Berkeley (as well as the community of oblates and laity) whose life of contemplative prayer, liturgy, and hospitality are a source of grace and friendship. Most especially, I want to thank Robert Ellsberg, who has guided *Julian's Gospel* through the editing and publishing process with the utmost care, expertise, and kindness. It has been a privilege to work with him.

Last, but certainly not least, loving gratitude is due to my actor/director husband of more than forty years, my technology executive son, and my theologian daughter, each of whom has firmly believed in this work from its inception to its completion, reading and commenting on various versions with boundless patience, perception, and passion. I could not have survived the challenges of spending four years immersed in Julian's fourteenth century without their unconditional faith and love.

A Note on Citations

My primary textual source has been the critical edition by Nicholas Watson and Jacqueline Jenkins, *The Writings of Julian of Norwich: A Vision Showed to a Devout Woman and A Revelation of Love* (Pennsylvania State University Press, 2006). I have made a new translation of the Middle English, yet retained old spellings for some of Julian's most frequently used words such as *shewing* (revelation), *evencristens* (fellow Christians), *seker* (secure), *wroth* (wrath), *werking* (divine working), *beseking* (beseeching in prayer), *noughting* (self-denying), *sinne* (sin), *homely* (intimate), *alle shalle be wele*, and so forth, in order to retain the sound of Julian's own voice and to suggest the unique meanings she gave these words and phrases in her text. In some cases, I have restructured the syntax slightly and inserted a few extra words, but only when absolutely necessary for ease of comprehension. For those wishing to compare my translation with the original Middle English in Watson and Jenkins, I have cited chapter numbers referring to Julian's Short Text (*A Vision*) in Roman numerals. In referencing Julian's Long Text (*A Revelation*), I have listed chapter numbers in arabic numbers.

I have also done my own translation of selections from *The N-Town Plays*, edited by Douglas Sugano, TEAMS Middle English Texts Series (Kalamazoo, Michigan: Medieval Institute Publications, 2007). I have retained some Middle English phrases for the sake of rhyme and texture.

Scriptural citations are from the New Revised Standard Version Bible, ©1989, Division of Christian Education of the National Council of the Churches of Christ in the United States of America. All rights reserved. Used with permission.

Introduction

> It seemed to me that I would have been present at that time with Mary Magdalene and with others who were Christ's lovers, that I might have seen bodily the passion that our lord suffered for me, that I might have suffered with him as others did who loved him. (2:7–10.125–27).[1]

What if Mary Magdalene and the "others who were Christ's lovers" had written their own account of the passion of Jesus of Nazareth? These were the women who knew him well, "who used to follow him and provided for him when he was in Galilee; and there were many other women who had come up with him to Jerusalem" (Mk 15:40–41). These women cooked for Jesus, served him his meals, washed and mended his robes, attended to his needs, accompanied him from place to place. What revealing details these "other women" could have given us about the historical Jesus: what he looked like, the texture of his skin and hair and beard, the beauty of his eyes, the timbre of his voice, the touch of his hand, the way he moved, what it felt like to be in his presence, day after day. What intimate stories they would have told us about how he comforted, encouraged, forgave, taught, healed, and expressed his love for them.

These women would also have shared with us, in painful detail, what they saw Jesus undergo during his passion and death by crucifixion. They would have described his infinite tenderness and mercy as he looked down upon them, hour after hour, as they stood at the foot of the cross, next to Mary, his mother, and the young disciple, John. These devoted friends of Christ would never have forgotten the exact words he spoke to each of them before he died—words unknown to Matthew, Mark, Luke, and unheard even by John, the Evangelist. No doubt they would have written of the excruciating sense of loss when they saw Jesus buried, the great stone rolled in front of the place where he lay in the tomb, followed by the darkest day of their lives, mourning their dead Master (Mt 27:59–61; Mk 15:45–47; Lk 23:55–56). They also would have shared with us their ecstatic joy when they came to the tomb at the break of dawn on Easter morning, found the stone rolled back and "two men in dazzling clothes" standing beside them, saying, "Why do you look for the living among the dead? He is not here, but has risen" (Lk 24:1–8; Mt 28:1–8; Mk 16:1–7; Jn 20:1–3). And the women believed the angels:

> . . . and returning from the tomb, they told all this to the eleven and to all the rest. Now it was Mary Magdalene, Joanna, Mary the mother of James, and the other women with them who told this to the apostles. But these words seemed to them an idle tale, and they did not believe them. (Lk 24:9–11)

What if we had been given such a gospel of Jesus Christ, told from the *women's* point of view, forever to balance and elucidate the men's gospels with which we are so familiar? Alas, these faithful followers of Jesus Christ in first-century Palestine could neither read nor write, so their voices remain forever silent.[2]

Yet in the latter part of the fourteenth century, another follower of Jesus Christ, Julian of Norwich, wrote the first book by a woman ever set down on parchment in the vernacular known as Middle English. She could not write Latin, the language of the churchmen, nor French, the parlance of nobility, but only her own "vulgar tongue," long considered the peasant language. And her remarkable book, largely unknown until the twentieth century, is now recognized as a classic of Western spirituality. Her book is precisely the sort of account the "other women" of Palestine might have written, namely, a woman's version of the gospel. It is Julian's own very personal story of seeing and hearing and coming to understand the living, dying, and risen presence of Jesus Christ.

Who Was Julian of Norwich?

Most books about Julian of Norwich contend that there is little or nothing we can know about her life. Many authors assume she must have been a Benedictine nun in Carrow Priory before she became enclosed as an anchoress . . . and then proceed to deal with her text. Such studies may list the major historical events that occurred during the latter half of the fourteenth century, *but they do not investigate the impact of these events on Julian's mental and emotional development.* Yet how can we understand the full import of what Julian wrote and why she wrote it (and under what difficult circumstances), if we do not make some effort to discover the woman behind the words? Christ did not appear to a person with no past, no hopes, no fears, no doubts, no burning questions, no personal conflicts, no sense of sin, no ties that bind. He revealed himself to a flesh-and-blood Englishwoman lying in bed in her home, surrounded by relatives and friends, so desperately ill that she was convinced she was at the point of death. He spoke to a woman who was very much a product of her time, her culture, her life experience—not an already-made saint. If the reader is willing to enter and explore Julian's world, then her text will become that much more meaningful. Who was the *real* Julian of Norwich? Eventually, she will be the one who reveals herself personally to you.

While it is true that Julian tells us very few facts about her life before receiving her visions, we can surmise a great deal about her parentage and the probable course of her upbringing through a detailed reconstruction of the political, cultural, and societal circumstances of her times. We can also employ the creative imagination, as does all biography, to suggest major influences on her intellectual and spiritual development. And then, when we delve into the text of her actual Revelations, we will uncover many hidden clues that further support our discoveries and allow us to get to know this extraordinary woman.

With this goal in mind, Part One will explore Julian's native city of Norwich and recreate the enclosed physical environment that determined her view of reality from an early age. We will discuss the class structure of feudal society to identify her probable parentage and deduce her family's social and economic status. We will suggest the atmosphere of her home and family life, describe medieval educational opportunities (or lack thereof) for girls and young women, explain the all-important network of craft and merchant guilds, and reveal the religious customs of Julian's time. We will define fourteenth-century views of marriage, the duties expected of a young wife, the risks of childbearing, and the challenges of child-rearing. From doctrinal teachings of the Catholic Church, contemporary devotional practices, the literature of medieval preaching and poetic works, as well as the enormously popular *Corpus Christi* mystery plays, we will propose some crucial influences on Julian's intellectual and spiritual formation. We will scrutinize the all-pervasive misogyny of the fourteenth century, instilled by the culture of the church since ancient times. In the process, we will be forced to ask some difficult questions concerning how much (or how little) Julian internalized these negative attitudes toward women. Such careful investigation into the social, educational, and cultural context of Julian's life will enable us, by inductive reasoning, to make strong arguments about what her state in life could *not* have been, and therefore, by implication, to discover what it might actually have been.

To understand the larger picture, it will also be necessary to place Julian in her historical milieu, against the political and religious backdrop of her time: the seemingly endless English conflict with France, eventually termed The Hundred Years' War (though it lasted even longer); the Papal Schism within the Catholic Church that sent shock waves reverberating throughout Europe; the heretical teachings of John Wyclif and his Lollard followers that planted the seeds for the English Reformation; the first Peasants' Revolt and its brutal aftermath, especially in Norwich. And finally, we must examine the most horrific plague that ever went around the earth: the so-called Great Pestilence that decimated populations from Asia to Europe, infiltrating the minds of people of all classes, even if it did not always kill their bodies. Every one of these seismic events would have impacted the psychological and emotional development of a young woman as sensitive and spiritual as Julian. Every one of them casts its shadow over the pages of her Revelations. Stroke by stroke, through the use of light and shade, we will endeavor to paint a rich portrait of Julian's *life*. This will be the focus of Part One.

In Part Two, we will examine the Long Text of Julian's *Revelations*, offering chapter-by-chapter commentary, with occasional references to the earlier Short Text as well. We will relate what we have uncovered in Part One about Julian's life context directly to her writings. We will be attentive to the multiple layers of meaning, both explicit and implicit, theological and mystical. We will focus especially on the inner dynamic of Julian's conflicts and questions, as well as on the search for understanding that motivates every word she writes. Thus we shall be able to illuminate the eventual transformation of the visionary by the vision.

First Appearance
We first meet Julian in 1373, at the age of thirty. She is near death, and over the course of twenty-four hours she receives "a revelation of love that Jesus Christ, our endless bliss, made in sixteen shewings" (1:1–2.123). These *shewings*, or Revelations, appear in vivid bodily sights of Christ on the cross, described in great detail; in locutions, that is, words heard in her inner ear; and in spiritual understandings that continue to develop throughout the rest of her long life. Through her vivid and heartfelt account of these Revelations, plus her subsequent contemplation of their deeper meaning, Julian reveals herself as a compassionate and loving woman. In fact, the only reason she spends several decades going to the great trouble of writing down her recollections not once, but three or more times, is because Julian feels compelled to express to her *evencristens* (fellow Christians) what the Lord so graciously revealed to her, much as the women of Galilee might have wished to do long, long ago, had they been able to write an account of the "good news" of Jesus Christ.

There is a crucial and as yet unsolved mystery that we must also try to unravel and it is this: how did Julian, self-described as an uneducated woman, "a simple creature unlettered" (2.1.125), ever manage to learn to read . . . and then, even more impressively for her time, to write? And how is it that a devout and orthodox Catholic laywoman dared to pen a book in the vernacular about her personal Revelations and then presume to interpret what she believed was the Lord's deeper meaning in each of these Revelations, *when it was strictly forbidden by the Catholic Church of her day to do so?* St. Paul had expressly denied women any right to speak up in church:

> As in all the churches of the saints, women should be silent in the churches. For they are not permitted to speak, but should be subordinate, as the law also says. If there is anything they desire to know, let them ask their husbands at home. For it is shameful for a woman to speak in church. (1 Cor 14:33-35)

During the Middle Ages, women were not allowed to open their mouths in church services except, along with the entire congregation, to say communal prayers and sing hymns. Neither were they permitted to preach or teach religion outside of church, except to their own children. They were forbidden to study theology or to write on spiritual or theological issues. A few brave and outstanding women on the Continent during the High Middle Ages (St. Hildegard of Bingen, St. Gertrude of Helfta, Hadewijch of Antwerp, Mechthild of Magdeburg, St. Catherine of Siena, St. Brigit of Sweden, Blessed Beatrice of Nazareth) had defied the *de facto* ban. They were firmly convinced that they were God's prophets, and they felt justified in their right to speak and/or write as the Lord compelled them. However, in the late medieval English world, a book of private mystical Revelations like Julian's, written in the vernacular, could be cause for ecclesiastical interrogation, excommunication, or worse. That Julian was willing to take such a risk in order to write and, by writing, *dare to teach*, immediately tells us that here is a woman who firmly believed God wanted her to make known her Revelations at any cost; otherwise she would not have had the courage to do so. She was also convinced she spoke only the truth.

Two Versions

Julian wrote her *Revelations* in two versions. The *Short* Text was presumably set down in the mid-to-late 1370s, or during the 1380s, both to record details of the visions and to reflect on their meaning in the process of writing. The only surviving copy of this Short Text is the British Library MS Additional 37790 (formerly known as Amherst MS, derived from the bookplate of its last private owner, Lord Amherst). This Short Text manuscript is found in the middle of a collection of contemplative works by late medieval writers and, judging by the style of the scribe's handwriting, dates from about 1450.[3]

The *Long* Text, penned during the 1390s and probably well into the 1400s, includes extended theological and spiritual commentary by a greatly matured Julian. There are three complete manuscripts of the Long Text: the Paris Codex and two manuscripts labeled Sloane (S1 and S2). The Paris version, Bibliothèque Nationale MS Fonds Anglais 40, is written in fine calligraphy. It was copied in the early seventeenth century, though it seems to be an elaborate attempt to reproduce the script of 1500, with blue initials at each chapter opening and flourishes in red ink.[4] This Paris copy may be the earliest of the complete Long Text manuscripts. Notably, it translates the original East Anglian dialect, in which Julian would have written, into the more standardized East Midland dialect of 1420.[5]

The remaining two manuscripts of the Long Text are both in the British Library: MS Sloane 2499 (S1), copied by English Benedictine nuns living in Cambrai in northern France, or at a newly established daughter-house in Paris, c.1650; and MS Sloane 3705 (S2), which seems to have been, in turn, copied from S1, either in the late seventeenth or early eighteenth century (with contemporary spellings).[6]

Additionally, there are two excerpts from the Long Text. One, termed Westminster Cathedral Treasury MS 4, is found in an English anthology of late medieval works on the spiritual life. Though heavily edited, this excerpt is actually the *oldest* version that we have of Julian's Long Text, penned by a professional scribe from a now-lost original or earlier copy, in a southeast Midlands dialect of the London area, sometime around 1500.[7] It is extremely valuable, since it predates (and miraculously survived) the dissolution of the English monasteries. (The dissolution occurred between 1536 and 1541 at the command of King Henry VIII, during which time more than eight hundred monasteries, friaries, and nunneries were disbanded and destroyed, along with their vast libraries.)

The other excerpt from Julian's Long Text was found in the Upholland Anthology, which resided at St. Joseph's College in Lancashire until its dissolution in 1999. The anthology may now be in private hands, or lost. This manuscript, like the Paris Codex and Sloane versions, was also probably copied by English Benedictine nuns. The Upholland may be contemporaneous with the Paris Codex (c.1650), or could even pre-date it (c.1630).

In reviewing this scant but intriguing textual history, we must acknowledge the enormous legacy of the nuns at Cambrai and Paris, who worked so diligently to preserve and copy the Long Text in its entirety for generations to come. Without their scribal expertise, Julian's Revelations might have been lost forever. We might consider these English nuns as "other women" friends of Julian, dedicated to preserving her work. Another "friend" of Julian was the English Benedictine, Fr. Serenus Cressy, chaplain to the nuns at the Paris house and later royal chaplain at the English court of King Charles II. Fr. Cressy seems to have discovered an older (now lost) manuscript of the Long Text while living in Paris and subsequently published the first printed version of Julian's *Shewings* in 1670, probably when he returned to England.

Alas, there are no surviving *original* manuscripts of either the Short or Long Texts, nor are there late fourteenth- or early fifteenth-century scribal copies of Julian's texts (unlike the many copies that survive of the writings of her male counterparts, Richard Rolle, Walter Hilton, William Langland, Geoffrey Chaucer, and the monastic author of the *Cloud of Unknowing*, among others). Furthermore, there seems to be no mention at all of Julian's Revelations in any list of either lay or monastic book bequests from the public record of English wills in the fourteenth or fifteenth centuries, as there are for the works of male writers.[8] After Fr. Cressy's seventeenth-century publication, Julian's work essentially lay dormant for two hundred years, waiting until the time was ripe.

In 1843, the Cressy Long Text was reprinted by G. H. Parker with some modernizations, although still in Middle English and therefore restricted to scholarly study. It was reprinted in 1864, and again in 1902 with a preface by the Jesuit priest Fr. George Tyrrell. It was not until 1877 that Henry Collins published the first modernized version of Sloane 2499 (S1), making Julian more accessible to contemporary readers. Even so, at the turn of the twentieth century, Julian's Revelations still remained largely unknown to the general public.

Modern Rediscovery

Then in 1901, Grace Warrack published her own modernized version of the Long Text (S1), with a beautifully written introduction that still deserves close attention. In 1905, Dean W. R. Inge produced his *Studies of English Mystics*, which included a section on Julian. In ensuing years, Evelyn Underhill drew attention to Julian in her own book on mysticism and characterized her as "the first English woman of letters" in the *Cambridge Medieval History*.[9] In 1942, T. S. Eliot referred to Julian's Revelations, using her words at the end of his poem, *Little Gidding*, the last of the *Four Quartets:*

> And all shall be well, and
> All manner of thing shall be well
> When the tongues of flame are in-folded
> Into the crowned knot of fire
> And the fire and the rose are one.[10]

All this time, the *Short* Text was thought to be lost, though mention of an anchoress named "Lady Julian," as well as the existence of her Revelations, had been made in 1745, in Francis Blomefield's history of Norwich:

> In the eastern part of this churchyard [St. Julian's] stood an anchorage, in which an anchoress or recluse dwelt until the Dissolution, when the house was demolished, though the foundations may still be seen. In 1393, Lady Julian was an anchoress here, a strict recluse, and had two servants to attend her in her old age . . . This woman, in those days, was esteemed one of the greatest holiness. The Rev. Mr. Francis Peck, author of the *Antiquities of Stanford*, had an old vellum MS, 36 quarto pages of which contained an account of the visions, etc. of this woman.[11]

Nothing else was heard or seen of this manuscript until 1910 when, somewhat miraculously, the Short Text appeared in the sale of Lord Amherst's library to the British Museum. At long last, in 1911, this *oldest manuscript* of all, dating from c.1450, was revealed to the world in Rev. Dundas Harford's modernization. The medieval scribe/copyist introduces the work in a short colophon:

> Here is a vision shewed by the goodness of God to a devout woman, and her name is Julian, who is a recluse at Norwich, and yet is on life [still alive], the year of our Lord 1413. In which vision are very many comforting words and greatly stirring to all those who desire to be Christ's lovers. (i.63)

We have no way of knowing if the scribe who wrote this colophon and transcribed the Short Text was working from Julian's now-lost original manuscript, or yet another copy, sometime in 1413. However, the colophon does confirm beyond the shadow of a doubt that when this transcription of the Short Text was made, Julian of Norwich was acknowledged as its undisputed author, was recognized as a female visionary, and was still very much alive at the age of seventy-one.

The second half of the twentieth century saw the proliferation of additional translations from the Middle English of both the Short and Long Texts. In 1976, Marion Glasscoe published a scholarly edition of the Sloane Long Text (S1), and in 1978, Frances Beer produced an equally scholarly edition of the Short Text. Also in 1978, Fr. Edmund Colledge, OSA, and James Walsh, SJ, completed the first critical edition of both the Long and Short texts, called *A Book of Showings to the Anchoress Julian of Norwich*, in two volumes, based on the Paris Codex, but working from all extant manuscripts.

In addition to numerous translations of both texts, there has been a multiplicity of scholarly and spiritual writings about Julian: theological investigations of her thought; feminist interpretations; psychological analyses; source studies; mystical treatises; prayer and retreat guides; music, art, and poetry inspired by Julian's visions and words; as well as post-modern textual criticism. Ever since Julian's writings first came to light over one hundred years ago, they have ignited the minds and hearts of those who study her in many different languages, and for good reason. The breadth and height and depth of the Revelations are always open to new interpretations, new approaches, and the cultivation of new themes; they provide, for scholars and spiritual writers alike, abundant material for theses, books, and articles. Julian's gospel never grows old.

Julian's Voice

Julian expresses herself in a woman's voice that sounds decidedly different from the exclusively male voices in which she would have been accustomed to hearing the gospel proclaimed. Her voice is not that of a celibate cleric, nor a canon law expert, nor an ecclesiastical judge. Nor does her writing have a monastic tone to it. Julian's book is full of a distinctly feminine sensitivity, along with incisive, analytical reasoning, rich imagery, and down-to-earth common sense. It is neither a treatise nor a catechism, nor is it a systematic guide to the spiritual life, yet it is full of rich teachings on prayer, the practice of faith, hope, and love, as well as personal advice on how to deal with one's own sense of sinfulness, recurring depression, life's suffering, and the fear of death.

Julian employs a circular, rather than a strictly linear, method of examining and interpreting Christian truths. She chooses favorite themes, words, and phrases, and returns to them again and again, layering them each time with ever-deeper meaning. This circularity does not in any way undermine her ability to analyze, argue, and categorize her teachings in a rational, linear mode when she so chooses.

She allows intuition to inspire her logic and rational explanations to support her mystical insights. Throughout, her moral angst drives her to probe relentlessly, to dare to make astounding theological leaps of thought and faith, but she has no desire merely to be clever, to impress, or to compete with the authoritative reasoning of the scholastics or the didactic sermons of the churchmen. In fact, she cuts through theological hair-splitting and well-accepted religious attitudes, "sharper than any two-edged sword" (Heb 4:12), revealing the hidden marrow of meaning. As Thomas Merton wrote of her in the twentieth century:

> Julian is without doubt one of the most wonderful of all Christian voices. She gets greater and greater in my eyes as I grow older... I think that Julian of Norwich is with [John Henry, Cardinal] Newman the greatest English theologian. She is really that. For she reasons from her experience of the substantial center of the great Christian mystery of Redemption. She gives her experience and her deductions, clearly, separating the two. And the experience is of course nothing merely subjective. It is the objective mystery of Christ as apprehended by her, with the mind and formation of a fourteenth-century English woman.[12]

Besides being a mystical theologian, Julian is willing to reveal her own inner battles, to admit her personal failings as well as her deeply felt longings. This quality sets her completely apart from fourteenth-century male writers like Chaucer and Langland, Rolle and Hilton, and the anonymous author of *The Cloud of Unknowing*, all of whom preferred to remain unexposed in their work. Julian may not tell us a lot of intimate details about her day-to-day life, but she does much more: she opens and entrusts to us her mind and heart. She discloses her mighty struggle to integrate her faith in the God she has been taught to believe in with the God of her mystical Revelations. She confronts her confusion head-on. One might even say she writes the first-ever *spiritual autobiography* in English.

Julian addresses the reader directly. She wants each of us to see as she saw, to hear as she heard, to understand as she came to understand. She speaks as a daughter, wife, mother, and concerned friend on every page of her work (more on this interpretation of her life status later on). She is, by turns, frankly emotional and searingly self-critical, profoundly tempted by doubt and buoyed up by hope. Julian's pressing questions are not limited to her time; they resonate in every age. They are the same metaphysical questions we keep asking, over and over again. Julian's asking of these questions, *our* questions, and her way of telling us how the Lord answered them, reveal a woman passionately concerned about the salvation and ultimate happiness of people she dearly loved. She also shows herself to be a woman of deep prayer, extraordinary faith, and prophetic powers.

Julian grows on us. For every man or woman, young or old, believer or skeptic, Julian has a gift. It is the gift of her questing spirit, her daring conviction. It is the gift of her personal witness to Christ's immense and incomparable compassion. Julian's *Revelations* were not written just for the *evencristens* of her time. Hers is a timeless gospel, composed over six hundred years ago, by one woman for *all* women and *all* men who long for the assurance of a love that can never fail. It would have been a very familiar story to the "other women" of Galilee.

Part One

Julian's Life

1
Norwich

Imagine a world in which everything, absolutely everything, was uncertain. Sun, wind, rain, snow, drought, flooding, heat, cold, and levels of humidity quite literally decided whether people would eat or starve. Julian's fourteenth-century world was nothing if not precarious, unsettled, full of danger. The hubris of kings and the in-fighting of nobles, the turbulence of a bloody Hundred Years' War with France, the onslaught of ghastly, untreatable plague, the high risks of death in childbirth and frequent infant mortality, plus a short adult life expectancy at best kept in check any fantasies she or anyone else might have entertained about feeling *seker*, a Middle English word that implies security and certainty. Violent assaults, drunken brawling, frequent dueling, murderous vendettas, and inter-family feuds were common. Every wealthy merchant in his townhouse or poor peasant in his cottage feared attack by domestic brigands, or sacking and burning by foreign invaders. Even the justice meted out by common law seems, to our modern sensibilities, barbaric.

A Religious People

A glimpse into fourteenth-century England reveals a feudal society lurching from one catastrophe to another and, at particular crisis points, falling into great despair. It was a society on the brink of dissolution. Paradoxically, it was also a world in which God was believed to be very close, sustaining the population through times of plenty and times of great want. The Roman Catholic faith, commonly held by all in England and throughout Christendom during the Middle Ages, expressed itself in oft-repeated Latin prayers, primarily the *Pater Noster* (Our Father), *Ave Maria* (Hail Mary), and *Credo* (I believe), as well as in the communal experience of attending Sunday

Mass as God's people. Citizens of every village, town, and city lived the same yearly liturgical cycle of fasting months and feasting days.

Advent repentance anticipated the coming of the Savior and led into the celebrations of the Christmas season, when Christ was born. Forty days of Lenten fasting (during which only one meal a day was permitted, without meat, eggs, dairy products, or alcohol), combined with penance and almsgiving, helped to create the appropriate disposition to enter Holy Week. This highpoint of the liturgical calendar commemorated Palm Sunday when Christ rode into Jerusalem on a donkey, Maundy Thursday when he instituted the sacrament of the Eucharist at the Last Supper, Good Friday when he died on the cross, and the vigil of Holy Saturday when he lay in the tomb, culminating in the most important feast day of all: the resurrection of Christ from the dead on Easter Sunday morning. Forty days later, the feast of the Ascension celebrated Christ's return to heaven, anticipating the rising of every redeemed soul in a glorified body at the end of the world. Then, fifty days after the ancient Jewish feast of Passover, came Pentecost, when the Holy Spirit appeared in tongues of fire to settle on the heads of the apostles gathered in the upper room, pouring the divine presence into their hearts. The reality of Christ's birth, death, and resurrection was a constant influence on people's daily lives. They lived in an all too real and threatening world, but they had, as it were, one foot in eternity at all times. They either hoped for the salvation that would bring them to heaven or feared the condemnation that would send them forever to hell.

Additionally, the church year was highlighted by such publicly celebrated feasts as Candlemas (February 2); the Annunciation to the Blessed Virgin Mary (March 25); St. George's Day (April 23); St. John the Baptist (June 24); St. James the Apostle (July 25); St. Michael the Archangel, also known as Michaelmas (September 29); St. Catherine's Day (November 25); and, very specially, St. Nicholas's Day (December 6). There was also the fairly new feast of *Corpus Christi* (Body of Christ), held on the Thursday, or the following Sunday, after Trinity Sunday, during which the holy Eucharist was carried in solemn procession through the streets of every large town and city. One of the most popular holy days was the ancient feast of the Assumption (August 15), commemorating the death of Christ's mother, the Blessed Virgin Mary, who was believed to have been taken body and soul into heaven, like her son before her.

The official feast days of the church were interlinked with planting and harvesting festivals, winter solstice lighting of candles, mounting of pageants and tomfoolery, the hearty singing of carols, May Day celebrations, popular songs both romantic and ribald, lighthearted and lusty dances, feasting and heavy drinking. These secular holidays (some with decidedly pre-Christian pagan elements), like the purely religious ones, bound families and communities together. They provided much welcome change from every day's hard work, boredom, loneliness, rain, dampness, and long winters of biting cold and frequent snow. They offered an excuse for high spirits, even in the darkest months. Likewise, in times of terror and tragedy, people developed rituals of dying, burying, mourning, and interceding for the souls of the dead. They had a sense of the "next world" pressing in on them, perhaps overtaking this world at any moment. They implored their patron saints to protect them from harm and a sudden death, and they prayed daily for their deceased family members to be released from the sufferings of purgatory.

This entire liturgical year of Masses, processions, feasts, and festivities created continuing cycles of communal preparation and celebration. It also conveyed to the body of the faithful that their own lives, no matter how harsh and uncertain, pain-filled and often tragic, contained a deeper human meaning within a much larger divine context. As the "mystical body" of Jesus Christ, the faithful themselves were born anew every Christmas, shared in the suffering and dying of Christ on the cross through the events of Holy Week, and hoped for their own resurrection on the last day.

Vernacular Teaching

The sacrifice of the Mass, the central liturgical rite, was sung and spoken by the celebrant entirely in Latin. Even the weekly epistle and gospel readings were proclaimed in the Latin Vulgate of the Bible. They could not be understood by the common folk, the rising merchant class, or even most of the upper gentry. In fact, by the mid-fourteenth century, very few people (except educated clerics) understood, much less read or spoke Latin. But the Bible stories, from both Old and New Testaments, were retold by preachers in paraphrased versions and rhyming verses in their English vernacular sermons. The congregation learned about Christ walking on water, feeding the five thousand with a few loaves and fishes, calming the winds in a violent storm so that the apostles' fishing boat would not sink... as well as about the fires of Gehenna waiting for those who sinned. They identified with the poor widow weeping over her dead son; with Martha and Mary pleading with Jesus to save their sick brother Lazarus; with the prodigal son begging for forgiveness. The secular and ecclesiastical overlords saw themselves as the wealthy tax collector, Zacchaeus, who promised to pay back, with interest, all he had swindled out of his people, because Jesus had just announced that he was coming to eat dinner at his home that very night.

Week after week, people of all ages and social levels could relate these gospel stories to their own life situations. *They* became the ones being touched and healed, chastised, forgiven, comforted, and redeemed by Christ. The faithful also heard sermons given by traveling friars in the church "preaching yard," or the town marketplace, that told of the man born blind, the woman with a hemorrhage, the leper, the deaf mute, the paralytic. They had special sympathy for Mary Magdalene, the alleged "woman of ill repute" who was forgiven by the Lord. They feared becoming another Judas, who betrayed Christ for thirty pieces of silver. Through popular outdoor sermons, a form of community entertainment, the laity experienced their own lives reflected back to them.

Also during the fourteenth century, in response to repeated papal and episcopal directives, homilists were required to preach regularly on the twelve tenets of the Apostles' Creed, the seven petitions of the Our Father, and the words of the Hail Mary, as well as on the seven sacraments, the seven deadly sins, and the seven corporal works of mercy. In this way, the major mysteries, doctrines, and moral teachings of the Catholic faith became implanted in the people. In addition to oral teaching, there was an abundance of visual instruction in the form of medieval art. Wall paintings filled every cathedral and parish church, offering a variegated palette of scenes from the Old and New Testaments. These colorful murals became the religious books of the so-called *lewed*, the illiterate, meaning those who could not read Latin. Frescoes, stained-glass windows, and sculptures and statues both inside and outside the churches enabled the stories and characters of scripture to come alive: the creation of the world, the fall of Adam and Eve, the giving of the Law to Moses, the annunciation by the angel Gabriel to the Virgin Mary, the nativity in Bethlehem, the visit of the three Magi, the presentation of the child Jesus in the temple, the baptism of Jesus, and of course, his passion, death, and resurrection. All the biblical personages were portrayed wearing medieval attire, from the Pharisees robed in ecclesiastical garb like bishops, to Roman soldiers dressed as medieval knights, to Christ's disciples in short tunics, to the women of Galilee in wimples, veils, and long, flowing gowns. These were images that people of every class could recognize and relate to personally.

Sacraments and Saints

The whole cycle of life and death was intricately bound up with the church's sacraments, from birth and baptism, to confirmation, and the rites of extreme unction to the dying. The commission of serious sins necessitated their confession to a priest in the sacrament of penance in order to receive absolution in Christ's name. In addition, all Christians were obliged to confess their sins at least once a year, usually during Holy Week, in order to be able to receive the Eucharist on Easter Sunday. Matrimony took place at the church door, under the guidance of a priest, and a "churching" ritual for the formal purification of the mother after childbirth had to be carried out before she could re-enter the church assembly. At the hour of death, the faithful looked to a priest to hear their final confession, receive the Eucharist if possible, and be anointed with the holy chrism (a mixture of olive oil and balsam). This was the same chrism they had received as babies at baptism.

Only those men who had received the sacrament of holy orders were trained (to a greater or lesser degree) in Latin, theology, and church doctrine. These men alone were empowered to administer sacraments, preach the word, grant absolution, and consecrate the bread and wine into the body and blood of Jesus Christ during the sacrifice of the Mass. However, participation in religious guilds by both men and women offered common folk a means of giving valuable service to the church. This was especially true of women, who were otherwise deprived of a voice in the pulpit or any presence on the altar.

On a personal level, Christians were well accustomed to seeking divine help in their hour of need. Those with sufficient financial resources made provision in their wills for "chantry priests" to sing memorial Masses for their own souls, as well as for the souls of their departed loved ones believed to be suffering in purgatory. Others, from aristocrats to peasants, embarked on arduous pilgrimages to holy shrines, usually the tombs of saints and martyrs, as a form of penance for sin, to have their petitions heard, or in the hope of gaining miraculous cures. Saint Mary, the Mother of God, and a panoply of patron saints were continuously beseeched for special protection. Knights prayed to be spared injury or death in mock tournaments or in real battle and asked for a quick victory in war or to return home safely. Women's guilds saw to it that large wax candles were kept burning in front of statues of St. Margaret of Antioch, patroness of women in labor, and St. Anne, mother of Mary, the model of all mothers.

This cult of the saints served a very real need of the laity, and prayers for assistance arose from the depths of the heart. According to contemporary records, 20 percent of women (who averaged five pregnancies each) died during or soon after childbirth, 5 percent of newborns died during labor and delivery, another 10 or 12 percent perished during the first month, and 20 or 25 percent succumbed during the first year. Even if they managed to survive through infancy, almost *50 percent* of children failed to reach their tenth birthday. Half the teenage population died before the age of twenty, and half of the remaining population died before reaching fifty. Only 5 percent of the fourteenth-century population could hope to live to see sixty-five.[1] (Julian was one of the rare ones; she lived to be at least seventy-four.) Given the frequency of infant mortality, accidents, wars, famines, and plagues, the prospect of being born, growing into adulthood, birthing a baby, and reaching maturity (much less surviving into old age), was a high risk venture.

Fear of God

Even with the rich liturgy and the great variety of devotional practices of the Catholic faith, there must have been many periods when God seemed to be distant and terrifying to the common folk. Hardline preachers portrayed the Almighty as a God of wrath who lay in wait to pass strictest judgment on those who had sinned, to cast them out of his sight forever and to condemn them to hell. For all of the long tradition of the church's salvific teaching, as well as abundant medieval devotional writings that stressed the love and mercy of Jesus Christ, surviving sermons in both Latin and English demonstrate that, all too often, the central message of the medieval church deteriorated into accusations and threats. The fear of death, the final judgment, and the strong possibility of eternal damnation were employed as a whip to beat goodness into the wayward. If one were to die in mortal sin (and a great many more offenses other than murder and adultery were considered mortal), it was believed that one's soul would instantly go to hell and suffer excruciating torments for all eternity. The Christian would be deprived forever of the sight and love of God and never hope to see his or her loved ones in the next life. Even if you confessed your sins and were *shriven* (that is, forgiven) and performed an earthly penance that could be quite severe, you were not truly free. It was taught that after death your soul would have to suffer a period of purification in purgatory in order to satisfy the just punishments due to the sins you had committed in your lifetime, even those that had already been forgiven in the sacrament of penance.

Furthermore, it was commonly held by medieval theologians that only those predestined to be saved by God could join the 144,000 listed in the Apocalypse (Rv 7:4) as worthy of meriting eternal life at the Last Judgment. The problem was, you had no way of knowing if you were one of the elect who had been chosen to be saved. You might live a fairly good and faithful Christian life, fail to persevere in grace to the end, and be damned; while someone else might live a sinful life and, at the last moment, respond to God's merciful grace and be counted among the saints. Salvation was supposed to be the one thing certain for a believing and practicing Catholic. Except when it was not.

The Divine Office

For residents of Norwich, the easternmost city in England, only the bells from Holy Trinity Cathedral that woke the city from its slumber every morning around 3:00 or 4:00 AM at the canonical hour of *Lauds*, or Dawn Prayer, could be considered certain.[2] The bells rang out all through the day and night to call the monks to choir for the *officium divinum*, or Divine Office, also known by the Benedictines as *opus Dei* (Work of God). Eight times a day they sang and read psalms, canticles, hymns, excerpts from scripture and accounts of saints' lives, all in Latin. After *Lauds* came *Prime* at 6:00 AM, *Terce* at 9:00, *Sext* at noon, *None* at 3:00, *Vespers* at 6:00 (at the lighting of the lamps at dusk), and *Compline* before retiring, about 9:00 PM. A rising chime for *Matins*, the Night Office at midnight or 2 AM, reminded the monks to "Keep awake therefore, for you know neither the day nor the hour" when death might arrive (Mt 25:13). The people of Norwich, and Julian herself, experienced the passage of time, not by looking at their watches, for they had none (although wealthy citizens might have old sundials or new water clocks), but by listening to the bells sound out the slow and steady increments of their lives, making them acutely aware that time passes and death approaches. It was their only certainty.

The Ancient Settlement

Julian's area of East Anglia was long believed to have been settled originally by Germanic tribes from Anglia (modern-day Angeln), which is in the northern part of Schleswig-Holstein. The assumption was that the "Anglians" migrated with the Saxons and Jutes to Britain in the fifth to sixth centuries. By 500 CE all of Norfolk was completely controlled by Saxon rule, the Romans having been successfully ousted after almost five hundred years. The Anglian area of settlement on the eastern seaboard included Norfolk (the north folk) and Suffolk (the south folk). Some modern archeological studies have disputed this scenario, however, by the discovery of numerous *fibulae* or brooches worn by women of earliest record in England. Most revealing is that cruciform-style brooches, found in east coastal and northern England, trace the women who wore them back to coastal Scandinavia and the whole of Denmark, as well as to the kingdom of Schleswig-Holstein and Pomerania. Whichever story is accurate (and it may be a combination of the two), we may conjecture that Julian's heritage was a mixture of Anglian, Saxonian, Scandinavian, and, after the Norman Conquest, French/Norman ancestors: bold, courageous, and decidedly independent people.

By the late fifth century, Anglo-Saxons had founded three distinct settlements in the area of East Anglia: Northwic (meaning north village or the village on the north creek), Westwic, and Thorpe. (*Wic* is an Old English word that could mean anything from a village, town, encampment, manor house, castle, or fortress, to a street, lane, bay, creek, or even a little port.) These three settlements were about five miles north of what is believed to have been a former Roman regional capital and main market town of the area, *Venta Icenorum*. It is conjectured that Northwic (eventually, *Norwich*) absorbed the citizens of the other two towns and quickly became a thriving center of trade. During the ninth, tenth, and early eleventh centuries, Danish Vikings repeatedly raided the East Anglian coastal region, destroying towns, villages, farms, monasteries, and churches. Yet in spite of such constant devastation, the Anglo-Saxon population continued to expand to such an extent that the Norfolk/Suffolk area became one of the most prosperous and densely settled areas in all of England, second in population and importance only to the great city of London.

The River Wensum

The River Wensum takes its name from the Old English adjective *wandsu* or *wendsum* meaning "winding." It flows down from the northwest directly into and through Norwich, almost slicing it in half, then changes its direction to move eastward and arches due south like a ballooning question mark. The Wensum defined the easternmost perimeter of the medieval town and was largely responsible for Norwich becoming a major import/export route, since it flowed directly into the River Yare and thence to Great Yarmouth, the official seaport of exit and entry for northeast England. For more than eight hundred

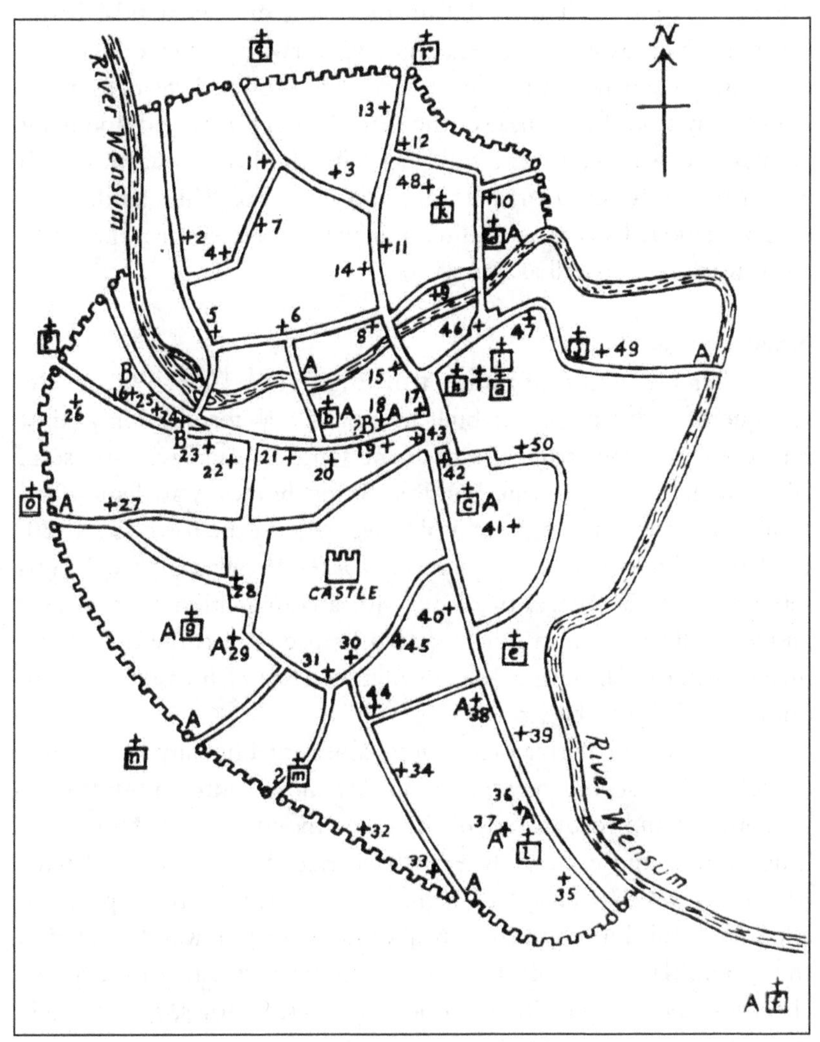

Map of Walls, Gates, Wensum River, and the Religious Institutions in Norwich, 1370–1532[3]

years, the River Wensum was the main traffic thoroughfare, carrying goods to and from Norwich in flat barges called *wherries*. By the tenth century, coins found all across Europe were conspicuously engraved with the word *Norvic*, having been minted right in Norwich during this Anglo-Saxon period and bearing witness to the flourishing trade between Norwich and the Continent.

Norwich citizenry took pride in considering themselves independent from the central government and even from the rest of England. Ever since ancient times, Norwich had been a land apart, separated by the vast expanse of marshes that formed its boundary on the west, sitting, as it then did, in the midst of a great tidal basin. Psychologically as well as geographically, Norwich was extremely isolated, situated at the easternmost part of the realm, 108 miles and a world away from London, ever the seat of royal power and dominant politics. Norwich had more solid ties with the Low Countries, with which it developed a brisk trade, and even the Rhineland, from which it enjoyed a constant influx of new ideas and controversial religious teachings, as well as fine wines.

Norwich Castle

Soon after his successful invasion of England in 1066, William the Conqueror ordered a castle built in Norwich as fortification against future attacks. The original settlement south of the River Wensum, which included almost one hundred Saxon homes, was demolished to mount a structure high on a hill, overlooking the town. By 1120, the large, almost perfectly square *donjon* (later called a "keep") was rebuilt as a royal palace, this time with a combination of local flint and stone from Caen in northwestern France. It was the only castle in East Anglia. All during Julian's lifetime, Norwich castle towered, quite literally, over the city.

Following the Norman Conquest, continental nobility and knights as well as industrious merchants quickly moved into the protected area around and to the west of the castle mound. The nobles established a new and exclusively French district in the previous Anglo-Saxon *Tombland* (open space), including an expanded marketplace. In addition to this bustling commercial center, Norwich was described in the Doomsday Book of 1086 as having approximately twenty-five churches, and a population of about six thousand souls, an extremely large settlement for its time.

Industry

From the early Middle Ages, Norwich became the veritable center of England's fast-growing wool trade. By the mid-thirteenth century, wool from East Anglia's sheepwalks had become the jewel of the realm. Flemish and Dutch craftsmen, traders, and weavers came to work and to settle, contributing extensively to the rise of wool manufacturing towns like Worstead. Then, from the fourteenth century on, a new type of cloth began to be processed from the long coarse strands of west Norfolk sheep: *worsted* wool. English wool was valued not only at home, but all over the Continent. Wool dealers from Scandinavia, Italy, and Spain arrived seasonally in the Norwich marketplace to examine and weigh the new wool, to bargain, and to strike deals. The Lord High Chancellor in the House of Lords sat on a large square sack of wool, appropriately called "the woolsack," so highly respected was this lucrative commodity. The woolsack custom persists to this day.

Norwich also experienced a major building boom. The proliferation of churches, homes, and especially the building of the Norwich Cathedral attracted architects and artisans from all over Europe. There were plentiful forests for timber and deep supplies of flint and chalk throughout the region, and the Wensum River turned multiple water-mills dating from Anglo-Saxon times. Since Norwich sat on a tidal basin, it presented an easily navigable route directly into the North Sea where herring fisheries were plentiful. Fish was a staple food in the Middle Ages, and herring was especially valued for its salt content, much needed in the medieval diet, so herring fisheries became a thriving industry. There were two quays for unloading fish in Norwich, one on the north bank of the Wensum in a section called Fishergate, the other in the western settlement, near the site of St. Laurence's Church. Growing up in Norwich, Julian would have been very familiar with the look, smell, feel, and taste of all kinds of fish, especially herring. (She will use this tiny fish as a powerful metaphor to describe an aspect of her visions.)

By the end of the thirteenth century, there were five bridges across the River Wensum within the city, providing foot and animal access to all parts of central Norwich. Rich merchants' homes and storage warehouses stood near the river, interspersed with wharves where goods were loaded and unloaded. (As we shall see, one of these might very well have been Julian's family compound.) The Wensum continued to be the lifeblood of Norwich, providing steady transportation of merchandise on its waters plus a profitable fishing trade along its shores. It also served as the necessary water source for industries such as leather working and the processing of woolen cloth.

The land around Norwich was gradually cleared of its natural forestation by peasant labor, and the marshlands were successfully drained for fertile farmland. With additional fields, some peasant farmers were emboldened to grow more than they needed for their families and owed in rent to their overlords, and so new agricultural markets opened up in the area. At the same time, more and more domestic and foreign goods began flooding into the city. It became incumbent on the local governing body to gain control over all points of entry and exit, not only as a protection against foreign invasion but also to regulate the collection of tolls on both land and river commerce. A new sense of power and business savvy demanded it.

Walls and Gates

Some time around 1294, work began on the total walling up of the city of Norwich on three sides. These walls, mainly constructed from local flint and mortar, were designed to form an unbroken line of defense encircling the city for approximately two and a half miles, on the north, west, and south. The River Wensum, outfitted with stronger gates to the north and south, was expected to provide a natural water barrier on the east. According to tax documents, the newly defined boundaries closely followed the line of previous ditch defenses, situating them on the inside of the walls.

The work on the walls and gates was not completed until the mid-fourteenth century, during Julian's lifetime. By that time, the entire city fortification system was considered a great communal achievement. Not only did the walls provide a new sense of security, they created a high degree of civic pride. Norwich could now inspire both respect and awe in visiting foreign merchants and dignitaries and strike fear in potential invaders. From the architectural remains, it is estimated that the massive flint walls were, in various places, from three to six feet thick, and stood from twelve to twenty-three feet high. The walls contained walkways between watch towers that held guards posted at the twelve city gates. (By 1385, Norwich could even boast a substantial arsenal of the new medieval artillery, since more than forty guns were mounted on its walls.) The city gates were now the only points of access into Norwich. They determined who should enter the city and who should not, and made the collection of tolls and taxes on merchandise much more efficient than its previous porous borders had. All goods brought over land were carried through the northern and western gates, and merchandise being transported by river came in and went out beneath the two Boom Towers in the south. There was also a giant Cow Tower (so called

Conisford Gate (later, King Street Gate)[4]

because cattle grazed in the nearby fields) in the northeast that, in addition to being an effective lookout, is assumed to have been a toll house to collect fees for the nearby monastery. It was rebuilt in the 1390s as part of the city's system of defense.

Each gate of Norwich had its own unique architectural design. Various coats of arms decorated the headings, and symbolic friezes were added in decades to come for splendor and show. The gates were also used to display the heads and body parts of those executed for various crimes, a repugnant medieval custom that was meant to strike the fear of God into any potential thief, murderer, or rebel. It did not, however, put an end to violent crime. At night, the portculises were lowered, keeping citizens in and strangers out, and watchmen were assigned to each gate. Even so, since there were no street lanterns, and since the danger of being attacked by thieves and vagrants was extremely high, it was considered dangerous for anyone to move about the city after the curfew.

In Julian's time, the walls, towers, and gates would have been visible from everywhere inside the city, dominating the horizon along every street. She would have traversed the walkway on the inside of the walls throughout her life, crossing from one part of the city to another. She would also have been keenly aware of the grey-stoned, imposing, and even claustrophobic limits of her approximately *one-square-mile* world. Except for the open-sided east, bordered by the Wensum River, it must have been like living inside a fortress. Julian never knew Norwich any other way. Growing up in a walled city must have had a lifelong influence on Julian's understanding of what it meant to feel enclosed, safe, protected. Also, the "holy city" would figure strongly in her *Revelations* as a metaphor for the inner sanctuary of the soul itself.

Julian's Marketplace

From its numerous docks to its bustling marketplaces, from north to south, Norwich was an overcrowded hub of business activity, producing wealth for merchants, employment for architects, builders, artists, and skilled craftsmen, and providing sustenance, however meager, for day laborers. Ever since Norman times, the Mancroft marketplace had been the center of buying and selling for the entire region of East Anglia. It operated under a license from the king, and the king's clerk had sole jurisdiction to collect the tolls and rents. Then in 1341 King Edward III ceded complete control over the marketplace, as well as the income from tolls and rents, to the city of

Norwich in perpetuity, which greatly increased the powers of the city bailiffs to regulate trade. The market was divided into separate stalls where merchants dealt in hay and grains, fish, meat, poultry, fresh fruit and vegetables, fine leather goods and metalware, clothes and shoes, rope, and last but certainly not least, prized English raw wool. There was a separate location for selling timber and livestock: pigs, cattle, sheep, and horses. This is precisely the marketplace where Julian's mother, and someday, Julian herself, would shop for their food, household items, and other supplies.

From earliest childhood, Julian would have absorbed the sights, sounds, and pungent smells of animals, fish, and traders from all over Europe speaking French, Italian, Spanish, Dutch, and German. Holding tightly to her mother's hand, she would have passed through narrow lanes of stalls with names like Glovers Row, Needlers Row, Spicers Row, Ironmongers Row, Apothecaries Row. Julian would have learned to identify the tall, narrow merchants' shops crammed cheek by jowl along the perimeter of the marketplace from the colorful pictures painted on their overhanging signs: vintners, candlemakers, copper and pewter potmakers, goldsmiths and jewelers, tailors, silk merchants, wimplemakers, lacemakers, parchment makers, pelterers, mercers (who dealt in expensive fine clothing as well as gloves, purses, belts, and needle cases made of leather), and cordwainers (shoemakers who fashioned the very finest shoes from soft cordovan leather). The list could go on and on.

Standing in front of a shop's fold-out display shelf, or entering its narrow interior, Julian would hear her mother ask for what she wanted, watch her examine the merchandise, turning it over and over, listen to the bargaining about price, and then observe her mother make a purchase or not, depending on quality and cost. Mother and child would set off again for the next shop, while a maidservant carried whatever merchandise had been purchased, maneuvering between hand-held steering carts stacked high with fruits and vegetables, packhorses laden with grains, and hawkers selling baked goods, meat pies, and *pesecods* (fresh, young green peas boiled, drained, and seasoned with butter, salt, pepper, mace, and white vinegar).

In the central area of the marketplace, Julian and her mother would have visited the bread market, the cheese market, the "flesh" market, the poultry market, the herb market, the many stalls of greengrocers, fruiterers, fishmongers, and egglers, all the while constantly on their guard amidst the heavy traffic of adult bodies shoving, shouting, arguing, spitting, cursing, and fighting. They would enjoy the music of traveling minstrels, stop to hear the town crier announcing the latest news, steer clear of drunken men emerging from the many alehouses, and pause to chat with friends amid the competing cries of street vendors, animals, and common folk. Julian would learn to be wary of pickpockets on the prowl, and to "mind" the herds of sheep, pigs, goats, and geese being led into or out of the marketplace, stepping carefully to avoid the dungheaps left behind on the dusty or muddy roadway. Going to market was nothing if not a vibrant, fascinating, and extremely noisy adventure, one that exposed Julian to a much larger world of people, languages, and attitudes than simply her one-square-mile city.

The *Brode Water*

The walls of Norwich, however high, and wide, and seemingly impenetrable, did not protect the city or its environs against the highly changeable weather of East Anglia. Dense fog and stiff winds blew in from the North Sea. They were cold, damp, and bone-numbing in winter; dense, humid, and cloying in the heat of summer. With the winds came "the brode water," the much-feared Norfolk Broads (which figure in Julian's early reflections), the devastating incursions of the sea onto the marshlands, inundating farmlands, homes, and barns. This extraordinary complex of inland waterways had been carved out in Anglo-Saxon times, when people dug the shoreline peat to fuel cooking fires and heat their homes. Masses and masses of peat were harvested for rich and poor alike. From the eleventh century on, the priory of Norwich, with its sixty monks in residence, needed 200,000 bales of peat a year just to keep the monastery running. It is calculated that, within two hundred years, some nine million cubic feet of peat had been harvested, in some places down to a depth of ten feet. This so gutted and depleted the protective coastal marshland that the massive peat pits filled with water and created more than three thousand acres of marshlands encircling the north and west of Norwich. Then, during the fourteenth century, the level of the sea rose, flooding the whole area. Thus "The Broads" were created, forming forty-one shallow lakes. In addition, there were, and are, 125 miles of rivers and streams in the area that can fill up The Broads in a matter of hours and cause severe flash flooding. By the early fourteenth century, there was even a shallow fjord from the North Sea into the easternmost part of England, leading right into Norwich.

In the second half of the fourteenth century, as Julian was growing up, England had endured summer after summer of heavy rains for some thirty years. It is reported that in 1362, during a once-in-a-century storm, the sea, driven by violent 100 mph winds, surged thirty feet above ordinary level, with fifteen feet of water inundating low-lying areas of Norwich.[5] No one and nothing was spared. Villages and towns between Norwich and Ely were trapped between creeks that had become raging rivers. Whole families drowned in their beds, their thatched houses toppling over and floating out to sea. Cattle and sheep fared no better, perishing by the thousands in the relentless waters. People tried to escape by climbing trees, clinging to each other the night long, holding out for days before being rescued. Their cries for help were drowned out by the endless howling of winds along the coastline.[6] These floods made a lasting impression on Julian. They figured so strongly in her psyche that at one point in her text she imagines herself being "led down into the sea ground" and contemplates being drowned "under the brode water" (10:15–19.159).

Survival

There was no central government agency to come to the rescue in times of natural disasters and during the resulting famines. Royal storehouses of wheat could be apportioned across the country if one or another area was in desperate need, but these allotments never lasted long enough. Further, transportation across the few bad roads, little better than horse tracks, deeply pitted from clay-digging by the peasants, was difficult at the best of times. Finally, the tolls demanded at almost every ford or pass were so oppressive that it was only too common for one district to starve while another district, a hundred miles away, might have sufficient resources.[7] Each district in England had to survive on its own and live from harvest to harvest, year after year. With a population surge that had begun in the first decades of the fourteenth century, there was never quite enough, especially for the poorest.

The people of Norwich, or any English city or town for that matter, relied solely on their own family resources in times of want. They counted on the kitchen garden or communal vegetable plot, as well as the hens, pigs, ducks, cow, or goat they kept penned up next to the house, even in towns and cities. Wheat, barley, and other grains for bread-making had to be bought at market, at least when it was available from the manorial farms. But if the Norfolk Broads overran the feudal farmlands, if there was too much rain in August so that the crops could not be harvested, if humidity was high and mold set in (rotting the grains and vegetables in the fields), if hoof and mouth disease raged through the cattle and sheep herds, *people did not eat.* Starvation, sickness, and sure death would follow. The importation of basic foods, canning and preserving of good crops for bad years, and of course, refrigeration, were still hundreds of years in the future.

Sanitation

Like every medieval city, especially one so intensely crowded and commercial, Norwich was dirty and putrid. People lived in such close proximity, both within and outside their homes, that the term "privacy" had little or no meaning. Raw sewage and stinking garbage clogged the ditches on both sides of the roadways; blood and offal flowed out from the open doors of butcher houses and turned the streets red; servants threw the contents of chamber pots out of the windows; and the stench of tanneries, as well as of tallow and parchment makers, filled the air. Dogs, hens, geese, and ducks wandered freely without restriction, and the constant traffic of noblemen and their entourage on horseback, and peasants pulling mule carts, added to the pile-up (and stench) of excrement. Farmers dug dung-heaps in the middle of the already rough roads, and the home-processing of fish oil made taking a deep breath almost unbearable.

When raw sewage was eventually collected from the streets, it was summarily dumped into the River Wensum. Local breweries then drew water directly from the river, right beside the fishing wharves and ship-building yards. River water in the city was anything but pure. In 1388, Parliament would issue a statute that, since

> so much dung and filth of the garbage and entrails be cast and put into ditches, rivers, and other waters . . . so that the air there is grown greatly corrupt and infected, and many maladies and other intolerable diseases do daily happen . . . it is accorded and assented, that the proclamation be made as well in the city of London, as in other cities, boroughs, and towns through the realm of England, where it shall be needful that all they who do cast and lay all such annoyances, dung, garbages, entrails, and other ordure, in ditches, rivers, waters, and other places aforesaid, shall cause them utterly to be removed, avoided, and carried away, every one upon pain to lose and forfeit to our Lord the King the sum of 20 pounds . . .[8]

Flies, fleas, rodents, and lice were also facts of life in England, both indoors and out. Domestic floors, even in merchant-class homes, were still made of white clay, covered over with rushes, and seasonally renewed on top, leaving the bottom layer to harbor "expectoration, vomiting, the leakage of dogs and men, ale droppings, scraps of fish, and other abominations not fit to be mentioned."[9] Herbs such as lavender, camomile, rose petals, daisies, and fennel were strewn in an effort to mask the bad smells, but were probably not very effective. Privies or lavatories, with wooden or stone seats, were built into the walls of castles, monasteries, convents, and wealthy merchants' homes. They were located as far away from the sleeping chambers as possible, with chutes to carry the waste matter down into a pit. Still, the lack of attention to the disposal of garbage and sewage would become a major contributor to deadly disease in the fourteenth century.

Norwich Cathedral

Towering over the skyline and thick walls of Norwich stood the Priory Cathedral of the Holy Trinity. Begun by Bishop Herbert de Losinga in 1096, it was made of local flint and mortar, and entirely faced with creamy limestone imported from Caen on the Norman coast of France. The cathedral was completed c.1145 and embellished by subsequent bishops over the course of more than three centuries. The Norman-style nave consisted of seven double bays, or fourteen separate compartments stretching from the great west entrance to the transept/tower crossing, where the choir or chancel screen divided the lay congregation from the choir and altar sanctuary, or presbytery. When completed, the entire length of the cathedral was 407 feet from west to east, making it one of the largest major churches in Europe. An organ would eventually be mounted on top of the choir screen, along with a loft for the choir, effectively blocking any vision of the choir and sanctuary by the laity, but no doubt adding to the acoustical excellence. Attached to the cathedral were the cloisters for the resident Benedictine monks. The monastic complex housed the Lord Prior, the sub-prior, sixty monks, a sacristan, sub-sacristan, bursar, chamberlains, almoner, refectorer, chaplains, chanter, sub-chanter, infirmerer, choristers, keepers of the shrines, lay officers, butlers, granerii, and hostelarii, and even a jailor, supported by the labor of hordes of peasants to keep the whole organization running smoothly. Surrounded by its own stone wall and

Norwich Cathedral Choir, looking east[10]

accessed during Julian's time by St. Ethelbert's Gate (1272) at the south end of the monastic enclosure, the vast cathedral and abbey functioned as a veritable city within the city.[11]

During the 1362 thunderstorm and tsunami-like flooding of the Norfolk Broads that caused so much devastation and death (accompanied by an earthquake that was felt throughout England), the wooden spire and parts of the tower of the cathedral were blown over and fell through the roof of the sanctuary. The roof was rebuilt during Julian's lifetime, with Gothic embellishments, and the dark Norman clerestory was opened up with large square windows to admit more daylight. Finally, in 1480, the present cathedral spire was built; at 315 feet, it is the second tallest in England.

Norwich Cathedral today is essentially the same structure in which Julian and her family would have worshiped from the time of her birth in November, 1342, at least until the thunderstorm in 1362, and then again, following the reconstruction. While she would also have attended a parish church near her family home, the entire Norwich community gathered in the cathedral when the bishop presided over the celebration of such great feasts as Christmas and Epiphany, and during the Triduum of Holy Thursday, Good Friday, and Easter Sunday. Julian would have been thoroughly familiar with the cathedral's stone floors, the massive Norman columns and arches, and felt the sacred presence in this holy place. As a child and throughout her life she might have watched the play of light through the clerestory windows, lingered before the vibrantly-colored frescoes of biblical scenes along the walls and in the stained-glass windows high above, and prayed in front of the many statues of saints. Here, in Norwich Cathedral, Julian would have experienced the majesty of the liturgy as well as the strangeness of not being able to understand a word of Latin. Nonetheless, the sheer grandeur of the vaulted space must have lifted up her mind and heart to God. And the organ, no doubt, stirred her soul to prayer.

It was also here that, as a young girl, Julian came to hear sermons from renowned Benedictine preachers such as Adam Easton (who later became a cardinal archbishop), as well as Dominican and Franciscan friars, all learned in theology and able to elucidate and interpret sacred scripture. They would read aloud the epistle and gospel in Latin, then preach in the vernacular on a selected passage, or on an aspect of faith or morals. Julian and her family sat on a hard bench, knelt on the cold stone floor, and stood for long periods of time. The choir stalls closest to the altar were reserved exclusively for the monks and canons, as well as those nobility and gentry who paid for the privilege of being seated within sight of the main altar. The layfolk who could not read or write Latin (however rich and respectable they might be) were restricted to the nave, most likely separated by gender on either side of the main aisle. Men exchanged news and views, talked and argued loudly, even did commercial business deals within the nave. Fashionable women eyed each other's clothing, comparing new styles from the Continent, and gossiped. Lowly peasants remained far in the back.

Julian's Churches

In addition to the cathedral, by the fourteenth century there were at least *sixty* parish churches as well as smaller chapels in Norwich, many of them financed by wealthy local merchants. (Thirty-two of these medieval churches, many of them very large, still survive, more than in any other northern European city.) Erecting a church to a favorite patron saint in return for commercial success, or favors granted, also served as a sign to the community of an individual's high status, or a group of merchants' financial ability to do so. A church was not only a monument to faith but also a testimony to civic pride; not incidentally, building a church was also thought to assure one's personal salvation. Men of power and status believed that the great monetary contribution necessary for the construction of a church or monastic house would commend their souls favorably to God in this life. It would also provide chantry chapels for masses and prayers to be said after their death, lessening the "time" their souls would have to spend in purgatory.

These churches were of various designs, from the Anglo-Saxon and post-Conquest Norman, to the newer Decorated and the later Perpendicular, all built of plentiful local flint. Julian's family might have attended the church dedicated to St. Peter and St. Paul (known in Julian's time as St. Peter of Gloucester), which had been built in 1075 by the Earl of Norfolk, who co-founded the city with William the Conqueror. (It was rebuilt in the mid-fifteenth century and then renamed St. Peter Mancroft during the Reformation.) Located in the center of the marketplace, it was by far the most populous and wealthy parish in the city, catering mostly to merchants and their families. Julian might also have prayed in St. Andrew's, the second largest parish church in Norwich; St. Edmund's, built to honor the

Pre-World War II photo of the Church of St. Julian in Norwich[12]

Anglo-Saxon king who was executed by the Danes in 870; St. Mary Coslany's, probably pre-1100; St. Clement's, again pre-Conquest, dedicated to the pope and martyr of c.100 CE and one of the first churches in the city to be erected on the north side of the river; St. Etheldreda's (c.679), on the site of an Anglo-Saxon settlement along the old Roman road.

Most certainly, Julian would have developed a deep connection to the Church of St. Julian, on King's Street, just off Southgate. The smallest of all the churches in the city, it consisted of a nave and chancel, with a Norman tower dating from the tenth century (quite possibly the oldest tower in Norwich). It is currently accepted that the original church was dedicated to the third- or early fourth-century St. Julian, bishop of Le Mans, France.[13] An earlier theory suggested that the church was named after the ninth-century St. Julian the Hospitaller, a local hermit who ferried people across the Wensum from a ferry landing close by the church. Either way, it is here, on these exact grounds, that Julian would choose in later life to become an anchoress, attaching herself, quite literally, to the side of the parish church by living in a small hermitage. Out of a desire for anonymity, she may have changed her real name to that of the church, though it is equally plausible that she was baptized *Julian* after her father, an uncle, or a family patron, which was a common practice in her time. Whatever the source of her historical name, it is adjacent to this little church that Julian would contemplate God and pray for her *evencristens.*

There was a medieval Norwich boast that the city had a church for every week of the year and a pub for every day. In addition to the sixty churches, there were some thirty-seven craft guild chapels dedicated to the spiritual life of their members throughout the city. Besides the Benedictines, Norwich also contained an abundance of monastic houses representing the black-robed Augustinian (or Austin) canons, the Franciscans (Grey Friars), the black-cloak-over-white-robed Dominicans (Black Friars), plus the stricter orders of Carmelites (White Friars) and Cistercians (White Monks) in an aggregate of some twenty-two religious houses crowded within the city, as well as eight more outside the city walls.

By 1342, when Julian was born, Norwich's population was approximately 13,000,[14] which made it the second largest city in the realm after London. It was a city abounding in religious, cultural, and commercial energy. It was here that Julian grew up. It was here that she would live out her life and die.

Now that we have sketched the history and topography of Julian's *physical* world, let us consider the structure of the feudal society into which she was born, in an attempt to deduce her parentage and social class. On these will depend her ability to learn to read and write.

2
Ancestry

The medieval feudal system divided all peoples into three estates. Everything about your sense of self, your family, dress, education, status, opportunity, wealth, and often health, was dependent upon your station in life. Thus it is imperative that we deduce into which estate, and into which class within that estate, Julian was most probably born. Also, by investigating those aspects of feudal society which figured prominently in Julian's life, we will better understand her references to the clergy, nobility, and peasantry that arise in her Revelations.

The First Estate

The first estate was comprised of the exclusively male clergy, from the pope, archbishops, bishops, abbots of monasteries and the monks, down to the lowliest parish priest or deacon in minor orders. This estate was considered the highest, in theory, because the clergy were supposed to be closest to God and to intercede continually for the Christian people. The clergy were further subdivided into two main categories: *regular* and *secular.*

The regular clergy were Benedictine, Cistercian, and Carthusian monks, who lived in enclosed monastic settings, such as Norwich Priory. Since the word *monk* comes from the Greek *monos*, meaning single, it was assumed that monks would not marry and would not own any personal property (although celibacy and poverty were not originally part of their vows). According to the guidelines laid down by St. Benedict of Nursia (480–543), monks took a vow of obedience to the Rule, a vow of stability (not to leave the monastic enclosure without permission of the abbot), and a vow of conversion in their way of life. All material things were supposed to be held in common and used according to need, as the early Christians had practiced poverty (Acts 2:44, 4:32). This lifelong commitment included the daily reciting of the canonical hours, the reading of scriptures, meditation and private prayer, as well as manual labor. Some Benedictine monks worked in the fields, the more scholarly copied and preserved ancient texts in the monastery's *scriptorium,* while others conducted schools for boy novices and clerics in training, teaching them how to read and write Latin and to sing plainsong. Monasteries also offered refuge and hospitality to wayfarers and pilgrims, medical treatment to the infirm, and food handouts to the poor. In the course of the Middle Ages, more and more lay (non-ordained) monks went on to study for priestly ordination so that monastery life changed radically from a community of laymen to a stratified society of abbot, prior, senior monks, choir monks, tonsured deacons, and boy scholars, all supported by the labor of serfs.[1] By 1348 there were some 650 monasteries throughout England (with an additional 200 friaries and 150 nunneries), totaling nearly one thousand monasteries, abbeys, and priories that housed a sum of twenty thousand men and two thousand women.[2]

Unlike the monks who lived on monastic estates, the *secular* clergy were ordained priests and deacons whose role it was to live in parishes and work in the world. They carried out the bishop's orders, dispensed justice in clerical courts, and ministered to the laity by baptizing, hearing confessions, offering Mass, officiating at marriages, giving spiritual guidance, and administering the last rites to the dying. In 1300, when the English population had reached a high of between five and six million people, approximately thirty thousand men were full-time secular clergy. These included parish priests, or curates (who had "the cure," or care, of souls); priests in seven hundred hospitals serving the sick, destitute men and women, and lepers; chantry priests who were hired to sing Masses for the souls of the faithful departed in purgatory; university chaplains, theologians, and scholarly priests, canon law priests, and priests who administered the sacraments to convents of nuns.[3]

Religious women lived in communities called priories or abbeys, just like monks. While nuns took solemn monastic vows of poverty, chastity, and obedience, and were obliged to chant the Little Office of Our Lady four times daily in chapel (*Matins*, *Lauds*, *Vespers*, and *Compline*), they were never allowed to be ordained members of the clergy, simply because they were female. Therefore, they were never actually considered members of the first estate. In fact, they had no ecclesiastical standing at all. Nevertheless, women religious often came from the ranks of the nobility and upper gentry. A prioress or abbess, like her male counterparts, was placed in charge of a large monastic church and estate, like Carrow Priory just outside the walls of Norwich, overseeing not only her nuns but also the servants and indentured serfs who worked the lands. A prioress could, at times, wield as much influence as any prior.

Reforms

During the High Middle Ages, the immense wealth and political influence of the church, plus the unbridled authority of the popes to make decrees and excommunicate any who dared to cross their will, led to great resentment among the secular powers. Additionally, monks and priests who had taken vows to live according to a high moral code fell into the vices of other men of their time: gluttony, gambling, drinking, and fighting. And while priests and monks had been strictly forbidden by canon law to marry or keep concubines since the First Lateran Council in 1123 (reinforced by the Second Lateran Council in 1139), that did not prevent them from indulging in licentious behavior.

In 1215, the Fourth Lateran Council instituted far-reaching reforms that affected both the clergy and the laity. The directives included the obligation of each Christian to make an annual confession of sins to a priest and to receive holy Eucharist at Easter, plus a host of regulations for the clergy regarding the selection and education of candidates, the frequency of preaching (at least four times a year), the administration of the sacraments, and the moral conduct of priests. The rules against holding multiple benefices (appointments to parishes and bishoprics, with their attendant stipends) were also renewed. Furthermore, the naming of local bishops, long a bone of contention between church and state, was to be made free of interference by lay lords. These reforms, though necessary, were slow to be implemented.

The Friars

Into the maelstrom of moral laxity, political dissensions, rampant heresies, and overall secularization came the Franciscan and Dominican friars. Founded by St. Francis of Assisi, and St. Dominic of Osma, these two orders of mendicant friars took entirely different approaches toward reforming the church, but both would bequeath their great faith to the ages. Francis called his dozen or so peripatetic companions the *Friars Minor.* They went forth two by two, in sandals and simple brown robes, singing the praises of the Lord and preaching repentance and peace to the people gathered in the marketplace, the town square, along the roadside. These friars worked alongside peasants in the fields, slept in barns, church porticos, and on the bare ground, begging for their food. Approved by Pope Innocent III in 1209 as a new religious order, their fame spread rapidly throughout the Continent and into England. Men of nobility, wealth, and education gave up everything to join their ranks.

Dominic's *Order of Preachers* would take up the Fourth Lateran Council's mandate to teach the truths of the faith to the laity, and to instruct those under the sway of heretical teachings (specifically, the Albigensian heresy then raging in France). Dominic's intention of training hordes of uneducated priests, both intellectually and spiritually, and then sending them out to preach Catholic theology in churches and at makeshift pulpits in the marketplace, even entering into open debate with heretics, was a thoroughly novel idea. The Dominicans would soon rival the Friars Minor (or Franciscans) for control of the minds and hearts of the laity.

Both orders sought to reform the church from the ground up: the Franciscans by teaching the imitation of Christ, his poverty, love, peace, and gentle courtesy; the Dominicans by preaching solid doctrine in terms that both the literate and the illiterate could comprehend, rooting out heresy along the way. Over the course of the thirteenth and fourteenth centuries, Dominicans and Franciscans passed each other on the highways and byways, heading toward every city, town, and village. Unlike monks and regular canons who might remain in one monastic settlement or urban house for a lifetime, the friars were everywhere at once, able to travel abroad to study, or be sent anywhere at any time they were needed. At first, this flexibility added to their popularity among the laity, while their superior preaching gained them an enthusiastic following. The friars were considered more accessible and perhaps more sympathetic in hearing confessions and giving spiritual counsel than the parish priests.

However, throughout the fourteenth century, the proliferation of lands donated and bequests made to the mendicant orders and the great houses and churches built by their increasing wealth (despite the strictures of their saintly founders) seriously compromised their teachings on poverty and the simple life of holiness. In addition, the papal privileges that allowed them to preach in *any* cathedral or parish church were seen by secular bishops, pastors, and priests as usurping their own parochial preaching role. Even the popularity of friars for hearing confessions, giving spiritual direction, and granting burial in their own friary cemeteries came to be seen as impinging on the provenance of the local hierarchy. Whatever fees went into the friars' coffers were considered "stolen" from the parishes. This conflict between local secular clergy and the ubiquitous friars was to fester. Eventually, the sheer numbers of Franciscans (much higher than the Dominicans) worked against them. Their power and presence became especially egregious when the friars were commissioned to go all over Europe, England, and Wales to raise funds for papal crusades by "selling indulgences."[4] This, perhaps more than any other activity, aroused deep resentment of the friars and would have disastrous consequences.

Curates and Canons

During Julian's near-death illness, a secular priest will come to her bedside to administer the last rites of the church, which included hearing her confession, giving her communion, and anointing her with holy chrism. Julian also records that, a week later, "My curate was sent for to be at my ending" (3:17–18.131). Finally, at the very end of her visionary experiences, Julian will be visited by "a religious person" (66:12.331), that is, either a Franciscan or Dominican friar, or perhaps an Augustinian (Austin) canon. This order consisted of well-educated priests and those in training for the priesthood who resided within the bishop's own household or in a separate friary within large cities like Norwich. Also known as Austin Friars, they served both to advise and assist the bishop's administration, to oversee the functioning of the cathedral, and to be accessible to the laity in the parishes. During Julian's lifetime there was a well-established friary of Austin canons directly across the road from the Church of St. Julian. Austin canons were admired for their erudition and maintained an extensive library of holy texts and commentaries, all in Latin of course. While Julian would not have been able to read (or borrow) such valuable books, she might well have had a confessor or known a family friend who was an Austin canon. Such an educated man might have taken it upon himself to answer Julian's theological questions and to instruct her in sacred scripture. He might even have given her spiritual direction. The very proximity of the Augustinian Friary to Julian's eventual anchorage invites speculation.

The Second Estate

Since men of religion were forbidden to marry, it seems highly unlikely that Julian's ancestry can be placed in the first estate. Let us then turn to the second estate, *those who ruled and defended* the kingdom. This estate was headed by the king who, with the nobility and the church, owned three quarters of all English lands. According to the ancient feudal system, the king gave his lords the right to rule his vast estates (called fiefs or manors), by which these lords amassed great wealth. Each large fiefdom granted to a duke or an earl by the king was again subdivided into smaller fiefs, ruled over by knights and lesser nobles who each in turn swore fealty to his superior lord. During the fifty-year reign of King Edward III (1327–1377), there were four dukes, three of them the king's sons; below them, seven to fourteen earls; beneath them, forty to seventy barons, all of whom ran their estates under royal patronage.

In exchange for this life of privilege, the lords gave solemn homage and fealty to the king, pledging under oath to serve at his will at court, in Parliament's House of Lords, and on the field of battle with the might of their arms. The lords also promised to defend the knights and other vassals under their authority. Likewise, every knight swore an oath to protect his liege lord, as long as the lord remained true to his oath to protect them. (This mutual promise was considered sacred and when it was perceived to have been broken, whether by king or noble or knight, the consequences could be lethal.) The second estate was a hierarchical corporate structure on which depended the entire organization, government, and defense of the realm.

In addition to protecting church and king, lords and lands, common people and the poor in times of invasion, the second estate had the right and obligation to uphold justice, to make laws and enforce them, and to maintain the peace. Ideally, lords and knights were supposed to defend the other two estates (the clergy and peasants) from civil uprisings and traitorous plots. Too often, however, they were themselves the instigators of political intrigue, frequently against each other and sometimes even against the king. During the fourteenth century, two kings were deposed by the machinations of their own nobles and knights: Edward II in 1327 (probably murdered in Berkeley Castle), and Richard II in 1399 (presumed poisoned in the Tower of London). No matter their oaths of allegiance, nobles and knights were not above carrying out vendettas, attempting to take over each other's estates, and fomenting internecine rivalries at home when not fighting abroad. Even kings feared their collective power.

Code of Chivalry

The code of chivalry that gradually developed over the centuries demanded that, however brutal a knight's conduct might be in actual battle, and however rapacious he might be in inflicting torture and death on his victims, he should always *appear* to be above reproach in his cultivation of Christian virtues. The knight was sworn to the ideals of "trouthe and honour, fredom and courteisie." It was the practice of these virtues that purportedly made the knight truly "noble," proving his spiritual lineage from the first knight of all, the archangel St. Michael. The virtues included gallantry in personal conduct, valor in military action, and absolute loyalty to his liege lord. The code of chivalry also encouraged the knight's comeliness (wearing a garland of fresh flowers, donning fashionable dress, lacing his sleeves, and sporting very pointed leather shoes so tight that common folk could not figure out how he got into them). It further prescribed a measure of personal cleanliness (especially brushing his teeth, combing his hair, and washing his hands and nails in the bowls made available before every banquet in the great hall). In addition to his oath of fealty to his lord, each knight promised to defend his fellow knights. Thus a chivalric brotherhood was born.

The rules of chivalry extended to what came to be known as "courtly love," a highly stylized code of behavior with rigid conventions. For example: a knight must woo a noble lady with whom he becomes smitten. He must conduct himself with the utmost courtesy, show her favors, defend her honor (however fanciful that might be in actuality), demonstrate his exceeding politeness, compose (or pay to have composed) ballads in her honor, play the flute and strings, sing to her (if he has a good voice), impress her with his graceful dancing, and promise her his undying faithfulness. Then he must set out to display his prowess in jousting tournaments, or go off to battle to prove his courage, wearing some token of her favor. Most importantly, he must return to tell his lady of his exploits. "If at arms you excel, you will be ten times loved."[5]

To complicate matters, the lady must always be a *married* woman, beyond the easy conquest of a knight, and therefore one for whom he must pine excessively, endure arduous tests (that his lady prescribes), and nearly die from unrequited love. Eventually, his feats of heroism, his good manners, his patience, as well as his witty conversation and/or romantic poems, must win his lady's acceptance of his attentions. The chivalric code was essentially an elaborate game of seduction and adultery, carried out right under the nose of the liege lord.

Lady Julian?

Was Julian born into the nobility? It has been suggested that she was an aristocrat, Lady Julian Erpingham, elder sister of the noble knight and lord Sir Thomas Erpingham, who was a close friend of King Henry IV and who fought in the Battle of Agincourt in 1415; and further, that she was the wife of Roger Hauteyn, who was presumably murdered in a duel in 1373, the same year in which her visions occurred.[6] However, there is absolutely nothing in Julian's text to indicate that she grew up in the rarified world of the aristocracy, internalizing the all-pervasive cult of the romantic knight and his lady and frequenting royal company. There is no sense of social superiority or elitism toward the common people, so characteristic of nobility, on a single page of Julian's writing. Nor is there any hint that Julian ever felt the least pang of guilt for enormous wealth and power over the common folk. On the contrary, Julian states expressly that she is writing solely for her *evencristens*, the *lewed*, whom she considers herself to be. And if we are to believe that Julian had no need to lie about her intentions, then by speaking openly of herself as "a simple creature unlettered" (2:1.125), she is clearly telling us she was *not* born into the aristocracy.

If she had been of noble birth or had married into it (a most unlikely scenario), from her earliest years she would have observed court life from the inside out. She would have experienced firsthand the deceit, vanity, pride, and not-so-subtle sexual games on the part of both men and women that the chivalric code condoned and even fostered. Courtly mores were part of an elaborate effort to idealize and praise the beauties and virtues of women through poetry, song, dance and witty conversation . . . to justify extra-marital lust. A perceptive young woman like Julian would have seen through the subterfuge and lamented the total lack of true courtesy and honor in social and personal relations. Likewise, if she had been raised in a noble lord's manor house, educated to become a knight's lady, both as a wife and secret lover, she would have written about *courtesie* from a disillusioned perspective.

As it is, Julian applies the courtly word *courtesie* to only one person, her Lord, Jesus Christ. She will assign to him all the attributes she has ever heard associated with the code of chivalry: purest love, compassion, mercy, exquisite kindness, and bending down to make the servant feel especially honored. Julian could have referred to Christ as her protective knight, her noble king. Instead, she describes Christ not according to the cult of knighthood or nobility at all but as a *mother*, always so considerate of her lowly estate. Julian speaks of the intimate *courtesie* of the Lord as a perfect metaphor for divine love, not only toward herself but toward all humankind.

Another point: throughout her work, Julian uses the most ordinary images and commonplace occurrences to describe aspects of her visions, such as rain dripping from the eaves of a house, the scales of herring, or the poor peasant laborer in his short, frayed *kirtel,* or tunic, worn down by sweat and toil. These are most certainly not the metaphors that would come most immediately to the mind of a noble lady living in a castle or manor house, attended by numerous servants, waited on hand and foot, who never once handled raw seafood in the marketplace or descended into the hot kitchen and cleaned fish scales. By telling us about the most humble daily observations and activities, by repeatedly using the word *homely* to mean the intimacy and informality of the Lord's demeanor, Julian is definitely not alluding to the "homeyness" of a sprawling manor house or castle. On the contrary, she is discreetly but unmistakably directing us toward her true parentage: that of the third estate. This is where we will find her *evencristens,* for whom she feels so deeply responsible and for whom she writes her book.

The Third Estate

By process of elimination, we must place Julian's ancestry in the third estate, which included everyone who *clothed, fed, and served* the kingdom, from the most prosperous wool merchants to the poorest indentured serfs working the land. Although the third estate comprised 90 percent of the population in any given medieval country, its vast numbers had no voting rights. The nobility did not even distinguish between various classes of the third estate, considering them all, from the well educated to the illiterate, as non-noble and therefore of servile degree. The fourteenth-century poet, William Langland, aptly described the sentiments of the poor peasant in *The Vision of Piers Plowman*:

That I shall labour and sweat and sow for us both
And other labours do for thy love all my life time
On condition that thou protect Holy Church and myself
From wastours [scoundrels][7] and wicked men that this world
destroyeth.[8]

Indeed, the great majority of the third estate consisted of peasants, both free and indentured. But this estate also included a growing and increasingly powerful *middle class* of skilled artisans, masons, artists, tradespeople, merchants, councilors, lawyers, judges, bailiffs, burgesses, and mayors living in the larger towns and cities.

Peasant Life

While outright slavery was no longer considered economically or morally viable and had died out in England by 1324, it is estimated that more than 50 percent of the population still remained indentured serfs.[9] The *villein* (a medieval peasant; through long association with disreputable qualities, *villein* came to mean a "villain") toiled and served for generations on great and small estates and was generally despised and considered by his master as having a value that was roughly equivalent to that of his beasts. The peasant's life was nothing if not miserable. He lived on land that belonged to his secular, ecclesiastical, or monastic feudal lord; he paid rent for his meager hut, covered with a roof of straw; he worked the lord's fields in all weather, year in and year out; and he personally owned nothing but his own skin. In return for this bondage, the villein and his family were supposed to receive protection from the lord in times of war or civil uprisings and be assured of food from his lord's stockpile during periods of famine. This was not always the case.

In addition to working on the *demesne* (the lands that the lord of the manor retained for his own farming and grazing purposes, worked by his serfs), the villein eked out a living from a small parcel of land allotted to him by the lord for his personal tillage, from which the villein had to give back the best part of his harvest to the lord as rent. Still, if the villein labored hard and had many sons to help him, he might gradually rent more land to farm, or pasture sheep, and make a small profit selling his crops or wool at market. But time was of the essence and the lord's bailiff frequently made unreasonable demands on the villein. As a field worker, the villein was required to plough the sod, sow the crops, trim the hedgerows, tend and harvest the crops, bind and thresh the wheat, clear forests, dig ditches, repair roads, fences, and bridges, drain swamplands, build and maintain walls and palisades, feed and care for farm animals, muck out the cowshed, cart produce and wool to and from market for his lord . . . all this before he could tend to his own field allotment.

The lord, meanwhile, held all property rights, not only to cultivate his fields, but also to graze his sheep and cattle and to hunt wild animals anywhere on his demesne (even if that meant allowing packs of dogs hot on the scent of a fox, and horses galloping in pursuit, to destroy a poor villein's meager crops or vegetable garden). The lord also held all forest rights to cut timber, shoot wild birds, or gather fruits, as well as all rights to fish from streams and to transport anything or anyone by water. If a villein were caught poaching, whether setting traps for small game, fishing in a stream at night, or cutting down large branches from a live tree to fuel his home, he would be severely beaten and heavily fined.

The villein had no legal right to refuse the lord any service whatsoever, on pain of punishment by the lord's bailiff. Further, if he was accused of a crime, the villein had no recourse to any court of justice except the lord's own manorial court, where the lord's judgment decided the law. Little differentiated from a plantation slave, the villein could never leave the land for more than one day without the lord's permission. He could not move his family elsewhere without first having found the means to buy his own and each of his family members' freedom at a price that would normally have been beyond his means. And so the feudal system of bondage persisted from generation to generation. Manumission (the freeing of a serf) was rarely given as a reward for good service, any more than freedom from slavery had been, since the lord required as many bodies as possible to get the best financial return he could from his estates. The lord's wealth was evaluated by the extent and income of his properties, which included both the land and those who worked the land. Villeins were, in essence, the lord's personal property. It is notable that the dirty, sweaty, impoverished image of the villein would play a major role in Julian's central parable of the lord and the servant.

Peasant Taxes

In addition to his life of servitude, the villein had to pay regular taxes to his lord on every one of his crops. The lord, whether the abbot of a monastery or the earl of an estate, always saw to it that his overseer took the best part of the villein's grain harvest, an extra dozen eggs from his chickens at Easter, and a goose at Christmas. The villein also had to submit a tithe of 10 percent on all of his scant earnings to the church. It was constantly preached, taught, and held inviolate that everyone, both rich and poor, was required to tithe. This law was based on the Old Testament directive to the Israelites: "Set apart a tithe of all the yield of your seed that is brought in yearly from the field (Dt 14:22).[10] The most destitute peasant had to pay tithes on his kitchen-garden, the honey collected by his wife, even on the grass growing by the wayside.[11] Not to do so was a mortal sin and worthy of damnation. Additionally, the bailiff of the manor or monastic estates, or the town parson, could rightfully claim tithes of every family for various types of lawful financial transaction or personal holdings, discounting the unlawful income of usurers, *jongleurs* (wandering poets, minstrels, clowns or jugglers), and prostitutes, unless they were penitent.[12] Tithes were figured on the gross proceeds of the harvest or any other transaction, without consideration of the human toil and financial outlay that produced it (which was reckoned to be half the going price). Therefore, the tithes actually added up to *20* percent rather than the prescribed 10 percent.[13] In addition, the feudal structure meant that the serf who labored on a monastic estate was paying secular dues to the abbot as his lord, as well as the required tithes to the church. Meanwhile, the church also stressed its own responsibility to provide alms to the poor in order to fend off impending starvation. (If a serf were dying of hunger and received alms, he did not have to pay tithes on the charity he was given.)[14]

Besides the onerous food taxes, the villein had to pay a *merchet* or marriage-fine if he wanted his daughter to marry, even for a marriage between manorial villeins. (If the husband-to-be was from another manor, the fine was called a *foremariage*, and if it was not paid fully, all the villein's goods would be confiscated.) The *merchet* was a much-hated fine, as it was an ongoing reminder of bondage in its requirement that the villein had to, in effect, "buy his own blood."[15] The *merchet* was fully enforced even on monastic and episcopal estates, and the prior's or bishop's consent was necessary for every marriage. The preference of lords, both religious and secular, to grant permission only for marriages *within* the manor complex led, inevitably, to frequent in-breeding, and this in spite of the fact that at the Fourth Lateran Council of 1215 the church had prohibited marriages to blood relatives within the fourth degree (that is, third cousins). Even on the larger manors, more than half of the peasant population was, at any given time, consistently inbred.[16]

Should a villein's daughter become pregnant out of wedlock, a *leywrite* penalty, a fine for sexual incontinence, had to be paid by the nearest male relative, usually the father. Finally, if a villein was so rash as to get sick or injured and then die, a *heriot* or death tax had to be paid to the lord for the loss of a worker. The landlord's bailiff or reeve (overseer) would come to the door of the villein's hut immediately following the funeral Mass and demand the tax. The bereaved wife would have to turn over her husband's best beast, be it ox, cow, horse, donkey, or goat, or his best movable possession, and at the same time the parish priest would take the second-best animal or piece of furniture as the church's rightful *mortuary* tax.[17]

For the villein's family there was no escaping taxes, even in death. Over the centuries, the tithes, mortuaries, and added penalties had become enforceable by customary law.[18] They were so burdensome and often brutal in their execution that they became more and more corruptive of the feudal relationship between the serf and his lord, whether that overlord was a nobleman or an abbot. The serfs' resentment was further fueled by their having to pay increasingly heavy "poll taxes" for the king's never-ending war with France. Peasants were also conscripted by poorer knights (or their squires) to go off to war in their stead. There seemed no end to the leeching.

However, it was not just the obligation of having to pay regular tithes and to offer the weekly Mass penny (which had once been viewed as voluntary), plus the marriage money, and the baptismal fee, and the burial price, in both money and property, that rankled with the peasants. It was the fact that these very offerings were supposed to be used to feed and clothe and care for the sick and hungry as well as the widows and orphans of the parish. For this purpose, the tithes might well have been justified. But too often the income went directly to subsidize the "squire parson" with his penchant for hunting, or the monks of the abbey who were wont to hold lavish feasts and hunting parties, or an absentee bishop. Tithe monies rarely stayed in the parish, nor were they seen to benefit those for whom they should have been collected. It can be estimated that as much as *two thirds* of the tithe monies might leave the parish, to go to nonresident bishops who held the benefices to vast estates or to absentee clerics who hired barely literate priests to serve the parishes in their stead.[19] Tithes were even handed over by unscrupulous priests as "bribes" to the nobility, to secure a position in the house of a lord and his lady, a position that would entitle the priest to food, fine living, and bodily protection. In this way, members of the clerical estate were viewed as available for a price to the lord of the manor. Indeed, the whole tithing system became rotten with greed, stealing from the poor to benefit the already-rich.

Of course, there was always the case where the town or village priest might be a poor barely-literate curate himself, scraping by on his stipend and totally dependent on peasant tithes and altar offerings to maintain the church building. He might well have seen the local cathedral chapter take what he considered his share of the mortuary, and so he might justify his confiscation of moveable goods from a poor widow as his rightful due. He deserved to be paid, after all, for his "cure" of souls. But these same souls deeply resented curates who demanded their due, and this and other practices (like taking possession of the very bed on which the dead person was brought to the church to be buried) only widened the breach between clergy and people.

To be clear, it was not one parson making excessive demands on widows or brewing beer in the rectory, or one monk using tithe money to entertain his friends, but *the entire feudal system* that was at fault for encouraging and permitting the rampant abuses of power and privilege. As Julian herself would indicate in her parable of the lord and the servant, the peasants' lot was extreme: they worked six days a week from sun-up to sundown, in all kinds of heat and cold and sleet and snow, bent under the triple yoke of servitude, drudgery, and boredom. Yet these uneducated, resentful—and often resented—peasants were the backbone of English society upon whom the entire feudal structure depended. The impending horrors of the fourteenth century, however destructive and deadly, would be the catalyst of transformative change for the villeins of England. After more than a thousand years of serfdom,[20] the peasants would do the unthinkable: rise up and demand their rights.

Julian's Estate

From the preceding description of the indentured villein, the poverty, the time-consuming manual labor, and the complete lack of opportunity for gaining the literacy and theological understanding necessary to write a book, we may assume that Julian was *not* of lowly peasant birth. Therefore, we may conclude that Julian must have been born into the home of a free man of the third estate, one of those in the more educated *merchant middle class* who effectively transformed Norwich into a thriving and affluent city. However, this deduction does not preclude the possibility that Julian's grandfather, or perhaps even her father, had been born of peasant stock, indentured to a lord or an abbot. Indeed, Julian's innate sympathy for the common folk could arise only because she felt vitally connected to the land and to the peasants, *since they were her own proximate ancestors.* But, given the strict feudal class structure, how is it that Julian's father or grandfather could have emerged from indentured serfdom into the merchant middle class?

Three Ways to Freedom

There were essentially three ways out of villeiny: *payment, education,* or *escape.* Perhaps Julian's grandfather saved enough money in good harvest years by dint of additional hard labor (growing seasonal crops to sell at market or raising pigs and sheep while his wife spun extra wool for local weavers in addition to all her other chores) to buy his way out of serfdom, paying as much as one quarter or one third of the value of his rented land and all his chattel to do so. However, even as a free man, if he wanted to relocate, rent from a more lenient feudal lord, work more fertile lands, or move to a city to become an artisan or merchant, he would still have been required to pay regular *heriots* and fines to his lord. And he would still have had to fear the lord's bailiff seizing him for non-payment of those taxes. It would take at least a generation for the freeman to feel truly liberated. And then he would hope and pray that no financial disaster would ever force him back into the clutches of his overlord.

A second way for a villein to obtain freedom was by getting a basic *education.* If Julian's grandfather obtained permission from his feudal lord to send his son (between the ages of seven and ten) to a public school, either in the village or in the nearest town or city (such as Norwich), he would again have had to pay the requisite fine, since the lord would lose the son's labor during the farming-intensive seasons of the year. But more and more peasant farmers were willing to make extraordinary sacrifices for their sons' education. After the twelfth century, public secular schools began springing up all over England and were termed, in order of advancement: reading or cathedral chantry (song) schools at the primary level, leading to grammar schools for the study of Latin grammar and accounting (necessary for a career either in the church or in international trade), thence to business schools or schools for higher studies, such as those of theology, arts, or the sciences.[21] It is quite possible that Julian's grandfather might have been able to pay the penalty for his son to receive a basic Latin education at the cathedral chantry school in Norwich. Even if the boy became tonsured as a chorister, once he learned to read and write he could have left the chantry school without being ordained in order to pursue a career in business. Many boys did.

A third method of gaining freedom was far more risky. A young, unmarried villein, not yet responsible for a wife and children, might chance all, leave his life on the land behind him and *escape* from the manor to a large, prosperous, and densely populated city like Norwich. Julian's grandfather might have concealed his son in a cart carrying goods to market, or simply left him behind in the city marketplace before returning home. Once on his own, a villein might be forced to enter into a life of crime just to survive (thus arose the alternate spelling, "villain"). But if he was an honest young man and if he could find manual work building town walls and repairing city gates, digging ditches, hauling and carting, caring for animals and mucking out stalls (all of which he would have done on the manor), and if he could secure some place to sleep over a stable or on the floor of a warehouse, he might just manage to keep body and soul together without resorting to theft. He might even find long-term manual work on one of the many new churches being constructed in Norwich. If he was strong in constitution and had acquired useful skills on the manor from his years in service to his lord, he might be taken on as an apprentice to a master artisan, stonemason, or craftsman and learn a new trade such as masonry, weaving, dyeing, painting, tanning, metalworking, or carpentry. In a similar fashion, a peasant who had sheared sheep for the lord of the manor, had a good eye for quality wool, a smart business sense, and a knack for trading might become an assistant to a wool merchant and learn how to make successful sales. If such a runaway villein could remain undiscovered for "a year and a day" in the belly of the city, he was henceforth considered a "free man." In any one of a number of possible scenarios, once the peasant blended into city life, his freeman's life could begin in earnest.

It is probable indeed, given the all-importance of the wool trade in Norwich, that Julian's father might have been just such an adventurous peasant boy who ran away from the overlord's manor as a young teenager, eager for a new life and freedom in the big city, and applied himself to learning a profession. Then, as now, if the will is strong and the time is right, it takes only one generation to rise in business. The fourteenth century, for all its chaos and recurring catastrophes, was just such an opportune time.[22] Julian's father could well have been what we now call a "self-made man," like those who rose up out of slavery to freedom within one generation in America.

Craft and Merchant Guilds

The road would be hard. In order to become a licensed craftsman or wool cloth merchant and to gain some measure of financial security and independence in the thriving commercial city of Norwich, Julian's father would have to earn the right to be accepted into a craft or merchant guild. That was a long and laborious process. Medieval guilds were associations of merchants and craftsmen geared to the orderly regulation of their trade or craft. The Saxon word, *gilden*, refers to the hefty dues each member had to pay to belong to the *gild*. Guild membership was absolutely necessary to practice a craft or to conduct business. It entitled the artisan or merchant to sell his wares at a retail price in the open marketplace; without membership, such commerce was strictly forbidden. Guilds created a monopoly for every product, set the standards of workmanship, and fixed the selling prices. In addition, guilds limited their membership so that supply did not outstrip market demand. Any illicit trading meant a stiff fine for those who were not members of guilds. Any member who violated his guild charter would also be fined. Even foreign merchants could sell only to bona fide guild merchants who then acted as middlemen, turning around and selling to the citizens, making a good profit in the process. If, on rare occasions, foreigners were allowed to sell directly to citizens, they had to pay a large tax to do so.

The advantages of guild membership included financial help if a member fell ill, funds for the singing of a funeral Mass and a dirge, burial arrangements, and the care of orphaned children. Guild donations also provided dowry monies for orphaned or poor girls and sometimes contributed funds for the education of both boys and girls. Guild members helped one another protect horses, wagons, and fungible goods as they moved along dangerous roads beset with thieves, vagrants, and soldiers of fortune. It was a mutual support system that not only proved very effective against robbers on highways throughout the realm but also helped to build a sense of interdependent community.

There were three stages to becoming a member of a craft guild. As already noted, Julian's father might have managed to become an *apprentice* in the workshop of a master cloth maker or wool merchant. There he would have performed the most menial tasks, watched the master, copied, practiced, gained expertise. In exchange, he would have been given rough lodging and a meager board. This would have continued for five to nine years, with no earnings. The boy would not have been allowed to marry until he had completed his apprenticeship, delaying any thought of wedlock until his late twenties or even thirties. Craftsmen and merchants regularly postponed marriage until later in life. Next came the stage of *journeyman*, during which time the artisan was finally paid for his work and was permitted to take on the support of a wife. In addition, on his own time, the journeyman labored to produce his "masterpiece," a representative creation that would prove his mastery of the craft. Then he would present the finished work to the guild in the hope of being accepted as a *master*, which was not at all certain. A great deal depended on how well the journeyman was respected by the leading members of the guild, and if he had saved enough money to pay the substantial fees for membership. Finally, if successful, the journeyman was accepted as a master and became entitled to join the guild, pay his dues, set up his own workshop and eventually take on his own apprentices. And so the cycle began again.

Wool and Taxes

Of all the craft guilds, that of cloth making (including wool, cotton, linen, flax, and silk) was by far the largest. There even developed separate guilds for each of the various groups involved in cloth manufacturing: spinners, weavers, fullers (who washed, shrank, and thickened the cloth), and dyers. The most prestigious guild was that of wool merchants who acted as the middlemen between the wool producers, the weavers, and the marketplace. The finest weavers of raw wool were in Flanders, especially Ypres and Ghent, and their own finished cloth-making industry became dependent on consistent supplies of English wool. To satisfy this demand, vast tracts of non-arable English land, and even formerly tilled acreage, were given over to raising sheep and nothing but sheep. Everyone in the realm, it seemed, from the Lake District and Pennines in the north, to the Cotswolds and West Country, across the Southern Downs and into East Anglia, counted personal wealth in terms of numbers of sheep.

By the mid-fourteenth century, King Edward III, married to a Flemish princess, was inviting highly-skilled Flemish weavers to come and settle in East Anglia. Thereafter, more and more Flemish artisans, their lives and business disrupted by the ongoing war with France, migrated to areas of Norfolk and Suffolk, as well as into the West Country, Yorkshire, and Cumberland. The resulting wave of immigration precipitated a massive rise in English *finished* cloth production. Norwich especially, which had enjoyed a steady influx of Flemish weavers since the twelfth century, again benefitted from this new wave of weavers. As demand for English finished cloth grew, more and more of the actual work was moved from the country cottage industry and organized professionally by cloth merchants in large town factories. Cloth making became a thriving metropolitan industry. With the invention of the Jersey spinning wheel around 1350, thread could be spun much more efficiently than by the old distaff process. Eventually, a foot treadle was added that powered the wheel and increased the speed of spinning. This all took place during Julian's lifetime.

The English cloth merchant gained ever-greater power and prestige as overseer of the entire chain of production, from sheep farmer, to factory worker, to final marketplace. And he reaped the concomitant financial rewards. In 1353, in order to maintain control over wool commerce, Parliament issued the Statute of the Staple, designating Yarmouth (the seaport for Norwich) as one of the staple ports, with exclusive rights to export English wool, provided that taxes were collected on every bale. The Mayor of the Staple had sole jurisdiction over the entire wool business, including the regulation of foreign merchants engaged in buying wool and the settling of disputes, debts, and breaches of contract. Through the Statute of the Staple, the state was able to keep a close eye on the collection of taxes for its "crown jewel" of English trade.

With its phenomenal financial growth as the wool and cloth center of England, Norwich felt an increased sense of pride and began to provide its citizens with a more professional and functional government. By the mid-fourteenth century, Norwich became the capital and regional administrative center of Norfolk County, one of the most prosperous and densely populated counties in all of England. A team of local bailiffs formed an official town council that appointed a treasurer, town clerk, and coroners. Norwich had finally gained respectability.

Evaluation

We cannot know for sure whether Julian's grandfather *bought* her father's freedom; whether her father became sufficiently *educated* to work his way up to earn his own freedom; or whether he *escaped* to freedom as a laborer/apprentice in the city of Norwich. Given the limited pathways out of villeiny, one of these storylines must come close. We have established that the primary industry of Norwich was textiles, particularly wool. We have deduced that Julian's text suggests not the elitism of the noble class or the desperation of the peasantry but rather the stability of the middle class. Also, Julian speaks explicitly of textiles in her visions, and she demonstrates an insider's familiarity with detail. Thus it seems to make sense that, living in Norwich and surrounded by the wool trade, she could easily have been a merchant's daughter.

The most convincing scenario is that by the time Julian was born in 1342, her father, then in his mid-to-late forties, was already an established wool merchant and finished cloth manufacturer. As a member of the emerging middle class, he would have prized his individual freedom (hard won as it had been), independent thinking, and the supreme value of being able to read and write as part of his priceless ticket out of poverty. He would have fostered these same values in his children, not only in his son(s), but also in his daughter(s). No one appreciates freedom and education more than the person who has had to break out of a repressive system to acquire them. And no one teaches his children the importance of reading to become self-educated more than the man who has had to learn to do so by dint of personal ingenuity.

3
Childhood

Julian might have grown up during her father's more successful years, living in a two-storied house, most likely in the southeast section of Norwich, called Conisford, near Ber Street, Conisford Gate, and the Royal Conisford highway.[1] This was the preferred area for the building of fine merchant homes, side by side, lining the main north-south artery through the city, though well-removed from the noisy, bustling, overcrowded Mancroft marketplace. Close to a big bend in the River Wensum, the Conisford location would have included a convenient dock, proximity to a storage warehouse (for the loading and unloading of merchandise), and easily accessible river transportation. The highway in front of the house ran through Conisford Ward, right past the Church of St. Julian, where we know Julian would spend the last decades of her life in an attached anchorage. Conisford might well have been Julian's neighborhood throughout the entire course of her life.

Julian's Home

What might her family house have looked like? Most probably it was a sturdily built two-story house made of post-and-beam (half-timbered) construction, with a wood-tiled and steeply raked roof, the upper story jutting out and overhanging the lower. On the ground floor, the house served as a commercial establishment, convenient to street traffic during the day and shuttered tightly at night. Adjacent to the oak entry door of the main house, another door led into the reception area of the shop, where men and women of the gentry could be seated to inspect the finest and most expensive fabrics, and where the merchant could conduct important business. In the rear of the shop, expert spinners, weavers, and tailors, as well as a clerk in a counting room, would have been hard at work from dawn till dusk, six days a week.

Directly behind the shop rose the two-storied great hall, the central living room of the merchant's private dwelling, used for all household dining and entertaining. By the middle of the fourteenth century it would have been heated by a massive stone fireplace with an overhanging hood (painted to look like expensive brick). The roof beams were exposed and blackened with soot, and the walls were whitewashed and covered with woven hangings. The room was furnished with a large cabinet (for storing silver plates, cups, and spoons) and a long wooden trestle table that was folded up after the main midday meal and put away for musical or dancing entertainment. At the side stood a low buffet chest (holding everyday pewter and pottery), along with wooden benches topped with colorful cushions.

On the clay or wooden floor were rushes sprinkled with lavender and fragrant herbs. These were changed often, but not often enough, considering the accumulation of food and pet animal droppings. (In the later fourteenth century, the floors of wealthier merchants' houses would be laid out in a checkerboard pattern with either dark green-brown or yellow glazed tiles, but probably not yet during Julian's childhood.) A high oriel window, protruding outward from the main wall and perhaps glazed with greenish opaque glass let in just enough daylight for the midday meal, while, in addition to standing oil lamps, torches were set in sconces against the walls to illuminate the rainy days and early evenings of winter.

Behind the great hall, at the back of the house, was the kitchen with another large fireplace, where the cook and servants prepared the food. A garbage pit was located off the kitchen area, along with a chicken coop, a pig sty, and a small herb, fruit, and vegetable garden. There was also a vaulted undercroft or basement area, often running the full length of the house, for cold storage of vegetables, a large "buttery" where mead, ale, and imported wines were kept, and a dry pantry for bread, spices, and table linens. Adjacent to the house stood the merchant's warehouse for the storage of raw wool and finished woolen cloth, with quarters directly above for cooks, servants, journeymen, and apprentices.

Off the great hall, a flight of stairs led up to the first-floor gallery. In the front bedroom, built over the shop and entry passage, the children slept in narrow trundle beds alongside their nurse's bed. In the back of the house, directly over the kitchen and away from the noise of the street, was the principal bedchamber. Both bedrooms, with oak floor boarding, were unheated and open to the roof beams. To let in maximum sunlight, they had large windows next to which women could gather and hold conversation while spinning, sewing, and reading aloud to one another. (All windows, whether glazed or not, would be shuttered against cold and inclement weather.) The principal bedchamber held a wooden framed bed crisscrossed with roping that supported one or two feather mattresses covered in canvas, topped with linen sheets, down pillow rolls, woolen blankets, and heavy quilts. The bed was canopied and could be surrounded by curtains for warmth and privacy. This is the very type of bed that Julian would be confined to during her illness and the entire time of her visions.

Principal bedchamber[2]

Iron hooks on the walls held a long bar for hanging garments, and a decorated wooden chest near the bed was used for storing linens, quilts, and additional clothing. One or two benches or backless folding stools, and perhaps a small table for writing, candlesticks, plus a washstand with a pitcher of water and a brass basin completed the furnishings. A *garderobe* for storing clothes was located off the bedrooms; in some houses, it also might contain a toilet alcove set over a chute that led to a pit in the basement, which a servant was required to empty regularly.

Since space was at a premium, each individual home stood flush with its neighbor. Streets in front of even the finest merchant houses were unpaved and deeply rutted, though the main Royal Conisford highway might have been improved somewhat by cobblestones. Even so, when it rained, as it did a great deal in Norwich, the water would run in thick mud puddles between the stones and pour into debris-littered ditches in front of the houses and along the city walls, creating impossible walking conditions for adults and children alike. This was the enclosed world of Julian's childhood.

Stages of Growth

By 1200, the church, as well as English law, recognized distinct stages of growth in children, from infancy (birth until weaning, at about two years), to childhood (two to seven years), stretching into adolescence (seven to fourteen for boys, seven to twelve for girls), thereafter arriving at adulthood. By this time the youth could go to the sacrament of penance, receive the Eucharist, get married, and become a parent. The adolescent was also obligated to pay church tithes, give donations, and fulfill his or her Easter duty. By the age of eighteen, youths could come into their inheritance, administer their business dealings, and govern their own property,[3] as well as be fully prosecuted for crimes.

The years of medieval growing up were short, but no less full of childhood games recognizable in every century. Playing ball, hopscotch, hide-and-seek, riding piggyback, jumping rope, chasing hoops with a stick, playing "follow the leader" or "hoodman blind" (a game of blindman's bluff, putting the child's hood instead of a blindfold over the eyes), juggling, turning somersaults, swinging on ropes, catching butterflies or snatching birds' eggs, see-sawing, spinning tops, blowing soap bubbles, singing nursery rhymes, concocting riddles, dressing up and pretending to be mythical characters and royal princes or princesses... all these were normal childhood activities, perhaps especially in times of upheaval and strife. Children still sang and played games, made up imaginary stories, jousted at mock-tournaments, and danced at make-believe balls, no matter what was happening in the world. For boys, the best game of all was playing at being a knight, riding on a wooden four-wheeled hobbyhorse, pulled along by two other children in harness, while using a long pole to tilt at a brightly colored board or *quintain* (a piece of cloth set on a stick or hanging from a tree to represent the opposing knight). For little girls, pretending to be a mother rocking a baby doll in a cradle, singing lullabies, and reciting nursery rhymes was much preferred. By 1300, various types of toys—like spinning tops, miniature figures of knights in armor, child-sized bows and arrows, soft animals, and stuffed dolls dressed in the latest fashion—were being manufactured for children.[4] Children also kept pet birds and piglets, hens and puppies. Boys trained fighting cocks (roosters) to engage in battle, much to the horror of their little sisters.

In her literate household, Julian would have loved hearing her father read and tell stories to the family gathered in the evening: *Aesop's Fables*, mythical tales about King Arthur and his knights of the round table, poetic romances translated from the French, and the *Lives of the Saints.* The young Julian would have listened attentively in order to soak up every word, image, sensation. And, like the older Julian, she would no doubt have asked many, many questions about the characters and the meanings hidden within the stories. It is arresting to consider that, if neither one of her parents had been able to read, there is little chance that Julian could have developed the skill needed to record her visions for posterity. The love of books was instilled in Julian at an early age—and that made all the difference.

War with France

There was another element that informed Julian's childhood: the long, protracted conflict with France that came to be known as the Hundred Years' War (although it actually lasted even longer, from 1337 to 1453). While the English expeditions took place primarily in France, Brittany, Gascony, and Normandy, the fact of growing up in a country almost continually at war must have been a defining aspect of Julian's psychology. She knew that an invasion of Norwich, despite its stout walls, boom towers, and massive gates, was always a very real possibility. And if, as suggested, her family's house was adjacent to the River Wensum, vulnerable to smaller French boats that might sail in by stealth at night, the danger of surprise attack must have been a source of great trepidation. Julian would live her whole life overshadowed by a war that never ended. A nation continuously at war, even in times of uneasy truce, always feels fear, no matter how successful this year's harvest or wool trading might be.

The seeds of the Hundred Years' War had sprouted in 1337, when King Philip VI of France decided to reclaim the vast and fertile fief of Aquitaine that had long been part of the English king's inheritance.[5] Not to be outdone, in 1338 the new English king, Edward III, countered the French king's claim by proclaiming himself to be not only *still* the Duke of Aquitaine, but actually the rightful king of France, through his French grandfather, King Philip IV. He would have to win this new title by starting a war, which he did in 1340 with a stunning naval battle that decimated the entire French fleet at the Flemish seaport of Sluys.

At first, English enthusiasm soared at the prospect of annexing France and national fervor stood firmly behind the English king. Noblemen, knights, and their attending squires, as well as the non-chivalric Welsh knifemen, Welsh and English yeomen adept at the use of the five- to six-foot longbow, pikemen, and indentured peasant foot soldiers joined horses, crates of arms, arrows, armor, livery, provisions, and caskets of wine that were loaded into ships to set sail in July 1346 for the coast of France. The French chronicler, Froissart, wrote of the English army: "There must have been four thousand men-at-arms and ten thousand archers, without counting the Irish and Welsh who followed his [King Edward's] army on foot."[6] In all, some fifteen thousand soldiers sailed to France for the *chevauchée* (essentially, the medieval "scorched earth" tactic of warfare meant to weaken and wear down the enemy by making a long promenade, or raid, through its territories while burning, looting and killing, thus instilling terror in the enemy).

However, when the English army finally faced the French army at Crécy, it was completely exhausted from the grueling march, its supplies of food, wine, and even shoes seriously depleted.[7] The French army, on the other hand, was fresh, well provisioned on its own soil, and numbered between 35,000 to as high as 100,000, according to different sources. Nevertheless, the English forces under Edward III and his eldest son, Edward, the Black Prince, decimated the superior French force, killing about eleven thousand, including twelve hundred French knights. The new English and Welsh longbow proved worth its weight in gold against the crossbow of the Genoese who were fighting for the French. The English archers literally mowed down the Genoese until the latter ran out of arrows. The Genoese then turned and retreated directly into the oncoming lines of French cavalry that proceeded to ride right over them. In the chaos and confusion, attack after attack by the French forces failed to break the staunch English lines of highly proficient English and Welsh longbowmen, with their unceasing onslaught of arrows piercing through row on row of horse and rider.

Crécy sent shock waves throughout Europe. The battle is considered the turning point in medieval warfare, not only because of the sensational use and effectiveness of the longbow, but also because of the strong showing by English *dis*mounted men-at-arms, fighting hand-to-hand combat.[8] Knights had always looked down (literally) on ground fighting, unless they were unseated accidentally, or their horses disabled. They despised the lowly archer or peasant who fought on his feet with bow or club, which was considered beneath nobility. Now it had been shown, beyond the shadow of a doubt, that ground combatants had superior mobility and could inflict devastating carnage. The one-on-one dueling of knights in shining armor, galloping toward each other on horseback while pointing their long lances, was already becoming obsolete. It was the beginning of the end of the pageantry of warfare.

After Crécy, King Edward laid siege to the prized commercial port of Calais (1346–1347). The ensuing year would prove extremely costly to the English populace. Repeated increases in taxation at home were needed to transport thirty thousand English reinforcements to join the siege, in addition to the commandeering of grain and cattle from English farmers to feed the men-at-arms and the ongoing requisitioning of English merchant ships to carry the army and supplies across the Channel. The disruption to the English wool trade at Calais reduced much-needed tax monies to the crown from English exports and cost the wool merchants, like those in Norwich, dearly. Finally, in August 1347, Calais capitulated (it would remain in English hands until 1558).

A truce was subsequently struck for four years. Knights, squires, pikemen, and archers returned home carrying their loot. The English nation rejoiced. With this new commercial foothold on the Continent, expectations rose that there would be more beneficial trading opportunities for merchants, more work for artisans, and increased prestige for the English crown. The Norwich Benedictine chronicler of the time, Thomas Walsingham, wrote:

> There were few women who did not possess something from Caen, Calais, or other overseas towns, such as clothes, furs, or cushions. Tablecloths and linen were seen in everyone's houses. Married women were decked in the trimmings of French matrons, and if the latter sorrowed over their loss, the former rejoiced in their gain.[9]

4
The Great Pestilence

A new kind of war would soon be fought, one much closer to home—and much more devastating. Julian may never have been able to trace the exact moment when she knew everything in her world was forever different: what kind of a day it was, what she was doing, how it started. All she remembered was that, suddenly, without warning, her childhood was torn apart. The terror blew in from the sea via trading ships, the same kind of merchant ships that carried her father's woolen cloth all over the Continent. It came like a thief in the night, or a dark cloud that settled on their home and never really left. It was the plague, called by many the Great Pestilence, or the Great Mortality. It did not become known as "black" until the sixteenth century, or as the "Black Death" until the early nineteenth century.

Spread of Infection

The disease came in waves, crossing sea and land. Current rumors were that this mysterious and terrifying epidemic had arisen in China in 1346 (and modern medical geneticists confirm this, as well as the fact that it was subsequently carried into Europe across the Silk Roads by Mongolian armies and commercial traders).[1] The plague infected most of Central Asia, then decimated the populations of India, Persia, Mesopotamia, Syria, Egypt, and all of Asia Minor. Pope Clement VI, reigning in his court at Avignon, calculated that the foreign death toll was almost twenty-four million. (This seems like an extravagant number, but it has been supported by modern research indicating that from 1332 to 1357 the plague killed twenty-five million Chinese and other Asians.)[2] No one, not even the pope, expected that it would devastate all of Europe.

In October of 1347, the Great Terror spread westward from the Black Sea port of Caffa (now called Feodosiya) in the Crimea by means of a cargo ship carrying infected Genoese traders back to Messina, Sicily. After being stricken by the plague, Messina closed its harbor to further vessels, so that other contaminated trading ships had to seek alternate ports, thus carrying the disease straight into Genoa and Venice. Thereafter, Italy, with an estimated population of ten to eleven million, possibly endured the heaviest toll in all Europe. Between February and May of 1348, the Great Pestilence cut a swath of death through Rome, Florence, Venice, Genoa, Milan, Naples, Palermo, Pisa, and the hinterlands. In Siena, more than half the population succumbed, and work stopped forever on the great cathedral, anticipated to be the largest in the world.

In January of 1348, the plague invaded France's southern coast through Marseille, was carried westward by ships along the coastal and river trade routes into Languedoc and Spain, and northward via the Rhone to reach Avignon by March. There, Pope Clement VI feared for his life and for the lives of those in his large court, many of whom quickly succumbed to the disease. At the advice of his personal physician, the highly respected Guy de Chauliac, Clement stayed enclosed in his private chamber, with large fires burning day and night even in the heat of summer to ward off the pestilence. He survived, probably because the infected fleas that carried the disease could not withstand the heat of the flames.

During the summer of 1348, the Great Mortality scaled the Alps into Switzerland and reached eastward into the heart of Hungary. It spread its infected arms westward into the area of Bordeaux, Lyon, and Paris, then north into Burgundy and Normandy. Eventually, it flowed up the Rhine into Germany. During the summer of 1348, the Great Terror crossed the Channel on ships sailing to England. According to a contemporary Grey Friars Chronicle, it arrived in Weymouth (then called Melcombe Regis), on the southwestern coast, in June:

> In this year 1348 in Melcombe, in the county of Dorset, a little before the feast of St. John the Baptist [June 24], two ships, one of them from Bristol, came alongside. One of the sailors had brought with him from Gascony the seeds of the terrible pestilence and through him the men of that town of Melcombe were the first in England to be infected.[3]

The weather had been unusually wet that summer, and grain was rotting in the fields, unable to be harvested. People expected severe food shortages. Instead, they were inundated by wave after wave of devastating disease. The effect was worst in the large cities, where overcrowding and the appalling lack of sanitation aided its rapid spread. Sometime early in November the plague reached London, where it is estimated that thirty thousand of the city's approximately sixty to seventy thousand inhabitants perished. The plague finally swept into Norwich in 1349. First it was just a rumor; then overnight, it was a rampage. *Julian was six years old.*

Back on the Continent, throughout 1349, the contagion spread from Paris to Picardy and Flanders. Biologists now believe that a separate strain of plague descended from Norway to infect the Low Countries.[4] It was reported at the time that a ship carrying a cargo of wool and an already dead crew ran aground near Bergen, after having drifted unmanned at sea.[5] Soon after, Sweden, Denmark, Prussia, Iceland, and even Greenland were afflicted by this disease. By mid-1350, it had ravaged most of Europe, though Bohemia was strangely isolated and unaffected. Russia was not affected until 1351.

Symptoms

The mysterious plague that was later termed the Black Death presented itself in three distinct forms: *bubonic*, *pneumonic*, and *septicemic*. The most frequent form in Europe was the first, the bubonic type, carried by rat fleas, a common household and shipboard nuisance, that had themselves become infected from biting diseased rats. The illness attacked the lymph glands, causing black swellings called *buboes*, each the size of an egg or even as large as a clenched fist, in the glands of the neck, armpit, or groin. These swellings oozed blood and pus, after which large boils and black discoloration from internal bleeding appeared. Symptoms also included a high fever (101–105° F), severe headaches, painful joints, nausea, and vomiting. Within eight days of the first symptoms, death occurred in 30 to 75 percent of cases.

As the plague grew rampant, a second pneumonic type appeared, with different symptoms, including an extremely high and continuous fever, severe coughing and sweating, the spitting of blood (rather than the appearance of black buboes), and eventually a bright red and free-flowing sputum. From 90 to 95 percent of victims died within three days or less. This form of plague was quickly spread through the air by coughing, sneezing, or just breathing, by person-to-person contact, much like the common cold. The fact that there were two strains of plague accounted for the high level of contagion and led to the devastating mortality rate. Every aspect of the disease, from the stench of the black buboes and the bloody excrement, to the foul breath and retching of its victims, to the contagious eruptions of blood-tinged sputum, made the plague (and the patient) revolting and terrifying to the onlooker.

Finally, there was septicemic plague, the least common but most deadly form of all, in which the bacteria entered the bloodstream directly, causing high fever and purple skin patches. The mortality rate for this form was almost 100 percent.

The lightning speed of this dreaded disease in its various forms brought severe mental trauma, physical pain, and emotional terror to the patient, as well as to all those attending the dying. There was no known method of prevention and certainly no remedy. No one, however young and healthy, was immune. The suddenness with which death overtook the victim stunned the medieval world. The Italian author, Boccaccio, described it in an eyewitness account:

> What gave the more virulence to this plague, was that, by being communicated from the sick to the hale, it spread daily, like fire when it comes in contact with large masses of combustibles. Nor was it caught only by conversing with, or coming near the sick, but even by touching their clothes, or anything that they had before touched...And indeed, every place was filled with the dead. Hence it became a general practice, as well out of regard to the living as pity for the dead, for the neighbours, assisted by what porters they could meet with, to clear all the houses, and lay the bodies at the doors; and every morning great numbers might be seen brought out in this manner, to be carried away on biers, or tables, two or three at a time; and sometimes it has happened that a wife and her husband, two or three brothers, and a father and son, have been laid on together...What numbers of both sexes, in the prime and vigour of youth...breakfasted in the morning with their living friends, and supped at night with their departed friends in another world![6]

Indeed, some died the very same day the symptoms first appeared; others went to bed seemingly unaffected and died that same night. Doctors attending patients caught the disease and expired even before their patients did, while priests called to deathbeds to administer the last rites of the church, by touching their patients with holy chrism, were themselves afflicted and struck down. Soon there were not enough priests to hear the confessions of dying men and women, and they were left unshriven, a horrifying thought to devout Christians. They faced not only a gruesome physical death but also the possible damnation of their souls. Their relatives (those who managed to survive) were ever after terrified that their loved ones who had died without confessing their sins or receiving the final anointing of the church had been condemned to hell. In January 1349 the lack of priests, monks, and clerics became so dire that Ralph of Shrewsbury, bishop of Bath and Wells, wrote his rectors, vicars, parish priests, and deans in their deaneries that

> either yourselves or through some other person you should at once publicly command and persuade all men, in particular those who are now sick or should fall sick in the future, that, if they are on the point of death and can not secure the services of a priest, then they should make confession to each other, as is permitted in the teaching of the Apostles, whether to a layman or, if no man is present, then *even to a woman.*[7]

Whether these lay men and women were empowered to grant the absolution of sins in Christ's name was not made clear. Still, it was an extraordinary admission on the bishop's part that the church's ability to care for its flock was undergoing a dire crisis. Additionally, the bishop wrote:

> The Sacrament of the Eucharist, when no priest is available, may be administered by a deacon. If, however, there is no priest to administer the Sacrament of Extreme Unction [the last rites of the church], then, as in other matters, faith must suffice.[8]

Pope Clement VI eventually granted the remission of sins to all who had died of plague, since so few could be absolved directly by priests. Extreme times demanded extreme measures. The emotional and psychological impact on anyone who witnessed this horror and survived must have been incalculable. Sorrow and mourning of such magnitude so gripped every city, town, and country that eventually a kind of self-protective emotional atrophy set in. Agnolo di Tura, a chronicler of Siena, noted that fear of the plague overtook every other human feeling:

> Father abandoned child, wife husband, one brother another; for this illness seemed to strike through the breath and sight. And so they died. And none could be found to bury the dead for money or friendship. Members of a household brought their dead to a ditch as best they could, without priest, without divine offices. Nor did the death bell sound. And in many places in Siena great pits were dug and piled deep with the multitude of dead. And they died by the hundreds both day and night, and all were thrown in those ditches and covered over with earth. And as soon as those ditches were filled more were dug. And I, Agnolo di Tura, called the Fat, buried my five children with my own hands. And there were also those who were so sparsely covered with earth that the dogs dragged them forth and devoured many bodies throughout the city. There was no one who wept for any death, for all awaited death. And so many died that all believed that it was the end of the world.[9]

The Plague's Toll

Jean Froissart, one of the most astute chroniclers of both France and England during the fourteenth century, commented sadly that "people died suddenly and at least a third of all the people in the world died then."[10] Froissart's figure has been verified by modern demographers to be much more than a good guess. Over four consecutive years, the death toll in France, Italy, and Germany combined ranged from a high of two-thirds to a low of one-eighth, depending on the area.[11] In the south of France, Spain, and Italy, the death toll may have been as high as 75 percent of the population.[12] The consensus seems to be that out of a pre-plague European population of approximately one hundred million, between twenty-four and twenty-five million people died in this first outbreak: *one quarter* overall.[13]

In England alone, within the space of just two years (1348–1350), it is generally agreed that the disease killed 25 to 35 percent of the total English population.[14] Even assuming a low estimate of that population at 4.2 million, that would mean at least 1.4 million people died.[15] If we accept the more commonly held higher estimate of the pre-plague population to be five to six million, the death toll could have reached as high as two million. Statistics may vary from country to country, but the scope of the suffering remains so horrible that the mind simply cannot grasp its enormity. And this was not the end. During the plague's repeated visitations up to 1400, *it killed half the European population*, more than all the wars fought in the fourteenth century. Devastation on such a massive scale seemed to warrant the biblical term: apocalyptic.

The Plague in Norwich

As we have seen, by the mid-fourteenth century, Norwich was a thriving metropolis, the second largest city in England, with a population estimated at thirteen thousand souls.[16] It was a proud city, "in the most flourishing state she ever saw, and more populous than she hath been ever since."[17] The Great Pestilence swept into Norwich sometime in March 1349, grew to its peak from May to July, and ebbed by autumn.[18] In that short period of time, more than seven thousand people in Norwich are said to have died.[19] Even allowing for medieval hyperbole and the lack of accurate death registers during such a calamity, it is generally agreed by modern scholars that at least *half the population* of Norwich perished from plague, a considerably higher percentage than in the rest of England.[20] The city was not to replenish its population until the end of the sixteenth century. It would never regain its prestige as the second largest and most prosperous city in all of England.[21]

In Norwich, as in every city, death carts were dragged through the streets. Bodies of husbands, wives, and children were thrown onto the carts or merely left on the street during the night to be picked up like refuse in the morning. Everything had to be done in great haste, without dignity or ceremony, as newly infected members of the family cried out for attention. Graveyards filled up so quickly that corpses had to be piled one on top of the other, high over the street level, or thrown into the river Wensum. Eventually mass burial pits were ordered to be dug outside the city, with no indication of names or dates of death. House after house in the city had a red cross painted on its door, warning visitors not to enter for fear of contamination. Thus, to the suffering and terror of such a horrific death was added total isolation in the hour of greatest need.

Local monasteries and nunneries were densely crowded. Consequently, as soon as they were infected, they became death traps for all. Some 44 percent of monks in the twelve most populous monasteries perished.[22] The entire population of the Friary de Domina (Friars of Our Lady), a begging order that lived in a house on the south side of St. Julian's churchyard, died during the Great Pestilence. Sometimes only a single monk would be left to bury the prior and all his fellow monks. For example, in Kilkenny, Ireland, a certain Brother John Clyn of the Friars Minor was all alone among dead men and kept a record:

> And in case things which should be remembered perish with time and vanish from the memory of those who are to come after us, I, seeing so many evils and the whole world, as it were, placed within the grasp of the evil one, being myself as if among the dead, waiting for death to visit me, have put into writing truthfully all the things that I have heard. And, lest the writing should perish with the writer and the work fail with the labourer, I leave parchment to continue this work, if perchance any man survive and any of the race of Adam escape this pestilence and carry on the work which I have begun.[23]

Like his brethren, he soon died, but his words on parchment remain as a testimony that he ever lived at all.

In addition to the high mortality rates for regulars (monks), estimates are that approximately 45 percent of English secular priests succumbed in the parishes.[24] Bishops seem generally to have escaped the same death rate of the lesser clergy, presumably because their episcopal estates were isolated from the rest of the population and the sanitary conditions were somewhat better. Nevertheless, the archbishop of Canterbury, John Stratford, and his two quickly appointed successors died one after the other, all within one year. And if eight hundred beneficed clergy (those receiving church stipends) were recorded as having died in East Anglia alone, then well over sixteen hundred *un*beneficed priests (those not listed in church registers as receiving regular income for the performance of spiritual duties) must also have died.[25] With a loss of over two thousand priests needed to perform the sacraments, the bishops of Norwich and Ely saw their parishes fall into dire straits. New priests had to be ordained with very little preparation. Unfortunately, as a result of the lowering of standards, too many totally unqualified, uneducated, and poorly trained young men were hastily consecrated as priests, men as young as twenty-one years old who could barely read or write, much less stumble through the Latin of the Mass. Their counseling skills were also sorely limited, and the laity suffered from lack of religious support precisely at a time when spiritual guidance was most desperately sought.

Julian's Family

Since we do not know Julian's surname, and there are so few surviving family records dating from this period anyhow, there is no way of verifying how many in her immediate or extended family actually perished. Did the plague carry off several older or younger brothers and sisters? Among wealthy merchant families, the birth rate tended to be higher than among the peasant class, but rarely exceeded twelve.[26] So many children died in infancy or before the age of five that even with multiple births, spaced two years apart, the typical medieval English nuclear family usually consisted of only two or three offspring plus two adults.[27] Given the estimate of the number of deaths that occurred during the plague in Norwich (one out of two or three), we arrive at the appalling realization that probably one-third to one-half of Julian's immediate family could have perished. And this is in addition to grandparents, aunts and uncles, cousins, perhaps a beloved nurse, household servants, and business employees. It remains conjecture, but even to imagine the depth of mourning in Julian's household and extended family is to draw closer to her personal suffering.

For a six-year-old to be suddenly encircled by the stench of death must have been terrifying. Julian would have caught sight of a brother and/or a sister covered in buboes, oozing pus, even though, at some point, she would have been told to leave the bedchamber. Brothers, sisters, perhaps even her father...whoever it was, there were certainly several people infected in her family. She could have awakened at night to hear the racked coughing, the agonized cries, freezing in fear until the end came. For one family member, it might have taken five days or even a week; for another, a mere twenty-four hours. She would have watched as the bodies were carried down the stairs and out the front door, covered in a sheet, the bed linens stripped and washed in scalding water, only to be put back in place for the next victim. *Julian might have been the only child to survive.*

Julian may have wandered alone through the great hall, once the scene of midday dinners, convivial conversation, music, storytelling, and dancing, now eerily silent. She may have tiptoed into and out of the empty upstairs bedchambers, once so full of life, now reeking of death. Upstairs, downstairs, upstairs again she went, perhaps making up stories about her favorite doll being taken ill, developing big lumps in her neck, armpits, and upper legs, turning black, coughing, wretching, crying out, dying, being carried out on a board, wrapped in a white sheet. Julian must have wondered when it would be *her* turn.

She might have heard her mother and father weeping, while offering prayers at their children's bedside, day and night, promising to make a pilgrimage to the nearby shrine of Our Lady of Walsingham, or St. Thomas Becket's tomb at Canterbury; to make donations for Masses to be said; to set aside funds for the building of a chantry chapel; to give more alms to the poor; to pay their back tithes; *anything,* if only their children might be spared. The little girl would have seen candles burning in the bedchamber and torches flaming in the great hall, both early and late, as the children's nurse and various servants came and went, until they were too ill to serve. Julian must have knelt and prayed just as she had seen the grownups do, imitating their words and gestures. She might have tried to remember the strange-sounding words of the *Pater Noster* or the *Ave Maria* that her mother had been teaching her. But she did not understand Latin. The words did not mean anything to her. She needed to talk to God in *English.* At some time during that dark spring and summer of desperation, little Julian must have been branded by a burning fire of suffering. Perhaps deep in her heart she made the connection between suffering and the need to pray. She did not understand it, but she would never forget it. It would return to haunt her years later, as she lay on her own deathbed.

No one would have had the time or energy to stop and explain to the little girl what was happening. Even if they had, no one could. A physician may have come and gone, himself dying the next day. If available, a curate would have arrived to anoint the adult victims, touching their eyes, ears, mouth, hands, and feet with holy chrism, as part of the sacrament of extreme unction. Then the priest left, never to return. If a victim was under the age of seven and sometimes even up to age twelve (for girls) and fourteen (for boys), the priest might withhold hearing their confessions, giving them the Eucharist and even conferring the last rites, since some clerics did not consider minors capable of the full intention necessary for mortal sin or criminal responsibility for their acts, and therefore condemnable to hell.[28] It might have afforded the family more comfort if the young victims had been allowed to make a final confession, receive communion and be anointed, assuring the survivors that their precious ones were in everlasting life.

The door to Julian's house and her father's adjacent shop would have been tightly closed against further contamination, though no one really knew how to ward off the contagion. If people had to go out to buy food or to conduct necessary business, they covered their mouths and noses in handkerchiefs, heavily scented with rosemary, lavender, and other fragrant herbs, or held a cloth to their faces with a "smelling apple" in it (a mix of black pepper, red and white sandalwood, rose petals, and camphor, pressed for a week in rosewater and then shaped with arabic gum into rounds like apples). Norwich citizens were convinced the evil pestilence was carried in the air, so every breath could become fatal. Streets were barred to all but those who lived there. A red cross might have been painted on Julian's own front door, as a warning to others to stay away.

Meanwhile, news continued to arrive of relatives and close friends and their children having died and been quickly carted to a churchyard. No one had time to say goodbye. Throughout Norwich, the list of names of the deceased grew longer . . . a nobleman, a neighbor's wife, a weaver, a shopkeeper, a fishmonger, another parish priest. No family, highborn or low, escaped the fury of the raging pestilence. Over and over again, Julian might have asked her mother if she could play with one of her friends, even after she had been told that the child was dead. She just could not comprehend what was happening—or that death was permanent.

Yersinia pestis

No parent could have imagined that the pestilent rat fleas were nesting *within* the house, in the very rushes and herbs beneath their feet, on the floor of the great hall, in the bedchambers, breeding on the pet pig, the geese, the chickens. (The cause of the plague, a bacillus not discovered until the late nineteenth century and named *Pasteurella pestis*, was renamed *Yersinia pestis* in 1967.) One by one, the animals also succumbed and had to be burned. There was no one left to prepare food in the kitchen; the servants' quarters grew silent. Soon, it was deafeningly quiet everywhere. The streets of Norwich seemed empty, except for the sound of the death carts at night, rumbling along on the Royal Conisford highway. Julian lay alone in her bed and recognized the sound of death.

How did Julian and her mother manage *not* to get infected? (There was slim hope of becoming infected and then recovering.) There is no telling. No explanation. Surviving records show that the eldest members of the population (over sixty) had a mortality rate of almost 40 percent, while those between fifty-six and sixty suffered the greatest incidence of mortality at 46 percent. On the other hand, those in the prime of life (from twenty-one to the mid-thirties in age) had significantly less mortality (approximately 20 to 28 percent). Amazingly, children, at least *some* children, had the least mortality. Only 7 percent of youths died in the six- to ten-year-old range, jumping to 15 percent in the eleven- to fifteen-year-old range.[29] Julian's youth and her mother's prime of life may have had a great deal to do with their survival.

We know her mother survived because, according to Julian's written account, she stood at the bedside, twenty-four years later, when Julian received her visions. Her mother must have deemed it a miracle that any of her family members remained. Some families were totally wiped out, parents as well as children. But survival also entailed carrying the burden of such a loss, being tortured by shocking memories of seeing so much pain and living in constant fear of its return.

Trauma and Guilt

A childhood trauma of this proportion, like the memory of being imprisoned in a concentration camp, repeatedly bombed in wartime, buried in an earthquake, barely surviving a fire or terrible accident, inflicts a deep wound that never completely heals. It may grow scar tissue, but the least reminder causes it to burst open again, the pus and pain of memory pouring out. It is a different kind of pestilence, this memory, a kind of living death. And for a child, it has untold consequences. Even as a six-year-old, Julian must have asked why a good and all-powerful God would allow this terrible disaster to descend upon her family and friends. What had they done to deserve this? Had all this horror and pain really been inflicted by the wrath of God, as the preachers insisted? Or was there some other reason why human beings suffer? These questions would continue to haunt Julian all her life. She would have to wait a long time for some light to filter through her darkness.

Over the ensuing months and years, Julian might also have harbored a deep guilt for surviving, when all those others did not. Why did God take them and not her? If she did something bad, would God strike her down, too? A child rarely thinks in any terms but black and white, pleasure or pain, punishment or reward. She would have determined more than ever to be a good girl and not get into any trouble. Indeed, if anything could have given the impetus to Julian to please her mother as best she could and never cause her any upset, helping her in every way with all the additional work in the household for lack of servants, being obedient and praying to God every day with all her heart, surviving the plague would have been it.

Survival

Meanwhile, Julian's father (if he was still alive) and her mother had to pull together more strongly than ever in order to go on once the tidal wave of death had abated. They would never be the same family, but they would learn to cope by accomplishing every day's chores, saying every day's prayers, completing every day's reading, work, and study. Julian would have been compelled to try to fill the shoes of whichever sibling(s) had died, to "make up" in some way to her parents, for the child or children lost (which, of course, she could never do). She might even have become the one her father now counted on, instead of an older brother or sister, to assist him in the cloth business, thus taking on adult responsibilities.

But who could help Julian survive the loneliness, the nightmares, the terrible fears of death that would not go away? Julian needed someone to lean on for strength and comfort. Someone she could be absolutely *seker* would take care of her and her family. A tragedy like this might have been the very catalyst for Julian learning how to pray in her own words and throwing herself into the care of the Lord. Perhaps, when she went to Mass with her mother, she looked up at the large rood (cross) hanging over the entrance to the chancel, mesmerized by the body of the crucified man on it, painfully graphic (according to fourteenth-century iconography), wearing a crown of thorns and with blood flowing down his face, his entire body bearing the marks of the whip. Maybe as she gazed she wondered: He suffered just like my family members suffered. Is that what it means to die for someone else?

Julian may have also accompanied her parents to church in the evening to pray the Office of the Dead, recited at Vespers. Everyone, it seemed, men and women alike, attended church more regularly now. They had all lost someone. Death was all the grownups talked about, in the churchyard, the marketplace, the streets. Life expectancy was short at best in the Middle Ages, and the fear of death had always been high; the plague magnified that fear a thousandfold. Daily life became even more morbid, a constant waiting for the sword of death to strike. There was a marked increase in pilgrimages to saints' tombs, days of fasting and penance, attendance at Mass, promises made to patron saints and town protectors. People prayed intensely for their deceased relatives and friends, even if they had confessed and received absolution of their sins before dying. Christians believed that the prayers of the faithful on earth could shorten the punishments of souls in purgatory.

Yet, for others, the sheer devastation and mental horror led to an even greater indulgence in violence and sexual license. Many men became cynical opportunists or went mad with despair. They lashed out at their fellow human beings. Murders, robbery, and every kind of attack on property and persons greatly increased. In the biblical Apocalypse, when the Evangelist describes the plague that kills one-third of mankind (Rv 9:15), he envisions that:

> The rest of humankind, who were not killed by these plagues, did not repent of the works of their hands or give up worshiping demons and idols of gold and silver and bronze and stone and wood, which cannot see or hear or walk. And they did not repent of their murders or their sorceries or their fornication or their thefts. (Rv 9:20–21)

So it was throughout Europe in the mid-fourteenth century. Some embraced religion with renewed fervor; others chose their earthly hells. It was a time of great extremes between strongest faith and darkest cynicism.

Seeking Explanations

While religious leaders blamed the deadly pestilence on the "wrath of God" (either as a punishment on all mankind for its sins or as a purification process to which all had to submit), medieval physicians believed in an ancient theory of bodily humors that controlled all human moods and endemic illness.[30] When imbalances develop in one of the four basic fluids (blood, choler, yellow or black bile, or phlegm), sickness inevitably occurs. As for *epidemics*, medical men tended to attribute them to sudden warm and moist weather patterns which putrified the air, causing a deadly *miasma* that infected the patient. Astrologers at the University of Paris linked the onset of plague to waves of just such polluted air and bad smells, caused entirely by the alignment of the planets more than three and a half years earlier, at precisely one o'clock on March 20, 1345. The medical community advised the burning of dry woods like juniper, ash, vines, rosemary, aloes, musk, laurel, and cypress to ward off contagion. Sweet-smelling plants were to be placed around the rooms, and the floors regularly doused with rosewater, and vinegar. Better still, if one could afford an amber stone, holding it might afford protection.[31] Sometimes potions of apples, lemons, rosewater, and peppermint infused with powders of precious metals like gold and quicksilver were prescribed,[32] enough to poison even a healthy patient. Bloodletting, the usual medical method of first resort, was highly recommended, as was breathing in the putrid smell of latrines, so that bad odors might eradicate bad air. Sex was to be avoided, since it created heat and disequilibrium in the body. Sadness was also to be shunned, even lamenting the deaths of loved ones, since melancholy generally cooled and depressed the intelligence.[33] Remedies were bizarre, but doctors had no cure. Guy de Chauliac had to admit:

> The plague was shameful for the physicians, who could give no help at all, especially as, out of fear of infection, they hesitated to visit the sick. Even if they did, they achieved nothing, and earned no fees, for all those who caught the plague died, except for a few towards the end of the epidemic who escaped after the buboes had ripened.[34]

It seemed there was no escaping an avenging God, the fetid air, or the alignment of the planets. The sense of futility felt by clergymen, physicians, scientists, and common folk alike must have been overwhelming. People died, no matter what anyone did or did not do.

Social Upheaval

Even as the upper classes were succumbing to the pestilence, in spite of medical advice, lower class serfs continued to die in the fields where they worked, or in the squalor in which they lived, unattended. Those who survived sank into deep depression, a resignation that the grim reaper would soon come for them, too. Sheep, goats, pigs, chickens, cattle and oxen, dogs and cats roamed wild, until they also fell dead in their tracks with the disease. Henry of Knighton, an Austin canon at the Abbey of St. Mary's of the Meadows in Leicester, a keen chronicler of the times, wrote:

> For want of watching many animals died in uncountable numbers in the fields and in bye-ways and in hedges throughout the whole country; for there was so great a shortage of servants and labourers that there was no one who knew what needed to be done.[35]

The devastation to prized English flocks of sheep and the subsequent effect on the kingdom's lucrative wool and cloth industry (and no doubt, on Julian's family income) was catastrophic. Wheat and barley corn were also in short supply. Inasmuch as all of England barely survived from harvest to harvest, the sudden scarcity of villeins and free laborers threatened the entire social structure. Lords and landowners, hit hard by the sharp cut in their peasant labor force, watched their fields go untilled and unplanted, their crops left unharvested, their cattle and sheep population decimated. The lack of farm workers became so critical that in Norwich wool weavers were forced to leave their highly skilled occupation to take up scythes and gather in the harvest, lest the entire city face starvation.

Meanwhile, those serfs who had managed to survive seized the opportunity to greatly improve their status. They demanded inflationary wages and even their freedom, a phenomenon previously considered unthinkable. Lords of the manor, both religious and secular, either had to acquiesce or see their serfs pick up and migrate to another area, where rates of pay were more generous. Prices for agricultural products and basic goods doubled overnight. The very fabric of medieval allegiance toward overlord and land, family and town, was torn apart by the strain of the plague. City merchants, too, lost almost half their skilled and unskilled labor force. Those who were left and able to work could name their price. Cheap labor became harder and harder to come by. As city wages rose, so did inflated prices for all kinds of manufactured goods. With rising fury, the landlords and merchants pressured Parliament to act. As early as June of 1349, Parliament issued the Ordinance of Labourers in an attempt to fix the skyrocketing wages. These new laws demanded that everyone under the age of sixty was required to work, that all wages had to return to what they had been *pre*-plague, that no employer could lure away servants from another household with the promise of higher wages, and that agricultural products were to be affordably and reasonably priced. The law was basically unenforceable, and inflation of both wages and prices continued.

In spite of the Ordinance of Labourers, there was no turning back the clock. Peasants and skilled workers increasingly became emboldened, moving from place to place to find work wherever they could get the best wages. Suddenly, mere villeins, long considered the scum of the earth, discovered their leveraging power. The entire social structure rumbled from its peasant base to its lordly heights. Peasant living standards rose so dramatically that villeins could now dress and eat and live more like skilled artisans in the cities, even like the local squires who served the knights. Landowners, desperate for field hands, offered food, drink, and many additional benefits (including new clothing) to lure laborers back to the farms. But it was not enough. Over a period of time, large tracts of land that had been cleared of trees and brush and successfully farmed for generations either returned to wilderness or were given over to the less labor-intensive pasturing of sheep. In addition, with the drastic fall in population, landowners no longer received the rentals and tithes from the peasants who formerly occupied their estates. Many landowners fell behind in paying their land taxes to the crown, thus being forced to sell or lease their lands at bargain rates to the industrious merchant class.

Then, in 1351, a new Statute of Labourers was passed to reinforce price controls, which were still skyrocketing, and again firmly fix wages at the pre-plague level, as well as to make any form of collective bargaining illegal. Attempts to form labor unions were forcibly stopped, and many workers migrating off the land against the new laws were caught, imprisoned, and fined. But this statute, too, was no bulwark against the rising tide of the English laboring class that found itself in a new and powerful bargaining position. Farm workers as well as all manner of skilled and unskilled laborers would continue to experience decades of increased prosperity, while the nobility and gentry would suffer grave losses to their cultivated lands and personal income. Therefore, even after the acute phase of the outbreak had passed, the effects of the Great Pestilence were felt not only in the loss of population but also in the political and social upheavals that occurred in English society itself. Even though the feudal structure remained fairly stable for some time to come, and the short-term prosperity for those who had survived the plague did not last, a window of opportunity had been opened: the heady air of individual freedom had been deeply inhaled. The peasant underclass would never forget.

5
Education

War or no war, pestilence or prosperity, parents had to educate the next generation. Basic literacy for daughters as well as for sons was much esteemed among fourteenth-century English merchants, not only to enable their children to help out in the family business and to make them more marriage-worthy but also to add to the family's pride and civic status. The successful merchant was especially eager to prove himself as good as any "gentleman to the manor born," who could afford to give all his children some education. Indeed, Julian's father must have been a major force in her life, a continuing example of the importance of setting goals and then working hard to achieve them. It might have been he who, very early, gave her the much-needed encouragement to commit to a life of reading, writing, and eventual theological study, at a time when both Latin grammar schools and university doors were tightly shut to women.

As the acute crisis of the plague abated in Norwich, surviving boys and girls around the age of seven returned either to the parish or the urban day-schools, sitting side by side on hard wooden benches. Julian might well have attended a parish school, taught by a local cleric, or a city school, headed by a master hired to tutor children of the middle class. Elementary students would learn to recognize the alphabet, read combinations of words in the English vernacular, sing hymns, and recite the basic three prayers—the *Credo, Pater Noster,* and *Ave Maria*—aloud in Latin. (Very few people ever read prayers or books silently; all reading was done in a low voice.) They would also receive a formulaic teaching on the tenets of the Catholic faith, using a simple catechism. They might also be taught to recognize numbers and do a little arithmetic. Julian makes a pointed reference, in her Long Text, to this learning period of her childhood. She uses the alphabet as a metaphor for the contemplative teachings she received over the years:

> ...I have teaching within me, as it were the beginning of an A.B.C., whereby I may have some understanding of our Lord's meaning. (51:28–30.285)

Learning to Observe

Additionally, if we place Julian's father in the textile business, this would suggest how Julian developed her keen "eye" for the details of color, shape, and texture in everything she records from her visions. Her visual skills had clearly been developed beyond the ordinary, long before her visionary experiences occurred. Such observation and retention ability does not develop overnight. Even as a little girl, Julian would have watched the techniques of spinners, dyers, and weavers (both men and women), as well as tailors (male only), laboring in her father's workshop. She would have followed the elaborate process of turning raw wool into woven cloth with a child's fascination and pride that this was the family business. As she grew older, Julian's mother would have taught her daughter how to card the wool,[1] spin it, and then weave it, as well as how to cut and sew the finished fabric to make her own clothing. Julian would have developed the ability to follow directions and remember a great many intricate steps to complete her work, and she would have acquired the awareness of color and texture and style that comes of being around finely wrought gowns and mantles, in richly dyed materials of red and blue and green and gold, as well as elaborately embroidered silks and velvets for the very wealthy. Through this training process, Julian would have developed an artist's eye, an able spinster's hand, a weaver's skill, and patience. This would explain her careful analysis of the symbolic value of clothing in the parable of the lord and the servant, in which she sees different fabrics as metaphors for human and divine qualities.

Julian's mother may have worked with the other women (as many middle-class women did) in her husband's shop, carding, spinning, weaving, and sewing, as well as tending to customers. It was generally permitted by the craft and merchant guilds for masters to teach their crafts to their children and wives. Then, if the master died, his wife could continue the practice of the craft and even retain her husband's apprentices. A woman was entitled to teach her own children, plus "the children of her husband" (i.e., her stepchildren), and "her brothers born of legal marriage."[2]

Women spinning, carding, dyeing, and weaving wool[3]

Adolescence

By the age of twelve, as puberty approached, boys would progress to the higher grammar school to study Latin grammar, rhetoric, and dialectic; but girls as young as ten years old would be strictly segregated and kept at home to learn the womanly arts of household management. This would include being responsible for younger siblings; planning, shopping for, and helping in the preparation of meals; setting a table; decorating the house for holidays; and instructing the maidservants. Girls also needed to apply their newly acquired reading, writing, and arithmetic skills to the task of assisting their mothers in business matters. While wives and daughters of the well-off merchant class, as against those of the laboring classes, did not have the financial need to ply a trade, they were urged by preachers to learn how to keep household accounts as well as to write, not for its own sake, but so that they could correspond with their fathers, brothers, and later, their husbands, who would often be abroad on business. English wives tended to know much more about their husbands' financial affairs than wives on the Continent, even to the extent of being able to take over the business contracts and manage the day-to-day dealings, should their husbands die.[4]

Indeed, medieval crafts and trades were valued areas where girls and women could exercise their skills even beyond those of household management. In the larger townships and cities, women could apprentice and learn a craft over many years just like men and, if they had the financial means to do so, pay to join one of the craft guilds open to women. If a woman became a guild member, bought or inherited property, or was married to a town citizen, she automatically became a "free citizen" herself. As such, a woman had the right to engage in commerce in the marketplace. Middle-class women could become tailors, carpenters, saddlers, and spurriers (makers of spurs). Many women became midwives, even barbers (in this capacity they sometimes acted illegally as "barber-surgeons," setting bones and stitching up wounds). Women functioned as bakers, brewers of ale, tavern-keepers, cloth dyers, and seamstresses, weavers of wool and silk. The dressmaking and lace-making guilds were made up of only women.

All told, women made an indispensable contribution to the life of medieval towns and cities. Even though, by right of primogeniture, eldest sons inherited their fathers' business and lands, daughters and younger sons were given the same rights of free citizenship. If there was no son, a daughter could inherit her father's or mother's properties and commercial shop, as well as farmlands bordering the town.[5] Thus it was in the fields of crafts and commerce that women, while never achieving social or political parity with men, were able to prove their financial worth. The laboring townswoman was, at least, a step up from the hard lot of her indentured ancestor and counterpart, the peasant woman who toiled with her husband (without wages) for the lord of the manor.

Yet no matter how intelligent, capable, and determined, or how well she could read and write, no female, whether of the noble or merchant class, could ever hope to be elected a member of the municipal council, hold any kind of public office, or be sent as a representative to Parliament. She could not train as a clerk or notary. No city woman was allowed even to attend an urban assembly, unlike some widows and spinsters in the villages who took part in rural assemblies.[6] Neither could a townswoman, however gifted, study to become a physician, lawyer, or judge.

Prymers

With her mother's help, Julian would have progressed in her reading skills by praying the psalms, morning and evening, from *The Prymer or Lay Folks' Prayer Book*.[7] This little manuscript, in common use during the fourteenth century, was usually in Latin, but sometimes Middle English, making it accessible to those who could not understand church Latin.[8] The *Prymers* were copied and translated from the Latin Breviary and Manual, which was recited daily by monks and priests. Even children as young as seven years old recited "our lady's matins and hours."[9]

In addition to the Hours of the Blessed Virgin Mary, the *Prymer* included the seven penitential psalms, the fifteen gradual psalms, the litany of the saints, the office for the dead, including Vespers, with additional psalms called "commendations." Some *Prymers* also contained Psalms 22–31, which were considered prophecies of Christ's passion. Occasionally, there were personal handwritten prayers and invocations inserted by the owner. Based on the number that survive, and the frequency of bequests of *Prymers* in wills, there must have been hundreds, if not thousands, available in scribal copies. (The earliest surviving full text of a *Prymer* dates from 1381, during Julian's lifetime.) Indeed, it is most likely that Julian acquired a great deal of her vernacular spelling and vocabulary from this familiar little book of psalms and prayers. Most of the *Prymers* had illuminations, ranging from pictures of the annunciation to the interior of a church where lay folk are singing the office for the dead. The commendations are preceded by a painting of a graveyard, with the graves open and the souls of the dead "being carried up in a large white cloth to the Almighty, who is depicted above."[10]

Lay Folks' Mass Book

On Sundays and feast days, Julian would have attended Mass, following along in the vernacular *Lay Folks' Mass Book*.

The worthiest thing, the most of goodness
In all this world, is the Mass...
When the priest speaks, or if he sings,
To him thou give good hearkening.
When the priest prays in private
Time of prayer then is to thee.[11]

The *Mass Book* did not translate or paraphrase the actual words of the Mass, but gave a running commentary on what the priest was doing at the altar. It also instructed the *lewed* folk when to mark themselves with the sign of the cross or lift up their hands, when to kneel or stand, when to join in the *Confiteor* (I Confess), or say the *Pater Noster* repeatedly, when to remain silent and listen attentively to the gospel (even though it was read in Latin), and when to recite the *Credo* in the vernacular. Following the Creed, the faithful were to go up to the front of the nave and offer a Mass penny to the priest, remembering the gold, frankincense, and myrrh offered by the three kings. And when the priest had prepared the bread and wine, he would turn to the congregation to ask for their prayers. At this point, the people were to beat their breasts, praying that the Holy Ghost might descend and rule the heart of the priest. While the celebrant washed his hands and begged to be made worthy to consecrate, all knelt and raised their hands and implored God to accept the offerings of both priest and congregation, to aid the living and the dead. Then the celebrant began the Preface to the Canon, the *secreta* part of the Mass, which he did not recite aloud, but under his breath. During this, and through the consecration, the people were to pray silently:

In world of worlds without ending
Thanked be Jesus, my king,
All my heart I give it thee
Right and just that it be so
With all my will I worship thee
Jesus, blessed may thou be...
Sweet Jesus, grant me now this
That I may come unto thy bliss
There with angels for to sing
This sweet song of thy loving:
Sanctus, Sanctus, Sanctus.[12]

After the *Sanctus* came prayers of intercession for all the estates of mankind, thanksgiving for gifts and talents, a healthy mind and safety in times of great peril, as well as a solemn request for the forgiveness of sins and for the grace always to do God's will, followed by petitions for the church, the pope, bishops, priests and clerks, for the safety of the king and queen and all the nobles. Prayers were also offered for friends, tenants, servants, old men, children, women, merchants, craftsmen, rich and poor alike, as well as for all living in sin or sorrow, the sick, those at sea, the banished, and the dispossessed. At the ringing of the bell, "Then is the time near of sacryinge," the consecration of the bread and wine. Worshipers were to kneel and hold up their hands, acknowledging the elevation of the host and the chalice with great devotion, praying the *Pater Noster*, *Ave Maria*, and *Credo* again, as well as their own private prayers of praise to Jesus Christ who shed his blood on the cross, died, and rose for their salvation. Prayers were recommended at this point for the souls of all the faithful departed, especially fathers and mothers, brothers and sisters in purgatory, that they might be remembered in the Mass and be released from their sufferings into eternal glory.

When the priest himself recited the *Pater Noster* aloud, the congregation joined in for the final petition: *sed libera nos a malo* [but deliver us from evil]. *Amen*. At the consecration bell, the faithful would rush up to the chancel screen, hoping to catch a glimpse of the host lifted high at the altar which, in a large church or cathedral, was almost invisible in the distance. Except at Easter, the reception of the Eucharist by the laity was not common or, at times, even permitted. Instead, the priest on the high altar kissed a *pax-brede*, which was, literally, a "peace board" made of wood, metal, ivory, glass, or, in wealthier parishes, gold or silver, encrusted with jewels. On it, the figure of Christ the Savior was either painted or engraved on a plate of copper and set in a frame, with a handle behind the board so that a deacon could hold it in front of the congregation. Everyone knelt and touched or kissed the pax board to signify a common bond of charity within the community. Each person was to recollect that one cannot be at peace unless one is in charity and charity is threefold: first it is the love of God, then the love of oneself, then the love of one's neighbor. During this time, the priest alone received the Eucharist under both species of bread and wine, and rinsed the chalice. Then final prayers were said for all who had been at the Mass, that they might be protected against any dangers during the day, and that if death were to come suddenly, the Mass itself would take the place of receiving a final absolution of sins and the sacred *viaticum* (holy communion). The faithful were instructed to kneel again and keep saying the *Pater Noster* until the Mass was ended. Afterward, came a final prayer:

> God be thanked for all his werks,
> God be thanked for priests and clerks,
> God be thanked for each a-man,
> And I thank God all I can;
> I thank God for his goodness
> And specially now for this mass
> And for all the prayers that here are prayed
> I pray to God that he be paid.
> In mind of God here I me bless [making the sign of the cross]
> With my blessing God send me his.[13]

Reading the *Lay Folks' Mass Book* enabled Julian to learn the sequence and understand the symbolism of the liturgy, as well as to develop a sense of wonder and reverence for the Holy Sacrifice. With its gentle rhymes and devotional guidelines, the *Mass Book*, like the *Prymer*, must also have helped Julian learn to pray. In this way, early literacy became a prime factor in Julian's spiritual growth.

Home Schooling

Julian's mother (assuming she was literate and had the leisure to do so) could have continued her daughter's schooling entirely at home. Alternately, a local cleric may have been hired as a private tutor, instructing Julian in the Ten Commandments, the order and meaning of the seven sacraments, the seven deadly sins, the seven virtues, along with the basic tenets of the faith, as stated in the *Credo*. Julian's mother would have seen to it that Julian recited her Latin prayers over and over again, until she knew them by heart. Julian also learned how to observe the fasting laws of the church, to say grace before and after meals, and to give food to beggars who came to the door. By twelve or thirteen, according to custom, she would have made her first confession of sins to a priest and received her first Eucharist at Easter. And if she had not already been confirmed at her baptism, or in the year following, she would have received the sacrament of confirmation at about the same time. It all depended on the availability and willingness of the residing bishop, for only he could administer confirmation.

Another source of learning for Julian might have been a strong mentor in her own family: an older nephew or cousin who had survived the plague and was already well advanced in grammar school. Julian might have begged him to recite his Latin conjugations, or copy out strange and mystifying sentences from the *Ars grammatica* of Donatus, the fourth-century teacher of St. Jerome. How fascinated she would have been by the dancing shapes and different sounds of the written words. A girl of Julian's later literary skill would have begun early to love language and its rhythms, to appreciate the nuances of meaning, the intonations of the voice, and to wonder at how scribbles with a stylus across a page of parchment can convey such tantalizing ideas.

If one of her close relatives happened to be a decade or so older than she, he might have been preparing for the priesthood at one of four colleges of secular priests located in Norwich: the Carnary College, the college of chantry priests in the bishop's palace, St. Giles's Hospital, or the college of St. Mary in the Fields. Alternatively, a cousin or friend of the family might have been a scholar at Oxford or Cambridge University, studying advanced theology and canon law. Either of these scenarios being the case, Julian would have had a first-hand resource for gathering knowledge of theological and moral topics. Whenever such a cleric came to visit, or returned to Norwich from the university, she would have questioned him about the scholarly texts he was studying. She might have begged him to translate and interpret a gospel story for her, or an epistle of St. Paul or St. John, savoring the words and later writing them down from memory. She also would have listened to the heated arguments in her household between scholars and businessmen discussing the resurgent neo-Platonic ideas of Greek and Latin writers, as well as the writings of the church fathers, from Origen to St. Augustine. No doubt she would have sat transfixed as they argued over scriptural interpretation or a point of Trinitarian theology, using the highly ordered scholastic method of *quaestio* (question and answer). Julian would have relished their heated debates as intellectual and spiritual nourishment for her hungry soul.

Reading Groups

As Julian grew older, she would most certainly have joined a women's reading group, alongside her mother. These highly valued opportunities for female companionship proliferated in the fourteenth century, especially among the wives and daughters of well-off craftsmen and merchants, who were not obligated to work full time in their husband's or father's shop. These women could afford the leisure time to listen to each other read popular romances like *Guy of Warwick* or *Floris and Blancheflour* (translated from the French); mythical stories of *Arthur and Merlin, Sir Tristrem*, and *Sir Orfeo*; scholarly works like *The Seven Sages of Rome* or *The Sayings of the Four Philosophers*; histories of Alexander the Great or Richard the Lionheart; and numerous collections of lyrical love poetry. These would have been available in parchment compendiums,[14] a single copy passed around in a circle, read by one woman after another, as the other women carded wool and spun it into thread by the hour.

Julian might also have grown up hearing tracts on mystical prayer, like *The Cloud of Unknowing*, or how to deal with moral and spiritual dangers, like William Flete's *Remedies Against Temptation* (written in Latin but translated, sometime in the second half of the fourteenth century, for those pursuing a devout spiritual life). Julian would also have heard her mother recount Bible stories from both the Old and New Testaments, told and retold from memory, as well as paraphrased by the preacher from the pulpit on any given Sunday. In addition, merchant families had excellent connections for borrowing books from one another and importing books from abroad, as well as the financial means to commission scribes to make copies of new and greatly desired works. A burgher prided himself on the number and quality of the books in his personal library. In fact, the books he was able to bequeath to his family in his last will and testament were a witness to a successful life, as well as a devout one.

We cannot know the exact scenario, of course, and which relatives inspired Julian to listen attentively, to read, to write, and to dare to think for herself. Given Julian's later vernacular literacy and her extraordinary grasp of complex theological concepts, we may assume that the seeds for these flowerings must have been planted in and around her parental home. If we posit at least one parent's literacy, we can assume the common practice of reading aloud to the family.

If we place Julian's family in the prosperous merchant middle class, we can explain her early access to and love of books. If we suggest that Julian, like many of her age, sought companionship in women's reading groups, we can imagine how she became a well-read young woman of her time. And when we come to examine the probing mind of Julian at work in her own book, then we may surmise that the habit of asking questions and seeking answers must have been developed in lively discussions with those who had received a Latin education.

Also, by placing Julian's family in the world of commercial and trading connections, we can be assured that there was a constant stream of business associates visiting from the Low Countries, even from Spain and Italy. Besides much-valued goods, these businessmen would have brought news of the Continent and its religious debates. They would have argued about the writings of the controversial Rhineland mystics: Meister Eckhart (1260–c.1327), Johannes Tauler (c.1300–1361), and Heinrich Suso (1295–1366). Theological and philosophical topics would have been discussed at dinnertime as heatedly as the economic situation, the progress of the war with France, and discussions of scientific experiments coming out of Italy. Putting the various pieces together like a puzzle, we can begin to envision Julian's home as a place where contemporary ideas flowed as freely as good ale and wine over dinner. Julian may have been expected "to be seen and not heard" (a warning that was originally applied to women, not children), but there is no doubt that her mind was being stimulated by ideas and trained in logic and debate within her own household, long before she received her visions and sought answers from the Lord himself.

Julian's father (if still alive) might have noticed his daughter's curiosity and grasp of difficult ideas, as well as her inordinate love of books. Even if he had been grooming his eldest son for eventual inheritance of his wool and cloth business, he might well have taken an interest in Julian's questioning mind as well. Likewise, Julian may have learned from observation that a daughter who reads and writes and asks intelligent questions could be (almost) as interesting, and even useful, to a father as a son. However, since girls were not taught Latin, Julian knew that, no matter how much she listened and learned in English, she would always be considered *lewed* and *unlettered*.

Womanly Arts

As Julian grew in age, her mother would have taught her to eat and drink only in moderation, not to use body lotions, nor to color her face with cosmetics, nor to indulge in fashionable clothing (or any other form of vanity), lest she fall into serious sin. Julian would also have been cautioned not to yawn too wide, nor laugh too loudly, to pay her tithes, give to the poor and bedridden, "bid her beads" during Mass,[15] and not *jangle* (chatter or argue) or gossip with her friends in church. She was never to scorn her elders, swear or get drunk, toss her head or shake her shoulders seductively when she walked, nor was she ever to allow any man to be so bold as to take her hand or kiss her cheek in public.

To preserve her reputation, Julian was warned never to attend wrestling matches or cockfights, never to be seen entering a tavern, and never to answer a man's question on the street or talk to strangers, lest she seem to be flirting or associating with bad company. When going out, even to market, she was always to be accompanied by a relative or female friend, for her own safety. And if a man were to woo her properly, with the intent of marriage, she would have been admonished never to scorn him, whoever he might be; but she was also never to sit or stand by him, lest proximity become an occasion of sin. Modesty, chastity, and obedience were highly prized virtues for a well-brought-up maiden, and Julian's mother would have gone to great lengths to protect her daughter's reputation, with an eye to making a good marital contract.

The church taught that daughters especially needed constant supervision, since their weakness of mind and penchant for frivolity would lead them into being easily seduced. In fact, Philippe de Novare was vehemently opposed to allowing girls to learn to read and write at all (except for novices in religious houses), because pubescent girls would only correspond with lovers and thus be led into sin. He even advised that daughters of the nobility and wealthy merchants should be taught to spin and weave in order to keep them from the idleness which would inevitably lead them into sinful behavior and also that they might appreciate the manual labor of poorer folk. The opposite viewpoint was voiced by Vincent de Beauvais, who argued that girls who learned to read and write would be able to keep their minds (as well as their hands) busy, and thus drive out sinful or foolish thoughts. He even believed that literacy could help noble daughters manage their estates and merchant daughters their household accounts, as we have discussed.

Nonetheless, no didactic writer or preacher *ever* suggested that girls be allowed to attend grammar school so as to learn Latin and the arts of rhetoric and logic side by side with boys. It was not even imagined that girls could be taught the *trivium* (Latin grammar, rhetoric, and dialetics) in a separate schoolroom from the boys. Nor could merchant daughters enter the business training school for merchant sons, or the daughters of lawyers ever hope to attend law school. That would have been unthinkable. At the level of higher education, the academic universities could not allow a young woman in their midst, as this would have posed grave temptation (and distraction) for the young men. Besides, what need had women, who were born to be wives and mothers, for higher education? It would only make them arrogant. This misogynist bias stemmed from the ingrained medieval belief that women were more highly sexed than men and deadly in their seductiveness. Eve, after all, had seduced Adam to disobey God's command. Ever since, mankind had suffered the effects of original sin. Thus, as we will see, women were punished from a very young age just for being the daughters of Eve.

Religious Formation

It has been suggested that Julian may have received her early education at a boarding school run by the nuns at St. Mary of Carrow Priory, the large Benedictine convent and church (founded in 1146, with a land grant from King Stephen), which lay just outside Conisford Gate.[16] This early connection to Carrow Priory has been posited as the source of Julian's reading skills as well as her supposed knowledge of Latin,[17] even though Julian herself flatly denies such a capability, referring to herself at the beginning of the Short Text as being "unlettered" (ii:1.125), that is, *unable to read Latin*. Suppositions like these can be questioned on many counts, starting with the fact that there is simply no documentation among the surviving registers of fourteenth-century Norwich that the nuns of Carrow ran a boarding school for young city children, either girls or boys.[18] While it was located just outside the walls of Norwich, Carrow Priory was more a rural than a city monastery, more involved with agriculture than learning (the Priory owned land in more than fifty villages as well as in Norwich and operated market stalls for which the city itself paid rent).

Not only did it have no school and no library, it did not even own a copy of the Bible in the Latin Vulgate (in fact, very few Bibles existed in parishes or convents throughout the whole of England). What few books Carrow did have were probably devotional treatises and a limited number of service books for chanting.[19] After the Great Plague, Carrow had only twelve nuns, and at the dissolution of the monasteries in the sixteenth century there were only eight nuns in residence. With so few nuns to share the many duties and daily chores of managing a large priory estate, in addition to their regular hours of prayer, it is highly unlikely the nuns would have had time to run a school for children. Unlike the Rhineland women mystics of the twelfth century, English nuns were not known at this time for their spiritual or theological erudition. They were respected for their embroidery.[20]

There is also no likelihood that, even if Carrow did accept students, the nuns would have been adept at teaching much more than basic vernacular literacy, since they (perhaps even the prioress) would have been less than fully literate themselves. Nuns could usually read Latin sufficiently well to recite the Little Office of Our Lady, but only by rote. They would not have been able to conjugate verbs and teach Latin texts to their students or even write simple letters in Latin or in English. A Latin-literate scribe was required for penning personal letters, drawing up contracts, and dealing with monastic correspondence. Writing was considered a separate and much higher skill than reading, and nuns were unable to offer much more than simple elementary-level A.B.C. reading skills, even for their own novices. One medieval scholar has written: "The sisters made no contribution to the scholastic philosophy and theology which were the main fruit of the culture of the High Middle Ages, nor to legal and scientific studies. The only sphere in which they made their mark was mysticism."[21] The convent day school in the fourteenth century was most definitely *not* a place for Julian or anyone else to obtain an education.[22]

Julian: Not a Nun

It has also been assumed that Julian had been a Benedictine nun at Carrow Priory before entering the anchorage sometime during her fifties.[23] This, too, seems highly unlikely. Very few townswomen of the merchant class became nuns during the fourteenth century. Because of the dowry customarily demanded of them,[24] nuns were most often from the nobility (usually younger daughters, for whom a suitable match could not be made), or the gentry (for whom a lesser dowry was available after an elder, or more beautiful, sister had been betrothed). In East Anglia, from 1350 to 1540, it has been documented that 32 percent of nuns came from the county gentry, 6 percent were considered parish gentry, 4 percent were from the nobility and yeomanry, and only 14 percent of varying income levels were from the towns.[25] There were also those from the poorer middle class who entered the convent as indentured servants and became "lay sisters." If Julian had ever been a nun, she would have spent most of her non-praying time repairing priests' vestments and altar cloths, embroidering, cleaning, cooking, and serving noble visitors, travelers, and important guests as well as caring for a vegetable garden. Carrow Priory was run like any other medieval manor house, though, like all female enclosures of the time, it was decidedly poorer than a monastery for men. Even with the help of lay sisters and villeins to farm the land and care for the animals, the nuns had to work hard to make ends meet. Julian would never have had the time for reading and studying, much less asking difficult questions of visiting clerics, in order to learn as much theology as she did. Neither would she have had the leisure to practice writing in order to gain proficiency. Carrow was not known to have produced any theological or mystical writings.

Given the fact that Julian wrote the first book by a woman in the English-speaking world, it seems plausible that she would have had to grow up *in the world* with access to a wide variety of books. She also had to have been involved in the discussion of theological ideas, to learn to express herself with such exceptional skill. She would have needed to meet well-educated and well-traveled clergymen and theologians, most likely friends of her family (as we have suggested), so that she could listen to them discuss doctrinal issues, ask pertinent questions, and dare to argue her viewpoints. She would have had to receive private tutoring by a knowledgeable scholar, and possibly gain verbal transmissions on the writings of St. Augustine and St. Bernard, as well as St. Bonaventure and St. Thomas Aquinas, from members of the religious orders themselves. She also would have required private time to think and record her thoughts (by keeping a diary, perhaps), without being under the supervision of a prioress who set the daily schedule for her life.

Arguments from the Text

There are several other clues from the Short and Long Texts that strongly suggest that Julian was not a nun. Sr. Benedicta Ward, a medieval scholar at Oxford, has determined that Julian's texts bear "no mark at all" of having been written in a monastery, or of having been copied in a *scriptorium* attached to a nunnery.[26] Julian never mentions any aspect of living in a convent as being either uplifting or burdensome, positive or negative (as would St. Teresa of Avila in her letters and autobiographical account of her visions in the sixteenth century or St. Thérèse of Lisieux in her *Story of a Soul* in the nineteenth century). There is simply no sense that Julian knew anything about the cloistered life.[27] She does not speak of a vow of poverty or praise its values. She does not mention having taken a personal vow of chastity as a young woman nor does she give any evidence of having a monastic mind-set that exalts the celibate life above the married life. She never alludes to a vow of obedience, which would have demanded that she obtain permission from her prioress and perhaps the bishop, just to be permitted to set quill to parchment. Neither does she suggest that anyone, either prioress or confessor, commanded her to write her book under a vow of obedience (as St. Teresa of Avila does, repeatedly). And she never writes anywhere that she humbly submits her work to her Mother Prioress, or her Father Confessor, to correct any unorthodox teaching that might have crept into her theology.

Furthermore, Julian never indicates that she is practicing a daily monastic schedule of prayer, work, and hospitality, according to the Benedictine Rule. Indeed, she never mentions that she obeys any monastic rule at all, or that she subscribes to a certain method of monastic prayer. Her text never hints that at any time before or immediately after her visions she chose to live as an ascetic, nor does she urge her readers to do so. In fact, Julian's work has nothing in it at all that suggests she is a nun writing only for a small community of nuns. On the contrary, as we have seen, she repeatedly mentions "my *evencristens*" as her audience, a term that probably meant her immediate circle of family and friends, her women's reading group, her parish community, or the people of Norwich, as well as the Christian world beyond. It is precisely for the laity, the *un*lettered, the *non*-monastic, that she writes; not for vowed religious. Far from discussing what it takes to be a good nun, Julian's work bears unmistakable testimony to her own experience of what it takes to be a good mother. No cloistered nun could have written (or would have chosen to write) about motherhood in the intimate and extended way that Julian does. For Julian, motherhood was sacred, a holy vocation in itself.

Julian's Mother

From another viewpoint, we can be quite certain Julian was not a nun at the time of her visions, since she mentions in her Short Text that "My mother, who stood among others and beheld me, lifted up her hand before my face to shut my eyes. For she thought I had been dead or else I had died. And this greatly increased my sorrow" (x:26–28.83). This statement is simply not believable if Julian had been a nun, lying on a straw cot in a tiny convent cell. She would have spoken instead of the presence of Mother Prioress and her religious sisters. Also, Julian makes mention of having received the last rites of the church (ii:3.65), noting that four days later "they that were with me sent for the parson my curate to be at my ending" (ii:19–20.65). This clearly refers to the local secular parish priest, not a regular monk attached to Carrow Priory. The curate came, "and a child with him, and brought a cross" (ii:20–21.65). Such an acolyte would not have been allowed to enter the cloister and visit a nun's cell. Besides, in a convent would there not have been a simple cross already hanging on the wall? Or, during her illness, would a cross not have been placed there by one of her religious sisters? There would have been no need to bring Julian an additional one. A standing altar cross, with a figure of Christ crucified on it, would have been brought only to a devout but *secular* merchant's townhouse, on the assumption that the family would not own such a crucifix. And only because Julian's family was respected and reliable (and had made generous contributions to the parish in the past) would the local pastor leave behind such a precious object to comfort the dying woman. The curate certainly expected to have the crucifix returned to the parish church for liturgical services once Julian had either recovered or died.

Near the end of both the Short and Long Texts, Julian indicates that a *third* cleric, probably a friar or a local canon, visited her: "Then came a religious person to me and asked me how I fared" (xxi:6.109). If she had been in the cloister, she would have been attended to by the priory's regular confessor, not a succession of one or two curates, plus a passing friar or Austin canon, whom it seems Julian did not even know. Also, as Sr. Benedicta argues, would not a monastic community with a resident nun who became deathly ill, recuperated miraculously, and then (perhaps at the request of her spiritual director), wrote about Revelations given to her by the Lord in a series of deathbed visions, have exerted all its influence with the bishop of Norwich to have the nun's manuscript preserved and copied in Norwich Cathedral Priory's own scriptorium?[28] Then, after she died, would not the nuns have petitioned to have Julian's remains transferred from the anchorage to be buried on the priory grounds and would they not have built a shrine to honor her memory? Such a shrine would have become a much-needed source of income and brought Carrow Priory great fame, attracting devout pilgrims from all over England. Julian's *Revelations* would have been well known, read, and revered throughout the country. No doubt, miracles would have been attributed to her intercession. Carrow would have been eager to plead her cause for canonization by the pope. Would not Julian's (full) name and family connections have surfaced in the process of gathering testimony about her sanctity from local witnesses who knew her?

As it is, none of these things occurred. Julian was not well known or documented in her life or after her death, except locally in a few wills allotting her some financial support for herself and her two maids. Her original texts were lost or perhaps burned during the dissolution of the monasteries, and very few copies could have been made during or following her lifetime. All this because Julian's connection to Carrow Priory was not as a nun whose writings would have been treasured, but as an occasional visiting member of the laity, marginal at best.

Julian's Choice

As we have suggested, it is entirely possible that Julian was the only surviving daughter (in her text, she never mentions any siblings standing with her mother at her bedside). Throughout her years of growing up, Julian might have oscillated between being an outgoing, loving, modest, dedicated adolescent, eager to learn everything she could and willing to engage in every way with other girls of her age, and a too-mature young woman, already scarred by suffering, whose childhood had been shattered and whose mind kept asking burning questions that gave her no rest. She would have been haunted by dark fears of a return of the plague and recurring nightmares of the devastation it had visited on her family. Like any girl going through puberty, she would also have had to cope with hormonal imbalances, migraines, mood swings from exuberant elation to debilitating depression, and the physical changes that made her question her attractiveness to men. Now she would need to please her family by marrying well. After the depopulation wrought by the Great Pestilence, marriage and children would have been understood by both parent and child as a familial, as well as a communal, responsibility.[29] There was not much time allowed for girls to become independent individuals before they became obedient and totally subjected to their husbands. Her youth was flying fast.

6
Marriage and Sexuality

While in medieval Italy the most common age of marriage for girls was thirteen, in England it was between fifteen and seventeen. Julian's betrothed could have been a cousin. She might have known him all her life. They may have played together as children. Or, he could have been the son of a neighboring merchant and have apprenticed with Julian's father, becoming a master in the same guild. He may have left Norwich for an extended period of time and traveled throughout Europe, as many merchants-in-training did in order to develop their commercial contacts and business acumen. Julian may already have had feelings for him at a very young age, long before he set out to explore the world—or she may barely have known him.

He was most likely older than Julian, even twice her age, as guild masters and merchants tended to postpone marriage, as we have seen, until their mid or late thirties. The English Dominican, Dr. John Bromyard, bemoaned the fact that male town dwellers put off marriage until they had gained not only entry into craft or merchant guilds but also financial independence, and could then offer their wives suitable homes. Bromyard preached that the delaying of marriage for men led to sinful patterns of fornication and adultery (as well as bastard children).[1] Still, the custom continued. A disparity of fifteen or twenty years between husband and wife was not at all unusual.

Betrothed at fifteen, married at sixteen, a mother at seventeen, mature at twenty-five, past her prime at thirty: this was a common scenario for a woman in fourteenth-century England. But how can we be sure that Julian was married? While Julian never mentions her marriage directly, we may surmise that she married because, more than thirty-five years later, Julian would write of motherhood and child-rearing with an intimacy and personal knowledge that could have come only from having borne and raised at least one child. She would also reveal the great pleasure she took in being a mother, as well as the total confidence she had in her maternal instincts and her understanding of a child's mind, down to its smallest needs. And when she extended the image of motherhood to reveal how Christ acts with regard to humankind, she did not develop her theology of the Motherhood of God as an academic study. It grew *organically* out of her most life-transforming awareness of what it is to conceive, carry, give birth to, nurse, teach, and love a child unconditionally. As with all Julian's mystical teaching, her convictions were planted deep in the soil of human experience.

The Marriage

The process of marriage, as formulated by the church, began with negotiations between the parents of the bride and groom and the settlement of an agreeable dowry. If the couple had reached the minimum age for marriage (twelve for girls, fourteen for boys), then the banns would be posted on the church door and announced from the pulpit for three consecutive weeks. Anyone who knew any reason why these two might not be joined in marriage (whether because of a previous marriage or because they were too closely related by blood) was under compulsion to come forward and speak. Then a suitable day would be decided upon, in accordance with church laws that forbade marriages during penitential times of the year (Advent and Lent) and on Sundays and certain feast days.

For a marriage to be considered legal, the bride and groom had to express their consent to wed one another, not merely at some future date, but in the present moment. According to ecclesiastical law, *mutual consent* was the only basis of the legitimacy of the marriage vows. Largely formulated by the canonist Peter Lombard at the end of the twelfth century, it was held that *consensus non concubitus facit matrimonium* (consent, not cohabitation, makes the marriage), not the social arrangement of the parents, nor the signed agreements to wed, nor even the consummation of the marriage in sexual relations. The dowry of the bride and the dower of the husband (from one-third to one half of all his assets that would go to his wife in the event of his death) also had to be agreed upon prior to the marriage and guaranteed at the ceremony.[2]

On the wedding day, Julian and her bridegroom, their relatives and friends, would have been met by the parish priest at the church door, where the actual marriage would then take place. According to the rubrics of the Sarum Missal, in use from the eleventh to the sixteenth centuries:

> The man should stand on the right hand of the woman, and the woman on the left hand of the man, the reason being that she was formed out of the rib in the left side of Adam. Then shall the priest ask the banns, and afterwards he shall say *in the vulgar tongue*, in the hearing of all, "Brethren, we are gathered together here, in the sight of God, and his angels, and all the saints, and in the face of the Church, to join together two bodies, to wit, those of this man and this woman that henceforth they may be one body; and that they may be two souls in the faith and law of God, to the end that they may earn together eternal life . . ."[3]

If no impediment was brought forth, then the husband would pledge to take this woman for his wedded wife, "to have and to hold from this day forward, for better, for worse, for richer, for poorer, in sickness, and in health, till death us do part, if Holy Church will ordain it: And thereto I plight thee my troth."[4] The wife repeated these words with an additional promise "to be gentle and obedient, in bed and at board, till death us do part."[5] After the blessing of the gold or silver ring, the bridegroom first placed it on the bride's thumb, saying, "in the name of the Father," then on the forefinger, saying "and of the Son," then on the middle finger, "and of the Holy Ghost," and finally left it upon the fourth finger, with an "Amen." It was believed that in the fourth finger of the right hand "there is a certain vein, which runs from thence as far as the heart; and inward affection, which ought always to be fresh between them is signified by the true ring of the silver."[6]

This was followed by various blessings, psalms, litanies, and prayers, including one comparing the state of matrimony "with the sacramental and nuptial union betwixt Christ and Church."[7] Thereafter, the couple entered the church and the solemn Mass of the Trinity was begun. After the *Sanctus* was sung, the wife was enjoined to be "as amiable to her husband as Rachel, wise as Rebecca, long-lived and faithful as Sara." The priest's prayer continued:

> Let not the father of lies [Satan] get any advantage over her through her doings; bound to thy faith and thy commandments may she remain united to one man; may she flee all unlawful unions; may she fortify her weakness with the strength of discipline. May she be bashful and grave, reverential and modest, well instructed in heavenly doctrine. May she be fruitful in childbearing, innocent and of good report, attaining to a desired old age, seeing her children's children unto the third and fourth generation; and may she attain the rest of the blessed, and to the kingdom of heaven. Through [Christ our Lord, Amen].[8]

It is notable that no such prayer was prayed for the man to remain faithful to his wife, to flee all unlawful unions, or to be willing to provide her with children. Nor did he ever promise to do so.

Following the Mass, a marriage feast—as lavish as Julian's family could afford—was given for the enjoyment of friends, neighbors, business associates, and the important town burgesses. These feasts often went on for days; in addition to course after course of fine foods and drinks, the celebrations included bawdy songs and entertainments, seductive games, clowning, and dancing (holdovers from ancient pagan mystery rites of copulation, over which the church, and even pious families, had little or no control). After her marriage, Julian moved out of her family home and into her husband's house, but since the marriage was likely to have been arranged within her family's merchant class, we may assume that this would have taken place right in Norwich. (Since merchants' homes tended to be built adjacent to one another, Julian's husband might have purchased a townhouse nearby.) Then, on the night following the wedding, when the bridegroom and bride had retired to bed, the priest approached the bedchamber and said:

> "Bless, O Lord, this chamber and all that dwell therein, that they may be established in thy peace and abide in thy will, and live and grow in their love, and that the length of their days may be multiplied."[9]

The bed was then blessed, the bride and groom were also blessed several times, and holy water was sprinkled on them. Then the priest departed.

Marital Duties

Julian would have been well-prepared for the transition to a new home by her mother. Still, being married would now mean taking on the sole responsibility of managing a household with servants, entertaining important visitors, and, most of all, catering to her husband's every wish. As stated in the marriage vows, she was bound to love, honor, and obey him in all things unquestioningly (as long as his request did not go against the commandments of God and the church). She was required not only to observe the sexual duties of marriage (known as the "marriage debt"), as was her husband, but also to remain totally faithful and chaste in her commitment and forever loyal to her spouse. Love was not expected before the arranged betrothal. However, it was viewed as a much-desired goal of a peaceful marriage and was seen as the *wife's* responsibility. She was expected to labor to prove herself worthy of her husband's love and to earn his affection. She could do this by being constantly attentive to him, ever docile, amiable, modest, patient, and forgiving.

There is a revealing document, a fourteenth-century compendium of everything a wife was expected to be and do, called *Le Ménagier de Paris* ("The Goodman of Paris").[10] It was composed by an older husband who was not of noble birth, probably a successful merchant who often traveled abroad, to instruct his fifteen-year-old Parisian wife concerning her wifely duties in the great hall, the kitchen, and the bedroom. The text instructs the young woman in the good habits of prayer and orderly dressing; in courteous behavior, as well as acceptable attire in public (and control of her gaze); in the sacrifice of Holy Mass and the examination of conscience before confession. There are sections on chastity, devotion, obedience to the husband and the care of his physical person; admonitions on keeping his secrets and protecting his reputation at all costs; directives for providing him with good counsel so that he refrains from sin or acts of folly; teachings on the value of hard work and virtue to attain and sustain his wealth; training in horticulture and in the selection and care of both servants and horses; tips on raising hawks; and finally, *Le Ménagier* includes an extensive cookbook with recipes for daily dinners as well as elaborate menus for festive occasions.

A contemporary text such as this indicates just what Julian was expected to accomplish, on a daily basis, in order to be considered a *goodwife*. She was to increase the prosperity of the household, gain friends, preserve possessions, and, by so doing, make the misfortunes that would come with old age easier to bear. In all things, the wife was instructed to be humble and obedient toward her husband, whatsoever he commanded her, "in earnest or in jest,"[11] whether of great or little importance, for everything he bade was to become important to her, as his wife. And if he has forbidden her to do "anything at all," she was required to obey.[12] She was never to be arrogant, or answer back, or contradict what he had said, especially in front of anyone else. If it was absolutely necessary, a wife was permitted to reprove her husband if he acted unwisely or sinfully, but she was always to do so with patience and respect, never with hostility.

The wife was also to attend to her husband's person, to "keep him in clean linen," for, she was told, "that is your business."[13] And even though a husband might often have to travel long distances on business in rain and snow, hail and wind, and become drenched, or full of sweat, sometimes chilled, poorly fed and lodged, he would always hold the hope of returning home to his devoted wife. She was to receive him joyously, wash his feet before a good fire, provide fresh hose and shoes, offer him dinner and look after him, prepare him a bed with white sheets and nightcaps, "well covered with good furs," and comfort him "with other joys and desports, privities, loves and secrets whereof I am silent. And the next day provide fresh shirts and garments."[14] Such attentions were necessary to encourage a man to want to return home to see his *goodwife*, and to remain distant with other women. And just as men provided fresh litter and sifted oats and tended to their horses, hounds, asses, and mules, when they returned after a long trip, "for pity of their labour," so was a woman to provide her husband with all manner of comforts on his returning to his own household.[15] Then, the husband's lodging in distant places would seem to him like a prison; he would be kept in mind only of the love he bore his wife. And their own home would seem like "a paradise" compared with any place else.

In the course of the husband's detailed instructions, the young wife was reminded of the old proverb that there were three things which could send the *goodman* running from his home: "a leaking roof, a smoky chimney, and a scolding woman."[16] Therefore, the prospective wife was enjoined to "bewitch and to bewitch again your future husband, and protect him from holes in the roof and smoky fires, and do not quarrel with him, but be sweet, pleasant and peaceful with him."[17] (The author fails to mention how she is to fix the roof and keep the chimney from smoking.) In winter, she was to keep her husband warm between her breasts in bed. In summer, she was to see that the chamber floor was fully covered with alder leaves to catch the fleas. She was instructed to set one or two loaves of old bread covered in glue or turpentine about the room, with a lighted candle in the center of each loaf so that the fleas would become stuck to the bait.

The detailed cooking techniques provide a glimpse into the medieval kitchen of the merchant class and suggest the enormous responsibility of a young wife who had to plan, purchase ingredients for, supervise the cooking of, and actually help prepare multiple courses and dishes for every noonday meal. Julian would have needed to know how to filet, bake, fry, or poach a variety of fish; cook venison or goose; stuff a capon and boil a rabbit; pluck and prepare mallards, larks, and partridge; roast a carcass of mutton, a loin of beef, a leg of pork . . . and then serve each with its appropriately spiced wine, fruit, vegetable, or herb sauce. She would have been expected to know how to bake the new "white bread" made from wheat, as well as light pastries and fresh fruit pies. The daily menu for a merchant's household would have been decidedly different from what Julian's peasant ancestors ate: brown rye bread, oat porridge, salt pork, root vegetables. The ever more rich and varied diet of the emerging middle class reflected their growing affluence. Food (like clothes, housing, and the number of servants) indicated what level of the third estate a family had attained, and how far from the old peasant ways their tastes had come.

Husband and Wife

What about the husband's duties? The husband was obliged to show his wife loyalty, although, as we have seen, male faithfulness was neither promised in the marriage vows nor commonly practiced. He was also directed to supply her with sufficient food and clothing.[18] Considering his wife's natural inferiority, moral laxity, and supposed rampant sexuality, the husband had the grave responsibility of teaching her how to behave and to obey in every situation, to keep her under control so she would not shame *his* good name. It was also incumbent upon him to try to improve her character. While the church did not actively condone wife beating, it did not totally condemn it either. A husband was free to punish his wife for misbehavior, as long as the punishment was not excessive; that is, he could not seriously injure, maim, or kill her.[19] Civic laws did allow a husband to beat his wife and some husbands did so regularly, and with impunity.[20]

Christ himself had taught that marriage was indissoluble: "What therefore God hath joined together, let not man put asunder" (Mk 10:9). Thus divorce was not canonically or legally permitted. However, because of the husband's impotence, violent physical abuse, or his squandering of jointly held assets, the wife's addiction to drink, or either partner's leprosy or heresy, separation was sometimes, but not always, allowed by ecclesiastical courts.[21] Remarriage, however, was never allowed. Annulments were granted only if the church tribunal was convinced that the marriage had been invalid in the first place because the partners were too closely related by blood, if either partner was already married, if the marriage had not been consummated as a result of the husband's impotence, or if there was irrefutable evidence that the marriage had been forced on the couple.[22]

Is it possible to intimate anything at all about Julian's personal relationship with her husband? Given the intensity of devotion we find in Julian's character, we may assume she tried to be a *goodwife* and to please her husband in every way. However, since she never refers directly to a husband in her text, we have no way of knowing if her marriage was a happy or an unhappy one.

Legal Rights

While a single man or woman of eighteen was considered an adult, having reached the age of so-called majority, a *married* woman like Julian was, from the day of her marriage, under the guardianship of her husband, as if she were a perennial minor. She could not take out a loan, draw up a contract, or go to court without her husband's permission, since her status as a married woman dis-entitled her to equality before the law.[23] As a wife, she would not have had the legal right to sell, pawn, trade, or exchange even her own inherited or personal property or goods without her husband's express consent, nor could she make a will without her husband's permission.[24] The thirteenth-century French jurist, Philippe de Beaumanoir (1250–1296), wrote that once a woman has entered into marriage, "she has no authority from her own will alone." He was adamant that "the dumb, the deaf, the insane, and the female cannot draw up a contract, neither alone nor through a representative, since they are subservient to the authority of others."[25] However, given her husband's consent, Julian would have been legally allowed to draw up a land or business contract, write her will, or sue in court, either directly or through a representative. A woman was permitted to take her husband to court for criminality, but only in cases of extreme physical abuse such as beating or rape or verbal abuse,[26] or if the husband had seriously mismanaged her personal property (that is, her dowry).[27] Since we do not know Julian's married name, we cannot learn from the surviving registers of Norwich courts whether or not she ever took such a course of action.

Joined but Unequal

It is obvious that the medieval marriage partnership was an unequal one. Both church and state considered woman essentially inferior to man. Well might we ask: How did these prejudicial teachings concerning women come about and why were they perpetuated, indeed consistently reinforced, by the church?

According to the Genesis account in the Hebrew Bible, woman was fashioned from the rib of man (Gn 2:21–23), not man from woman. She was made as an afterthought of God, because man needed a helpmate. Furthermore, the woman listened to the serpent, ate the apple, and then seduced the man into disobeying God by also partaking of the forbidden fruit of the tree of knowledge of good and evil (long interpreted to be symbolic of sexual initiation). Thus, the woman was considered personally responsible for original sin, the greatest disaster ever to befall humankind. From then on, even though the man also ate of the fruit, the woman was considered the cause of his downfall. As a direct result of her sin, Eve was made forever subject to Adam, even though both man and woman had been created in the "image and likeness" of God (Gn 1:27). Henceforth, Eve (and by extension, all women) would have to undergo greatly increased "pangs in childbearing." God said to her: "In pain you shall bring forth children, yet your desire shall be for your husband, and he shall rule over you" (Gn 3:16). Because of his own sin, the man, now named *ha-Adam*, would have to till the ground to produce his food. God's words to him were: "By the sweat of your face you shall eat bread until you return to the ground, for out of it you were taken; you are dust, and to dust you shall return" (Gn 3:19). The man named the woman, *Havvah* (Eve), which, in Hebrew, means, "the mother of all living" (Gn 3:20). And since both Adam and Eve had sinned against God's command, both were cast out of the Garden of Eden forever and deprived of the sight of God (Gn 3:23–24).

Marriage was considered by St. Paul as a remedy for the weak, the sinful, the tempted; in short, for those who were not able to commit to a celibate life as he had, completely devoting himself to the love and service of God. In his first epistle to the Corinthians, he wrote:

> Now concerning the matters about which you wrote: "It is well for a man not to touch a woman." But because of cases of sexual immorality, each man should have his own wife and each woman her own husband. The husband should give to his wife her conjugal rights, and likewise the wife to her husband. For the wife does not have authority over her own body, but the husband does; likewise the husband does not have authority over his own body, but the wife does. Do not deprive one another except perhaps by agreement for a set time, to devote yourselves to prayer, and then come together again, so that Satan may not tempt you because of your lack of self-control. This I say by way of concession, not of command. I wish that all were as I myself am [celibate]. But each has a particular gift from God, one having one kind and another a different kind. To the unmarried and the widows I say that it is well for them to remain unmarried as I am. But if they are not practicing self-control, they should marry. For it is better to marry than to be aflame with passion. To the married I give this command—not I but the Lord—that the wife should not separate from her husband. (1 Cor 7:1–10)

Since earliest Christianity, matrimony was viewed as the lesser way to holiness; the chaste life of consecrated religious was esteemed as the higher way. Ever since the time of Plato, philosophers had thought that, for a woman to be worthy of the male pursuit of the mystical life, she had to give up procreation and all attachments to the functions of her own body. The mystical life (for a woman) was deemed impossible within the state of marriage. However, according to men, for a woman *not* to marry required a much greater sacrifice than it did for the man. Unlike the man, whose nature was considered "inherently spiritual," and whose sexuality was not considered compromised by remaining unmarried and not producing offspring, the woman in search of a mystical life had to relinquish *precisely that which defined her as woman*, namely, her ability to bear children. If she did not marry, she had few alternatives. In order to remain chaste, she had to become a nun. In short, women were so identified with their sexual organs that it was considered no less than heroic for them to sacrifice their drive to procreation in order to dedicate their lives to God. It was almost inconceivable to St. Paul, the church fathers, or theologians and canonists of the Middle Ages that a woman (like Julian) could cultivate a mystical life . . . *and still be married.*

The main thrust of church teachings on marriage concerned the wife's subordination and therefore, total obedience to her husband. The author of the Epistle to the Ephesians had exhorted women: "Wives, be subject to your husbands as you are to the Lord. For the husband is the head of the wife just as Christ is the head of the church, the body of which he is the Savior" (Eph 5:22–23). The writer balanced this directive by addressing men in kind: "Husbands, love your wives, just as Christ loved the church and gave himself up for her" (Eph 5:25). And again, "In the same way, husbands should love their wives as they do their own bodies. He who loves his wife loves himself" (Eph 5:28). The early church taught that since both men and women have eternal souls, men and women are equally able to be saved. St. Paul wrote that in Christ, "There is no longer Jew or Greek, there is no longer slave or free, there is no longer male and female; for all of you are one in Christ Jesus" (Gal 3:28). However, the man was believed to have been saved *directly* by Christ, the second Adam, with whom he could identify as a man, while the woman would be saved *by bearing her husband's children*:

> I permit no woman to teach or to have authority over a man; she is to keep silent. For Adam was formed first, then Eve; and Adam was not deceived, but the woman was deceived and became a transgressor. *Yet she will be saved through childbearing*, provided they continue in faith and love and holiness, with modesty. (1 Tm 2:12–15, italics added)

Tertullian (c.160–220), considered the father of Latin Christianity, reinforced the primordial shame of women. All women were responsible for the evil in the world, and were required to do unceasing penance for their "wicked mother," Eve.

> And do you not believe that you are [each] an Eve? The sentence of God on this sex of yours lives in our times and so it is necessary that the guilt should live on, also. You are the one who opened the door to the devil; you are the one who first plucked the fruit of the forbidden tree, you are the first who deserted the divine law; you are the one who persuaded him [Adam] whom the devil was not strong enough to attack. All too easily you destroyed the image of God, man. Because of your desert, that is, death, even the Son of God had to die. And you still think of putting adornments over the skins of animals that cover you?[28]

St. Jerome (c.331–420), revered as the most learned of the Latin fathers of the church, wrote in a Letter to Eustochium:

> Let those take wives and procreate who were condemned by the curse of "in the sweat of thy brow shalt thou eat bread and the earth shall produce thorns and thistles"; my seed [remaining celibate] shall bear fruit one hundredfold.[29]

Like most patristic fathers, Jerome viewed sexual desire as synonymous with human evil. Sex, even in marriage, was "vomit" and, according to him, "women with child offer a revolting spectacle."[30] But the woman who put off her sexuality could become truly *manly*, that is, spiritual: "As long as a woman is for birth and children she is different from man as body is from soul. But when she wishes to serve Christ more than the world, then she ceases to be a woman and will be called a man."[31]

St. Augustine of Hippo (354–430) came to disagree with his predecessors who said that because of their sexuality, women were not to be considered images of God. He affirmed that, according to the Genesis account, God created male and female in his own image—the *imago Dei* (image of God).[32] Augustine explained that human beings are the *imago Dei* insofar as we are a reflection of God's rational mind. Since women have "a like nature [to men] of rational intelligence in the mind," they are truly images of God.[33] In addition, since rational creatures are made children of God through Christian baptism, "Is there anyone then who would exclude females from this association seeing that together with us men they are fellow heirs of grace . . . ?"[34] Nevertheless, Augustine drew the line at viewing women as *independent* images of God or as being fully equal to men. In Book 12 of *De Trinitate*, he writes:

> I believe . . . that *the woman with her husband* is the image of God in such a way that the whole of that substance is one image, but when she is assigned her function of being an assistant, which is her concern alone, she is *not* the image of God; whereas in what concerns the man alone he is the image of God as fully and completely as when the woman is joined to him in one whole.[35]

Augustine equates the higher rational mind, when it contemplates the truth and seeks to know the eternal reasons of things, with man as the image of God. However,

> when something is drawn off from [contemplating truth] and assigned or directed in a certain way to the management of temporal affairs, it is still all the same the image of God as regards the part with which it consults the truth it has gazed on; *but as regards the part which is directed to managing these lower affairs, it is not the image of God.*[36]

Augustine clearly identifies this distracted, diverted, and "temporal" functioning of the mind with women (who are involved with the bringing forth and nurturing of children), and he warns that "too many advances into this lower territory are dangerous."[37] Therefore, a woman's rational activity, which is primarily occupied with bodily and temporal things, "ought to have authority over its head (1 Cor 11:10); this is indicated by the [head] covering, which symbolizes its need to be curbed."[38]

> Well, it is only because she differs from the man in the sex of her body that her bodily covering could suitably be used to symbolize that part of the reason which is diverted to the management of temporal things, signifying that the mind of man does not remain the image of God except in the part which adheres to the eternal ideas to contemplate or consult them: and it is clear that females have this as well as males. So in their minds a common nature is to be acknowledged; but in their bodies the distribution of the one mind is symbolized.[39]

In spite of his admission that the woman has a right to use her rational powers as much as any man in the pursuit of eternal truth, Augustine agrees with St. Paul that "the man ought not to cover his head because he is the image and glory of God, while the woman ought to because she is the glory of the man (1 Cor 11:7)."[40] Augustine considers this division valid solely because of a woman's *sexual* nature. He interprets this passage of St. Paul allegorically to mean that woman, in her "diverted" mind, must always remain submissive to man's natural authority, signified by her head being covered with a veil.

Procreation

Regarding marriage and procreation, Augustine challenged the general denigration of women in his time and counterbalanced some of the more demeaning views held by his fourth- and early fifth-century contemporaries (Jerome in particular). Since human beings are essentially social, Augustine taught that God preordained that they should be connected by ties of kinship. He considered man and wife as "the first natural tie of human society,"[41] a mutual bond based on love through which family, friendship, and community are created. Thus he stresses the *procreation* of children as the primary good of marriage and "the only worthy fruit... of sexual intercourse."[42]

However, Augustine admits that marriage is good not solely because of the procreation of children "but also because of the natural companionship between the two sexes."[43] And so he defines the second good of marriage as *fidelity*. "Therefore, married people owe each other not only the fidelity of sexual intercourse for the purpose of procreating children... but also the mutual service, in a certain measure, of sustaining each other's weakness, for the avoidance of illicit intercourse."[44] He concedes that for the married "to have sexual intercourse even without the purpose of creation" is not actually permitted because of the marriage, "but because of the marriage, it is *pardoned*."[45] While "intercourse for the purpose of generation has no fault attached to it," he considers the satisfaction of concupiscence with the spouse as being "a venial sin; adultery or fornication, however, is a mortal sin."[46]

The third good arises from the nuptial pact as *sacramentum*, a sacred sign "of something greater than that which could arise from our weak mortality."[47] And because of this unifying symbolism, Augustine holds that marriage must be both monogamous and indissoluble.

While Augustine writes that true marriage can be a loving friendship, and that such a spiritual union redeems the sexual act from being mortally sinful even if it lacks a specific desire to produce offspring, he still argues, like St. Paul, that the celibate life is superior to the married state: "marriage and continence are two goods, the second of which is better."[48] This is because, as St. Paul says: "...the unmarried woman and the virgin are anxious about the affairs of the Lord, so that they may be holy in body and spirit; but the married woman is anxious about the affairs of the world, how to please her husband" (1 Cor 7:34). Therefore the unmarried woman has a greater sanctity "than [that] of the married woman, and a more ample reward is due to this sanctity because it is better than the other good, because she thinks only of this, how she might please the Lord."[49] Augustine considered that if Christians marry, it is only because they do not have the self-discipline necessary for a life of continence.[50]

> Let married people put the unmarried above themselves; let them acknowledge that they are better; let them respect in them what they do not have in themselves; and in them let them love Christ.[51]

In his later works, Augustine develops the idea that "since the goodness of marriage is the good use of an evil [*libido*, lust, or concupiscence of the flesh], it does not surprise us that the evil that is original sin is derived from the evil of concupiscence, which the goodness of marriage uses well [to propagate children]."[52] He deems the passionate excitation and "loss of control" during sexual intercourse to be the penalty for Adam's disobedience and the very means by which the stain of original sin is transmitted from one generation to another.[53] Therefore, according to Augustine, there must be a good reason *outside* of the sexual act that makes it permissible, even in marriage. That reason, again, is to procreate.

> The union of male and female for the purpose of procreation is, then, the natural good of marriage. But one makes a bad use of this good if one uses it like an animal so that one's intention is directed toward the pleasure of sexual desire, but not toward the will to propagate.[54]

Near the end of his life, writing his *Retractiones* (*Revisions*, c.426–428), Augustine clarified that he had never actually condemned marriage, but had always held it to be a great good, and that God's command to "increase and multiply" was, indeed, a directive to be fruitful in the flesh.[55]

Why must we consider St. Augustine's views? Simply because his theology and ethics exerted tremendous influence on the medieval church; indeed, they do so even today. During the thirteenth and fourteenth centuries, his autobiographical book of *Confessions* was copied and read all over Europe. St. Augustine's theological and polemical works were discussed and debated in the universities, and they dominated the development of Christian thought. His interpretations of scripture were preached far and wide in the marketplaces and pulpits of Europe, especially by the Order of Franciscan Friars.[56] In Norwich, the Augustinian canons would have been steeped in his teachings and disseminated his viewpoints. Therefore, we may assume that Augustinian attitudes toward women, marriage, and procreation suffused the air Christians breathed . . . and that Julian would have been exposed to them all her life.

The Sacrament of Marriage

By the eighth century, the church had officially established marriage between Christians as a sacrament, thus defining the union of a man and a woman as a source of God's grace. However, in the twelfth century, the renowned codifier of canon law, Gratian, condemned the man who was too passionate a lover of his wife as an adulterer.[57] The canonical purposes of marriage were defined as three: to avoid the sins of the flesh, to procreate children, and to provide mutual companionship. In the late twelfth century, the Italian canon lawyer, Huguccio, stretched the teaching on sex in marriage to the point of absurdity, saying that pleasure during intercourse, *even to procreate a child*, was still a sin.[58]

St. Thomas Aquinas (c.1225–1274) described marriage as a true union of hearts (as well as bodies) that could not be broken. Agreeing with Augustine, Aquinas wrote that marriage should be a perfect friendship, and since friendship requires some measure of equality, women cannot be made slaves (as in polygamous unions), and marriage must always be monogamous.[59] Aquinas also stressed the *naturalness* of marriage, in accordance with the laws of nature as laid down by Aristotle.[60] This was all to the good, insofar as it acknowledged respect for the role of woman in marriage and rooted the sacrament in the law of nature. Yet Aquinas also insisted that, "good order would have been wanting in the human family if some were not governed by others wiser than themselves." He concluded that "woman is naturally subject to man, because in man the discretion of reason predominates."[61] And this is for the woman's own benefit and good. He even taught that the father should be *better loved* than the mother (because the father's role in conception was more active, and the mother's merely passive).[62] Therefore, the child's obligation to the father was, according to nature, greater. "Now it is evident that the upbringing of a human child requires not only the mother's care for his nourishment, but much more the care of his father as guide and guardian under whom he progresses in good both internal and external."[63]

In her teachings on the Motherhood of God, Julian will utterly refute this lip-service to the work of motherhood, speaking instead of the mother's service as "nearest, readiest, and sekerest [securest]: nearest, for it is most of nature; readiest, because it is most of love; and sekerest, for it is most of truth" (60:12–13.313). It is also worth noting that, in the entire course of her Revelations on the Motherhood of God in Christ, Julian never once mentions the role of the human father. Nor, in her explication of the parable of the lord and the servant (which is a direct analogy to the fall of Adam), does she ever allude to a woman called Eve. Even though age-old misogyny suffused medieval society and was reinforced and perpetuated from the pulpit, Julian seems to have been determined to write her *Revelations* from a *woman's* point of view.

Medical Viewpoint

The medieval medical community based its knowledge of sexual intercourse on the renowned physician, philosopher, and surgeon Galen (129–c.200/216 CE). He wrote that the wombs of women are naturally "cold" and require the "hot" male sperm to warm them; in fact, if women lacked regular sexual activity, Galen warned that their "seed" might coagulate and clot the womb, greatly endangering women's health.[64] Therefore, Galen explained that women needed to copulate frequently, suggesting that the satisfaction of both male and female lust can "indebt" the husband and wife to each other. Neither husband nor wife should refuse the payment of this "marriage debt."

Following Galen's teachings, physicians became convinced that the woman must reach orgasm in order to produce her own ejaculation of "female semen" that was believed to fertilize the egg. This contemporary gynecological science was applied by theologians in cases of alleged rape, in which the victim was known to have conceived a child. Legally, such an instance was deemed *no rape at all*, since the woman must have enjoyed the act in order to conceive.[65] There is no indication that the medical and ecclesiastical experts ever disagreed on the necessity of the woman's sexual satisfaction in order to conceive.

Mary and Joseph

Throughout the Middle Ages, women continued to be viewed as sexually insatiable and, as such, the direct cause of everyman's sin. Nevertheless, the church generally taught that sexually active married people could still be saved, as long as procreation was the sole reason for intercourse. Some clergymen even sought to give a more positive image to the married state. They became increasingly aware of the importance of the layfolk in the church and preached on Mary and Joseph, their mutual love and devotion, as well as the purity of their lives (no doubt referring to their total abstinence from sexual intercourse). Mary and Joseph became the beloved and revered models of sanctity in marriage, with the Christ Child completing the holy family. The nativity scene, as well as depictions of Mary nursing her baby, were favorite themes of medieval painters, sculptors, and book illuminators, revealing a new acceptance in religious iconography of the natural functions of a woman's body. Husbands and wives were urged to imitate the virtues of this perfect family (if not the total abstinence), and so come to holiness themselves. Marriage, then, could be considered a worthwhile role in life, a vocation certainly not as high or as respected as that of the priesthood, or as holy as the consecrated religious life, but nonetheless (with serious reservations), a salvific path in itself.

There was always this double message. On the one hand, marriage was viewed favorably. After all, it had been personally blessed by Jesus himself, who performed his first public miracle at the marriage feast at Cana by changing water into wine for the wedding guests when the wine had run out (Jn 2:1–11). And, according to St. Paul, as we have seen, marriage imitated the bond between Christ and his church. On the other hand, marriage sanctioned a necessary evil; it was an institution perpetuated to keep carnality within societal bounds, whereas, "in the resurrection from the dead neither [men or women] marry nor are given in marriage" (Lk 20:34–35).[66] It seems that every positive statement about marriage came with a warning label: to experience sexual pleasure is to sin.

A Young Wife

Julian must have heard the full gamut of positive and negative teachings on marriage and received all the dire warnings against taking carnal pleasure in sex. The priest was directed to instruct women repeatedly in the confessional against engaging in sexual activity for any reason except procreation. In sermon after sermon, Julian would have been reminded that woman is fleshly and weak, lacking self-control, and intellectually inferior to man; that a wife needs constant supervision and strict disciplining by her husband so that she does not fall into sin; that sex, even in holy marriage, could be the "near occasion" of sin. How must these restrictive and negative attitudes have affected Julian's marital relations? How deeply did she internalize the all-pervasive misogyny? Was she terrified of displeasing her husband, or even more terrified of being sexually mistreated herself? Or might she have fallen in love with her husband, dared to express her love in the sexual act, and then felt guilty for having sinned grievously, even to the point of needing to confess her sins of pleasure?

One wonders if Julian's recurring preoccupation with sin (as apparent in the *Revelations*) did not stem, at least initially, from her sense of having led a double life, as a devout Christian and as a young, passionate wife. Given the threats of hellfire and brimstone, it must have taken heroic mental stamina for her to balance the imbalance between what she was taught and what she experienced. Julian may have been haunted by fears of sexual transgressions, impure desire, imperfect intention to leave every sexual act open to the procreation of a child (even during the two-year period of lactation). The psychological, emotional, and spiritual conflicts involved in this internal struggle must have been especially intense for a woman as sensitive and honest as she. One can only hope she was able to confide in her reading circle of "other women," as well as her mother, a childhood friend, a female relative. She could not have unburdened her soul freely to any parish priest and hoped to receive anything but a penance.

Many women were so terrified of sex and so fearful of sexual abuse, as well as of the possibility of becoming pregnant and dying in childbirth, that they fought their family's betrothal arrangements with all their might, to the point of self-mutilation, in order to be rendered ineligible for marriage. Even those medieval mystics known to have been wives and mothers severely punished themselves for either being forced to undergo sex in marriages they hated (Mary of Oignies, Rita of Cascia, Dorothy of Montau, Catherine of Genoa, among others),[67] or for having actually enjoyed it (Angela of Foligno, La Beata Umiltà, Margery Kempe, and St. Elizabeth of Hungary, who was, by all accounts, deeply in love with her husband).[68]

Julian's Sexuality

Unlike the majority of medieval mystics, Julian never reveals any hint of self-loathing about her own body. At no point in her text does she ever express revulsion toward her sexuality or degrade the natural desires and functions of human physicality in any way. She never exhorts her reader to punish the flesh in order to ward off or expiate sin, or to engage in extreme ascetical practices as the path to mystical experience. This strongly indicates that she did not follow such practices herself. On the contrary, her book exudes *a sense of wonder* about being made in the image and likeness of God. Repeatedly, Julian expresses her delight in the full range of motherly feelings and even praises the miracle of bodily processes such as digestion and excretion. She does not seem like a woman who denied her sexuality in order to devote her life to God. She speaks of sensuality as a natural function of the soul, albeit the "lower" part. True to the Augustinian teaching predominant in her time, she views reason, memory, and will as the "higher" parts of the soul. But in all her explanations, neither the higher nor lower parts of the soul are, in any way, *sexed*. Both are absolutely essential to form a whole human being.

Indeed, Julian seems to have inherited from her mother a healthy sense of the "female" elements, that is earth and water, as being every bit as necessary as the "male" elements, fire and wind. She accepts her sensual nature, yet she does not deny her right to use her rational mind to delve into the mysteries of her faith. She considers humanity in all its aspects as the very flesh with which Christ clothed himself in the incarnation. This does not mean that she is naïve about the dangers of lust, the selfish desire for sexual pleasure; she is very clear that the body is able to cast us down as well as lift us up. But there is no trace in her text that woman, as a sexual temptress, is the cause of original sin.

As we shall see, Julian's book is a constant struggle to counteract the misogynist teachings of her time. She deals with these views not in an obviously combative way, but very subtly, by substituting an entirely different paradigm, one that greatly ennobles both women *and* men. Her conviction of the sanctity of the physical and spiritual in humankind is crystal clear, and provides the strongest possible assertion of a woman's right to express her love: physical, emotional, and spiritual.

7
War and Childbirth

The war with France was not proving worth its cost. Even though some had made fortunes from plunder, trade, and ransom, by far the majority of people in the English nation groaned under the weight of ever-increasing taxation on top of several bad harvests and the lingering aftermath of the Great Pestilence. Since 1354, the unanimous cry for a permanent peace treaty had been heard in the House of Commons. Rich merchants were reluctant to give more money to the crown, seeing that their outstanding loans were unlikely to be repaid. Parliament even put strictures on the king's ability to raise a new army. Meanwhile, the Turks had entered Europe by seizing Gallipoli and the old, sickly Pope Innocent VI was urging a permanent settlement between France and England precisely so that these two nations could focus their combined energies on waging a new crusade against the Ottoman Empire.[1]

The Flower of Chivalry

France, however, persistently refused to accept the English terms of peace, which motivated King Edward III to convince Parliament to fund yet another war. He placed his eldest son, Edward, the Black Prince, also known as "the flower of chivalry," in charge of the army headed for Bordeaux. A second army was bound for Normandy, under the leadership of Henry, Duke of Lancaster, revered as the "father of soldiers," because he had been fighting the king's battles for forty-five years.[2] Before setting sail for France, the Black Prince and the duke were installed into the newly founded Royal Order of the Garter (created by King Edward as a fellowship of knights to rekindle the mythical brotherhood of King Arthur's knights of the round table). The chivalric club took as its motto *Honi soit qui mal y pense* [Shame on him who thinks ill of it], and the twenty-four members became the highest ranking knights in the kingdom.

Once they had landed on French shores, the Black Prince and his army headed east and proceeded to plunder and pillage their way through Languedoc to Narbonne. They then returned in like manner through Bordeaux, once again sending shock waves throughout France. The British prince intended to teach the local population an unforgettable lesson, namely that his father, Edward III, meant to rule these lands, and that their continued allegiance to the French crown was traitorous and would result in destruction and death. The Black Prince and his army, now some nine thousand strong, slaughtered men, women, and children with impunity; they killed cattle, pigs, and chickens and feasted on them. They burned bridges, cities, towns, granaries, and barns; they drank the local wines, then destroyed the wine vats and incinerated the ancient vineyards as well.[3] It was a mindless exhibition of rape, robbery, and murder of helpless, mostly unarmed civilians, spearheaded by the so-called "flower of chivalry."

Poitiers

Then, in 1355, the new French king, Jean II, amassed the largest army of the century, led by his four sons, a constable, two marshals, 26 counts and dukes, 334 bannerets, and almost all the lesser lords of France. (Estimates of the total numbers range from a high of eighty thousand to a low of sixteen thousand, which is probably closer to the actual number.)[4] They confronted the exhausted army of the Black Prince at a fork in the road, near the village of Poitiers. Once again, an English force would engage in battle with a French army twice its size. Contemporary accounts of the resulting bloodshed, mutilation, and carnage are horrifying. After six hours of battle, with most of his French forces either dead or fled, King Jean, badly wounded and bleeding profusely, handed over his glove and finally surrendered to the English. It was the decisive and devastating turning point. The remaining French army took flight to the city, pursued by the English who captured every soldier they could get for future ransom. It is estimated that several thousand Frenchmen were killed that fateful day, over two thousand nobility alone.[5] The loss of prestige to the French aristocracy from such a defeat was incalculable. All of Europe was stunned by the capture of King Jean and conspiracy theories abounded. The French nation was demoralized, the nobility in shambles, the lack of leadership only too apparent.

The Black Prince, on the other hand, returning to England in 1357, was greeted as a national hero. The celebrations that followed his arrival in London were the largest the nation had ever seen, confirming to the vast crowds assembled an unmistakable victory for English national pride. Royal favors abounded, wine and cash flowed freely. Henry of Lancaster used the fortune he had gained from the French campaigns to build his Savoy Palace in London, while William Berkeley, three generations later, would recount that his own manor house was "builded out of the ransom that his great-grandfather took on the field of Poitiers."[6]

Coastal Raids

But the war would soon come closer to England. French privateers ravaged the English Channel, preying on English merchant ships.[7] In March of 1360, when Julian was seventeen, a French raiding party sailed to the south coast of England, seeking to make its way to Lincolnshire to free King Jean by stealth and force. Landing at Winchelsea, the French plundered and raped citizens, even breaking into churches and murdering worshipers at Mass. At Rye, they defeated a small force of English and burned the town. The local population assembled reinforcements of about twelve hundred, which convinced the small raiding party to escape back to France.[8] After that, every coastal town, including Norwich, was filled with fear that the French would return, wreaking the same kind of havoc on the English that King Edward and the Black Prince had wrought on them.

Julian's husband and cousins might well have been called up to regular military duty in the defense of Norwich. Every household would have laid in supplies and made defensive plans for a long siege in the face of another coastal attack. This is likely the origin of the first of four fears Julian would refer to in her Long Text more than thirty years later: "dread of afray" (74:1–2.355), the sudden attack. The preparations for war on the home front must have made a strong impression on the young wife, one that she never forgot.

Additionally, the uncertainties and disruptions of war, along with several bad harvests, would have seriously affected the availability of goods and supplies as well as prices and profit margins. Such fluctuations must have made every married couple feel financially and physically vulnerable, no matter how steady their business dealings or heavy the iron bolt on the front door. At any moment, Julian's husband might be conscripted to go to war abroad. How could Julian, a new bride, support and manage the household and the servants as well as maintain her husband's business affairs all by herself while he was gone? Many a young wife took on just such responsibilities before she was out of her teens. It was a tenuous time to be starting a family.

Pregnancy

During 1359–1360, Julian might well have been pregnant with her first child (a vision of a child will figure dramatically in her *Revelations*, as we shall see). Pregnancy for every woman was a time of joy and trepidation, given the threats to both mother and child during gestation and birth. Julian, like all women her age, knew the dangers. The poll and hearth taxes of the period show that the death rate for women between twenty and forty years of age was *higher* than that of men (even given the rate of male war fatalities), no doubt due to the risk of dying in childbirth as well as the greater susceptibility to disease among nursing mothers.[9]

In popular *fabliaux* (short, comic, often bawdy, popular tales told in verse by *jongleurs*, or minstrels, in France, which became popular in England during the fourteenth century),[10] as well as in canon law and theological treatises, there is little or no attention paid to pregnancy and parenting. All the contemporary teachings focused on marriage, the relationship between husband and wife, and the responsibilities of the wife toward her husband, but *not* on those of becoming a mother to his children. (Even *Le Ménagier de Paris*, which covers every aspect of a wife's behavior and extensive duties, never instructs his fifteen-year-old spouse about her future role as a mother.)[11] A father was held accountable for the financial care of his offspring, both legitimate and illegitimate (a wife was also obliged to care for her husband's bastards). The father was especially responsible to provide his children with a religious education.[12] In fact, St. Thomas Aquinas considered the primary good of begetting children was that they might be educated to worship God.[13] Unlike religious writers, didactic writers tended to stress the value of parenthood for a father in perpetuating his family name and assuring an heir for his estate and business properties. But no one seemed to think it necessary to dwell on training young women for the role of motherhood.

The Blessed Virgin had long been revered as the Mother of God and was a prominent figure in Western painting and sculpture of the High and Late Middle Ages, as we have seen. Mary was depicted as giving her consent to become the Mother of the Savior at the annunciation by the angel Gabriel; as noticeably pregnant; and as visiting her cousin, Elizabeth, also large with child, the future John the Baptist. Mary was shown holding her newborn baby in her arms for the shepherds and three Magi to adore and, as previously mentioned, nursing her infant son, her breast exposed. Every aspect of Mary's motherhood and, by extension, all motherhood was made holy and beautiful and worthy of veneration by medieval artists.

There was even the story of Mary's holy house in Walsingham, a village very near Norwich. In 1061, it was believed that Mary had appeared in a vision to Richeldis de Faverches, a Saxon noblewoman, and asked her to build a simple structure of wood, similar to the house where Mary had been living at the time of the annunciation in Nazareth. The house was duly built (later, a priory for Austin canons was erected there as well), and became a shrine of great popular pilgrimage and the working of miracles. English kings from Henry III to Henry VIII and his wife, Catherine of Aragon, made pilgrimages to Walsingham, the latter king praying for a male heir.

Occasionally a sermon would touch on the duties of motherhood. More often, it accused mothers of becoming too caught up in the managing of their households to worship God properly; or of being too attentive to their children's needs and loving them too much "according to the flesh alone," or of spoiling them with material goods instead of teaching them to worship God.[14] Other sermons viewed children as a burden, a distraction, even a cause of sin, in that peasants refused to pay tithes because of their children's upkeep, or parents worked their whole lives merely to support their children and thereby neglected the worship of God.[15] Eustache Deschamps, the French poet and melancholic author of *Le Miroir de Mariage* writes:

> Blessed is the man who has no children, for infants are nothing but wailing and smells, a source of sorrow and anxiety. They must be

> clothed, shoed, and fed. There is always a danger that they will fall and injure themselves or sicken and die. When they grow up they may go to the bad and be cast into prison. They can bring no happiness which can compensate for the fears, trouble and expense of their upbringing.[16]

Philippe de Novare was one of the rare commentators who affirmed that the joy parents felt in children was the greatest wealth of all. Yet there was always the deep-seated fear among parents that children, though given by God, were "conceived in sin" and could be taken away by God as a punishment. The rate of infant mortality was so high in the Middle Ages that this terror of losing one's baby had strong foundations.

It has been estimated that in English noble families between 1330 and 1479, 36 percent of boys and 29 percent of girls died before reaching their fifth birthday[17] (and this with the highest level of care, attention, and good food that money could buy). While there are no figures for the frequency of stillborns or deaths immediately postpartum, it is assumed the number was extremely high.[18] From several parish records in sixteenth-century England, it becomes painfully clear that even in the Renaissance, 30 percent of infants died during delivery and 50–60 percent of infants who died in the first year succumbed in the first month.[19] Yet, in spite of the warnings about suffering in childbirth, of the burdens of motherhood, of homiletic chastisements of mothers who love their children too much, and of the ever-present fear of maternal or infant mortality, women got pregnant and bore children in abundance. And they prayed.

Early in her pregnancy, Julian might well have gone on pilgrimage to Walsingham to pray for a safe delivery and a healthy baby. In addition to prayer, Julian would also have talked at length with her circle of women friends who had already borne a child or two and learned from them what she most needed to know: which foods to eat during pregnancy, which to avoid, and which saints to implore for special protection. She would have heard the warnings about not lifting heavy objects or overworking lest she suffer a miscarriage. As her pregnancy advanced, the women would have tried to predict the sex of the child: a clear, rosy complexion on the pregnant mother meant she was carrying a boy, since boys were considered healthier than girls. Additionally, the male child was believed to lodge on the right side of the womb and the female on the left (implied in Genesis). If the fetus moved more energetically on the right side, it was definitely a boy.[20]

Julian most probably consulted several midwives, longtime friends of the family with many years' experience, and engaged two or three of them to deliver the child, since physicians were not trained in obstetrics. There were so many possible complications during delivery, then as now, that midwives instructed expectant mothers to pray for a safe delivery to the Blessed Virgin Mary and St. Margaret, patroness of childbirth, and against *mors improvisa* (unexpected death).[21] If a son were strongly desired, women were advised to pray to St. Felicitas who, according to legend, had given birth to seven sons.[22] Before she went into labor, Julian would have received a blessing both for herself and her fetus, and been encouraged by her parish priest to confess her sins and receive holy Eucharist, in case she should die.[23]

Childbirth

Delivery took place at home for both the nobility and for middle-class merchant wives. (No one would think of going to a hospital, which was only for the poor and destitute, unwed mothers, or the homeless.) During the course of labor and delivery, Julian would have been surrounded by a small group of female relatives and friends as well as her mother, to assist the midwives. The scene would have been similar to the very one Julian will describe in her text when she lay dying, just before she receives her visions. In fact, these may have been the very same *evencristens* who would stand watch around Julian's bedside more than a decade later.

A family "birth girdle,"[24] used by generations of female relatives who had had successful births, would have been placed around Julian's abdomen. Saints' relics were also brought from the parish church to be placed on the mother. One of the women may have put coral rosary beads into Julian's hands (coral was believed to have healing powers); another might have placed a pendant around her neck containing an image of St. Anne (the fecund mother of Mary and a much-revered patroness of childbirth);[25] yet another may have pinned up a brooch showing an icon of St. Margaret; and someone else might have hung charms and amulets around the bedposts and sprinkled the bed with water from Mary's holy well at Walsingham. These acts may seem superstitious, but the church chose to overlook such practices as long as the right prayers were said at the same time.

The Infant

When Julian's child was finally born, it was slapped on its buttocks to induce the first cry, its mouth and throat cleared of amniotic fluid or mucus, and its naked body laid on her abdomen. Then the midwife severed the umbilical cord and tied it off with soft woolen thread, leaving four fingers-width of cord. The cut ending of the cord was rubbed with the ash of a snail, saliva, cumin or cicely and bandaged in cotton previously soaked in olive oil. The baby was then bathed by the fire in a tub of warm water, with rose petals, salt, and olive oil. According to contemporary recommendations, the midwife washed the baby's tongue with warm water so the child would speak well, placed honey on its gums and palate to make it nurse effectively, massaged the head and face to improve its shape, and stretched out its legs and arms so they would grow straight. If the baby felt hot and thin it was considered sanguine or choleric, according to the medieval system of bodily humors, and rubbed gently with oil. If it seemed cool and flabby then it might prove melancholic or phlegmatic, and a more astringent, even stinging, ultra-fine salt rub was advised to stimulate the skin and protect it against cold, heat, and infection. Nostrils and ears were cleansed by use of the little finger (with the nail cut short) dipped in oil.[26] After this cleansing, oiling, and salting, the midwife dried and swaddled the baby in long linen strips tied with bands to straighten out the limbs[27] and gave the baby back to Julian to nurse. Later, the baby was placed in a sheltered area of the room, protected from daylight and loud noises, so that its eyes and ears would not be adversely affected. In colder months, great care was taken to set the baby's cradle near the fire in the great hall for warmth, but not so near as to risk burning from a random spark or falling log.

After Julian had been bathed, the bed linens changed, and her husband summoned to view the child for the first time, she must have been exhausted but radiant. She would have looked down at the sleeping infant in her arms, "the fruit of her womb," and felt the greatest joy of her life. Many years later, she would recall this joy of joys, the miracle of giving birth, in relation to Christ's own joy in giving birth to all humankind on the cross, the new beginning that would never end (63:40–42.321). Yet, for all her joy, Julian knew the dangers of the first few months and years. She and her husband would have been cautious about celebrating too much, lest, according to common thinking, their joy might seem presumption and the infant die.

Baptism and Churching

Under normal circumstances, the godparents and the midwife brought the baby to the parish church a week after its birth for the ceremony of baptism. The infant was completely undressed and held over a baptismal font. The priest poured water over the baby's head and recited the words of the sacrament: "God's creature, I hereby baptize thee in the Name of the Father, the Son, and the Holy Ghost."[28] The baby's head and body were anointed with holy oil and a pinch of salt was placed on its tongue. Afterward, the infant was covered in a white cloth to signify his or her new life in God. Speaking for the child, the godparents recited the *Credo* and *Pater Noster*, rejected Satan and all his pomp and all his works, invoked the intercession of the saints in a long litany, and promised to teach the child the holy faith of the Catholic Church. It was commonly held, though not part of official church teaching, that once a child was baptized its chance of survival greatly increased; it could be cured of illness or handicaps and live a healthy life.[29] Even if it died in infancy, before it could commit any sin, it would go straight to heaven. Some medieval preachers tried to console the parents of baptized infants (who later died) with this thought.[30]

What of the mother? Mothers were not allowed to worship in church until they had been ceremonially cleansed forty days after childbirth. According to the ancient Jewish custom of purification, a woman was unclean because of the contamination of retained menstrual blood (in which it was believed the child had been nourished *in utero*) after delivery. In Luke's gospel, the presentation of Jesus in the temple forty days after his birth was also the occasion of the purification of the Blessed Virgin Mary (Lk 2:22–40). By the Middle Ages, this rite of purification was called *churching*. According to custom, Julian presented herself to her parish priest and gave thanks for a safe delivery and a healthy child. She was spiritually cleansed of her impurity and received a blessing. She was then allowed to re-enter the community of the church.[31]

Mother and Child

It is most likely that Julian nursed her baby for at least two years, the recommended time before weaning. While Julian would write of the role of a *nurse* in her text, she was probably referring to the nurse who assisted her in daily child care, rather than to a wet nurse. Only English nobility tended to employ wet nurses, and authors of medical and secular works repeatedly advised *against* hiring a wet nurse and in favor of maternal nursing. Mother's milk was preferred for the child's physical development, and nursing was acknowledged to be emotionally satisfying both for child and mother. Preachers and writers of manuals for confessors generally censured women who did not nurse their own infants, calling them remiss in their maternal duties, even accusing them of unnatural behavior.

However, since even preachers and confessors knew that some women suffered from breast sores and inflammations, depression and other postpartum illnesses, or simply did not produce enough milk, they had to make allowances for mothers who could not nurse, or who delivered twins, as well as for babies whose mothers had died in childbirth.[32] Wet nurses were then deemed necessary, since animal milk was known to cause bad reactions in infants. But there was always the fear, with a live-in hired wet-nurse, that she might put her own child to the breast more often than the newborn in her care. And for an urban mother to send her newborn away for two years to a wet nurse in the country would mean loss of all emotional attachment during that crucial period of development. From everything we read in Julian's tender and intimate description of the mother and child interaction, it becomes clear that she would have nursed her own child and been a loving and attentive mother.

Medieval medicine held that the blood which had nourished the child *in utero* flowed after parturition into the arteries and veins leading to the breasts and there was turned into mother's milk. The breasts, in fact, purified the blood.[33] The church had long used the image of the female pelican who feeds her chicks with her blood by piercing her own breast as a symbol of Christ who saves his people through the bloody sacrifice of the cross. Julian must have grown increasingly sensitive to the power of such devotional images as she suckled her infant. We may assume that the maternal instincts developed in Julian through the carrying, delivering, and nursing of her child would later become the foundation for her understanding of the Motherhood of Christ, the core of her mystical theology.

A World of Brigands

Meanwhile, following the Treaty of Calais in October 1360, ending the first phase of the war, English men-at-arms started returning home from France. These lesser knights and soldiers of fortune, some of whom were former criminals, had become accustomed to murder, rape, and pillage during their long sojourn in France. Now they began to terrorize their homeland, effecting the same atrocities on their own countrymen as they had on the enemy. Everyone feared being attacked at any hour of the day or night. Wealthy merchants as well as whole villages were captured and held for ransom. Travelers, male or female, were not safe on English roads; traders and peasants carrying goods to market were easy targets for bands of robbers. At times it was the king's own knights who, under royal orders, fanned out in every direction to extract payment of material goods in return for protection from the marauders. Commoners complained in Parliament that lawless companies of men and archers, often under the command of a knight, "do ride in great routs in divers parts of England." They were said to burn manor houses and rape women, and "beat and maim and slay the people for to have their wives and their goods." They stirred up riots, disturbing the peace of the kingdom, "to the great mischief and grievance of the people."[34] Such an invasion by English armed thugs brought the brutality of the war in France close to home.

By 1362, an English statute would impose on justices the duty of gathering information on the peasant plunderers who were not willing to return to normal work and lawful living. However, the king and Parliament would do little or nothing to rein in the knights who led these lawless companies, since the nation counted on them to fight the next stage of the war with France.[35] In two separate bulls (*Cogit Nos* and *Miserabilis Nonullorum*) issued in 1364, Pope Urban V excommunicated the companies, calling them "unbridled in every kind of cruelty."[36] The bulls were meant to put a stop to anyone providing for or collaborating with the so-called companies, but they had very little effect. Even the promise of plenary indulgences (of all punishment due to sin) for those who died in combat against the companies did not put a stop to them.[37] The brigands continued to roam, terrorize, and wreak havoc both in France and, to a lesser extent, in England, for years to come. No one, whether lord or peasant, could ever feel safe.

All of these very real threats must have clouded Julian's experience as a new mother. She lived on the edge of terror for her child's security every day. Her many responsibilities no doubt kept her mind focused, and the joy of her new baby must have been a great consolation. Yet, like any parent who brings forth a child during wartime,

Julian must have asked herself repeatedly: *What kind of world will my child inhabit?*

The Mortality of Children

In the late spring of 1361, Julian was eighteen and very likely the mother of an eighteen-month-old toddler, not yet weaned. She may also have been pregnant with her second child, since breast feeding was considered to be the only (but never reliable) method of spacing births in the Middle Ages. Any form of birth control or, of course, abortion, was strictly forbidden by the church.

Julian and her husband had lived through the years of war, the constant threat of coastal invasions by French ships, piracy attacks on English merchant ships and the rapid decline of the wool trade, and they were trying to resume their lives with some sense of peaceful regularity. The English production of finished cloth was rapidly replacing the export of raw wool, and now that the port of Calais was ruled by the king of England, there was hope of improved commercial activity through Calais to Bruges and beyond.

Then the unthinkable happened. The dreaded plague descended again in 1361 and continued into the spring of 1362. It was termed the *Pestis Secunda*, the second pestilence, or more graphically, "the mortality of children." The overall death rate, estimated at 20 percent of the population, while not as great as the first time around, was disproportionately high among children born after the Great Pestilence, and among men.[38] There is no explanation for this; we know only that, from existing records, it seemed to be so. Women were first robbed of their children, then their husbands. To alleviate their suffering, women became so desperate to procreate that, it was said, they "took any kind of husbands, strangers, the feeble and imbeciles alike, and without shame mated with inferiors."[39] This reads like a gross exaggeration, but it is certainly an indication of the biblical desperation of the times: "A voice was heard in Ramah, wailing and loud lamentation, Rachel weeping for her children; she refused to be consoled, because they are no more" (Mt 2:18).

We can only imagine Julian's terror, the renewed memories and fears of her childhood now multiplied a thousandfold by being a wife and mother. She must have prayed day and night: *Lord, please don't let my child die! Lord, don't take my husband!* She would record in her text, many years later, in an oblique way, a visionary version of what had happened:

> And in this time I saw a body lying on earth, which body appeared heavy and fearful and without shape and form, as if it were a bog of stinking mire. And suddenly out of this body sprang a full fair creature, a little child, perfectly shaped and formed, swift and lively and whiter than the lily, which sharply glided up into heaven. The bog of the body betokens great wretchedness of our deadly flesh, and the littleness of the child betokens the cleanness and the purity of our soul. (64:24–30.325)[40]

This child, we may conjecture, was her firstborn, the darling of her heart. She must have spent the rest of her life mourning this baby, reassuring herself that since it had been baptized, its soul had flown straight to heaven. But there was little consolation for the mother who had been left behind. Julian may also have lost her husband at this time, since he is never mentioned in either of her texts. Perhaps only the pregnant Julian and her mother were left. At some point, Julian's mother probably came to live in Julian's home. And it is likely that Julian gave birth to her second child, a daughter, in the same bed in which she would later receive her visions.

How may we surmise there was, indeed, a *second* child who lived? And on what basis may we suggest it was *a daughter*? Julian would one day write about a mistake she made during the time of her Revelations from the Lord:

> And when God almighty had shewn me plenteously and fully of his goodness, *I desired of a certain person whom I loved, how it would be with her* [what her life would be like]. And in this desire I letted [hindered] myself, for I was not taught in this time. (xvi.12–13.97, italics added)

She is given a spiritual instruction that no private information will be given her about anyone with whom she has such a close, personal attachment. Might this not reasonably have been her second child? If Julian gave birth to her daughter during the winter of 1361–1362 (soon after the deaths of her husband and first child), then this *second* child would have been approaching puberty when Julian received her visions in May of 1373. Julian would have been concerned about her daughter's spiritual life, as well as doing everything she could to safeguard her virginity for marriage. She might even have been thinking about a marriage arrangement for her daughter at this time. Of all people who would have come to Julian's mind during her visionary experiences, would it not have been her own child? She clutches at the opportunity to ask the Lord about "a certain person whom I loved," more precious to her than anyone else in the world, and begs the Lord to tell her, in essence: *Will she live a holy life?* Almost immediately, her reason tells her that she is overstepping the bounds of what she has a right to know. By seeking to discover the future, she is creating an obstacle for herself and hindering the flow of grace. She is profoundly humbled when she realizes the audacity of her petition and understands that she must care about every child as much as her own flesh-and-blood daughter.

From 1369 to 1373

Julian's visionary experiences are yet to come. Let us now consider the year 1369: Julian is perhaps a young widow of twenty-six (her birthday did not fall until November), with a seven-year-old daughter in her care. In addition to being a single parent, she may be managing her husband's textile business as *femme sole*: an unmarried or widowed woman who owns her own property, who can sue or be sued in court, and who maintains the right to make binding contracts and conduct trade. She would have needed to work in order to support her mother, daughter, employees, household servants, and apprentices as well as herself. As we saw, guild rules allowed the wife of a merchant or craftsman to assume her husband's business on his death, *if* she had already worked with him for many years and had learned the requisite skills. She could not take on any new apprentices (other than her own child), but she could keep training those in the household at the time of her husband's demise. Merchants' wives were often known to continue their husband's international trading businesses, importing and exporting finished cloth and a wide variety of other merchandise.[41]

We may assume that, during this period, Julian chose not to remarry, although the pressure to do so must have been very great. Very few spinsters or young widows remained unmarried for long, especially after the plague had so decimated the population. And Julian was, after all, still considered a young woman . . . at least, until she turned thirty. On the other hand, Julian might have preferred her newfound independence as a single woman, owning her own business and making all the household decisions. It was an independence that no married woman under her husband's control could ever enjoy.

Then, for the *third* time in her short life, Julian's world imploded. The plague returned to England in 1369: "It was great beyond measure, lasted a long time and was particularly fatal to children."[42] At the same time, an epidemic of cattle disease decimated the herds.[43] In addition, the harvest of 1369, following years of bad harvests due to exceptionally rainy summers, was deemed the worst in half a century, making wheat and grains of every kind scarce and very expensive. Could anyone doubt that the "wrath of God" had descended upon the land? Preachers insisted that people, animals, and crops were suffering as a direct result of waging war on France, rampant immorality, violence, and the love of luxury at home.

Julian's Ordeal

Julian must have lived in great fear from day to day, year to year. She never knew where or when the dreaded pestilence would strike next . . . or whom. Would she lose her second and only surviving child? Like someone under constant bombardment, she could not find any peace in living her life. She attended more funerals of relatives, servants, friends, and neighbors, in a fog of mourning so intense it seemed like not feeling anything at all. Life seemed so cruel, so unfair. And God so far away. There is a reason why the fourteenth century appears obsessed with Domesday, of which Julian herself would speak. The Dance of Death was a daily occurrence. And even when there was a pause for celebration, people dreaded the coming appearance of the four horsemen of the Apocalypse (Rv 6:1–8).

Julian's resilience must have been breaking down, no matter how hard she prayed for strength to endure . . . to go on believing in a loving and protective Creator. If "God so loved the world that he gave his only Son so that everyone who believes in him may not perish but may have eternal life" (Jn 3:16), then *why? why? why* was there still so much death? Julian's mind became overshadowed by sorrow; she sank into a long, excruciating dark night of the soul. Old childhood fears resurfaced; new terrors closed in upon her. Was all this suffering a divine punishment for sin, as the preachers repeatedly said it was, or

Satan's testing of humanity's faith in God, like the temptations visited on Job? Was God's wrathfulness toward sinners greater than his love? Had she committed some terrible offense to bring down God's fury on her family? Was God angry with *her*? In addition to the unbearable grief of losing one child and the dread of losing another, an all-pervasive sense of guilt, fed by medieval attitudes, must have suffused her soul. Yet instead of *blaming* God for her suffering, she begged forgiveness for herself and all her *evencristens*, buried her terror, and sank into a deeper depression. Would the black cloud of pestilence come again and again until it took her, too? The Book of Revelation (often quoted by medieval preachers) warned that death would arrive "like a thief" (Rv 16:15). Christ himself had told his followers to be watchful:

> Then two will be in the field; one will be taken and one will be left. Two women will be grinding meal together; one will be taken and one will be left. Keep awake therefore, for you do not know on what day your Lord is coming. But understand this: if the owner of the house had known in what part of the night the thief was coming, he would have stayed awake and would not have let his house be broken into. Therefore you also must be ready, for the Son of Man is coming at an unexpected hour. (Mt 24:40–44, cf. Lk 17:35, Mk 13:32-37)

When we examine Julian's text, we will attempt to follow her spiritual ordeal, from falling headlong into a deep ditch of physical pain, to being pulled up, up, up from certain death by the love of Christ. She will not only experience Christ on the cross, she will come to understand, at least intuitively, the value of human suffering. And in Christ's ultimate sacrifice, she will glimpse its power to radically transform the human condition itself. She will begin to identify her own suffering with Christ's and, most of all, experience not the wrath but the *compassion* of a Savior who loves so much, he insists: "If I might suffer more, I would suffer more" (22:41–42.197). Julian will be able to imagine this inordinate love because she herself was a mother who would do *anything*, even give her life, to save her only child.

Some interpreters of Julian's text jump to the end of her twenty-plus years of reflection on her Revelations and call her naturally optimistic, or "a happy saint," as if she had been that way from the very beginning.[44] Given the tragedies of her lifetime and the pain-filled questions that arise in her text, this appellation does not seem plausible. In fact, considering the personal losses and mental anguish she endured, we may reasonably posit a psychological basis for her own near-death illness in 1373, at the age of thirty, following the third wave of plague. Whatever her unnamed disease was, it was most certainly *not* a figment of her imagination, nor brought on by female hysteria. Yet the conditions for her physical breakdown may have had their foundation in many years of spiritual darkness. The twisted roots of inconsolable mourning, coupled with corrosive guilt, will eventually take their toll on a person's mental and physical health. The symptoms may not show up for months, even years. But eventually, these roots will invade the immune system. In Julian's case, they would have invaded the very immune system that had already withstood *three cycles* of the Great Pestilence.

Recent research has shown that deep emotional scarring (such as the shock of a husband's or a child's death, or clinical depression endured over many years) actually alters the chemistry of the brain. Likewise, post-traumatic shock affects the variations in levels of stress hormones and chemicals that carry information between the nerves. Severe stress may even cause lesions in the brain that can lead to pulmonary edema.[45] While scientists still do not know the actual cause of Post-Traumatic Stress Disorder (PTSD), or what triggers it in some people and not in others who undergo the same or similar experiences, they do know that it involves psychological, genetic, physical, as well as social factors. Could a syndrome such as this have been the catalyst for Julian's mysterious illness?

Throughout her text, Julian will refer repeatedly to her tendency to sloth, considered one of the seven deadly sins. It is the failing she confesses and fears the most. The medieval concept of sloth, which in Latin was termed *acedia,* meant a general apathy toward life, a physical or spiritual laziness, even to the point of postponing (or not doing) what one knows to be God's will. In its most extreme form, it is the total absence of caring about anything at all. Julian will reveal, in a startling and very modern tone of voice, that during her grave illness, "I felt a great loathesomeness to die, but for nothing that was on earth that I wanted to live for" (3:5–6.131).

What a classic expression of emotional depression! She had a young daughter, yes, but she does not mention her until much later in the text. Her mother also stood at her bedside; there were friends and relatives gathered around her, the *evencristens* for whom she would eventually write her book. Yet the severity of Julian's language suggests that, just before her visions began, her remembered state of depression was so extreme that she simply did not care whether she lived or died. In the spring of 1373, Julian had carried her emotional and psychological burdens for twenty-four years, ever since she was six years old. She felt worn out and ready to die at the age of thirty.

8
Schism, Heresy, and Revolt

Beginning in 1309, seven consecutive French popes had resided at the Palais des Papes in Avignon instead of in the eternal city of Rome. The Spiritual Franciscans (those who followed St. Francis's teachings on poverty most strictly) compared this period of church history to the captivity of Israel in Babylon.[1] However, the Avignon popes were far from being held captive by anyone but their own curia of cardinals, bishops, canon lawyers, theologians, and a vast army of clerics. They held court in the grand manner and lived a shamelessly lavish lifestyle, comparable to that of the richest kings and the Holy Roman Emperor. While Avignon in the south was fairly independent of the French king's rule in the north, these French popes nevertheless came to be more and more under the monarchy's power, military protection, and sphere of influence.

From Avignon, the papacy appointed personal favorites to be cardinals, archbishops, and bishops, granting them manor houses and vast lands throughout England and on the Continent, in addition to the customary benefices (church properties and incomes given to individual clerics for the performance of some spiritual service) that were attached to each position. The pope received tithes from every town and country in Europe, plus the first year's income from the estates of every newly appointed bishop and other taxes raised for crusades. Additionally, he accumulated fees from the granting of indulgences, marriage (and other) dispensations, and regular parish collections for Peter's Pence. As a result, popes could afford to finance the building of elaborate cathedrals, monasteries, and churches as well as the grand expansion of the papal palace at Avignon (which eventually covered more than two and a half acres). They also acquired luxurious personal wardrobes, silver, gold, and jewels, and they entertained regularly at banquets for kings, princes, foreign dignitaries, and fellow ecclesiastics. In its ever-increasing effort to expand its power, influence, and financial resources, the papacy was accused of corruption and heavy-handed political maneuverings. It was also seen as siding with France during the Anglo-French war. In short, the papacy became, for those who found fault with the Church, the crux of the problem.

The English, especially, resented the exorbitant payments made yearly to a French pope, payments that amounted, it is said, to more than the entire income from English taxes. John Wyclif, the Oxford don, calculated it to be £100,000[2] per year. Even in the papal court at Avignon, it was joked that "the English are good asses, for they carry well all the loads laid on them."[3] Although under the direct influence of French politics, the Avignon popes must be credited with having made repeated attempts to make peace between the two warring nations.

The Papal Schism

Finally, in 1376, at the urging of Catherine of Siena, Pope Gregory XI agreed to return to Rome, hoping to win back church lands that had already been lost in recurring civil wars and to reestablish the papacy in the city of St. Peter. After Pope Gregory's death, within a mere two years, chaos ensued. Roman mobs demanded that the college of cardinals choose a Roman pope, or at least an Italian one. Under great pressure and fear of bodily harm, the cardinals duly elected a little-known Neapolitan monk, Urban VI, who proved to be a disastrous choice. Almost immediately, he appointed a rash of Italian cardinals, greatly reducing the control of the French cardinals over the papacy. He then proceeded to castigate in no uncertain terms all the cardinals for their despicable morals, upbraid them for their love of pomp, and demand an end to their holding multiple bishoprics and abbeys which produced the enormous incomes that supported their indulgent lifestyles. While the new pope was determined to make much-needed reforms, his belligerent manner antagonized everyone. Given to violent outbursts of temper, he was exceedingly tactless, rude, and undiplomatic. The French cardinals, along with three Italians, convened in secret to elect a new (and politically expedient) pope, Robert of Geneva, a cruel and conniving despot. As papal legate in 1377, Robert had ordered troops to massacre thousands of men, women, and children in Cesena, which resulted in his receiving the appellation

"Butcher of Cesena." Now this man became the first *antipope*, Clement VII. He returned from Italy with the French cardinals to re-establish the court at Avignon.

Thus the catastrophic Papal Schism of 1378–1417 was launched. It marked the end of the medieval papacy as the acknowledged unifying spiritual leader of all the nations of Catholic Europe. For the rest of the fourteenth century and into the fifteenth, Europe would divide its allegiance to the papacy along strictly nationalistic lines: England, Ireland, Flanders, Denmark, Norway, Sweden, Poland, Hungary, Portugal, northern Italy, and the Holy Roman Empire vowed tribute to Urban VI and his successors; while France, Aragon, Castille and Léon, Scotland, Spain, Cyprus, Burgundy, Savoy, Naples, and Albania paid allegiance to Clement VII (and, after him, to Benedict XIII). The Roman papacy became dependent on whichever powers would support its claim to hold the chair of St. Peter. Excommunications were issued by Pope Urban VI against antipope Clement VII and vice versa, as well as toward everyone in the countries supporting them. Urban VI called on all of Christendom "to gird themselves for a crusade against the damned schismatics," meaning the French.[4] He counted on England to lead it. The religious tensions between the two nations were further exacerbated by a strong movement in England to resume the war against France. To support the English cause, an Act of Parliament declared Urban the rightful pope and it became treasonable to side with Clement. The next phase of the English war with France would become no less than "a religious quest," not only to unseat King Charles, but to do away with the Avignon antipope.

It was written that during those nearly forty years of schism, "Kingdom rose against kingdom, province against province, cleric against cleric, doctors against doctors, parents against their sons, and sons against their parents."[5] There were calculations that the Papal Schism caused the deaths of some two hundred thousand people in the ensuing carnage throughout Europe. Hyperbole, perhaps, but John Wyclif attested that "so general strife as now is among many realms was never heard of before from the beginning of the world."[6]

A Cloth in the Wind

Until the end of her life, sometime after 1416, Julian would live with two popes (three would later follow) vying for political power, with parallel excommunications causing spiritual chaos, religious wars raging among princes over which pope was valid, amidst a wounded, bleeding Christendom. This "kingdom divided against itself" (Mt 12:25) would no doubt be one of the driving forces behind Julian's internal struggle to maintain adherence to orthodoxy at all costs and to work unceasingly for the integration of her mystical experiences with the traditional teachings of the Catholic Church. There was so much at stake. She knew what the tragedy of schism looked and felt like. She prophesied that "Holy Church shall be shaken in sorrow and anguish and tribulation in this world as men shake a cloth in the wind" (28:4–6.211). She felt the lack of a single, authoritative, and trusted leadership. She witnessed the loss of faith and the brutality of brother against brother resulting from not one but two "holy, catholic, and apostolic" churches.

In addition to schism, *heresy* was the stiff wind violently shaking the fragile fabric of the church. Four decades of papal polarization would serve to disillusion and anger both educated and common folk alike. The papal schism introduced the volatile element of doubt into the long-held belief in the absolute spiritual and temporal authority of the pope. It created the controversial medium for Christians to question papal bulls that were issued from either side and to raise serious questions about the whole concept of divinely instituted leadership. When once these doubts and questions gained momentum, some Christians began to think the heretofore unthinkable: they questioned the need for allegiance to any pope at all.

As Julian set down and interpreted her visions from the Lord, she knew she had to do so with the utmost care, reiterating her faithfulness to the church with the greatest humility lest she, too, lead her *evencristens* astray. And that she never wanted to do.

The Wyclif Factor

John Wyclif, the most renowned preacher and doctor of theology at Oxford University, became the predominant English voice of opposition to the papacy. In his two treatises, *De Domino Divino* and *De Civili Dominio,* delivered first as Oxford lectures between 1374 and 1376, Wyclif developed a theory of lordship that vigorously opposed any religious authority that is inherently evil.[7] Wyclif insisted that an "unrighteous lord" is not to be obeyed, be he priest, bishop, cardinal, or even pope. *Dominicus* (that is, lordship, dominion, authority) belongs to God alone, and it is God alone who grants lordship (and properties) to kings, and through kings to the aristocracy, and thence to clerics. In fact, Wyclif insisted that clerics received their spiritual as well as their temporal authority *from royalty*, not from the papacy, effectively turning upside down the doctrine of the divinely appointed supremacy of the Catholic Church. He also asserted that if an ecclesiastical lord (either pope or bishop) proves himself immoral, corrupt, simoniacal, and unable to manage his earthly holdings, he is guilty of mortal sin; therefore, his lordship becomes invalid, he may be deemed a traitor to the king, he forfeits his authority, and ipso facto, all his ecclesiastical property may be confiscated by the state.[8] It was an incendiary idea.

Wyclif went even further. Since, in fact, *every* man is a sinner, no monk, friar, or secular priest, not even those deemed by others to be "righteous," should ever hold temporal possessions. He called it an evil to do so.[9] In his scathing sermons and writings, he railed against the immorality, wealth, and worldliness of both the monastic and secular clergy. He advocated a church *entirely without property* and demanded that all clerical lands that had been previously bequeathed by wealthy lords to the church be disendowed and returned to the state. Wyclif also called for the total abolition of payments of English gold to the papacy in Avignon, since they drained England's coffers and fed those of its enemy, France. Of course, the English king welcomed such an argument. (It is notable that in 1373, Wyclif had received a "prebend," or paid post equivalent to that of a canon, from Pope Gregory XI, along with income from a collegiate church at Oxford, as well as another substantial benefice as "absentee cleric" at the church in Lutterworth, Leicestershire. These positions and payments notwithstanding, Wyclif maintained that he abhorred benefices of any kind.)

Wyclif's initial intention, namely, to chastise and shame the hierarchy into a radical reformation, may have been sincere. No doubt the wealth and moral hypocrisy of the higher clergy stood in stark contrast to his awareness of the scriptural teachings of Jesus Christ on poverty and humility, which Wyclif insisted God's servants *should* be practicing. However, his written and preached diatribes against the clergy grew more and more vengeful. He called the secular clerics "devils," and accused regular monks of a self-satisfied un-spirituality which he dubbed "a religion of fat cows."[10] He castigated the papacy as "full of poison" and called the pope a "horrible fiend" who was not even necessary to the church: "he is not the head, life, or root except perchance of evil doers in the Church."[11] The pope himself was the antichrist, and Rome "more cursed than Sodom or Gomorrah."[12]

Wyclif became convinced that since every man had Christ to protect him, no man needed either pope or bishop to attain salvation.[13] He railed against the granting of papal indulgences as a heresy that men should flee.[14] The more he railed, the more numerous his political friends became, especially in London, both among anti-clerical lords who hoped to confiscate church properties and among poor clerics who resented their ecclesiastical superiors' great wealth. Wyclif knew how to play upon the grievances of his various audiences and, having taken on the role as the defender of the English king's authority over that of the pope, he pushed his condemnations to the limit. He taught that there was only one, true, universal church, that of the elect in heaven and those predestined to heaven, though still on earth. However, he categorically denied that the pope, any pope, was the true head of that church of the elect. Only Jesus Christ is head of the church. Since no pope can prove that he is a predestined and a truly *elect* member of the church, no pope can be considered the unique representative of Christ on earth or head of the "church militant." Still, Wyclif upheld the commonly accepted medieval belief that there was no possibility of salvation outside of the Catholic Church.[15]

When Wyclif's treatises on the Church (*De Ecclesia*, 1378) and on the power of the papacy (*De Potestate Papae*, 1379) were published, his extreme positions overstepped the bounds of what even his most ardent followers at Oxford and at the king's court in London were willing to support.[16] By questioning the validity of the Catholic Church on earth, the authority of the pope, and the office of the priesthood, Wyclif struck at the core of the hierarchy itself. He further inveighed against the very existence of monastic orders and denied that these religious "sects," as he called them, had any foundation in the Bible or provided any service whatsoever to the church. He called for the immediate destruction of all "chantries, abbeys, and houses of prayer"[17] and the restoration of all monastic lands and riches to the poor and to the state. More was to come.

In his treatise on the Eucharist (*De Eucharistia*, 1379), Wyclif flatly and publicly denied transubstantiation, the doctrine of the sacramental presence of the body and blood of Jesus Christ under the appearances of bread and wine.[18] He called the sacred host a figurative "sign" or "holy signification," but not real presence.[19] He wrote: "The consecrated host is neither Christ nor any part of him, but the effectual sign of Him."[20] Wyclif tried to modify his heretical view by defining the eucharistic miracle as *con*substantiation: that is, *both* the substance and accidents of bread and wine remain *and* Christ's presence appears. He explained that "Christ lies hidden in the elements" (as in a tomb) and that "by faith" we can see him there.[21] But that teaching totally vitiated church doctrine on the nature of the Eucharist, as well as the long-held belief in a radically altered reality.

Wyclif went on to attack the priesthood itself as extraneous, since he held that no priestly intermediary was needed between God and man. Even the Eucharist was not dependent on the words of the priest, as they were only its "occasion."[22] According to Wyclif, the only requirement of orthodoxy was adherence to *Goddes Law*, as given by the authority of the Bible; not papal teachings, not the writings of the church fathers, nor the ecumenical councils' definition of doctrine. But who was to interpret the Bible's rule of law for the uneducated laity, the *lewed*, if not educated clerics? Wyclif believed that simple, unlearned men (most of whom could barely read) could understand the meaning of scripture on their own.[23]

Wyclif further obviated the need for the sacrament of penance, deeming that any confession to a priest who was in mortal sin was ineffective, and who could know which priest was or was not in mortal sin?[24] For Wyclif, sins were to be confessed only in private, directly to God. Wyclif considered that since all men are predestined to heaven and eternal blessedness or to hell and eternal damnation, nothing one does during one's lifetime, even committing mortal sin, can change God's will.[25] Curiously, Wyclif did hold to the existence of purgatory as a place of purification for those predestined to go to heaven, and he believed in hell for the greater part of mankind that would be damned.

Wyclif sought to sweep away, in addition to the sacraments, the role of the teaching authority of the *magisterium*, and he discounted the abiding presence of the Holy Spirit in the church, which had been promised by Jesus Christ (Jn 14:16–17). Wyclif set up an impassable divide between the *holy* church (which included the "church triumphant" in heaven, as well as that elect "congregacion of trewe Cristene men"[26] on earth who are predestined to salvation), and the *false* church (the pope as the antichrist, or the devil incarnate, who presides over the church of the damned). In doing so, Wyclif raised many of the same philosophical doubts and theological denials that would be taken up by the Reformation.

Thus Julian's prophecy of the church being "shaken in sorrow and anguish and tribulation in this world as men shake a cloth in the wind" (28:4–6.211) would be fulfilled, not only in her own lifetime, but again during the Reformation more than one hundred years later, when the very fabric of Christendom would be torn and shredded into many divergent sects.

The Peasants' Revolt

In the midst of the ongoing papal schism and the spread of Wyclif's heresies, King Edward III died in June 1377, after a fifty-year reign (following his son, the Black Prince, who had died in 1376). He was the only king most of his subjects, including Julian of Norwich, had ever known. By the time of his death, the territorial gains in France ever since Crécy and Poitiers (primarily the lands of Aquitaine and Gascony) had been irretrievably lost. Only the towns of Bordeaux and Bayonne, in addition to the important commercial Port of Calais, were still under English rule. The new king, Richard II, son of the Black Prince, was ten years old and placed under the wardship of John of Gaunt, Duke of Lancaster, Edward's third surviving son. John of Gaunt ruled England during Richard's minority and managed to alienate most of the aristocracy. He was by far the richest, most powerful, and possibly the most ruthless man in England.

By 1380, in order to support the exorbitant lifestyles of King Richard's inner circle of royal uncles, lords, councilors, and prelates (as well as John of Gaunt's personal ambitions in Spain), the third poll-tax in four years was levied against every English citizen over fourteen years of age. Each time the tax rate had increased, antagonism had mounted. Peasant farmers, city laborers, and local artisans simply could not afford the burden of extra taxes year after year. The merchants also resented it mightily, especially since, in every village and town, the well-off had to make up for the allotment the poor could not pay. In addition, the tax collectors were empowered to inquire into every aspect of people's personal lives. It was reported that some of the tax collectors raped wives and young girls. Deceit and evasion, as well as briberies to the tax collectors to undercount household members, became so rampant that, on the ensuing tax records, the population appeared to have fallen by one-third from 1377 to 1381.[27]

Strikes erupted all over England, signaling the first organized social protests in the realm's history. The situation grew ripe for revolution. Towns in Essex on the east coast, north of London, refused to pay and turned to violent protest. At the same time, a large contingent of peasants and yeomen, carrying picks, axes, poles, scythes, longbows, swords, and knives gathered farther south in Kent, where they sacked private homes, burned manor houses, and invaded monasteries, destroying records of villeinage and debt. Since the villeins had no right to bring legal charges against their oppressive overlords in court, they summarily killed the most hated lords and chief justices, sticking their heads on poles. Moving north to Rochester, the Kentishmen forced the surrender of the castle, liberated a runaway villein, and arrived at Maidstone, where they chose Wat Tyler, a seasoned veteran from the wars in France, as their leader. Then they headed toward Canterbury. There, the angry mob invaded the cathedral during Mass and demanded the release of John Ball (a renegade priest and probably a follower of Wyclif) from the archbishop's prison. John Ball became the official spokesman of the peasant army, preaching incendiary sermons to the crowds, urging them to throw off the hated burden of villeinage and to destroy all those in positions of authority, so that all Englishmen could be of equal ranking, freedom, and power.[28] It is possible that he spoke the words that became a ringing cry for the peasant cause thereafter:

> When Adam dug, and Eve spun, who was then a gentleman? From the beginning all men by nature were created alike, and our bondage or servitude came in by the unjust oppression of haughty men. For if God would have had any bondmen from the beginning, he would have appointed who should be bond, and who free. And therefore I exhort you to consider that now the time is come, appointed to us by God, in which you may (if ye will) cast off the yoke of bondage, and recover liberty.[29]

Led by Ball and Tyler, the rebel hordes, estimated by contemporary chroniclers at twenty thousand men, marched toward London, traversing the seventy miles on foot in just two days. Partisan sympathizers opened the London city gates, and the rebels poured in, demanding the heads of sheriffs, tax collectors, judges, lawyers, abbots, bishops, lords, and dukes.[30] Drunk on power and lusting for blood, the mob liberated Marshalsea prison, then descended on the archbishop's house at Lambeth, where they burned official chancery records. From there, they marched to Fleet prison, set fire to the lawyers' hated deeds and records at the New Temple, and destroyed the treasurer's house. They murdered Sir John Cavendish, the chief justice of England, and proceeded to raid the bishop of Lichfield's palace. They also sacked and burned the lavish Savoy palace of John of Gaunt, Duke of Lancaster, blowing up all its art treasures with gunpowder found in storage, pounding his precious jewels with axe heads and throwing his rich furnishings into the Thames. Throughout London, prisons were opened, convicted felons set free, lawyers, judges, and other representatives of the royal court beheaded. The hospital of the Knights of St. John in Clerkenwell was set afire and burned for seven days.[31] Tyler and his army also hunted down and murdered so-called *aliens,* mostly Lombards and Flemings, along with rich city burghers and merchants. Anyone who symbolized the ruling or wealthy class had to be slain. Tyler boasted that "in four days' time all the laws of England would be issuing from his mouth."[32]

The leaders finally acquiesced to meet with the fourteen-year-old King Richard II at Mile End on the next day, June 14, 1381. Accompanied by the mayor of London and a small coterie of lords and knights, the king, sitting high astride his white horse, robed in royal purple, wearing his golden crown and carrying a scepter of the realm, approached the peasant army. The crowd, awestruck at seeing their young king in the flesh, knelt and acknowledged him as their sovereign, but they demanded that all those they deemed to be traitors be surrendered into their hands. Richard agreed, but only if these individuals were first tried and convicted in a court of law. The rebels then petitioned for the complete abolition of all villeinage and the hated poll taxes; the end of all servitude to their lords; the right to rent land belonging to the lord's demesne at fourpence an acre; and the freedom to hunt and cut in the forests, along with the ability to form free labor contracts at will.[33] The king, under mounting pressure, agreed to all their demands, granting charters written and signed, then and there, by thirty clerks.[34] He even consented to having all suspected traitors in the realm brought directly to him, so that he could personally guarantee they would be brought to justice.

Meanwhile, the king's own castle, the Tower of London, was being invaded by Wat Tyler's men, and the king's garrison of six hundred men-at-arms and six hundred archers was subdued without a fight. The mob entered the royal bedchambers and sacked the privy wardrobe, which contained the royal arms. In a most deplorable act, Archbishop Sudbury, together with Sir Robert Hailes (the king's chancellor and treasurer), various other royal councilors, and the Duke of Lancaster's personal physician were hauled out to Tower Hill and executed in front of cheering crowds. Their heads were mounted on pikes, marched in procession throughout the city, and finally stuck up on London Bridge.[35] The carnage continued throughout the next day, while King Richard confronted yet another mob, led by Wat Tyler, demanding a charter granting even more stipulations to be signed and sealed then and there. The demands included the eradication of all lordships (except for the king) in favor of total equality of men throughout the realm; the confiscation of the great estates of the church, to be apportioned out to the common people; and the end of all bishoprics, save one.[36]

With amazing calm, Richard agreed to all these astonishing demands, but Tyler was still not satisfied. The situation grew heated, angry words were exchanged between Tyler and the king's squire. Tyler drew a dagger. The mayor of London drew his sword, pulled Tyler down from his horse, and killed him on the spot. The king was in extreme danger from the mob, but to his great credit, he did not turn and flee. He rode directly *into* the angry crowd, now bereft of their leader and ready to attack the king's entourage. Richard cried out: "Sirs, will you shoot your king? I am your captain, I am your king, follow me." Amazingly, under the spell of royalty, the rebel host followed him as he rode his horse away from the city. A hastily gathered army of knights in full armor soon surrounded the leaderless rebels, but the king would not allow them to be slaughtered. He did, however, take Tyler's head and ordered it placed on London bridge in place of Archbishop Sudbury's.[37]

The revolt was not yet over. Uprisings, murder, and carnage continued to fan like wildfire into villages and towns outside of London.

The greatest violence erupted in the eastern counties by out-of-control villeins turning on their masters, even on abbots of monasteries, with a vengeance.[38] At Cambridge University, peasants and townsmen destroyed Corpus Christi College, seized priceless parchments documenting the history of the university, and burned them in Market Square.[39]

Violence in Norwich

In East Norfolk, mobs pillaged and looted recklessly. Geoffrey Litster, called "king of the commons" by his rowdy army of peasants, assembled on Mousehold Heath, forced open the gates of the city of Norwich and installed himself in Norwich Castle, feasting and drinking with his men, served by "captive" knights. Meanwhile, Litster's mob of rebels plundered and devastated the city, its cathedral and churches, burning rolls on which tax and other records were kept. The townsfolk, wealthy burghers, merchants and their families, Julian among them, must have bolted their doors, praying that their homes and businesses would escape looting and burning. From his Norwich castle mount, Litster dispatched rebels to nearby villages and monasteries, as far as Yarmouth, twenty miles away, with orders to loot and burn. Mock trials and real executions were carried out under his authority.[40]

On June 20, Litster sent two knights sympathetic to the peasants' cause, along with three peasants, off to London. They carried a large amount of money with them, extracted from Norwich citizens, to petition for a general pardon and to secure "a charter more special than the charters granted to other counties."[41] The entourage was stopped at Newmarket by Norwich's Bishop Despenser, just returning from his defense of Peterborough Abbey and the crushing of peasant mobs in Huntingdon and Cambridge. Despenser pardoned the two knights, as being of his own noble class, but executed the three peasants on the spot. Traveling on toward Norwich, Despenser learned that Litster and his band of men had already fled the cathedral city. Hot in pursuit, Despenser caught up with them at North Walsham, where his horsemen surrounded and destroyed the rebels' primitive defenses of carts and stolen furniture.[42] The bishop confronted Litster, heard his confession, gave him absolution, and promptly had him hung, drawn and quartered. Despenser brought

Litster's head back to Norwich and set it high over a city gate as a warning to any other peasants who might think of rebellion.

Random resistance sputtered, then died out over the next few months. Rebel leaders were hanged, but the great hordes of peasants, with their promise of pardons, eventually returned home. King Richard appointed a commission of aldermen to secure the future safety of London and its suburbs. When a representation of men arrived from Essex to petition the king to keep his solemn promise made at Mile End to abolish all villeinage, Richard reportedly retorted: "Villeins ye are and villeins ye shall remain."[43] Indeed, the king revoked all the pardons that he had granted under duress to the peasants and called for a lengthy juridical inquiry. Thereafter, the king and his new chief justice visited the devastated areas of the kingdom. The trials were many, the punishments swift and severe, but they stopped short of a general massacre.[44] The remaining leaders of the uprising were condemned to death. Among them was John Ball, who was hanged, drawn, and quartered at St. Albans in the presence of King Richard himself. The preacher's head joined those of the other rebels on London Bridge.

Julian's Reaction

Julian must have been horrified, not only at the breadth of murder and destruction in the city of Norwich, but at the population that had caused it. These were the same peasants and artisans, skilled laborers and common workmen with whom she did business on a daily basis in the marketplace, in the cloth business, in her home. These were the people she knew by name, with whom she talked regularly, attended Mass, walked in processions on holy days. Perhaps some of her own apprentices had taken part in the riots, or perhaps her cook's husband. There were even some Norfolk knights and other landowners who, out of their extreme discontent with the central government, had supported the peasants' rebellion.

Julian would have listened often to the peasants' grievances and, like many others, sympathized with their plight. She was herself only one or two generations removed from being a villein. She understood the mentality; she sympathized with the anger, their frustrations, the longing for freedom. Perhaps she remembered her father's stories of his own childhood escape to Norwich, and recalled her grandfather's hardened, wizened look from having been a laboring villein all his life, subject to the will of his lord and master. These men who had rioted, looted, and burned were her own people, her *evencristens.*

Julian, a mere woman born into the merchant class, had no power to change the labor laws or repeal the poll taxes in order to make the peasants' lives any easier. The poll taxes were a burden on her own household as well as on every other. She had always tried to be fair and charitable toward her servants and apprentices, caring for them in good times and bad. She had relied on them to be faithful to her in return. Yet some of these same people with whom she felt such affinity must have betrayed her, turned against her family as well as against other well-off merchants. Almost overnight, lawyers, judges, merchants, anyone with power in the city, had become the enemy. The mob had looted and destroyed property, even murdered, in the name of justice. How could she look any of these peasants in the face thereafter?

When Litster's head was brought back triumphantly by Bishop Despenser to Norwich and set up at the end of a long pike over one of the city gates, Julian might have joined the crowd of men and women who stood and watched in stunned silence. Like most of the onlookers, Julian had probably known Litster, a well-liked local artisan. For a short while, he had been hailed the *idolus Northfolkorum*, a leader with dreams of obtaining a king's charter for artisans like himself who wanted the freedom to work wherever they wanted to work, for wages they could negotiate, without the heavy restrictions of the Statute of Labourers. Many citizens must have sympathized with his passionate energy for social change, even wished his emissaries well as they set off for London to present their petitions to the king, before they were intercepted by Bishop Despenser and murdered. Now it was excruciating to gaze on Litster's disembodied head. No matter what he had done, did he deserve this fate? The blood was not yet dried where it had dripped down the side of his matted hair. The death mask was tortured, the last moment of agony before he breathed his last. Had Litster been truly repentant for all his misdeeds when he made his confession, just before the bishop had him slain? Was the face on the pike that of the good thief crucified next to Christ, or the bad thief? In her Long Text, Julian would write:

> That there are many evil deeds done in our sight and such great harms suffered, that it seems to us that it would be impossible that it ever could come to a good end. And upon this we look, sorrowing and mourning therefore, so that we can not rest ourselves in the blissful beholding of God as we should do. (32:8–11.221)

Was she referring directly to this horrific sight? That a bishop should order a man (to whom he had just granted absolution) killed without trial under the law was surely one of these "evil deeds." And everyone knew that the bellicose bishop was more comfortable encased in armor astride a war horse than clothed in vestments on the altar. The chronicler Walsingham described Despenser as "young, unbridled and insolent . . . endowed neither with learning nor discretion, experienced neither in preserving nor bestowing friendship."[45] History does not record the extent of Despenser's acts of butchery in putting down the peasant hordes in Yarmouth and North Walsham, but he must have led a typically brutal reprisal. His outrage against the presumption of villeins rising up against their lords was that of a nobleman against his serfs, not that of a bishop willing to go to any lengths to save his flock. Having seen their bishop show no mercy, how were the faithful to honor and obey him? No doubt, Despenser's swift retribution against rebellious peasants, which went on for months, caused a crisis of faith for many, including Julian. Public reaction was so violent against Bishop Despenser that the next year there was even a plot to murder him, but it was foiled.

After the Peasants' Revolt and the bishop's violent suppression, could Julian ever feel safe in Norwich again? The thick, protective walls had been breached, not by a French attack, but by an unruly peasant population with strong sympathizers among townfolk and clerics, who simply let them in through the gates. The "dread of afray" (74:1.355), or general raising of the alarm, which Julian would mention in her text, related not only to outside attack by French invaders from the sea; now, it became fear of Norwich *even-cristens* attacking one another inside the city walls.

The Short Text

At this very time, Julian must have been grappling with the parable of a lord who had a servant (a villein) who ran off and fell headlong into a ditch. This parable had appeared to Julian in the course of her visions eight years before. Perhaps, in 1381, she was still in the process of writing her first version of her *Revelations*; more likely, she had already finished the Short Text at the time of the Peasants' Revolt. Either way, it is important to notice that she deliberately *omitted* any reference to the mysterious parable that would assume a central position in her Long Text. Julian admits that it took twenty years before she was able to understand it (51:73.277). Could it be that her conflicted feelings over the Peasants' Revolt (sympathy with their cause and abhorrence of the measures they took to achieve it) made the process of interpreting the relationship of the noble lord with his servant all the more difficult? Though in 1381 Julian could not yet plumb the deeper meanings hidden in the parable, she must have sensed its profound relevance to the social upheavals of her time. She had seen with her own eyes the plight of the anguished peasants and their failed leaders, their mutilated bodies trapped forever in the burning pit, their heads hoisted up on the city's walls. What did the parable mean in relation to such sin and suffering? Had it been a prophecy? What was she to learn from it? How could she explain it to her *evencristens* if she could not comprehend it herself? Could Christ transform *even this* horror into something meaningful? She would have to wait another twelve years for the answers.

Denunciations of Wyclif

Following the Peasants' Revolt of 1381, the English aristocracy more and more associated the religious tenets of Wyclif with the insurrectionists and grew convinced that the heretics represented a dangerous *political* as well as religious movement. King Richard II, formerly supportive of Wyclif's ideas, became an outspoken opponent of the Oxford don and his followers and ordered them completely suppressed. As early as 1382, civil authorities were given power to detain suspected heretics for eventual investigation by church courts. Knights and nobles who had once been sympathetic to Wyclif's views also closed ranks against any wandering Wycliffites who might breed further sedition. They saw their own estates and political power threatened by Wyclif's anti-establishment and equalizing tenets. If Wyclif's demands for the disendowment of the holdings of the rich could cause enraged peasants to burn manor houses and monasteries once, they could do it again. Bishop Despenser, determined to maintain authority and orthodoxy in his diocese, vowed to eradicate heretics with the same violence he had shown toward Norfolk peasants. Walsingham wrote of the bishop's tactics:

> He swore, moreover, and did not repent of what he said, that *if anyone belonging to that perverse sect should presume to preach in his diocese, they should be taken to the fire or beheaded.* Consequently, having understood this, no one belonging to that tendency had any desire to embrace martyrdom, with the result that, up to now, the faith and true religion have remained unaffected within the bounds of his episcopal authority.[46]

The combined power of church and state stood firmly against the poor and disenfranchised. The peasants' grievances were not addressed, nor was freedom granted. But economic forces beyond the control even of bishops and nobles were already at work, seeding the changes that revolution could not effect.

To his final days, Wyclif was unwilling to alter any of his heretical opinions; in fact, he went further still and, in 1381, issued his staunchly heretical *Confessio*.[47] By May of 1382, the new Archbishop of Canterbury, William Courtenay, called a synod of bishops, theologians, and canonists at Blackfriars, the Dominican House in London, to examine twenty-four propositions drawn from Wyclif's published texts. These included his opinions on the sacraments of Eucharist and penance, the authority and jurisdiction of the papacy, and the relationship between lordship and grace.[48] At the end of four days of heated deliberation (interrupted by a major earthquake that seemed to signal divine justice deciding the matter), the so-called Blackfriars synod issued a unanimous denunciation of all the propositions as containing either outright heresy or grave error. Unaccountably, Wyclif himself was not called to stand trial. He was, however, henceforth forbidden to teach or preach at Oxford. Already retired to his parish at Lutterworth and suffering speech paralysis from a stroke, he nevertheless continued to write indefatigably: pamphlets, treatises, sermons, and tracts.[49]

Wyclif was summoned to Rome by Pope Urban VI but either refused or was physically unable to go. While hearing Mass in his church on December 28, 1384, he suffered a second stroke and died on New Year's Eve, alone but not totally forgotten. Thirty years later, at the Council of Rome (1412–1413) and again at the Council of Constance (1414–1418), the church *magisterium* would censure Wyclif's works in no uncertain terms, citing 45 propositions that had already been condemned by the universities of Paris and Prague as well as 260 grave errors. His writings were ordered to be collected and burned, and his body was to be exhumed and denied a resting place in consecrated ground. This was not actually carried out until 1428, when Wyclif's remains were dug up, burned, and thrown into the nearby River Swift, with the expectation that this would be the end of the spread of his heresies. It was not.

The Vernacular Bible

In the years 1378 to 1384, while making his attacks on the papacy as well as on the doctrines and sacred traditions of the church, Wyclif had raised the Bible to the position of sole, final, and absolute authority in all matters. The Bible became for him the one and only authority that taught *Goddes Lawe*.[50] In writing on the truth of sacred Scripture (*De Veritate Sacrae Scripturae*, 1378), Wyclif fiercely defended the Bible against friars and other academics who focused on its errors, inconsistencies, and contradictions, and who claimed that the scriptures could not be taken seriously as a practical guide for life.[51] Wyclif insisted that every Christian of whatever rank must hear, know, and learn the gospels *in the vernacular*, if he or she was to follow Christ and the rule of faith for salvation. Further, he demanded that bishops and priests study the whole law of scripture (primarily in the Old Testament) in order to fulfill their responsibility to preach the New Testament effectively to the faithful.[52] He strongly disagreed with official church policy that illiteracy and lack of theological education were sufficient justification for not allowing the people to hear or read holy scripture. Following St. Augustine, he argued that any man, no matter how infirm or sinful, should rather run to hear Christ speaking to him in the gospels.[53] He upheld the classic fourfold levels of interpreting scripture (literal, allegorical, moral, mystical), but insisted that the *literal* meaning is the primary and authoritative one and that all other scriptural meanings derive their authority from it.[54] To make the Bible available to every Christian, Wyclif put forth an ambitious program of translating the Old and New Testaments into Middle English. For all the controversy it would create, his vision of a vernacular Bible was no less than prophetic. Unfortunately, he never did learn how to win over the opposition to his side. Wyclif labeled those friars who attacked his plan as impractical, "foolish modern heretics."[55]

Why, we may ask, were the Franciscan and Dominican friars so averse to the translation of sacred scripture into the vernacular? Since their explicit mission was to preach to the people in the "mother tongue" in a way that even the uneducated could understand (in order to bring them all to God), why did the thoroughly orthodox scholars who taught at Oxford and Cambridge not instigate a vernacular translation of the Bible themselves? Why, in short, did the medieval church frown on the literal translation of the Bible from the Latin Vulgate?

The answer is that, traditionally, the Latin Church (unlike the Eastern Orthodox Church which had long employed the vernacular in reading scripture and in the recitation of the Divine Office) felt compelled to protect the sanctity and the mystery of sacred scripture from the large majority of the population that was uneducated. No one made this clearer than Pope Gregory VII in 1079, when he wrote:

> For it is clear to those who reflect often upon it, that not without reason has it pleased Almighty God that holy scripture should be a secret in certain places, lest, if it were plainly apparent to all men, perchance it would be little esteemed and be subject to disrespect; or it might be falsely understood by those of mediocre learning, and lead to error.[56]

There was a prevailing (and highly warranted) fear that a vernacular Bible, however well translated, would be copied repeatedly and, in the process, *mis*copied by careless scribes and give rise to grave mistakes (this, in the days before the printing press). And if the literal text were mistranslated or miscopied, then scripture itself would be misunderstood, thus leading to heretical viewpoints. There was the further danger that a vernacular Bible could be preached by unlearned and non-ordained common folk, effectively removing the interpretation of scripture from the exclusive domain of learned Latin clerics. Also, such a Bible could be read to or read by the *lewed* in the privacy of their own homes, without a priest to help them understand its meanings according to the four levels of scriptural interpretation. It was assumed that, without university training in theology, philosophy, and the dogmatic teachings of the church fathers, the uneducated would not be able understand the "glosses" or commentaries that accompanied scriptural texts The laity would be liable to misconstrue the correct import of sacred scripture and this, in turn, would give rise to the spreading of heretical doctrines (as indeed it did). At the Synod of Toulouse in 1229, official church position stated that:

> Lay people shall not have books of scripture, except the psalter and the divine office: and they shall not have these books in the vulgar tongue. Moreoever we prohibit that lay people should be permitted to have books of the Old or New Testament, except perchance any should wish from devotion to have a psalter, or a breviary for the divine office, or the hours of the blessed Virgin: but we most strictly prohibit their having even the aforesaid books translated into the vulgar tongue.[57]

Two Translations

In spite of the long history of condemnations, Wyclif, with the help of a small coterie of Oxford scholars and devoted scribes, initiated his life's most important legacy: the production of a complete English Bible. The first translation of the Old Testament, along with almost all of the New Testament, was completed in 1384 (the year Wyclif died) by a team of five Oxford scholars led by Nicholas Hereford, an esteemed colleague of Wyclif's and an early and passionate follower. This initial version was an extremely literal and very stilted translation of St. Jerome's Vulgate, following the order of the Latin word for word, resulting in a hopelessly unreadable text. Its very literalness meant the text did not flow like spoken language, making it impractical for traveling preachers who needed a vernacular translation that both they and their *lewed* audiences could easily memorize.[58]

The second version of the English Bible, completed sometime after 1395 (more than a decade after Wyclif's death), was a much freer and more colloquial translation, adjusting the sequence of words into recognizable and easily understandable Middle English sentences. This text read like a living language and became the preferred translation until the Reformation. It is generally believed that this second translation was the work of the eminent scholar John Purvey, one of Wyclif's trusted associates who followed him from Oxford to his parish at Luttersworth to serve as his personal secretary and who became the leader of the scholarly Wycliffites after his master's death.[59]

Wyclif's followers copied and disseminated the translation in small pamphlet formats. They then traveled the highways and byways of England, preaching the gospels openly in the vernacular tongue so that every man and woman might hear and learn them by heart.[60] They called themselves "poor priests," although they were only unlicensed laymen who had received no formal theological training or priestly ordination. In 1382, an Irish Cistercian monk, Henry Crump, first dubbed these peripatetic preachers "Lollards," naming them after contemporary Flemish lay preachers who wandered from town to town, preaching heresy and mumbling the gospels to one another. Such a pejorative appellation caused a sensation at the time, but the name stuck. Gregory XI, in his bull of condemnation, also called these pilgrims "Lollards." Wyclif's followers countered by using the term freely about themselves, in the sense of the Middle English *loll* (meaning to lounge or sprawl). They claimed that Christ was, in truth, "the most blessed Loller," in that "he lolled between two thieves."[61]

Condemnation of Lollardy

By 1399, King Richard, deposed and betrayed, had been murdered in the Tower of London. John of Gaunt, Duke of Lancaster, had also died, and his son, Henry of Bolingbroke, was crowned Henry IV. In 1400, the new king directed the enforcement of the erstwhile law that no chaplain or secular priest lacking a benefice should be permitted to preach in London.[62] The rapid spread of Lollardy had quickly become not only a religious issue, but a cause of political unrest as well.

Archbishop Arundel of Canterbury could feel the hot winds of heresy blowing out of control as Lollard tenets continued to be openly discussed, argued, attacked, and defended. By 1401, the archbishop began to take offensive action. He was the driving force behind the parliamentary statute, *De Haeretico Comburendo*, directed against those who thought "damnably" of the sacraments and presumed to "preach and teach these days openly and privily divers new doctrines, and wicked heretical and erroneous opinions contrary to the same faith and blessed determinations of the Holy Church."[63] The statute authorized any bishop to arrest, imprison, and within three months prosecute suspected heretics in an ecclesiastical court. If convicted, the heretics could be fined and imprisoned. If the heretics did not recant, or if they later relapsed, they were to be handed over to the local sheriff who was to receive them, and "before the people in an high place cause [them] to be burnt, that such punishment may strike fear into the minds of others."[64] The statute was granted by King Henry, sanctioned by the House of Lords, and supported in the House of Commons.[65] It was the first such law against religious offenders in England's history. In that same year, under the king's personal command, William Sawtre, the vicar of St. Margaret's Parish in Bishop's Lynn (forty-four miles west of Norwich), was the first Lollard burned alive for his heretical views.

Thereafter, in 1407, Archbishop Arundel called a provincial council at Oxford at which Thirteen Constitutions were passed, which strongly condemned Lollardy and acted decisively against its spread. These were published as the *Constitutions* of 1409. They reiterated that all preachers were to be licensed to preach and there was to be no more unlicensed preaching, "either in Latin or in the vulgar tongue," either in a church or the church-yard (that is, the cemetery). Further, no preaching by any secular or monastic priest was to take place without his first undergoing an examination of competence and orthodoxy by diocesan representatives and obtaining a letter of authority to preach. Additionally, if any parish curate allowed a visiting preacher to preach in his parish without such credentials, he was to be severely censured. Strict punishments were set out for those who did not conform. Sermon topics of even licensed priests were henceforth to be limited to the *Credo*, the *Pater Noster*, the *Ave Maria*, the Ten Commandments, the seven sacraments, the seven deadly sins, and so forth. It was further forbidden for any mere master of arts or grammar even to discuss the sacraments, nor could he examine holy scripture (except as a Latin grammar exercise) in the course of instruction to his young students. In direct condemnation of the Lollard Bible, Arundel formally declared:

> No one shall in future translate on his own authority any text of holy scripture into the English tongue or into any other tongue, by way of book, booklet, or treatise. Nor shall any man read this kind of book, booklet or treatise, now recently composed in the time of the said John Wycliffe, or later, or any that shall be composed in future, in whole or part, publicly or secretly, under penalty of the greater excommunication . . . Whoever disobeys this, let him be punished

> after the same fashion [as has been indicated above] as an abettor of heresy and error.[66]

No person was allowed to dispute these constitutions or any articles of the church. No chaplain could celebrate Mass in the archbishop's diocese without letters of testimony, and the University of Oxford was to hold examinations each month concerning these constitutions. Penalties were specified and procedures defined. Finally, the archbishop convicted the University of Oxford of bringing forth the wild and bitter grapes of Lollardy and setting the children's teeth on edge throughout the whole Church of England.[67]

In 1414, Parliament's own statute against heresy was further strengthened to allow all *secular* justices to examine suspected heretics and then turn them over to the ecclesiastical courts for trial. With this new authority, heresy became a punishable *civil offense* against the common law of England; secular as well as ecclesiastical courts were empowered to proceed aggressively against heretics.[68] Thereafter, at least seventy convicted heretics were hanged or burned at the stake. It was a new plague: religious persecution.

Julian and The Lollard Bible

Even after the extreme strictures of the Arundel *Constitutions*, there must have been many aristocratic and wealthy merchant households that still possessed these new English Bibles, just as their ancestors had retained French Bibles, though the church had never sanctioned those either. Since the Wyclif Bible was the *only* English Bible at this time, this would have been the version copied by scribes and widely disseminated, even among the orthodox. There was no listing of those who had done the translation, nor any scribal signature given on the pamphlets. In fact, the Wyclif Bible could have been read and studied by the most devout Catholics without their making any association with Lollardy.[69] If a learned spiritual director or a venerable doctor of theology verified the orthodoxy of a translation and considered it spiritually beneficial for a particular soul in his "cure," he could obtain a special license from the bishop for a certain individual to read the scriptures in the vernacular. This, of course, would have been more likely among the upper classes who retained personal curates to say Mass in their private chapels and who had confessors with the right connections.

It is entirely possible that during the early 1390s, before she was enclosed as an anchoress, Julian, like so many other faithful Christians, heard excerpts from the Old and New Testaments being preached in the open air by Lollard preachers and assumed that the translations had been sanctioned by the church. After her enclosure, Julian could also have been given a pamphlet of the vernacular New Testament by a confessor (one with enough influence to obtain the necessary ecclesiastical license), without having any idea that it was a "Lollard translation." And because of the popularity of the new English Bible, even the priest who gave it to her might not have known of its Lollard origin. It would indeed be comforting to think that Julian was able to hold scriptural texts in her hands and read them in her native tongue during the 1390s and early 1400s. Unfortunately, it may have been less likely than we would wish. According to existing documents, there is no record of any non-royal person bequeathing an English Bible in a will between 1408 and 1526. King Henry IV did not have one, nor did his son, Henry V. Henry VI, however did own one manuscript, which he gave to the Carthusians of Sheen monastery. And Henry VII also possessed a copy.[70]

Lollards, on the other hand, were known to have English Bibles, as would be expected. In fact, according to evidence from their trials, ownership was fairly frequent. From the more than 250 manuscripts of the Wyclif Bible that have survived, this text seems to have been the most commonly produced work in the Middle English language. Yet, among the orthodox, English Bibles of "unknown" or "suspected" Lollard provenance had to be kept carefully hidden. This was true especially after Arundel's *Constitutions* were promulgated, lest such an unauthorized book be discovered by the authorities and severe penalties imposed on the owner.

Lewed Learning

In times of war, plague, famines, peasant revolts, murders of archbishops and kings, amid the constant fear of invasion, people tend to flock to the newest and the most easily accessible preachers of any popular movement. It was no different in the 1390s and early 1400s. There was an apocalyptic foreboding repeatedly preached by the Lollards that branded the pope as the antichrist, signaling the end of days. And the fact that the Wyclif Bible was taken up and championed by the "poor priests" of the Lollard movement was more than sufficient to condemn it as heretical, as much as the fact that it was in the vernacular. Perhaps if an *orthodox* group of Oxford friars had translated the Bible, it would have been received with some trepidation, but not instantly labeled heretical. It certainly seems plausible.

Still, the question arises: if the full texts of the gospels and epistles were not allowed to be translated into English and read aloud at Mass, and there was no approved vernacular Bible available for the laity, how did the *lewed* hear and reflect on the story of their salvation, from the Old Testament to the New? We will consider this important question, which relates directly to that of how Julian learned what she learned during her formative years, in the following two chapters.

9
Preaching and Poetry

Medieval scholars generally agree that in the larger, more cosmopolitan towns and cities (like Norwich), 1350–1450 was the golden age of English sermonizing. It was a period of "concentrated, systematic, vigorous, and rhetorically crafted sermon literature" like nothing that had preceded it.[1] There was certainly a sermon to suit every taste, from high- to low-brow, and as many styles of preaching as there were preachers. Additionally, the vast record of homiletic literature that has been uncovered from the fourteenth and fifteenth centuries, both in Latin and in English, attests to the fact that the responsibility of preaching the gospel was taken very seriously, both by bishops and by the educated clergy.[2] A major reason for the explosion of popular and vernacular sermonizing was the growing demand by the emerging middle class of literate laity for scholarly preaching that would satisfy their hunger for intellectual stimulation. Men and women, separated both by gender and by class into different seating sections of the church, "sitten all [in] a rewe"[3] in carved and reserved pews, or on roughly hewn benches, or standing in the back, learned more about the doctrines of the faith and the moral law during the later medieval period than had been possible since the time of Charlemagne (742–814).

The Ancient Sermon

During Charlemagne's reign only bishops, not priests, were commissioned to preach on Sundays and feast days. They used the "ancient" sermon form, called *homily*, drawing on Latin collections of the sermons previously given by revered church fathers (St. Augustine, Caesarius of Arles, St. Gregory the Great, etc.), recopied many times and eventually translated into the vernacular languages of the Empire.[4] These ancient Latin texts were quite literally *vulgarized* to appeal to the non-Latin-speaking aristocracy as well as to the uneducated common folk. The scriptural text would be translated and examined in the vernacular, line by line, phrase by phrase, and often, word by word. "In preaching in the vulgar tongue to the common people, the gospel is expounded bit by bit."[5] This was St. Augustine's preferred method of sermonizing, as it was St. Gregory's, in imitation of Christ's own simple and direct way of explaining and interpreting his parables to the disciples. The ancient form was considered the most pedagogically effective, the most emotionally compelling, and by far the most suitable approach for preaching to the common folk.

Preaching of the Friars

As the mendicant friar revolution swept throughout Europe in the mid-thirteenth century (the Dominicans arrived in England in 1221, the Franciscans by 1224), a new form of popular preaching in the vernacular caught fire: the *sermo modernus*, the "modern sermon." The friars wrote and circulated among their brethren a series of thematic collections that would suit the sermon to the Latin scriptural readings of the day in a much more complex way than had been done in the past. They gave these modern-styled sermons at Masses on Sundays, feast days, during Advent, and daily during the holy season of Lent, in preparation for receiving the Eucharist at Easter. The ubiquitous friars also preached at marriages and funerals, for visiting dignitaries, at church dedications, and at any time the local bishop or pastor was indisposed or unavailable to fulfill his duty. They spoke from church pulpits, in cemeteries and open courtyards, on monastic or convent properties, on public greens, and in bustling marketplaces. They gathered a mixed audience of nobility and common folk at village crossroads, where "preaching crosses" (raised structures constructed either of wood or elaborately carved stone) were used as open-air pulpits.[6]

Such outdoor Sunday sermons were regularly available for all citizens of Norwich at Le Greneyard preaching cross, near the cathedral.[7] If there was no such elevated preaching cross, friars would mount a makeshift scaffold or portable wooden pulpit that had been carried out into the church yard or cemetery for the occasion, in order to gain the necessary elevation, then proceed to preach in the vernacular to the crowd seated on crude benches or on the ground. Distracting noises from rumbling carts, yelping dogs, and crying children as well as loud quarrels over commercial dealings going on in the background posed a constant problem of concentration for both sermonizer and listeners. The preacher needed to possess a resounding voice, clear articulation, and a dramatic mode of delivery to hold his audience's attention and to drown out the ever-present hecklers in the crowd. He had to be, in fact, an accomplished orator.

In spite of the difficulties, much-needed instruction was gained by the people from these outdoor sermons. No matter the wind, rain, or cold, the press of the crowd or the numerous other entertainments that might be had of a Sunday afternoon, the laity flocked to the mendicants' sermons, sometimes hearing one sermon at Mass in the morning and then, following the main Sunday family meal taken at noon, another sermon that lasted from one to three o'clock. And if the preacher was especially renowned, with a reputation for insightful teaching and the ability to evoke the passion and death of Christ in an affecting manner or to describe a harrowing account of the apocalyptic "second coming" of Christ at the end of the world, crowds would swarm to hear him. And if, during his discourse, he delivered political and social criticism with biting sarcasm, recounted personal tales of adventures abroad or stories of miraculous cures, even told the occasional rude jest, the crowd would endure any weather and weariness to hear him speak. One Oxford doctor, the Carmelite William Badby, who flourished in the later fourteenth century, was so esteemed that people flocked to him "as to a show."[8]

The *Sermo Modernus*

Just what was this *sermo modernus* that caused so much excitement during the fourteenth century? First developed by the friars at the universities, the modern sermon was constructed according to a well-worked scholastic formula originally meant for an audience of clerics and scholars. These academics viewed the ancient homiletic style of St. Augustine as suitable only for "addressing the common people in the vulgar tongue,"[9] whereas the modern sermon was the preferred form for "educated and intelligent listeners."[10] In fact, the very complexity of the *sermo modernus* made it impossible for less educated clerics even to attempt. It became associated with highly qualified friars who were capable of holding many divisions, which were then subdivided and subsubdivided, along with a multitude of *distinc-*

tiones (subtle distinctions), in their heads at once, even if some of them used a written text, or spoke from scribbled notes.[11] To hear such a sermon must have been like watching a street juggler keep multiple rings in the air without dropping any of them. It was precisely this mental tour de force that made the modern sermon so popular among the more sophisticated clerical and lay audiences.

Through the preaching of the friars, the technique of the *sermo modernus* spread all over England. It was imitated and elaborated as a high art form in itself. For the critics, however, the *divisiones* and *distinctiones* became so numerous, the investigations into ever finer shades of meaning, the constant stream of scholarly allusions, the pious references to the appropriate authorities, and the multiple biblical concordances so distracting, that they often obfuscated and shredded the text, rather than serving to illuminate it. The controversy over structure raged between the friars, who preached the modern sermon, and the Lollards, who espoused the ancient form, with no possibility of compromise on either side. While the ancient sermon was still being preached by monastics as well as by most secular parish priests, and even enjoyed a resurgence in popularity toward the end of the fourteenth century,[12] the *sermo modernus* definitely assumed primacy of importance. As we shall see when we encounter her text, Julian's own skill at choosing a theme, making clear divisions of her theme (she usually chooses two, three, or five), and then developing each idea in turn, bears strong witness to her having internalized the modern sermon technique and accommodated it to her own purpose.

John of Bromyard

The Dominican abbot John of Bromyard (died c.1352), a doctor of divinity, was the modern sermon writer and preacher par excellence in England during the first half of the fourteenth century. Bromyard's four surviving works, exclusive of his five lost texts, amount to almost two million words. He compiled every conceivable type of sermon into his Latin masterpiece, the *Summa Predicantium* (Compendium of Preaching), which thereafter became the consummate handbook on the art of preaching. Bromyard's 189 sermon topics were listed alphabetically, with over one thousand *exempla* (short stories) marked by index letters and numbers for easy cross-referencing.[13] Friars and secular priests of successive generations made generous use of these well-wrought compositions, translating and freely paraphrasing them in English. These, then, are the kind of sermons, in multiple variations, that Julian would have heard throughout her lifetime.

The abbot's sermons are cultural treasures. He is a master of sacred rhetoric and offers rich commentary on scriptural texts. Throughout his discourses, he makes ample use of quotations from the Bible as well as classical authors, stretching as far back as the Greek and Arabic sages. He traces a line of scripture from its earliest interpretation by Latin and Greek church fathers to that of St. Gregory the Great, St. Bernard, St. Thomas Aquinas, and St. Bonaventure. He references the scholastic theology of St. Thomas, based on medieval interpretations of Aristotelian principles. He even calls on the most contemporary scientific knowledge to dispel common myths concerning occurrences in nature.

Yet Bromyard, like all popular preachers of his time, is not averse to telling short morality tales or long and quite fantastic fables to drive home his points and to entertain (or terrify) his audience. He creates succinct rhyming verses and refers to common proverbs as aids to memory. He inserts an aspect of canon law to substantiate Christian doctrine. Whether preaching about heaven or hell, he has recourse to the *five wits*, or physical senses, to stimulate the listeners' imagination and to increase the very human appeal of his words. There is no technique of oratory, whether incitement, hyperbole, self-deprecation, anger, pleading, disgust, or derision, that he will not use in order to make an impact on his audience. He became, in fact, the primary mentor of all subsequent late medieval preachers.

The abbot deals extensively with the moral aspects of life. He gives plenteous examples of the seven deadly sins as well as the vices and peccadillos that so distinctly color a nation's people. He is not loath to describe the deplorable habits of secular clerics high and low; of the rich nobility; of avaricious and deceitful merchants; of coarse, irreverent, and unruly peasants; and, inevitably, of vain and loose-tongued women. Bromyard chronicles the seemingly infinite variety of sins and self-justifications as well as the humor of his people. At the same time, he bemoans the fact that parents push their sons into the priesthood not so that they may apply themselves to the study of philosophy or theology but rather in order that they may succeed in civil law or gain positions as secretaries and notaries in the king's court. He asks the damning question: "Why does the Law

School have a hundred or two hundred pupils, where the School of Theology has not even five?" He answers that the reason is the unbridled avarice of the times, the insatiable pursuit of power, wealth, and status, which, like the Great Pestilence, spreads its contagion to all classes of society.[14]

He inveighs against merchants who profiteer in corn, who deceive with false weights and measures, who tip the balance of scales with the touch of a hand or finger, who mix goods with sand, or even wet them to add to their weight, who mingle old merchandise with new, rancid with fresh, displaying goods in a dark place so that customers are fooled as to their quality. He especially cites "cloth drapers, mercers, and many other such [guild members]."[15] Criticism like this must have been especially hard for Julian to hear as a young girl, when her father was still alive. Perhaps she feared that he, and later, her husband, resorted on occasion to such deceptive techniques.

Citing the critical times, Dr. Bromyard singles out for special blame the skeptics who no longer believe in the power of prayer but who come to church to deride the pious and devout. "They say that never were there such evil times nor so many tempests as have occurred since men of religion, and those who pray for the world, were multiplied throughout it."[16] Bromyard also does not fail to castigate friars of his own Dominican order who preen their erudition before the masses. How can they condemn those who take pride in their fine clothing when they themselves are bedecked like peacocks in elaborate pulpit robes that belie their sermons about avoiding worldly vanity? How can the preacher reproach the rich for their gluttony and proclaim the poverty of Christ when his own "fat belly and ruddy cheeks" are the result of too much food and wine?[17] Alas, the persistent dichotomy between the friars' Rule of Life, according to their saintly founders' intentions, and the self-indulgence some of them actually practiced became a cause of mockery among the laity.

Doom and Damnation

In an impassioned effort to reach those so bored by the harangues of the preacher that they no longer felt remorse for sin, Dr. Bromyard, like most medieval homilists, resorted to threats of the "wrath of God." He cites the many dire forms of suffering in hell if sins are not confessed and evil ways of life not amended. Bromyard was not one to sugar-coat the pill, pamper his audience, nor dwell long on the virtues of the saints already in heaven. On the contrary, his motto was: "First, argue frequently; second, implore urgently; third, rebuke persistently."[18] His main task was to attack the seven deadly sins of luxurious extravagance, gluttony, greed, despair, wrath, envy, and pride, in addition to the all-too-common lechery, adultery, usury, cheating, swearing oaths, bearing false witness, sloth in one's religious duties, fighting and shedding blood, bear-baiting, bull-baiting, thievery, murder, and so forth. He spared no pains to put the fear of God into those who persisted in these vices.

Notably, Friar Bromyard considered those fourteenth-century preachers who stressed the *mercy* of God over his *wroth*, as performing the devil's work:

> "Howsoever great thy sins may be, greater is His mercy." *And in this... he [Satan] deceives man, nay rather well-nigh the whole world. And therefore more preaching is to be made against this deception of the devil's, and little or nothing of the mercy of God.* Because, as against a hundred who attend preaching, and sin in presuming over much upon the Divine mercy, there is not one who sins in desperation.[19]

Bromyard believed it an outright fallacy that God would be so merciful he would not punish a man's sins or condemn him to hell for "a light oath." The Dominican warned that, even for the healthiest, the body would inevitably age, the back bend over, sight and hearing fail, limbs fall into disuse, the breath turn sour and putrid. Then death would arrive unannounced like "a thief in the night" and bring with it the "greatest and most grievous temptations, and such as they never had before in all their life."[20] Bromyard describes the pathetic sinner as

> so feeble that scarce can he think of anything but his own weakness, or utter a last confession to the priest, or even move a limb. Not merely does he see a crowd of grinning demons waiting to snatch away his soul with their infernal claws, but hard by his own friends and executors waiting too with "adhesive fingers" to burst open his coffer and his money-bags, and carry off his worldly possessions...[21]

With burning words, the preacher painted stark pictures of the unrepentant sinner on his deathbed, devils taunting him, hiding in doorways, ready to attack, rip him to pieces, and bear him away to hellfire, where his five wits would be tormented for all eternity (all this inspired, no doubt, by the Inferno wall paintings in medieval churches). Satan is graphically depicted as strange-looking and dark-skinned, with a pointed nose, a hate-filled face, fire flashing in his eyes, flames thrusting out of his mouth, burning men's throats with brandishing irons, bearing boiling cauldrons full of worms and adders. Following her visions, Julian would experience just such a fiendish presence in a nightmare (67:1–8.333). Her vivid description strongly suggests the influence of such "hellfire and brimstone" preaching.

Bromyard also gave apocalyptic sermons on the fifteen days of signs and portents that would precede Domesday (which included the sea turning to blood, fishes flooding the land, rocks and castles falling, earthquakes erupting, tempests raging, fires covering the earth, constellations appearing in the sky, graves opening, dead men walking, the living going mad in fear).[22] And then would follow the fierce description of Christ the Judge, sitting in glory but "wooden in his fury,"[23] demanding of the living and the dead an account of their stewardship, sending sinners away to the gaping hell-mouth, or welcoming the blessed into his kingdom. The impact of such sermons must have been terrifying, as indeed it was meant to be. No wonder Julian cried out, when she thought she was dying: "It is today domesday with me" (8:25.151).[24]

Preaching about Women

Attitudes toward women in sermons, as in literature and in life, were not generally positive, even though this was reputed to be the age of chivalry that championed, at least in popular romances, the idealization of the female sex. It was mostly just that: popular romance. In the real world of sermonizing, women were singled out for every kind of vice, from lechery to harlotry, from superstition to witchcraft, from gossiping to slander, from disobedience to shrewishness, from envy to anger and physical fighting. As a woman had been responsible for the fall of man by opening her mouth and tasting an apple, so women were still considered sinful just by opening their mouths in lies, hypocrisy, and words of seduction.

Julian would have heard the oft-repeated theme that "the women of our time, when they are at home with their husbands, take no trouble over their adornment, but when they display themselves in public, they wish to go forth adorned—and yet they say that they adorn themselves for the benefit of their husbands."[25] In spite of his scientific knowledge, Bromyard directly relates women's vanity to reverses in war, implying that women's sins at home prevent victory in France!

On the other hand, preachers were usually ready to offer a prayer for women during childbirth and were also wont to list the responsibilities of parents toward their children and children toward their parents. Friars gave recognition to a mother's tenderness; however, they cautioned against the showing of too much affection lest it spoil the child, or too little corporal punishment lest it allow the child to fester in its sins. Directives about strict child-rearing practices were summed up in easy-to-remember quatrains:

> Chastise your children while they are young
> Of werk, of deed, of speech, of tongue.
> For if you allow them to be bold
> They will grieve you when they are old.[26]

As we have mentioned, if a child died, preachers generally warned the parents not to grieve too much or too long, since the baptized child had gone to heaven, which should have been a cause for rejoicing. It must have been a very "hard saying," particularly for a mother like Julian.

Preaching at Norwich Cathedral

At Norwich Cathedral Julian would have heard sermons from university-educated Benedictines, like the highly esteemed scholars Adam Easton (d.1397) and Thomas of Brinton (a.k.a. Brunton, d.1389). Adam Easton, doctor of divinity, future cardinal and staunch defender of the faith, was the kind of top-quality fourteenth-century scholar-monk that Norwich Priory could produce. Thomas of Brinton, doctor of canon law, was made bishop of Rochester in 1373 (the same year as Julian's visionary experiences) and became renowned throughout England as the quintessential monk-bishop and preacher from 1373 to about 1382. Both were resident monks at Norwich Cathedral Priory during Julian's younger years. They not only preached, they trained other monks to preach as well, though they probably preferred the "ancient" form of preaching to the *sermo modernus.* Since the Benedictine monks were in direct competition with the popular preaching of the friars, it was imperative that the monks give superlative sermons in their own style.

In the midst of plague, famine, and drought, with war raging abroad and political unrest brewing at home, Bishop Brinton scorned those who attributed all the suffering to the position of planets and constellations in the sky. He saw a direct connection, instead, with the nation's *sins*:

> Therefore, since the corruption of lust, and designs of wickedness are greater to-day than in the days of Noah—for a thousand fashions of vice which assuredly did not exist then are rife to-day . . . since too, greater to-day is the cruelty of the lords than in David's time, let us not impute *the scourges of God* to planets or elements, but rather to our own sins, saying, "Worthily do we suffer these things, for we have sinned."[27]

Brinton's remedy for sin (and more disasters) was the confession of sinners, "For how should the scourge of God cease at the people's prayers, while a third part of them are in mortal sin?"[28]

> For words that Christ spoke in the gospel about the future have quite plainly been fulfilled in our days, namely: "Nation shall rise against nation, and kingdom against kingdom; and there shall be pestilences, and famines, and great earthquakes in places. And all these are the beginnings of sorrows." (Mt 24:7–8)[29]

It was precisely this persistent teaching that God was essentially furious at humankind which Julian's Revelations would directly challenge. Nevertheless, Bishop Brinton must have been a powerhouse presence in the pulpit and Julian would have taken every opportunity to listen to him preach. In addition to hearing sermons from Benedictine monks at Norwich Cathedral, Julian would also have searched out highly respected preachers in the many churches staffed by Austin canons, Dominicans, and Franciscans, all of whom, as we have seen, were educated in theology and in the art of preaching the *sermo modernus.*

Religious Literature

An additional source for Julian's exposure to sacred scripture and theological concepts would have been religious literature. There were *historical poems* based on biblical topics (written between 1350 and 1400); *morality poems* featuring Old Testament characters (written between approximately 1370 and 1380); translations from the French of *rhymed gospels*, complete with homilies; and *verse plenaries* that recounted the Sunday gospel stories, along with their appropriate homilies. These latter texts were often combined to form a sequential life of Christ and became known as *gospel harmonies.* They were highly sought after for private study at home, or to help less-educated parish priests prepare their Sunday homilies.[30] By the late fourteenth century, old collections of Latin sermons written in the ancient style were also being translated into the vernacular for secular priests and pious laity to read in private.[31] These translations included the *Mirror*, John Mirk's *Festial*, and some anti-Lollard sermons by Benedictine monks.[32]

We have no way of knowing if Julian owned, borrowed, or read verse gospels or vernacular sermons, whether before or after she entered the anchorage. While scholarly dating of manuscripts remains tentative and dependent on a variety of factors,[33] it seems reasonable to conjecture that at least some verse plenaries and gospel harmonies would have been copied and spread abroad by orthodox preachers during the 1390s, specifically to counteract the proliferation of Lollard preachers. And Julian might well have read these texts.

Meditation Manuals

Other manuscripts that might have come into Julian's hands were not sermon collections per se, but sermon-like *meditation manuals*, written or translated specifically for the edification of the devout lay reading public. Because they were so expensive, these manuscripts were often passed around by small communities of like-minded individuals, whether guild members, women's reading groups, or neighbors. By far the most revered religious manual was *Meditationes Vitae Christi*, which provided daily meditations on the earthly life of the Lord. Parts of it pertaining to the passion account were translated from Latin into Middle English rhyming couplets early in the fourteenth century, then into a later abridged prose translation that may have influenced Richard Rolle's own *Meditations on the Passion.* A closer translation was made in southern England and finally the entire work was translated into English prose around 1400, as *The Mirrour of the Blessed Lyfe of Jesu*, by Nicholas Love.[34] In fact, this last was the *only* English book on the life of Christ that was officially sanctioned as orthodox by Archbishop Arundel. It became the most desired book of spiritual devotion for the next two hundred years. At some point during her later life, Julian must have obtained a copy of this extremely popular manual.

An abundance of vernacular translations of older religious treatises, as well as new works written in Middle English, also appeared throughout the fourteenth century in direct response to a high demand by literate lay folk for religious instruction, spiritual guidance, and devotional texts. The most widely circulated included: *Handlyng Synne* (1303); Richard Rolle's first-ever English *Psalter* (1340s); *The Lay Folks' Catechism* (1357); *Instruction for the People: The Book of Vices and Virtues* (1375); *Chasteau d'Amour* (Castle of Love), in a 1390s English translation from the original Anglo-Norman; and finally, *The Chastising of God's Children* (c.1380s or 1390s), adapted from the works of Jan van Ruusbroec, a fourteenth-century Flemish monk and contemplative. Julian could very possibly have read several or all of the above texts, filled with doctrinal teachings and spiritual insights. It is even conceivable that the descriptions of Ruusbroec on the procession of the soul from God and its return into God through love might have exerted a strong influence on Julian's own mystical theology.

Poetry and Prose

Also during this time period we find several *allegorical poems* and *prose treatises*, originally written in English that appealed to the literate laity with the leisure time to read. Around 1300, an unknown cleric penned the encyclopedic *Cursor Mundi* ("Runner of the World") that divided the entire Bible and the history of salvation into seven ages, describing them in thirty thousand lines of poetry. An anonymous author contributed the very popular *Pricke of Conscience* (c.1350), a ten-thousand-line poem in English rhyming couplets dealing with the sufferings of mankind and the afterlife. Most importantly, an unnamed monk wrote *The Cloud of Unknowing* and *The Book of Privy Counseling*, both in Middle English prose, to instruct a young novice in monastic and meditation practice. (To this day, these two books are hailed as being among the greatest works of Christian mysticism, having influenced generations of priests, religious, laity, saints, and contemplatives from St. John of the Cross in the sixteenth century to Fr. Pierre Teilhard de Chardin, SJ, in the twentieth.)

While Julian's own mystical theology does not derive directly from *The Cloud*, since hers is based on the vivid use of an inspired imagination (which *The Cloud* author insisted should be denied), it is quite likely that Julian read these widely circulated treatises on the advice of a woman friend, a relative who was a priest or monk, or her confessor.

In the early 1380s, Walter Hilton composed the *Scale of Perfection*, originally directed to an anchoress. However, this two-part masterpiece on the spiritual life was copied repeatedly and popularized by the devout laity. It is a book Julian must have known. At about the same time, the *Abbey of the Holy Ghost*, written by a man for a lay woman, was translated from the French. It suggests the ways in which this woman might see the whole world as her convent, like a mystical abbey of the Holy Ghost, where she can live a spiritual life of great depth and prayer even as she remains faithful to her worldly duties. One can imagine the impact such a book might have had on Julian, who tried to do exactly this before she became an anchoress. Since there were so few books addressed specifically to lay (single, married, or widowed) women in the world, this little book might have become another incentive for Julian to write her own Long Text.

At some point Julian must have obtained a copy of the early thirteenth-century Middle English *Ancrene Riwle* ("Anchorite's Rule"), originally composed by an anonymous male author for three lay sisters pursuing the enclosed life. The *Riwle* was consistently transcribed throughout the fourteenth century and became a model both of external behavior and the inner life of contemplative prayer prescribed for hermits. One wonders if Julian was attracted to becoming an anchoress by reading this seminal book.

Langland and Chaucer

Finally, among the most circulated works of all (and this brief survey does not begin to cover the profusion of vernacular poetic and prose works of the fourteenth century), we come to the two most outstanding authors of their time: William Langland and Geoffrey Chaucer. Langland's magnificent allegorical poem, *The Vision of Piers Plowman,* was written, like Julian's own book, in three expanding versions, between 1362–1367 and his death, probably around 1386.[35] The poem tells of a young man, Will, who falls asleep in a "fair field full of folk," and who, in a series of dream-like visions and waking interludes, sets out in quest of intellectual truth and great "wonders to hear."

Guided by the "Poor Plowman" of the title, Will wanders the world, seeking "Dowel" (Do-Well), "Dobet" (Do-Better), and "Dobest" (Do-Best). In his old age, after many adventures, the narrator comes to understand the nature of love and spiritual wisdom. He vows to "walken as wide as the world lasteth" in search of Piers Plowman, the figure of Christ.

Geoffrey Chaucer's enormously popular *The Canterbury Tales* (composed in the 1380s) recounts the competitive stories, both in verse and in prose, of an eclectic group of pilgrims on their way to pay homage at the tomb of the martyr, St. Thomas Becket, at Canterbury Cathedral (the best story would win its storyteller a free dinner). The tales told by such diverse characters as the Knight, Miller, Reeve, Cook, Lawyer, Wife of Bath, Friar, Summoner, Clerk, Merchant, Squire, Franklin, Physician, Pardoner, Shipman, Prioress, Monk, Nun's Priest, two Nuns, Canon's Yeoman, Parson, and so on present a panoply of both likeable and eminently dislikeable contemporary English personages and attitudes. In the course of recounting their tales, the pilgrims are so colorfully, critically, and ironically drawn that they continue to be recognizable human types, even today.

These two masterpieces demonstrate the fact that late medieval writers came to prefer Middle English over Latin, not only as an appropriate language for religious treatises and manuals of devotion but also for works of literature. Among these fourteenth-century authors, there is one, and only one, woman who has been compared to Chaucer: namely, Julian of Norwich.

Julian's Sermon and Literary School

It becomes abundantly clear that Julian was able to enjoy a wide range of opportunities for hearing brilliant sermons as well as reading literary and scripturally-based texts. These formed the foundation for her writing skills, the very "schooling" Julian needed to begin recording the mystical insights she had received from the Lord. Thus, if we ask how Julian acquired the sense of *solid structure* she would one day need to organize her book, the answer is: from hearing the modern sermon and reading vernacular sermon collections. If we wonder how she gained the *theological foundation* that enabled her to defend her mystical teachings in the confident way that she does, we may answer again: from the *sermo modernus* that included commentaries by church fathers and scholastic theologians as well as from a wide variety of vernacular instructional treatises. If we inquire how Julian developed the *exegetical skills* needed to interpret the visions and locutions she received from the Lord with such clarity, we need look no further than to the four levels of meaning she heard preachers use to illuminate scriptural texts: the literal, allegorical, moral, and mystical. And if we question why Julian focused so much of her *spiritual quest* on understanding the nature of sin and the "wrathfulness" of God, on divine blame, judgment, and the threat of damnation, even on her role as a woman, then we can be sure she had done interior battle with viewpoints expounded upon by preachers and writers on these very topics.

From expert homilists, Julian learned how to choose a *thema* for each of her chapters, make divisions, develop her themes with careful attention to details and distinctions, and interpret the various layers of the meaning of Christ's words to her. She also realized the value of using *exempla* to illustrate spiritual intuitions that came to her in contemplation. From reading gospel harmonies, Julian discovered how to ruminate on a single word or phrase, turning it over and over again in her mind, examining the significant aspects of a passage, applying them to her own life, and then allowing Christ's words to filter deep into her soul. She practiced the ancient monastic art of *lectio divina* (divine reading), and it served as her guide in writing her Revelations.

Indeed, the central parable of the lord and the servant, which Julian tells us she meditated on "for twenty years after the time of the shewing, save three months" (51:73.277), was made clear to her only after she had worked through layer after layer of exegesis from the literal, to the allegorical, to the tropological (moral), and eventually to the anagogical (mystical) content. Her final explanations, theologically stunning and heartbreakingly beautiful, are a laywoman's sermon, written on parchment, every bit as brilliant and compelling as any she might have heard preached from a pulpit.

The frequency of sermonizing in Norwich would also explain how Julian memorized passages from the gospels and epistles, so that she could reference them without actually having an English text of the Bible in front of her. She, like many of her *evencristens*, was able to commit to memory a vast number of scriptural quotations merely by hearing them read, paraphrased, turned into verse, and explicated in sermons Sunday after Sunday, year after year, from the pulpits in Norwich. There exists a thirteenth-century record of someone's memory at work: "[I] learned by heart within that year *40 Sunday gospels* ... and other extracts from sermons and prayers."[36] A statement like this seems daunting to us in an age of immediately accessed (and just as quickly forgotten) quotations; but, like this anonymous layperson with a good memory, Julian stored up gospels, epistles, sermons, quotations from St. Augustine, as well as excerpts taken from the writings of Bede, Bernard, Aquinas, and Bonaventure. Bit by bit, she became learned in sacred scripture, theological principles, and the art of exegesis in the only way a woman could during that time: by osmosis.

Simultaneously, Julian absorbed the cadences of educated oratorical speech. She discovered the techniques of alliteration, allusion, and antithesis, the use of repetition and paradox. She became practiced at juxtaposing simile and metaphor for richness of style; using synecdoche as well as personification. She picked up stylistic details, such as rhetorical questioning, comparison and contrast, making sudden switches of mood, and so on. She had no Latin education like the friars and clerics, or like the royal courtier and diplomat Geoffrey Chaucer, or like the deacon William Langland. But Julian was able to acquire techniques of compelling writing by having drunk deeply from the literature of her time. We may conclude that, by hearing sermons and reading vernacular theological and literary works, Julian developed her extraordinary ear for language, logic, and elucidation. What she would need was the divinely inspired motivation to write, as well as decades of practice, like any true artist, to perfect her skills.

A Room of Her Own

She will write in secret, taking refuge in her bedchamber at the top of her house, as far away as she could get from the noise of servants, tradesmen, and the steady rumble of carts over cobblestones. She will sit at a small writing desk near a large, leaded-glass window. She may only write for a few hours a day, reliving her Revelations, keeping a diary of her thoughts and feelings, and receiving spiritual insights into everything the Lord had shown her. She will read what she writes to a very few intimates, maybe her close circle of women friends, her mother among them. She will not dare allow her Short Text to get into the wrong hands. She must have been aware that there were Lollard women throughout East Anglia who were holding "secret conventicles" at which they freely quoted biblical texts in support of their heretical doctrines. These women were also appealing to *evencristens*, just as Julian wanted to do with her own book of Revelations. If Julian read her work aloud or presumed to teach, even to a small gathering of women, she could easily be accused of being a Lollard. And if, by chance, selections of her text were read out of context, they could be totally misunderstood and bring her under clerical scrutiny.

Simply that she was a *laywoman* who wrote in the *vernacular* would have made her doubly suspect as a heretic, not to mention the fact that she claimed sixteen private Revelations from the Lord! If anyone had gossiped, Julian could have been called into the office of Bishop Despenser for questioning. As we have seen, the bishop was known to be more of a bellicose knight than a benevolent shepherd. In 1383, at the urging of Pope Urban VI, Despenser convinced Parliament to let him lead a crusade against the followers of Louis II of Flanders, a supporter of the antipope Clement VII. The campaign, though heavily funded, lacked military leadership, sufficient troops and supplies, and proved a disastrous failure for the English army. After returning to England, Despenser was impeached in parliament, and all his properties were confiscated. However, the bishop managed to regain his lands and income as well as to earn great favor with the eighteen-year-old Richard II during the king's first campaign to Scotland in 1385.

Such a tyrant as Bishop Despenser would not have tolerated a *lewed* woman like Julian who dared to usurp the teaching and preaching roles of Latin-educated, ordained, and duly licensed male clergy. He would have immediately cut off any possibility of a cult developing around this so-called "visionary." He would have forbidden Julian to write or speak another word about her Revelations, under threat of excommunication.

An Anchoress

At some point in the early 1390s Julian must have realized that her position in the world was growing more and more untenable. She may have considered that becoming an anchoress (in essence, giving up her household, handing over the reins of the textile business, and removing herself from the world to go into hiding) was preferable to being vulnerable to scrutiny by the bishop. She may also have grown tired of the daily demands on her time and energies, as well as the burden of financial responsibilities she bore as a *femme sole*. Why should she continue to manage a home and servants and apprentices, being responsible day to day for running a business, if it was no longer necessary? Her daughter would have been in her early thirties by this time, long since married and raising her own children. Julian was free to make the radical choice to become an *anchoress* (from the medieval Latin, *anchorita*, meaning to retire or withdraw).

There is another possibility to consider: the devastation wrought by successive returns of the Great Pestilence. A *fourth* outbreak of plague began in the south of England in 1374 (just a year after Julian received her Revelations). Then: "In 1375, the weather was scorching, and there was a great pestilence that raged so strongly in England and elsewhere that infinite numbers of men and women were devoured by sudden death."[37] By 1378, the fourth pestilence arrived in York, lasted for over a year and, like the second cycle of 1361, decimated the population of children. Then:

> In the summer of 1379, due to a hostile configuration of the planets, plague broke out in the north country on a scale never seen before. The mortality waxed so powerful that almost the whole region was rapidly stripped of its best men; and among the middle classes it was said that nearly every house was deprived of its residents and left standing empty. Even large families were wiped out by the plague, with not one person left alive.[38]

Still, it was not over. In 1381–1382, the plague erupted in the Midlands. Again in 1383 and 1387, there were consecutive outbreaks in East Anglia, Kent, and Essex, which especially affected those in the seven- to twenty-two-year-old age range. (If, as we have conjectured, Julian's daughter was born during the winter of 1361–1362, she would have been in her early twenties during these plague-ridden years and therefore particularly vulnerable.)

Then came the *fifth* pestilence: "In 1390 a great plague ravaged the country," and "in 1391 such a great mortality arose in Norfolk and in many other counties that it was thought as bad as the great pestilence. To take only one example, in a short space of time 11,000 bodies were buried at York."[39] Could it have been that during one of these recurring cycles, *Julian lost her only surviving child?* As difficult as it is to speculate, the possibility remains that Julian entered the anchorage in 1392 or 1393 after her daughter was dead.

Whatever threats of persecution or tragic events might have occurred recently in her life, it is clear that, at the advanced age of fifty, Julian longed for the physical and mental freedom to pray and contemplate deeply. She must have assumed that, once more, she was nearing the end of her life. She had been receiving spiritual teachings from the Lord and had greatly developed her theology and writing skills since the 1370s and 1380s, when she had composed her Short Text. Now she needed the total privacy and silence (rare commodities in the fourteenth century) to undertake the writing of the expanded version, which would become her Long Text. Furthermore, as an enclosed anchoress, she knew that no one, not even the bishop, would enter her sacred space and investigate what she was writing.

History has assumed that Julian of Norwich freely chose to become an anchoress. And most probably, she did. But there is also the distinct possibility that, like emigration for the persecuted, enclosure in an anchorage offered Julian a necessary and timely "way out" of the public arena, as well as the "way in" to the life of a contemplative. This suggestion in no way denies that Julian felt a call to become a solitary hermit, wholly dedicated to God. Nor does it question the level of deep prayer that Julian practiced in her anchorage, or undermine the wise and saintly woman she became in her cell. It only suggests that *external*, as well as internal, pressures may have contributed to her decision to become an anchoress. Julian knew that God had given her a holy work to do and that she had limited time and leisure in which to do it. Becoming an anchoress would enable her to fulfill that vocation.

Enclosure

Ironically, to be permitted to be enclosed as an anchoress, Julian would have needed to obtain permission from none other than Bishop Despenser. Given her memory of his brutal suppression of the peasants during the Norwich uprising, this must have been a difficult process for her. She would have had to submit to an ecclesiastical examination of her strength of mind and body, her freedom from debts, and her financial stability to support herself as an anchoress so that she would not become a burden to the bishop. (Presumably, she would have sold her house to have sufficient resources for years to come, and/or she received regular income from the rental of her property.) And, most importantly, she would have had to be tested on her orthodoxy concerning doctrinal matters. One doubts that in the course of this examination Julian ever mentioned having received or written about her Revelations. It is conceivable that the bishop never found out.

Once Julian was granted permission to become an anchoress (the first one recorded in Norwich since 1313),[40] it would most probably have been Bishop Despenser who performed the Rite of Enclosure ceremony. This included a Requiem Mass (henceforth, the anchoress was to be considered "dead" to the world), followed by a procession to the anchorage, which was "anchored," or attached, to the side of the church. The bishop would have entered the anchorage and blessed the room that Julian would occupy. It was approximately nine and a half feet by eleven and a half feet[41] and contained a narrow bed with a straw-filled mattress, linens, blankets, a quilt, a trestle table and an open-backed stool, a small altar covered with a white cloth holding a crucifix and an icon of Christ's mother, perhaps a kneeler for prayer, a few hooks for hanging clothes, a storage chest, a wash bowl, pottery, cups, utensils, rush lights, and an enclosed candle lantern. The floor was flattened earth, covered with rushes and fragrant herbs that were changed seasonally. The anchorage was probably unheated, like the church itself, although a small brazier burning wood or coal might have afforded Julian some warmth during the coldest months. (An adjacent room was reserved for Julian's maid who prepared her meals, as well as for a servant girl who ran errands.)

After the room was blessed by the bishop, Julian was led inside to her "living grave," where she received the sacrament of extreme unction as she had some twenty years previously, when it was thought she was dying. Now, these last rites were both symbolic and final: she was dying to the world. The bishop sprinkled her with ashes and commanded her to remain enclosed for the rest of her life, under threat of excommunication. The door was then bolted from the outside, as a solemn sign of her isolation. However, this may have been more symbolic than absolute. The concept of the "cell" was often extended to include a small enclosed garden or cemetery adjacent to the anchorage.[42] Julian's servant could unbolt the door so that Julian might walk in privacy and breathe the air, reciting the Little Office of Our Lady when no one else was around to see her.

Like most medieval anchorages, Julian's cell had three narrow windows. One was a "squint" window opening into the church interior, enabling Julian to follow the liturgy of the Mass and receive the Eucharist from the hands of the priest on feast days and at Easter as well as to focus her attention during times of prayer on the hanging pyx containing the Blessed Sacrament suspended over the altar. Another window allowed Julian's cook to pass her food and thin homemade ale, and a domestic servant to give her books, writing parchment, quills and ink, fresh sheets and clothing (as well as to remove her waste bucket on a daily basis). A third window opened out to a small parlor, sheltered from the rain, where a visitor who wanted to seek Julian's advice on spiritual matters or any problem troubling his or her soul could sit. *The Ancrene Riwle* advised that this window should have a double layer of black cloth hung over it, with the shape of the cross cut through the center, revealing a piece of white cloth in between.[43] Behind this cloth Julian's face would remain forever hidden from her visitors, especially if they were men. Even a confessor, spiritual advisor, abbot, or prior visiting an anchoress was well advised to bring a witness with him (albeit standing at a respectable distance) to protect against any sexual impropriety.[44]

Bequests

We know that Julian was already enclosed as an anchoress by the early 1390s from the testimony of four bequests written in wills and spanning a period of more than twenty years. The earliest mention in a will of either 1393 or 1394 (the date on the document has been compromised) is that of Roger Reed, rector of St. Michael's Coslany, Norwich, who bequeathed two shillings to "*Juliane anachorite* at [the] church of St. Julian in Norwich."[45] The second gift (1404) is from Thomas Emund, a chantry priest from Aylesham in Norfolk, leaving twelve pence to *Juliane anachorita* at the Church of St. Julian in Norwich, and "to Sara [her maid] living with her 8d [pence]." The third record (1415) is from the will of John Plumpton of Conisford, who bequeathed "to the anchoress in the Church of St. Julian's, Conisford in Norwich, 40d, and to her maid 12d."[46] He also gave twelve pence "to Alice her former maid." The fourth bequest (1416) is that of a noblewoman, Isabel Ufford, countess of Suffolk, who distributed to "Julian recluse at Norwich 20s."[47] It is significant that there are so few extant bequests and that those we have indicate a wide range of people (a local vicar, a chantry priest, a merchant, and a very wealthy countess) who had received spiritual guidance from Julian and wanted to express their gratitude in their last wills and testaments. It is also notable that none of these four bequests makes reference to Julian as *domina* or *dame*, the title most often given to nuns and occasionally, to holy laywomen.[48]

The Long Text

It is assumed that during the twenty-plus years Julian spent in the anchorage (c.1393–sometime after 1416) she produced two or three versions of her Long Text. However, except for the scribe who penned the colophon on a manuscript copy of the *Short* Text in 1413, which refers to Julian as being still "on life" (i:63), *there is no mention by a single contemporary that Julian ever wrote a book*. Did anyone even know about the Long Text? Those who left her stipends in their wills alluded to her being an anchoress, not a visionary or an author.

The all-pervasive atmosphere of suspicion hanging over any layperson (male or female) writing mystical theology in the mother tongue must have had a strong impact on Julian's own manner of setting down her Revelations. She would have had to be careful about how many memorized paraphrases of scriptural passages she used, for fear of seeming to be a Lollard who had access to an English Bible. She would also have felt compelled to reaffirm her orthodoxy every time she presented an unconventional or mystical interpretation in her work, lest she seem to stray from the traditional teachings of the church. She had to work assiduously to reconcile what she understood directly from her Revelations with what she had learned since her childhood in church. In the Short Text, Julian had both acknowledged and questioned *why* a woman had no right to teach:

> But God forbid that you should say or take it so that I am a teacher. For I do not mean it so, nor have I ever meant it so. *For I am a woman, lewed, feeble, and frail.* But I know well, this that I say I have received it from the shewing of him who is sovereign teacher. But truthfully, charity stirs me to tell it to you. For I would

God were known and mine evencristens helped, as I would be myself, to the greater hating of sin and loving of God. *But because I am a woman should I therefore believe that I should not tell you the goodness of God, since I saw in that same time [of the Revelations] that it is his will that it be known?* And that you shall see very well in the same matter that follows afterward, if it be well and truly taken. Then shall you soon forget me, who am a wretch . . . and behold Jesus who is the teacher of all. I speak of them that shalle be saved, for in this time God shewed me none other. But in all things I believe as holy church teaches. For in all this blessed shewing of our lord I beheld it as one in God's sight. And I never understood anything therein that stunned me, nor kept me from the true teaching of holy church. (vi:35–49.75, italics added)

It is remarkable to note that, by the time Julian wrote her Long Text, she *removed* this strong protestation from her book. By then, she did not dare defend her right to speak about God as a laywoman, lest she be considered a Lollard. Julian might have heard that an anchoress of Leicester named Matilda had been physically removed from her cell sometime between 1389 and 1393 and called in for questioning by the authorities. Another anchoress, a nun, and a laywoman were also put in prison for "consorting with Lollards." The East Anglian chronicler, Thomas Walsingham, recorded "the clergy's alarm at the intrusion by heretical lay people and above all *heretical women* in the sphere hitherto strictly reserved for the ordained ministry."[49] In such dangerous times, even an anchoress was not above suspicion.

Julian would have learned from a visiting cleric about the 1401 parliamentary edict against heretics; about the burning the same year of the Lollard curate, William Sawtre, in Bishop's Lynn; about Archbishop Arundel's 1409 *Constitutions* against the unlicensed reading or preaching of the vernacular Bible (or any other vernacular religious books, like her own); and about Parliament's 1414 statute authorizing secular courts to seek out heretics. What must it have been like for her to know that if either text of her *Revelations* was ever read by an unsympathetic priest or friar, or found its way into the hands of the bishop of Norwich, it would most certainly have been investigated by Archbishop Arundel; and that anyone who was *lewed*, presuming to record personal Revelations from Jesus Christ in the vernacular, could be brought for interrogation into a church court, censured as a heretic, imprisoned, and condemned to die?

Julian must have feared that just sitting down to write every day in her anchorage was a high-risk undertaking, especially since she was both *lewed*... and a woman.

Scholars have suggested that Julian's self-deprecating phrases, like the one quoted above, were removed from her Long Text because by that time she had grown in her sense of authority as a woman and assumed her right to teach without having to justify or apologize for it. On the contrary, it seems more likely that Julian excised such protestations out of her great fear of being labeled (even after her death) as a Lollard heretic. In fact, in the Long Text, Julian went so far as to cut out *all references to herself as a woman.*

Margery Kempe's Visit: 1413

There is other compelling evidence that Julian did not speak openly about her visions or her book, even to those *evencristens* who came from near and far to seek her spiritual counsel. Sometime in 1413, toward the end of Julian's life (when she was more than seventy years old), a forty-year-old woman named Margery Kempe from Bishop's Lynn visited Julian at her anchorage. Margery was a laywoman, born the year Julian received her visions (1373), married at twenty, and the mother of fourteen children. Margery claimed that after the birth of her last child she had begun receiving visions of Our Lord and his mother and felt that God was calling her to a life of total chastity. She needed to convince her husband to accept mutual renunciation of sex and then to accompany her on pilgrimage to the holy sites in England, as well as those in Rome, Spain, and Jerusalem. Margery had been summoned to Norwich to answer questions posed by Bishop Despenser's officers about the orthodoxy of her visions, as well as her decidedly unorthodox and peripatetic way of life. She was, in fact, strongly suspected of being a Lollard.

While under investigation in Norwich, Margery was "bidden by our lord" to seek the advice of *Dame Jelyan* the *ankres.* Margery *shewed* Julian "the grace that God put in her [Margery's] soul of compassion, contrition, sweetness, and devotion," along with "holy meditation and high contemplation," even sharing "very many holy speeches and dalliance that our lord spoke to her soul, and many wonderful revelations which she shewed to the ankres to know if there was any deceipt in them, for the ankres was expert in such things and could give good counsel."[50] Margery, identifying herself throughout her *Book* as the "creature," dictated her account of the meeting.

> The ankres [Julian], hearing the marvelous goodness of our lord, highly thanked God with all her heart for his visitation, counseling this creature [Margery] to be obedient to the will of our lord God and fulfill with all her might whatever he put in her soul if it were not against the worship of God and profit of her evencristen, for if it were, then it was not the moving of a good spirit, but rather of an evil spirit.[51]

According to Margery's report, Julian also instructs her that: "The holy ghost never moves a thing against charity, and, if he did, he would be contrarious to his own self, for he is all charity."[52] Likewise, the Spirit inspires chaste living, since "chaste lovers are called the temple of the holy ghost, and the holy ghost makes a soul stable and steadfast in the right faith and the right belief."[53] Julian urges Margery not to doubt her own revelations, for the one who doubts is "like the flood of the sea, which is moved and born about with the wind."[54] The *ankres* tells Margery that "when God visits a creature with tears of contrition, devotion, or compassion, he may and ought to believe that the Holy Ghost is in his soul,"[55] reminding her that abundant tears give greater torment to the devil than all the pains of hell. Julian also remarks that "Holy scripture says that the soul of a righteous man is the seat of God," adding: "and so I trust, sister, you are."[56] Finally, Julian prays that God would grant Margery perseverance and patience, reassuring her that "the more despising, shame, and reproof that you have in the world, the more is your merit in the sight of God."[57] All of this sounds very much like Julian's voice.

However, inasmuch as Margery's *Book* was dictated to two different scribes some *twenty years after* the actual meetings with Julian, there is no verification that Julian's words were faithfully quoted. Given Margery's penchant for consulting friars, priests, and hermits who might advise her about what she felt called to do, it seems quite possible that Margery documented Julian's counsel in order to reinforce her decision not to have any more children, and even to authenticate her visions and locutions.

While there is no way to know what Julian actually told Margery, it is intriguing to consider what she did *not* tell her. There is nothing in Margery's account about Julian being a visionary herself, or about her having written a book, or about her reading parts of her *Revelations* aloud. Yet the two women spent, according to Margery, many days together in "holy dalliance . . . through communing in the love of our Lord Jesus Christ."[58] There could be some allusions to Julian's text in Margery's use of words like *evyncristens* and *revelacyons*, but these terms were commonly employed by preachers and playwrights as well as by popular spiritual writers like Walter Hilton. And even Julian's image of the soul as "the seat of God" is not conclusive, as this was a familiar figure of speech used by mystics since the early Middle Ages. Perhaps Julian had some reservations about Margery's possible Lollard tendencies, especially since Margery was under investigation by the Bishop of Norwich. And, given Margery's tendency to talk freely, it is very likely that Julian did not want to discuss her own Revelations for fear of being misquoted. Julian would certainly have listened to Margery with great compassion, advised her about the workings of the Holy Spirit, and spoken honestly, woman to woman, about the value of a chaste life, but she may have kept silent about her Revelations. Margery, in her fulsome recording of her own spiritual life, does not mention *a single word* that Julian spoke about herself. Still, we must be grateful to Margery Kempe for documenting her visit and thus preserving the only firsthand account we have of *Jelyan* the *ankres.*

10
Corpus Christi Plays

Besides Julian's sermon and literary schooling, there was another and perhaps even more emotionally affective influence on her spiritual formation, namely, the annual presentation of the Corpus Christi plays in Norwich. These came to be called "mystery plays" (from the French, mystère) which had little to do with the mystery of the faith and more to do with the secret and mysterious crafts of the professional guilds. The Corpus Christi plays offered the spectator dramatized and engaging presentations of stories from the Old and New Testaments, in rhymed and often alliterative verse, that were readily accessible to all because they were written in the vernacular.

To see and hear these plays performed and be able to enter into them as part of a closely knit community of believers became a powerful way for the laity not only to learn the truths of their faith but also to identify with biblical characters whose dramatic predicaments reflected their own. They saw themselves as Adam and Eve, disobeying God's commandment and suffering the consequences; they could sympathize with Joseph, the doubting spouse, and the plight of Mary, the lamenting mother who watches her son die. They could choose to consider themselves among those who loved and ministered to the Lord or who betrayed him, even those who crucified him. Christ was impersonated by a human being, so it was made physically clear that he was "one who in every respect has been tested as we are, yet without sin" (Heb 4:15). He walked and talked and suffered and died on the cross for the audience's salvation.

It is truly astonishing that even in our post-modern secular age the frequent re-stagings of the Corpus Christi mystery plays in York and Chester, among other places, have been so highly acclaimed and attended by thousands of people. Such popularity certainly bears witness to the plays' continuing power to involve even the most hardened skeptics. It is said that "those who had come to gaze, even to mock...in an almost literal sense...stayed to pray."[1] We may also have experienced the raw power of drama to make a religious story come alive in a way no sermon could ever do. Good drama affects us emotionally, at the very core of our being. We suspend disbelief and become, more readily, *believers.*

Pageant Wagons

Julian was fortunate enough to grow up precisely during the time of a profusion of religious theatre in medieval city streets, during the second half of the fourteenth century. Mystery plays were an annual summer event (when the English weather was warmer and daylight hours longer) in at least twelve medieval towns and cities, from York in the north to Coventry in the south, from Chester in the west to Norwich in the east. These sequential plays sought to dramatize no less than the entire history of salvation, from the creation to the fall, from the giving of the Ten Commandments and the Old Testament prophecies of a Savior, to the birth, life, death, resurrection, and ascension of Jesus Christ...even to the final judgment. Local actors impersonated biblical characters: Adam and Eve, Cain and Abel, Noah, Abraham and Moses, the Blessed Virgin, St. Joseph, Jesus Christ, the apostles, Mary Magdalene, and the nameless "other women" who followed Jesus, as well as Judas, Herod, Pilate, Annas, Caiphas, and a host of other likable and dislikable characters. Satan always played a major role.

The plays were performed on large, thick-wheeled and covered pageant wagons, fifteen or more feet in length, that were dragged and pushed by men through city or town streets from pre-announced station to station. (In the Norwich inventory of stage properties, six "horse cloths" are listed, so horses may have been utilized to pull the pageant wagons from place to place.)[2] At each stop, some two hundred people of every age and social class would assemble to see each successive play. These moving stages had to be sturdily built and high enough to contain rudimentary sets or painted backdrops, a seating area for the actors, plus room for some activity, however limited. Most wagons had an interior roofing with a proscenium overhang, suitably painted and decorated, from which stage effects like Noah's dove and God's rainbow, the Magi's Star in the east and hand-crafted angels, operated by windlasses, could descend on golden wire "shafts of light" and be hoisted back up to heaven again in due course. On the actual stage, there might be a decorated "tree of knowledge" for the Garden of Eden and a makeshift front wall or low curtain to cover Adam and Eve's nakedness; a nativity stable with a manger, plenty of straw, even a live sheep or two.

These wagons were probably equipped with curtains that could open and close along the front (audience) side of the stage, both to mask the carriage wheels when standing stationary and to create some below or backstage space where the actors could change costumes and from which they could make their entrances. Alternatively, curtains may have opened and closed over three sides of the playing area, allowing audience members to stand in a semi-circle and view the stage from more than one angle. There were also drop-down steps for the likes of Herod to descend from the wagon and rant and rave both "in the pageant and in the street."[3] On the floor of the stage, there was the requisite trap door for the actor playing Satan to rise out of, or to descend back into, the "hell mouth."

The Feast Day

Two hundred or more individual pageants were known collectively as Corpus Christi plays because they were first performed as part of the feast day processions to honor the Eucharist, the "Body of Christ." The feast of Corpus Christi was a fairly new one in the early fourteenth century, having been confirmed by the Council of Vienne in 1311. The feast was designated an important holy day in the Archdiocese of Canterbury by 1317.[4] The following year, the first recorded procession was held. Corpus Christi became a much-anticipated annual occasion for communal religious expression and civic pride. The feast was, and is, celebrated on the Thursday after Trinity Sunday, any time from May 21 to June 24. The bishop, processing under a canopy held by four acolytes, would carry the host, visible within a gold and glass enclosure, or monstrance, held high for all to see. Monks and priests, friars and deacons walked behind the host, followed by dignitaries of the city, town merchants, local artisans and their apprentices, shopkeepers, and finally peasant families of all ages. The long circuitous line proceeded from the gates of the local abbey, priory, or church through the main streets, stopping at designated sites or stations along the way for prayers, blessings, the singing of hymns, and moments of adoration before arriving at the cathedral for benediction and adoration at *Vespers* in the evening.

It is conjectured that *tableaux vivants* of actors on moving floats, depicting static scenes from the life of Christ, were included very early in these Corpus Christi processions. And by mid-century, during Julian's childhood, lay sponsorship through craft guilds provided the needed impetus for the creative explosion of indigenous "mystery playing."[5] By then, articulate monks and friars as well as chaplains who served the guilds were engaged in writing dramatic plays on biblical texts solely for the purpose of enactment during the Corpus Christi procession. The feast day would have been considered a prime "teaching moment" for the clergy to instruct the laity about Jesus Christ. Patriarchs and prophets were also included in the cycles, because they had long been considered by church fathers as precursors of the Messiah. Every Old Testament story was viewed as an allegory about Christ as well as a prophecy that Christ would fulfill. The plays were designed to present the full arc of mankind's relationship with God, from Genesis to the Book of Revelation.

Laicization of the Plays

No one could have predicted the social and commercial success of the plays or the subsequent lay assumption of control over the entire venture. The civic authorities and local craft guilds saw in the feast day a golden opportunity to create stronger social bonds through the collaborative effort involved in production and performance. The guilds also welcomed the plays as a form of popular devotion, independent of Latin rituals of the church, which were always under the control of the priests. It was a chance for the *lewed* to enter more deeply into the mysteries of the faith side by side with their relatives, friends, and neighbors. Gradually, the laity took charge of creating settings, costumes, and, no doubt, developing more dramatic methods of speaking the verse rhymes. Soon the sheer enthusiasm of the crowds for the Corpus Christi plays all but overshadowed the focus of the feast day procession itself. Religious drama became a favorite source of family entertainment as well as religious instruction. It was a complete communal celebration.

The intimacy and proximity of the "street theatre" experience made the plays both appealing and emotionally affecting. Hearing biblical texts dramatized in English liberated the crowds from Latin as the preferred language of religion, much as the populist friars had staged their own revolution when they brought vernacular sermonizing right into the marketplace. All people, whether educated or not, could understand and sympathize with the biblical stories. Even though the plays contained subtle and sophisticated points of theology to intrigue the elite, the spiritual meanings and moral messages could have been grasped by any person with a basic knowledge of the faith. The Corpus Christi plays presented the drama of salvation as if it were happening at this very moment in time, in this very city, enacted by people everyone knew. The man, Jesus, could be seen, heard, touched, and felt.

When the burghers of the towns and cities witnessed the power of the plays to entice large crowds, they rose to the challenge to give them ever more sophisticated productions. The guilds rivaled one another to beg, borrow, steal, or commission the best versions of the plays from whatever source they could. Many a script was lent out from one town to another; alternately, spies were sent from one city to another, to see, copy, and report on what the competition was doing. In the surviving collections of plays from different cities, we find repeated instances of considerable "borrowing" from one text to another. Cycles from Chester and Wakefield rely on that of York for as much as one-third of the verse in any given play.[6] Since there were no copyright laws, plagiarism was not an issue. In fact, it was a mark of appreciation. Plays were rewritten, enlarged, divided from one into two, so that more than one guild could participate, or condensed because a certain guild could no longer afford to produce its assigned play.[7] No wonder that it is nearly impossible to reconstruct which version of the plays any given town saw and heard on any given date. There is also no way of knowing who actually wrote the plays, since medieval playwrights did not put their names on texts. Either they were known locally and a signature was considered unnecessary or they honored the usual tradition of anonymity; or the source materials (the scriptures) were considered so sacrosanct that no monk or cleric would have presumed to take credit for paraphrasing and dramatizing the stories. That would have been like claiming authorship of the Bible itself.

In addition to assembling play scripts, guilds were responsible for auditioning, selecting, and rehearsing actors in their roles (as well as providing abundant rehearsal food and drink). It was imperative that the local men chosen to act large roles have good, strong voices (in order to be easily heard out-of-doors, over the din of the crowd) and at least some dramatic sensitivity (later, traveling actors with these qualities would be in great demand). The main actors also had to be basically literate and have excellent memories in order to learn and retain the intricate rhyming verse. Choice parts were most likely assigned to leading guild members as well as to wealthy merchants who made large financial donations. There were also many small roles that were taught to illiterate men by repetition. Several different actors played Jesus, Mary, Judas, Pilate, Herod, and so forth as the wagons rolled by and presented a new play involving these same personages. It is likely that a prompter stood below or in front of the stage, whispering the lines just before the actors said them aloud in performance just in case someone got stage fright.

Production

While the town councils of Norwich or York, Lincoln or Chester might issue the command for the plays to be performed, they did so at little, if any, expense to the municipality. It was the craft and religious guilds that shouldered the full financial burden as well as the physical ones. A city corporation would be set up to assign individual plays to guilds according to their ability to produce and perform them. A levy or tax was charged to each guild craftsman and journeyman.[8] We know that in Norwich, the grocers' guild was responsible for the creation of the world and the fall of mankind. (Having easy access to a wide variety of fruits and vegetables as well as an abundance of grains and nuts, even animals and birds, the grocers' guild would have been well suited to provide an appropriate setting for the Garden of Eden.) In York, however, it was the tanners' or barkers' guild (who were used to working with foul-smelling manure and sulphur as well as fire as part of the tanning and parchment-making processes) who were called upon to stage the creation and the fall of Lucifer. The tanners were also adept at dyeing animal skins as close to white flesh-color as possible for Adam and Eve to wear, suggesting primeval nudity. The York fullers' guild (consisting of those who washed, sheared, and finished woolen cloth) were chosen to clothe Adam and Eve after their fall from grace. In Coventry, the fullers had originally come together as the Guild of the Nativity, so this is the pageant they always staged.[9]

Generally, the shipwrights' guild built Noah's Ark as a model ship that was wheeled through the town, while the fishmongers pooled their efforts to gather enough water to simulate the flood. The tile-thatchers "put forth" the journey to Bethlehem and constructed the dilapidated stable for Mary and Joseph, with the requisite hole in the roof for the star to shine through when the child was born. The goldsmiths and goldbeaters played the three Magi in gold-threaded costumes (and exhibited their prized golden plates, cups, and bowls at the same time, along with the required frankincense and myrrh), while the guild of barbers (who also served as surgeons) staged the baptism of Jesus because their specific religious fraternity was dedicated to St. John the Baptist.[10] The bakers were in charge of the Last Supper scene and were later known to throw out free loaves of unconsecrated altar bread to the members of the audience at the end of their play. The shearers (of sheep) led Christ "like a lamb" to the cross, while it fell to the pinners (who made nails) and the butchers (who had access to ample supplies of blood) to be in charge of the realistic enactment of the crucifixion. The carpenters staged the resurrection, because they first came together as the Holy Fraternity of the Resurrection,[11] and the tailors (perhaps to fashion an extravagant celestial robe for Christ's return to heaven) designed the ascension. The drapers (cloth and dry-goods workers) supplied the material for Mary's shroud, while the ostlers (stablemen able to handle horses for a suitable procession) performed Mary's assumption and coronation as queen of heaven. The cooks commonly produced stunning "fire and smoke effects" for the harrowing of hell (Christ's descent into the realm of Satan before his resurrection), and the mercers (rich textile merchants) staged the last judgment, suggesting to the audience that they were to be viewed as eminently just and honest-dealing men, the most responsible among citizens, who would sit at the right hand of God because of their financial support of these Corpus Christi plays (and other works of mercy) in their proud city.

In addition to building the wagons and stage settings, guild members had to create the necessary properties and mechanical effects needed for their respective plays, including hoists to raise Christ at the ascension and, later, his mother, at the assumption. Costumes for the characters were paid for and created by the guilds, though some were rented and others came from clergy willing to lend vestments, chalices, and a "doctor's weed"[12] (university dress). Local gentry contributed body armor, visors, swords, boots, and gloves. (It is notable that the various craftsmen/actors wore gloves to show due respect for the holy work of the mystery play at hand,[13] and perhaps also to cover up the permanent skin stains, scars, burns, and blemishes acquired by the practice of their crafts.) Authenticity was not to any biblical period, but only to the proper medieval station in life. Thus Annas, the high priest, though historically Jewish, was to be arrayed like "a bishop of the old law in a scarlet gown. And over that, a blue tabard furred with white and a mitre on his head after the old law, with doctors [of the law] standing by him in furred hoods, and one before them with his staff of state. And each of them [has] on their head a furred cap with a great knob in the crown, and also on [one] standing before as a Saracen, the which shall be his messenger."[14] Meanwhile, church choristers (and secular minstrels) were in great demand to perform the singing and musical interludes at certain key points in the drama, whether to intone *Hosanna* at the nativity or the *Te Deum* at the end of the world.[15]

The more acclaimed a given cycle of plays and its production values might be, the larger the crowds a metropolis could draw, and the greater its local standing and prestige at home and abroad. Smaller towns must have pooled resources, both financial and creative, to produce their own cycles. City merchants and artisans certainly capitalized on the magnetic pull of these plays to attract large audiences. Performance days became a lucrative opportunity for increased commerce. It has been suggested that the plays even brought many new craft guilds into existence, as artists and artisans who shared a common trade undertook to organize and publicize themselves by funding and performing a play in their town cycle.[16] The Corpus Christi event soon became a complex mix of social bonding, vernacular religious worship, and civic pride, plus an annual source of financial gain.

There was also the necessity of advertising, so the "banns" had to be composed (also in rhyming verse), announcing which plays would be performed each year, as well as when and where. Runners were sent out among neighboring towns and villages, summoning all people to the plays on the prescribed day and at the proper hour. Eventually, each guild appointed a pageant master whose duty it was to collect donations from individual guild members, oversee the storing and maintenance of the guild wagon, choose the actors (as well as play a part himself), and probably direct the production as well. Then he was obliged to organize a guild feast for the accounting of all funds.[17]

Performance

It is conjectured that some play cycles began at the first light of summer dawn, as early as 4:30 AM, with the creation of the world.[18] (Notably, this was the same time at which Julian's own visionary experiences would begin.) If all the plays were to be performed in one day, they would have continued late into the night, when torches and hellish bonfires being prepared for the damned would light up the last judgment. The city of York performed its forty-eight separate plays on one such marathon day. Each individual pageant had to be played between twelve and sixteen times, at each successive station, from dawn to dusk. In Chester, the complete cycle was divided into a more manageable time frame and took three consecutive days. The banns announcing the N-Town plays set the performance time "at 6 of the bell,"[19] a more agreeable 6 AM. Either way, those who attended all or even most of the plays had to be hardy souls, every bit as hardy as the actors themselves.

As the plays multiplied, gaining in length and complexity as well as audience appeal, crowd control must have become quite a problem. It seems more and more doubtful that the plays could have remained connected to the actual Corpus Christi procession for very long, since the host would have had to wait for each play to be performed at each separate station before being carried to the next. There was even the sacrilegious aspect introduced by boisterous and drunken groups in the streets around the play stations, jostling and shouting back at the performers and using foul language in front of the host, not to mention the normal hustle and bustle of buying and selling wares in the nearby marketplace. And since it became impossible to perform the ever-longer cycle of plays in a single day and still arrive at the cathedral in time for the culminating Corpus Christi liturgy at *Vespers*, it was inevitable that the plays had to separate from the actual Corpus Christi procession. Some municipalities (Norwich included) eventually moved the performances to Whitsun (Feast of Pentecost) and the day following. In other cities, the plays won out as the main Corpus Christi celebration, with the procession being held on the following day.

The Norwich Cycle?

Historic dating of both texts and performances is always problematic, but references seem to indicate that the performance of actual plays (not just tableaux) was already well established in Beverley, Ipswich, Kendal, Hereford, Lincoln, Newcastle-on-Tyne, Worcester, Dublin, Chester, and York by the second half of the fourteenth century. The most intriguing group of plays for our purpose is the *N-Town Collection*, so-called by the opening banns announcing the name of the town where it would next be performed. (This collection is actually an assortment of three much older, individual scripts that were edited and transcribed by an especially able scribe in the mid-fifteenth century.)[20] Because the N-Town plays are such an eclectic compendium drawn from many different sources and not a coherent working script, they are unlikely ever to have been performed as a complete dramatic cycle from start to finish. They have been identified as written in the East Anglian dialect, probably from the area of Norfolk, and were indicative of plays performed throughout the East Midlands, perhaps even by traveling actors.[21]

Could N-Town (possibly for *N*orwich, which scans perfectly in the verse of the banns) be, in fact, the "lost" Norwich cycle of plays?[22] We cannot be sure. However, we may conjecture that a prosperous commercial city like Norwich, abounding in religious fervor, artistic creativity, and financial resources (with a Cathedral Priory full of educated monks and friaries replete with highly literate Franciscans, Dominicans, and Austin canons) would have commissioned dramatists to write its own mystery cycle, if only to compete with York, Lincoln, Chester, and Beverley! It is probable that Norwich lent out its scripts and even its players to neighboring towns for their smaller local productions through a network of creative collaboration and mutually beneficial remuneration. Perhaps most of these scripts were never returned, or were lost, or were later destroyed. It is also plausible that Norwich craft and merchant guilds (with the help of monastic and clerical creativity) managed to borrow and absorb, edit and rewrite, plays from many different parts of East Anglia, making possible an amalgam of scripts for eventual collecting, such as that of the *N-Town Collection*. We may assume that this collection of plays is, at the very least, indicative of the type and content of the lost Norwich Corpus Christi cycle, that is, the very plays that might have been seen and heard by Julian. Further, as we shall see, Julian's references in her text to specific aspects of the N-Town plays lend strong credence to the likelihood that she saw some version of these plays performed.

Passion Plays

In addition to the pageant wagon mystery plays, there were separate "passion plays" that dealt exclusively with the passion, death, and resurrection of Christ.[23] However, because of their length and complexity, these plays were usually performed in two- or even three-year cycles. It is interesting to note that in the *N-Town Collection* the two passion plays are structurally independent, both from the rest of the mystery plays and from each other. Therefore, they needed their own separate productions. The sheer technical and dramatic demands, as well as the numerous detailed stage directions, suggest that these plays could not have been performed on moving pageant wagons. In addition to having large casts and multiple sets, they have simultaneous action occurring in separate playing areas, as well as a total lack of the distinct breaks between scenes that were so typical of pageant wagon presentations. Rather than having been written as a series of separate scenes, each complete passion play was clearly meant to be experienced as a unified whole, with a cumulative dramatic effect.

***Platea* and Scaffold**

An alternate method of staging had to be developed, that of "*platea* and scaffold," to create a more spacious, cohesive, and also stationary playing area.[24] The *platea* was a central open space suitable for fixed stage performances. In Norwich, we may imagine the open *playne* of Tombland being utilized, or the large central *Greneyard*. Sizeable stage platforms were erected on top of several raised wooden scaffoldings set up in a semi-circle around a central *platea* to define specific areas of dramatic and continuous action. (Chaucer refers to "holy Absolon" who played Herod "on a high scaffold.")[25] Additionally, the imposing facade of the wealthy merchants' Church of St. Peter and St. Paul might have served for God to appear "in a high place," or to ascend into the "clouds," while a natural or intentionally raised area might have been designated for the Magi's entrance, or "a place like to a park"[26] used as the Garden of Olives where Jesus went to pray before his arrest.

Much of the dramatic action of the N-Town "Passion of Christ" takes place on the central *platea*, with characters coming and going repeatedly from a scaffold on one side to a scaffold on the other (from the Jewish council chamber to the Last Supper, from the court of Pilate to that of Herod, from the bowels of hell to the heights of heaven during the last judgment). Stage scaffolding not only provided better audience viewing for all of this activity and intrigue and afforded more prominent focus on the main characters and their actions, but it also allowed the guilds to produce spectacular mechanical effects from *behind* the scaffold structures. In addition, scaffolds helped to delineate the medieval sense of a well-ordered universe: heavenly (and earthly) courts passing judgment from high on the scaffolds; humankind in the middle-space on the *platea*; and the eternal fires burning from within the traditional, monstrous "hell mouth" underneath the scaffolding, complete with chains, a windlass, flames, smoke effects, and no doubt, a barrel to roll for the resurrection earthquake.[27] This multi-level solution enabled several scenes to happen at once, both on the *platea* and on and under the scaffolds. For *platea*-and-scaffold plays, additional platforms were also built for audience seating, as they were for jousting tournaments, at least for the gentry and merchant elite of the city. The villeins sat on the ground.

Julian's Theatre

Julian would have seen mystery plays performed on individual pageant wagons as well as passion plays acted out in a *platea*-and-scaffold setting. She might well have been a member of the audience from her early adolescence right up until such time as she became enclosed as an anchoress. Perhaps her father, as a respected merchant guild member, had played a major role in an earlier (now lost) Norwich cycle: God in the *Paradyse* play, or *Moises* expounding the Ten Commandments, or one of the *three kinges* in the Nativity Play. We can only assume that Julian, like all people who feel a kinetic attraction to live drama, could not wait for the next performance.

Imagine the excitement of preparations for the plays every summer in Norwich. Wagons had to be refurbished; viewing scaffolds constructed; stage platforms set up; sets, backcloths, and front curtains painted or repainted; and multiple costumes sewn and mended. Props had to be carved, gilded, painted; some from previous years, others newly fashioned each spring season. Everyone in the craft and religious guilds, women included, helped in some way. Perhaps Julian herself sewed Mary's veil, or wove her dress, or placed beading on her cape. Maybe Julian mended Christ's tunic, as "the other women" of Galilee once had done. Many a family evening would have been spent learning lines with the help of literate family members acting as prompters. Julian might well have been much in demand to "hold the script" in her household; in the process, like all young people with prodigious memories, she would have committed the verses (many of them literal gospel passages) to memory much more easily than her older male relatives. How she must have longed to play a part, any part, but women and girls were not allowed to rehearse and perform alongside men.

Then, after much anticipation, the announced performance day(s) would arrive. Julian would have risen early to get a prime position in the street, before the wagons started rolling through town, or to find a good place in the seating area of the *platea.* Merchants vied (and paid) for the wagon stations to be located near their shops, so as to publicize their support for the pageants and do a brisk business while the crowd waited for the next wagon to arrive. Then, when all was ready, in the emerging light of a summer dawn, Julian would see the actor playing God appear, his face painted gold like an icon, wearing a royal crown and long flowing robes. She would hear the first words (similar in all the cycles) that signaled the start of the first play:

Deus. *Ego sum alpha et oo, principium et finis.*
[I am the First and the Last, beginning and end.]
My name is known, God and king
My work to make, now will I undertake.
In myself rests my reigning:
It has no beginning nor no end.
And all that ever shall have being,
It is enclosed within my mende [mind].
When it is made at my liking
I may it save; I may condemn
After my good pleasure.
So great of might is my power
All things shall be wrought by me.
I am one God, in persons three
Knit in one substance.
I am the true Trinity
Here walking in this place.
Three Persons, myself I see
Locked in me, God alone.
I am the Father of Power;
My Son within me proceeds

My Spirit is grace in majesty
Wielding wealth in heaven's throne.
One God in three I am called
I am Father of Might
My Son keepeth Right [Justice]
My Ghost hath light
And grace withall.

Thus begins the *N-Town Play of the Creation and Fall* (first of the angels, then of Adam). Angels sing a canticle of praise, and Lucifer asks whether their song is to reverence God or himself; he is swiftly cast out for his colossal pride. God creates heaven, brings forth the first day and night, water and the firmament. He parts the waters from the earth and gives life to "every growing thing"; he places the sun and moon and stars in the sky, and the creeping things and fish and birds and beasts on the earth. Finally, God creates man, "Adam by name." Later, God brings forth Adam's wife, telling Adam she is "flesh of thy flesh and bone of thy bone." They are both full of gratitude and walk in a pleasure paradise, promising to keep God's directive to "touch not this tree that is of knowledge." The story of the fall is told succinctly as the Serpent, appearing as "a fair angel" of light (the better to disguise himself) convinces Eve to eat the apple with the promise that she will become "as wise as God." She then tries to get Adam to eat it, with the enticement it will make him "God's equal to be always/ All his wisdom to understand." But Adam will not touch it: "If that we do this sinful deed/ We shall be dead by God's judgment." Yet after some insistent reassurances from Eve (delivered, no doubt, with seductive charm), Adam finally gives in, takes the apple, tastes it, and immediately repents his sin of disobedience. He discovers them both to be naked, searches for some fig leaves, and bids Eve to "lay this leaf on thy private parts/and with this leaf I shall hide myself."

God appears and chastises them both mightily, according to the Genesis account. Adam immediately blames the woman:

The woman that thou gave to me
She brought me thereto.
It was her counsel and her advice
She bade me do the same deed.

Nevertheless, Adam is told by God to:

> Go till thy meat with swynk and swoot [toil and sweat],
> Unto thy life's end;
> Go naked, hungry and barefoot,
> Eat both herbs, grass, and root:
> Thy suffering has no other relief,
> As a wretch in the world thou goest.

And Eve is likewise condemned:

> Woman, thou soughtest this sinning
> And bade him break my bidding
> Therefore shalt thou be an underling,
> To man's bidding bend.
> What he biddeth thee, do thou that thing,
> And bear thy children with great groaning,
> In danger and in death dreading,
> Unto thy life's end.

Therefore, according to medieval exegesis, the full blame is placed on Eve for the fall of Adam and, by extension, the whole human race. Her sin/seduction is also the reason given for Eve's subjugation by man, as well as her bearing of children with "great groaning" and the fear of death; all because she "soughtest this sinning." Julian and every other woman (and man) of her time had been indoctrinated by this teaching ever since their earliest years. So it will be all the more astounding that, in the parable of the lord and the servant, Julian will envision a representation of the play of Adam's fall very, very differently.

Thereafter, the plays of Cain and Abel, Noah and the Flood, Abraham and Isaac, Moses and Laws, and the Play of Jesse, follow in biblical order. Moving into the New Testament, Julian would have seen the play of the annunciation, of Joseph's doubts, of Mary's visit to her cousin Elizabeth, of the nativity with the visit of the shepherds, of Herod and the three kings, followed by Mary's purification and presentation in the temple, and the slaughter of the innocents. After this, there was always a leap in time (as in the gospel narrative) to the appearance of the adolescent Jesus in the temple and his being questioned by the doctors of the law, then another leap to the baptism of the adult Jesus, followed by his temptation by the devil in the wilderness. Finally, this section of the *N-Town Collection* concludes (like the collections of York and Chester) with a play about the woman taken in adultery, and all the cycles enact the raising of Lazarus from the dead.

The Passion

The first-year N-Town passion play begins with the conspiracy against Jesus by the council of the Jews, who are concerned that so many of the populace are following this teacher, Jesus. Christ enters into Jerusalem on a donkey, followed by a large crowd waving palm branches and spreading their cloaks on the ground. Thereafter, the Last Supper scenes are interspersed with further scenes of the conspiracy and with Judas's betrayal. Then Christ's agony in the Garden of Olives is played, followed by his arrest. A final procession of saints ends the first passion play.

In the second year of the passion play, Julian would have heard a short prologue delivered by the figure of *Contemplatio*, who beseeches the audience "that your wills be good/To keep the Passion in your mind that shall be showed here," thus urging the very same "true mind in the passion of Christ" that Julian would specify that she longed to have (2:16.127). Then the trial of Jesus begins, with Herod and Pilate, Annas and Caiphas, appearing on their separate raised scaffolds. Jesus is dragged from one court or council chamber to another, back and forth across the *platea* many times, bound with ropes like any common criminal on his way to the gallows in Norwich. At the interrogation by the high priests Annas and Caiphas, one of the Jews strikes Jesus on his cheek while others beat him "about the head and the body, and spit in his face, and pull him down, and set him on a stool, and cast a cloth over his face." The torturers play a game of blindman's bluff, similar to that played by children, turning Jesus round and round, striking him on the head, daring him to identify his torturers by crying out: "What! Thou Jhesus, who gave thee that?" It must have been unbearable to watch.

The apostle Peter, out of fear of capture, denies three times to a mere servant woman that he even knows this Jesus. Then the cock crows and the stage directions indicate: "Peter shall weep," saying:

I have forsaken my master and my Lord Jhesu
Three times as he told me I should do the same
Wherefore I may not have sorrow enough!
I, sinful creature, am so much to blame.

Annas and Caiphas bring Jesus to Pilate, while Judas returns the blood money he was given to betray Jesus. Then Judas goes out and hangs himself. Pilate questions Jesus, trying to find out if he really is the Son of God, "Lord of earth and of all things." Then, according to the stage directions, the Jews take "Jhesu and lead him in great haste to the Herod. And the Herod's scaffold shall unclose, showing Herod enthroned in state, all the Jews kneeling except Annas and Caiphas." Herod has heard of the "wonder-werkings" of this man, and begs him: "Now, Jhesu, I pray thee—let me see/One miracle wrought in my presence!" As recounted in the gospels, "Jesus shall speak no word to the Herod." The king becomes furious at the insult, ranting and raving, demanding that the soldiers pull off Jesus' clothes and beat him with whips to make him speak. Jesus, all bloodied, is dragged back to Pilate.

Meanwhile, Pilate's wife comes "running off the scaffold, and her shirt and her kirtel [tunic] in her hand, and she shall come before Pilate like a mad woman." She tells Pilate of her dream (inspired by Satan, who wants to keep Jesus from dying and thus saving the world and emptying out hell).

A fiend appeared before me,
As I lay in my bed sleeping fast.
Since the time that I was born,
Was I never so sore aghast!
Like wildfire and thunder blast,
He came crying unto me.
He said, "They that beat Jhesus, or bound him fast—
Without end damned shall be!"

Pilate thanks her:

Gramercy [many thanks], my wife, for ever you are true!
Your counsel is good, and ever hath be [been].
Now to your chamber, do you go
And all shall be weyl, dame, as ye shall see [italics added].

And all shall be weyl...

It is indeed startling to read the best known and most-quoted phrase in all of Julian's writings emerge out of the mouth of Pilate! The only explanation must be that the phrase was simply not unique to Julian. "Alle shalle be wele" (in Julian's spelling) must have been a colloquial saying in the fourteenth century, for the same phrase is found several times in Walter Hilton's book, the *Scale of Perfection*, written in the 1380s.[28] It may have been as common a phrase in the late fourteenth century, as "Everything's going to be all right" is to modern ears. These sound like the soothing words a mother might say to her child, or the comforting reassurance a husband, even Pilate, might offer his wife in a moment of terror. However, what Julian *heard* in this everyday phrase, when spoken to her directly by the Lord, was more than soothing, comforting, or reassuring. The Lord's meaning is ultimate, not momentary; complete, not partial. Still, the presence of these words in the N-Town play demonstrates that, in speaking to Julian, the Lord used familiar, colloquial phrases to convey the most profound mystical meanings.

Pilate's Condemnation

When Jesus will not answer Pilate in his own defense, the procurator speaks to Jesus with a direct quotation from the gospel of John (Jn 19:10–11):

> **Pilate.** What sayest, Jhesus? Why speakest thou not to me?
> Knowest not I have power on the cross to put thee?
> And also I have power to let thee go forth.
> What canst thou say here?
> **Jhesus.** Power over me thou hast rightly none,
> But that which my Father hath granted thee beforn.
> I came, my Father's will to fulfill,
> That mankind should not spill [perish].
> He that hath betrayed me to thee at this time,
> His trespass is more than is thine.

Though Pilate tries to find a way to release Jesus, he finally condemns him, under great pressure from the "doctors" (that is, doctors of the law) and the crowds. The doctors bring the murderer, Barabbas, and the two thieves on either side of Jesus, bare-legged and wearing only their shirts, up to the judgment bar. At the same time,

Annas and Caiphas go into the council-house when Pilate sits down to pass sentence. The murderer, Barabbas, is freed (for the paschal day), while Jesus is sentenced to be nailed upon a cross, as the crowd cries out with a loud voice: "Ya! Ya! Ya!" The two thieves are condemned to die alongside Jesus, but Pilate directs that only those who are "knights and gentlemen born" be permitted to strip Jesus of his clothes. After Jesus is bound to a pillar and scourged for a second time, the stage directions state:

> *And when he is scourged they put upon him a cloth of silk, and set him on a stool and put a crown of thorns on his head with forks.*[29] *And the Jewys kneel to Christ, taking him a sceptre and scorning him. And then they shall pull off the purple cloth and put on again his own clothes and lay the cross on his neck to bear it and draw him forth with ropes. And then shall come two women weeping and with their hands wringing.*

Jesus speaks to the daughters of Jerusalem, as quoted in the gospel of Luke (Lk 23:27–31):

> **Jhesus.** Daughters of Jerusalem, for me weep not,
> But for yourself weep, and for your children, also.
> For the days shall come that they have sought after,
> Their sin and their blindness shall turn them to woe.

While being dragged by ropes in a circle around the *platea*, Jesus meets Simon, who is forced to help Jesus carry his cross. He also encounters Veronica:

> **Veronica.** Ah, ye sinful people! What are you doing?
> Because of sweat and blood, he may not see!
> Alas, Holy Prophet, Christ Jhesus!
> Sorrowful is my heart for thee!
> *And she wipes his face with her veil.*
> **Jhesus.** Veronica, thy wiping does me ease.
> My face is clean that was black to see.
> I shall keep those from all suffering
> That look on thy veil and remember me.

Julian will refer to the "holy vernacle" during her vision of the passion (10:30–32.159). It is apparent that the medieval story of Veronica's veil, believed to have been housed in St. Peter's Basilica in

Rome, had made a great impression on her. It is also revealing that the N-Town cycle is the *only* one of the extant passion plays that includes this episode of Veronica wiping the face of Jesus. Could Julian have first learned of Veronica's veil from this very passion play? Whatever the case, the presence of this episode indicates the highly devotional character of East Anglian spirituality, and once again, strongly suggests that Julian may have seen this N-Town version.

The Crucifixion

> *Then shall they pull Jhesus out of his clothes and lay them together. And there they shall pull him down, and lay him along on the cross, and after that, nail him thereon.*

Completely contrary to the gospel account, in the N-Town passion play it is "the Jewys" who nail Christ to the cross, not the Roman soldiers. The torturers worry that the pre-drilled nail holes are too far apart for Christ's hands and feet:

> **Judeus 4.** This is right—take good heed.
> Pull out that arm to thee, hard!
> **Judeus 3.** This is short—the devil take him—
> By a large foot or more!
> **Judeus 2.** Fasten on a rope and stretch him out,
> And I shall pull against thee.
> Spare we not these strong ropes
> Though we burst both flesh and vein.
> **Judeus 3.** Drive in the nail anon! Let's see
> And look if the flesh and sinews will hold.
> **Judeus 4.** That I grant, so may I suffer.
> Lo, this nail is driven very well and deep!
> **Judeus 1.** Fasten a rope, then, to his feet
> And pull him down long enough.
> **Judeus 2.** Here is a nail that's both good and long!
> I shall drive it through, I swear!
> (*Here shall they leave off and dance around the cross shortly.*)

The pulling of Christ's arms and legs to fit the nail holes was a traditional stage device, perhaps to mask the need to tie the actor's wrists and ankles to the cross while pretending to hammer in the nails. (Possibly, the actor playing Jesus was surreptitiously strapped with wristbands containing pre-fixed nail heads; he would also have had to rest his feet on a small platform to support his full body weight.) Still, the brutality of stretching the Lord's limbs so as to tear every sinew, burst every vein, and cause the utmost torture, as well as the cold-heartedness of the executioners, the celebratory dancing around the cross, the taunting of Christ to prophesy, while crying out "Hail, King of Jewys, if thou be!" seem too painfully graphic. The executioners then set up the other two crosses, hanging the two thieves by their arms on either side of Jesus, and cast dice for his clothes, exactly as in the gospel account.

> *And in the meantime shall our Lady come with three Marys [Mary Magdalene, Mary the mother of James, and (Mary) Salome, as in Mk 16:1] with her, and afterward John with them, setting themselves down at the side before the cross, our Lady swooning and mourning and saying slowly:*
> **Maria.** Ah! My good Lord, my son so sweet!
> What hast thou done? Why hangest now here like this?
> Is there no other death to thee now fitting,
> But the most shameful death among these thieves?
> Ah! Out my heart! Why do you not burst?
> For thou art maiden and mother and seest thy child die.
> How may thou abide this sorrow and this woeful thought?
> Ah, death, death, death! Why wilt thou not kill me?
> *Here our Lady shall swoon again.*

What woman in the audience would not have wept at Mary's *planctus*, her tears of lamentation? How much Julian could identify with Mary's agony, her swooning, her desire to die herself rather than watch her child die. The reality of Christ on the cross became, not a gospel read from the pulpit, nor an article of faith discussed in a sermon, nor a painted mural on a church wall, nor even a holy rood hanging high above in church. In this dramatic re-enactment it was happening here and "now" (twice reiterated in these lines alone). There was no way the audience could escape the horror of God's Son dying such a death to take away their sins. Jesus speaks the words of forgiveness from the cross:

> **Jhesus.** Oh! Father almighty, maker of man,
> Forgive these Jewys that make me suffer!

Forgive them, Father. Forgive them then.
For they know not what they do.

Mary, his mother, cries out for a word, any word, from her son.

Maria. Oh, my son, my son, my darling dear!
What? Have I offended thee?
Thou hast spoken to all those that are here,
And not one word thou speakest to me!
To the Jewys thou art fully kind;
Thou hast forgiven all their misdeeds.
And the thief thou hast in mind—
For once asking mercy, heaven is his reward!
Ah, my Sovereign Lord, why wilt thou not speak
To me that am thy mother, in pain for thy wrong?
Ah, heart, heart! Why wilt thou not break,
That I were out of this sorrow so strong?

Christ answers and entrusts Mary to John for her safekeeping: "Ah, woman, woman! Behold there thy son." He also reminds Mary that it is his Father in heaven who sent him:

Jhesus. To take this manhood of thee, Adam's ransom to pay.
For this is the will and my Father's intent:
That I shall thus die to deliver man from the devil's prey.

This was a consistently held medieval view of salvation, that the Son of God took his mother's flesh and blood in order to "pay the price" to extricate humankind from the clutches of Satan. The moment is so touching, even the stage directions strike a compassionate tone:

Here our Lady shall rise and run and embrace the cross.
Maria Magdalena. Ah, good lady, why fare you thus?
Your sorrowful face now grieves us sore.
And for the pain of my sweet Lord Jhesus,
That he sees in you, it paineth him more!
Maria Virgo. I pray you all, let me stay here
And hang me up here on this tree
By my friend and son that to me is so dear,
For where he is, there would I be!

Johannes. Gentle lady, now leave your mourning
And go with us now, we you pray,
And comfort our Lord at his departing,
For he is most ready to go his way.
Here they shall take our Lady from the cross. And here shall Pilate come down from his scaffold, with Caiphas and Annas and all their retinue and shall come and look on Christ.

After Pilate writes: *Hic est Jhesus Nazarenus Rex Judeorum* ["This is Jesus, King of the Jews"], he mounts the ladder himself and sets the inscription above Christ's head. Then Pilate, Annas and Caiphas return to the scaffold. At this point, Christ cries out in agony:

Heloy, heloy! Lamazabathany! [Mt 27:46]
My Father in heaven on high!
Why dost thou forsake me?
The frailty of my mankind
With strong pain, it begins to pierce!
Ha! Dear Father, have me in mind,
And let death my sorrow slake! . . .
So great a thirst did never man take
As I have, man, now for thy sake.
For thirst, asunder my lips gin crake [begin to crack];
For dryness, they do cleve (split apart].
In manus tuas, Domine [Into your hands, Lord]. [Lk 23:46].
Holy Father, in heavenly see [on heaven's throne]
I commend my spirit to thee,
For here now endeth my fast.
I shall go slay the fiend, that freak.
For now, my heart begins to break:
No word more shall I speak—
Nunc consummatum est [Now it is finished]. [Jn 19:30]

In her vision, Julian will experience the terrible thirst of the Savior for all humankind. She will become acutely aware of the drying out and splitting apart of his skin. She will hear Christ tell her, referring to his sacrifice, "herewith is the fiend overcome" (13:4–5.169). It is precisely at this moment in the passion play that Julian would have experienced the agony of the cross *as if* she had been one of the three Marys, standing with the Blessed Mother and John in the great open *platea*, watching Christ die. Like them, she would have felt utter helplessness to do anything to relieve the Lord's sufferings.

After the Roman soldier, traditionally named Longinus, plunges his spear into Jesus' side and pronounces him dead, Joseph of Arimathea arrives to request the body of Jesus from Pilate. Given permission, and with the help of Nicodemus, Joseph takes Jesus down from the cross in full view of the audience and lays him in his weeping mother's lap, the living *Pieta* that would depict the sufferings of the *Mater Dolorosa* for generations to come.

Artistic Representation

The fourteenth century may seem macabre, even melodramatic, to our post-modern viewpoint. Its realistic presentations of the crucifixion, both in the passion plays and in contemporary paintings, leave little to the imagination. Christ's countless wound-holes bleed profusely, his face is contorted, his mouth droops, his hair is matted with spittle and blood, his hands are clenched around the nails, his body is bruised from the beatings, his legs are twisted in agony, and the lance-mark in his side is a gaping hole. In fourteenth-century art, Christ was no longer painted as the already triumphant king, bloodless and without pain on the cross, his wounds merely symbolic, as he had been in the thirteenth century. Likewise in the passion plays, the literalness of the language and the gory depiction of the crucifixion were conceivable only by the fourteenth century.

Why this change? No doubt it emerged as a result of the recurring horrors of the Great Pestilence and the ongoing disasters of the Hundred Years' War. No family had escaped suffering. Playwrights, poets, homilists, painters, sculptors, could no longer *sanitize* the crucifixion. Christ on the cross needed to embody the very tortures and gruesome deaths that people knew firsthand. For these audiences, anything other than total realism would have made Christ appear less than human. Similarly, the depiction of the agony of women (Christ's swooning mother, the grieving three Marys, the weeping women of Jerusalem, Veronica offering Christ her veil to wipe his face full of blood) gave recognition to women as having suffered along with Christ, at the foot of the cross, while all the apostles except for John had fled.

The Harrowing of Hell

While the dead body of Christ is wound in cloth and placed in the sepulcher, another actor depicts the *Anima Christi* (Soul of Christ) descending into hell to lead forth Adam, Eve, Abraham, John the Baptist, and all those who died in good grace in ages past and who were awaiting the coming of the Savior. This was the long-anticipated scene, the "harrowing of hell,"[30] based on an account from the apocryphal *Gospel of Nicodemus.* In this oft-told story, the Spirit of Christ descends into hell and binds Satan and all his devils (with real ropes and chains) and consigns them there forever, while Satan's prisoners are led from the inferno to freedom. It was one of the most consistently performed plays in the Middle Ages, much to the enthusiasm of the cheering audience. No doubt everyone whose family members had died "unshriven" during the Great Mortality must have prayed that this very same "harrowing" would happen for their own dear departed. The scene would have created an immense cathartic release for the whole audience. *This* is what salvation looks like!

Julian's Reactions

As a devout young woman, Julian would have heard the many episodes from the story of salvation preached from the pulpit and then meditated on them in private, especially on Christ's passion. But each time she saw the mystery and passion plays, her meditations took on a new reality. No matter that Julian knew the Blessed Virgin was being played by a young boy with a veil over his head, and that the baby in her arms was a doll in swaddling clothes; when Mary laid the baby in a manger, Julian remembered placing her own infant in the cradle and rocking her to sleep. Julian tells us that she wanted to be like Magdalene, the converted sinner who washed Jesus' feet with her tears and dried them with her hair. She wanted to go with "the other women" who followed Jesus across the *platea* to Calvary and stand with Mary, his mother, at the foot of the cross. Julian knew the re-enacted crucifixion had to be simulated with ropes and animal blood. Nevertheless, seeing a human Jesus figure endure such unspeakable beatings and humiliations from the hands of the soldiers and then hang, naked and bleeding, on a wooden cross right in front of her eyes meant to her that *Christ was dying*, in this very moment, just as in the gospel story.

We may imagine the tears that rolled down her face as Julian heard Jesus utter his last words and give up his Spirit. Every performance she ever saw brought back the dying she had watched during the Great Plague in her childhood, and again, as a young wife and mother. Seeing the passion play reopened her own spiritual wounds that bled like Christ's physical ones. And she must have felt every word of Mary's lament for her lost child as the sword of remembrance pierced her own heart. Julian longed to stand, like Mary Magdalene, in front of the empty tomb, weeping for her lost Lord... and then hear Jesus call her name after he rose from the dead on Easter morning.

The Final Play

The Play of Judgment Day or, as it was more commonly called, Domesday, was the very last. It depicts the end of the world. The Archangel Michael announces: "*Surgite*! All men arise! *Venite ad judicium* [Come to Judgment]!" The Archangel Gabriel calls forth to this Day of Doom both pope and princes, priests, kings, Caesars and knights. Anyone found to be guilty, "In endless hell he shall be destroyed/His deeds, his death shall bring about." Demons rise from the ground crying: "Harrow and out!... Alas! Harrow! Is this that day to endless pain that we must pass?"

God appears and calls to himself the blessed who were his faithful servants on earth, and St. Peter welcomes them through the gates of heaven. But the souls of the damned cry out:

> Ha! Ha! Mercy, mercy we cry and crave!
> Ah, mercy, Lord, for our misdeeds!
> Ah, mercy, mercy! We rub! We rave!
> Ah, help us, good Lord, in this need!

God the Judge is depicted as just, strict, and unbending:

> **Deus.** How would you wretches any mercy have?
> Why ask you mercy now in this need?
> What have you wrought, your soul to save?
> To whom have you done any merciful deed,
> Mercy for to win?

As in the gospel parable of the end of the world, God lists all the ways in which the souls of the damned have failed to do the seven corporal works of mercy: they did not feed the hungry and give drink to the thirsty, welcome the stranger, clothe the naked, visit the sick, or relieve those in prison (Mt 25:34–46). Neither have they buried the dead poor man who could not afford his own grave.

Deus. For your love I was rent on rood [the cross],
And for your sake I shed my blood.
When I was so merciful and so good,
Why have you wrought against my will?

The accusations of the seven deadly sins are listed by the demons themselves: pride, covetousness, wrath, envy, sloth, debauchery, gluttony (including drunkenness). And the damned cry out:

Ah! Mercy, Lord, great of might!
We ask thy mercy and not thy right [to judge],
Not after our deeds, so us requite!
We have sinned! We are to blame!

The rest of the N-Town Domesday play is missing, but it may be assumed that, like similar plays of Chester and York, the Lord God (in the human figure of Jesus Christ) explains that in the "time of grace" these souls failed to act. And even though Mary and all the saints prayed for them to repent, now it is too late. Therefore, they must go into the eternal hellfire. The devils carry them off amid loud screams, wailing, and the gnashing of teeth. There is final rejoicing high in heaven, however, even as the damned cry out from below. The music of angels fills the air and the story of salvation is ended.

Julian's Questions

Julian must have walked home from the plays overcome by love, sadness, hope, and burning questions for which she had no answers. Why was Eve always blamed for the fall of Adam? If God is love, why is God portrayed as wrathful toward his creatures? Does he continue to love us, or does he turn away and leave us to be punished and to suffer alone? How much sorrow for sin, how much suffering, is enough sorrow and suffering to be completely forgiven? If the soul keeps on sinning because of its bad habits and sinful desires, how could it ever be saved from damnation? Yet why would God create countless souls only that they be damned? How can a soul in hell, testifying to "God's justice," give glory to God? On the contrary, if Christ suffered to prove God's unconditional love, how could *anyone* be damned? Yet what about the thieves, the murderers, all those criminals who were dragged through the streets of Norwich, then hanged, drawn and quartered, their heads stuck high on the walls as a warning to passersby? Could they be saved? Could one of them be like the good thief who stole into heaven at the last minute? Or did they never repent their crimes in time to be forgiven in eternity? Yet if Christ died that terrible death on the cross to save sinners, why some and not all?

Every time Julian heard a sermon that said people would go to hell for their unconfessed sins, she became afraid. How could she be sure who was in heaven: her siblings and other relatives who had died from the Great Pestilence, her childhood and adult friends? Faces flew past the eyes of her memory: the creased and haggard faces of peasants bringing their crops to market... men and women haggling over the prices of vegetables and fish... merchants making deals with foreigners in strange languages... nobles, knights, and yeomen leaving for war and never coming back. Where were they now? When they died, were they in a state of grace? Were they in heaven? Were they in hell? When the plays ended every summer, Julian must have become so immersed in the stark reality of the human drama that the images never left her mind. Her questions, too, continued to multiply and to plague her. Who would give the answers her soul craved?

Julian's Parable

There is convincing evidence of the direct influence of the mystery plays on Julian: her vision (which she will describe near the end of her *Revelations*) of the parable of a lord and a servant. It appears to her in a flash and burns into her memory, though she admits that it took "twenty years less three months" (51:73.277) for her to understand its meaning. It unfolds before her eyes as a series of pictures or *tableaux*, as precisely staged as the scenes of any mystery play. She will be led to examine every aspect of costume, demeanor, action, and motivation of the two characters. Indeed, her analysis will reveal just how poignant and theatrical the parable is meant to be. It is, in fact, Julian's vision of the fall of Adam. However, in her version, there will be no Garden of Eden, no lushness, no forbidden tree of knowledge, no apple, and—most amazingly—no mention of Eve seducing Adam and willfully disobeying God's command. On the contrary, the creation revealed to Julian will be a wide open, barren, and deserted space, much like the open-air *platea*. And her mind's ability to go deeper into the parable will no doubt be influenced by the dramatic storytelling that had been a part of her formation.

This is just one example from Julian's text that suggests the impact that the Corpus Christi plays must have had on her development. From her adolescence, she had expressed a wish for a more intense involvement in the passion of Christ: to "have been present at that time [of the crucifixion] with Mary Magdalene and with others who were Christ's lovers" (2:7–8.125). By enabling her to undergo a dramatic purgation, a *catharsis* in the classic sense, the passion plays would have opened her spiritual "heart," just as the sermons she heard and the manuals she read helped shape her inquisitive mind. It is conceivable that, until her Revelations, the Corpus Christi plays were Julian's most visceral experience of the suffering Christ—and an essential preparation for seeing her visions.

Part Two

Julian's Revelations

11
Three Gifts

> This is a revelation of love that Jesus Christ, our endless bliss, made in sixteen shewings. (1:1–2.123)

Julian prefaces the Long Text with a summary of its contents, describing briefly what each of the sixteen Revelations will contain. In the Short Text, Julian had called all her visionary and verbal experiences *shewings*, an older English word meaning "manifestations." Now, in the Long Text, she will employ a fairly new Middle English word for what she saw and heard that came into use only in the 1380s: *revelations.* This word could imply both visions and prophecies assumed to be of divine origin. In Julian's text, it refers to the sixteen separate Revelations and to the complete work as a whole.[1]

Julian may have begun the writing of her Short Text based on jottings in a journal set down during a period of convalescence after her illness and in the years following her visions. Like so many mystical writers, she may have used the private diary form to work out what the original *shewings* meant to her personally, as well as to come to a greater understanding of their meaning for her *evencristens.* She may have allowed her Short Text to be read by a trusted confessor who urged her to write more. Later, she must have become convinced that the Lord was directing her to expand her text with the fruit of "twenty years less three months" of further theological and contemplative understanding (51:73.277). And then, at some point during the 1390s, with grace-filled inspiration (and no doubt, some trepidation), Julian started to write a more extensive document that came to be known as the Long Text.

A Simple Creature

Julian begins her Revelations by introducing herself to the reader very directly, simply, and with a personal disclaimer.

> These revelations were shewn to a simple creature that could [read] no letter the year of our Lord 1373, the eighth day of May,[2] which creature desired before three gifts of God. The first was mind of his passion. The second was bodily sickness in youth at thirty years of age. The third was to have of God's gift three wounds.[3]

We have already seen that when Julian speaks of herself as "a simple creature *unlettered*" (or, as in the Sloane manuscript quoted above, "a simple creature that could no letter"), she does not mean to imply she was unable to read or write English, but that, according to medieval usage of the phrase, she could not read or write *Latin*. Thus she makes very clear that she is no scholar, no theologian, no well-educated member of the aristocracy. She never uses her name directly, nor (in the Long Text) does she anywhere indicate that she is a woman.[4] She is simply God's *creature*, a term she will use at least seventy times in her Revelations, both to refer to herself and to all men and women.[5]

While Julian will not tell us anything about the facts of her life before her visions, nevertheless, at the beginning of both the Short and Long Texts, Julian does offer the reader an astonishing glimpse into her mind and heart during her early formative years. It is the only strictly biographical information she provides. She must have felt that this aspect of her spiritual life was deeply pertinent to the eventual unfolding of her grave illness and subsequent Revelations. Julian may also have thought it was necessary for the reader to understand the extreme nature (perhaps even spiritual recklessness?) of her soul. She tells us that, at some point, most likely during early adolescence and well before her marriage, she desired three gifts: "mind of the passion," a "bodily sickness in youth at thirty years of age," and "three wounds."

The First Gift

> For the first, it had come to my mind with devotion: it seemed to me I had some measure of feeling for the passion of Christ, but yet I desired to have more, by the grace of God. It seemed to me that I would have been present at that time with Mary Magdalene and with others who were Christ's lovers, so that I might have seen bodily the passion that our lord suffered for me, that I might have suffered with him as others did that loved him. And therefore I

> desired ***a bodily sight***, wherein I might have more knowing of [understanding of and sympathy with] the bodily pains of our savior, and of the compassion of our lady, and of all his true lovers that were living at that time and saw his pains. For I would have been one of them and have suffered with them. Any other sight or shewing of God I never desired, until the soul was departed from the body, for I believed myself to be saved by the mercy of God. This was my intention: because I wanted afterwards, because of that shewing, to have the more true mind of the passion of Christ. (2:5–16.125–27, italics added)

Julian reveals quite candidly that, even in her youth, she had "some measure of feeling for the passion of Christ." Yet she was convinced that her ability to enter into the Lord's sufferings did not go deep enough. She wanted to feel more, to suffer more, in order to have a truer understanding of what Christ underwent to save the world from sin. She hoped that if she received a vision, the reality of Christ's "bodily pains" would become so physical, so visceral, so immediate that she could experience them as fully as if she had been standing in front of Christ on the cross, next to Mary, his Mother, and Magdalene, and the "others who were Christ's lovers." She wanted to be a living figure in the scene of the crucifixion.

Given Julian's history of personal tragedy from the age of six, one might argue that she knew only too well the experience of personal suffering. She had seen the horror of the Great Pestilence firsthand. She had stood at the bedside of the dying, surrounded by the uncomprehending grief of others, and lost many loved ones. As a little girl, she must have prayed passionately that she and her family might *escape* suffering. Why, as an adolescent, would she ever pray to undergo more suffering? Quite simply, in order to become Christlike—and to have a personal experience of Christ's presence that would forever transform her life.

Affective Devotion

Throughout the Middle Ages, and especially during the fourteenth century, "affective devotion" was the most favored form of meditative prayer. As early as the twelfth century, in his *Sermons on the Song of Songs*, St. Bernard (1090–1153), abbot of Clairvaux, had urged his monks to focus their powers of imagination on specific scenes from the life of Christ in order to develop "the love of the heart" for

Christ, albeit a "carnal" love of his humanity which was the same love that the apostles themselves felt for his physical presence.

> The soul at prayer should have before it a sacred image of the God-man, in his birth or infancy or as he was teaching, or dying, or rising, or ascending. Whatever form it takes, this image must bind the soul with the love of virtue and expel carnal vices, eliminate temptations and quiet desires.[6]

In the *Golden Epistle,* William, abbot of St. Thierry (1080–1148), taught his novices to meditate on "God in human form . . . so that as long as his faith does not separate God from man he will learn eventually to grasp God in man."[7] Aelred, abbot of Rievaulx in Yorkshire (1109–1166), suggests in his *Rule of Life for a Recluse* (composed for his sister) that she use her imagination to place herself, quite literally, in the events of Christ's life.[8] And St. Francis of Assisi (1181?–1226) centered his great devotion and that of his friars on experiencing every aspect of the Lord's life. Franciscan spirituality urged the daily imitation of Christ in poverty, humility, and prayer that would lead to a personal intimacy with Christ's joys and, most especially, his sorrows and sufferings. Francis was also the first recorded saint to receive the stigmata of Christ's five wounds while in a state of rapture before the cross of Christ on top of the mountain known as La Verna, thereafter bearing the physical imprints of the crucifixion on his own body. For generations of devout souls, physical identification with the sufferings of Christ became the goal of the mystical life. St. Bonaventure (1221–1274), who followed in Francis's footsteps as minister General of the Franciscan Order of Friars Minor, maintained that:

> Since fervor of devotion is nourished and preserved in us by a frequent return of our thoughts to the passion of Christ, anyone who wishes to keep the flame of ardor alive within himself should frequently—or rather, incessantly—contemplate in his heart Christ dying upon the cross.[9]

Likewise, in Julian's fourteenth century, meditation manuals for parish priests and the literate laity strongly enjoined the faithful not just to think about Christ's suffering from a safe distance but to enter into the actual scenes of suffering. *Meditations on the Life of Christ*, as we have seen, were translated from Latin into English for use in sermonizing as well as in private devotions. They also deeply influenced the writing of the passion plays. These meditations were intensely visual and emotionally charged, in accord with Franciscan spirituality:

> ...to make yourself more deeply compassionate and nourish yourself at the same time, turn your eyes away from his divinity for a little while and consider Jesus purely as a man. You will see a fine youth, most noble and most innocent and most lovable, cruelly beaten and covered with blood and wounds...Imagine yourself present and consider diligently everything done against your Lord and all that is said and done by and regarding him...With your mind's eye, see some thrusting the cross into the earth, others equipped with nails and hammers, others with the ladder and other instruments, others giving orders about what should be done, and others stripping him.[10]

Richard Rolle, the hermit of Hampole, wrote his own English-language *Meditations on the Passion.* He tells a combined story of the passion from all four gospel accounts, providing highly visual (and often gruesome) images of the sufferings of Christ, and includes fervent prayers directed to Christ on the cross. These are intended to arouse in the reader a deep sorrow for sin and the intention to devote his or her life to God.[11]

Julian must also have heard the words of St. Paul:

> *Let the same mind be in you that was in Christ Jesus,* who, though he was in the form of God, did not regard equality with God as something to be exploited, but emptied himself, taking the form of a slave, being born in human likeness. And being found in human form, he humbled himself and became obedient to the point of death—even death on a cross. (Phil 2:5–8, italics added)

Mind of the Passion

The "mind" Julian asked for as her first gift, then, would have been both the agonized mind of Christ's mother and the "other women" standing at the foot of the cross, helplessly watching the Savior die and a deeper understanding of the "mind" of Christ Jesus himself, pouring out his blood for the salvation of the world. One can begin to understand how the urgent message of Franciscan affective spirituality as conveyed in popular sermons, in graphic meditation manuals depicting the sufferings of Christ in all five of his senses, and in the use of prayers for spiritual healing, would have exerted a powerful influence on an impressionable girl like Julian. She would have been led to believe that if only she could "see" Christ in the flesh, then she could suffer with him much more deeply and truly than she could in her imagination.

Of course, it was rash for the young Julian to request such a "bodily sight" of the crucifixion, however holy the impulse might have seemed at the time. Had she mentioned her desire to her parish priest in confession or to a Franciscan friar, he would have warned her that such a vision was *not* something for which she should pray. Indeed, a prayer like that might arise out of pride and be the devil's own temptation! Visions, however seemingly the work of God, were always considered suspect as the work of Satan, who was well known to disguise himself as an "angel of light" (2 Cor 11:14). Christians were customarily taught that no one should ever ask to have a vision of Jesus Christ, not even in order to sympathize more deeply with his sufferings on the cross. Even to conceive of such a request could indicate a lack of humility and was clearly against all acceptable forms of the prayer of the church. Holy men and women did not request visions; they came unbidden.

The Second Gift

> For the second [gift], it had come to my mind with contrition, freely without any seeking: it was a wilful desire to have by God's gift *a bodily sickness.* I would that that sickness were so hard as to be like the death, so that I might in that sickness undertake all my rites of holy church [extreme unction], expecting myself that I should die, and that all creatures might suppose the same that saw me. For I would have no manner of comfort of fleshly nor earthly life. In this sickness, I desired to have all manner of pains, bodily and ghostly [spiritual], that I should have if I should die, all the dreads and tempests of fiends, and all manner of other pains, save the out-passing [from the body] of the soul. And this was my intention: for I would be purged by the mercy of God, and afterward live more to the worship of God because of that sickness, for I hoped that it might be a help to me when I should die. For I desired to be soon with my God and maker. (2:17–27.127–29, italics added)

We read this and cannot help but draw back. Is this the ardent love-longing of a deeply pious girl to be united with Christ in his sufferings and death on the cross, or is it a self-destructive instinct bordering on the pathological? Did it come to her as a grace "freely without any seeking," or was it a compulsive desire to suffer something extraordinary for God? If it seems morbid in the extreme, Julian would not have been alone in her near-death wish. Throughout the history of Christianity, the *imitatio Christi* demanded that devout disciples should be willing to suffer with Christ, even to death on the cross. Some interpreted this as a call for self-immolation, a kind of living death, a "white martyrdom" in place of the "red martyrdom" of Christians who were killed for their faith. The extremism of the Middle Ages was reflected in the lengths to which the practice of mortification could go.

Fasting and Mortification

While male mystics like St. Francis starved and beat their bodies into submission in an effort to gain control over their desires for power, wealth, and sex, female mystics and visionaries, on the other hand, more often sought self-control over their desires for *food*. Taught by their culture that women were much more sensual creatures by nature and thus more prone to lust than men (because it was believed that their wombs craved sex to prevent their female organ from "wandering" aimlessly throughout their bodies), girls who wanted to remain pure needed to quell sexual desire more aggressively than did men. And since lust had long been associated with the desire for food, many medieval adolescent girls (like modern-day anorexics) became obsessed with the thought of food, the preparation of food, the specific contents of food, and the compulsive feeding of others but refused to eat themselves. Gradually, through the combination of fasting, bingeing, and vomiting, they destroyed their digestive tracts and were unable to metabolize food at all. They also became incapable of distinguishing basic bodily sensations like heat or cold. These fasting women were also known to starve themselves of sleep (or suffer from chronic insomnia as a result of excessive fasting), walk barefoot in the snow, wear coarse hair shirts, burn and cut their skin, bind their bodies tightly with rough and knotted hemp ropes, thrust thorns into their heads and nettles into their breasts, flagellate and mutilate themselves, sometimes experiencing the *temporary euphoria* of seeming to cast off bodily imprisonment entirely, until their mood plunged into paranoia, self-doubt, and often despair. In fact, Blessed Angela of Foligno (d.1309), St. Catherine of Siena (d.1380), and Blessed Jean Marie de Maille (d.1414) associated their inability to eat with the deadly sin of *acedia*, or sloth, brought on by their own severe depressions.[12]

Such women could not know and did not consider the cost of these practices on their overall body chemistry. Even if they had, it would probably not have changed their minds regarding the value of physical mortification. They firmly believed that the more they suffered, the more they became like Christ and the early martyrs. In their search for an experience of spiritual union with God, many female mystics longed to destroy any sense of personal identity and to punish their bodies in order to be in a continual state of pain, linking such extremism to ecstatic states. Rather than practicing moderate forms of fasting and self-denial as a means of acquiring self-discipline (as prescribed by the church-sanctioned fasting days during Advent and Lent), fasting became an end in itself for the paranormal results it often produced. It became a spiritual addiction.

Anorexia mirabilis (marvelous fasting) women like Blessed Ida of Louvain (d.1139), St. Margaret of Ypres (d.1237), Blessed Beatrice of Nazareth (d.1268), and St. Rita of Cascia (d.1457) rejoiced when severe starvation and thirst led them to cease menstruating but start bleeding spontaneously from the nose and mouth.[13] They and others were convinced that the wounds that erupted on their flesh were symbols of Christ's five wounds in his hands and feet and on his right side: the holy stigmata. They went so far as to fashion for themselves crowns of thorns, they drove nails into their flesh, they stood with arms outstretched for excruciatingly long periods of prayer in imitation of Christ on the cross. The trances they experienced, partially induced by hunger, thirst, and exhaustion, were assumed to be divine visitations. This is not to deny the personal sanctity of these and so many other medieval mystics, but only to question the drastic and dangerous means they took to achieve that sanctity. Some women, like Blessed Angela of Foligno and St. Catherine of Genoa (d.1510), were fortunate enough to recover, more or less, from the prodigious fasting syndrome; numerous others, like St. Catherine of Siena, Blessed Elsbet

Achler (d.1420), and Blessed Columba of Rieti (d.1501) starved themselves into early deaths.[14]

While church officials vigorously disapproved of and continued to denounce such practices as flagellation, continual fasting, self-mutilation, sleep-deprivation, and so on, the hagiographers who wrote the accounts of saints' lives (and freely stretched and elaborated their stories to make the case for sainthood), as well as the popes who canonized them, tended to view such mortifications as signs of extraordinary holiness, especially when fasting women like Catherine of Siena claimed to survive only by receiving the Eucharist. And those who had known these women during their lives were eager to attest to supra-normal manifestations of sanctity: levitations, floating over walls, the working of miracles, healings, and other favors granted by them in life and after death. In this way, the medieval cultivation of self-induced suffering fed on itself, producing ever more morbid practices.

Julian and Suffering

Julian must have heard frequent sermons extolling such saintly heroics, as well as descriptions of holy men and women being granted severe illnesses from God (as opportunities to atone for their sins and the sins of others) from which they miraculously recovered. Did she want just such an illness and recovery as a sign of God's preferential love? Given her vulnerability, could she have become fascinated, even obsessed, with a desire for physical suffering? At the Good Friday liturgy, a passion play, or during a particularly explicit homily on the agonies of Christ on the cross, might she have been overwhelmed by remorse for her sins? Could she have felt compelled to offer God the greatest self-sacrifice she could think of, to make the kind of petition she imagined the saints themselves might pray? Might she have wanted to emulate the mystics and visionaries she had heard about, crying out to heaven to take notice of her, because she, too, was longing to do something great for God?

This second request for the gift of a sickness "as hard as to be like the death," seems to be just such a prayer. Everything she read or heard quoted from *Meditations on the Passion* must have convinced her that unless she was willing to suffer to the utmost (including "all the dreads and tempests of fiends, and all manner of other pains"), she did not really love her Savior enough. Just as she had asked for the *mind* of the passion in her first request, so here, in asking for an illness, she wanted to experience the pains of the *body* of the passion. Add to this Julian's acknowledged need for spiritual cleansing. What terrible sin could such a devout girl have felt she needed to "be purged of by the mercy of God"? Adolescent sexual fantasies? A debilitating depression (equated with the sin of sloth), brought on by hormonal changes for which she felt acutely responsible? Physical exhaustion that made her lax in her religious duties? A questioning of God's love amid the stark reality of human suffering? Perhaps the shameful doubts she harbored deep in her heart that seemed to blame God for allowing tragedy to happen?

Or could Julian's great guilt have been the burden she had carried within her since the age of six, a secret guilt that, in spite of her searing childhood experience of watching her loved ones suffer excruciating deaths during the Great Pestilence, *she* had not suffered enough? *She* had not gotten sick with the oozing buboes, burning fever, bloody retching, and asphyxiating cough, and then expired "with no comfort from bodily or earthly life," as had her family members and friends. *She* had been spared. She did not know what such physical agony or dying actually *felt* like. Did the young, sensitive Julian actually convince herself that, in order to be relieved of her burden, she must go through what she had seen others suffer, get as close as she dared to dying herself, so that afterward she might "live more to the worship of God because of that sickness"? *Was she consumed with the guilt of being a survivor?* Julian's prayer for a near-death illness, if prayed often enough and with Julian's passionate nature, could have brought on a serious psychosomatic illness by itself.

Mercifully, Julian managed to avoid medieval excesses. Remarkably *un*like many of her contemporaries, Julian in her writing makes no mention or recommendation of any practices of mortification whatsoever. Nor is there any indication of pathological behavior, self-mutilation, extreme fasting, and the like. Quite the contrary. Julian presents a much more balanced, healthy, and wholesome approach to the body/mind than do most medieval mystics. She also espouses a theology that is about *transcendence* rather than indulgence in suffering for its own sake, as we shall see. Through her personal experience, she will suggest that the devout Christian does not need to self-inflict ever greater physical and mental pain in order to be a true imitator of Christ. Suffering will come in the course of living, regardless: "Today's trouble is enough for today" (Mt 6:34). Julian will understand that Christ does not die on the cross to *increase* our sufferings, our personal agonies, but rather to offer us his infinite help in bearing our own inevitable griefs, with the confident hope that we will see every one of them transformed into glory by his own resurrection.

Youthful Demands

In describing her prayers for a vision and an illness, the mature Julian shows great candor and humility in presenting her inordinate desires exactly as she remembers feeling them in her youth. She even allows the reader to notice that there was something *extremely demanding* about her immature requests. She uses the phrases "I desired," "I would have," "I would be purged," "I should have," "I hoped," in quick succession. In so doing, she reveals herself as having once held a decidedly solipsistic view of the spiritual path. She wanted to suffer in a bold, dramatic, and quite public way. She requested that her dying experience take place in exactly the manner *she* would plan it. She expected to receive the last rites of the church, usually administered only to those actually dying, even though she fully expected to recover. She welcomed all kinds of pains and temptations (she would later admit that she did not know what she was asking for), and specified that "all creatures" standing around her bedside should be convinced she was dying. Why? So that they would weep for her as she had wept for her siblings who perished? She wanted everyone to take her "death scene" very, very seriously. Yet for all her protestations of desiring to almost-die in order to experience what the worst kind of death might be like, something in Julian did not really wish to go through with it. She wished to *seem* to be dying, but then survive to live a holier life.

With this second request, Julian is testing the limits of what she can demand . . . like an adolescent girl who climbs to the top of a bridge and threatens to jump off, hoping against all hope that someone will rescue her before it is too late. Perhaps she thought she needed such a complete dress rehearsal for death to convince *herself* how much she was already suffering emotionally and spiritually, even more than she needed to convince God of her love. Clearly, she is crying out for help in this morbid passage, but presumably she did not share her intention with anyone, so that no one heard her cri de coeur. Except the Lord.

In modern terminology, we might say that what Julian was seeking from such a near-death experience was a personal kind of shock therapy, to be jolted by the sheer horror of extreme suffering into changing her life completely and then to rise from her deathbed so transformed that thereafter she would live the kind of saintly life she felt she was *not* living. She was praying for a "deathbed conversion," an "instant enlightenment," a "fast track" to holiness. She would discover that even divine revelations do not make a sinful soul into an overnight saint. The work of the Holy Spirit cannot be accelerated one iota. Neither can the process be demanded of God, nor brought on by sheer human willpower.

> The wind blows where it chooses, and you hear the sound of it, but you do not know where it comes from or where it goes. So it is with everyone who is born of the Spirit. (Jn 3:8)

In Julian's case, it would take a very long lifetime to come to terms with the slow process of transformation. Yet she will, by her patience and willingness to learn, reveal a whole new and liberating spirituality based not on self-loathing and the desire for sacrificial self-destruction but on a child's love and trust in Christ, its Mother.

On Condition

> These two desires of the passion and of the sickness that I desired of him were *with a condition*. For it seemed to me this was not the common course of prayer. Therefore I said: "Lord, thou knowest what I would want. If it be thy will that I have it, grant it to me. And if it be not thy will, good lord, be not displeased, for I will not but as thou wilt." (2: 28–31.129, italics added)

Julian quickly tells us she harbored her own doubts about her first two requests. Even as an adolescent, a healthy instinct for self-preservation rose up in her that would not allow her to pray *un*conditionally: "Please God, let me (almost) die for love of you," even though she "desired to be soon with my God and maker." Julian's basic good sense and the touch of divine grace gave her a strong warning signal. She became aware she was overstepping the bounds of spiritual propriety. She realized she was "tempting God" by her rash demands.

Writing as an adult, in the aftermath of her visions, Julian admits in this passage that she recognized the danger of her tendency to spiritual extremism. She recalls that she had used the caveat in the *Pater Noster* that she had been told must accompany every prayer: "Thy will be done." It was the Lord's own caveat prayed in the Garden of Gethsemane the night before he died, when he sweated blood in anticipation of what he would have to go through in his passion and cried out: "My Father, if it is possible, let this cup pass from me" (Mt 26:39). (How different Christ's prayer was in that moment from Julian's: even the Son of God, as a fully human being, did not *want* to suffer and die.) But then, in the next breath, Christ submits: "yet not what I want but what you want" (Mt 26:39, cf. Lk 22:42). Fortunately, Julian also submitted her reckless prayer to the will of God.

Thirty Years Old

Still, some inner force was driving her to make her request and pushing her mind and body to the brink of... revelation. She even set an exact date for her near-death illness:

> This sickness I desired in my youth, that I might have it when I was thirty years old. (2:31–32.129)

Julian is clear that she asked for this sickness before she knew any better, *in her youth*. In so saying, she acknowledges that it was, again, an inordinate desire. But she also reveals, astonishingly, that she specifically stipulated she wanted this to happen when she was "thirty years old"; not while she was still young, not then... but later, much later. Thirty was the age at which it was traditionally believed the Lord began his public ministry. It was also the turning point for medieval women, from youth to middle age. To a girl of thirteen or fourteen, thirty must have seemed very old indeed, more than *twice* her present age, like the birthday that one expects will never come. In fact, women were only half as likely as men to reach the age of thirty. As we have mentioned, childbirth took a greater toll on young women than all the casualties of war did on men. It is also possible that Julian chose this age of thirty because someone especially dear to her had died of the plague or in the war, or had some terrible accident, or had been murdered, precisely at thirty. Perhaps an older brother on whom she had doted, a beloved nurse, a devout parish curate. Thirty was a symbolic age in every respect. The number three was, of course, evocative of the Trinity, followed by the sign of God: the infinite circle. It was the age beyond which Julian might not have expected to live much longer anyway, even if she did recover from her illness.

The Third Gift

> For the third [gift], by the grace of God and the teaching of holy church, I conceived a mighty desire to receive *three wounds* in my life, that is to say, the wound of true contrition, the wound of kind [natural][15] compassion, and the wound of wilful longing for God. (2:33–36.129, italics added)

In the Short Text, Julian included a very revealing story that precipitated the desire for this third gift. In that first version, she tells us:

> For the third [gift], I heard a man of holy church tell of the story of Sainte Cecille, in which shewing I understood that she had three wounds with a sword in the neck, with which she suffered to the death. By the stirring of this, I conceived a mighty desire, [etc.]. (i:36–39.65)

The apocryphal story surrounding the martyrdom of the second- or third-century St. Cecilia was familiar to medieval Christians from a hugely popular text, *The Golden Legend*, by Jacobus de Voragine.[16] The gruesome account of her martyrdom would have been oft-repeated in sermons for her feast day, November 22, and was the theme of many wall paintings in medieval churches. Cecilia was thought to have been a Roman noblewoman whose husband and brother were martyred c.230 under Emperor Alexander Severus. (Later research showed she probably died in Sicily sometime between 176 and 180, under another tyrant, Emperor Marcus Aurelius.) When the soldiers arrested Cecilia, they tried to boil her alive, but she survived. Then they tried to behead her with a sword and failed three times. According to tradition, she lay dying from her three wounds for three days, giving away all her possessions and asking that her house be preserved as a church, which it was. She did not succumb until she received the holy Eucharist. She is one of only seven women, in addition to the Blessed Virgin Mary, who is mentioned in the canon of the Mass.

That a stirring sermon by "a man of holy church" was the impetus behind Julian's third request confirms the devout impressionability of the young girl (and the impact of medieval sermonizing). She conceives "a mighty desire" to have three wounds just like "Saint Cecille." This third desire is really three-in-one, so there are five requests in all, like the five wounds of Christ, a much revered medieval devotion. But, unlike the self-mutilating ascetics, Julian's final prayer was for *spiritual* wounds, not physical ones. Rather than fastings, flagellations, and sleep deprivation, she seeks contrition, natural compassion, and a great longing for God, hoping these three will break open her heart to healing and love and joy.

> Right as I asked the other two with a condition, so I asked this third mightily without any condition. (2:36–37.129)

Julian knows that her final request is in perfect keeping with the acceptable graces for which every soul should pray daily. Christians were admonished to make frequent acts of "true contrition" for venial sins and immediately to seek the sacrament of penance for the forgiveness of mortal sin. They were taught to say the Act of Contrition devoutly, to express their detestation of sin because of God's "just punishments," but most of all, "for having offended Thee, my God." This Act of Contrition was deemed absolutely necessary for the forgiveness of any transgressions. To feel great sorrow for sin was the first of Julian's three desired "wounds."

As for the second, Julian was asking for the grace to perform the corporal and spiritual works of mercy with a loving heart. These works, appropriate for the laity, were all about "kind compassion": feeding the hungry, giving drink to the thirsty, clothing the naked, visiting the sick, sheltering the traveler, bearing wrongs patiently, forgiving offenses willingly, comforting the afflicted, and praying for the living, the sick, and the dead. By asking for the wound of compassion, Julian sought to live more fully the teaching of Christ to "love your neighbor as yourself" (Mt. 22:39, Mk 12:31, Lk 10:27).

And third, in asking for a "wilful longing for God," Julian was expressing her desire to obey the first and greatest of all commandments, to love the Lord God with all her heart, with all her soul, and with all her mind (Mt 22:37, Mk 12:30, Lk 10:27, Dt 6:5). Thus there was no reason to offer a caveat for her tri-part request, since she was sure it was already in accordance with the will of God.

The Forgetting

> The two desires said before passed from my mind, and the third dwelled continually. (2:37–38.129)

After the intensity of the preceding spiritual requests, this matter-of-fact remark is stunning. Julian *forgot* about her desire to have a vision of the passion! She *forgot* about her desire to receive an illness with the greatest possible suffering that would lead her to almost-die! Julian gives no explanation for *why* she forgot. She only states that the third desire became her usual and acceptable way of prayer, that is, her regular spiritual practice. Every day, she asked pardon for her sins, prayed for the grace to be compassionate and loving toward her fellow human beings, and longed with all the force of her will to love God with all her might. Julian's own testimony that she forgot makes it clear, yet again, that she was neither a nun nor an ascetic, fixated on seeing a vision or wanting to suffer *in extremis* to prove her love for God. If she had been in a nunnery or anchorage as a young woman, she would have had every opportunity to nurture her requests for visions and extreme mortification practices, whether sanctioned by the church or not.

It seems obvious that the reason Julian's first two requests "passed" from her mind was because she became occupied with other all-consuming events happening in her adolescent life: she was betrothed and married, gave birth to her first child (who, as we have suggested, most likely perished in the second wave of the plague), had a second child, and, if her husband also perished in the plague or in the war, became a single mother in her early twenties. She no longer thought of asking for a vision of Christ on the cross or a severe illness. She no longer doubted that she had suffered enough. By this time, Julian had suffered more, much more, than she ever could have imagined as a young girl. She was carrying her own heavy cross every single day.

The startling fact (which Julian never directly alludes to in her text) is that the first two requests *would be granted* after all, and at *exactly the age* she had originally intended, even though she had totally forgotten about them. She wants us to know that, for all the immaturity and rashness of her adolescent prayer, there was also something miraculous at work even then; a premonition, if you will, of the way in which the Lord would one day visit her. Who can say how grace works in us to plant seeds that may lie dormant for decades only to sprout from an earlier inspiration in a time of crisis? This was certainly to be the case with Julian.

Dying

> And when I was thirty years old and a half, God sent me a bodily sickness in which I lay three days and three nights, and on the fourth night I took all my rites of holy church, and thought not to have lived until day. And after this I langorid forth [went on languishing, growing weaker] for two days and two nights, and on the third night I often thought to have passed [died]; and so thought those who were with me. (3:1–5.129–31)

Julian lay dying. As we have seen, the date was either the first or second week of May 1373, and Julian was, by her own testimony, "thirty years old and a half." (Therefore, we know she was born in November 1342.) All the elements of her second request are there: her precisely-desired age; a bodily sickness unto death; her reception of the last rites of the church; and even a group of friends, including her mother, gathered around her bed. All were convinced she was dying. She lay in bed for three days and three nights "and on the fourth night" (which means there must have been another day in between) a priest came and heard her confession while she was still able to speak and gave her Eucharist while she could still swallow. Usually, the final anointing of the eyes, ears, lips, hands, feet, and heart with holy oils (the sacrament of extreme unction) did not take place until the victim was in the last moments of death, or had just died, so that no further sin could be committed and the soul could fly straight to God. But it seems that Julian received all the last rites at this time, including the final anointing. Still, she did not die. She lingered on for two more days and nights. . .then another day. . . and on the third night after that (totaling seven days and nights of severe illness), she felt certain she was dying.

> And yet in this I felt a great loathesomeness to die, but for nothing that was on earth that I wanted to live for, nor for any pain that I was afraid of, for I trusted in God of his mercy. But it was because I would have lived to have loved God better and for a longer time, that I might, by the grace of that living, have more knowing and loving of God in the bliss of heaven. For it seemed to me that all that time that I had lived here so little and so short a time in comparison with that endless bliss. I thought: "Good lord, may my living no longer be to thy worship?" And I understood in my reason and by the feeling of my pains that I should die, and I assented fully with all the will of my heart to be at God's will. (3:5–13.131)

Julian felt a great depression at the thought of death, not because there was anything (or anyone) compelling her to remain on earth, but because she ached to live longer in order to worship and serve God for a greater period of time. It was believed that the more numerous one's works of mercy were here on earth, the greater one's reward would be in heaven. Compared to eternity, thirty-and-a-half years did not seem so long a life after all.

> Thus I endured till day, and by then my body was dead from the middle downward, as it felt to me. Then I was moved to be set upright, supported with help, to have more freedom of my heart to be at God's will, and think about God while my life would last. (3:14–17.131)

Somehow, she survived that seventh night. She had lost all feeling from her waist down. Her heart was racing. . . pumping erratically. . . and her breathing was becoming more and more labored. Those attending to her lifted her body into a semi-sitting position and propped her up with stuffed pillow rolls supporting her back; they placed cloths under her head and applied cool, damp compresses on her forehead to ease her fever. This adjustment enabled her to breathe a little more easily and took some pressure off her exhausted heart. It also allowed her to concentrate more fully on thoughts of God while she was dying.

Medical Diagnosis

We must pause to ask: What was Julian dying *of*? We do not know. Perhaps Julian herself never knew. Thus we can only surmise. It could have been congestive heart failure, meaning her heart was not pumping blood efficiently to the rest of her body, hence her description of overall weakness and the subsequent paralysis of her lower torso and legs. Alternately, Julian may have been suffering from pneumonia with a high fever that produced chills and sweating, and again, poor heart functioning and lack of circulation to her lower body, especially her legs and feet, explaining the numbness. Whatever the symptoms, was anything done for her? Was she seen by a physician? Again, we can only surmise from known medieval practices.

Julian does not mention having been visited by a physician who diagnosed and treated her condition. Yet it seems highly implausible that her mother and other relatives and friends would not have made every effort to seek the help of a responsible medical expert. Julian may not have remembered his consultation or wanted to recall his treatment (many people mistrusted physicians as charlatans and extortionists). Regardless, in her written account, Julian was so focused on the work of the Divine Physician, the true healer, that she had no reason to mention any other.

Yet, presumably, just as the priest was summoned to give Julian the last rites of the church, so a physician was called in at some point to observe her condition, especially when she did not rally after the first few days of home remedies. A medical person would have been consulted only after the patient had been *shriven*. Since 1215, the church had required that all those seeking medical help had to first confess their sins, receive absolution, and promise to do penance if or when they recovered. Likewise, all physicians were supposed to confess their sins before attempting to treat a patient. It was believed that no healing of the body could ever take place unless and until the soul of both patient and healer had been cleansed of sin and become acceptable in the sight of God. Therefore, the spiritual malaise of the patient had to be treated *before* the physical ailment could be addressed. And always, for priest or physician (and most academically trained physicians were also priests), the unspoken assumption of healing was: if it be God's will.

University-trained physicians, however, were few and far between in fourteenth-century England, often unavailable even to those middle-class merchants who could afford to pay their exorbitant fees. Outside of London, physicians had to travel long distances to see a royal or aristocratic patient. Fortunately, Norwich was a large and thriving cathedral city, and we know from infirmary records at Norwich Priory that the local *medicus* (physician) was called in regularly to treat the monks.[17] So Julian may well have been seen by a respected Norwich man of medicine as well as a man of the cloth. However, if a reputable academically trained physician was *not* available, then a local surgeon belonging to the Norwich Barbers' Guild might have been brought in to give a diagnosis.[18] While these skilled practitioners were usually in the business of setting and binding dislocated joints and broken bones, closing flesh wounds with stitches or hot irons, staunching hemorrhages, "couching" cataracts, cutting out infections, cauterizing skull wounds, lancing boils, treating unsightly rashes and sores, burning cankers, extracting teeth, surgically removing anal fistulas, *leeching* (applying leeches on the skin to suck out bad blood), and *letting* (drawing) blood and the like, they also had the same basic understanding of humoral medicine that academically trained physicians possessed, albeit on a more practical level. Barbers had to undergo a minimum of five to six years of apprenticeship under a master before admittance into the Barbers' Guild, and were usually quite expert at both diagnosis and surgery. Since they were *not* priests, deacons, or sub-deacons (forbidden by canon law to draw blood), barber-surgeons were licensed to make incisions, let blood, and perform any and all types of cauterization and surgery.[19] Thus a local barber-surgeon (one on whom Julian may have relied previously) might have been called to her bedside to diagnose and treat her condition.

Either way, Julian's case must have been deeply mystifying. There seem to have been no visible signs of infection. She herself describes no cut or burn through which infection might have entered, no rash, no pustules, no swelling, bruising, or discoloration of the skin. Her symptoms were apparently internal, yet she remains vague even about these. She mentions "shortness of breath," heart pressure, total numbness from the waist down (and later in her upper body as well), a great deal of unspecified pain, "lack of power" to hold up her head or hands near the end, and a general sense of "failing of life." Nevertheless, the procedure of a physician or barber-surgeon in arriving at a diagnosis would have been substantially the same, regardless of whether the sickness presented externally or internally.

Urine, Pulse, and Blood

First, the medical practitioner had to determine the nature and cause of Julian's illness by "reading" her overall condition. Since he was not allowed to examine a woman's body, even with other women present in the room, he had to *observe*, and observe carefully, her temperament or "complexion," not by looking at her skin, but by examining the color and smell of her urine in order to decide which of her bodily humors was out of balance. As we have seen, medieval medicine was based almost entirely on Galen of Pergamon's second-century principle of bodily humors needing to be in balance for health to prevail. Otherwise, illness occurred. However, it was not always immediately apparent *which* humors were out of balance. The same disease might result from an excess of blood, yellow bile, or black bile in one person, or the production of excessive phlegm in another, depending on the individual's "natural" temperament (sanguine, choleric, phlegmatic, or melancholic). Uroscopy, the examination of urine, was the primary means of diagnosing humoral imbalance and, hence, disease. Twenty or more types of urine color, sedimentary deposits, and possible substances in the urine were described in medieval Latin scholarly texts. These texts were translated into English in the later fourteenth century so that non-university (non-Latinate) medical practitioners like barber-surgeons could consult color charts, read the accompanying vernacular texts, and make their diagnoses.[20]

In addition to examining the urine, the physician or barber would feel the patient's pulse. Since accurate time-measuring devices were unknown (as was the principle of blood circulation), the counting of beats was interpretive at best, determining merely rapid heartbeat or arrhythmia, which could indicate high fever or blockages. Galen had listed nine "simple" and about thirty "complex" pulses as a guide to the patient's condition, but these could never lead to a definitive diagnosis. Additionally, the feces might be inspected for "blood or putrid phlegm," coloration, texture, parasites, and other signs of disease.[21] The practitioner would have inquired of those present in her room about Julian's general diet and the exact day and hour she first became ill, since these were often telltale signs of humoral imbalance.

The next step would be bloodletting, the draining of blood for diagnostic examination. (This could be performed either by a physician who was *not* a cleric, a barber-surgeon, or even by a female phlebotomist. All were commonly called *leeches.*) Again, the blood sample would be scrutinized for color, texture, heat, and smell—and sometimes even taste.[22] Bloodletting was a frequent practice in the Middle Ages, recommended seasonally (especially after winter and before the start of Lent) as a method of maintaining good health for monks, hermits, anchorites, and laity alike. Julian would probably have been bled from the basilic vein in her arm, by the elbow, not once but several times, for diagnostic purposes as well as to ease any feverishness. However, the letting of blood may have added acutely to Julian's muscle pains and severe physical weakness. Loss of blood might also explain her self-described paralysis: extremely low levels of potassium in the blood (or lack of blood containing sufficient potassium) can compromise and then destroy nerve cells in the spinal cord or brain, in turn causing temporary or permanent paralysis, and sometimes, if not remedied by blood transfusions, even death. In the Middle Ages, since blood transfusions were unknown, death often resulted from repeated bloodletting.

Heavenly Signs

After examinations of the urine, feces, and blood were complete, astrological signs had to be interpreted. Before prescribing a course of treatment, Julian's physician or leech would have been duty-bound to consult his chart that showed the signs of the zodiac. While the church was categorically opposed to the use of astrology in any attempt to predict the future, it could not deny the practice of university-trained physicians and barber-surgeons to consult the heavens when calculating the most propitious time for performing certain medical procedures. Medieval belief, based on Aristotelian writings, held that the earth was a microcosm of the universe, and man was a microcosm of the earth. Influences that affected the heavenly bodies would necessarily impact human life as well. As long as astrology never crossed into the realm of religion and did not undermine belief in the patient's free will or in God's power to work miracles of healing beyond those of any man of medicine, the consulting of astrological tables by physicians, barber-surgeons, and phlebotomists was considered prudent, if not absolutely necessary.

Medieval science maintained that the moon, which controlled tides and the water element, had a constant fluctuating power over the human body. The moon could affect the humors either positively or negatively at different times of the month. Consulting the phases and positioning of the moon in the astrological "houses" was considered imperative in both the diagnosis and cure of disease. Women especially (who were considered "cold" and "wet" by natural temperament, and whose menses were influenced every month by the phases of the moon) lived under constant lunar influence. This is also why women were considered "lunatic" and became "crazed" by lunar cycles.

Likewise, the placement of stars and planets also determined the best (or worst) time to initiate (or avoid) treatment of a patient. When an individual became ill, he or she was supposed to notice the phase of the moon and the exact hour at which the first signs of illness began. The patient also had to reveal the date and hour of his or her birth, so that a horoscope chart could be consulted. Charts assigned each body part and each disease to a different astrological sign. The so-called "zodiac man" showed the portrait of a man with twelve signs of the zodiac, according to the month, painted on twelve areas of his body. Every medical person consulted it when visiting a patient. If the moon happened to be in the particular "house" of the body part that was diseased, any treatment on that area was considered extremely dangerous. Since Julian was, by her own indication, born in November, ruled by Scorpio (which governed the genitals), *if* the moon happened to enter that "house" when Julian became ill, no localized treatment or surgery could have been performed in that area. This could have meant she received no laxatives, enemas, bloodletting, cupping, or cauterizing in her lower abdominal region.[23] (It is of interest to recall that, at the crisis point in her illness, Julian described her body as "dead from the middle downward.") Additionally, the particular phase of the moon was considered predictive: if Julian became ill on the *second* day after a new moon, she would have been expected to make a full recovery. However, if she took sick on the *third* day, there was little hope of survival, despite the physician's best efforts.[24]

We have encountered this strange marriage of medieval medicine and astrological divination before, in considering the "heavenly causes" of the Great Plague. Add to this the persistent teaching of the church that sickness was sent directly by God (as a Job-like test of the faith of the sufferer, as a judgment on the patient's sinful way of life, or as a "visitation" to specially chosen holy victims), and the mix of cosmic and supernatural causes of disease becomes well-nigh indecipherable. This is not to say that Julian herself necessarily believed in astrological signs and portents or feared to die because she may have been taken sick on the third day after a new moon. Similarly, there is no suggestion that Julian ever considered her illness a test, a punishment, or a divine visitation. In fact, she never tries to *explain* it at all. The medieval connections between the sun, moon, stars, parts of the human body, and the diseases affecting them tell us more about how a leech or physician would have proceeded to treat Julian than about what Julian herself thought. Perhaps that is why she never bothered to mention any purgatives, restoratives, or curatives. Whatever unpleasant or painful procedures she was made to undergo, Julian knew they could not be the direct cause of her healing. Her mind and heart were elsewhere.

Procedures

After deciding whether the moon was in a favorable position, the physician or barber-surgeon would initiate a course of action. First, he would suggest *a preparatyffe*, a warm and soothing cream (or even a soothing herbal bath) to strengthen the body's own defenses. Second, he would order *a purgatyfe*, that is, an herbal laxative or *clyster* (enema) to drive unhealthy matter from the body. Third, he would prescribe a *proper sanatyff*, specific foods and potions containing stronger herbal medicines to speed recovery.[25] If Julian's case was diagnosed as *rheume* or pneumonia, for example, she would have been given cold compresses and cooling salves to bring down her high fever, as well as cool herbal baths to remove the flush-color from her skin and restore equilibrium. Then she might have been cupped and/or cauterized in her chest area (this would have been carried out by a licensed *female* phlebotomist) to reduce her coughing and chest pains, and given a strong medicinal potion if there was blood in her urine. Her face might also have been covered with cloths heavily soaked in musk as a measure for invigorating her vital organs, improving her breathing, reducing the production of phlegm, and stimulating circulation. (It is possible that the "cloths" Julian mentions were placed underneath her head when she sat up had been saturated in strong-smelling aromatic herbs.)

Other remedies might include the use of *maturatives*, extremely cold poultices (made of swine's grease and oil in a plaster of wheat) that forced the body to produce its own heat to overwhelm the excessive humors. Aggressive plasters and waxes called *repercussives* were even colder. These were applied to the skin to prevent internally produced heat from escaping through the pores, forcing it deeper and deeper into the diseased (lung) area where it could attack the infection. The strongest of these treatments, called *stupefactives*, were considered extremely dangerous. They could, if not used with caution, bring on bodily numbness such as Julian experienced and lead to total paralysis and death.[26] We may wonder if Julian was subjected to one or all of the above.

Any image of Julian being untreated, undisturbed, and unattended in her misery as she lay in her bed for a full week, is simply untenable. Everything possible would have been done for her, from the application of professional ointments and medicines, to the administration of herbal remedies prepared by womenfolk. Whether they did more harm than good is another question entirely.

Herbal Remedies

The medieval belief in humoral theory, namely, that nature is made up of fire, air, water, and earth, which correspond to the four fluids in the body (blood, yellow bile, black bile, and phlegm), had applications to herbal remedies. Since disease was believed to be caused by an excess of one humor over another, herbal treatment was used to realign the body's natural heat and moisture balance. Herbs, like the four humors themselves, were listed as hot, cold, moist, or dry. Herbal remedies were employed not only to purge the body of excessive and destructive liquids but also (if used correctly) to restore humoral balance and health to the whole body.

Depending on the physician or surgeon's diagnosis (infection of bloody humors affecting her heart? Preponderance of yellow or black bile causing infection? Over-production of phlegm producing *rheume*, or pneumonia?),[27] Julian may have been forced to swallow a diuretic drink or a vile-tasting horehound cough syrup. She may have been given other concoctions to thin out the mucus in her sinuses, as well as gargles for her throat, and a variety of putrid-smelling herbal poultices for her chest. Perhaps coltsfoot (used to relieve asthma, bronchitis, or coughs since ancient times), licorice, and hyssop were brewed as an expectorant, the leaves and roots of *Angelica archangelica* boiled with those of *Matricaria chamomilla* to lessen her fever, and the floral petals of *Calendula* mixed in a hot broth or tonic especially suited for strengthening the heart. These herbs had to be picked from the pharmacologist's garden at specific times of day and at exactly the right stage of growth. The repeated recitation of the *Pater Noster* and *Ave Maria* was recommended for the gatherer of the herbs so that they would retain their full effectiveness.[28] The leaves were then ground or boiled or pressed into a plaster. Alternately, remedies were frequently made from herbs grown by every medieval wife. No doubt Julian had her own herbal garden to provide for the many treatments she had administered to her family, friends, and servants over the years. Now she counted on her women friends to pick, pray over, and prepare the leaves for her.

Herbal remedies are potentially mind-altering. Some have analgesic power, others cause vivid dreams, still others can induce sleep. Could medicinal herbs have produced vivid images in Julian's brain? Could they have been instrumental in producing her visions? There is no evidence at all that Julian was "drugged" or "sedated" at the time of her visions. On the contrary, her high level of physical pain, her complete alertness of mind, and her total ability to remember each and every detail of what she experienced bear abundant witness to the fact that the herbal medicines she was receiving did not have much, if any, effect on her brain power. They certainly did not reduce her pain or put her into a long, deep sleep (she was awake during the night, so near death that the parson was sent for again, to be with her in her last moments). She was not drowsy, confused, or hallucinating; neither was she out of her wits with fever. She was completely lucid. Furthermore, the experiences Julian would describe arose in a mind and heart made even more crystal clear and single-focused by the long bout with physical suffering and by the absolute conviction that she was about to die.

Prayers

All through that week in May, Julian's mother, family members, and friends would have been taking turns lighting candles in her parish church and requesting that Masses be said to speed her recovery. They would have burned incense in her room to ward off polluted spirits and purify the air. Quite possibly, according to custom, these women also took a measurement of Julian's body with a candle wick which they then fashioned into a wax candle of exactly the same length as her height to burn continually before Our Lady's altar in church. (Broken arms and legs were often measured in this way, and the wax or silver casts of injured limbs were placed before a favorite saint's shrine.) Such practices were considered potent visible signs of deeply felt prayers for healing. Rosaries, prayers, and various incantations would also have been recited around Julian's bedside, as they had been when she delivered her children.

No doubt, Julian was never left alone. Her mother and closest female relatives and women friends would have been sleeping on the floor of her room, keeping watch at all hours, to be available to her should she call out (as indeed, she recounts she did on several occasions). The *social aspect* of illness was a major part of its cure. A strong and loving female bonding, expressed by the constant praying and whispered murmurs at her bedside, must have brought great comfort and courage to the suffering Julian. She had specified, in her second request for an illness, that these "other women" would be around her at all times, convinced that she was dying. And so they were.

The Curate and the Cross

Julian was probably awake for most, if not all, of that fateful seventh night, reciting the psalms from *Matins* and *Lauds* that she knew so well from her *Prymer*:

> Lord, open thou my lips!
> And my mouth shall tell thy praising.
> God, behold thou come into my help!
> Lord, hasten thou to help me![29] . . .
> God, my God! I wake to thee full early.
> My soul thirsteth for thee; my flesh thirsteth for thee full manifold;
> In a land forsaken, without any way [meeting of the roads] and without water

So I appeared to thee in the sanctuary, that I should see thy virtue and thy glory.
For thy mercy is better than life; my lips shall praise thee.
So I shall bless thee in my life; and in thy name I shall raise my hands . . .
So I had mind of thee on my bed;
In the morningtide I shall think of thee, for thou art my helper.[30]

She lay motionless, in a linen nightgown, her hair caught up in a nightcap, feeling alone in the darkness. She was in great pain, unable to move or adjust her body at will. How she longed for daylight to drive away the thick shadows of demons in the room! At last, a slow-spreading dawn broke through grey-white fog from the Norfolk Broads and marshlands, sending faint streaks of light across the River Wensum through the cracks in the shutters into Julian's room. At that time of year, this first light could have appeared as early as 3:30 AM.[31] Would this be her last daybreak?

Julian must have murmured or cried out, prompting her mother to come quickly to her side. The patient seemed weaker, more fragile than ever, her face bathed in sweat, yet her body shivering in the damp spring chill of the room. By the light of a single candle her mother could see that her daughter's skin was unearthly pale, the gaunt cavities around her eyes browner and much deeper than the day before. Quite possibly, Julian's fingers, hands, and feet were swollen, and we know her breathing was shallow and labored. She could not speak clearly or respond to questions. She tells us herself that her eyes were frozen, unmoving. Julian's mother, a woman of at least fifty who had survived the plague only to mourn the loss of her husband and possibly several children, knew the look and feel of impending death. She whispered to the other women, one of whom ran to get the parson.

And they that were with me sent for the parson, my curate, to be at my ending. He came, and a child came with him, and brought a cross, and by then I had fixed my eyes and could not speak. (ii:19–22.65–67)

If, as we have suggested, Julian lived close by the Church of St. Julian, the priest could have arrived from his house within ten minutes. It was his priestly responsibility to come quickly at the call of the dying. He brought with him a boy, a tonsured acolyte of nine or ten, who served as altar boy at Mass each morning, reciting the Latin responses. The boy carried a cross, or more precisely, a *crucifix* (with the figure of the Savior nailed to the cross), ahead of the priest as he mounted the steep wooden staircase to Julian's bedroom. This crucifix must have been the *dallye* (daily) cross, made of brass or copper (perhaps from a side altar where daily Mass was said), about twenty inches high and fifteen inches wide. It could *not* have been a processional cross, a large brass, or silver and gilt engraved crucifix, set atop a long staff or handle extending ninety inches, since this would have required a heavy and nonportable pedestal to support it in Julian's bedroom. Nor could the crucifix have been a small hand-held one; these were extremely rare, and anyway, Julian would have been too weak to hold it raised in front of her face (and she would later testify that she kept her eyes focused on the crucifix for the next twelve hours). Therefore, the crucifix must have been of an easily portable size, not too heavy for a small boy to carry, and able to stand upright on its own base.

After showing Julian the crucifix close to her face, the boy placed the cross on a trestle table or blanket chest at the foot of her bed, facing toward her. Julian remembered the exact words the parson said to her, for she had heard them many times before in her life. They were not his personal words of comfort. They come directly from the Sarum Missal greeting for the dying:

> The parson set the cross before my face, and said: "Daughter,[32] I have brought thee the image of your savior. Look upon it, and comfort yourself with it in reverence of him who died for you and me." It seemed to me then that I was well [already in a good position to die] for my eyes were set upwards into heaven, whither I trusted to come. (ii:22–25.67)

Julian wanted to keep focusing *upward* to the familiar high-beamed roof of her bedroom. Perhaps one of the women had opened the shutters to let in fresh May morning air, and the palest light streaked into the room. Julian longed to gaze out of the high window into the boundless sky, where she expected to go . . . toward heaven. Momentarily, she objected to the curate's request for her to look *directly* at the crucifix. It meant a difficult adjustment of the positioning of her head, as it had become impossible for her to move any part of her body without pain. Even refocusing her eyes required an enormous effort and a decisive act of the will. Every breath felt like her last.

> But nevertheless I assented to set my eyes in the face of the crucifix, if I might, in order to endure longer unto the time of my ending. For it seemed to me I might endure longer by looking forward than upwards. (ii:26–28.67)

Out of humility and obedience, Julian did as she was told by her curate. She was still sitting partially upright as before, her head supported by pillows and cloths. When she managed to force herself to look straight ahead, her eyes would have been more or less at the level of the crucifix.

> After this my sight began to fail, and it was all dark around me in the room, and as murky as if it had been night, except in the image of the cross, wherein there remained a natural light, and I never knew how. All that was beside the cross was ugly to me, as if it had been much occupied with fiends. After this the other part of my body began to die, as to my feeling. My hands fell down on either side, and also for lack of power my head settled down on one side. The most pain that I felt was shortness of breath and failing of life. Then I thought truly to have been at the point of death. (ii:29–36.67)

Her area of vision closed down to a small, intense circle of light (where it came from, she never knew) that illuminated the figure of Christ on the cross. She had just seen the first light of dawn, but now the whole room darkened as if it had become night again. Conditioned by medieval sermons and meditation manuals, Julian believed that during the process of dying, fiends lay in wait to tempt the soul to sin mortally and then drag it down into hell. She needed to be on her guard, alert, awake, praying constantly. Meanwhile, the general numbness below her waist spread to her upper body, her hands dropped down from her chest to the bed, her head fell to one side, even as Christ's head leaned to one side on the crucifix before her. Yet still she kept her eyes fixed on the cross. Her heart beat erratically. Her breathing grew short and rapid; she was gasping for air. She fixed every aspect so keenly in her memory that she was able to recall these details in her later account. She was watching herself in slow motion, dying.

Healing

> And in this moment, suddenly all my pain was taken away from me and I was completely whole, and especially in the upper part of my body, as ever I was before or after. I marveled at this change, for it seemed to me that it was a private werking of God, and not of nature. (ii:36–39.67)

All at once, Julian's pain ceased, her erratic heartbeat returned to normal, she could breathe easily. She was amazed by this sudden and unexpected "change" and was convinced it was not due to any natural causes (or herbal medicines), but only to the intervention of God. It was as if Christ himself had taken her by the hand and said to her, as he had to the twelve-year-old girl who everyone thought had just died of fever: "*Talitha kum*!" ["Little girl, get up!"] And the girl arose from her bed (Mk 5:38–43, cf. Mt 9:23–25, Lk 8:49–56). Julian felt *healed*.

Yet she did not cry out with joy and gratitude at the miracle taking place within her. She did not speak at all. None of the women gathered around her bed saying prayers, or those whispering to each other in the corner, or those coming and going in the bustle of morning chores, bringing fresh water and cloths, suspected there was any change in her condition. Why did Julian not shout for joy and let everyone know what had happened?

> And yet despite the feeling of this ease, I trusted nevermore that I should live, nor was the feeling of this ease fully ease for me. For it seemed to me that I would rather have been delivered from this world, for my heart was willing thereto to die. (ii:39–42.67)

The miraculous healing and feeling of ease (as against dis-ease) came from deep within her soul, spreading throughout her body. Julian was sure of it. She did not need to test its efficacy by moving her head or raising her arms or even, like the girl in the gospels, getting up out of bed and walking. But the physical healing did not bring spiritual peace, what she describes as "full ease," to her. Julian still did not think she would live. In fact, the sudden easing of all her pain and immobility felt like a bitter disappointment. After having suffered so much, her heart longed to be delivered from the trials of this world forever. She was ready to die.

She may also have considered her sudden healing as a transitional stage on her journey into the next life, before the last temptations would attack her from all sides. She knew she needed to remain vigilant, not distracted by letting anyone know what was really transpiring within her, lest she fall into pride because of the women's excitement over her healing, or slip into despair if she was then to be fiercely tempted. Julian had no desire to emerge from her meditative focus on the Holy Face, like those in the gospels who could not take their eyes off Jesus. Her body felt as if it was slipping away from her, gently, like layers of clothing she no longer needed. There was no turning back now. Her soul hung naked, suspended in the darkness, stripped of all attachments to this life, as Christ's body hung on the cross in front of her. She kept her eyes firmly fixed on the image of her suffering Savior. He was her only hope during this last rite of passage.

> And suddenly it came to my mind that I should desire the *second wound* of our lord's gift and of his grace: that he would fill my body with the mind and feeling of his blessed passion, as I had prayed before. For I would that his pains were my pains, with compassion and afterward longing for God. Thus I thought I might, with his grace, have his wounds that I had desired before. (iii:1–6.67, italics added)

Julian refers to this request as the "second wound" of the three wounds she had desired of the Lord without condition (that is, "the wound of natural compassion"). The way she phrases it, however, her petition sounds more like the "first gift" she had asked for so long ago, that of "a bodily sight," that she might see the passion that the Lord suffered for her. Was she asking once again for a vision? She is quick to clarify:

> But in this I never desired neither a bodily sight nor any manner of shewing of God, but *only compassion*, as it seemed to me that a nat-

> ural soul might have with our lord Jesus, that for love would become a mortal man. (iii:6–8.67, italics added)

She is very firm that this time she did *not* ask for a vision (using the triple negative in the original Middle English: never-neither-nor). Neither is she asking for the "second gift," a sickness well nigh unto death. She has already undergone that. She simply wants the compassion to experience as much of Christ's suffering as she can possibly bear, so that when she dies, she will die with him.

> With him I desired to suffer, living in my mortal body, as God would give me grace. (iii:8–9.67)

12
The Vision

Julian heard the chimes on Norwich Cathedral strike 4 AM for *Lauds.* It was the "day belle." She remembered the time and will refer to it later in her account. Those gathered around her bed began to pray the psalms together, keeping vigil until she had passed. The priest and the boy had since departed from the room, leaving the crucifix in place at the foot of Julian's bed. Julian gave no sign to anyone that she was no longer in pain. Neither did she move. She expected to die very soon. All around the bedroom it was dark, murky, and menacing, as if demons were gathering to tempt her into hell.

Her meditation may have begun as a somewhat reluctant, eventually obedient, effort to concentrate on the crucifix while struggling with her fear of the invisible fiends all around, and distracted by her sudden awareness of being healed, yet not at complete "ease." Nevertheless, an unearthly light still shone from the crucifix and this is where Julian continued to focus her eyes with all the love in her heart. She was inspired to ask for the "wound of compassion" as she had done since adolescence while meditating on Christ's holy cross, hanging high above the congregation in church. All through the years, she had tried every means she knew to evoke in herself a deeply felt sympathy for the suffering Savior, like the women in the gospel story. Yet her ability to enter into the passion in her imagination had always fallen short of her longing to *be there.*

Then, after being healed of her deadly illness and its acute suffering, quite suddenly, her mind drops into a vast and spacious contemplative zone. This is the nonspecific place of boundless, though supremely concentrated, energy. Her mind, in fact, enters an altered state, an intense realm of psychic experience often described in mystical literature, where there is only one distinct and all-consuming reality. This is the inner stillness where revelation occurs, beyond the mind's self-conscious control. In this mystical space, Julian's mind becomes able to maintain focus without distraction, and her understanding expands effortlessly beyond all previous boundaries. Without warning, and for no reason that she could ever trace, Julian becomes a recipient of divine *shewing*.

The First Revelation

> And in this state of mind, suddenly I saw the red blood trickle down from under the garland [crown of thorns], hot and freshly, plentifully and vividly, exactly as it was at that time that the garland of thorns was pressed on his blessed head. (4:1–3.135)

Given Julian's lifelong devotion to the passion of Christ and her conviction that she was nearing her own death, it seems perfectly plausible that, at this critical moment, an apparition would arise from the depths of Julian's subconscious that looked to her as lifelike as any other image she had ever seen: that of Christ bleeding from underneath his crown of thorns. As a young girl she had prayed to have the "mind of the passion." Could this ardent longing engender an actual vision? It had long been promised that in the last days:

> I will pour out my Spirit upon all flesh, and your sons and your daughters shall prophesy, and your young men shall see visions, and your old men shall dream dreams. Even upon my slaves, both men and women, in those days I will pour out my Spirit; and they shall prophesy. (Acts 2:17–18, cf. Jl 2:28–29)

Well might we ask what Julian actually *saw*. Was it a waking dream? A vivid lifelike picture conjured up by her imagination? A hallucination brought on by fever, illness, hunger, dehydration, low blood sugar, or too-intense longing? An out-of-body transport like those of the "fasting women"? A temporary mental derangement? A fantasy? A phantasmagoria? Or was it exactly what Julian says it was: red blood dripping down from under Christ's crown of thorns on the cross? There is no sure way of knowing what Julian actually experienced, except by her own testimony. And there is no way of explaining how the vision happened in psychological or scientific terms. Even if we could, there is no guarantee that such an explanation would convince anyone. Julian herself does not know how it happened. She does not try to explain. Nor does she give any more salient details of the vision, at least for now. She simply describes what she "saw," vision by vision, revelation by revelation, as she experienced it. The very simplicity of her account renders it remarkably credible. She never comments that she is actually having a vision, that her long-forgotten request for "a bodily sight" has finally been answered. At that timeless moment, she was utterly *un*self-conscious.

Seeing and Grace

Still, we might try to imagine just how Julian's visions could have developed, always acutely aware that without the extraordinary grace of the moment, we are merely skimming the surface of what *really* happened. We know that Julian, obedient to the parson's directive, had focused her eyes straight ahead, staring at the crucifix. There was, by her own account, an inexplicable light shining from within it. This precise area of bright light, against the dark and murky background of the bedroom, could have created the optical illusion that the crucifix was growing larger and larger, more and more distinct, while everything around became engulfed in darkness and fell away.[1] As Julian's mental awareness, infused by grace, transformed the dead metal or wood of the twisted figure into the appearance of the living flesh of the Savior, the vision began to expand in dimension, proximity, and intensity. It grew all-absorbing, literally blocking out every other visual or auditory impression. There was nothing else in the room that could possibly distract Julian. Christ on the cross suspended in front of her bed was *all there was for Julian to see.* Though she was still sitting somewhat upright, immobile, she felt herself placed at the foot of the actual cross. Every image, thought, inspiration, and reaction Julian will experience in the course of her visions will arise from the wellspring of her subconscious, prepared for by her entire life experience, her sufferings, her capacity for joy, her ardent prayer, her intense longing and spiritual practice. No doubt, the crisis of Julian's illness (coupled with her conviction that she was dying) acted as the immediate catalyst for such mystical phenomena. Nothing focuses the attention like thinking one is about to die. But many come near to dying and then die without seeing visions. In Julian's case, something markedly out-of-the-ordinary occurred.

It is imperative to note that the various psychospiritual elements that had to converge to produce Julian's visions (as well as the accompanying Revelations contained within those visions) could only have coalesced in that time and place through an extraordinary infusion of divine grace. What happened within Julian was a dynamic and explosive process that propelled both her body and mind into a supra-sensual sphere of being. As Julian's body became anaesthetized and stiffened (and, by her own account, lost all physical sensation, even that of her previous pain), and her eyes became frozen and fixed on the crucifix, all her spiritual energies were channeled into one immense uprising and outpouring of love. In that extreme moment, the scales of limited human sight fell from Julian's eyes and, for an extended period, she was graced to perceive Christ's presence on the cross at a level of awareness far beyond what any of us would call "reality."

As unimaginable as this may be, we might also consider: Is Julian's vision of the suffering Christ so radically different from Mary Magdalene's vision of the resurrected Christ on Easter morning? To Julian, Christ showed himself as a small carving of a man, his head crowned with thorns and leaning to one side, his hands and feet nailed to a cross. To Magdalene, Christ appeared, at least initially so as not to frighten her, disguised as a common gardener (Jn 20:11–18). Is wood or metal more difficult than human flesh (or bread or wine, for that matter) for Christ to transform into the reality of his Divine Presence? And should Julian's "seeing" Christ on the cross be considered any less authentic than Magdalene's seeing the Savior standing before her, risen from the dead?

We simply do not know, because Julian never tells us, when the figure of Christ on the cross ceased being brass or wood and actually took on human features before her eyes. Did the actual carving of the figure remain the same size, perhaps ten or twelve inches high? Did it appear to move on the cross, or was it stationary throughout the length of the Revelations? And when Jesus spoke to Julian, as he would many times, did she hear the voice coming from the direction of the mouth of the living figure or did it arise from within her own heart? Julian herself will be our best guide here. She will be very careful to differentiate between what she saw as a "bodily sight" (a physical presence), a "ghostly" sight (an imaginative vision), and an "even more ghostly" sight (an intellectual understanding, developed after years of meditation).

Further, she will specify which of Christ's words she heard spoken distinctly within her mind, and which words arose in her mind "as if" Christ were addressing her directly, according to what she understood to be his meaning. She will try to be as clear as she can, lest she mislead the reader in any way. This endearing fact may reassure the skeptic that at no point was Julian out to deceive, but sought only to convey the truth of her experience as far as she was able. It is as important to her as it is to the reader that she report *rightly*. And when she does not tell us pertinent details, it must be either because she did not think them important or because the particular experience was so far beyond description that words completely fail her.

It is understood that during her visions no one else around her could see what Julian saw. When her mind engaged in a voiceless, interior dialogue with Christ, no one else heard. To those in the room, Julian still lay dying, her eyes fixed, her body stiffened and unmoving. Perhaps the women drew the thick drapes around the sides of her bed so that she could die in peaceful contemplation of the crucifix standing before her.

Mystic Creativity

The normal human mind creates, projects, and labels sights, sounds, smells, tastes, and a seemingly infinite variety of tactile sensations into a recognizable and functioning "world" of people, places, and things. Likewise, the creative imagination of the artist "sees" the shapes and colors of the painting within the imagination before they appear on canvas, senses the contours of the human figure within the inert block of marble, anticipates the architectural design even as the hand lifts to draw, choreographs the flow of dance movement on an inner stage. The artistic mind also "hears" musical phrases, cadences, whole symphonies within; listens attentively to poetic rhymes and rhythms that demand to be written down; overhears the dialogues and silences while watching the actions and reactions of characters in dramatic situations, long before they take scripted form on the page. Every art emanates from within the human psyche, and the artist struggles to give full expression to these inner visions and locutions with more or less success.

In a parallel way, the mystic mind is graced by Divine Reality to be able to experience a heightened level of awareness that is ordinarily beyond human capacity. In order to "incarnate" these sublime contacts, divinity infuses the human mind with visions and voices that can be seen and heard, felt and contemplated. Yet the real value of such experience does not lie in the actual visions or even in the precise words of the locutions. The incalculable worth lies in the fact that Transcendent Reality *animates* such symbols to make its presence known to the visionary. This intimate contact between divine and human is the ultimate creative experience.

Tests of Authenticity

How can we know if the experience of a vision is genuine . . . or the product of an unbalanced mind? Though "tests" may not categorically prove anything to a particular individual, it may be salutary to consider the various aspects of extraordinary experience frequently used to establish the authenticity of a vision or locution.[2]

First, the authentic vision arrives suddenly and unbidden, without human effort or contrivance. It is immediately experienced as proceeding from a superior source. It carries the weight of divine authority. Sometimes by means of sight and/or sound the mystic is given a directive for action, a precise warning, an instantaneous clarity about a decision to be made, or is shown a prophetic vision of an event that is bound to occur in the future. Often the visionary is graced by an infusion of wisdom and spiritual insight that he or she could not have attained by ordinary methods of study or human effort. At other times, the visionary may be absorbed in a trance in which he or she becomes privy to things not able to be described in human language, as was St. Paul, who "was caught up to the third heaven" (2 Cor 12:2–4). The sublime experience may be seen either through a lifelike apparition *exterior* to the visionary, or as a compelling *interior* picture occurring in the recipient's imagination, or as a purely *intellectual understanding* that arises all-at-once, without recourse to specific images or words. In whatever form the visionary receives the divinely inspired revelations, they have a veracity about them that is incontestable. For the recipient to deny that such an event ever took place would be akin to denying the truth of his or her own existence.

Likewise, the voice and words of *locutions* may be heard as coming from the outside, or as emanating from within, or as purely intellectual inspiration received from the divine source. In any case, it is generally agreed that all visionary and verbal transmissions, if they are genuine, must be distinctly formed, whether by a convincing physical, imaginative, or intellectual illumination, or by means of understandable words. The authentic vision is not confusing, distracting, or obfuscating in its effect on the recipient's mind. It is reassuring, affirming, sometimes cautionary, even demanding, but always precise. The truth-filled words are clearly spoken in the visionary's language, and their effect is profoundly empowering, much more so than if the same words had been spoken under normal circumstances. Both image and words are thereafter indelibly imprinted in the person's memory and can be recalled at will. As St. Teresa of Avila wrote of her own locutions: "For the Lord makes the words stay in the memory so that we cannot forget them, whereas those that originate in our own minds are like a first stirring of thought that passes and is forgotten."[3] Yet even though the original experience cannot be forgotten, there may be a significant delay in the mystic's full understanding of the meaning of the revelation.

Another and most important indication of authenticity is that the visions and locutions of Christian mystics conform to holy scripture and to the most sacred teachings of the church. They do not contradict revealed truth. They also produce a lasting change in the recipient's state of mind, enabling the will to act on the directives given, thus dramatically altering the visionary's course of life greatly to the good. And while the revelations may seem at the time full of mystery to be contemplated for years to come, both visions and words continue to produce a sense of ineffable joy and profound peace. *The visionary is forever transformed by the vision and the listener by the words.*

Julian's visions and locutions meet all the above qualifications. Her vision of Christ on the cross appeared suddenly as she lay dying, shortly after all her pain had inexplicably ceased. She specifically records that she saw Christ on the cross, "without any meane" (4:5.135), that is, not mediated through the intervention of an angel or saint, and appearing completely lifelike. She was absolutely convinced that he who revealed himself to her was truly Jesus Christ, the Son of God, bearing all the weight of divine authority. He answered questions that had tortured her soul for many years and deepened her understanding of the nature of the Trinity, the incarnation, the passion, and the resurrection, as well as the divine attitude toward sin, judgment, and personal suffering. In her sixteen Revelations, Julian was given extraordinary wisdom and divine teachings she never could have figured out on her own, but for the grace of the *shewings.* She was also granted a prophetic intuition concerning the future state of the church. And, like St. Paul, she was "lifted up into heaven" (14:2–3.173), and there she was abundantly graced with knowledge of mysteries that, by her own account, "no heart can speak, no word can tell" (11:1.163; 20:5.191).

Throughout, Julian's visions were distinctly formed, either when manifesting in a "bodily sight in the face of the crucifix" (10:1.157), or when being conceived in "ghostly sight" (9:25.157) in her imagination, or when arising "more ghostly" and all-at-once "in a point" (11:1.163) of profound understanding while she was poised in contemplation. Likewise, Julian understood the words spoken in her own Middle English language, with no sense of obfuscation. Whether heard as words formed in her soul, "without voice and opening of lips" (13:3–4.169), or "as if" Christ were speaking directly to her mind in "words formed in my understanding" (9:24–25.157), these locutions were incontrovertible in their truthfulness and power. They brought clarity and peace to Julian's troubled mind. Most certainly, the visions and locutions that unfolded during the course of the Revelations were indelible. Julian never lost sight of what the suffering or the glorious Christ looked like, nor did she forget the words he spoke to her. She was compelled to write about them all her life. These divine illuminations expanded Julian's spirit, opening up a level of faith, hope, and love in her heart previously unimaginable. They re-interpreted familiar and firmly held doctrines of the church and pushed the boundaries of what could be thought or written about the mercy and love of God.

Julian's Doubt

What about Julian's own faith in her Revelations? Did she ever doubt them herself? It is true that, in a moment of aberration at the very end of her visions, when her former physical pain returned in full force, Julian told a friar who came to visit her that she "had raved today" (66:12–13.331). Does this imply she negated her own experience? In that moment of torture, perhaps. But the effect on her psyche was like a denial of the truth of her own existence. She became instantly mortified and overcome by shame at her total misrepresentation of the extraordinary graces she had received. Like St. Peter after he denied even knowing Jesus Christ (Lk 22:54–62), she felt she had betrayed the Lord precisely because she *knew* that he had been really present to her. She then underwent a nightmare during which she saw herself violently attacked by a devil. Obviously, her guilt had overwhelmed her. Only later, when she was given full reassurance by the Lord that her visions were *not* ravings, did she feel forgiven for her moment of doubt. Then, for the rest of her life, her certainty that her visions were of divine origin never left her.

Just as those who saw Christ after his resurrection became transformed from petrified followers hiding in an upper room behind locked doors (Jn 20:19) to passionate disciples ready to suffer martyrdom for the sake of the gospel, so Julian became a changed woman by virtue of what she had seen and heard in the course of her Revelations. From these encounters she developed a mystical theology that stands second to none in the fourteenth century or since. And this "simple creature, unlettered" (2:1.125, vi:36.75), was given the grace and courage to write the first book in English by a woman. As we have discussed, two decades after her visions she will enter an anchorage to devote the remainder of her life to prayer, silent contemplation, and the spiritual guidance of her *evencristens.* Perhaps, most convincingly, Julian will experience a spiritual joy that, in spite of hardships, nothing could ever take away from her. Julian knew who had appeared to her and spoken with her, as surely as did Mary Magdalene on Easter morning. And Julian, like Magdalene, longed to spread the good news of her very personal gospel.

Arguments

Some scholars have argued that Julian's visions and locutions could have been produced by her own fevered imagination and that, after a life of meditation on the passion story, she was able to conjure Christ's sufferings so vividly that they seemed to her to appear lifelike; then she put her own words in Christ's mouth and later wrote them down. However, the fallacy in such an argument lies in the fact that it is impossible to explain how a "lewed creature" could develop a mystical theology as authoritative and comprehensive as Julian's unless she had been graced with divine wisdom through immediate contact. *Only because of what Julian saw and heard was she empowered to write what she wrote.* Such luminous insights do not arise from an attempt to deceive, or from a diseased or disoriented mind. Julian is far too disarmingly honest, outspoken, and level-headed, far too demanding in her own unrelenting search for truth, to be considered anything but sincere in recounting what she saw and heard.

A final consideration: Julian records insights into the gospel message that would have been so unusual, perhaps even shocking, for her intended audience of *evencristens*, that she would not have dared write them down if she had not trusted the authenticity of her visions. There was too much at stake. As we have seen, she was under constant threat of persecution for being an uneducated laywoman writing mystical theology in the vernacular. Only a fool is willing to die for a lie. It was precisely Julian's absolute faith in whom she had seen and what he had said that gave her the courage to commit her Revelations to parchment.

Right So!

> Right so, both God and man, the same who suffered for me. I conceived truly and mightily that it was Christ himself who shewed it to me, without any meane. (4:3–5.135)

Julian's first reaction to the vision is an exclamation of wonder at the unexpected delight of seeing Christ on the cross, alive before her eyes. "Right so!" is a cry of affirmation, of sheer exhilaration. This is what the Christian longs for, the experience of convincing divine presence. Astonishingly, Julian implies that she was not at first horrified by Christ's sufferings, nor did she recoil from the flow of blood, nor express sorrow for her sins, nor ask pardon for the sins of all humankind. No, her recollection is that she was struck to the heart by the undeniable appearance before her of Jesus Christ, who is both God and man.

> And in the same shewing, suddenly the trinity filled my heart most full of joy. And so I understood it shall be in heaven without end, to all who shall come there. For the trinity is God, God is the trinity. The trinity is our maker, the trinity is our keeper, the trinity is

> our everlasting lover, the trinity is our endless joy and our bliss, by our lord Jesus Christ and in our lord Jesus Christ. And this was shewed in the first sight and in all [the other Revelations]. For where Jesus appears the blessed trinity is understood, as to my sight. (4:6–12.135)

Immediately, Julian is given an insight into the most difficult of all Christian doctrines, that of the Trinity: one God in three Divine Persons. In a great rush of exuberance, she experiences and extols the Trinity as the "maker" (creator), "keeper" (preserver and protector), and "everlasting lover" of all it creates. Thus, the Trinity is our "endless joy and our bliss." And all this is done "by" and "in" Jesus Christ. Julian acknowledges that the trinitarian activities of creating, keeping, and loving were shown to her in this first and subsequently in all of the sixteen Revelations. She will also affirm that the Blessed Trinity was continually made present in Christ, through all the physical and spiritual aspects in which he appeared to her throughout the visions. Indeed, Trinity-in-Christ will be a central theme of her book. Christ is the entry point into the trinitarian doctrine. For Julian, all the Revelations will show aspects of God's dynamic inter-relatedness.

Trinity

The word *Trinity* is taken from the Latin *trinitas*, meaning three-in-one. St. Augustine, in his magnificent work, *De Trinitate*, wrote that all the church fathers and expounders of sacred scripture, from the earliest days of Christianity, teach this doctrine:

> that according to the scriptures Father and Son and Holy Spirit in the inseparable equality of one substance [essence] present a divine unity: and therefore there are not three gods but one God; although indeed the Father has begotten the Son, and therefore he who is the Father is not the Son: and the Son is begotten by the Father, and therefore he who is the Son is not the Father; and the Holy Spirit is neither the Father nor the Son, but only the Spirit of the Father and of the Son, himself coequal to the Father and the Son, and belonging to the threefold unity.[4]

St. Augustine was well aware that many in his time gravely misunderstood or misinterpreted this doctrine to mean that there were three separate gods, since they "seemed" to work independently, as recorded in the gospels. He makes clear that this is *not* the orthodox meaning:

> It was not however this same three . . . that was born of the virgin Mary, crucified and buried under Pontius Pilate, rose again on the third day and ascended into heaven, *but the Son alone*. Nor was it this same three that came down upon Jesus in the form of a dove at his baptism, or came down on the day of Pentecost after the Lord's ascension, with a roaring sound from heaven as though a violent gust were rushing down, and in divided tongues as of fire (Acts 2:3), *but the Holy Spirit alone*. Nor was it this same three that spoke from heaven, "You are my Son," either at his baptism by John (Mk 1:11), or on the mountain when the three disciples were with him (Mt 17:5), nor when the resounding voice was heard, "I have both glorified it [my name] and will glorify it again" (Jn 12:28), but it was *the Father's voice alone* addressing the Son; although just as Father and Son and Holy Spirit are inseparable, so do they work inseparably. This is also my faith inasmuch as it is the Catholic faith.[5]

Augustine reaffirms that there is only *one* God, in three distinct and co-equal Divine Persons. Although in scripture "some things are even said about the persons singly by name," he explains that this is done in order to make us more aware of the Trinity. Augustine verifies that this singular activity does not exclude the other persons, since where one Divine Person acts, the other Divine Persons are equally present, "because this same three is also one, and there is one substance and godhead of Father and Son and Holy Spirit."[6] Therefore, when Julian saw Christ on the cross, she was given immediate insight into the unfathomable mystery of the Trinity: where Jesus Christ is, there is the Father and there is the Spirit, since "the divine utterances have many ways of saying things about them individually which belong to them all, on account of the *indivisible operation of their one and the same substance*."[7]

Further speaking of Jesus Christ, St. Augustine affirms: "It was in the form of a servant that he was crucified, and yet it was the Lord of glory who was crucified. For that 'take-over' was such as to make God a man and a man God."[8] And again, even more specifically: ". . . and yet the Lord of glory was crucified, because *it is quite correct to talk even of God being crucified*—owing to the weakness of flesh, though, not to the strength of godhead."[9]

From her childhood training, Julian certainly knew the basic trinitarian doctrine contained in the Latin *Credo*:

> I believe in one God, the Father Almighty, maker of heaven and earth, of all things visible and invisible. I believe in one Lord Jesus Christ, the Only Begotten Son of God, born of the Father before all ages. God from God, Light from Light, true God from true God, begotten, not made, consubstantial with the Father, through him all things were made . . . I believe in the Holy Spirit, the Lord, the giver of life, who proceeds from the Father and the Son, who with the Father and the Son is adored and glorified, who has spoken through the Prophets . . .[10]

This creed was recited in Latin by the celebrant (and also by the laity) at every Mass. Julian would also have heard Austin canons preach intricate sermons on the doctrine of the Trinity. But in that moment of both physical and intellectual vision, Julian was graced with an *experience* of the Trinity existing within Jesus Christ that no sermon could possibly have given her. Even so, by the time Julian came to write the Long Text, she must have consulted a scholar on what she could rightly say in dogmatic terms concerning the Trinity. It was one thing to experience a trinitarian oneness in a vision of Christ on the cross. It was quite another to know how to express it in an orthodox manner on parchment.

Benedicite!

> And I said: "Benedicite dominus!" This I said with reverence in my meaning, with a mighty voice. And full greatly was I astonished, for wonder and marveling that I had, that he that is so reverent and so dreadful will be so homely with a sinful creature living in this wretched flesh. (4:13–16.135–37)

Julian cannot contain herself for joy! She cries out in a loud voice with the greatest reverence, astonishment, wonder, and marveling, the equivalent of: "Bless me, Lord!" though revealingly, she uses the wrong Latin syntax. She should have said and written: "*Benedicite, Domino!*" (which are the closing words of the office of *Prime*). A similar greeting was customarily said by Benedictine monks and nuns whenever they met each other, the younger asking for a blessing (*Benedicite*) and the older religious responding: "*Dominus te benedicat.*" (May the Lord bless you).[11] Julian had often heard the invocation and responsorial in current use, and simply combined the first words of each: *Benedicite... Dominus.* (Likewise, "Bless me, Father, for I have sinned" was, and is, the usual greeting spoken to a priest before making a confession of sins.) Julian would also have used the word *Benedicite* in greeting members of the many religious orders living in Norwich. But the fact that Julian, in her eagerness for a blessing from the Lord, gets the Latin wrong is a clear indication she was *not* fluent in the language and yet another proof she was not a Benedictine nun, accustomed to using the correct greeting on a daily basis.

Those in the room must have been thoroughly startled at Julian's sudden vocal Latin outburst; this, from a dying woman! They must have rushed to her bed, taken her hand, wiped her brow, asked her questions, rejoiced in the strength of her "mighty" voice. But Julian did not, could not, respond to them. She was utterly focused on the Lord. She was overcome with emotion that Christ who is to be revered and dreaded (in the sense of inspiring fear and awe) would stoop so low and become so approachable, so "homely" with her, "a sinful creature." *Homely* is a delightful medieval word that means, literally, "like home," simple, plain, familiar, intimate. It implies everything comfortable that we would associate with being utterly at ease with someone. (We may say "homey" about a place that is non-imposing, in which we feel relaxed and welcome.) In its medieval sense, *homely* also suggests a way of treating another person, no matter how subordinate he or she may be, as an equal. This is one of Julian's favorite words throughout her text (she uses it almost thirty times),[12] and it conveys the moving impression of Christ *lowering himself* to become completely familiar with Julian, even deigning to treat her as an equal.

Julian assumes that Christ has come to comfort and strengthen her during her time of temptation before she dies. At this point, she has no idea of the Revelations that will follow. All she knows is that, as long as she has a physical sight of his "blessed passion" (and a new spiritual understanding of the Trinity), she and "all living creatures that would be saved" would be strengthened "against all the fiends of hell and against all ghostly enemies" (4:22–23.137).

Saint Mary

However, Julian receives no temptations, at least not at this time. Instead, Christ brings "our lady Saint Mary" (4:24.137) to her understanding. She does not see Mary in the flesh as she does Christ, but "ghostly, in bodily likeness" (4:25.137). This implies that Julian saw Mary appear suddenly and distinctly *in her imagination*, without any effort on Julian's part to conjure her. Mary is young, not much older than a child, small and meek and in the position of prayer that she had taken at the time of her conception of the Savior. (It was a common medieval belief that at the annunciation, Mary was fifteen years old.) Julian is granted a glimpse into the beauty of Mary's soul and the holy awe in which she contemplated God:

> Also God shewed me in part the wisdom and truth of her soul, wherein I understood the reverent beholding in which she beheld her God, that is, her maker, marveling with great reverence that he would be born of her who was a simple creature of his making. For this was her marveling: that he who was her maker would be born of her who was made. And this wisdom and truth, knowing the greatness of her maker and the littleness of herself that is made, made her say so meekly to Gabriel: "Lo me here, God's handmaiden." (4:26–33.137)

In this meditation, Julian is keenly aware that Mary is, like herself, "a simple creature," uneducated, and without any earthly nobility. Yet Julian understands truly that Mary is more worthy than all other creatures God has made, because she was conceived without sin. All other creatures are therefore below her. And above her is "nothing that is made but the blessed manhood of Christ, as to my sight" (4:35.139).

Our Clothing

Julian returns to the sight of Christ's bleeding head. She tells us that at the same time she had the *physical* sight of the blood, she was given an *intellectual* understanding of the good Lord's "homely loving."

> I saw that he is to us all things that are good and comfortable to help us. He is our clothing, that for love wraps us and winds us, embraces us and totally encloses us, hanging about us for tender love, that he may never leave us. And so in this sight I saw that he is all things that are good, as to my understanding. (5:2–6.139)

The sight of the Lord's bleeding head never becomes for Julian a cause for fear or guilt. On the contrary, it is a reason for rejoicing in the Savior's overwhelming and all-inclusive love. Julian realizes that he is everything "good and comfortable" in the entire universe, everything good we believe in, hope for, sacrifice for, work for, take care of, enjoy, cherish, nurture, create, and strive to preserve. He is everything and everyone she has ever loved. Christ's arms are outstretched on the cross to embrace the entire world. And his delight is to be with the sons and daughters of humankind (Pr 8:31). For Julian, he is not a distant Savior, not a harsh master, but one who loves every person so intimately that he stoops down to get as close to us as *the very clothing* we put on our skin. Julian uses a series of encircling terms: "wrappeth . . . windeth . . . halseth [embraces] . . . becloseth [encloses]" in an effort to describe the all-surrounding tenderness she feels Christ exuding from the cross. The paradox is that Christ, who hangs before Julian, has been *stripped* of all his own clothing, his flesh exposed to the harsh elements. Yet he wants to go on "hanging about us" out of his tender love for us. He never wants to leave, discard, or cast us off.

We may consider what clothing implies, not as fashion or status symbol, but simply as bodily covering: it is protection against sun and heat, wind, cold, rain, and snow, and sometimes, of necessity, it becomes the very blanket under which we sleep. To medieval women, clothing was the modesty of a veil or a wimple to cover their heads, the comfort of a soft linen tunic close to their flesh, the warmth of a woolen over-tunic. To men, clothing meant a short tunic and woven hose, a jacket and heavy sur-coat and a thick scarf around the neck. Clothing included a brightly colored shawl inside drafty homes, or an all-encompassing woolen cape against fierce winter winds. From being swaddled in linen cloth and wound 'round with bands in infancy, to being encased in the required woolen shroud in the coffin, clothing wrapped medieval people from birth to burial. As we have suggested, Julian had dealt with wool all her life: carding, spinning, weaving, and dyeing it to make cloth and then sewing it into clothing. She had draped and hung material on customers, family members, friends. She knew how wonderfully protected they (and she) felt when enclosed in beautifully woven, richly colored, and expertly tailored tunics, sideless tabards, woolen capes, and cloaks. Now, clothing arises in her mind as an all-embracing metaphor to describe the indescribable love of Christ for his people. By becoming human, God clothed himself *in our very skin*. And Christ is the *lamb* of God who allows himself to be shorn and then lays down his life to "enclothe" his people. He is our own flesh and blood.

St. Paul had long ago urged Christians to "put on the Lord, Jesus Christ" (Rm 13:14), also using the image of clothing to signify a radical change of heart. And Julian may have recalled Richard Rolle's imagery of Christ as our clothing from his *Meditations on the Passion*:

> Therefore, I will *clothe me* in the wounds and the passion and the reproofs of Jesus Christ *as in a clothing*, and then his passion, inasmuch as I need, shall fight for me against the flesh, the world and the fiend, and all my enemies. It were possible that if I were well transformed into Christ crucified, that I should be his heir in heaven.[13]

Unlike Rolle, however, Julian does not envision herself being clothed in "the wounds and the passion and the reproofs" of Jesus Christ as in an impregnable suit of medieval armor in which to do battle against "the flesh, the world and the fiend, and all *her* enemies." Rather, Julian, in a distinctly feminine way, experiences Christ's outpouring of love on the cross as the most comforting and comfortable clothing, supremely gentle to the touch.

The Hazelnut

> And in this [sight], he shewed a little thing the quantity of a hazelnut, lying in the palm of my hand as it seemed to me, and it was as round as any ball. I looked therein with the eye of my understanding, and thought: "What may this be?" And it was answered generally thus: "It is all that is made." I marveled how it might last, for it seemed to me it might suddenly have fallen into nought for its littleness. And I was answered in my understanding: "It lasteth and ever shall, because God loveth it. And so hath all things being by the love of God." (5:7–13.139)

From clothing as metaphor for the insights she is receiving, Julian's mind moves to cooking, the other activity that has occupied her whole life. She is suddenly shown, through an imaginative vision, a perfectly round hazelnut lying in the palm of her hand. How many times she had held, cracked, and eaten raw or roasted hazelnuts, ground them with a mortar and pestle to make a paste or sauce, pressed them to produce flavorful hazelnut oil, followed a recipe calling for a quantity of butter or lard "the size of a hazelnut," or saved one half of the nut covering to use as a makeshift measuring spoon for salt and spices. The uses of hazelnuts were so many and frequent, the trees on which they grew so ubiquitous throughout the countryside that one would pick the hazelnuts up off the ground as one walked among the hedgerows between fields. Hazel tree branches were used to make wattle and daub homes, farm fencing, even strong but flexible bows for arrows. In fact, the hazelnut had been around so long (since 7000 BCE, during the Mesolithic Period) and had become so commonplace, *so utterly ordinary*, that Julian did not understand what the import of its imaginary presence in her palm could possibly mean. She looks more deeply with the inner eye of her understanding and asks the first of many questions in her text: "What may this be?" She makes very clear that she was answered not specifically from the Lord's mouth but in a general way, through an illumination given directly to her mind. The response was short, direct, precise: "It is all that is made."

The moment is stunning in its simplicity and grandeur. Julian realizes in a flash how precious the little nut is, simply because *it exists*, and, as such, it encapsulates "all that is made." But how could it be "all that is made" if it is so small and so innocuous? Why, it could so easily fall into "nought," or complete nothingness, because of its very littleness, disintegrate into the earth unnoticed, as Julian had seen so many hazelnut casings turn to compost in the garden. It is as if Julian's inner eye became a floating telescope, zooming out to view infinite space, revealing the minuteness of planet Earth in the immensity of the cosmos. What power allows such a tiny thing to exist at all and cares enough to sustain it in existence? She is approaching the ultimate metaphysical question: *How is there anything at all?* Again, she is answered not by externally spoken words but by a voice within: "It lasteth, and ever shall, because God loveth it." And in the same way do all things exist or "have being" from moment to moment, solely because of the love of God.

Some people, as they lie on their deathbeds, see their lives pass before them in a flash. Julian sees all creation enclosed in the symbol of a little hazelnut, as miniscule in God's eye as a tiny round ball floating in space. Nevertheless, the smallness does not mean the hazelnut is any less loved by God for being so little and so ordinary. It is loved equally with suns and moons and stars, all the wonders of nature, and the uniqueness of human beings. In the course of future Revelations, Julian will experience again and again this ever-present, all-pervasive reality of love that alone sustains creation. Rather, creation is nothing else but the expression of Divine Love. Here Julian is given a glimpse into a universe upheld not by physical matter, whether in microcosm or macrocosm, but by the *fact* of the all-pervasive love of God.

As we have suggested, Julian might have read the *Scale of Perfection*, a popular book on the spiritual life written by an Augustinian abbot, Walter Hilton (c.1340/45–1396). In it, he referred to the prophet Ezekiel's vision of the heavenly Jerusalem:

> He says that he saw a city upon a hill toward the south, that to his sight when it was measured was no more of length and of breadth than a rood [cross], that is, six cubits and *a palm of length*. But as soon as he was brought into the city and looked about him, then thought he that it was wondrous great, for he saw many halls and chambers, both open and secret; he saw gates and porches, without and within, and many more buildings than I now speak of, and it was in length and breadth many hundred cubits, so that it seemed a wonder to him that this city was so long and so large within, which seemed *so little to his sight* when he was without. The city betokens the perfect love of God set upon the hill of contemplation, which to the sight of a soul that without the feeling of it travels in desire toward it seems but a little thing, no more than a rood, that is, six cubits and a palm of length. By six cubits are understood the perfection of man's work; *by the palm* [is understood] *a little touch of contemplation*. He sees well that there is such a thing that passes the deservings of all the workings of man, like as a palm is surpassed by six cubits, but he does not see within what it is; yet if he can come within the city of contemplation, then sees he much more than he saw at first. (Ez 40:2)[14]

This excerpt from the *Scale* provides a revealing insight into Julian's own vision. Ezekiel's rood "was so little" to the prophet's sight; yet once he entered within, it became the city that "betokens the perfect love of God, set upon the hill of contemplation." Likewise, Julian was shown "a little thing the size of a hazelnut, lying in the palm of my hand." The *palm*, which was a medieval measurement of three inches, may also have been a common English term to mean: "a little touch of contemplation." Julian might have understood the little hazelnut appearing in the palm of her hand as the "entry point" into mystical revelation. Once inside, the hazelnut (like the Holy Rood upon which Julian gazed), would reveal its "many halls and chambers, both open and secret." The prophet Isaiah had dared to suggest that the image of every human being is permanently etched on the palms of God's hand: "Behold, I have graven thee upon the palms of my hands . . ." (Is 49:16). And of course, the wounds of the nails through the hands of Christ on the cross are a shocking physical sign of God's love.

Three Properties

Julian understands three properties of the hazelnut. Not its hardiness, usefulness, and tastiness. Rather, "the first is that God made it, the second is that God loves it, the third is that God keeps [protects] it" (5:14–15.139). This trinity of hazelnut attributes strikes her mind with great clarity. Still, she is not sure what the meaning of its sudden appearance in her imagination could be, here and now, *for her*: "But what is that to me?" she asks, in internal dialogue (5:15.139). The answer comes immediately: "Truly, the maker, the keeper, the lover" (5:16.139). It is important to note that here, in the Long Text, either Julian or a later scribe switched the order of terms from the Short Text, which reads: "Truly, the maker, the lover, the keeper" (iv:16.69). Either way, consideration of the humble hazelnut raises her mind once again to the contemplation of Trinity as creator, protector, and eternal lover revealing itself not only in the reality of Jesus Christ, but in and through *everything that is made*.

Now, in a rush of ardor, Julian expresses her life's longing for God, the third of the "three wounds" she had once requested. She laments that until she is "substantially oned" (5:16.139), that is, united to God in the very ground of her being, with nothing created interposing itself between herself and God, she cannot have any rest or peace. She feels she must become "fastened" (in her heart) to Christ on the cross, so that there is nothing standing between her and him. This may seem a startling conclusion. Is Julian suddenly *denying* the holiness and goodness of the "hazelnut," which she has just understood represents all of creation? How could she? She has seen that it is created, protected, and loved in being by God. But she knows that it is still *not* God, nor can it ever be. And no matter how good and true and beautiful creation appears, it can never satisfy the soul's yearning to be "oned" with the One by whom all is created. No creature can ever become God for her. She cannot substitute a hazelnut for a heaven.

Julian is echoing the thought of St. Augustine here: "Thou hast made us for thyself, O Lord, and our hearts are restless until they rest in thee."[15] This was a common theme in medieval literature. Julian knows only too well that we continually grasp at what we can see, hear, taste, touch, and hold in the palm of our hands. Too often, what we seek after with such inveterate determination distracts us from the love and service of God, our ultimate destiny. Our ever increasing earthly needs and goals can mount up like a thick wall between the soul and its Creator. We think we are striving after what will make us happy until we either get it and realize it cannot satisfy our fundamental longing, or we lose it and start craving something else. Yet somehow, even though we know our wants always exceed our needs, we start the process over and over again.

Noughting

> Of this each man and woman needs to have knowing who desires to live contemplatively, that he desires to nought all things that are made in order to have the love of God that is unmade. For this is the cause why they who are occupied willfully in earthly business, and evermore seek worldly wele [being], are not completely at ease in heart and in soul: for they love and seek here rest in this thing [the hazelnut] that is so little, where no rest is in [within], and know not God, who is all mighty, all wise, and all good. For he is very [true] rest. (iv:37–43.71)

Julian discerns that all creation, even in its most awesome beauty, is only the size of a hazelnut in the sight of God. She realizes that the very "littleness" of the hazelnut (i.e., the world) shows us it is necessary to *nought* everything that is made "in order to have the love of God that is unmade." Only God is great enough to satisfy our soul's deepest desire. What does Julian mean by this word, *nought*? The word was not known before the twelfth century, when it meant, literally, "nothing."[16] In medieval mystical literature, *noughting* implied the deliberate letting go of attachment to self, as well as the renunciation of worldly goods and concerns, in order to attain a deeper spiritual union with the divine.[17] *Noughting* was the essential way of purgation, before illumination and spiritual union with God could be achieved. *Noughting* was considered a direct response to Christ's injunction:

> "If any want to become my followers, let them deny themselves and take up their cross and follow me. For those who want to save their life will lose it, and those who lose their life for my sake, and for the sake of the gospel, will save it. For what will it profit them to gain the whole world and forfeit their life?" (Mk 8:34–36, Mt 16:26)

The sense in which Julian uses the word implies a self-denial, a turning away from human selfishness and its obsession with finite, ever-changing, always-decaying goods that can distract the soul from seeking the infinite, unchangeable, and everlasting good. In modern terms, we could say *noughting* involves a negation of self-centeredness in order to become more focused on the "other," an absolutely necessary component of learning to love.[18] For Julian, it means letting go of the unnecessary in order to focus on the one thing needful (Lk 10:42).

Norwich and *Noughting*

Julian knew her bustling, materialistic, and competitive city of Norwich only too well. It is possible that much of that same restless activity had driven her own life, out of necessity. Her responsibilities for maintaining a household, being a good wife, raising a child, running a commercial business, caring for servants, family members, friends, and apprentices plus the never-ending cycle of shopping for and overseeing the preparation of meals, spinning, weaving, sewing, and bookkeeping must have kept her mind and body mired in the duties of being a working woman, yet ever aching in her heart to "live contemplatively," as she calls it . . . a life that finds its rest in God alone.

We must also consider that, at this point, Julian still believes she is about to die. She is lamenting that she has not done enough to know God in this life. Her mind is straining to try to figure out *why* her imagination perceived a hazelnut at this critical moment. What is its portent? Could it be to inspire her to hand over to God (like the hazelnut she sees herself holding in her palm) "all that is made," all that she has ever loved in this life, as well as her own body and soul, before she dies? One thing she knows for sure: at this point of death, she cannot allow herself to be bound to earth by ties of attachment, or responsibility, even human love. She must dare to become *noughted*, utterly stripped of all she holds dear, like Christ on the cross.

Yet it must be clearly noted that nowhere in her text does Julian ever denigrate love of this world, or the worthy goals for which human beings strive, the knowledge we gain, or the talents we develop and use to such creative purpose, much less the love we bear one another and the care and protection we strive to give our families and friends. Julian is most decidedly not one of those medieval mystics who urges "flight" from any and all involvement in earthly endeavors and human love as the sole means of attaining to God. Neither does she despise "homely" pleasures, as do so many of her mystical contemporaries. She does not develop a dualistic theology based on the neo-Platonic incompatibility of flesh and spirit, matter and mind. Even in later life, when she becomes an anchoress and to all appearances, "cuts herself off" from the world, she does not turn her back on her *evencristens* or their very human concerns. On the contrary, even in the midst of profound contemplative prayer, she is always readily accessible to friends, neighbors, and strangers at her anchorage window. And because of her own *self-noughting*, she becomes better able to guide their anxious, restless souls toward the God of "spiritual rest."

Julian's tone, in writing about the essential *noughting* of the spiritual life, is never disparaging, but always gentle and encouraging. She tells the reader that God "wills" to be known, and "liketh that we rest ourselves in him" (5:24–25.141). Julian will use this intimate term, "liketh" (meaning "enjoys"), often in her text. It is her way of conveying the certainty she feels that God was speaking to her mind directly, telling her what to impart to her *evencristens*. She adds that the Lord derives very great pleasure from an innocent soul that comes to him "nakedly, plainly, and homely" (5:29.141). This is the kind of *noughting* Julian means: dropping every distraction and becoming a little child again, rushing into the arms of its loving parent and resting there: "for this is the natural yearning of the soul by the touching of the holy ghost, as by the understanding that I have in this shewing" (5:29–31.141). Inspired by this meditation, Julian pours out all her heart's longing in prayer:

> God, of thy goodness give me thyself. For thou art enough to me, and I may ask nothing that is less that may be full worship to thee. And if I ask anything that is less, ever will I be wanting. But only in thee do I have all. (5:31–33.141)

Julian is sure that this petition is most comforting to the soul and completely in union with the will of Our Lord. She also tells us that the ultimate gift of God's goodness, for which she prays, extends to all his creatures and all his holy works, and will continually surpass itself for eternity. Then, again in words reminiscent of St. Augustine's, she writes:

> For he is eternity, and he has made us only for himself and restored us by his precious passion, and ever keeps [protects] us in his blessed love. And all this is of his goodness. (5:36–38.141–43)

In *noughting* herself, Julian anticipates receiving, in exchange, the boundlessness of God.

Intermediaries

And now the ordinary manner of praying comes into her mind, the way she and her *evencristens* normally have recourse to *meanes*, or intermediaries, because they do not sufficiently know or trust the limitless goodness of God. She examines the custom of calling on the Blessed Virgin and one's patron saints to intercede:

> Then I saw truly that it is more honor to God, and truer pleasure, that we faithfully pray to himself in his goodness and cleave thereto by his grace with true understanding and steadfast belief, than if we used all the meanes that heart may think. For if we use all these

> meanes, it is too little and not full worship to God. But in his goodness is all the whole, and there nothing is lacking. (6:4–8.143)

This is a bold statement. It calls into question the all-pervasive medieval devotions to saints and their shrines; the accumulation of prayers of petition and thanksgiving, the lighting of candles, the adorning of statues, the use of relics; the offering of money, gifts, jewelry, and other personal items, including wax casts of body parts that are in need of healing or that have been healed through the saints' intercession. If we read it literally, this new insight of Julian's could seem positively iconoclastic, agreeing with Wyclif's own denunciation of devotion to the saints.

However, it seems Julian is aiming at something deeper than a mere critique of excessive (and potentially superstitious) devotional practices. She certainly does not mean to deny the spiritual power of the communion of saints in heaven, forever helping, consoling, teaching, and strengthening the church here on earth. Yet, she is aware that if *evencristens* focus all their energies in prayer on devotion to the saints as intermediaries, they may fail to give "full worship to God."

Furthermore, Julian affirms that even the ability of the saints to intercede for us in heaven comes from the goodness of God. She illustrates the common medieval practice of praying to God by "his holy flesh," or "his precious blood," or "his holy passion," or "his dearworthy death and worshipful wounds" (6:9–11.143). She is struck by the fact that "all the blessed kindness and the endless life that we have because of all this, it is because of his goodness" (6:11–12.143). And if Christians pray for "his sweet mother's love that bore him," and all the help she gives us, "it is of his goodness" (6:12–13.143). And if they pray to the holy cross on which Christ died, and all the help and graces that are received from the cross, they also come from God's goodness. Likewise, all the "help that we have from special saints and from all the blessed company in heaven," as well as their love and friendship, "it is of his goodness" (6:15–18.143). She declares that the highest intermediary of all is the blessed human nature that God took from the Virgin Mary, his mother; that is, Jesus Christ himself. And all the patriarchs and prophets who came before Christ, and all the saints and martyrs who have come since, are also helpful to us because of God's goodness. Therefore, Julian does not *deny* the spiritual value of praying to the Virgin Mary and all the saints, but she stresses that all "the holy endless friendship that we have from them" (6:17.143) is precisely the overflow of God himself, working in and through all intermediaries. It is God who makes them so grace-filled.

> For the goodness of God is the highest prayer, and it comes down to us, to the lowest part of our need. It quickens [revives] our soul and brings it into life, and makes it grow in grace and virtue. It is nearest in nature and readiest in grace. For it is the same grace that the soul seeks and ever shall, til we know our God truly, who has us all in himself beclosed. (6:25–29.143)

God comes down to us in Jesus Christ, to the very smallest and most mundane of our human needs, to the level of our most basic, intimate prayer. Christ inhabits the souls of the faithful, enlivening them in baptism, pouring grace into their hearts through the sacramental life of the church, enabling them to grow in grace and virtue. Because Christ is fully human, he knows exactly what each person's emotional and spiritual requirements are at every moment. And because he is God, he can give every soul the precise help it seeks until each can know itself fully enclosed, *and clothed*, in Christ.

The Purse

Even more astonishing, Julian sees the goodness of God providing for our most basic and intimate *bodily* needs; namely, digestion and excretion. Julian considers that "a man goes upright, and the soule [food] of his body is sealed as in a very fair purse" (6:29–30.143).[19] When the time of his "necessity" comes, the purse is "opened and sealed again very cleanly" (6:31.143). And it is by the goodness of God that this is done because, as she has written above: "he comes down to us, to the lowest part of our need." Julian explains further that God does not despise anything that he has made, nor does he disdain to do us the simplest service "that belongs to our body by nature, for love of the soul that he has created to his own likeness" (6:33–35.145). She refers back to the metaphor of clothing:

> For as the body is clad in the cloth, and the flesh in the skin, and the bones in the flesh, and the heart in the bowke [chest],[20] so are we, soul and body, clad and enclosed in the goodness of God. (6:35–37.145)

How different this attitude is from that of the medieval "fasting women" who despised their bodies, starved and exhausted, beat and mutilated them, in an effort to induce "out-of-body" experiences. And how diametrically opposed to the tone of the *Ancrene Riwle* that held the body in contempt as being a *vas stercorum*, literally a "bag of shit."[21] Julian's holistic approach to the body is the polar opposite of extreme self-mortification and self-loathing as a means of reaching God. Rather, she espouses ever-increasing wonder and gratitude for the overwhelming goodness of God that reaches to every part of our bodies and to every natural human function, however lowly it may be. "Yea, and more homely!" (6:38.145); that is, God is even more intimately close to us than our own bodies. For while the body will waste and wear away, the goodness of God will remain forever whole and nearer to us than anything else we can imagine.

> For truly our lover desires that the soul cleave to him with all its might, and that we be evermore cleaving to his goodness. For of all things that the heart may think, it pleases God the most, and soonest benefits us. For our soul is so preciously loved by him that is highest, that it overpasses [transcends] the knowing of all creatures: that is to say, there is no creature that is made that may know how much and how sweetly and how tenderly our maker loves us. And therefore we may, with his grace and his help, stand in ghostly beholding, with everlasting marveling in this high, overpassing, unmeasurable love that our lord has for us because of his goodness. *And therefore we may ask of our lover, with reverence, all that we will.* For our natural will is to have God, and the good will of God is to have us, and we may never cease from willing nor from loving till we have him in fullness of joy. And then we will no more will. For he wills that we be occupied in knowing and loving till the time comes that we shall be fulfilled in heaven. (6:39–53.145, italics added)

Thus in this very first Revelation, Julian already declares what she will realize fully only in the last chapter: the "lesson of love" that all the following Revelations will show. "For the strength and the ground of all [the revelations] were shewn in the first revelation" (6:54–55.145). Julian also pauses to comment that:

> For of all things, the beholding and the loving of the creator makes the soul seem least in his own sight, and fills it most with reverent

dread and true humility, and with plenty of charity for its even-cristens. (6:55–58.145)

This, then, becomes the essence of *noughting* for Julian. When the soul learns to rest in adoration and love of the goodness of God, it does not have to perform any drastic self-mortifications to make itself feel small, humble, and insignificant. It is so overwhelmed with reverence and humility at the disparity between Creator and creature and, at the same time, so filled with an awareness of God's stupendous love that the soul actually *rejoices* in its own littleness that makes it so utterly dependent on God, like the hazelnut itself. Julian declares that the spiritual vision of Saint Mary was the best teaching she had on this point. Mary's high wisdom in contemplating God, "so great, so high, so mighty and so good," filled her with deep and "reverent dread" (7:4–5.145).[22] Even Mary, the Mother of God, conceived without sin, saw herself "so little and so low, so simple and so poor in comparison with her God, that this reverent dread filled her with meekness" (7:6–7.145). Therefore, she was made full of grace beyond any other creature. Julian sees that Mary's humility is like the hazelnut. It is her very "littleness" that makes her irresistible to God.

The Bleeding

Julian writes that all during this time, as she was considering the hazelnut and the humility of Mary in a "ghostly sight," the bodily sight continued "of the plenteous bleeding of the head" (7:10.147).

> The great drops of blood fell down from under the garland like pellets, seeming as if it had come out of the veins. And in the coming out they were brown red, for the blood was very thick. And in the spreading abroad they were bright red. And when it came out at the brows, there the drops vanished. And notwithstanding this, the bleeding continued till many things were seen and understood although the fairness and the vitality continued in the same beauty and liveliness. (7:10–16.147)

Even though the bleeding seemed inexhaustible, and could have been overwhelming, Julian was struck by its beauty and vitality. It must be clearly noted, according to Julian's testimony, that this is *not* a spiritual vision, but a realistic appearance in flesh and blood that conveys to Julian both the suffering and the inconceivable vividness of the Savior. In fact, the physical bleeding is so very graphic, so abundant, and so real, that Julian tries to compare it to other things she knew well. In their plenteousness, the drops of blood coming from the crown of thorns seem like the dripping of water from the thatched eaves of a house after a heavy rain shower, drops "that fall so thick that no man may number them with any bodily wit" (7:18–19.147). In the roundness of the drops of blood as they emerged and spread in perfect formation across the forehead, Julian is reminded of "the scales of herring" (7:19–29.147).[23] She identifies three things that the drops of blood brought to mind: pellets in the roundness of their emerging, the scales of herring in the ordered circularity of their spreading, and drops of rain in their plenteous falling. She tells us that this *shewing* was at the same time "quick [full of life] and lively, and hideous and dreadful, and sweet and lovely" (7:23–24.147).

Julian affirms that in this bleeding, as in every sight, the Lord did not mean to frighten her. Throughout, he appeared "so homely and so courteous" (7:25–26.147). And in spite of the suffering it conveyed, the vision filled her with the greatest delight and confidence within her soul. In order to meditate further on this, she was given an "open," or everyday, example about a servant who wonders what more honor and joy his noble lord could give him than to be so *homely* as to teach him, both openly and privately, the meaning of his noble words (this is the first of several allusions to a lord and a servant). The servant's heart becomes so ravished with joy that he almost forgets he is a servant, for joy of this great homeliness. "Truly, it is more joy and pleasure to me than if he gave me great gifts and was himself strange [aloof] in manner" (7:32–33.147). Like the servant she describes, Julian's heart feels that the greatest conceivable joy lies in the fact that Christ, who is "highest and mightiest, noblest and worthiest" stoops to become "lowest and meekest, homeliest and most courteous" (7:37–38.147–49). She is sure that Christ will show this marvelous joy of his familiarity to each one of us, when finally we see him in heaven.

> And our good lord wills this: that we believe and trust, rejoice and take delight in, comfort and solace ourselves, as much as we may with his grace and with his help, until the time that we see it truly. For the greatest joy that we shall have, as to my sight, is this marvelous cour-

> tesy and homeliness of our father who is our creator, in our lord Jesus Christ who is our brother and our savior. (7:39–44.149)

Julian explains that no one may know the wisdom of God the Father in this life, except by a special *shewing* of the Lord, or through an infusion of immense grace by the power of the Holy Spirit (as was given to Mary at the annunciation). Nevertheless, she is convinced that humble faith and charity will deserve such a reward eternally in heaven. And while a revelation may be made to anyone to whom God wishes to show himself in order to illuminate private points pertaining to the faith, Julian asserts that this private *shewing* urges the very same faith that is taught to everyone in the open by the church. This is especially true, because, as Julian admits, when the time of the *shewing* was completed (and she could no longer see the Lord in the flesh), it was precisely her faith that preserved it, by the grace of the Holy Spirit, until the end of her life.

Space and Time

Julian sums up this first Revelation by saying she came to understand six things: the "tokens" of the blessed passion in the symbol of the crown of thorns and the abundant shedding of Christ's blood;[24] the worthiness of the maiden who is Christ's mother; the blissful trinitarian Godhead "that ever was and is and shall be; all mighty, all wisdom, and all love" (8:7–8.149); everything that God has made (symbolized by the hazelnut) that is "great and large and fair and good" (8:10.151), even though it appears so insignificant in the presence of the Creator who made it; that all things are made out of love and by that same love are sustained without end; and finally, that "God is all things that are good, as to my sight. And the goodness that all things have, it is he" (8:16–17.151).

> And all this our lord shewed in the first sight, and gave me space and time to behold it. And the bodily sight stinted [ceased], and the ghostly sight dwelled in my understanding. And I abode with reverent dread, rejoicing in what I saw, and desiring as I dared to see more, if it were his will, or for a longer time, the same. (8:18–21.151)

At this point, Julian was also greatly moved in love toward her *evencristens*, no doubt those who were taking care of her during her illness, as well as all those who came to her mind. She longed for them to be able to see and know what she was seeing so that they, too, might be comforted. Julian was convinced that the vision was not given to her "specially," or because she had suffered patiently, or as a reward for any good service done in her lifetime. The vision was meant in general, for everyone. She felt that she was merely a conduit, a messenger of the gospel.

Perhaps because the physical sight of Christ's bleeding head has just ceased, Julian feels able, for a moment, to reach out to those in the room around her.

> Then I said to those who were with me: "It is today domesday for me." And this I said for I expected to have died. For that day that a man or woman dies, he is deemed as he shall be without end, as to my understanding. This I said for I would they loved God the better, in order to make them be mindful that this life is short, as they might see in my example. For in all this time I thought to have died. And that was a marvel to me and partially a grief, for it seemed to me this vision was shewn for them that should live. (8:24–30.151–53)

Here again Julian reiterates her conviction that she is about to die. She wishes she could have revealed her vision, with its loving reverberations, to the womenfolk gathered around her bed. But she could not at this point, so she cries out, in essence: "I'm dying. Take heed! Life is short! You will die soon, too!" What a shock it must have been for the other women to hear Julian declare her impending day of doom. Julian seems to be referring to the *particular* judgment that the church taught would take place for every soul immediately after death. As we have seen in the passion plays, the much-feared Domesday was actually the *last* judgment, when Christ would appear and receive those into eternal glory who had welcomed, clothed, and given food and drink to the stranger, visited the sick and imprisoned, while condemning to hell those who had failed to do these things: "Then he will answer them, 'Truly I tell you, just as you did not do it to one of the least of these, you did not do it to me'" (Mt 25:45). Julian felt an imperative, not only for those who were in the room at the time of her visions, but as she wrote her account years later, for her future readers as well. She wants it understood that anything she says about herself or about what the Lord revealed to her personally is meant to apply to all her *evencristens.*

> And therefore, I pray you all for God's sake, and counsel you for your own profit, that you leave the beholding of a wretch who it was shewn to, and mightily, wisely and meekly contemplate God who of his courteous love and endless goodness would shew it generally in comfort of us all. *For it is God's will that you take it with as great joy and delight as if Jesus had shewn it to you.* (8:33–38.153, italics added)

Julian implores her readers to make all the Revelations extremely personal, to take them to heart and to be attentive to their true meaning. She wants us to see and hear the *shewings* "as if" they had been revealed directly to each and every one of us, not only to her. She remarks further that she is not good simply because she was gifted with a visionary experience, but only if she loves God better because of it. Likewise, if her readers love God better because of the Revelations, then the visions could apply even more to us than to herself. Julian is not addressing those who are learned and wise, but rather she is speaking to the commonfolk here: "you who are simple, for ease and comfort" (9:3.153). She includes those who never think of themselves as "worthy" of receiving God's extraordinary graces. "For we are all one in love" (9:3–4.153). Julian insists that she was never shown that God loved her any better "than the least soul who is in the state of grace" (9:5.153). In fact, Julian is *seker*, absolutely certain, that "there are many who never had a shewing nor sight but of the common teaching of holy church who love God better than I" (9:5–7.153–55).

Once again, Julian reveals her disarming honesty and profound humility. She is not boasting of being chosen by God for particular favors. She knows herself to be but a "sinful creature" (vi:4.73). This lack of pride bears witness to the truth of her Revelations throughout her book. She does not want the reader to think highly of *her*, but only of God. Julian firmly believes that if she looks within herself, she is "right nought," truly nothing at all (9:7.155). Even though she regards herself as nothing, Julian hopes that she is one in charity with all her *evencristens.*

> For in this oneness stands the life of all mankind that shall be saved. For God is all that is good, as to my sight, and God has made all that is made, and God loves all that he has made. And he who generally loves all his evencristens for God, he loves all that is. For in mankind that shall be saved is comprehended all: that is to say, all

> that is made and the maker of all. For in man is God, and in God is all. And he who loves thus, he loves all. (9:8–14.155)

In this passage, Julian states her firm belief that all who will be saved (*whoever* they may be) are one in God. And he (or she) who loves all *evencristens* for God's sake, in fact loves all that is, for God dwells in every man, woman, and child. This in itself is a bold statement. Is Julian suggesting that all who love shall be saved? Julian quickly clarifies that "I speak of them that shalle be saved because in this time God shewed me no other" (9:16–17.155–57). She was never taught in her visions about what might happen to those Christians who died in mortal sin, nor about non-Christians and pagans, nor was she ever given a vision of any souls in purgatory or in hell.

Them That Shalle Be Saved

Julian's frequent use of the phrase, "them that shalle be saved," seems to imply that some, but not all, will be saved. Thus she raises the problematic belief in predestination. Throughout the ages, just what predestination means has been much debated. Since this teaching on predestination will become an underlying theme in Julian's book (and the phrase, "them that shalle be saved," will recur twenty-five times in her writing),[25] it is worthwhile to examine it further. St. Paul's epistle to the Romans raised the issue by saying:

> We know that all things work together for good for those who love God, who are called according to his purpose. *For those whom he foreknew he also predestined* to be conformed to the image of his Son, in order that he might be the firstborn within a large family. And those whom he predestined he also called; and those whom he called he also justified; and those whom he justified he also glorified. (Rom 8:28–30, italics added)

Likewise, we read in the epistle to the Ephesians:

> Blessed be the God and Father of our Lord Jesus Christ, who has blessed us in Christ with every spiritual blessing in the heavenly places, *just as he chose us in Christ before the foundation of the world to be holy and blameless before him in love.* He destined us for adoption as his children through Jesus Christ, according to the good pleasure of his will... (Eph 1:3–5, italics added)

While acknowledging the providence of God in preordaining all things, the early church fathers upheld the idea that the human will remained free to choose good and to avoid evil for the sake of salvation. St. Augustine agreed that the essential freedom to choose good or evil did not perish with original sin; however, humanity no longer had the complete freedom to be righteous as Adam was before the fall.[26] In his writings against the Pelagians (who denied that original sin had impaired the will's freedom to choose the good), Augustine argued that the human will had been so *damaged* by original sin that it had lost the total freedom it once enjoyed. After the fall, it was beyond the capacity of the will to perform the good actions necessary for eternal life. The will could no longer turn toward God of its own accord and freely choose the good; in fact, even though the will remained free in principle, Augustine claimed it would incline more readily to evil than to good.[27]

In order to choose the good, then, the will requires a *direct infusion of sanctifying grace* from God: "But to believe in Christ belongs to faith, and none can believe in him, that is, come to him, unless this gift has been given to them."[28] Augustine defines the active nature of this grace, a grace that was fully operative in the soul of Julian: ". . . God produces in the hearts of human beings, not merely *revelations that are true*, but also *wills that are good*. He does this not through the law and teachings that strike our ears from the outside, but by his marvelous and ineffable power that is internal and hidden."[29] Grace, then, actually implies the indwelling of the Holy Spirit. Augustine believed that without this divine gift, this intervention of grace, which is first received through baptism and then sustained through the life of the sacraments, no one could even *desire* to choose the good. In fact, according to Augustine, without the grace of mercy that spares the saved from the just condemnation of God, all Adam's descendants would deserve to be one *massa damnata* (literally, a "lump," or mass, of perdition).[30]

Grace, for Augustine, became the indispensable enabling power that operates within the soul to direct it to do what is right and to avoid what is wrong. Grace does not stifle or take away the free choice of the will (a person can always refuse to receive it, or fall from grace-once-given); rather, if accepted, grace empowers the will's fragile freedom and perfects it. By cooperating with grace, the individual can freely choose the very end for which he or she was created: eternal life in God. And when the will acts in accordance with a divine infusion of grace, good works may be done with great ease, the utmost pleasure, and will merit a heavenly reward. Then the will delights more in doing good works than in evil ones. It begins to enjoy *libertas*, true freedom.[31] Thereafter, it becomes incumbent upon the individual to persevere in living a good life in faith, hope, and charity, in accordance with the directives of the church, in order to partake in the redemption of Jesus Christ.

Predestination

St. Augustine further argued that since God is all-good and the soul is made only for God, the only truly *free* choice is precisely to choose the good. And God alone knows who will do so. Since God is omniscient, God has total foreknowledge of all that will happen in the course of human history, who will be saved and who will be damned. Does God's foreknowledge take away the freedom of the individual to choose? According to Augustine, absolutely not. Each person is free to accept or reject God's grace and to perform good or evil works. However, Augustine taught that God prepares the wills of those God knows in advance will freely respond to his call and motivates them to make the right choices and to perform the good works they truly desire to perform.[32] He writes:

> Would anyone dare to say that God did not foreknow those to whom he would give the gift of believing, or whom he would give to his son, so that he should lose none of them? This and nothing else is the predestination of the saints, namely the foreknowledge and the preparation of God's kindnesses, whereby the Elect are most certainly delivered, whoever they are that are delivered.[33]

St. Thomas Aquinas also taught that God does indeed predestine since everything that happens is under the control of his Divine Providence which directs all that exists toward its proper end. This end, Thomas writes, is twofold: one that is proportionate to the created nature (and may be reached by human powers), and one that *exceeds* the possibilities of created nature (that is, life eternal and the vision of God which, according to Thomas, is above the capacity of every creature). Since human nature cannot possibly attain to the vision of God and eternal life by the power of its own fallen nature, then humanity must be directed to this ultimate end by God, in whom the reason for that direction pre-exists. Only God can place in the mind of rational creatures a desire for life eternal and this, for Aquinas, is called predestination. "For to destine is to send. Thus it is that predestination, as regards its object, is a part of providence."[34]

Well might we ask, if Christ died on the cross for the salvation of *all* (2 Cor 5:15), does not God desire "everyone to be saved and to come to the knowledge of the truth" (1 Tm 2:4)? If so, then why does God's providence not direct *every* soul toward eternal life by intervening with sanctifying grace just at the moment a person might sin mortally, to prevent that soul from being damned? That, theologians argue, would be to undermine the individual's freedom of will to choose between good and evil. And St. Augustine is firm that, since the gifts and graces of God are neither the natural *right* of humankind nor the *reward* of human effort, they cannot be demanded or earned.

Yet the question persists: how is it that the apostle Peter is given the grace of repentance after he denies three times that he knows Christ, and then becomes head of the church, while Judas Iscariot, the betrayer, falls into total despair and hangs himself? How is it that some people are born into faith in Jesus Christ and others never hear his name preached their whole life long? Why do some criminals repent and remake their lives, while others do not? Augustine would answer:

> Furthermore, who is so irreligious and foolish as to say that God cannot turn to good any of the evil wills of men he wishes, when and where he wishes? When he does this, he does it by mercy, and when he does not do it, it is by judgment that he does not do it, since *he has mercy on whomever he chooses, and he hardens the heart of whomever he chooses* (Rom 9:18).[35]

Augustine admits that the reason why God gives the gift of salvific grace to some and not to others is simply beyond human knowledge: "But as to why [God] sets free this person rather than that one, *his judgments are inscrutable and his ways unsearchable* (Rom 11:33)."[36] To the end of his life, Augustine remained convinced that God had long ago decreed "an unshakeable number of the Elect" who shall be saved, and that the true sons of God had been "permanently inscribed in the archive of the Father,"[37] a number precisely equal to the number of angels that had fallen from grace.

This is the general doctrine of predestination Julian would have heard preached since childhood. It is all the more astonishing then, that she will dare to develop her own nuanced interpretation of God's foreknowledge as the most tender and maternal providence that loved humanity before he created it, and that continually works, through mercy and grace, to save and not condemn. This compassionate and inclusive teaching would be based entirely on her vivid experience of Christ on the cross.

Protestation of Orthodoxy

Julian affirms that during the whole time of her visions, she always clung fast to the faith that had been instilled in her from an early age.

> But in all things I believe as holy church preaches and teaches. For the faith of holy church, which I had beforehand understood—and, as I hope, by the grace of God willfully kept in use and custom—remained continually in my sight, willing and meaning never to receive anything that might be contrary thereto. And with this intent and with this meaning I beheld the shewing with all my diligence. For in all this blessed shewing I beheld it as one in God's meaning. (9:17–23.157)

Julian was well aware that demons might try to tempt her away from orthodox belief at the very moment she was receiving these blessed Revelations from Christ. If she saw or heard anything that suggested she abandon any teaching of the church, she was certain it would have been a grave sin to do so. She must remain constantly on her guard. She has held on to the faith through years of conflict and tragedy. She will not reject or leave it now. And she cannot believe it possible that the Lord would show her anything contrary to his own revealed truth.

One wonders, however, if Julian is stating her case rather insistently here, in order to declare her total orthodoxy on all aspects of Christian faith before she discloses the rest of her Revelations (or perhaps at the later suggestion of a confessor or spiritual guide). As we have discussed, the Church repeatedly warned that a vision or message from God could be judged true only if it was not "inclined to any error of holy church, of the faith, or any wonder or new thing."[38] By strongly affirming that she is a faithful daughter of Holy Church, Julian places this, and every *shewing*, within the context of official church doctrine. She sees the insights of the Revelations and her faith in orthodox teachings as never being contradictory, but "as one in God's meaning." Nonetheless, there will be occasions when the *apparent dichotomy* between what the Lord was showing her in the Revelations and the way in which church doctrine was currently being preached would cause Julian great personal anxiety.

Julian completes this section by reiterating that she was shown everything in three distinct modes: "that is to say, by bodily sight, and by words formed in my understanding, and by ghostly sight" (9:24–25.157). She admits that the ghostly, or spiritual, sights cannot and may not be told as openly or as fully as she would have liked. She simply cannot find words to convey what is beyond words. But Julian trusts in the Lord, that because of his goodness and his love of the reader, he must "make you to take it more ghostly and more sweetly than I can or may tell it" (9:27–28.157). She is about to record her astounding Second Revelation.

13
The Passion

The Second Revelation

> And after this, I saw with bodily sight in the face of the crucifix that hung before me, in which I beheld continually a part of his passion: contempt, spitting, soiling, and buffeting, and many languring [exhausting] pains, more than I can tell, and often changing of color. And one time I saw how half the face, beginning at the ear, was spread over with dried blood till it beclosed the middle of his face. And after that the other half was beclosed in the same way, and thereafter it vanished in this part, even as it came. (10:1–7.157–159)

This new vision of the shame and brutality of Christ's sufferings includes aspects of the scourging and the crowning with thorns prior to the crucifixion. Julian observes that the flow of blood has become so thickly clotted that it completely encloses first one side, then the other, of Christ's face. Perhaps his head, hanging down to the right side, turns in anguish to the left and then falls again to the right, as the blood blinds his eyes and pours into his nose and mouth and coagulates on his skin and beard. His skin changes color as his bodily fluids are being poured out and death approaches. His arms and legs, hands and feet become mottled, purplish, then turn bluish-white. His lips and nails, if not caked in dried brown blood, appear blackened.

The gruesome experience is so intense that Julian cannot describe the many impressions it has on her. She simply attests that she saw this sight of the passion "bodily, sorrowfully, and obscurely," not with the exultant joy she first had in seeing Christ come to life before her eyes (10:8.159). Now she is watching Christ die an agonized death. Yet even as she is totally involved in the hyper-reality of the vision, she has not lost touch with where she is. She is fully aware that the increasing darkness in the bedroom around the area of the cross is preventing her from observing the vision as fully as she would have liked. She desires "more bodily light" to be able to see Christ's face more clearly (10:8.159):

> And I was answered in my reason: "If God will show thee more, he shall be thy light. Thou needeth none but him." (10:9–10.159)

Whereas before a "natural light" had shone on the cross, now all around Julian is darkened, as on Calvary: "From noon on, darkness came over the whole land until three in the afternoon" (Mt 27:45). She is straining to define Christ's Holy Face, even in its disfiguration. She wants to see better, behold longer. Once again, Julian's impetuous nature almost leads her into presumption. But her reason warns her that she may be asking too much. She must submit her intense longing to God's desire. If it is his will, he will show her more . . . and more clearly. If not, she must count on him and him alone to be her "light" and inner vision.

Seeing and Seeking

> For I saw him and sought him. For we are now so blind and so unwise that we can never seek God till that time that he of his goodness shows himself to us. And when we see anything of him graciously, then we are stirred by the same grace to seek with great desire to see him more blissfully. And thus I saw him and sought him, and I had him and wanted him. And this is and should be our common werking in this life, as to my sight. (10:10–15.159)

Julian is full of gratitude for what she sees, but also feels unbearable longing for what she cannot see. It strikes her that, because of human blindness and lack of wisdom, even the initial desire to seek God must come through his goodness already revealing itself to the soul before the soul knows how to ask. This is the work of what has been called "prevenient grace." And then, when the soul "sees" a little, it may be stirred by grace to see and seek even more. Julian must have known that Christ had said to his followers: "Ask, and it will be given you; search, and you will find; knock, and the door will be opened for you. For everyone who asks receives, and everyone who searches finds, and for everyone who knocks, the door will be opened" (Mt 7:7–8, Lk 11:9–10). What she had not realized before was that it is *God's own goodness* that impels the soul to ask, to search, to knock. She understands that this is the way the spiritual path must always proceed: forever seeking and seeing, then *not* seeing (or losing), and seeking again. She admits that even in her vision when she "saw him," she continued to seek him. And when she "had him" visibly before her, she "wanted him" even more.

There is great significance in the fact that while Julian tells us what she sees, she never mentions what she wanted *to do* in response to beholding her Savior before her eyes. Julian must have felt like Magdalene whose initial impulse was to throw herself at the feet of the risen Lord and embrace him, holding on to him with all her might. Yet she was told:

> Do not hold on to me, because I have not yet ascended to the Father. But go to my brothers and say to them, "I am ascending to my Father and your Father, to my God and your God." (Jn 20:17)

Julian, too, is physically prevented from reaching out and touching the suffering Christ on the cross before her... from grasping his feet with both her hands... from wiping off the clotted blood and mud with her tears and drying his feet with her hair... from offering a veil, like Veronica, to cleanse his face. She feels paralyzed, not by her illness, but by the very nature of the vision itself. She can only look on her Lord and receive as much or as little as he wishes to reveal to her. She is so close to seeing him totally, "to have and to hold," as in the marriage vow. Yet she knows the vision may disappear momentarily and she will not have seen it well enough to last a lifetime. Will he appear to her again? Will she ever touch him? She is like the distraught bride in the Song of Songs:

> Upon my bed at night I sought him whom my soul loves; I sought him, but found him not; I called him, but he gave no answer. "I will rise now and go about the city, in the streets and in the squares; I will seek him whom my soul loves." I sought him, but found him not. (Sg 3:1–2)

The Sea Ground

In the midst of describing her spiritual conflict of seeing and seeking (and yet not being able to touch), Julian suddenly recalls another experience:

> One time my understanding was led down into the sea ground, and there I saw green hills and dales, seeming as it were overgrown with moss, with debris and gravel. Then I understood thus: that if a man or woman were there, under the brode water, and he might have sight of God—since God is with a man continually—he should be safe in soul and body, and take no harm. And even more, he should have more solace and comfort than all this world may or can tell. (10:16–22.159)

At first it seems like a non sequitur, to leave the seeing and the seeking of Christ on the cross and dive down in her imagination to the depths of the sea floor under the Norfolk "brode water." (This diversion may have been a reflective entry that Julian inserted at a later date. Or it may have been intimately connected to the vision at this very moment.) All Julian tells us is that "one time" her understanding was led down into the bottom of the sea, as if she had dropped from a great height into the darkness of the abyss. Still, what Julian is imagining here (in a "ghostly" vision, not a physical one) is an extreme case of seeking God in impossible circumstances, a case with which she would have been familiar: drowning. Growing up, Julian must have feared the storms and giant waves that rose up from the North Sea and inundated the marshlands, causing the Wensum River to overflow its banks, sweeping houses and families away in a sudden rush of floodwaters up and down the coastline. She must have heard about fishermen who had drowned in the sea, as well as sailors and soldiers lost in the English Channel while crossing to and from France. She herself may have had a great terror of drowning, since few people in the Middle Ages knew how to swim. Deadly stories of the dangers of the sea were the stuff of nightmares for children and grownups alike.

All the more amazing, then, that Julian discovers that even when being "led down" by a spiritual vision into this dreaded "sea ground," she still finds God there, since God is ever-present within the soul. She feels a sweet bliss that nothing could come between her Savior and herself, and she is quite certain she would be safe "in soul and body, and take no harm" even should she drown. We must remember that at this point in her Revelations, Julian is still anticipating her own imminent death. She seems to be testing the waters, quite literally. What will death be like: drowning, falling down, down, down into the bottomless seabed? Her immediate realization is that she feels *absolutely no fear* at the prospect, but only solace, because wherever her soul goes, God will be there.

There is another "sea ground" Julian intimates here, that of meditation in the fathomless depths of God's presence where there is "more solace and comfort than all this world may or can tell." If we read this passage as her awareness of "one time" being led down into the "ground" of her own being, there in the primordial sea where all life is spawned, we may perceive that Julian is opening up her Revelations to us on many levels at once. She is seeing and hearing *both* fleshly and ghostly. She is experiencing and contemplating the specific objects she is being shown (a hazelnut, clothing, drops of blood, the depths of the sea ground) at an imaginative *and* a mystical level. Her mind is being guided, through these sequential meditations, into ever deeper caverns of single-pointed concentration to prepare her for what is yet to be revealed.

> For he [God] wills that we believe that we see him continually, though we think that it be but little, and in this belief he makes us evermore to gain grace. For he will be seen, and he will be sought, and he will be abiden [waited for] and he will be trusted. (10:22–24.159)

In reliving this extraordinary inner journey years later, Julian feels compelled to tell the reader (as if speaking to us, face to face) that it is God's will that "we believe we see him continually" in every aspect of our lives: in *this* blessed event, in *this* hard labor, in *this* triumph, in *this* disappointment, in *this* falling in love, in *this* birth, in *this* betrayal, in *this* illness or accident, in *this* tragic occurrence, here and now. Under normal circumstances, we do not do this by having extra-sensory visions, but only by the inner sight of persevering faith. She explains further that even though we may think our faith is "but little" and wavering, fragile and sometimes sorely tested, yet through the constant practice of daring to believe in God's presence when it is hardest to do so we will gain great grace. Julian is adamant that God wants to be seen (implying an eternal desire to reveal himself), and he wants to be sought (suggesting that he wishes us to find him), and he wants to be waited for, longed for, and expected. And, perhaps most of all, he wants to be *trusted*. Every day Julian had prayed in the *Pater Noster*: "Thy will be done." Now she is beginning to understand what that Divine Will really desires.

Great Travail

There is something else occurring in Julian's mind now: confusion. The outlines of the vision are becoming blurred, the details appearing less and less certain. Julian begins to be in "great travail," or uncertainty, about whether, in fact, "this second *shewing*" is indeed a *shewing* at all. It was "so low and so little and so simple," so basic, that her spirit became troubled in the process of the "mourning, dreading and longing" that filled her heart as she meditated on the passion. "For I was sometimes in a fear whether it was a shewing or not" (10:25–27.159).

Is Julian feeling doubt, a doubt that will return with a vengeance later on, concerning the authenticity of what she is, in fact, *seeing*: Christ suffering on the cross? Yet Julian's confusion seems only natural for someone who does not think herself worthy of such an extraordinary grace. She considers herself more like the *evencristens* who never receive visions than a mystic who might. Perhaps she is even afraid that, in the process of dying, her mind is indeed playing tricks on her because of her great longing to "see" the Lord in the flesh. Julian's nature, even during a protracted death meditation, always seems to question, examine, review, analyze, lest she convey an impression or give an interpretation that is not fully truthful. Hence, her admission here (preserved even in the later recording of her visions) of momentary doubt. Yet almost immediately, she reassures us:

> And then diverse times our lord gave me more sight whereby I understood truly that it was a shewing. It was a figure and a likeness of our foul, black, dead skin which our fair, bright, blessed lord bore for our sinne. (10:27–30.159)

Perhaps this is the source of her confusion. Because Christ's face looked so much like the "foul, black, dead skin" of those dying of the Great Pestilence, she was convinced that she had conflated all the terrible deaths she had seen in her lifetime with the one that the Lord was enduring before her eyes. Her mind recoiled from having to view again the foulness, the blackness, the deadness of the sloughed-off skin of those she had seen dying. She began to doubt whose death she was actually "seeing." She realized Christ was suffering all those other deaths when he endured his own death on the cross. All the dying were present in Christ's dying. Christ's "foul, black, dead skin" becomes, for Julian, the skin of all humankind.

The Holy Vernicle

Julian is reminded of the Holy Vernicle (that is, Veronica's veil, which we have encountered in a scene from the passion play). According to a legend dating from the late fourth century, an unknown woman (named Veronica after the event), felt such compassion for Christ as he carried his cross on the way to Calvary that she wiped the blood and sweat from his face with her own veil. It was later believed that, in gratitude, Christ imprinted the image of his suffering face on the cloth.[1] Though documented as a relic from 1011 CE and residing in the Vatican, the Vernicle, or "true image" (from the Latin *vera icona* or the Greek *eikon*), only came to be identified with the passion account in the fourteenth century. In the Holy Year of 1300, the Vernicle was displayed to the public in St. Peter's Basilica and was acclaimed as one of the wonders of Rome. Authentic or not, it had a powerful impact on those who made a pilgrimage to view it. Julian must have heard details from travelers who had actually beheld the image, which seemed to appear or disappear as well as to change color at different times of the day, depending on how the light might strike it. Perhaps Julian had even seen paintings depicting the Vernicle. It was certainly revered as one of the holiest relics in Christianity, because it was believed to have touched Christ's face and retained traces of his blood and sweat. Yet Julian wonders how the face of the Son of God could appear so horribly disfigured.

> Of the brownness and the blackness, piteousness and leanness of this image, many marveled how that might be, understanding that he portrayed it with his blessed face, which is the beauty of heaven, flower of earth, and the fruit of the maiden's womb. Then how might this image be so discolored and so far from beauty? I desire to say as I have understood by the grace of God. (10:32–37.159)

Imago Dei

Julian begins her explanation by referring again to the Trinity, reminding her *evencristens* that

> We know in our faith and in our belief, by the teaching and the preaching of holy church, that the blessed trinity made mankind to his image and to his likeness. (10:38–39.159)

This ancient teaching derives from the creation account in Genesis:

> Then God said, "Let us make humankind in our image, according to our likeness; and let them have dominion over the fish of the sea, and over the birds of the air, and over the cattle, and over all the wild animals of the earth, and over every creeping thing that creeps upon the earth." So God created humankind in his image, in the image of God he created them; male and female he created them. (Gn 1:26–27)

Medieval theologians taught that the "image" of God (*Imago Dei*) resides in the human being's powers of reason and free will, which reflect God's own infinite wisdom and divine will. This image is imprinted on the soul at creation and can never be erased, since it is the very essence of what defines a human being. The "likeness" was considered by St. Irenaeus in the second century as a spiritual endowment, a ***donum superadditum***: supernatural attributes given ***on top of nature***, to enable the human being to be more like God. These are the moral virtues.[2] The "likeness" is what makes a human person whole, holy, and capable of being divinized. It is also the "likeness" that could be, and most certainly was, stained and lost by sin, beginning with the fall (Gn 3:1–24). Julian briefly summarizes the well-known biblical story in which "man fell so deep and so wretchedly by sinne, there was no other help to restore man but through him that created man," that is, by the Creator (10:40–41.161). She adds that, with the same love by which God created mankind, so he would restore it to the same bliss, even "overpassing [transcending]" the state of happiness humankind had enjoyed in the beginning (10:41–43.161).

> And right as we were made like to the trinity in our first making [creation], our maker willed that we should be like to Jesus Christ, our savior in heaven without end, by the virtue of our re-making. (10:43–45.161)

However, this could only happen at the greatest possible cost.

> Then between these two makings he would, for love and for honor of mankind, make himself as like to man in this deadly life, in our foulness and in our wretchedness, as man might be without guilt. Whereof it means, as is said before: "It was the image and the likeness of our foule, black, dead skin" wherein our fair, bright, blessed lord hid his godhead. (10:46–50.161)

Through this concise account, Julian explains why the Lord, who was deemed the most beautiful man who ever lived, had to become radically changed by "travail and sorrow, passion and dying," as pictured in her vision and in the Vernicle (10:52.161). In St. Paul's words, "For our sake he made him to be sin who knew no sin, so that in him we might become the righteousness of God" (2 Cor 5:21). Therefore, Christ on the cross was seen to be the ugliest of men, disfigured by the effects of humanity's sin. Long before, the prophet Isaiah had written:

> For he grew up before him [God] like a young plant, and like a root out of dry ground; he had no form or majesty that we should look at him, nothing in his appearance that we should desire him. He was despised and rejected by others; a man of suffering and acquainted with infirmity; and as one from whom others hide their faces he was despised, and we held him of no account. Surely he has borne our infirmities and carried our diseases; yet we accounted him stricken, struck down by God, and afflicted. But he was wounded for our transgressions, crushed for our iniquities; upon him was the punishment that made us whole, and by his bruises we are healed. All we like sheep have gone astray; we have all turned to our own way, and the Lord has laid on him the iniquity of us all. (Is 53:2–6)

Atonement Theory

Julian's teaching in this section is based on the medieval atonement theory of St. Anselm (1033–1109), which was developed to explain *why God became man*. While Julian could not have read Anselm's Latin text, she would have heard this theory preached year in and year out, as it was the most common explanation of why the incarnation of Christ was necessary. According to Anselm, when Adam disobeyed God's commandment not to eat of the tree of knowledge of good and evil, his sin was so dire (because he, a man, had dared to set his own will in opposition to the divine will and thus offended the supreme dignity of Almighty God) that no mere mortal could ever make restitution to God for the deadly offense. Through this initial disobedience, all of mankind that followed Adam had incurred a "debt" to Divine Justice that it could never repay: original sin. Only God could atone to God for his offended honor and make satisfaction for human sin. According to Anselm's theory, God was compelled by his own love to send his only-begotten Son to earth as a sinless man to take on the debt of sin, to repair the offense to the Father through his perfect obedience on the cross, and to restore humanity to its original likeness to God. Anselm held that Christ's death not only *repaid* the debt of original sin and *repaired* the injustice done to Divine Justice, but, because it was free and voluntary, *provided superabundant satisfaction* to God: "His merits are infinite, hence superabundant and available for man's rescue" and "his death outweighs the number and greatness of all sins."[3] And again: "The life of this Man was so exalted and so precious, that it may suffice to pay what is due for the sins of the whole world, and infinitely more."[4] This, perhaps, is the cause for the "overpassing" bliss to which Julian has referred (10:41–43.161).

The view of sin-as-debt that can only be redeemed by an appropriate suffering pervades medieval church teaching. The concept of a "just punishment due to sin" extended to every mortal or venial sin a person might commit. In order to be forgiven, the penitent needed to be truly sorry for the offense and then confess the sin(s) to a priest, who acted in the person of Christ to show mercy. If the penitent was deemed by the priest to be heartily sorry, the priest recited the words of absolution,[5] and then the penitent had to carry out, to the best of his or her ability, the penance prescribed for the offense and recommended by the priest. These penances were often done publicly, such as appearing in the marketplace wearing only a tunic and covered in ashes, sitting motionless for days in the public stocks, being submerged in a bucket of cold water, walking barefoot in procession around the parish, fasting and begging for mercy at the door of the church, or even being flogged within the cathedral.

Some penances needed to be public, not only as a warning to others of the wages of sin but also because sin was seen to be an offense against one's neighbor as well as God. Hence, during the Lenten season of penitence, the priest might accompany the penitent to his enemy's door to ask forgiveness. Financial debts had to be repaid, restitution of land, sheep, cattle, or crops had to be made, and brother reunited with brother, if pardon was to be complete. If a murder was committed, a debt had to be paid to the victim's family. If a theft, likewise. Besides the usual Advent and Lenten periods of prayer, solemn penance, and fasting, going on pilgrimage was often demanded to reduce the time spent in purgatory to satisfy the "just punishment" for the offense. This pilgrimage could be to a saint's tomb, or even, if the offense had been severe (such as heresy or apostasy), all the way to Rome or Jerusalem. Penance was seen as a *communal* sacrament, even if the actual sins were confessed in private. And it was well known that the priests consulted manuals that prescribed certain penances for certain sins. No one was immune, except perhaps a wife who had confessed her act of adultery to a priest and who might be sorely beaten and disfigured by her husband if he found out the reason she was doing public penance. In such a case, the priest was advised to give her a private penance, like fasting before feastdays, to save her life and limb.[6] Even the rich and powerful had to promise to make just amends in order to receive absolution.

Seek, Suffer, and Trust

> And this vision was a teaching to my understanding that the continual seeking of the soul pleases God very greatly. For it [the soul] may do no more than seek, suffer, and trust. And this is wrought in every soul that has it by the holy ghost. And the clearness of finding, it is because of his special grace when it is his will. The seeking with faith, hope and charity pleases our lord, and the finding pleases the soul, and fulfills it with joy. (10:57–62.161)

After an examination of the cause of Christ's disfigurement, Julian returns to her theme of seeking and seeing. She reiterates her understanding that God wants the soul to keep seeking even if, and especially when, it is "in travail" (which can also mean "in labor," as a woman labors to give birth). At these times the soul does not feel God's presence, yet it must continue to seek and walk by faith through the "dark nights." Julian considers this "seeking" of God every bit as important as "seeing." And she is sure that God will show himself to the soul through a special grace if it is patient, and when it is the Divine Will to do so. Then God himself will teach the soul how to "have" him in a graced contemplation. And this beholding is the highest honor and reverence human beings can give to God, and extremely profitable to souls, producing the greatest humility and virtue, "with the grace and leading of the holy ghost" (10:67– 68.161). For the soul "that only fastens itself onto God with true trust, either in seeking or in beholding," gives him "the most worship" (10:68–69.161). Julian defines two distinct *werkings* that become apparent from this vision and its attendant revelation. One is seeking, the other beholding. Seeking is the common lot, given as a grace to all by the teachings of holy church. Beholding, or mystical seeing, however, is only in the provenance of God.

Julian also considers three aspects of seeking which are conducive to seeing. First, one must seek willfully and diligently, without becoming lazy, disheartened, or depressed by the effort. Rather, one must seek "gladly and merrily, without unskillful heaviness and vain sorrow" (10:75–76.161). It is notable that Julian gives an inkling here of her own lifelong battles against these very human tendencies to sloth, depression, and sorrow. She knows only too well that such often self-indulgent moods are not those that will most please God and give him worship. She goes so far as to call them "unskillful," meaning unreasonable, unproductive, and even destructive of the spiritual life. How different her approach is from those "fasting women" and self-flagellants who deliberately induced starvation, physical exhaustion, and self-mutilation, courting chronic sadness of mood. For Julian, the true seeker is a glad-hearted and hope-filled soul, not because it is free from suffering, but because it trusts in the One it seeks. Such a person comes to believe that the Ultimate Answer to every *Why?*... loves us.

The second way of seeking is that "we abide [wait for] him steadfastly because of his love, without grumbling and striving against him unto our life's end, for it shall last but a while" (10:76–78.161–63). Julian warns her fellow seekers that grumbling against God is to be avoided at all costs. (The onomatopoeic Middle English word she uses is *gruching*, very close to "grouching.") That, and "striving against him" (which would be outright disobedience) are deadly to seeing.

The third way of seeking is that "we trust in him mightily, with full, seker faith" (10:78–79.163). The Middle English word *seker*, which Julian uses repeatedly in her text, connotes *absolute security* that the soul is protected from all danger, is not at any risk, is spiritually safe, and is even among the already saved.

> For it is his will that we know that he shall appear suddenly and blissfully to all his lovers. For his werking is private, and he wants to be perceived, and his appearing shall be very sudden. And he wants to be believed, for he is very pleasant, homely, and courteous. Blessed may he be! (10:79–82.163)

Julian ends this section with the promise that these three ways of seeking will have blissful results, when one is least expecting them. God will work in the soul in a secret manner, yet his own great desire to be perceived and to be believed will make him suddenly appear (not necessarily in a vision, but by granting a spiritual sense of his intimate presence). And then the soul that has been seeking, suffering, and trusting will, for a suspended time, be filled with joy, as was Julian.

The Third Revelation

> And after this, I saw God in a point—that is to say, in my understanding—by which sight I saw that he is in all things. I beheld with avisement, seeing and knowing in that sight that he does all that is done. (11:1–3.163)

Now, in the Third Revelation, Julian's mind experiences God in a single-pointed meditation and with the greatest clarity. She is granted the "beholding" she had just been seeking so ardently and receives it with *avisement*. This Middle English word (in use only after 1369) implies deep contemplative concentration, giving the most deliberate consideration to what one sees. Julian is struck by the blissful experience of God's presence in all things, flowing out from a single point at their center. Is this, like the hazelnut, an imaginative vision that accompanies her focus on Christ's sufferings? Or is it still more "ghostly"? Does she see this "point" at the center of Christ on the cross? Is she experiencing a mind-searing beam of whitest light? A dark vanishing point of sheer absence? An infinite vortex from which all rushes forth and into which all returns? A point-of-no-return into which her mind drops, where there is total rest and incomparable peace?

Most likely, she is not "seeing" anything at all, even in a *ghostly* sense through her imagination. Rather, in this moment of sudden, spiritual clairvoyance, perceived in her contemplative "understanding," Julian knows without a doubt that God truly exists in all that is. It is a revelation of boundless joy. She not only *believes* in God's all-pervasive presence, now she *experiences* it. Time stops. Julian's mind is suspended in space. For that precious instant, she understands that God IS the Infinite Reality behind all that is, and that he does "all that is done" in heaven and on earth. Julian cannot help but be exhilarated by the vastness of God's effusive power, feeling a holy fear at the sheer magnificence of being immersed in Divine Presence. Such a moment is akin to that of Moses seeing the fire burning within the bush, without consuming it, and hearing a voice:

> God said to Moses, "I am who I am." He said further, "Thus you shall say to the Israelites, 'I AM has sent me to you.'" (Ex 3:14)

Moses asked for and was told the sacred name of Jehovah, the One who is, who was, who will be, the One who makes it possible for anything at all to come into and to remain in existence, the eternal "I AM."

We are perhaps accustomed to thinking of supra-normal visions and voices as the highest art forms of the mystic. However, it is precisely this flash of unmediated, internal, incontestable, realization of Divine Truth that is the purest mystical experience. In such a visitation, the Holy Spirit infuses the mind directly, without the use of images or successive words. The transmission happens in an instant. It conveys its wisdom whole, complete, and all-at-once. It produces an intellectual certainty that was never possible before, along with an ecstatic joy of heart. Such an experience is its own confirmation of authenticity.[7] Yet it can also be profoundly disorienting. Julian recalls:

> I marveled in that sight with a soft dread, and thought: "What is sinne?" (11:3–4.163)

We may remember that when Julian saw a hazelnut appear in the palm of her hand in the First Revelation, her initial reaction was: "What is this?" as if to ask: "Why am I being shown this?" At that time, she was told that God creates, protects, and loves all creation as much as the little, helpless hazelnut. Now, in this Third Revelation, Julian sees "in a point" that God not only creates, protects, and loves his creation, he is continually present and active *within* all things. This time, Julian is drawn to ask: if "all that is" is suffused with the presence and divine activity of God, then... "What is sinne?" *Can sin also be the presence of God?* Julian's contemplation of the immanence of God in all creation throws into sharp relief the one thing that is in direct opposition to all that God is, all that God does; that is, sin. The thought stuns her. As if to dispel the distraction, Julian quickly proceeds to elaborate the actual *shewing* that "God does all thing, be it ever so little" (11:4–5.163).

Happe and *Aventure*

> And I saw truly that nothing is done by happe [good fortune] nor by aventure [bad accident], but all by the foreseeing wisdom of God. If it be happe or aventure in the sight of man, our blindness and our lack of foresight are the cause. For those things that are in the foreseeing wisdom of God exist from without beginning (which rightfully and honorably and continually he leads to the best end as it comes about) appear to us suddenly, ourselves unknowing. And thus, by our blindness and our lack of foresight, we say these things come to be by happes and aventure. Thus I understood in this shewing of love, for well I know in the sight of our lord God there is no happe nor aventure. Wherefore it behooved me to grant that all things that are done are well done, for our lord God does all. (11:5–15.163)

Julian understands that if an event *seems* to us to be a stroke of good or bad fortune, that is only because of our blindness and lack of foresight. We just do not see where things are coming from, or how and why anything arises in our consciousness and our experience. So we give it a label and call it "good luck" or "bad luck." However, in the sight of Divine Providence, there is never any such random luck, either good or bad. All things that are done by God are *well* done.

This may seem at first reading like an unacceptable viewpoint, considering the agonized struggles of all creatures, the sin prevalent in the world, and the traumas and tragedies that occur in each individual's lifetime. Is God the *cause* of these? Julian explains that "For in this time the werking of creatures was not shewn, but of our lord God *in* the creature" (11:15–16.163, italics added). Whatever choices human beings make, for good or for ill, Julian understands that God's presence in the soul is always good. At this point, Julian rejoices in God's immanence in all things as the purest *fact* of creation.

Sinne Is No Deed

> For he is in the mid point of all things, and does all things, and I was seker that he does no sinne. And here I saw truly that sinne is no deed, for in all this, sinne was not shewn. (11:16–18.163)

The thought of sin returns like a malign shadow in the background of Julian's mind, the unanswered question. She reiterates a commonly held theological tenet that she would have been taught and heard preached from her childhood: that sin is *not* created by God, because sin is evil and God, who is defined as being good, cannot bring forth evil. Further, Julian explains that, in comparison with the goodness of all of God's creation, sin is not even a "deed" that is done, as if it was produced through the agency of a separate evil power, apart from the thoughts, feelings, and actions of a particular person. Julian clearly states that "sinne was not shewn" to her in this still-point of God's holy presence. How could it be?

However, the question inevitably arises for us, as it will for Julian: If sin is to be considered "no deed," what *is* that which we experience as being sinful, or pure evil? St. Augustine described evil as a *privatio boni*, that is, an absence, or removal, of the good.

> Nor would Almighty God... in any way allow anything evil to exist among his works were he not so omnipotent and good that he can bring good even out of evil. *For what else is that which is called evil but a removal of good?*... In the same way all evils that affect the mind are removals of natural goods: when they are cured they are not moved to somewhere else, but when they are no longer in the mind once it has been restored to health, they will be nowhere.[8]

Writing against the Manicheans, Augustine also termed evil a *corruption* of the good:

> For who can doubt that the whole of that which is called evil is nothing else than corruption? Different evils may, indeed, be called by different names; but *that which is the evil of all things in which any evil is perceptible is corruption*. So the corruption of an educated mind is ignorance: the corruption of the prudent mind is imprudence; the corruption of the just mind, injustice; the corruption of the brave mind, cowardice; the corruption of a calm, peaceful mind, cupidity, fear, sorrow, pride. Again, in a living body, the corruption of health is pain and disease; the corruption of strength is exhaustion; the corruption of rest is toil . . . Enough has been said to show that corruption does harm only as displacing the natural condition; and so, that corruption is not nature, but against nature. And if corruption is the only evil to be found anywhere, and if corruption is not nature, no nature is evil.[9]

Since God who is all-good cannot create any nature that is evil, it must be that human beings *corrupt* something that is good, and thus commit sin and produce evil. And they do so through the wrong exercise of their free wills. Augustine further held that since evil is a deprivation of the good that should be operative in the human person, evil clouds the mind. It is an all-encompassing fog that cuts off the intellect from the contemplation of Divine Truth.[10] Evil is also a moral defection of the will that "consists in the will's turning away from the changeless good [that God is] and in its turning to goods that are changeable."[11]

> For when the will, abandoning what is above it, turns itself to something lower, it becomes evil because the very turning itself and not the thing to which it turns is evil. Therefore, an inferior being does not make the will evil but the will itself, because it is a created will, wickedly and inordinately seeks the inferior thing.[12]

Augustine argued that the evil of original sin is inherited: "The child is born a sinner—no sinner as yet by its own act, a new sinner by its birth, and old sinner in terms of its guilt."[13] Therefore, Adam's willful sin of disobedience darkened not only his own soul but also the souls of all his progeny. It turned humankind away from the primary good of obedience to God's command.

Following Augustine, medieval theologians continued to consider evil as a non-thing, a privation of good, that which does not exist, the very opposite of the good that *is*. While evil seems to appear as an irresistible force, it has no intrinsic reality. Metaphysically speaking, evil cannot even "exist" anywhere, just as darkness cannot exist in the universe of perfect light that God continually creates. To love evil, writes Augustine, is actually to love nothing.[14] Evil is the quintessential lie, the distortion of truth. Christ himself said of Satan:

> He was a murderer from the beginning and does not stand in the truth, because there is no truth in him. When he lies, he speaks according to his own nature, for he is a liar and the father of lies. (Jn 8:44)

Yet human beings repeatedly fall for "the big lie" under the appearance of this or that false good. They continue to choose instant gratification based on pride, lust, power, greed; the seductive, shiny apple that the serpent promises will open their eyes and make them "like God, knowing good and evil" (Gn 3:5). And this they choose instead of obedience to God's will in imitation of Christ's own obedience that alone enables the direct infusion of divine wisdom, which would make them *truly* godlike.

While Julian accepts the contemporary Augustinian teaching of sin as the absence of a good thought, feeling, or action that should exist, she continues to wrestle with the appearance of evil as an all-pervasive and seemingly independent reality. Sin as "no deed" may be technically correct, according to medieval theology, but such an abstract, intellectual definition does not answer her basic dilemma about the *experience* of evil as only-too-real, both within the heart and "out there" in the world, causing continual suffering in every person's life. The wounds of her childhood and adulthood will flood her mind during the course of her visions and eventually erupt in a volcano of questions. This eruption will reveal that Julian's encounter with Christ was not only physical, imaginative, and spiritual. It was also, and perhaps most fiercely, emotional. She had suffered too much and waited too long for answers and now, on her presumed deathbed, she felt she had a right to some explanations.

Rightfullehede of God

Julian will confront the experience of sin and suffering in depth, but at a later time. (As she has just mentioned: "in all this, sinne was not shewn.") Now, she is drawn to contemplate God's *rightfullehede*, which includes rightfulness, righteousness, justice, and perfection. *Rightfullehede*, Julian observes, has "two fair properties: it is right and it is full" (11:21–22.165). All of God's works are righteous and fully just, needing neither mercy nor grace to make them so. (Julian mentions that eventually, when God showed her the nature of sin "nakedly," he would reveal the workings of mercy and grace that come to the aid of the sinner.) Furthermore, Julian is convinced that God discloses his righteousness because he wants us to behold himself and his works constantly, for they are good and his judgments are "easy and sweet" (11:28.165).[15] In fact, the contemplation of God's good works brings the person who has been mired in seeing only the blind (and sinful) judgments of humankind into the "fair, sweet judgment of our lord God" (11:29.165).

> For man beholds some deeds as being well done and some deeds evil, and our lord beholds them not so. For as all that has being in nature is of God's making, so is everything that is done an aspect of God's doing. For it is easy to understand that the best deed is well done. And as well as the best deed is done and the highest [deed is done], as well is the least deed done, and all in the manner and in the order that our lord has ordained it from without beginning. For there is no do-er but he. (11:30–35.165)

Here Julian is talking about the perfection and order of all that is part of natural existence. She is being shown only positive, divine Revelation. She is seeing creation from *God's* point of view, not from the distorted view of humankind that defiles its own human nature and destroys the beauties of the natural environment. She is also giving the reader a taste of her future Revelation concerning the workings of Divine Providence. In God's ultimate purpose, all that is done is *well* done. This teaching echoes the creation story in Genesis: "God saw everything that he had made, and indeed, it was very good" (Gn 1:31). The letter of James the apostle speaks the same wisdom:

> Do not be deceived, my beloved. Every generous act of giving, with every perfect gift, is from above, coming down from the Father of lights, with whom there is no variation or shadow due to change. (Jas 1:16–17)

Julian also acknowledges that she "saw full sekerly" that God *never changes* his purpose in anything, "nor ever shall without end" (11:35–37.165). How could he? Change-of-mind would imply indecision, imperfection, incompleteness. These are human faults, not Divine Wisdom. On the contrary, in God's providential plan, everything has been "set in order before anything was created, as it should stand without end, and no manner of thing shall fail of that point" (11:38–40.165). That is, nothing God creates will fail to fulfill its preordained goal. Seen from God's point of view, everything ever created is, and always has been, *perfect.* "For he has made all thing in the fullness of goodness, and therefore the blessed trinity is ever fully pleased in all his works" (11:40–41.165). Could this be the divine point-of-it-all?

See!

> And all this he shewed full blissfully, meaning thus: "See, I am God. See, I am in all thing. See, I do all thing. See, I never take my hands from my werks, nor never shall without end. See, I lead all thing to the end that I ordained it to, from without beginning, by the same might, wisdom, and love with which I made it. How should any thing be amiss?" (11:42–46.165)

Suddenly, Julian hears an outpouring of words that seems to express the hidden "meaning" of her wordless vision of God-in-a-point. This magnificent litany is biblical in its parallelism, poetic in its lyricism, dramatic in its escalation of emotional energy. The words were not heard through the ear, but perceived through direct spiritual intuition. How did Julian experience (and remember) such perfect cadences? St. Teresa of Avila tells us:

> . . . when God speaks, the voice is so clear that not a syllable of what He says is lost . . . the soul finds itself addressed in grand speeches that it could not compose for itself . . . and at the first word, as I have said it [the soul] is completely changed. How, since it is in ecstasy and its faculties are suspended, could it possibly understand things that have never come into its mind before?[16]

The words Julian heard Christ speak ("See, I am God") seem to echo the Book of Revelation:

> It is done! I am the Alpha and the Omega, the beginning and the end. To the thirsty I will give water as a gift from the spring of the water of life. (Rv 21:6)

In summary, Julian's "God-in-a-point" epiphany enabled her to experience not only that God IS, but that God is the underlying Reality of all things, whether or not she is able to "see" how this could be so . . . that God does all that is done, but that he "does no evil" . . . that God never removes his "hand" from that which he creates, nor ever has, nor ever shall . . . that God leads every single thing to the ultimate end for which it was created in the beginning . . . that God does all this with the same trinitarian "might, wisdom and love" with which he creates all that is. And finally, since such God-ness eternally IS, "How should any thing be amiss?"

Julian is hearing the Spirit within her mind describe the world as it is forever being created by perfect Wisdom, not as it is falsified and corrupted by the ignorance and sinfulness of humankind. In this ecstatic experience of Divine Reality, everything is immaculate, blissful, perfectly ordered to its appropriate end. All is accomplished through God's infinite power, wisdom, and love. Every tree is a divine image, every creature reflects its Creator, every human being walks in the garden of God's love. There is no evil, no sin, no disorder. All is as it was created to be. Such is the kingdom of God.

Tested

> Thus mightily, wisely, and lovingly was the soul tested in this vision. Then I saw truly that it behooved me to assent with great reverence, enjoying God. (11:46–48.165)

As sublime an insight as this was, Julian admits that her soul was greatly *tested* in this vision. How could she call such a glorious Revelation "a test"? Perhaps because the two world views, one of the heavenly kingdom, and the other of the earthly existence Julian knew only too well, could not be reconciled in her mind. The teaching that all that is done on earth is done by God for the best possible "end" was still incomprehensible to her; it was not her *normal* way of viewing evil in the world. Given her life experience, she could not readily discount the violence and grave injustices she had seen, the sufferings she had undergone, the terrible toll of the plagues on her family and friends, the maimings and deaths of war, the pains of childbirth, the scandals of the papal schism, the Lollard heresies rampant in the church, the violence of the peasants' revolt, the adultery, brutality, cheating, lying, and corruption of her *evencristens* in Norwich; the quarrels and jealousies within her own family; her own deep sense of wretchedness. There seemed to be no end to the many faces of cosmic evil and personal sin.

One senses that, in spite of her absolute certitude concerning the truth of this Revelation of "God in all things," Julian simply could not fathom *how* God might be working in and through the evils of sin, suffering, and death to lead all things to a perfect ending, according to his divine purpose. She must have heard the rhetorical question in her mind: "How could any thing be amiss?" with a burst of joy one minute, and, in the next, been hit hard by the realization that obviously so much all around her *was* sorely amiss. And we must remember that all during this Revelation, Julian was still facing Christ on the cross, suffering for the sins of humankind. How could such agony have been part of God's plan from all eternity?

Julian implies here that she felt deeply mired in the human condition while God was showing her a *divine* dimension, a transcendent perspective beyond anything she could have imagined. And in this blessed moment she felt she was being tested, in the sense of challenged to break open her mind to an entirely different plane of reality. Throughout the *shewings*, Julian's daring spirit will fly directly into the burning sun of divine revelation, only to fall back to earth like a blinded bird. True illumination never happens without a struggle, an intense contest between two versions of reality, human and divine. Julian's *agon* was no different. She could not yet grasp the full implications of what God was revealing about the righteousness of all his works. Even so, Julian knew well that it *behooved* her to assent to the import of the vision "with great reverence," whether or not she understood it, because she believed it to be true. St. Paul spoke of faith as "the assurance of things hoped for, the conviction of things *not* seen" (Heb 11:1, italics added). Julian does not see or comprehend. Thus her faith is being tested.

She feels called simply to rest for a while, and *enjoy* God. "Be still, and know that I am God!" sings the psalmist (Ps 46:10). "See! I am God," cries the Spirit within Julian. The hardest challenge was yet to come: to hold onto the divine viewpoint of the *rightfullehede* of all God's works even when plunged into a shattering vision of human suffering.

The Fourth Revelation

> And after this I saw, beholding the body plenteously bleeding in seming of the scourging, as thus: the fair skin was broken very deep into the tender flesh, with sharp smitings all about the sweet body. The hot blood ran out so plenteously that there was neither skin nor wound, but as it were all blood. And when it came to where it should have fallen down, there it vanished. Notwithstanding, the bleeding continued awhile till it might be seen with avisement. And this was so plenteous to my sight that it seemed to me, if it had been so in nature and in substance for that time, it should have made the bed all full of blood, and have passed over all about. (12:1–8.167)

In the Fourth Revelation, Julian's contemplation shifts abruptly from the bliss of "enjoying God" to a shocking vision of Christ's body bleeding plenteously, "in seming,"[17] or in resemblance of, the scourging, when the Savior was tied to a pillar and brutally beaten before his crucifixion. The Middle English word *seming* (or *semyng*) may also suggest the deep furrows made by the plowman's gashes in the soil as prophesied in Psalm 129:3: "The plowers plowed on my back; they made their furrows long."[18] If this is Julian's meaning, the long seams or wounds inflicted on Christ's body would have been from the repeated use of whips, knotted and tipped with animal bone or lead.[19] In Julian's sight, these wounds become torrents of "hot blood," flowing now not only from the crown of thorns on Christ's head, but erupting all over his "sweet body," which Julian can barely see for the abundance of blood. In Christian theology, the "sharp smitings" in Christ's flesh atone for the seven deadly sins (lust, gluttony, greed, sloth, anger, envy, and pride) into which humankind falls again and again. They are the deep gashes of every kind of temptation to which human beings succumb, the wrong thoughts that inflict so much suffering on themselves and others. Julian sees the blood from these wounds of sin as pouring out of every pore of Christ's body, from which he is literally bleeding to death.

She remarks that the bleeding "continued a while" so that she could consider its import "with avisement," in deepest contemplation. Lifelike as the experience was, Julian recalls with great precision that when the blood reached the perimeters of her "visionary field," it suddenly vanished. Otherwise, she comments, if Christ's blood had been flowing all during the time of her vision the way blood flows naturally (as it must have flowed out of Julian when she was being bled by the barber-surgeon), it would have covered her entire bed and the whole room, "over all about," in a river of blood. Quite unexpectedly, the abundant outpouring of blood suggests to Julian's mind the plenteous, baptismal-like waters God provides over all the earth "to our service, and to our bodily ease, because of the tender love that he has for us" (12:9–10.167). She freely associates the profusion of blood with the waters that rain down and feed the earth, filling the rivers, lakes, and streams, as well as the waters that clean and heal and satisfy the thirst of all creatures. Yet she draws a distinction:

> But yet he likes it even better that we take full wholesomely [healingly] his blessed blood to wash us of sin, for there is no licuor that is made that he likes so well to give us. (12:10–12.167)

For Julian, the cup of Christ's blood is the "licuor," or healing medicine, that saves humanity from sin. She evokes Christ's giving of his precious blood to his disciples at the Last Supper, which is re-enacted in the sacrament of the Eucharist:

> Then he took a cup, and after giving thanks he gave it to them, saying, "Drink from it, all of you; for this is my blood of the covenant, which is poured out for many for the forgiveness of sins." (Mt 26:27–28)

The Precious Plenty

> For it is most plenteous, as it is most precious, and that by the virtue of the blessed godhead. And it is our own nature, and all blissfully overflows onto us by the virtue of his precious love. The dearworthy blood of our lord Jesus Christ, as truly as it is most precious, so truly is it most plenteous. (12:12–16.167)

Julian envisions the outpouring of Christ's blood on the cross as "plenteous" and "precious," precisely because it is the boundless blood of the Son of God. It is also "our own nature" because it is very *human* blood, just like ours. And as precious as it is, so is it plenteous, sufficient to cleanse every and all sin, if only humankind will allow itself to be purified by it.

> Behold and see the virtue of this precious plenty of his dearworthy blood! It descended down into hell and burst their bonds and delivered them, all who were there who belong to the court of heaven. The precious plenty of his dearworthy blood overflows all the earth, and is ready to wash all creatures of sinne who are of good will, have been, and shall be. The precious plenty of his dearworthy blood ascends up into heaven in the blessed body of our lord Jesus Christ, and there is in him, bleeding, praying for us to the father, and is and shall be as long as we need. (12:17–23.167)

In a paean of praise to the "precious plenty" of Christ's "dearworthy blood," Julian imagines the blood descending deep into the bowels of hell and rising up, in Christ's resurrected body, into heaven. She even suggests that the resurrected Christ is *still* "bleeding" (that is, pouring out his blood metaphorically in heaven) as he prays unceasingly for humanity to the Father, for as long as we shall need. This is an evocation of the Lamb eternally slain upon the altar of the Apocalypse:

> Then I saw between the throne and the four living creatures and among the elders *a Lamb standing as if it had been slaughtered*, having seven horns and seven eyes, which are the seven spirits of God sent out into all the earth. (Rv 5:6, italics added)

There is another aspect Julian ponders, one that goes beyond her previous statement concerning "them that shalle be saved." She understands "the precious plenty" of Christ's blood as being ready to wash "*all* creatures of sinne who are of good will," in times past and future. She makes no differentiation between *evencristens* and Jews or pagans, an extraordinary statement for her time. Julian would not have dared prophesy "universal salvation" outright, as this would have been opposed to the medieval church's teaching of salvation only for those who believe in Jesus Christ, were baptized, kept his commandments, and died in the state of grace. Nevertheless, she dares to write that the "precious plenty" of Christ's salvific blood "overflows all the earth" with its perfect cleansing. St. Peter taught that "Christ also suffered for sins *once for all*, the righteous for the unrighteous, in order to bring you to God" (1 Pt 3:18). Various translations have suggested the original meaning is "once for all *time*," or "once for all *people*." In her inclusive interpretation, Julian implies that Christ's outflowing blood will reach all and save all who are touched, in some mystical way, by its liberating power.

Similarly, the letter to the Ephesians declares that "In him we have redemption through his blood, the forgiveness of our trespasses, according to the riches of his grace" (Eph 1:7). The Book of Revelation also says that the blood of the sacrificial Lamb of God will bring peoples of *all nations* to salvation, through their own experience of redemptive suffering: "These are they who have come out of the great ordeal; they have washed their robes and made them white in the blood of the Lamb" (Rv 7:14). Julian completes this apocalyptic vision, seeing the blood of the Lamb of God as divine energy flowing evermore throughout heaven, "enjoying the salvation of all mankind that is there and shall be there, fulfilling the number that faileth" (12:24–25.169). As we have seen, it was generally believed that the predestined number of souls of the elect to be saved would equal the number of angels that had dropped out of heaven when, because of pride, Lucifer fell "like a flash of lightning" (Lk 10:18). According to St. Augustine, only God knows who and how many there will be.[20]

The Fifth Revelation

Julian was given a period of time in which to behold the passion of the Lord and to meditate on the first four Revelations. Now, in the Fifth Revelation, she hears Christ speak directly to her again, in distinct, interior words:

> Then he, without voice and opening of lips, formed in my soul these words: "Herewith is the fiend overcome." (13:3–5.169)

Julian is extremely careful to note that there was no external, audible voice coming from the cross, nor was there any movement of Christ's mouth. One is reminded of Isaiah's fourth "Song of the Servant," in which he spoke about the Savior to come:

> He was oppressed, and he was afflicted, yet he did not open his mouth; like a lamb that is led to the slaughter, and like a sheep that before its shearers is silent, so he did not open his mouth. (Is 53:7)

The precise words Julian hears within her soul ("Herewith is the fiend overcome") give voice to the vision of the outpouring of blood she sees before her, by which the power of Satan is forever vanquished. These particular words do not appear in the synoptic gospel accounts of the seven last words of Christ from the cross. They are directed specifically to Julian and form part of her particular gospel account. However, the locution does evoke Christ's parting words to his disciples as recorded in the gospel of John:

> I have said this to you, so that in me you may have peace. In the world you face persecution. But take courage; *I have conquered the world!* (Jn 16:33, italics added)

Sin as Bondage

For some time now, Christ has been showing Julian the bleeding wounds of his passion, revealing the enormity of suffering that was needed to repair the evil that Satan unleashed upon the world. The power of the devil was greatly feared in the Middle Ages, as it had been from ancient times. Sin had long been considered a state of bondage to devils, a spiritual captivity from which humankind had no power to free itself. In addition to the debt that must be paid to God, souls had to be ransomed from the grip of evil by the payment of a debt to Satan: "For you were bought with a price" (1 Cor 6:20).

In the second century, St. Irenaeus developed the idea that the Son of God, out of his own perfect justice, had to "buy back" humanity from Satan:

> The mighty Word and true Man reasonably redeeming us by His blood, gave Himself [as] a ransom for those who had been brought into bondage. And since the Apostasy [Satan] unjustly ruled over us, and, whereas we belonged by nature to God Almighty, alienated us against nature and made us his own disciples, the Word of God, being mighty in all things, and failing not in His justice, dealt justly even with the Apostasy itself, *buying back from it the things which were His own.*[21]

St. Augustine also taught that

> The Redeemer came, and laid down the price; He poured out his blood and purchased the whole round world . . . The price paid was Christ's blood. What is worth a price like that? What else but the entire world? What else but all the nations?[22]

Augustine goes even further. He depicts the cross as the "trap" into which Christ placed his blood as "bait" which "caught" Satan and held him prisoner, thereby defeating him and forcing him to release his human captives from bondage. (This is the so-called "mouse-trap" theory of atonement.)

For over a thousand years, church teaching expounded such debt and entrapment theories. It was understood by common Christians that just as a prisoner of war could be freed only by the payment of a ransom to the conqueror, so Christ had to "pay a debt" directly to Satan in order to liberate humankind from his clutches. It was St. Anselm's new theory of atonement in the eleventh century that radically altered this debt-to-Satan theory. For Anselm, as we have seen, it would take a Redeemer who was both God and man to effect complete atonement. As man, Christ could suffer as a human being in place of all human beings; as God, he could make full satisfaction to Divine Justice.

However, in the thirteenth century, St. Thomas Aquinas, as well as most later medieval scholastics, *rejected* the idea that Christ's death on the cross was absolutely necessary to appease Divine Justice. He postulated that sin could have been forgiven in other ways than by Christ's passion and death. He viewed the restoration of humankind into the good grace of God as a free act of mercy and kindness on God's part. But since Christ did choose to suffer and die, then St. Thomas agreed that it was fitting for there to have been a God-man who could bring about redemption from sin and give full satisfaction to the Divine Majesty. And because the least action or suffering of Jesus Christ was infinite in its power to effect salvation, "By suffering out of love and obedience, Christ gave more to God than was required to compensate for the offense of the whole human race."[23]

Christ's Victory

By showing Julian the abundance of his "dearworthy blood," Christ also demonstrated to her "a part of the fiend's malice, and fully his *un*might, for he shewed that his passion is the overcoming of the fiend" (13:6–7.169, italics added). St. Paul tells us that Christ "became obedient to the point of death—even death on a cross" (Phil 2:8). Satan is understood to be utterly impotent against Christ's total sacrifice of love and his example of perfect obedience to the Father's will. Thus Christ robbed Satan of any illusory power he might have had over humankind. Notice that Julian does not quote Christ as saying the fiend "*will be* overcome" but "*is* overcome." *Christ's victory is already complete.* Humanity is already ransomed by his blood. And in the unbloody sacrifice of the Mass, Christ, the great High Priest, unceasingly offers his suffering and death to the Father so that every person of every generation may be incorporated into the salvific act.

Julian is fully aware, however, that human beings have yet to see Christ's victory completed on earth. The Lord reveals to her that the fiend still has the same malice and evil intentions that he had before the incarnation. And he works as hard as ever to ensnare souls, especially when he sees that those souls that are saved "escape him honorably by virtue of Christ's precious passion" (13:9–10.169).

> And that is his [Satan's] sorrow, and he is terribly emptied of his power, for all that God suffers [permits] him to do turns for us to joy and for him to shame and pain. And he has as much sorrow when God gives him permission to werk as when he does not werk. And that is because he may never do as ill as he would, for his might is all locked in God's hand. (13:10–14.169)

Julian does not mean to imply that Satan is *literally* locked in God's hand, or that God is in any way complicit in the devil's evil, only that ultimately the "hand" of God destroys the might of evil and leads his people forth as he did the Israelites out of Egypt, by the power of his arm: "You have a mighty arm; strong is your hand, high your right hand" (Ps 89:13). Christ spoke of himself as the Good Shepherd whose sheep hear his voice and follow him: "I give them eternal life, and they will never perish. No one will snatch them out of my hand" (Jn 10:28). And the Book of Revelation predicts that in the final days God will send an angel to bind up the devil:

> Then I saw an angel coming down from heaven, holding in his hand the key to the bottomless pit and a great chain. He seized the

> dragon, that ancient serpent, who is the Devil and Satan, and bound him for a thousand years, and threw him into the pit, and locked and sealed it over him, so that he would deceive the nations no more, until the thousand years were ended. (Rv 20:1–3)

This, as we have seen, was enacted in the popular scene from the passion plays, when a figure of Christ's Spirit descended into the depths of hell and released the souls of patriarchs and prophets and faithful followers of the Judaic Law, while all the devils were chained and bound together on stage and thrust into the fiery "hell mouth."

No Wrath

> But in God may be no wrath, as to my sight. For our good lord—endlessly having regard to his own worship and to the profit of all them that shalle be saved—with might and right he withstands the reproved [the demons] who out of malice and wickedness busy themselves to counteract and go against God's will. (13:14–18.169)

Here, in the Fifth Revelation, is also the first mention that Julian saw "no wrath" in God, a profound insight that will become central to her theology. By recording this mystical realization, Julian dares to challenge the numerous biblical references to God's "wrathfulness," as well as prevalent medieval views of an avenging God, ever threatening to pour out "fire and brimstone" on those who sin.[24] The Old English word *wroth* connotes intense anger and moral indignation. Wrath was considered an attribute of God, an aspect of his righteousness through which he shows his Divine Justice and eternal glory.

In *The City of God*, St. Augustine interpreted numerous scriptural passages to prove that all the sufferings that God permits to occur in "this most wretched life" are caused by his terrible wrath: "For God's wrath is this mortal life, in which man is made like to vanity, and his days pass as a shadow."[25] And again, "His wrath is manifesting itself in this miserable corruption."[26] As we have discussed, many medieval sermonizers, in an effort to urge sinners to repent, fulminated about the *wroth* of God to the near-exclusion of his mercy, as shown by the sufferings of his Son on the cross. Considering such a mindset, it must have taken immense courage for Julian to write that "in God may be no wrath, as to my sight."

Julian simply does not "see" any trace of wrathfulness in God, neither in his just judgment against the devils, nor in his attitude toward human beings who have sinned. In her vision, Christ, the God-man, does not hang on the cross pouring out his blood upon the whole world *because he is angry at humankind*. Rather, the Savior is only concerned with the worship of the Father and the ultimate good of all those for whom he is dying. By giving his life to expiate the sins of the world, Christ offered himself as the sacrificial *lamb*, not the butcher. As the Son of God, Christ withstands "with might and right" all that is against his Father's will, but he does not condemn anyone in *wroth*, any more than he condemned the woman taken in adultery (Jn 8:1–11). Instead, he repeatedly counsels repentance, faith, and the amendment of one's life. In so doing, he forever fights *for* the soul of the sinner and *against* the evil wiles of the "demons" who seek to do great harm to others.

What is Julian suggesting here? That the idea of an angry, avenging God (even if wrath might be considered an aspect of Divine Justice) is inconsistent with his merciful goodness? That the view of a wrathful God is simply untenable theologically? Julian knew that, according to scripture, "God is Love" (1 Jn 4:8). God cannot help but be loving. God cannot stop pouring out love. That is why, in Julian's understanding, God cannot become vindictive and seek revenge and inflict punishment in emotional anger as human beings do. God does not change in his attitude toward his creation, loving one minute and wrathful the next. *People* change in their receptivity to, or refusal of, God's love. If human beings obey the divine imperative to love God and each other, they will recognize God as the source of all love. If they refuse and suffer the consequences of their loveless actions, they will experience God as "wrathful."

Scriptural Allegory

In both the Old and New Testaments, the use of "wrath" to personify God's "hatred" of sin is a literary and pedagogical device to impress upon people the paramount importance of obeying the divine commandments for the sake of their eternal happiness. *Wroth* is a metaphor, not a divine attribute. Even St. Augustine acknowledged that scripture uses bodily images and signs, like Adam and Eve *hearing* the voice of the Lord God "walking in the garden at the time of the evening breeze" (Gn 3:8),[27] and analogies with human emotions (like *lov-*

ingkindness, mercy, wrathfulness), in order to convey important teachings (and warnings) about the nature of God. Augustine explained that when truths are embodied in figures of speech, they can excite our love (or fear) of God in ways that symbolic truths set out in abstract fashion cannot. "But no one disputes that it is much more pleasant to learn lessons presented through imagery, and much more rewarding to discover meanings that are won only with difficulty."[28]

However, Augustine cautioned that these analogical images can never tell us the true nature of God, nor can God reveal himself in his Divine Essence in any bodily image or likeness, whether in a dream or a waking vision.[29] Neither can the human mind deduce insights into Divine Wisdom on its own; these may only be received through direct illumination from God (as were Julian's mystical Revelations). Then the human mind creates images and symbols, expressed in spoken and written words, to try to convey what it has learned mystically and intellectually, however imperfect these "labels" may be. *Wroth* is just such an imperfect human label used to describe the incomparable *rightfullehede* of God.

Scorning and Noughting

> Also I saw our lord scorne his [Satan's] malice and nought his unmight, and he wills that we do so. (13:19–20.171)

The Middle English word *scorne* implies total rejection, absolute disdain . . . to the point of utter disregard. This is how Julian understands the Lord's attitude toward evil: he scorns the devil's malice because he did not create it. Julian replaces the customary *wroth* analogy with this figure of speech, *scorne*, to express a strong insight she received about God's attitude toward evil. And by adding the word *nought*, Julian further implies that the Lord sees Satan's "*un*might" as impotence that should be thoroughly derided. She indicates that Christ wants all human beings to scorn the devil in the same way. For when souls are purified by Christ's cleansing blood, sin no longer exists: it is obliterated. And "Herewith is the fiend overcome." This scorning of and derision at the devil's malice by the Lord was such a liberating vision that Julian tells us:

> For this sight, I laughed mightily, and that made them laugh who were about me, and their laughing was a pleasure to me. (13:20–21.171)

Suddenly, Julian (believed by all to be in the last stage of dying) is laughing out loud! The women around her bed must have laughed nervously in reaction to the sheer incongruity of a dying woman suddenly bursting into laughter without any idea of what had made her laugh. Obviously, Julian could not tell them at that time. However, she mentions that she wanted all her *evencristens* to see Christ scorning the devil as she did, because then they would have known exactly what she was laughing about and been able to laugh along with her, no doubt with great relief. Julian adds: "But I saw not Christ laugh" (13:23.171). Indeed, no medieval artist had ever painted the Man of Sorrows laughing. Nevertheless, Julian was convinced that human beings may laugh to comfort themselves and to express joy in God because "the fiend is overcome" (13:25.171).

To clarify this Revelation even more, Julian explains that her understanding was led deep into the Lord in contemplation when she saw him *scorne* the devil's malice. Like the words spoken from the cross, this inward *shewing* of truthfulness was given without any change in the Savior's countenance. Christ's *scorne* was not seen by Julian as a sudden outburst of emotion, or any change of facial expression, but rather as a "worshipful property that is in God, which is durable," that is, unchanging (13:28.171). In his divine goodness, God *eternally* scorns Satan. According to medieval theology, so do the saints:

> For I saw that he [Satan] shall be scorned at domesday generally by all that shall be saved, for whose salvation he has had great envy. For then he shall see that all the woe and tribulation that he has done them shall be turned into increase of their joy without end. And all the pain and the sorrow that he would have brought them to shall endlessly go with him to hell. (13:36–41.171)

The Sixth Revelation

After this, Julian hears Christ speak to her interiorly, in distinct words:

> "I thank thee for thy service and for thy travail [labor] and namely of thy youth." (14:1–2.173)[30]

It seems as if Julian is indeed at the end of her short life, experiencing her own judgment day, hearing God thank her for her years of labor, devotion, and good works. And he thanks her *namely* (that is, especially) for having been faithful to him during her youth. What an astounding moment, that God should be so *homely* as to thank Julian for her life!

> And in this word, my understanding was lifted up into heaven, where I saw our lord God as a lord in his own house, which lord has called all his dearworthy friends to a solemn feast. Then I saw the lord taking no place in his own house but I saw him royally reign in his house, and filling it all with joy and mirth, endlessly gladening and solacing his dearworthy friends himself, very homely and very courteously, with marvelous melody of endless love, in his own fair blessed chere [facial expression]. Which glorious chere of the godhead fills all heaven with joy and bliss. (14:2–9.173)

Whereas before Julian has envisioned aspects of Christ's suffering on the cross, here she is invited to experience a new level of mystical awareness: that of Christ's ineffable courtesy as host of the heavenly banquet. This vision indicates that her consciousness is expanding to be able to anticipate her own salvation. She is being given a taste of the bliss awaiting her in heaven when she will see the resurrected Christ face to face. In the gospel of Matthew, Christ told the parable of the wedding banquet that a king gives for his son, and in Luke, he used the metaphor of a great supper at which the lord himself seats and serves the invited guests, to describe the heavenly kingdom (Mt 22:1–4, cf. Lk 14:16–24). Long ago, Isaiah had depicted heaven as the divine banquet: "On this mountain the Lord of hosts will make for all peoples a feast of rich food, a feast of well-aged wines, of rich food filled with marrow, of well-aged wines strained clear" (Is 25:6–8). And the Book of Revelation also portrayed union with Christ in glory as a great marriage supper (Rv 19:6–9, 17). All these images would have been familiar to Julian, so it is natural that her glimpse of heaven would come in the form of a "solemn feast." The Spirit uses the metaphors most familiar to the mystic's mind to reveal hidden meaning. This type of vision usually appears to the inner eye in a flash, completely formed and incomparably clear.

Three Degrees of Bliss

Julian is shown "three degrees of bliss that each soul shall have in heaven that willfully has served God in any degree [station in life] on earth" (14:10–11.173). The first is the abundant honor and thanks (such as Julian has just heard Christ give her) that the soul shall receive from God when it is free of all pain, perhaps even alluding to the pain of purgatory. Julian writes that this thanks is so overwhelming that it seems the soul could not be filled any fuller with honor. It appears to Julian that all the pains and travails that might be suffered by all the living would not have deserved the thanks that even one person who served God shall receive in heaven. The second degree of bliss is that all the blessed creatures "shall see this honorable thanking" (14:17–18.173). The image is of a great homecoming with the citizens of paradise gathered to greet the new arrival, and to hear the Lord welcome the soul and make "his service known to all who are in heaven" (14:18–19.173). Julian was shown an example of a king who thanks his subjects, who therefore feel honored. But if the king makes his appreciation known to all the realm, then the subject's glory is increased that much more. The third degree of bliss is that the king's thanks "shall last without end" (14:23.175).

> And I saw that homely and sweetly this was shewn: that the age of every man shall be known in heaven and be rewarded for his willful service and for his time. And especially the age of those who willfully and freely offer their youth to God, are rewarded surpassingly and wonderfully thanked. For I saw that, when or at what time that a man or woman is truly turned to God for one day's service to fulfill his endless will, he shall have all these three degrees of bliss. And the more that the loving soul sees this courtesy of God, the readier he is to serve him all the days of his life. (14:23–30.175)

It is notable in this passage that Julian quite naturally speaks of "a man and a woman," side by side, in a culture in which nearly all theological and spiritual teachings were directed to "men" alone. She also suggests that anyone who truly serves God for *even one day* will begin to anticipate God's courteous reward and will want to serve him for a lifetime.

The Seventh Revelation

After this, Christ grants Julian "a supreme, ghostly delight" in her soul (15:1.175). She feels full of eternal "sekernesse, mightily fastened without any painful dread" (15:2–3.175). This euphoria is "so glad and so spiritual" that she is in complete peace, ease, and rest, so much so that there was "nothing on earth that could have grieved me" (15:3–4.175). She is experiencing a contemplative state of stillness and joy, the prayer of exquisite quiet in the presence of God. This sense of presence, while utterly spiritual, is more convincing than any physical sight. But it is ephemeral.

> This lasted but a while, and I was turned and left to myself in such heaviness and weariness of my life and irkenes [irritation] with myself, that I could barely have patience to live. There was no comfort nor any ease to my feeling, but faith, hope and charity, and these I had in truth, but very little in feeling. (15:5–8.175)

A sharp and sudden shift occurs. Julian feels as if she has been dropped out of heaven. Left alone on earth, she is full of sadness, weariness, and *irkenes*, that is, acute annoyance with herself. She scarcely has the patience to go on living. What a drastic change! Yet this shock and dismay at feeling suddenly abandoned by God is a familiar one in the mystical life. It is a classic example of the return of the visionary from the heights of contemplation down to the harsh fact of her still-separateness from divinity and a very human dissatisfaction with herself. The thirteenth-century poem *The Chastising of God's Children* had called it: "The play of love [which is] joy and sorrow, the which two come sundry times one after another, by the presence and absence of him that is our love."[31] All that Julian could hold onto was her faith, hope, and love, and this she did "in truth," but without any sense of consolation.

> And soon after this, our blessed lord gave me again the comfort and the rest in soul: delight and sekernesse so blissful and so mighty that no dread, nor sorrow, nor any bodily nor ghostly pain that might be suffered could have unsettled me. And then the pain shewed again to my feeling, and then the joy and the delight, and now that one, and now the other, diverse times, I suppose about twenty times. And in the time of joy, I might have said with Saint Paul: "Nothing shall separate me from the love of Christ." And in the pain, I might have said with Saint Peter: "Lord, save me, I perish." (15:9–16.177)

This excruciating oscillation between the utmost bliss and extreme turmoil recurs some "twenty times." One minute she feels totally at peace in the presence of God, the next she is like a little boat being tossed about on the high seas. She is reminded of sacred scripture, but her references are inaccurate. She conflates two gospel passages: Matthew 8:25 ("Lord, save us! We are perishing!"), spoken *not* by Peter alone, but by all the disciples to the sleeping Jesus in the boat during a storm; and Matthew 14:30 ("Lord, save me!"), cried by Peter on another occasion when he began to sink after walking toward Christ on the water. This confusion strongly suggests that Julian did not own or have access to a copy of the new Wyclif English translation of the gospels. But she did know the essential *meaning* of these passages, having heard them quoted in English sermons, and also from a lifetime of meditation. Thus it was natural for her to identify the dramatic swings of feeling with the extremes of ecstasy described by St. Paul in his letter to the Romans (Rom 8:38–39) and the agony voiced by St. Peter and the other disciples. Julian is convinced that she had to undergo these spiritual extremes in order to learn that it is profitable for souls to be unmoored in this way:

> . . . sometimes to be in comfort, and sometimes to fail and to be left to themselves. God wills that we know that he keeps [protects] us ever in the same seker [security], in woe and in wele [well-being]. And for the profit of man's soul a man is sometimes left to himself, although sinne is not always the cause. For in this time, I sinned not for which I should be left to myself, for it was so sudden. Also, I deserved not to have this blissful feeling, but freely our lord gives it when he wills, and suffers us to be in woe sometimes, and both are one love. (15:18–24.177)

The analytic understanding of this Revelation must have come a long time after the experience itself. Reflecting on "What does this mean?" yet again (as with the hazelnut), Julian is led to appreciate that both well-being and woe, common aspects of human existence, must be borne with patience. But the Revelation is clear that *woe* is not always the result of sinful behavior (Julian was convinced she had not sinned "in this time"), nor is the *wele*, that is, the graced sense of God's presence, ever deserved. It is gift, pure and simple. The one reality we can be sure of is that both states of mind are "one love." By seeming to come close and then removing himself, God teaches us not to crave blissful feelings over blind faith. God wants us to *believe* in his presence, whether we feel it or not: "For it is God's will that we hold ourselves in comfort with all our might" (15:24–25.177).

Julian is fully aware that bliss will be everlasting and that earthly pain is merely passing and "shall be brought to nought for them that shalle be saved" (15:26.177). But while we are trapped in this earthly mode of swinging between the two extremes, she is adamant that it is *not* God's will that we pay undue attention to the feelings of pain and allow ourselves to sorrow and mourn over them, "but quickly pass over them and hold ourselves in the endless delight that is God" (15:28.177). Unlike the common medieval spiritual directive that the faithful should see their pains and sense of abandonment as direct punishments from God, or as signs of God's disfavor which they should bear with a heavy heart, Julian's conviction is that God wants his people to cling in faith to the fact of his love, *even* and *especially* in the midst of great suffering.

14
The Dying

The Eighth Revelation

> After this, Christ shewed a part of his passion near his dying. I saw the sweet face as it were dry and bloodless with pale dying; and afterward more deadly pale, languring; and then [it] turned more deadly into blue; and afterward more brown blue, as the flesh turned more deeply dead. For his passion shewed to me most explicitly in his blessed face, and especially in his lips, there I saw these four colors—those lips that were before fresh and ruddy, lively and pleasing to my sight. This was a terrible change, to see this deep dying. And also the nose withered together and dried, to my sight, and the sweet body waxed brown and black, all changed and turned out from the fair, fresh, and lively color of himself into dry dying. (16:1–9.179)

Now, Julian is led into a realistic vision of the terrible dying of Jesus Christ. She describes the death process through the four colors of his face, but most especially the lips: bloodless pale, more deadly pale, deathly blue, and finally, brownish blue. She is watching Christ expire in front of her, as she watched loved ones die in wave after wave of the Great Pestilence. She knows the shriveling of the nose, of the whole body, the progression of color from the blue of deep bruising to brown and thence to black, as the bodily fluids dry up, the blood clots and ceases to flow. This Revelation is both a concrete image of Christ's unique death and a reliving of all the individual deaths Julian has ever witnessed. There is more:

> For in that same time that our blessed savior died upon the rood, it was a dry, bitter wind, wondrous cold as to my sight. And at the time all the precious blood was bled out of the sweet body that

> might pass therefrom, yet there dwelled a moisture in the sweet flesh of Christ, as it was shewn. Bloodlessness and pain dried from within, and the blowing of the wind and cold coming from without, met together in the sweet body of Christ. And these four, two without and two within, dried the flesh of Christ over the course of time. And though this pain was bitter and sharp, yet it was very long-lasting, as to my sight. And the pain dried up all the lively spirits of Christ's flesh. (16:9–17.179)

The wind blew frigid, as if blasting from the North Sea, across the *brode* waters and into Norwich. Julian knew the biting saltiness and searing coldness of that unrelenting wind, and it seemed to be howling that day on Calvary. The wind and the bitter cold are nowhere documented in the gospels, nor are there any details of the endless bleeding and descriptions of Christ's great pains. In fact, *the four gospel accounts do not describe his sufferings at all.* This is Julian's own gospel, told with great attention to the drying up of Christ's face, lips, and all the life-elements of his body. She is finally and truly "there," in the midst of the passion, as she had longed to be. And it is more dreadful than she ever could have imagined.

> Thus I saw the sweet flesh dry in my sight, part after part, drying with marvelous pain. And as long as any element had life in Christ's flesh, so long he suffered pain. This long suffering seemed to me as if he had been seven nights dead, dying, at the point of outpassing [when the soul departs the body], always suffering the great pain. And where I say, "it seemed to me as if he had been seven nights dead," it indicates that the sweet body was so discoloured, so dry, so withered, so deadly, and so piteous, it looked as if he had been seven nights dead, continually dying. And it seemed to me the drying of Christ's flesh was the most pain, and the last, of his passion. (16:18–24.179)

Julian had been slowly dying for seven days and nights herself. Yet she saw Christ dying in her stead. It seems endless, not just from noon to three, as recorded in the gospels (Mt 27:45, Lk 23:44). Because he looked so pitiful, he seems to have been dying this way, his body discoloring, drying, withering, nearly dead, for a week. Yet Julian knows very well that Christ did not hang on the cross for a full seven days and nights, nor did he die at night. What she is describing in such distinct detail is how it appeared, and most of all, *how it felt* to her. Of all the pains, it was the "drying of Christ's flesh" that seemed to be the most excruciating for him to endure . . . and for Julian to watch. She is convinced it is the last pain of his passion.

The Thirst

> And in this drying was brought to my mind this word that Christ said: "I thirst." For I saw in Christ a double thirst: one bodily, and another ghostly. This word was shewn for bodily thirst, and for the ghostly thirst was shewn as I shall say after. And I understood by the bodily thirst that the body had lack of moisture, for the blessed flesh and bones were left all alone without blood and moisture. (17:1–5.181)

Julian becomes fixated on the "drying" of Christ's body. It reminds her of, and partially explains, the words spoken by Christ and recorded by St. John, "I am thirsty" (Jn 19:28). At this moment in Julian's vision, as on Calvary, all the fluids in Christ's body have dried up. He is parched, with a terrible human thirst. His tongue is stuck to the roof of his mouth, his lips are swollen, cracked and bleeding. What a pitiful cry Julian hears from the Son of God, who is himself the "fountain of living water" (Jer 2:13), the Savior who Isaiah wrote would "pour water on the thirsty land, and streams on the dry ground" (Is 44:3). This is the same Lord who told the Samaritan woman at the well, "If you knew the gift of God, and who it is that is saying to you, 'Give me a drink,' you would have asked him, and he would have given you living water" (Jn 4:10). And this is the Teacher who had cried out, saying, "Let anyone who is thirsty come to me, and let the one who believes in me drink" (Jn 7:37–38). Now, he was like the psalmist, David, in the wilderness of Judah, crying out:

> O God, you are my God, I seek you, my soul thirsts for you; my flesh faints for you, as in a dry and weary land where there is no water. (Ps 63:1)

Julian might have recalled the scene from the N-Town passion play, when Christ spoke from the cross:

> For thirst, asunder my lips gin crake;
> For dryness, they do cleve . . .
> I shall go slay the fiend, that freak
> For now my heart begins to break.

It has cost Christ everything to "slay the fiend." And he who has, in Julian's vision, been pouring out his "dearworthy blood" on all creation, is now desperately *thirsty.* Even more than his human thirst, the Son of God is agonized by his divine thirst for the salvation of humankind, as Julian will explain later on. For now, she can only watch and wait.

The Physical Agony

> The blessed body dried all alone a long time, with the wrenching of the nails and weight of the body. For I understood that because of the tenderness of the sweet hands and the sweet feet, by the largeness, hardness, and grievousness of the nails, the wounds waxed wide. And the body sagged because of its weight from a long time hanging, and piercing and scraping of the head, and binding of the crown, all baked with dry blood, with the sweet hair clinging the dry flesh to the thorns, and the thorns to the flesh, drying. And in the beginning, while the flesh was fresh and bleeding, the continual pricking of the thorns made the wounds wide. And furthermore, I saw that the sweet skin and the tender flesh, with the hair and with the blood, were all raised and loosened above by the thorns, and broken in many pieces, and were hanging as if they would hastily have fallen down while they had natural moisture. How it was done I saw not, but I understood that it was with the sharp thorns and the rough, grievous pushing on of the garland, not sparing and without pity, that all at that time broke the sweet skin, with the flesh and the hair, and loosed it from the bone. For which reason it was broken in pieces as a cloth and sagging downward, seeming as if it hastily would have fallen for heaviness and for looseness. And that was great sorrow and dread to me, for it seemed to me that I would not for my life have seen it fall.
>
> This continued a while, and after it began to change, and I beheld and marveled how it might be. And then I saw it was because the flesh began to dry and lose a part of the weight that was round about the garland, and so it was encircled all about, as it were garland upon garland. The garland of thorns was dyed with

> the blood. And that other garland and the head, all was one color, as clotted blood when it is dried. The skin and the flesh that seemed part of the face and of the body was slightly wrinkled, with a tawny color, like a dry board when it is aged, and the face was more brown than the body. (17:5–30.181–83)

Julian does not spare us any aspects of what she saw in her vision. This is perhaps the most graphic account of the crucifixion in medieval literature. It is filled with details that remained indelibly imprinted in Julian's memory as a result of her keen observation. There is the inexorable "drying" of the body, the enlarging of the wounds in the hands due to the great sagging of the body, with hair clinging to the flesh and thorns, and the thorns mingled with flesh and hair, all caked with dried blood. She also remarks on areas of skin above the crown of thorns on Christ's head that opened to the bone and then hung down with the flesh and hair like pieces of torn cloth. She could not understand how the flesh did not break off and fall down, it seemed so loose and heavy. After watching it for a long time, she realized it did not drop off because it, too, had dried up, losing much of its weight. It piled up like many other garlands, above the garland of thorns, row upon row of torn, hanging, and shriveled flesh.

Julian's repeated use of the word "garland" for the crown of thorns (ever since its initial appearance in the First Revelation) and for the crumbled flesh, is painfully ironic. A garland was associated in medieval times with the crowns given to victorious knights after a joust, and with the May Day flowers worn by young girls. Julian herself would have worn such a garland over loose-flowing hair in her youth. Therefore, her description of "garland upon garland" of ripped and bleeding flesh piling on top of the crown of thorns, the thorns and head all becoming one color of clotted blood, evokes an image of the face of the suffering Christ like no other. She also tries to convey the drying and browning of Christ's torn and sagging pieces of skin as "small rumpelde" (that is, slightly rumpled or wrinkled). His matted hair, his dark brown face, his body caked with dried blood, all take on the color of "a dried board when it is aged," like the wood of the cross itself.

Four Manners of *Drying*

Julian pauses to describe "four manners of drying" which she observed (17:31.183). This focus on *drying* is especially poignant.

(In fact, "drying" can be so easily interchanged with the word "dying" that in the Sloane manuscript the latter actually replaces the former, whether by scribal mistake or conscious intent.) The first *drying* was due to *blodlesse*, that is the loss of blood and the withdrawing of all moisture from Christ's body, as his fluids were emptied into the cross itself. The second *drying* was the "pain following after" this shriveling and withering of Christ's flesh, as if time sped up and aged his body into a living corpse. The third *drying* occurred because Christ was hanging high up in the air, "as men hang a cloth for to dry" (17:32–33.183). This is the same Christ whom Julian had much earlier understood so tenderly as "our clothing." Now Julian saw that Christ was literally hung out to dry in the bitter cold wind with his arms spread wide over his head, as laundry is made taut on a line with clothespins, or as a parchment-maker hangs out strips of wet parchment.[1] The force of gravity pulled down his entire bodily weight and stretched out his joints and rib cage to such an extent that every intake of breath became torture; the pain in his hands, and up and down his arms, grew unbearable; and the helplessness of being *nailed* in this position, both hands and feet, made it impossible for him to do anything to alleviate his own condition. The fourth *drying* resulted from the fact that Christ's "bodily nature needed licoure," or liquid, "and there was no manner of comfort ministered to him" (17:33–34.183). The greater Christ's dehydration, the more acute his suffering became. *Drying* was, in Julian's eyes, the source of his unquenchable thirst, both physical and spiritual.

Death by Crucifixion

As gruesome as Julian's depiction of Christ's physical sufferings may seem, it is still not as detailed as that offered by modern doctors and medical examiners who have studied the physical process of death by crucifixion. These experts provide a long list of the tortures and affronts to Christ's body. The night before he died, Christ prayed in the Garden of Gethsemane in full realization of what he would have to suffer: "And being in an agony he prayed more earnestly; and his sweat became as it were great drops of blood falling down upon the ground" (Lk 22:44). This phenomenon is a symptom of acute stress called *hematidrosis*, during which tiny capillaries in the sweat glands burst asunder and mix with sweat. The person literally sweats blood and experiences extreme weakness.

Then, during the long night of questionings by the leaders of the Sanhedrin, the supreme council of the Jews, by Pilate, by Herod, then back to Pilate, Christ underwent scourgings by *both* the temple guards and the Roman soldiers. Hebraic law permitted forty lashes, but the Pharisees restricted the beating of a prisoner to thirty-nine lashes lest the temple guards inadvertently break the law. The Romans, however, had no such restrictions. The soldiers stripped Christ naked, positioned him facing a pillar in the tribunal, and tied his hands over his head. Then they beat him until they, themselves, grew tired. Scourging was not done in place of crucifixion but as part of the normal legal preliminary procedure *before* crucifixion.[2] The soldiers used a *flagrum* or whip with a short handle, equipped with several long leather thongs tipped with lead balls or sheep bones. The force of these thongs first caused massive bruises and ripped open the skin. After repeated blows, the lead balls and sharp bones tore into subcutaneous tissue, cutting deep gashes in Christ's flesh. Muscle tissue erupted through the open wounds, falling outside the skin. Blood poured from capillaries and large veins lying deep within the muscles.[3] Great chunks of skin hung off Christ's back and buttocks and there was blood all over his body, legs, and arms. The heavy bleeding, both externally and internally, led to fluid build-up in Christ's lungs even as he continued to sweat blood, shivered uncontrollably, and endured horrific nerve and muscle pain.[4] As a result of the bleeding and sweating, Christ lost vast quantities of bodily fluids and was left severely weakened, with a desperate thirst. The increasing dehydration may have precipitated an early stage of traumatic shock. The centurion in charge stopped the scourging only when he feared the victim might die before he could undergo crucifixion.

The Roman soldiers, in a sadistic locker-room show of mockery toward the "King of the Jews" wove a crown of large thorns, probably from the common lote-tree, called the *Zizyphus spina Christi*.[5] The crown might actually have been a skull cap of spiney thorns, each an inch and a half to two inches long, covering Christ's entire scalp. The soldiers pressed this cap of thorns deep into Christ's head with reeds, piercing the trigeminal and greater occipital nerves in his cranium and forehead, causing excruciating head and facial pain. During the long process of interrogation and scourging, Christ also received sharp blows from the soldiers' fists, and was struck repeatedly with reeds on his head and across his face (Mt 27:30). His eyes swelled shut, his nose bled profusely, and his lips were torn to shreds by the clamping down of his own teeth. The hematomas under his skin turned his face and entire body a purplish blue and brown.

After his condemnation by Pilate, already extremely weakened and barely able to stand, Christ was forced to walk barefoot the 650 yards of rough and uphill road, the Via Dolorosa, to Calvary, carrying (not dragging) the heavy crossbeam, called the *patibulum*. (This five- or six-foot horizontal beam would eventually be inserted into the vertical beam, the *stipes*, on Calvary, to become the instrument of his own crucifixion.) The *patibulum* weighed between 75 and 125 pounds and was either placed on Christ's back and balanced by his outstretched arms or strapped to his back with ropes around his chest, arms, and hands.[6] Christ must have fallen repeatedly from stumbling on stones, his eyesight impaired by swelling and blinded by blood and stinging sweat dripping from the skullcap of thorns. Each time he fell, the heavy weight of the crossbeam crashed down on his back and neck. Since he was growing visibly weaker due to the great blood and fluid loss, and could barely rise after each fall, the Roman soldiers in charge of his execution had a duty to make sure he lived long enough to be crucified. According to gospel accounts, the soldiers enjoined Simon the Cyrenean to help Christ carry the *patibulum* (Mt 27:32, Mk 15:21, Lk 23:26).

Once on Calvary, Christ, already extremely weak, pale, and death-like, was stripped of his linen tunic, heavily stained with clotted blood from deep gashes. The rough stripping reopened those wounds. Then the soldiers forced him to lie down and stretched out his arms at a 90 degree angle on the *patibulum*. They drilled holes (or, as in the passion play, stretched his arms and feet to fit pre-drilled holes) and then leaned heavily on top of his body as they drove large, square, iron nails through his upper palms, at the wrist. The affront of soldiers exerting pressure on Christ's chest would have caused unbearable pain, due to his internal wounds from the scourging. The hammering in of the nails in the upper palms of both hands severely damaged the many branches of the median nerves, shooting electric shocks through his arms, into the spinal cord, and up into the brain. This syndrome, known as *causalgia*, is considered the most acute pain possible.[7]

The horizontal *patibulum* was then lifted up by four soldiers and inserted into a pre-existing groove at the top of the *stipes crucis*, or vertical stake of the cross, which weighed about 125 pounds. Christ was referring to this lifting up when he said: "And I, when I am lifted up from the earth, will draw all people to myself" (Jn 12:32). The stationary *stipes* was probably about six feet, eight inches high; when the *patibulum* was in place, it added another foot or so of height and formed a T-shape, or *Tau*, which was the normal design of Roman crosses.[8] After being lifted into a hanging position, Christ's arms sagged to a sixty-five degree angle, with the full weight of his body pulling down on his nailed palms. (If he weighed close to 174 pounds, the downward pull would have been about 66/67 pounds per hand.)[9] His feet were then placed flat against the *stipes*, left over right, pointing downward, and one nail was driven into the arches of both feet. This action would have ruptured the plantar nerve, producing shooting pains up the length of the legs and acute cramping of the leg muscles. The nailing of hands and feet was the fulfillment of the ancient prophecy in the psalms:

> For dogs are all around me; a company of evildoers encircles me. My hands and feet have shriveled; I can count all my bones. They stare and gloat over me; they divide my clothes among themselves, and for my clothing they cast lots. (Ps 22:16–18)

Given the full length of the cross (approximately seven feet, eight inches), if Christ's standing height was somewhere between five feet, ten inches, and six feet, then, allowing for the slight bending of his knees, his feet would have been about eighteen to twenty inches off the ground. Hence, even if he spoke his last words in a dry, hoarse whisper, as he exhaled, he could have been heard by those standing near the foot of the cross.

During the three hours of his crucifixion, every time Christ moved in the slightest way, the pressure on all his wounds increased his torture . . . and his bleeding.[10] Each day, the normal heart pumps approximately two thousand gallons of blood through more than sixty thousand miles of blood vessels, both large and small. Throughout the passion, Christ bled and clotted, bled and clotted, hemorrhaging all over his body from the deep lashes. And he bled copiously from the nail wounds in his hands and feet. He also experienced excruciating pains in his chest cavity due to the hematomas and fluid build-up from the scourgings. In addition to the traumatic shock from his injuries, he suffered hypovolemic shock, which is initiated by a steep drop in blood volume due to continued hemorrhaging and loss of body fluids and salty sweat.[11] This caused acute dehydration and a terrible thirst. Again, the psalmist prophesied this thirst:

> I am poured out like water, and all my bones are out of joint; my heart is like wax; it is melted within my breast; my mouth is dried up like a potsherd, and my tongue sticks to my jaws; you lay me in the dust of death. (Ps 22:14–15)

Added to this suffering was the Savior's shame of nakedness and loss of control of bodily excretions, as well as the cramps in every muscle of his arms, legs, back, and neck, the ongoing stretching and tearing of tendons and ligaments, the agonizing pain in his shoulders from holding his arms outstretched for three hours, and the affront to his central nervous system.

> After this, when Jesus knew that all was now finished, he said (in order to fulfill the scripture), "I am thirsty." A jar full of sour wine was standing there. So they put a sponge full of the wine on a branch of hyssop and held it to his mouth. When Jesus had received the wine, he said, "It is finished." Then he bowed his head and gave up his spirit. (Jn 19:28–30)

According to medical experts, his head did not fall to one side, as depicted by so many artists through the ages. When his body sagged in death, the massive muscles on either side of his neck would have locked in a symmetrical and rigid position, his head falling straight forward onto his sternum.[12]

Joseph of Arimathea, a wealthy and respected member of the Sanhedrin, went to Pilate and requested Christ's body (Mk 15:43–45). The Roman procurator was astonished to find that Jesus was already dead, but he gave his permission for Joseph to take down the body. In order to release the body to family and friends for burial, however, Roman regulation required that the crucified be pierced with a lance in order to make absolutely certain that the criminal was dead, lest he be taken down by family members *before* his death and escape punishment.[13] Hence, the Roman executioner, traditionally named Longinus, followed orders and raised his five- or six-foot infantry spear over his head to pierce Christ's heart. The lance blow entered from the right side through an interspace between the ribs, perforated the pericardium, the fluid-filled sac that surrounds the heart, and struck the heart in the right auricle.[14] "And at once blood and water came out" (Jn 19:34). St. John's eyewitness report suggests to modern post-mortem analysis that, due to Christ's injuries, an excess of watery fluid had accumulated in the pericardium, causing severe constriction of his heart which, combined with both traumatic and hypovolemic shock, led to cardiac arrest.[15] Thus, when the Roman soldier pierced the body with his lance, Christ had already died of heart failure.

Two Pains

Julian, of course, was not a physician, not even in the medieval sense. However, it is well worth noting that *her visionary account details many of the very same aspects of death by crucifixion* that modern forensic scientists have articulated: severe and changing discoloration of the face and body due to the heavy blows and profuse internal bleeding; deep gashes from repeated whippings, like the *semys*, or furrows, that ploughing makes in the ground; the clotting of blood and the hanging of flesh from open wounds; extreme loss of blood and fluids resulting in a lack of bodily moisture and an overall withering and drying out of his body, leading to an unbearable thirst. Julian further observed "two pains that shewed in the blessed head" (17:36.183). The first came from the terrible drying out of his wounds, which must have produced a stabbing and throbbing migraine of incomparable proportions. The second pain resulted from the slow but continual withering and drying out from the

> blowing of wind from without that dried him more and pained him with cold more than my heart can think—and other pains. For which pains, I saw that all is too little that I can say, for it may not be told. (17:38–40.183)

In her vision, Julian experienced the cold wind as the final affront to Christ's flesh, a bitter, biting, merciless movement of air across his exposed wounds that caused additional torture. Given Julian's lack of medical knowledge, the remarkable accuracy of her description of the deterioration of Christ's face and body lends enormous credence to her account. How else but through a bodily sight of the passion (and Julian's own extraordinary ability to *observe* and *recall* everything she saw) could she have recorded such details, not to be scientifically documented for another six hundred years?

True Compassion

Julian confesses she is at a loss to say what it was actually like to watch Christ die. She can write only that, "The shewing of Christ's pains filled me full of pains" (17:41.183). She knows that Christ suffered "once for all" (Heb 10:10),[16] but she also believes Christ showed it to her "as if" she had been there, so that he could "fill me with mind [of the passion], as I had before desired" (17:42–43.183). Now, at last, she is experiencing Christ's agony in her own body, with true *com*passion for Christ on the cross. She is literally suffering with him. This was, of course, the first of three gifts she had requested so long ago:

> It seemed to me that I would have been at that time with Mary Magdalene and with others who were Christ's lovers, that I might have seen bodily the passion that our lord suffered for me, that I might have suffered with him as others did who loved him. And therefore I desired a bodily sight, wherein I might have more knowing of the bodily pains of our savior, and of the compassion of our lady, and of all his true lovers who were living at that time and saw his pains. For I would have been one of them and have suffered with them . . . For I would after, because of that shewing, have more true mind of the passion of Christ. (2:7–16.125–27)

Julian declares that "in all this time of Christ's presence, I felt no pain but for Christ's pain" (17:43–44.183). It must have been a great deal worse than anything she had ever experienced in her life, even during her own seven days of dying. She humbly admits that she had never imagined what compassion such as this would involve:

> Then I thought, I knew very little what pain it was that I had asked for. And like a wretch, I repented my request, thinking if I had known what it had been, I would have been loath to have prayed for it. For it seemed to me that my pains surpassed any bodily death. I thought: "Is any pain in hell like this?" And I was answered in my reason: "Hell is another pain, for there is despair. But of all

> pains that lead to salvation, this is the most: to see thy love suffer. How might any pain be more than to see him who is all my life, all my bliss, and all my joy suffer?" (17:44–50.183)

In the moment, she actually regrets that she ever prayed for such suffering. The depth of her pain convinces her this must be hell; it cannot get any worse. But her reason tells her that being in hell means experiencing hopeless despair, for hell's suffering is deemed eternal. Still, she cannot imagine any suffering "that leads to salvation" that could be more terrible than seeing the one who is "all my life, all my bliss and all my joy" suffer in this way. She had watched many loved ones die. She thought she knew what the process was like. Seeing Christ crucified surpassed the pain of all other deaths she had ever witnessed.

> Here I felt truthfully that I loved Christ so much above myself that there was no pain that might be suffered like to that sorrow that I had to see him in pain. (17:50–52.183–85)

Our Lady's Love

Instinctively, Julian identifies with the suffering of Mary, Christ's mother. She also knows from her own experience that when a child suffers, the mother suffers:

> For Christ and she were so oned [united] in love that the greatness of her love was the cause of the magnitude of her pain. For in this I saw the essence of natural love, increased by grace, that his creatures have for him, which natural love was most fulsomely shewn in his sweet mother, overpassing [all others]. For as much as she loved him more than all others, her pain surpassed all others. For ever the higher, the mightier, the sweeter that the love is, the more sorrow it is to the lover to see that body in pain that he loved. And so all his disciples and all his true lovers suffered pains more than their own bodily dying. For I am seker, by my own feeling, that the least of them loved him so far above themselves that it surpasses all that I can say. (18:1–10.185)

No one who has ever loved and watched the loved one die can fail to identify with Julian's words. What she describes is so very human, so touching in its expression, so easily understood. Mary loved Christ more than did anyone else on earth. He was her son, flesh of her flesh, love of her life. She was *oned* with him, both in body and in spirit. Hence, she suffered watching him suffer. And those who stood at the foot of the cross, Christ's "true lovers," also suffered more than those who were not there to see him die. Except for the disciple John, and possibly some men among those who "stood at a distance, watching these things" (Lk 23:49), the onlookers specifically recorded by the four evangelists as being present at the crucifixion were *all women*:

> There were also women looking on from a distance; among them were Mary Magdalene, and Mary the mother of James the younger and of Joses, and Salome. These used to follow him and provided for him when he was in Galilee; and there were many other women who had come up with him to Jerusalem. (Mk 15:40–41; cf. Jn 19:25, Mt 27:55–56)

Perhaps, as she entered into Mary's suffering as well as Christ's, Julian recalled "Mary's Lament" from the passion play:

> **Maria.** Oh, my son, my son, my darling dear!
> What? Have I offended thee?

And she may have remembered the moment when Mary, in desperation to touch her dying son once more, ran forward and embraced the cross:

> **Maria Virgo.** I pray you all, let me stay here
> And hang me up here on this tree
> By my friend and son that to me is so dear,
> For where he is, there would I be!

We have suggested that Julian, too, was a mother who had watched her beloved child die. She writes not only about Mary, mother of all mothers, but about herself and all those, both male and female, who suffer irreparable loss:

> Here I saw a great oneing between Christ and us, to my understanding. For when he was in pain, we were in pain, and all creatures that might suffer pain suffered with him: that is to say, all

> creatures that God hath made to our service, the firmament and earth, failed for sorrow in their nature in the time of Christ's dying. (18:11–14.185)

Julian becomes acutely conscious that all the pain of her life, and of everyone's life, is united with the pain of Christ on the cross. And this is because, in becoming human, Christ took on all manner of pain as his own (Heb 2:9–18). Therefore, "when he was in pain, we were in pain" with him. She might have added: "When we were in pain, *he* was in pain." St. Paul even dared to write that "in my flesh I am completing what is lacking in Christ's afflictions for the sake of his body, that is, the church" (Col 1:24).

Additionally, Julian realizes that not only "all his true lovers," but "all creatures" shared in the agony of Christ's dying. This inextricable connection between the inner life of human beings and the state of the natural world had long been perceived. St. Paul was convinced that the physical earth as well as its creatures are involved in the great struggle of salvation: "We know that the whole creation has been groaning in labor pains until now; and not only the creation, but we ourselves, who have the first fruits of the Spirit, groan inwardly while we wait for adoption, the redemption of our bodies" (Rom 8:22–23). Julian believes that all earth's creatures naturally recognized the Lord, "in whom all their virtues stand" (18:15–16.185). Thus when the Lord died, it behooved creatures out of kindness to die with him, "in as much as they might, for sorrow of his pains" (18:17.185).

The Sacrificial Lamb

There was also a deeply symbolic connection between the death of Christ on the cross at the ninth hour and the daily ritual at which birds and animals were slain in the temple in Jerusalem and their blood sprinkled on the high altar to atone for sin (Lv 4:5–6, 17:11). The day Christ died is believed to have been the preparation day for the Sabbath and the Jewish feast of Passover (Mk 15:42, Lk 23:54, Jn 19:31). As part of this most-important ritual, commemorating the exodus of the Jewish people from slavery under Pharaoh, a lamb was sacrificed and its blood sprinkled on the altar as a holocaust offering for sin. St. Paul writes: "Indeed, under the law almost everything is purified with blood, and without the shedding of blood there is no forgiveness of sins" (Heb 9:22). It was about "the ninth hour [3 PM]" that the temple priest customarily blew his ram's horn from the temple ramparts, announcing that the priests within had just completed the slaying and burning of the lamb for the sins of the world. And according to scripture, at the very moment when Christ "yielded up his spirit," the heavy curtain that enclosed the Holy of Holies where the sacrifice had just been offered was ripped asunder:

> At that moment the curtain of the temple was torn in two, from top to bottom. The earth shook, and the rocks were split. The tombs also were opened, and many bodies of the saints who had fallen asleep were raised. After his resurrection they came out of the tombs and entered the holy city and appeared to many. (Mt 27: 51–53, cf. Mk 15:38)

Julian would not have been aware of the interconnection between the Jewish Passover sacrifice of the lamb in the ancient temple and the Lamb of God who died on the cross, shedding his blood for all. However, she certainly understood that, when Christ took on all flesh in himself and "failed," his entire creation failed with him, animals as well as humans, out of "sorrow for his pains" (18:16–17.185). Even "they who knew him not suffered for failing of all manner of comfort" (18:19.185). And here Julian bears witness to a profound truth: *that the fates of humankind and the entire creation are intimately connected.*

> God of his goodness, who makes planets and the elements to werk in their natures to the benefit of both the blessed man and the cursed, in that time [of the crucifixion] it was withdrawn from both. Wherefore it was that they who knew him not were in sorrow at that time. Thus was our lord Jesus noughted for us, and we stand all in this manner noughted with him, and shall do so till we come to his bliss, as I shall say after. (18:26–30.187)

Throughout this section, Julian shows her great empathy with plants and animals, as well as with the earth that continually groans, and quakes, and labors like a woman about to give birth (Mt 24:7–8, Mk 13:8, cf. Lk 21:11). She reveals wonder alike for heavenly planets and the elements (earth, air, fire, and water) that, according to medieval astronomy, ruled and sustained all life.

Time, Revelation, and Language

In the course of her Revelations, Julian interchanges the concepts of time, seeing, and understanding. She uses the word, "time" ("one time," "at that time," "for that time,") over two hundred times: "in this," meaning a Revelation that occurred in time, one hundred and fifty times; "I saw," one hundred and sixty times; and "I understood," in countless ways to mean a more contemplative "seeing."[17] She is constantly aware that there was a definite progression to what she was seeing and hearing, though the actual Revelations occurred in short, discrete, and seemingly eternal "instants." By her own account, after each *shewing*, Julian was given considerable "time" to ponder and evaluate what was being revealed to her, step by step, so that she might better understand its hidden meaning. And then, over the course of many decades, she further contemplated the Revelations, adding a third layer of insight. Julian weaves these aspects of her experience seamlessly, now describing what she saw or heard in the moment of the Revelation, then her understanding of it "at the time," then articulating her later intuitions about the deeper meaning.

We have seen that, quite often, Julian has recourse to commonplace images (a hazelnut in her palm, rain dripping from the eaves, the scales of a herring, a dried-up wooden board, a cloth hanging in the wind) to give a concrete picture of what is for her essentially indescribable. She often admits that she simply cannot find the words to express what she experienced or what she came to understand. At other times, she alludes to apocryphal stories she believed, as did most of her contemporaries, were true. Simply because the form of expression, or the example chosen to prove her point, may seem less-than-exalted does not indicate that the Revelation that prompted it was less-than-profound. Julian, like all writers, was forced to use the language, metaphors, and even the commonly held assumptions of her time to record transcendent illuminations. Sometimes her form of expression is sublime; at other times, less so. While the revelations of true mystics are always clear, distinct, and indelible, the language of mystics is often imperfect, tentative, even confusing.

Add to this, in Julian's case, a writer's unfamiliarity with a still imprecise and inelegant language in which she was forced to describe the ineffable in commonplace phrases, and we may appreciate the impossible task she set herself. Julian was literally learning to write (and to spell) an unformulated and constantly evolving vernacular even as she was working out her mystical theology. Sometimes, it seems as if Julian is composing a stream-of-consciousness monologue or rehearsing an interior dialogue with Christ. At other times, she seems to be speaking aloud as she writes, addressing herself to an intended audience of *evencristens*, known personally to her. Then her writing becomes more oral than literary, like the spontaneous transcription of a conversation. It is only by listening well to her living speech, and perhaps even speaking it aloud as we read, that we may unravel the deeper sense of her words.

This understood, we may forgive Julian a few scriptural inaccuracies, her occasional recourse to popular religious culture (such as *The Golden Legend*, with its largely apocryphal tales of the lives of saints), her sometimes convoluted sentence structure, and even small contradictions. Language, at the best of times, is merely an imperfect attempt at labeling inspirations, thoughts, and emotions that cannot be confined to any word or phrase. Words are the eternal bane, as well as the blessing, of the writer. We must be grateful that Julian pressed on, attempting in whatever way she could to use the language of the *lewed* to express the inexpressible.

Julian's Choice

> In this time I would have looked from the cross, and I dared not, for I knew well that as long as I beheld the cross, I was seker and safe. Therefore, I would not assent to put my soul in peril, for beside the cross was no sekerness, only ugliness of fiends. (19:1–4.187)

The torture of seeing and feeling Christ's pains, in some measure, made Julian want to look away from the cross on which she had been focused since the First Revelation. She longed to fly up to heaven (she had already enjoyed a glimpse of the heavenly banquet) and have all this suffering be finished. Instinctively, however, she knew this desire was a temptation from the fiends that were believed to gather at the bedside of the dying. If she did as the fiends suggested, she might sin mortally and put her soul in peril. She was convinced that only by keeping her eyes focused on the crucifixion, like the "other women" at the foot of the cross, would there be security and safety from the devils.

> Then I had a proposition given in my reason, as if it had been friendly, say to me: "Look up to heaven to his father." And then I saw well, with the faith that I felt, that there was nothing between the cross and heaven that might have disturbed me, and either it behooved me to look up or else to answer. I answered inwardly with all the might of my soul, and said: "Nay, I may not! For thou art my heaven." This I said for I would not look up. For I had rather have been in that pain till domesday, than have come to heaven otherwise than by him. For I know well that he that bound me so sorely, he should unbind me when he would. (19:4–11.187)

The tempter tried again: "Look up to heaven to his [Christ's] father." This seemed to be a "friendly," even holy, suggestion. However, Julian quickly realized that this too was a temptation, to get her to break her total concentration on the dying Christ. We must recall that when the crucifix was first brought to Julian by her curate, her eyes were already looking up toward heaven, where she thought she soon would go. It was the curate who told her to look directly at the cross and, though it required a great effort on her part, her obedience set the stage for the first and all the following Revelations. Julian is determined to remain faithful to that initial instruction. She also realizes that there is nothing between the cross and heaven that could disturb her.

Julian answers her mental tempter with the emphatic inner response: "Nay I may not!" She switches immediately to address Christ: "For thou art my heaven." She testifies that she is willing to suffer with him in his pain until the end of the world and Domesday, rather than try to escape to heaven (if it were possible) in any way other than through a share in his death. And she counts on the fact that if Christ has bound her to himself through suffering, then he, and he alone, will unbind her when it is his will to do so.

> Thus was I taught to choose Jesus for my heaven, whom I saw only in pain at that time. I wanted no other heaven than Jesus, who shall be my bliss when I come there. And this has ever been a comfort to me, that I chose Jesus to be my heaven, by his grace, in all this time of passion and sorrow. And that has been a teaching to me, that I should evermore do so, to choose Jesus only for my heaven in wele and in woe. (19:12–17.189)

Julian does not want to desert Christ and leave him alone, as the disciples did, by looking away from the harshness of his sufferings, even for a single moment. She desires no heavenly vision that is without Jesus and, paradoxically, to be with Jesus, even in his terrible suffering on earth, becomes heaven for her.

In Julian's mind, this is a major turning point. Earlier, she had longed to be out of her suffering and go quickly to heaven. Now she understands that there is no way to reach that exalted place except through a share in the sufferings of Christ and through the transformation of the soul that this compassion effects.

> But if we have died with Christ, we believe that we will also live with him. We know that Christ, being raised from the dead, will never die again; death no longer has dominion over him. (Rom 6:8–9)

By bearing her own suffering in faith and patience, Julian realizes she will finally be like him who "humbled himself and became obedient to the point of death—even death on a cross" (Phil 2:8). And by electing to remain focused on the suffering Christ, she also chooses to go on living on earth, no matter how painful, and uncertain, and long it might be, rather than giving in to the blessed release of death. By this emphatic decision "to choose Jesus for my heaven," Julian also registers her willingness to stay with Mary and the "other women" at the foot of the cross on Calvary and with the *evencristens* beside her bed, fingering their rosary beads and praying on her behalf. If Christ wants her here, here she will stay. When he wants her to go, she will be willing to go. This choice releases something in Julian at which she had still been grasping, even in the self-*noughting* process of watching the passion unfold, namely, her great desire for heaven. She finds lasting comfort in the fact that she has been able, by the power of grace, to endure "all this time of passion and sorrow." And she affirms that this was an important life teaching for her: "to choose Jesus only for my heaven in wele and in woe."

Flesh and Spirit

Julian recalls that earlier she had wished that she had never prayed to experience Christ's sufferings. At that time, "like a wretch," she had wanted to take back her prayer. She recalls with stunning candor that she had thought: "If I had known what pain it would be, I would have been loath to have prayed for it" (19:17–18.189). Now, she sees truly that what had so frightened her and caused her momentary revulsion was the "begrudging and resistance *of the flesh* without assent of the soul" (19:19.189, italics added). Hence, since she did not refuse to suffer by an act of her free will, God assigned her no blame. She reflects that her regret (for having prayed to suffer with Christ) and her deliberate choice (the one she has just made, choosing Jesus for her heaven), are two contraries, "which I felt both in one at that time" (19:21–22.189). She understands the one is outward, that is, having to do with the mortal flesh, which is now in pain and in woe that she experienced greatly during this time. And that is the part of her that recoiled from suffering. However, the other, the inward part, was the foundation of her soul. There she felt secure that she had chosen her Lord over herself.

> The inward part is a high and blissful life, which is all in peace and in love, and this is more privately felt. And this part is that in which mightily, wisely, and willfully, I chose Jesus to be my heaven. And in this, I saw truly that the inward part is master and sovereign to the outward, not reckoning nor taking heed of the will of that outward self. But all the intention and the will of the inner part is committed endlessly to be oned to our lord Jesus. That the outward part should draw the inward to assent was not shewn to me. But that the inward part draws the outward part, by grace, and both shall be oned in bliss without end by the virtue of Christ, this was shewn. (19:25–32.189)

Here, Julian gives a description of the duality of flesh and spirit, body and soul, that has long been perceived as two separate parts of the self, co-existing in one person. She gains a great insight, that the resistance of the will of the "outward self" (that is, the will of the flesh) to suffering, no matter how strong the impulse may be, does *not* make us culpable of sin or betrayal. Only the will of the "inward part" truly chooses. Julian extols this inner will as "a high and blissful life, which is all in peace and in love." She believes "the intention and the will of the inner part" are essentially good and ever long to be "oned" to Jesus Christ. Further, she maintains that it was precisely the "inner part" of her spirit that, through the gift of grace, enabled her "outer part" to "mightily, wisely, and willfully" choose

Jesus to be her heaven. (Julian will develop these thoughts when she later discusses the nature of the soul's substance and sensuality.)

The *Languring*

> And thus I saw our Lord Jesus languring [growing weaker] a long time. For the oneing with the godhead gave strength to the manhood for love to suffer more than all men might suffer. I mean not only more pain than all men might suffer but also that he suffered more pain than all men of salvation that ever were, from the first beginning unto the last day. No tongue may tell, or heart fully think, the pains that our saviour suffered for us, taking into account the worthiness of the highest, worshipful king and the shameful, pitiless and painful death. For he that is highest and worthiest was fullest noughted and most utterly despised. (20:1–8.189–91)

Julian is stunned by how long Christ continues to languish on the cross and wonders how he could possibly endure it. She understands that it was only because his divinity gave strength to his humanity that he was able to suffer more than all humankind that has ever lived, or will live. Words fail her here. Even the love in her heart cannot express the pains he went through, especially because he who was the king of all creation "humbled himself" (Phil 2:7–8) to endure such a "shameful, pitiless and painful death." Julian continues to reflect on "the height and the nobility of the glorious godhead" of Jesus Christ and on "the preciousness and tenderness of the blissful body which are together oned" (20:12–14.191). She also considers how much human beings (like herself) are loath to undergo pain. But Christ was not. He was willing to suffer for the sin of every person who shall be saved. And Christ saw and sorrowed for every person's "desolation and anguish," out of "kindness and love" (20:17–18.191). He also suffered for his mother, though she was without sin.

> For inasmuch as our lady sorrowed for his pains, that much he suffered sorrow for her sorrow, and more over, inasmuch as his sweet manhood was more noble in nature. For as long as he was able to suffer, he suffered for us and sorrowed for us. And now he is resurrected and no longer able to suffer, yet he still suffers with us, as I shall say after. (20:18–22.191)

"Beholding all this by his grace," Julian realizes that the love Christ has for souls was so strong that he willfully chose suffering "with great desire, and patiently suffered it with *great joy*" (20:23–25.191, italics added). This is an astounding insight that cuts through and completely transforms Julian's personal pain at watching Christ suffer. She is convinced that any soul that is "touched by grace" in watching Christ's passion shall see that his pain surpasses all human pains, that is, all those pains that "shall be turned into everlasting joy by virtue of Christ's passion" (20:25–28.191). (It is notable that Julian does not consider the pains of hell.) She perceives that there are *three ways* of beholding the passion. The first, which she has been experiencing by the power of grace, is by looking at the "hard pain that he suffered, with contrition and compassion" (21:2–3.191). She will consider the other two later.

15
Transformation

> And I looked for the departing of life with all my might and expected to have seen the body completely dead. But I saw him not so. And just in that same time that it seemed to me, by all appearances, that his life might no longer last, and the shewing of the end must needs be near—suddenly, as I beheld the same cross, *he changed in blissful chere* [his face changed into a joyful expression]. The changing of his blissful chere changed mine, and I was as glad and merry as it was possible to be. Then our Lord brought this merrily to mind: "Where is now any point of thy pain or of thy grief?" And I was completely merry. (21:5–11.191–3, italics added)

She waited and waited, but Christ did not die as in the gospels; as in the pitiful paintings she had seen of the lifeless Savior on the cross, with his head dropped down; or as she had seen in the passion play. Instead, as she looked steadily into the cross, Christ's face was transformed before her eyes. His countenance looked so exquisitely joyful that it caused Julian's own expression to change. Suddenly, she became "glad and merry," implying happy, cheerful, ebullient, almost giddy—as if she might laugh out loud once again, as if she had never had a pain in the world. And the locution that spoke within her mind in that moment was equally startling: "Where is now any point of thy pain or of thy grief?"

In that instant, she experienced the radical *changeability* of even the worst suffering. (We recognize the feeling: when we start laughing aloud in gratitude and relief that some near-tragedy has just been averted, even as hot tears still flow down our faces.) Historically, we know Christ did not escape death. He really "bowed his head and gave up his spirit" on the cross (Jn 19:30). His side was really pierced with a soldier's lance (Jn 19:34). He really was taken down from the cross and wrapped "in a linen cloth"; his body really was laid "in a rock-hewn tomb where no one had ever been laid" (Lk 23:53, Mk 15:46). However, Julian's unique gospel account of Christ's passion and sudden transformation is based on a lifelike *vision* happening before her eyes. Moment by moment, her mind has been inspired by grace to experience the sensory images, the words, the vivid impressions, the intellectual understanding, and the emotional reactions. Like the images we project and perceive every moment of our lives, none of these mental images is absolute and unchanging. Therefore, every situation, every emotion, can (and does) change eventually. For Julian, in a mysterious and wonderful way, the image changed in an instant.

By her faith, Julian knew Christ had already died and the resurrection had already occurred. Therefore, even in her vision, she could not actually *see* Christ die, because she believed from Christian teaching that he cannot die again:

> We know that Christ, being raised from the dead, *will never die again*; death no longer has dominion over him. The death he died, he died to sin, once for all; but the life he lives, he lives to God. (Rom 6:9–10, italics added)

In this Revelation, Julian's mind leapt into eternity. In that sublime moment, she saw Christ's face utterly transformed into a radiant expression, like the instant when Peter, James, and John saw Christ transfigured before their eyes on Mt. Tabor, "and his face shone like the sun, and his clothes became dazzling white" (Mt 17:1–2, Mk 9:3). It was as if Julian herself had died, letting go of all her assumptions about earthly reality and the inevitability of death. Her mind was privileged to glimpse the glory of Christ's reality in the bliss of heaven, where sorrow and suffering do not exist.

> I understood that we are now, in our lord's intention, on his cross with him in our pains and in our passion, dying. And we, willfully abiding on the same cross, with his help and his grace, into the last point, *suddenly he shall change his chere toward us, and we shall be with him in heaven*. Between that one [the pain on the cross] and that other [being in heaven] shall all be one time, and then shall all be brought into joy. And this is what he meant in this shewing:

> "Where is now any point of thy pain or of thy grief?" And we shall be fully blessed. (21:12–17.193, italics added)

By the sheer suddenness Julian suggests what a holy death might be like: one moment in pain, the next in bliss. She understands that not only has Christ overcome the fiend through suffering, he has eradicated the mighty grip of death altogether: "Where, O death, is your victory? Where, O death, is your sting?" (1 Cor 15:55). For some, death might even be ecstatic:

> because God did not make death, and he does not delight in the death of the living. For he created all things so that they might exist; the generative forces of the world are wholesome, and there is no destructive poison in them, and the dominion of Hades is not on earth. (Ws 1:13–14)

Death and Life

In seeing that death is as evanescent as any given moment of life, Julian not only believes, she *experiences* that death is not final in any ultimate way, either for Christ or, because of Christ, for all of humankind. It is a passage from one form of life to another, not an end, but a beginning. "So you have pain now; but I will see you again, and your hearts will rejoice, and no one will take your joy from you" (Jn 16:22).

In heaven, the saints become one-in-Christ who creates the "new heavens and the new earth" (Is 66:22, Rv 21:1). The transformation happens beyond time. Christ said to the good thief who was crucified beside him: "Truly I tell you, *today* you will be with me in Paradise" (Lk 23:43, italics added). However, the thief on the other side of Christ (in a prophetic simulation of the Last Judgment), having no fear of God, cursed and mocked Jesus: "Are you not the Messiah? Save yourself and us!" (Lk 23:39). Likewise, the leaders of the people also jeered and scoffed at him: "He saved others; let him save himself if he is the Messiah of God, his chosen one!" (Lk 23:35), and "Let the Messiah, the King of Israel, come down from the cross now, so that we may see and believe" (Mk 15:32). The soldiers, standing guard by the cross, also derided him: "If you are the King of the Jews, save yourself!" (Lk 23:37). According to the way we have chosen to live our lives, death will either be a blissful liberation from pain and suffering into unimaginable joy or a self-inflicted damnation into a mental hell.

Right now, according to Julian's understanding, we abide in the reality of the cross; we are living existentially *within* the passion of Christ, "in our pains and in our passion, dying." In fact, when we look at the cross, we "see" what sin really looks like by the suffering it causes. We also recognize in Christ's sufferings what our own suffering feels like. Yet Julian envisions that, at the last moment of our lives, suddenly Christ will "change his chere toward us, and we shall be with him in heaven." By this she means that Christ will instantaneously convert all our suffering into joy, *simply by transforming our mind's ability to perceive him.* Julian insists that between the time of suffering and the time of joy will be "all one time"; that is, in medieval terms, no time at all. St. Paul also wrote:

> Listen, I will tell you a mystery! We will not all die, but we will all be changed, in a moment, in the twinkling of an eye, at the last trumpet. For the trumpet will sound, and the dead will be raised imperishable, and we will be changed. (1 Cor 15:51–52)

Julian had a premonition of this "twinkling of an eye" in her vision. So great is the glory of the transformed Christ that Julian imagines that if he were to reveal his blissful countenance to each one of us, here and now, there would be no suffering on earth that could cause us grief; rather, everything would be pure joy and bliss. But he must show us now the countenance of his passion because, until we are purified and sanctified by the catalyst of suffering, we will not be able to "see" his blessed face. Therefore, we are still in great distress and labor with him for our salvation.

Adoption

Most importantly, in Julian's understanding, "the cause of his suffering is because he wills out of his goodness to make us the heirs like him in his bliss" (21:22–23.193). Hers is not a theology of *atonement* like St. Anselm's; it is a theology of *adoption* like St. Paul's:

> For all who are led by the Spirit of God are children of God. For you did not receive a spirit of slavery to fall back into fear, but you have received a spirit of adoption. When we cry, "Abba! Father!" it

> is that very Spirit bearing witness with our spirit that we are children of God, and if children, then heirs, heirs of God and joint heirs with Christ—if, in fact, we suffer with him so that we may also be glorified with him. (Rom 8:14–17)

Julian is convinced that we are Christ's own children for whom he has labored long and hard, like a woman enduring a painful childbirth, in order to overcome our mental and emotional fiends and give us new life. Therefore, he is personally responsible for us, like a good parent who will never give up on his child. This is a theme to which Julian will return in much greater depth at a later time, when she speaks of Christ's Motherhood.

> And for this little pain that we suffer here, we shall have a high, endless knowing in God, which we might never have without that pain. And the harder our pains have been with him on his cross, the more shall our honor be with him in his kingdom. (21:23–26.193)

With great understanding, Julian is only too aware that the reality of Christ's triumph over each individual's death, and the soul's liberation into resurrected bliss, is yet to be made manifest in each person's experience. Meanwhile, the length of days and nights of suffering persists and the large stone that keeps us walled up in our minds and bodies seems too big and heavy ever to be rolled back. Death seems so final, for ourselves and for those we love. We are like the "Three Marys" on their way to the tomb on Easter morning:

> When the sabbath was over, Mary Magdalene, and Mary the mother of James, and Salome bought spices, so that they might go and anoint him. And very early on the first day of the week, when the sun had risen, they went to the tomb. They had been saying to one another, "Who will roll away the stone for us from the entrance to the tomb?" When they looked up, they saw that the stone, which was very large, had already been rolled back. (Mk 16:1–4; cf. Mt 28:1–2, Lk 24:1–2, Jn 20:1)

Julian bears a similar witness that, in no time at all, we will experience that the great stone of our suffering and death has already been rolled back... indeed, pulverized. It will be no more. Darkness has been obliterated by the light of Jesus Christ. And for "this little pain that we suffer here" (no matter how devastating it may be for us to endure here and now), we shall bask forever in the radiance of his Holy Face.

The Ninth Revelation

> Then said our good lord, asking: "Art thou well apaid [well satisfied] that I suffered for thee?" I said: "Ya [yes] good lord, gramercy [grand mercy, great thanks]. Ya, good lord, blessed may thou be." Then said Jesus, our good lord: "If thou art satisfied, I am satisfied. It is a joy, a bliss, an endless liking [delight] to me that ever I suffered my passion for thee. And if I might suffer more, I would suffer more." (22:1–5.193–95)

In this new Revelation, the implications of Julian's spiritual dialogue with Christ are vast. With his words, "Art thou well apaid?" the Lord seems to invert the traditional teaching that the Son of God became man to make atonement *to God* for the disobedience of original sin and the sins of all humankind. As we have seen, whether theologians saw this atonement as the settlement of a "debt" to Divine Justice or a "buying back" of humankind from the clutches of Satan, the basic logic stayed the same: the goodness and majesty of God had been offended by human sin, humanity was ensnared in evil, restitution had to be made, and only the God-man could do so. Thus the incarnation was necessary: Christ, the Son of God, had to suffer and die on a cross to overcome the fiend and, more importantly, to make amends and repair the debt to the Father.

Yet here Christ is asking Julian directly if *she* is "well apaid" or sufficiently satisfied (and even pleased) that he suffered as he did "for thee," *as if restitution for sin had to be made to sinners*! And the "for thee" is singular, not plural, yet is individually applicable to every person who ever lives. In her answer, Julian seems astonished by Christ's overwhelming courtesy and humility in asking her this profound question, in essence: *Is she satisfied with the crucifixion?* She hardly knows what to say. She stammers colloquially: "Ya, good lord, gramercy," as if she already comprehends what Christ means by these extraordinary words. Then, still searching for a way to respond, she adds another "Ya, good lord," and finally a short, common expression of praise: "blessed may thou be."

The upheaval does not end there. Christ lets Julian know that if she is satisfied with his payment of the great debt, both to the Father and to her, then so is he, as if he had waited to find out how *she* felt about his passion before being fully satisfied with it himself! Christ continues: "It is a joy, a bliss, an endless liking to me that ever I suffered my passion for thee." Julian has just been watching him endure inconceivable agony...and Christ calls it a joy, a bliss, an endless *delight*? Christ even adds: "And if I might suffer more, I would suffer more."

This line seems to echo Isaiah's Song of the Vineyard: "What more was there to do for my vineyard that I have not done in it?" (Is 5:4). Similar words appear in the liturgy for Good Friday: "What more should I do for you and have not done?"[1] Yet in Julian's locution, Christ is not asking what more he *could* have done, but saying how much more he *would* have done if it had been possible. As it was, the Son of God could not have suffered any more than he did. His passion was and is the complete and perfect sacrifice for all time. But Christ insists that he wants Julian to be as pleased and joyous and blissful about it as he is; otherwise, he will not consider his suffering fully satisfactory.

Christ's Mind

Julian had sought "mind of the passion," by which she meant a deeper compassion in her own mind and heart for Christ's sufferings and death. She had never expected to hear Christ reveal to her *his own mind* about why he suffered. From this locution, she becomes acutely aware that he endured his passion to convince her of his love and of his great compassion for *her* sufferings. The realization is heart-stopping. What Julian is telling her readers is that everything we suffer is not a loss, not pointless, and will never be forgotten by Christ. He considers our trials and agonies as part of his own. He took them on, even as he took on our flesh and blood. Christ's suffering became, in a very real sense, his initiation into what human beings endure. And Julian understood that because of Christ's stupendous sacrifice on the cross, every physical pain, every emotional loss, every spiritual torture, whether small or great, becomes part of the process of our salvation. In fact, the only existential "mind of the passion" that we can have is through our personal sufferings. Our pain-filled lives, even more than our meditations on the passion, are our truest union with Christ on the cross. And Christ, by suffering within us and for us, radically changes the very *meaning* of human suffering from incomprehensible tragedy to transformation in glory.

By asking, "Art thou well apaid that I suffered for thee?" Christ was forcing Julian to examine how completely she accepted his sacrifice on the cross. He was saying to her, in effect: "Are you finally convinced that I loved you *this much*?" It will take Julian years to fully appreciate the magnitude of Christ's gift and the depth of his compassion, much less to be able to accept it with all her heart: "Ya, good lord, gramercy."

Three Heavens

The inexpressible joy of this divine dialogue allowed Julian's vision to expand to such a degree that, "In this feeling, my understanding was lifted up into heaven" (22:6.195). Unlike St. Paul's description of being "caught up to the third heaven" (2 Cor 12:2), Julian writes that she saw "three heavens" (22:7.195). She greatly marvels that all three heavens consist of different aspects of the glorified manhood of Christ. And she attests that no single heaven is more or less, or higher or lower, but all are equally alike in bliss.

> For the first heaven, Christ shewed me his father, in no bodily likeness, but in his property and in his werking [in his attributes and activity]; that is to say, I saw in Christ that the father *is*. The werking of the father is this: that he gives mede [reward] to his son Jesus Christ. This gift and this mede is so blissful to Jesus that his father might have given him no mede that he might have liked any better. (22:9–13.195, italics added)

Julian is again gifted with an intellectual vision of the Trinity, which is seen existing, as at the very beginning of her Revelations, "wherever Christ appears." First, Christ showed Julian the Father, not in any physical form, for he has none. The physical representations of God the Father as an old man with a long white beard, both in Eastern Orthodox icons and Western medieval paintings, had long been considered theologically wrong. (The mystery plays, however, continued to depict God the Father as a man with a gilded face, wearing a halo and long flowing robes.) Julian understood the Father through his properties, or attributes, and as being *pure existence*:

"That is to say, I saw in Christ that the father *is*." In the glorified humanity of Christ, Julian is privileged to contemplate the Father, He-Who-Is, Jehovah. She realizes that the Father's *werking* is to give his Son a reward, the *mede*. And this gift is so abundantly satisfying to Christ that it could not be any more so. St. Paul had written that:

> Therefore God also highly exalted him and gave him the name that is above every name, so that at the name of Jesus every knee should bend, in heaven and on earth and under the earth, and every tongue should confess that Jesus Christ is Lord, to the glory of God the Father. (Phil 2:9–11)

This first heaven, the pleasing or delight of the Father, was shown to Julian as a heaven in itself; "and it was completely blissful" (22: 15.195). She will explain the other "two heavens" subsequently.

> For he [the Father] is fully pleased with all the deeds that Jesus hath done for our salvation, by which we become his not only by his buying of us, but also by the courteous gift of his father. *We are his bliss, we are his mede, we are his worship, we are his crown.* (And this was a singular marvel and a fully delectable beholding, that we are his crown!) This that I say is such a great bliss to Jesus that he sets at nought [discounts] his travail and his hard passion, and his cruel and shameful death. And in these words—"If I might suffer more, I would suffer more"—I saw truly that as often as he could die, so often he would, and love would never let him have rest till he had done it. (22:15–23.195, italics added)

Astonishingly, the *mede* Julian beholds the Father giving the Son is none other than "us." According to this Revelation, we become Christ's reward not just because he bought us back from Satan, but as a "courteous gift" from the Father. We, for whom Christ labored and died, are his bliss, his honor, his crown. The garland of thorns has been transformed into the crown fit for a king, and human beings are its diamonds, pearls, rubies, emeralds, and sapphires. Julian is ecstatic at this Revelation. Further, she understands that Jesus is so completely blissful in receiving this gift of the salvation of humankind that he totally discounts all that he had to endure in order to achieve it. She intuits that if he could die over and over again for each individual who would accept salvation, his "love would never let him have rest until he had done it." It may seem to us incomprehensible that the greatest gift the Son could receive from the Father is *ourselves.* But that is why Christ was born into the world: "I came that they may have life, and have it abundantly" (Jn 10:10).

Then Julian, with disarming curiosity, reveals that she tried "with great diligence" to behold *how often* Christ would have died if he could (22:24.197). She admits the number so far surpassed her understanding and her wits that her reason could not comprehend it. Yet she knew that, even then, if Christ had died an infinite number of times, he would still have "set it at nought for love," for he would consider all that suffering but little in comparison with his love (22:27.197).

> For though the sweet manhood of Christ might suffer but once, his goodness may never cease to offer himself; every day he is ready to do the same, if it might be possible. For if he said he would for my love make new heavens and new earths, it would be but little in comparison. For this might he do each day, if he wanted, without any travail. But to die for my love so often that the number passes creatures' reason—this is the highest offering that our lord God might make to man's soul, as to my sight. Then he means thus: "How should it then be that I should not for thy love do all that I might? Which deed grieveth me nought, since I would for thy love die so often, having no regard for my hard pains." (22:28–36.197)

Here, Julian suggests the way in which Christ offers himself to the Father in the daily sacrifice of the Mass. In this *un*bloody re-enactment of the sacrifice of the cross, Christ does indeed "die so often" for love "that the number passes creatures' reason." In the Short Text, Julian was even more explicit: "I saw truly that *if he might die as often as once for every man who shall be saved*, as he died once for all, love would never let him have rest until he had done it" (xii:20–22.87, italics added). The church believes that, throughout the world, the Lamb of God is being immolated on the altar for the salvation of humankind until the end of time. He allows himself to be bound under the appearances of bread and wine so that he might be truly and mystically present to those who receive him in Eucharist. Julian understands that he does all he can possibly do to show his love, even more than creating "new heavens and new earths." He continually enters into the midst of every person's suffering, in every time and place, having no regard for the cost. And he does it all "for thy love."

The Second Beholding

Earlier, Julian had mentioned three manners of beholding the passion of Christ. The first was to contemplate the terrible pain that he suffered, "with contrition and compassion" (21:2–3.191). (These were also two of the "three wounds" Julian initially desired.) Now, she reveals the second way of beholding the passion: by recognizing that "the love that made him suffer it surpasses all his pains as far as heaven is above earth" (22:37–38.197).

> For the pain was a noble, precious, and honorable deed done at one time by the werking of love. And love was without beginning, is, and shall be without end. For which love he said very sweetly this word: "If I might suffer more, I would suffer more." He did not say, "if it were *needful* to suffer more" but, "if I *might* suffer more." For though it was not needful, if he might suffer more, he would. (22:38–43.197, italics added)

Julian makes a fine and poignant theological distinction here. As we have seen, medieval scholastics, following St. Thomas Aquinas, were generally agreed that it was *not* absolutely necessary for Christ to suffer and die. Being God as well as man, Christ could have chosen any other way to redeem humankind from sin and satisfy Divine Justice. But he chose to suffer and die. And Julian is very careful to draw the distinction between it being *necessary* to suffer (which it was not) and Christ being *willing* to suffer (which he was).

> No one takes it [my life] from me, but I lay it down of my own accord. I have power to lay it down, and I have power to take it up again. I have received this command from my Father. (Jn 10:18)

Julian adds that Christ's death and our salvation "was ordained as well as God could ordain it and it was done as worshipfully as Christ might do it" (22:44–45.197). And because of the perfect sacrifice of Christ's death, Julian saw a fullness of bliss in Christ that was unsurpassable. And she knows that his bliss could not have been as complete if he could have wrought our salvation any better than he did.

> And in these three words—"it is a joy, a bliss, an endless liking to me"—were shewn three heavens, as thus: for the joy, I understood the pleasure of the father; and for the bliss, the worshipping of the son; and for the endless delight, the holy ghost. The father is pleased, the son is worshipped, the holy ghost is delighted. (23:1–4.199)

Here, Julian finally adds the other "two heavens" to the "first heaven" she described earlier, the Father's perfect joy in Christ his Son, which was revealed at Christ's baptism in the Jordan: "This is my Son, the Beloved, with whom I am well pleased" (Mt 3:17, Lk 3:22). The second heaven is Christ's own personal bliss in being so greatly honored by his Father: "If I glorify myself, my glory is nothing. It is my Father who glorifies me" (Jn 8:54). And the third heaven is the Holy Spirit of Christ Jesus himself, who takes "endless delight" in the Savior, even during the worst moments of his passion. In this triple joy, bliss, and "endless liking," Julian extols the three persons of the Trinity as "three heavens" which are, in fact, one.

The Third Beholding

> And here I saw the third beholding in his blissful passion: that is to say, the joy and the bliss that made him take pleasure in it. For our courteous lord shewed his passion to me in five ways: of which the first is the bleeding of the head, the second is the discolouring of his blessed face, the third is the plenteous bleeding of the body in the wounds of the scourging, the fourth is the deep drying—these four as it was said before as shewing the pains of the passion—and the fifth is this that was shewn for the joy and the bliss of the passion. (23:5–11.199)

Now Julian identifies the third way of beholding the passion as seeing Christ's own exquisite joy and bliss that he took in undergoing it. Using the *sermo modernus* formula she knew well from the pulpit, Julian sums up the *five ways* in which the Lord had shown her "the pains of his passion": the bleeding of the head, the discoloration of the face, the bleeding of the wounds from the scourging, and the deep drying, as she has explained before. The fifth is the present one to which she is referring: the passion as being a "joy and bliss" for Christ to suffer, not a tragedy. It appears as incomprehensible to

Julian as it does to us. Yet Julian insists that it is God's will that we *delight* with Christ in our salvation, and that we take great comfort and find strength in it as well. It is with this attitude, even more than one of sorrowing (repeatedly urged in medieval meditations on the passion), that he wishes "merrily, with his grace, that our soul be occupied" (23:13.199). Julian continues:

> For we are his bliss, for in us he delights without end, and so shall we in him with his grace. All that he has done for us, and does, and ever shall, was never cost nor charge to him nor might be, but only that he did it in our manhood, beginning at the sweet incarnation, and lasting to the blessed resurrection on Easter morrow. (23:13–17.199)

Julian is making a distinction here between the work of Christ as God and as man. Nothing he did as God cost him anything in the way of expenditure of effort or difficulty. Only in his *humanity* did Jesus have to pay the "cost" and satisfy the "charge" of our redemption (she is using a medieval monetary and theological metaphor here). Yet she is convinced that Jesus wishes us to attend to the joy "that is in the blissful trinity because of our salvation," not only to the suffering he endured on earth to achieve it (23:19–20.199). She even declares that our delight in our own salvation should be "like to the joy that Christ has because of our salvation," at least as much as this is possible while we are in this life (23:22.199). She affirms that the whole Trinity worked in the passion of Christ, "ministering an abundance of virtues and fullness of grace to us by him. But only the maiden's son suffered," that is, Mary's son (23:23–24.199). And in this, the whole Trinity endlessly rejoices. Julian understands this joy as the deeper meaning behind Christ's earlier words: "Art thou well apaid?" and "If thou art apaid, I am apaid." She explains that it was "as if" Christ had said to her:

> "It is joy and delight enough to me, and I ask nought else of thee for my travail but that I might apaye [satisfy] thee." (23:27–28.201)

According to this Revelation, Christ wants us to take endless delight in his hard labor for our salvation. We cannot and need not try to earn or merit being saved. It has already been accomplished. We are invited to receive the gift and to rejoice in what the Savior has done for us. Julian is reminded here of the "glad giver" who does not take notice of the thing he gives, because "all his desire and all his intention is to please him and comfort him to whom he gives it" (23:29–31.201).

> And if the receiver takes the gift gladly and thankfully, then the courteous giver counts as nought all his cost and all his travail, for the joy and delight that he has, for he has pleased and solaced him whom he loves. Plenteously and fully was this shewn. (23:31–34.201)

In speaking of the "glad giver," Julian provides an *exemplum*, like any good preacher, to further illustrate her point that Christ wants no payment for his gift of salvation except humanity's joy and thanksgiving. She reiterates that this was shown both plentifully and completely. She advises her reader to "Think also wisely of the greatness of his word: '*Ever*'" (23:35.201, italics added). She is referring back to the locution in which she heard Christ say: "It is a joy, a bliss, an endless liking to me, that *ever* I suffered my passion for thee" (22:3–4.194–95, italics added). In that one word, "ever," Julian was shown "a high knowing of love that he has in our salvation" (23:36.201). Christ rejoices that he *ever* did it "in deed," that is, at a certain time in history, and that "he shall no more suffer" (23.37–38.201). He rejoices that he *ever* "bought us from the endless pains of hell," that is, from the wages of sin (23:38–39.201). And finally, he rejoices that he *ever* "brought us up into heaven and made us to be his crown and his endless bliss" (23:39–40.201).

Ecstasy

Since this Ninth Revelation is startling in so many ways, it is perhaps wise to pause and consider: How did Julian gain such realizations, and how did she have the confidence to be able to write about them? What does Julian mean when she says she was "lifted up" and saw "three heavens"? How can she be so convinced of all she saw and heard and understood? How does she know for sure that Christ, "the courteous giver," wants nothing else from humanity for all his sufferings, except to see that we are well satisfied, and that we, like him, take great joy in his gift? How can she be so certain of having experienced a "high knowing," an exalted realization, of the infinite love of Christ himself and of the total delight he takes in humanity's salvation? *How does a simple human being contemplate such divine mysteries?*

Much has been written about the states of trance, ecstasy, or ravishment. The fourteenth-century hermit, Richard Rolle, explained:

> Ravishing, as it is showed, in two ways is to be understood. One manner, forsooth, in which a man is ravished out of fleshly feeling; so that for the time of his ravishing plainly he feels nought in the flesh, nor what is done to his flesh, and yet he is not dead but quick, for yet the soul gives life to the body. And on this manner saints are sometimes ravished, to their profit and other men's learning; as St. Paul was ravished to the third heaven... And many others as we read of.[2]

In the sixteenth century, St. Teresa of Avila felt at a loss to describe her states of union with God, and especially her experiences of rapture or ecstasy:

> I wish I could explain, with God's help, the difference between union and rapture, or elevation, or flight of the spirit, or transport—for they are all one. I mean that these are all different names for the same thing, which is also called ecstasy. It is more beneficial than union, its results are much greater, and its very many other effects as well. Union seems to be the same at the beginning, the middle, and the end, and is altogether inward. But the ends of rapture are of a much higher nature, and their effects are both inward and outward... In these raptures, the soul no longer seems to animate the body; its natural heat therefore is felt to diminish and it gradually gets cold, though with a feeling of very great joy and sweetness. Here there is no possibility of resisting, as there is in union, in which we are on our own ground... Against union, resistance is almost always possible though it costs pain and effort. But rapture is, as a rule, irresistible.[3]

And again:

> ... this complete transformation of the soul in God is of short duration. While it lasts, however, none of the senses perceives or knows what is taking place. We can have no way of understanding this, while we are on earth at least—or rather, God cannot wish us to, since we have not the capacity for such understanding. *This I have learnt for myself.*[4]

However difficult these states of mystical transport may be to explain, St. Teresa was sure of one thing: that she had truly *experienced* both union and rapture. And she struggled to report them as honestly as she could, always allowing for the failure of language to describe the ineffable.

Julian, too, had learned for herself that there was no way she could fully understand or communicate to others the "complete transformation of the soul in God" that had happened to her. She had first experienced a sensory perception of Christ on the cross in front of her and felt an overwhelming emotional compassion for his sufferings. This was the most profound and realistic meditative involvement in the passion she had ever undergone. Then, just when she thought she would see Christ die in front of her, suddenly his countenance was changed into a vision of glory and she was "lifted up" in a "flight of the spirit." It was not a physical levitation, nor an imaginative "lifting up." It was much more. In her transported state of mind, Julian enjoyed an infusion of graced wisdom that enabled her spirit to expand within an inner sky of boundless awareness. There she entered into a mystical union with God that took her out of time and space. Her attention became totally focused on the divine interaction. Nothing could possibly disturb or distract her. Her imagination lay dormant, her memory was stilled, her reasoning faculty silenced. In the deepest ground of her being she enjoyed the presence of Christ. *Ego dormio et cor meum vigilat*: "I slept, but my heart was awake" (Sg 5:2). In this state of sublime intimacy, she was given an understanding of Trinity as "three heavens," all equally glorifying Christ's resurrected humanity. She heard Christ's heart-to-heart words more clearly and memorably than any words she had ever heard spoken aloud. In this great expansion of her spirit, she perceived what she could not explain: a "high understanding" of the boundlessness of Christ's love for humanity. Such pure perception cannot be learnt, earned, or argued. It is divine gift. Her ecstatic joy in Christ's joy was, indeed, a foretaste of heaven.

To those standing watch around her bedside, Julian's body lay immobile, her limbs rigid, her extremities cold, even more so than before. She could not speak or make a sign to anyone, even if she had wished to do so. Her circulation slowed considerably, her breathing could not be detected. To all physical appearances, she was truly at the point of death . . . or had already died. It was not a fantasy or a hallucination. Neither was it a dream. It was more real to her than earthly existence could ever be. Her "lifting up" was a purely intellectual phenomenon, though not in the rational, analytical sense. She did not "think" her way into the Revelations that followed. Like Rolle and Teresa, she *experienced* them in a super-sensual state of mind that transcended all normal ways of perceiving. Her soul became enraptured by God.

Whether the ecstasy was of short duration, or seemed blissfully long, when she emerged from its peak intensity she was absolutely certain of the truth of what she had experienced. Her entire consciousness had been plunged into contact with the Divine. The illumination had so absorbed and focused her whole being that it was incontrovertible. And afterward, as she returned to "normal" levels of sensory awareness, she realized it was for one purpose only: to bear witness to the love and joy she had experienced and to speak the good news of what she had heard to all who would listen, like the women at the tomb on Easter morning.

The Tenth Revelation

> With a glad chere our good lord looked into his side and beheld it, enjoying. And with his sweet looking he led forth the understanding of his creature by that same wound into his side, within. And there he shewed a fair, delectable place, and large enough for all mankind that shalle be saved to rest in peace and in love. (24:1–4.201)

In the Tenth Revelation, while Julian is still immersed in the contemplative state, Christ on the cross gazes into the wound on his right side with a joyous expression. Through this shift in the focus of Christ's eyes, Julian understands that he is inviting her to enter mystically, through the open wound, into the depths of his Sacred Heart. It is such a magnanimous gesture, like the resurrected Christ showing his five wounds to Thomas and inviting him to touch and "do not doubt but believe" (Jn 20:27). Yet it is even more intimate than that. Christ is offering Julian a profound insight into the abundance of divine love *within* his human heart. Her mind passes through the physical cleft in his flesh into "a fair, delectable place," a spiritual heaven, that is "large enough" not only for herself, but "for all mankind that shalle be saved to rest in peace and in love." While he walked the earth, Christ had offered this same invitation: "Come to me, all you that are weary and are carrying heavy burdens, and I will give you rest" (Mt 11:28). Here, Christ allows Julian to experience, very personally and very tenderly, another dimension of heavenly bliss: the ineffable joy of entering into the Heart of God.

The Sacred Heart

Devotion to the Sacred Heart had its foundation in Benedictine and Cistercian monastic life of the eleventh and twelfth centuries. It was believed that Christ's wounded Heart of love could be approached through contemplation of the physical wound in his side. William of St. Thierry (d.1148) wrote that he longed to come "to the most holy wound of His side . . . that I may put in not only my finger or my whole hand, but enter wholly into the very Heart of Jesus, into the Holy of Holies."[5] St. Bernard of Clairvaux (d.1153) taught that the piercing of Christ's side shows forth his goodness and the love of his Heart for us. And Richard of St. Victor (d.1173) believed there was no tenderness comparable with that of the Heart of Jesus. In the thirteenth century, the *Ancrene Riwle* for enclosed women counseled the wounds of Christ as the refuge against temptation:

> Name Jesus often, and invoke the aid of his passion, and implore him by his sufferings, and by his precious blood, and by his death on the cross. *Fly into his wounds; creep into them with thy thought.* They are all open. He loved us much who permitted such cavities to be made in him, that we might hide ourselves in them. And, with his precious blood, ensanguine thine heart.[6]

St. Bonaventure (d.1274) wrote frequently on the Sacred Heart: "Who is there who would not love this wounded Heart? Who would not love, in return, him who loves so much?"[7] And St. Gertrude (d.1301) had profound revelations concerning the Heart of Jesus. In one vision she received on the feast day of St. John the Evangelist, Gertrude recorded that she was invited to "lay her head" near the wound in Christ's breast, where she heard the beating of his Sacred Heart. She became bold enough to ask St. John if, at the Last Supper, when he lay his own head on Christ's breast, he had felt the delightful pulsing of the Lord's Heart and if so, why had he never recorded it in his gospel. He replied, "Because I was charged with instructing the newly-formed Church concerning the mysteries of the Uncreated Word."[8] St. John then told Gertrude that the grace of learning of the Sacred Heart was reserved to her century, to rouse it from its lethargy so that it would be inflamed with the great worth of Divine Love.

Throughout the thirteenth and fourteenth centuries, Franciscans, Dominicans, and Carthusians prayed to the Sacred Heart of Jesus, but only as a personal and contemplative practice. The Five Wounds of Christ on the cross (in both hands, both feet, and in his heart) as we have seen, were often acknowledged in prayer as symbols of his great suffering and salvific love. But there was no liturgical movement in the church encouraging devotion to the Sacred Heart, and it was not yet at all common among the laity. Julian's Revelation, while in a long and completely orthodox tradition of private devotion, suggests a fresh and poignant invitation by Christ to see the wound in his side as both the physical and mystical entry point into his Sacred Heart. Julian writes:

> And therewith he brought to mind his dearworthy blood and his precious water which he let pour all out for love. And with the sweet beholding he shewed his blissful heart split completely in two. And with this sweet enjoying he shewed to my understanding, in part, the blessed godhead, to the extent that he wished to at that time, strengthening the poor soul to understand what can be said: that is to mean, the endless love that was without beginning, and is, and shall be forever. (4:5–10.201)

It is important here to distinguish between Christ's *physical* heart, which poured out blood and water from the cross, and his *symbolic* heart as unconditional love, forever emptying itself and pouring forth mercy and grace. The physical piercing by Longinus with a lance split Christ's human heart "completely in two." By this act, Julian recognizes the Savior's love being symbolically pierced by sin and apathy in every age. "But he was wounded for our transgressions, crushed for our iniquities; upon him was the punishment that made us whole, and by his bruises we are healed" (Is 53:5). The gaping wound from the spear in his flesh becomes the graphic image of Christ's broken heart, which in turn becomes the spiritual dwelling place for all humankind.

Lo, How I loved thee

> And with this, our good lord said full blissfully: "Lo, how I loved thee," as if he had said: "My darling, behold and see thy lord, thy God, that is thy maker and thy endless joy. See thine own brother, thy savior. My child, behold and see what delight and bliss I have in thy salvation, and for my love enjoy it with me." (24:11–14.203)

Julian hears a direct locution in which Christ speaks, in five words, everything that could be said from his Heart to Julian's: "Lo, how I loved thee." And yet, for Julian, the layers of meaning keep pouring forth, as if Christ had told her his love over and over again, as lovers do, in countless different and intimate ways. She tries to find words to express the inexpressible:

> And also, for better understanding: this blessed word was said, "Lo how I loved thee," *as if* he had said: "Behold and see that I loved thee so much, before I died for thee, that I wanted to die for thee. And now I have died for thee, and suffered willingly whatever I can. And now is all my bitter pain and all my hard travail turned to endless joy and bliss to me and to thee. How should it now be that thou should pray to me for anything that pleases me, but that I should full gladly grant it thee? For my pleasure is thy holiness and thy endless joy and bliss with me." (24:15–21.203, italics added)

Julian's use of paraphrase here reaches a fever pitch. It is "as if" Christ had said there is nothing he would not have done to show his love for her, as for every person. From eternity, he knew he would die for love. Then he "suffered willingly" and did die for love. And now, he is in "endless joy and bliss" and wants nothing so much as to share his love with all those for whom he has died. This is the love, past, present, and future, that Julian understood "was without beginning, and is, and shall be forever." Here, for the first time, she introduces the topic of prayer in connection with Christ's love. *Why should he refuse anything that she asks for, if it is pleasing to him?* Out of love, he will grant it if it will lead to her holiness and eternal joy. How could he not? Julian will continue this theme of prayer at a later point in her text. Like so many of her contemplative intuitions, it takes time for them to come to analytical fruition.

The Eleventh Revelation

> And with this same expression of mirth and joy, our good lord looked down on the right side, and brought to my mind where our lady stood at the time of his passion, and said: "Wilt thou see her?" And in this sweet word, it was as if he had said: "I know well that thou wouldst see my blessed mother, for after myself she is the highest joy that I might shew thee, and the most pleasure and worship to me. And she is most desired to be seen of all my blessed creatures." (25:1–6.203)

In medieval paintings of the crucifixion, Mary was most often depicted standing to the right, beneath Christ on the cross, with St. John the Evangelist on the left. Likewise, on the wide beam that stood atop the rood screen (spanning the chancel arch and separating the main altar and the monks' choir stalls from the nave and the laity), a carving of Mary, stationed on the right side of the crucifix, usually faced the congregation.[9] Julian would have looked up at just such a rood, raised high in Norwich Cathedral, or in her parish church, with or without a solid screen below. Countless times, while deep in prayer, her eyes would have moved from the central crucifix down to Mary, standing in sorrow, her hands clasped together, and then over to the disciple John, "the one whom Jesus loved" (Jn 13:23).

Just as Christ had gazed toward the wound in his right side in the Tenth Revelation, now, in the Eleventh Revelation, Julian notices him look further down beneath the crucifix, toward the general area where his mother would have been standing on Calvary. Julian's great devotion to Mary is apparent here, as her heart longs to see Christ's mother at the foot of the cross. And Christ is well aware that Julian, like "all my blessed creatures," longs to see her. Saint Mary was considered to be the most compassionate and powerful mediatrix between sinful human beings and her son. Julian would have sought her intercession in every crisis or moment of need.

> And for the marvelous, high, and special love that he hath for this sweet maiden, his blessed mother, our lady Saint Mary, he shewed her highly rejoicing, which is the meaning of this sweet word, as if he had said: "Wilt thou see how much I love her, that thou might rejoice with me in the love that I have in her and she in me?" (25:6–10.203)

Previously, Julian has contemplated Mary standing beneath the cross, suffering with Christ, lamenting her great loss. Now Julian sees Mary *rejoicing* in eternal bliss with her Son, delighting in his love and he in hers. She understands that the words the Lord spoke to her were intended "in love to all mankind that shalle be saved, as it were all to one person" (25:11–12.203). It was as if he had said to Julian and to everyone:

> "Wilt thou see in her how thou art loved? For thy love I have made her so exalted, so noble, so worthy. And this pleases me, and I want it to please thee." (25:13–14.205)

In the love Christ has for Mary, Julian recognizes how much Christ loves each and every human being. In fact, Christ has made Mary so highly glorified, honored, and worthy in order to be an inspiration for all women and men. He has raised her body into glory to be with his own. He has crowned her queen of heaven and earth. She gives the Lord the greatest worship and pleasure and he wants everyone to take great pleasure in her, too. Yet Julian becomes acutely aware, through an inner teaching, that she is *not* being encouraged to long to see Mary in a physical presence while here on earth. She is to contemplate her spiritually, in "the virtues of her blessed soul—her truth, her wisdom, her charity," whereby Julian might learn to know herself better and more reverently fear and serve God (25:16–17.205). Even so, when Christ asks Julian if she wants to see Mary, Julian answers eagerly: "Ye, good lord, gramercy. Ye good lord, if it be thy will" (25:19–20.205). She admits, with striking candor, that she has often prayed for just such a vision, and on this occasion, "I expected to have seen her in bodily likeness," just as she saw Christ on the cross: "But I saw her not so" (25:20–21.205).

Rather, when the Lord asked the question ("Wilt thou see her?"), in that very moment, Julian was shown "a ghostly sight" of Mary, similar to the imaginative vision she had had of her as a girl, little and simple, at the time of the annunciation. Mary appeared this time "exalted and noble and glorious and pleasing to him [Christ] above all creatures" (25:22–23.205). Julian is sure that Christ wills it to be known that everyone who "likes" (an even more intimate form of the word "love") and delights in him must also truly "like" her, with all the connotations of delighting in everything about her. And Julian realizes that this very "liking," this most familiar manner of loving, is the purest form of "bodily *like*ness" that she could possibly have experienced.

Julian was not disappointed that she was not allowed to enjoy Mary in a physical manifestation, as she did Christ. And in all her Revelations, she saw no one else "spiritually" or "individually" but Saint Mary. In this *shewing*, Julian was deeply touched that Christ had confided to her his own love for Mary as a young maiden, as a suffering mother, and now, as an exalted and noble lady in heaven. In revealing to Julian his great love for Mary, by extension Christ was showing, in yet another way, his great love for Julian.

The Twelfth Revelation

Now Julian's spirit is lifted up even higher in contemplative wonder and she sees Christ in greater glory than before. She is so full of ecstatic joy and gratitude, and yet she knows she will never experience true rest until she comes to the beatific vision of Christ in heaven. He alone is the fullness of eternal happiness. And in this he is simple and familiar as well as regal and courteous; and always the source of true bliss and true life.

> Oftentimes our lord Jesus said: "I it am, I it am. I it am that is highest. I it am that thou lovest. I it am that thou likest. I it am that thou servest. I it am that thou longest for. I it am that thou desirest. I it am that thou meanest. I it am that is all. I it am that holy church preacheth to thee and teacheth thee. I it am that shewed myself before to thee." (26:4–8.207)

This litany of holy names that Christ pours out of his glory in revelation to Julian, not once, but "oftentimes," evokes an endless stream of ways in which he is present to the human mind and heart. Various scholars have translated Julian's seemingly awkward syntax, "I it am," as "I am He,"[10] or "It is I."[11] However, Julian must have deemed her exact words important, since she repeats them again and again. Thus it seems imperative to honor and retain her transcription of the precise phrases she understood Christ to say. What is the *it* to which the *I* of Christ refers? To consider this, we must recall Julian's First Revelation in which she understood that:

> The trinity is our maker, the trinity is our keeper [protector], the trinity is our everlasting lover, the trinity is our endless joy and our bliss, by our lord Jesus Christ and in our lord Jesus Christ. And this was shewed in the first sight *and in all.* For where Jesus appears the blessed trinity is understood, as to my sight. (4:8–12.135, italics added)

The *it*, therefore, is the Blessed Trinity: Father, Son, and Holy Spirit. The *it* is also Jehovah, the eternal "I AM" revealed to Moses. And wherever Jesus appears, God, three-in-one, is understood. Thus the *it* also refers to Christ himself, he who is highest, he whom Julian loves, he whom she personally and intimately *likes* (and in whose image and *like*ness she is made). Christ is he whom Julian serves and for whom she longs, he whom she desires, the one her heart "means" when she thinks or speaks of God. Christ tells Julian that he is "all" she could possibly long for, love, or ever need. He is the one whom "holy church" preaches to her in the gospels and teaches her to know, love, and serve. He is the one who has been showing himself to Julian all this time.

Earlier in her Revelations, Julian had understood that Christ is our clothing . . . the sea ground of our very existence . . . the Creator of the simple hazelnut in her hand that symbolizes all that is made . . . the still "point" out of which all that is comes forth and to which it returns. Christ has revealed to her: "See, I am God!" (11:42.165). Now, he reiterates the numerous ways in which he is power and presence to her. Because Christ is both God and man, the *it* applies to every divine and human activity of Christ as creator, protector, and lover that Julian could possibly imagine. He might have added: *I it am* who enables you to live, and move, and have your being (Acts 17:28). *I it am* who walks and runs and sings and dances and grows up within you, laughs with you, cries with you, teaches you, listens to your heart, speaks to you in the innermost recesses of your mind, guides and encourages your every choice. *I it am*, your creativity, your knowledge, your courage, your gentleness, your loving heart, your truthfulness. *I it am*, your capacity to envision and enjoy a sunrise, to cherish the tenderness in your beloved's eyes, to delight in your child's smile or funny word, to work and serve others unselfishly. *I it am*, the thrill of achievement and the hard-but-necessary lesson learnt only through failure. *I it am* present in your deepest worry, fear, agony, betrayal, or shame, and who sustains you through the darkest nights of body and soul. *I it am* comforting you in tragic loss, tending you in sickness, protecting you in times of danger, and sending you help from the most unlikely source just when you need it most. *I it am* who sustains you even when you fall into sin. *I it am* close by who picks you up, forgives you, embraces you, and sets you on the path again. *I it am*, your awareness of being alive. *I it Am Who Am*... Christ Incarnate, long ago, now, and forevermore: your creation, birth, life, death, and salvation. By becoming human, Christ took on all these variations of human thought and feeling, joy and suffering, longing and love. Indeed, Julian writes:

> The number of the words [Christ spoke] passes my wits and my understanding and all my powers, for they were in the highest number, as to my sight. For therein is comprehended I cannot tell what. But the joy that I saw in the shewing of them surpasses all that heart can think or soul may desire. And therefore these words are not declared here. But every man, after the grace that God gives him in understanding and loving, receives them in our lord's meaning. (26:8–13.207)

The Divine Names that Christ reveals to Julian are numberless, as are his manifold works in us. Julian is at a loss to count them... or to recount them. She cannot declare in writing all that she heard and understood that Christ showed her. It is beyond what "heart can think or soul may desire." It is beyond what any "poor creature" such as Julian could possibly record. She simply attests to her inexpressible joy in realizing Christ's manifestations. Like John the Evangelist, she understood that "All things came into being through him, and without him not one thing came into being" (Jn 1:3). The Divine Nature becomes incarnate in and through all creation and all creation is the eternal extension of Christ. *I it am* is, in truth, all that exists.

In her great desire for her readers to understand this Revelation, Julian encourages "every man" (and by extension, every woman) to receive these words and make them their own, as the Lord will personally give them grace to do so. In each individual's life, *I it am* will mean something entirely unique, a personal revelation.

16
Making All Things Well

The Thirteenth Revelation

> And after this, our lord brought to my mind the longing that I had for him before. And I saw that nothing letted [prevented] me but sinne. And so I beheld this generally in us all, and it seemed to me: "If sinne had not been, we should all have been as clean and like to our lord as he made us." And thus in my folly before this time, often I wondered why, by the great foreseeing wisdom of God, the beginning of sinne was not letted. For then I thought that alle would have been wele. (27:1–6.207–9)

Julian recalls the third of the "three wounds" she had been praying for, over the course of many years: that is, "the wound of wilful longing for God" (2:35–36.129). At last, her longing has been fulfilled beyond anything she could have imagined. She has been experiencing a blissful union with God in the person of Jesus Christ. She longs with all her being to stay forever in contemplation of the vision. And yet, in this moment of pure ecstasy, the thought arises that nothing is hindering her from remaining in such delight *except sin*. This is the cause of her suffering and the cause of the suffering of all human beings generally, since it is sin and only sin that prevents people from seeing and enjoying God.

This thought about the problem of evil had arisen before, in the Third Revelation: "I marveled in that sight with a soft dread, and thought: 'What is sinne?'" (11:4.163). Now, even as she beholds Christ in glory, that unanswered question arises from the depths of Julian's soul in a slightly different form. This time she does not ask, "what?" but "why?": *Why* is there sin at all? If sin had never happened, we would all be as pure and perfect as God created us to be. We would be like Adam and Eve in paradise before the fall. We would be on intimate terms with God; our intellect would have no limitations; our will would be inclined to virtue and possess the complete freedom *not* to sin; our body would be entirely subject to our will and immune from all physical suffering; we would be clothed by God in a state of perfect grace, beatitude, and enlightenment; we would be fully able to persevere in doing God's will; we would never have to die.[1]

Julian admits that to question this matter of sin is "folly," though she has done it many times in her life, wondering: Why did God, in his "great foreseeing wisdom," not prevent the very beginning of sin? If God knew in advance that sin would so severely damage his magnificent creation and bring untold suffering to human beings, why did he allow it to happen? For if sin had never been allowed, then, according to Julian's very human perspective (shared by philosophers, theologians, and commonfolk in every age), "alle would have been wele."

> This stirring was much to be rejected, but nevertheless I mourned and sorrowed over it, lacking reason and discretion. (27:7.209)

Alle Shalle be Wele

> But Jesus, who in this vision informed me of all that I needed, answered by this word and said: "Sinne is behovely, but alle shalle be wele, and alle shalle be wele, and alle manner of thing shalle be wele." (27:8–11.209)

In answer, Julian hears a simple and profoundly reassuring statement by Christ: "Sinne is behovely, but alle shalle be well . . ." It seems to have been prompted by Julian's own suggestion that "alle *would have* been wele," *if* there had been no sin. However, Christ does not agree with her reasoning. He tells Julian that "sinne is behovely, *but* alle shalle be wele": that is, all shall be well *in spite of* sin. *Behovely* in Middle English bears the connotations of "useful," "necessary," even "advantageous." These startling meanings as applied to sin bring again to mind the ancient *Exsultet*, the hymn of praise sung before the paschal candle at the Easter Vigil, which describes the sin of Adam as: "O happy fault, O necessary sin of Adam which has gained for us so great a Redeemer!" The word *behovely* also suggests St. Paul's teaching that God made Christ "to be sin who knew no sin, so that in him we might become the righteousness of God" (2 Cor 5:21). It *behooved* Christ to do so. Could the concept of sin as the gravest affront to God and the curse of humanity become so transformed in Christ that it might be deemed useful, necessary, even advantageous? St. Paul wrote: "We know that *all things* work together for good for those who love God, who are called according to his purpose" (Rom 8:28, italics added). And St. Augustine was convinced that "[God] can bring good even out of evil."[2]

For Julian, the idea of the usefulness of sin was summed up in the words: "but alle shalle be wele." This is the first time she writes these words that have become so identified with her Revelations as a whole. We have seen in Part One that this saying might have been quite common in the fourteenth century, perhaps equivalent to our current "Everything's going to be all right." It is a phrase that indicates deep sensitivity to the other person's pain or grief, that desires to give comfort, and that offers reassurance that this suffering will not persist interminably. The colloquial nature of this Middle English phrase should not surprise us. When Christ speaks to the soul, it is always in the familiar language that the recipient understands and in terms that will carry the clearest significance. Christ's words to Julian were those that would have been the most easily memorable and the most helpful to her individual psyche.

They were also the words that would answer her heart's greatest longing: *to be sure*. In fact, from the precise way in which Christ spoke to Julian, we can learn what was most pressing on Julian's mind: the horror of sin, the suffering it causes, and how all things can possibly be well if sin is "allowed" to persist. Since the Middle English *wele* was a form of weal, it meant not only "well" in our modern sense, but the greatest happiness and prosperity; hence, "well-*being*." More than anything else in her life, Julian needed the reassurance that well-being in an ultimate sense was possible, no matter how many terrible things happened in her world. And this is the phrase Christ used to teach and promise her that it is.

The Naked Word

> In this naked word "sinne," our lord brought to my mind generally all that is not good, and the shameful contempt and the utter noughting that he bore for us in this life, and his dying, and all the pains and passions of all his creatures, ghostly and bodily. For we

> are all in part noughted and we should be noughted following our master Jesus, till we be fully purged: that is to say, till we be fully noughted of our mortal flesh, and of all our inward affections which are not very good. (27:11–17.209)

Julian considers the "naked word 'sinne,'" and is reminded of what Christ looked like in his own naked passion and dying; the wounds, the bleeding, the deep drying, and the humiliations he suffered when he who was sinless "became sin" to atone for humanity. She also sees sin as the "pains and passions" of all creatures, animals as well as people. She is keenly aware that we are all ***noughted*** in varying degrees in this life. We suffer trials, troubles, and failures as well as physical pains and spiritual tribulations. And she is sure that we ought to allow ourselves to be ***noughted*** and to suffer afflictions, following in our Master's footsteps, until we are completely purified. By sharing in Christ's humiliations and sufferings, we will be fully purged of our sins of the flesh, and of the emotional attachments that are not good for us.

> And the beholding of this, with all the pains that ever were or ever shall be—and for all this, I understood the passion of Christ to be the greatest pain and overpassing [all other pains]—was shewn in a touch, and readily passed over into comfort. For our good lord does not want the soul to be frightened by this ugly sight. (27.18–22.209)

Julian is granted an instantaneous image of the history of suffering that has been endured because of sin, but she sees that the passion of Christ was the most all-encompassing agony that ever was or ever could be. Still, the Lord did not allow her to dwell on the pains of humankind, nor even on his passion on the cross, as before. She envisions this universal suffering "in a touch," a mere glimpse, and is immediately given comfort lest the physical and emotional impact plunge her soul into terror.

> But I saw not sinne. For I believe it has no manner of substance, nor any part in being, nor might it be known *except by the pain that it causes.* And this pain, it is something, as to my sight, for a time. For it purges and makes us know ourselves and ask mercy. (27:22–25.209–11, italics added)

In her momentary glimpse of universal suffering, Julian does not "see" sin. As she already mentioned in the Third Revelation, this is because she has learned that sin has no essence or substance and, thus, no real existence: "And here I saw truly that sinne is no deed, for in all this, sinne was not shewn" (11:17–18.163). We have considered that, according to St. Augustine, evil is a lack of a good that should exist, a *privatio boni*. Evil cannot be seen because it is a darkening or primordial ignorance of the mind, blocking out the light of God. The evil of sin can only be known, as Julian realizes, "by the pain that it causes."

Maimings and murders, poverty and homelessness, wars and social unrest, even famine, drought, and the outbreak of deadly pestilences as well as fires, earthquakes, and floods are all results of the sins of human beings toward each other which, in turn, cause catastrophic upheavals in nature. The evil of sin perpetrates every form of violence and abuse visited on the young and the strong, on infants and the aged, on the infirm and the weak. It penetrates to every level of our physical environment, infects every aspect of our daily life. Sin destroys families and disrupts governments, sets one nation against the other and casts down empires. While sin itself may be technically *no*-thing, lacking any form of real existence, the pain it causes is *some*-thing, inasmuch as it is undergone and suffered, as Julian testifies. Still, she affirms that this suffering, great as it may be, is only "for a time" in the eternal scheme of things. And in that time, it humbles and purifies us, teaches us our fatal flaws and weaknesses, and brings us to our knees in search of God's mercy. As such, sin can be *behovely*, useful, necessary, even fitting and good, as Christ has said. It can, by a miraculous alchemy, have a positive outcome. St. Paul writes in a similar vein:

> I consider that the sufferings of this present time are not worth comparing with the glory about to be revealed to us. For the creation waits with eager longing for the revealing of the children of God, for the creation was subjected to futility, not of its own will but by the will of the one who subjected it, in hope that *the creation itself will be set free from its bondage to decay and will obtain the freedom of the glory of the children of God*. (Rom 8:18–21, italics added)

According to Julian, this transformation of sin and decay into glory is possible only because the passion of Christ strengthens us to endure the effects of sin, and it is precisely Christ's "blessed will" that his passion should do so. Even more, the tender love of the Lord comforts us "readily and sweetly" in our sufferings, constantly reassuring us (27:27.211):

> "It is true that sinne is the cause of all this pain, but alle shalle be wele, and all manner of thing shalle be wele." (27:28–29.211)

No Manner of Blame

> These words were shewn full tenderly, shewing no manner of blame to me, nor to none that shalle be saved. Then it would be a great unkindness of me to blame or wonder at God for my sinne, since he blames me not for sinne. (27:29–32.211)

Here Julian introduces a theme that will reverberate throughout her text. While she never denies or mitigates human responsibility for sin, she also never sees Christ on the cross attaching any blame to human beings for their sin. It is a striking concept, a seeming contradiction of the ancient and medieval teachings on the terrible "wrath of God" ready to strike down sinners and send them to hell. Yet at no point does Julian *deny* God's sovereign right to judge, or even possibly to condemn sinners to eternal punishment. She simply recounts what she saw and heard in her Revelation; namely, that God shows only tenderness and not blame toward those "that shalle be saved." Again and again, in one way or another, Julian specifies that those who turn to God humbly and in contrition for sin will surely feel his tender mercy. As for those who refuse to seek God's mercy, Julian simply *did not see them*, any more than she saw sin.

There is no way of knowing if, by her use of the phrase, "none that shalle be saved," Julian was suggesting that there will be some who will not respond to salvation, or if eventually "*alle* shalle be saved." (It is interesting to note however, Julian's preference for inclusiveness: she uses the word "alle" more than six hundred times in her *Revelations.*)[3] Generally, it may be said that Julian wrote of salvation from the all-encompassing divine perspective that she was privileged to see, not the specifically human one. In a rush of insight, Julian realizes she has no right to "blame or wonder at God" for her sins, since God does not blame her. It is an astounding realization.

> And in these same words, I saw a high, marvelous privity [a glorious secret], hidden in God, which privity he shall openly make known to us in heaven. In which knowing we shall truly see *the reason why* he suffered sinne to come, in which sight we shall endlessly have joy. (27:33–36.211, italics added)

While Julian receives an intimation of a wondrous secret God will reveal in heaven (which will explain why he permitted sin to come into the world), she is fully aware that she cannot know this *privity* now, as long as she is still on earth undergoing the purgative effects of sin. But she is heartened that someday, in that knowledge "hidden in God," we will understand how "alle shalle be wele," and this will bring everlasting joy. Here Julian alludes, for the first time, to a mystery she will explore more fully in the future. Could it be that humanity's overwhelming gratitude for Christ's salvific death on the cross will make us love, praise, and delight in God even more than we would have if we had *not* sinned?

Christ's Compassion

> Thus I saw how Christ has compassion on us because of sinne. And just as before in the passion of Christ I was filled with pain and compassion, so in this I was in part filled with compassion for all my evencristens. For full well does he [Christ] love people that shalle be saved: that is to say, God's servants. (28:1–4.211)

Julian feels that Christ not only does not blame us for sin, he has compassion for us because of the curse of sin and all the sufferings it produces in our lives. And now the sympathy that Julian had felt for Christ's pain is transferred, at least in part, to that of her fellow Christians: the recurring outbreaks of plague, the ongoing papal schism, the war with France, the Lollard heresies, the peasants' revolt and its aftermath. She is consumed by the thought of how much Christ loves and pities his "people that shalle be saved." The following appears only in the Long Text, which was probably not written until the mid or late 1390s:

> Holy church shall be shaken in sorrow and anguish and tribulation in this world as men shake a cloth in the wind. (28:4–6.211)

Julian sees this shaking of the church and its people happening all around her, at present and in the future. The great sufferings of her *evencristens* and the deep wounds inflicted on the church reflect Christ's own passion, during which his body hung on a cross and was shaken by a bitter, cold wind, like a cloth hung out to dry. In the last decade of the fourteenth century there was a heightened anticipation of the appearance of Antichrist, the forerunner of the Last Times, the Final Days, signaling death, destruction, and the apocalyptic end of the world. But according to Julian, the Lord reassured her:

> "Ah, a great thing shall I make hereof [out of this suffering] in heaven with endless worship and everlasting joy." Yes, I saw even as much as this: *our lord enjoys the tribulations of his servants*, with pity and compassion. And to each person that he loves, in order to bring them to bliss, he lays on them some thing that is no blame in his sight, whereby they are blamed and despised in this world, scorned and abused and cast out. And this he does in order to prevent the harm that they might take from the pomp and the pride and the vainglory of this wretched life, and make their way ready to come to heaven, and raise them up in bliss without end everlasting. (28:7–15.211–13, italics added)

The idea that the Lord "enjoys the tribulations of his servants" may seem, at first, abhorrent to us, considering his tender pity and compassion. Does God *enjoy* our sufferings? To explain this problematic passage, we must recall that Christ has told Julian how much he rejoiced in his *own* sufferings and would endure them all over again for every single soul that ever lived. On the night before he died, he compared himself to a woman in childbirth, dreading that her hour had come, but then rejoicing that her suffering has brought forth new life into the world (Jn 16:21). And we know that Christ told Julian: "If I might suffer more, I would suffer more" (22:4–5.195). Christ in his wisdom sees our suffering not from a human and limited point of view but from an eternal one. He knows within our pain the glory that will certainly come of it; in the midst of our great mourning and sorrow, he anticipates the wiping away of every tear and the great reward. This is what God in eternity *enjoys*.

However, it must be clearly stated that in no way does this Revelation ennoble abuse or brutality, nor does it make pain a value to be cultivated for its own sake, as some interpretations might assume. Neither does it make God seem unjust for "allowing" suffering, since each and every soul must share in Christ's suffering in some incomprehensible way in order to be incorporated into his glory. Julian even suggests that Christ "permits" public shame, rejection, and outright persecution to arise as strong *preventive* measures for those souls who might otherwise be tempted by the love of riches, pride, and the misuse of power. It is a hard saying. Yet Julian firmly holds that suffering can become the loving discipline of a Savior who does not merely desire the soul's temporal satisfaction, which is passing and full of disappointment, but rather its eternal salvation. And whatever trials his servants must suffer, Christ has already incorporated these into his own passion. He has experienced every aspect of them. Thus, these trials should not become a cause for despair but for rejoicing. For in dying with him, his faithful servants will surely rise with him (Rom 6:4). The paradox of the cross being *both* suffering and glory, death and life, will continue to be a cause of great confusion, even of disbelief: a sign that shall be contradicted (Lk 2:34).

> For he sayeth: "I shall alle to breke you [tear you away] from your vain affections and your vicious pride. And after that I shall gather you together, and make you meek and mild, clean and holy, by oneing you to me." (28:15–17.213)

Julian may be paraphrasing Psalm 2:9 here: "You shall break them with a rod of iron, and dash them in pieces like a potter's vessel." She understands that since all humanity must undergo this painful process of purification in order to be made "clean and holy," every natural feeling of pity that one man (or woman) has for another in charity, "it is Christ in him" (28:18.213). And every kind word or deed done out of compassion is Christ's own comfort. Julian realizes that each type of humiliation that the Lord endured in his passion was, in fact, a sign of his great compassion for what we, as human beings, must suffer. She notices especially "two ways of understanding" his meaning here (28:20.213). First, Christ knows the everlasting bliss to which he will bring us, and he wants us to *enjoy* the fact of our salvation, in anticipation. Second, even when we must be "broken" before being healed, he gives great comfort to us in all our present pains.

> For he wills that we know that it shall all be turned for us to worship and to profit by virtue of his passion. And that we know that we suffer not at all alone, but with him, and see him as our ground. And that we see his pains and his noughting surpass so far all that we may suffer that it may not be fully thought. And the right beholding of this will save us from grudging [begrudging] and despair in the feeling of our pains. And if we see truthfully that our sin deserves it, yet his love excuses us. And out of his great courtesy, he does away with all our blame, and beholds us with compassion and pity as children, innocent and not loathesome. (28:22–30.213)

Here, Julian intimates another theme she will develop further on: that of Christ as a loving Mother, ever compassionate and forgiving toward his children, always viewing us in the best possible light, because of his great love, no matter what we may think of ourselves. Out of his gracious courtesy, he even does away with our self-loathing.

Anxiety and Fatigue

> But in this I stood [my ground], contemplating generally, anxiously, and mournfully, saying thus to our lord in my meaning with the greatest dread: "Ah, good lord, how might alle be wele for the great harm that has come by sinne to thy creatures?" And here I desired, as far as I dared, to have some more open declaring [more teaching that was not of a private nature] wherewith I might be eased in this. (29:1–5.213–15)

Even with all this reassurance about the potentially positive results of sin and suffering, Julian is not easily distracted from her previous question: "Why, by the great foreseeing wisdom of God, the *beginning* of sinne was not letted?" She has long endured the effects of sin in her own life and has seen its all-pervasive damage around her. And now, a deeply buried fear arises to the surface of her consciousness, dimming the joy of her vision of Christ in glory. From an ecstatic realm of absolute certainty, she drops down into a tortured state of soul where old demons, long-held doubts, and primal terrors of damnation resurface, every bit as real to her as her visions and locutions. By her own account, she contemplates the human condition "generally, anxiously, and mournfully" because she cannot understand *how* all things might "be wele," either for herself or for all humanity. Her inability to accept Christ's affirming words immediately and without question causes yet another layer of self-recrimination. She descends into a darkened night of the soul.

It seems that Julian is suffering from *psychic fatigue*, an inevitable result of the suspended state of ecstatic contemplation that she has enjoyed. Her nervous system cannot sustain such divine intensity much longer. She is, after all, still in need of purification, still acutely conscious of being trapped in the flesh, still full of mental afflictions, still mortal, even though her spirit longs to remain in rapture. Her desperate need to know how all could possibly "be wele," if it is so obvious that sin devastates God's creatures, simply overwhelms her. At an earlier point, she had buried her doubt, when Christ assured her "how should any thing be amiss?" (11:45–46.165). Then she felt she was being "tested" to accept God's intervention in good faith and to rest content, enjoying God. Now, she becomes so consumed with fears about the human condition that she must question the Lord further. She longs for some direct declaration that is not a "secret" teaching, known only to those in heaven. She craves some reassurance *here and now*.

Adam's Sin

> And to this our blessed lord answered very meekly and with a totally loving expression, and shewed that Adam's sinne was the most harm that ever was done or ever shall be done to the world's end. And also, he shewed that this is openly known in all holy church on earth. Furthermore, he taught that I should behold the glorious atonement. For this act of atonement is more pleasing to the blessed godhead and more honorable for man's salvation, without comparison, than ever was the sinne of Adam harmful. Then our blessed lord meant thus in this teaching, that we should take heed of this: "For since I have made wele the greatest harm, then it is my will that thou know thereby that I shall make wele alle that is less." (29:5–14.215)

Christ is not in the least offended by Julian's persistence. He welcomes it, gently and with great love. He tells her that the greatest sin that caused the most harm to humankind was original sin, according to open church teaching, because from this sin of disobedience all other sinfulness followed. But rather than focusing on this devastating sin, Christ wants Julian to contemplate his own glorious act of perfect obedience by which he effected complete *at-onement* between God and humanity. Christ's reparation was so much more pleasing to God than Adam's sin was ever harmful, and the Savior raised humanity to a nobility so much higher than it had before, that the two acts, Adam's sin and Christ's atonement, cannot even be compared. Christ wants this teaching completely understood and devoutly taken into account in every situation: If he has "made wele" the greatest harm ever done to human nature, then he can and will "make wele" every other lesser harm done, every mortal sin ever committed. No evil is too great (or too small) to be "made wele" by Christ's redemptive power.

It is imperative here that we not conflate "Adam's sinne" with the mere eating of an apple, lest we doubt that such an act could, in any way, be considered "the greatest harm" ever done to humankind. The eating of a forbidden apple is a biblical metaphor for the grave disobedience of the creature toward its Creator. It has been understood as a sign of what happens when a mere human being thinks he knows better than God what is for his own good. It may be seen to represent the act of grasping at the sensory and intellectual delights of the earthly Garden of Eden as if they were goods that existed independently, without any need for a Divine Reality to create or hold them in being. According to this interpretation, the taking of the apple becomes the primordial act of defiance, as the serpent suggested it to Eve, a not-so-subtle decision to usurp and displace divine power altogether and become "like God." It is the consummate act of pride.

Finally, insofar as Adam, the first man, was created to be the most noble of all creatures, with a will completely free to do good, so his choice to commit sin becomes the worst possible offense against God.[4] In fact, that blatant disrespect was so heinous that it rippled into the moral downfall of all Adam's progeny, making them both innately sinful and able to conceive only sinners. According to St. Augustine, as we have seen, humanity became a *massa damnata*; literally, a "condemned lump" of sin, everlastingly doomed, except for the grace of Christ.[5]

According to church teaching, the first sin thoroughly distorted the relationship between God and humankind as well as between creatures and the creation itself. Original sin blinded human reason and weakened the human will so drastically that it could not differentiate illusory and temporary goods from ultimate good, nor deceptive appearances from eternal truth. It was the first sin that led to the first act of hatred, represented by Cain killing his brother Abel: "For where there is envy and selfish ambition, there will also be disorder and wickedness of every kind" (Jas 3:16). It was the first sin that introduced the first suffering, anguish, fear of loss, terror of retribution, guilt, and helplessness, and that erupted into the first cry for forgiveness in humanity's heart. The first sin showed humankind its total blindness without the light of God; its tendency to anger, deceit, violence, and war, without the grace of God; its futile grasping to itself as a god-substitute that is at the root of every other sin.

> Those conflicts and disputes among you, where do they come from? Do they not come from your cravings that are at war within you? You want something and do not have it; so you commit murder. And you covet something and cannot obtain it; so you engage in disputes and conflicts. You do not have, because you do not ask. (Jas 4:1–2)

The first sin was not just "a" sin. It was Sin itself: the result of a totally distorted view of how everything comes into existence. Sin turned everything upside down and inside out, producing an Alice-in-Wonderland version of reality.

God is, was, and will be, the one and only Reality that enables anything-at-all to be. But by that first sin, according to the biblical account, the first *homo sapiens* we call Adam negated the truth of his own existence by attempting to set himself up as independent, instead of recognizing his utter dependence on the Creator for his very life and breath. In so doing, he cut off his very capacity to experience the blissful paradise in which God had intended him to dwell. Yet what Julian understands from this Revelation is that if Christ was able to overcome the catastrophic upheaval of the first sin by his death on the cross, he could and would transform *every other sin* human beings could possibly commit. As the God-man, he could restore and re-create creation, making all "wele" and whole and good again, by radically re-orienting the human mind and heart.

Whether we accept the story of Adam and Eve and the doctrine of original sin as revealed truth, consider it a primordial myth intended to "explain" the origin of suffering, or dismiss it entirely as an outdated model that simply does not "work" with evolutionary science, we cannot escape the reality of brokenness and pain in our world. Where do these come from? Do the everyday experiences of inner conflicts, betrayals, and brutality flow from the perfect creation of an all-loving, all-good God? Or are they more properly the result of *human* activity? Christ himself said:

> For it is from within, from the human heart, that evil intentions come: fornication, theft, murder, adultery, avarice, wickedness, deceit, licentiousness, envy, slander, pride, folly. *All these evil things come from within*, and they defile a person. (Mk 7:21–23, italics added)

If so, then how can God save humanity from itself? These are some of the questions Julian was asking in 1373, questions as crucial to our own tumultuous times as they were to hers. She summed them up in her longing to know "how might alle be wele for the great harm that has come by sinne to thy creatures?"

Two Parts

Julian writes that the Lord then gave her an understanding of two categories of truth concerning our salvation. (Most likely, this objective analysis did not occur until some time later, although she includes it in her text at this point.) The first part is what has already been revealed about "our savior and our salvation. This blessed part is open and clear and fair and light and plenteous" (30:1–3.215). All human beings of good will who ever were or shall be are included in this part. It concerns knowledge of Christ as redeemer, the entire spectrum of moral and theological truths, as well as the sacraments of grace that lead to salvation. Through these, we become bound to God and taught inwardly by the Holy Spirit and outwardly by holy church. Christ wants us to be completely occupied and content in this part, "rejoicing in him because he rejoices in us" (30:6–7.215). And the more we immerse ourselves in these truths of revelation, "with reverence and humility," the more thanks we will receive from Christ and the more benefit we will have for our souls. Julian tells us that, in this part, we may say joyfully: "Our part [portion] is our lord" (30:9.217).

The second part, which concerns what is *not* directly pertinent to our salvation, is kept hidden and locked away from us: "For that is our lord's prevy councelle" (30:11.217). Using the metaphor of an earthly monarch and his privy council of advisors, Julian explains that the royal lordship of God has the right to keep his secret counsels in peace and his servants must be obedient and reverent in not wanting to know them. She remarks:

> Our lord has pity and compassion on us, because some creatures make themselves so busy about them [the counsels]. And I am seker that if we knew how much we would please him and ease ourselves to leave it alone, we would. The saints in heaven, they will to know nothing but that which our lord wills to shew them, and also their charity and their desire is ruled by the will of our lord. And thus ought we to will to be like them. Then we shall not will nor desire anything but the will of our lord, just as they do. For we are all one in God's intention. And here I was taught that we should only rejoice in our blessed savior Jesus, and trust in him for alle thing. (30:13–21.217)

With these words, Julian interposes a note of caution to her readers. By placing it at this point in her narrative, she implies that at the time, she, herself, was one of those creatures who "make themselves so busy" about what belongs solely to the Lord's privy council. She knows only too well how desperate human beings can become to know not only *that* Christ saves (the open part of revelation), but *when* and *where* and *how* and *whom* Christ saves (the secret part). She is taught that the Savior does not want us wearying our souls in such speculation, but rather desires us to become like the saints in heaven who "will to know nothing but what our Lord wills to shew them," enjoying and trusting in the Savior for everything.

Christ's Answer

> And thus our good lord answered to all the questions and doubts that I might make, saying very comfortingly: "I may make alle thing wele, and I can make alle thing wele, and I wille make alle thing wele, and I shalle make all thing wele. And thou shalt see thyself that alle manner of thing shalle be wele." (31:1–4.217)

In spite of "all the questions and doubts" that arose in her mind (and it is clear that at this point her mind was being tossed in a sea of arguments), the Lord took pity on Julian and yet again gave her the promise of his unfailing power. Escalating into a crescendo, as if answering each objection arising in Julian's heart, Christ tells her *five ways* in which he makes "alle thing wele." For Julian, these are clear and concise. And each is layered with deeper meaning. First, Christ *may* "make all things well" because he is Supreme Power, able to do all that needs to be done. Second, he *can* (from the Middle English, *cann*, meaning he knows the best way to do it), because he is Divine Wisdom and understands how to perfect his own creation. Third, he *will* (in the sense that he *chooses* to do so), since the Father's Will *will* be done. Fourth, he *shall* (an even stronger auxiliary verb than *will*), and this word expresses Christ's absolute intention to make everything well. And fifth, Christ promises Julian, in no uncertain terms, that she shall *see* herself that this shall be done.

Julian explicates further. By "I may," she understood the working of the Father; by "I can," that of the Son; by "I will," that of the Holy Ghost, and by "I shall," the unity of the Blessed Trinity, "three persons and one truth." And in the saying, "thou shalt see thyself," she understood not only herself, but "the oneing of all mankind that shalle be saved into the blissful trinity" (31:5–9.219). In these five words (*may, can, will, shall* and *shall see*), "God will be enclosed in rest and in peace," when Christ's own spiritual thirst for souls is finally quenched (31:10–11.219).

> For this is the ghostly thirst of Christ: the love-longing that lasts and ever shall till we see that sight at domesday. For we that shall be saved, and shall be Christ's joy and his bliss, some are yet here, and some are to come, and so shall some be until that day. Therefore this is his thirst: a love-longing to have us all together, whole in him to his endless bliss, as to my sight. For we are not now as fully whole in him as we shall be then. (31:11–16.219)

Christ's spiritual thirst is defined as a "love-longing," like that of a human parent who wants to have the whole family gathered together, safe and happy, never to be parted again. So Christ aches to have all his children made whole and one within himself, enjoying endless bliss. Until such time as we are brought up to heaven and united with Christ, we will never be completely whole.

Christ as God and Man

Julian is quick to differentiate here between Christ as God and Christ as man. As God, he is "highest bliss, and was from without beginning and shall be without end" (31:18–19.219). And this bliss cannot ever be raised or lowered in himself, nor suffer any thirst, or anguish, or pain of unfulfilled or unrequited love. Julian reminds the reader that this was amply shown in the Twelfth Revelation, when he said: "I it am that is highest" (26:4–5.207; 31:21.219). But the church's creed states that Christ *as man* suffered great pains and died out of love in order to bring us all into his glory. And this was shown in the Ninth Revelation, when Christ declared it had been "a joy, a bliss and an endless liking to me that ever I suffered my passion for thee" (22:3–4.193–95; 31:25–26.219). Thus, as regards his *divinity*, Christ always was and is "impassible," which means incapable of suffering. However, as regards his *humanity*, "he is not yet fully glorified nor completely impassible" (31:30.221). Julian makes a strong statement here, that until all those for whom Christ thirsts have been brought into heavenly bliss, as regards the "whole Christ" (both head and members in the Mystical Body), *he is still capable of suffering.*

> For the same thirst and longing that he had up on the rood tree—which desire, longing and thirst, as to my sight, were in him from without beginning—the same has he yet, and shall into the time that the last soul that shall be saved is come up to his bliss. (31:30–33.221)

Julian is so convinced of this realization that she declares: "as truly as there is a property in God of compassion and pity, as truly is there a property in God of thirst and longing" (31:34–35.221). And we are obligated to long for Christ as he does for us, because without this yearning, "no soul comes to heaven" (31:36.221). According to Julian's understanding, Christ's longing and thirst, as well as his pity, arise from his goodness, even though these seem to be separate properties. And the point of his spiritual thirst, which will continue as long as we are in need during this life on earth, is to draw us up into heaven. The humanity of Christ will *always* have compassion on us, which will only cease at Domesday. Likewise, he has the greatest love-longing to have us enclosed within himself, but "his wisdom and his love do not allow the end to come till the best time" (31:44.221).

Julian writes that at one time the good Lord said, "'Alle manner of thing shalle be wele,' and another time he said, 'Thou shalt see thyself that alle manner of thing shalle be wele'" (32:1–3.221). In this variation, she perceives different meanings. On the one hand, Christ wants us to know that he notices and will make well not only noble and great things, but also things little and small, low and simple. This is why Christ spoke of "*alle* manner of thing," not just some things. According to Julian, even "the least thing shall not be forgotten" (32:7.221).

Evil Deeds

On the other hand, "there are many evil deeds done in our sight and such great harms suffered that it seems to us that it were unpossible [impossible] that ever it should come to a good end" (32:8–9.221). Julian simply cannot see how the problem of evil could be "made wele."

> And upon this [evil] we look, sorrowing and mourning therefore, so that we can not rest ourselves in the blissful beholding of God as we should do. And the cause is this: that the use of our reason is now so blind, so low, and so simple, that we can not know the high, the marvelous wisdom, the might, and the goodness of the blissful trinity. (32:10–13.221)

Julian cannot forget the brutalities that have torn apart the very fabric of her life. She has not been a cloistered nun or a distant observer of the sufferings of her age. She has seen peasants bound by ropes and dragged through the streets, hanging from the back of horse-drawn carts. She has watched severed heads be raised atop pikes on the walls of Norwich. She has witnessed the hands of thieves cut off as punishment. She knows about the evils perpetrated by immoral clergy and nobility alike. She has heard the stories of rape, murder, and pillage from the war. She has held her disconsolate *even-cristens*, crying aloud in her arms. She has spent years "sorrowing and mourning" and been unable to rest "in the blissful beholding of God." More than once, she must have asked the question that has no human answer: *how could such evil deeds ever come to a good end?*

Julian is painfully aware that the presence of evil impacts all who look on it, listen to it, smell it, touch it. The effects of evil deeds wreak havoc in our emotional lives and test our faith in the goodness of God. The seeming triumph of evil that, for a time at least, goes unpunished, raises severe questions about God's lack of intervention. The terrible sufferings produced by evil wear down our hope in ever being set free from its clutches. Evil disillusions and embitters our hearts, making us unable to love or trust God as we should. Evil arouses annoyance, fuels anger, feeds the desire for revenge. And in all this, we become unable to pray, to praise, and to give glory to God as we ought to do. We cannot rest in contemplating the pure *goodness* of God. We are worn out with weeping. Julian is admitting here that she knows this debilitating process only too well. She has looked on evil and been shaken to the core by her contact with it.

Yet she refuses to blame God for evil. She insists that the cause of our despair over the all-pervasiveness of evil is that our reasoning minds are "so blind, so low, and so simple." What she means is that we simply cannot comprehend the transcendence of the Trinity in its glorious wisdom, might, and goodness. We may find it easier to believe that God may *not,* can *not,* will *not,* and shall *not* save all humankind, and that we shall *never* see him make "alle manner of thing wele." This is due to our inability to comprehend who God is and what God is capable of accomplishing. It is also symptomatic of our lack of faith. It takes a long time for us to allow God's promise to filter through our fears and find a home deep in our injured psyches.

> And thus, this is what he means where he says: "Thou shalt see thyself that alle manner of thing shalle be wele," as if he had said: "Take heed now, faithfully and trustingly, and at the last end thou shalt see truly in fullness of joy." And thus in the same five words before said—"I may make all thing wele" [etc.]—I understand a mighty comfort because of all the deeds of our lord God that are to come. (32:13–18.221–3)

Julian insists we must take sharp notice of what Christ is saying. We must have faith and trust in his promises, most especially because we *cannot* see how this or that particular evil could ever "come to a good end." We must hang on Christ's words, counting on him to make all things well at the end of time, even though we have no idea how he will ever do it. We must believe that he can and wants to do it. Such belief does not arise easily. It is an acquired habit. It takes continual and determined practice. But if we do practice such belief, then "at the last end," we will be able to "see truly in the fullness of joy" how Christ has done it. With great insistence, Julian acknowledges the imperative of each of the "five words," or separate clauses: *may, can, will, shall... and thou shalt see.*

Fulfillment or Prophecy?

Are these "five words" of Christ a statement of fact about what has been fulfilled, or prophecy concerning what will be accomplished at the end of the world? Both. In God's sight, salvation is already accomplished. "It is finished," were Christ's last words before "he bowed his head, and gave up his spirit" (Jn 19:30). With his perfect sacrifice, Christ has overcome the fiend, every fiend. Evil is fully routed. In the mind of God, all has already been made "wele."

From our side, however, these words are prophecy, full of promise and hope, but not yet fulfilled *for each one of us.* We wait to see, trusting, yet not knowing, how the transformation of all things into "good" will be accomplished, "for we walk by faith, not by sight" (2 Cor 5:7). In our blind ignorance, we cannot possibly behold the way God beholds, nor imagine how God could make things well that are obviously not well to our way of seeing right now.

Unfortunately, the words "alle shalle be wele" and their variants have become so popular and over-used in our time that they have lost much of their startling and apocalyptic significance. The greeting card sentimentality that has grown up around them, reducing them to an instant panacea for everything that is currently wrong in our lives, is an erroneous interpretation. Christ did *not* promise "alle manner of thing shalle be wele" tomorrow... or the next day... or next year... or at any time during the course of our lives on this earth. And Julian did not imply immediate solutions to life's problems when she recorded Christ's words for posterity. To interpret his words as meaning he will "fix" everything to our liking, mend our broken relationships, land us the perfect job, heal our aches and pains, end all world conflicts, even dispense justice in the way we think it should be dispensed, is to vitiate the Revelation. Yes, Christ will be with us in every step, every breath, of our life, helping us to make good decisions and to bear our crosses. And we will feel his strength and grace as he works in small ways and large to transform all our struggles and sufferings into his perfect joy. But that metamorphosis will not, cannot, be fully experienced by us here and now. We simply do not yet have the minds to "see."

Christ is speaking to Julian of the *ultimate* "alle shalle be wele," not the temporary one. We will not be able to envision how he converts evil into good as long as we ourselves are bound by our ignorant views, our sinful habits, our grasping to self. The only way "alle manner of thing" can possibly be fulfilled is through our complete transformation through death and rebirth into Christ. Only when our minds and hearts are illuminated within a state of perfect knowing and perfect loving, when we enter into the beatific vision, will we be able to comprehend what truly IS, in the light of God. Then, and only then, on a completely glorified plane of existence, *shall we see ourselves* "that alle manner of thing shalle be wele."

17
The Great Deed

> There is a deed which the blissful trinity shall do in the last day, as to my sight. And what the deed shall be and how it shall be done, is unknown by all creatures who are beneath Christ, and shall be till it shall be done. The goodness and the love of our lord God wills that we know that it shall be. And his might and his wisdom, by the same love, will conceal and hide it from us, what it shall be and how it shall be done. And the reason why he wills we know it thus is because he wills we be the more eased in our soul and at peace in love, leaving the beholding of all tempestes [agitations and tumults] that might prevent us from truly rejoicing in him. This is the great deed ordained by our lord God from without beginning, treasured and hidden in his blessed breast, known only to himself, by which deed he shall make alle thing wele. For as truly as the blessed trinity made alle thing of nought, right so the same blessed trinity shalle make wele alle that is not wele. (32:19–30.223)

The monumental Revelation that Julian received concerning the Great Deed does not explicitly answer her questions about *why* evil was allowed to come into the world, nor how sin is *behovely*, nor how evil will finally be overcome. This crucial section does not even appear in the Short Text. Yet it became paramount in Julian's soteriology (her understanding of how God saves) over the course of several decades of contemplation on the Thirteenth Revelation. And the fact that she places it here, after the famous "five words," connects it directly to what Christ will do to "solve" the problem of evil.

Julian specifies that the Great Deed "is unknown by all creatures who are beneath Christ." The Blessed Virgin does not know, nor do the angels and saints know, what the Great Deed will be and how it will be done. Yet Julian is sure that Christ wants everyone to know *that there will be such a deed* that will finally make all things well. In his trinitarian might, wisdom, and love, Christ does not wish us to speculate about what it is and how it will be accomplished because he does not want us consumed by torturous imaginings "that might prevent us from truly rejoicing in him." Simply receiving the Revelation that there will be a Great Deed should give sufficient comfort to our souls and enable us to be at peace and live in love.

The Great Deed has been ordained "from without beginning," and while we know by faith that Christ's passion, death, and resurrection make all things well ultimately, it seems Julian is implying another divine action here. It has been suggested that she might be anticipating a decree of universal salvation and the emptying out of hell. But Julian in no way hints at or dares to imply this possibility, much as we might like to read such an interpretation into her text. On the contrary, she does not speculate at all and perhaps neither should we. Suffice it to say that Julian compares the Great Deed with the act of creation itself: as the Trinity creates all things from nothing, so the Trinity "shalle make wele alle that is not wele."

Two Realities

The key to Julian's ongoing explanation is that the Lord is showing her two separate realities. The one, human reality, we experience mentally, physically, emotionally, and spiritually every day, with both its joys and its sufferings, its blessings and its curses. This reality is constantly in flux, ever-changing from moment to moment for good or for ill. Therefore, it is always fraught with uncertainty, hidden dangers, the pain of dissolution. Nothing lasts. In this reality, we think and feel and make countless choices, some right, some wrong. We try to create safe havens of light and peace and love, but at the same time we are tossed about by conflicts, within and without, over which we have no control. This is what we call our "life." But it is only one way of existing. This earthly life is not the whole of reality. And it is continually darkened by our deep ignorance about the other *Divine* Reality.

Divine Reality is God's own life in trinitarian bliss. When we are wrenched away from what we call our "life" and resurrected as members of Christ's Mystical Body, our minds will become illuminated through and through with God's life. Then we will be able to see and experience the ever-new creation as it pours forth from the Word of God in perfect wisdom and love. Then it will be made clear what we cannot possibly fathom now: how the resurrection (Christ's, and ours-to-come *in* Christ) has changed everything. Then we will truly have "the mind of Christ" (1 Cor 2:16, cf. Phil 2:5) to be able to witness the Great Deed, whatever it will be, and to see that "alle manner of thing shalle be wele." Once our minds and hearts are completely transformed and incorporated into Christ's own mind and heart, we will be able to rest in contemplation of the central mystery of the Trinity. This alone is eternal happiness.

Yet even now our efforts to persevere in hope can enlighten our minds and reassure our hearts. Faith can enable us to believe that this, *even this,* illness or tragedy will be transformed by Christ. Even now Divine Reality is constantly impinging on human reality through the outpouring of grace, like shafts of sunlight reaching deep into the thick, dark forest of our minds. During her Revelations and in the years-to-come of contemplation, Julian glimpsed this Divine Reality and gained profound insights concerning its nature. But she could not rest in the promise Christ gave her concerning this Reality until she had first allowed him to calm the raging *tempestes* of doubts and terrors that plagued her very human soul.

The Damned

> And in this sight I marveled greatly, and beheld our faith, meaning thus: our faith is grounded in God's word, and it belongs to our faith that we believe that God's word shall be preserved in all things. And one point of our faith is that many creatures shall be damned: such as angels that fell out of heaven because of pride, who are now fiends, and men on earth who die outside of the faith of holy church—that is to say, those who are heathens—and also men who have received christendom [been baptized] and live un-christian lives, and so die out of charity [die without love]. All these shall be damned to hell without end, as holy church teaches me to believe. And understanding all this, it seemed to me that it was unpossible that alle manner of thing should be wele, as our lord shewed in this time. (32:31–40.223)

Here Julian states medieval church teaching concerning those who shall be damned. But she does so to point up the fact that, given her vision of Christ's "dearworthy blood" covering all the earth, she simply cannot understand how Christ can assure her "alle manner of thing should be wele," if even one single soul is damned for eternity.

> And as to this, I had no other answer in this shewing of our lord but this: "That which is unpossible to thee is not unpossible to me. I shall save [preserve] my word in all things, and I shall make althing wele." And in this I was taught by the grace of God that I should steadfastly hold myself in the faith as I had before understood, and in addition to that, I should stand firm and steadily believe that alle manner of thing shalle be wele, as our lord shewed in that same time. (32:41–46.223–25)

Christ responds to Julian's inability to comprehend that some might be damned and yet all would be well with a direct reference to the gospel of Luke. In a startling teaching that Christ once gave to his disciples he remarked that it was easier for a camel to pass through the eye of a needle than for a rich man to enter the kingdom of heaven: "Those who heard it said, 'Then who can be saved?' He replied, 'What is impossible for mortals is possible for God'" (Lk 18:26–27). Now Christ affirms that his word will be preserved and fulfilled in all things. He will not go back on a promise, or a prophecy: "For truly I tell you, until heaven and earth pass away, not one letter, not one stroke of a letter, will pass from the law until all is accomplished" (Mt 5:18).

In this crisis, Julian feels she is being directed to stand firmly in an unresolvable dichotomy between two extremes. On the one hand, she must believe the church's doctrine predicting damnation for unbaptized non-believers as well as those who "live unchristian lives" and die in mortal sin. On the other, she must embrace Christ's incontrovertible promise that "alle manner of thing shalle be wele," that all creation shall be brought to perfect fulfillment and bliss. In her mental torment of not knowing how to do this, Julian is focusing more on her own psychological dilemma than on Christ's surpassing love. What has happened to the joy she experienced when Christ spoke the "I it am" litany? Where is her delight that surpassed "all that heart can think, or soul may desire" (26:10–11.207)? It has fled, it is nowhere to be found. This is the invasion by doubt that Julian herself alluded to as being so destructive of the blissful contemplation of the Lord.

Dogma and Mysticism

For all her warnings to the contrary, Julian becomes entrapped in her own questions. What is at the root of Julian's turmoil? It would appear that it is the essential conflict between her total adherence to the dogmatic teachings of the church on damnation and her equally total faith in the visions and locutions she is receiving from the Lord in which she *does not see* God's wrath, blame, or condemnation of any kind, only pity and compassion for the great sufferings our sins cause us. It is the problematic distinction between dogmatic and mystical ways of understanding and interpreting divine revelation.

No doubt, Julian knew that the doctrines recited in the Apostles' Creed had been revealed by God through sacred scripture and apostolic teachings, formally defined by the *magisterium* of the church and made binding for all the faithful. On the one hand, the Creed demands absolute belief if one is to be called a Christian (though, significantly, it does *not* include any mention that souls who die in original or mortal sin will be condemned to hell for all eternity). On the other hand, the Creed specifies that after Christ died and was buried, "he descended into hell: the third day he rose again from the dead." It was generally believed that Christ brought out of hell all those patriarchs and prophets, men and women of good will of the Old Testament, who had waited patiently for his coming. Pope Benedict XVI illuminated this startling passage. The "descent into hell," he said,

> should not be imagined as a geographical or a spatial trip, from one continent to another... it mainly means that Jesus reaches even the past, that the effectiveness of the Redemption... *embraces the past, all men and all women of all time...*[1]

We have seen the "harrowing of hell" as the most raucous scene in the passion play, following the bloody enactment of Christ's death on the cross. The flames and clouds of smoke, the sulphurous smells, the banging of chains and drums, both terrifying and liberating, suggested to a medieval audience that Christ *could* release previously damned souls, not only from the interim place of purgatory, but also from the bowels of hell itself. And although orthodoxy compels belief in the existence of hell for the damned (as a theological parallel to heaven for the saved), *the church has never taught definitively that any single soul is actually in hell.*[2] On the contrary, the tradition is consistent in teaching that no one can know the final state of an individual soul at the moment of death. Christians have always been reminded that God desires "everyone to be saved and to come to the knowledge of the truth" (1 Tm 2.4), that God is able to save all, and that God will never abandon anyone who did not hear his word. Indeed, Christians have also been exhorted *to hope* that all shall be saved.

Julian heard Christ tell her: "Herewith is the fiend overcome" (13:4–5.169). She firmly believed that there was nothing Christ's passion, death, and resurrection could not overcome. She hoped that Christ's promise that "alle shalle be wele" would be fulfilled. However, in this moment, she is deeply concerned that if people continue to live dissolute lives, if they do not repent of their sins, if they are "heathens" who have never heard the name of Christ preached to them, or if they refuse to believe in the Savior for whatever reason . . . and then, if they die unshriven, with the double stain of original and mortal sin on their souls . . . in short, if they do not take advantage of the mercy and graces of Christ's passion . . . *how could even Christ's salvific death save them from hell?* Would not Christ's Divine Mercy be superseded by his Divine Justice that demands eternal punishment for unrepentant sinners? Did not Christ's own parable concerning Domesday describe how the Great Judge would separate the wheat from the chaff, that is, those who had performed the works of mercy during their lives from those who had not? And did the parable not predict that God would welcome the saved into his kingdom but say to those who are accursed: "depart from me into the eternal fire prepared for the devil and his angels" (Mt 25:41)?

As we have discussed, these and other references to eternal damnation were regularly preached from pulpits by Dominican and Franciscan friars as well as by parish priests. They issued dire warnings to urge sinners to make acts of contrition and confess their sins, especially when times were dangerous and death seemed imminent. All these seemingly incontrovertible teachings about the sufferings in hell for both believers and unbelievers must have struck real terror into Julian's heart, as no doubt they did into the hearts and minds of many other *evencristens* of her time. Did not Julian have family members who had died unshriven during the plague? In the war in France? Perhaps in the very act of committing violent crimes? Did she not have relatives who had left the church and turned their backs on the sacraments altogether?

There is an additional cause for Julian's anxiety: her own *shewings*. In her visions, and in every word she heard the Lord speak to her, Julian experienced Christ's overwhelming and unconditional love. He told her in no uncertain terms, not once, but in five distinct ways, that "alle shalle be wele," strongly implying that *all* shall be brought to eternal happiness, otherwise how could he make such a prediction? And he gave her the additional assurance that she would "see" this Great Deed happen herself. After this Revelation, how could Julian deny the certainty of what she had heard and experienced in her heart? Yet, by accepting the veracity of her visions and locutions, was she perhaps embracing *an alternate vision of truth* from that which the medieval church commonly taught and preached? Could she be falling into grave error? Could her vision of Christ's all-inclusive love be coming from the devil-in-disguise, to lead her into heresy?

True mystical experience never contradicts the revealed truths of Christian faith. It is *a deeper experience* of these truths. Mysticism may, and often does, present a new interpretation, a different layer of meaning, leading to a more profound understanding of divine mystery, stretching the boundaries of what was previously thought possible, addressing an imbalance or outright prejudice in the way the teaching is currently being presented. And this is precisely what Julian's Revelations do, in a most incisive and orthodox manner. However, at this point in her mystical experience, Julian was not yet sure of her own mind. She had plunged from her state of ecstasy into a tempest of inner conflict. Julian admits she had no other clear answer in this *shewing* but a reminder of the message from the gospel: "For nothing will be impossible with God" (Lk 1:37).

Hell and Purgatory

> For this is the great deed that our lord God shall do, in which deed he shall save his word in alle thing and he shall make wele all that is not wele. But what the deed shall be, and how it shall be done, there is no creature beneath Christ who knows it, nor shall know it, till it is done, according to the understanding that I took of our lord's meaning at this time. (32:46–50.225)

In her great longing for clarity, Julian perceived that the Great Deed must ultimately have something to do with a *different way of interpreting* the church's teaching on those condemned to hell. This new way of "seeing" would not conflict with the personal Revelation she had received concerning Christ's total lack of wrath. Julian's great hope is that, at the end of time, Christ's overpowering and all-forgiving love will somehow make all non-believers and sinners, even those who have died in grave sin, completely "wele."

The instructions on hell and purgatory are necessary, in Julian's words, "for the same end that holy church teaches" as long as we are in this place and time (33:3–4.225). Such divergent concepts as good and evil, right and wrong, heaven and hell, serve as paradigms and warnings that both reveal and hide much deeper truths. For example, there is the level at which we have all been, at one time or another, "cast down into hell" and felt the burning of its spiritual fires, its agony of despair and helplessness. We thought it would last forever. We have also been in a continual process of "purgation" on the treacherous road to illumination. We strive to be fully cleansed of our ignorance, sin, and suffering so that we might finally "arrive" in the heavenly place of the heart. Hell, purgatory, and heaven are extremely potent concepts that define our spiritual alternatives and continual mental oscillations, even in this life.

Still swirling in the maelstrom of her mind, however, Julian dares to desire a sight of hell and purgatory, not to "test" the truth of their actual existence as defined by the church, but to have more teaching "in all things that belong to my faith, whereby I might live even more to God's worship and to my profit" (33:5–6.225). However, just as earlier in the Thirteenth Revelation, she "saw not sinne" (27:22.209), now she is shown neither hell nor purgatory. *She simply did not have the spiritual disposition to be able to see them.* Julian insists that even though the whole Revelation showed only God's goodness, "in which was made little mention of evil," she was not "drawn thereby from any point of the faith that holy church teaches me to believe" (33:12–14.225). That is, she was not inclined to *reject* the literal existence of hell and purgatory.

Torn by her need to confront such painful issues, yet always desiring to remain a faithful daughter of the church, Julian expresses her hope that she will remain in the mercy and grace of God until her life's end. She believes it is God's will "that we have great regard for all the deeds that he [Christ] has done" already and in such profusion, because then we will more readily "know, trust, and believe all that he *shall* do" (33:23–24.225, italics added). Yet we must, as she has said before, stop trying to conjure up what the Great Deed will be and become more like the saints in heaven who want nothing but what God wills.

> Then shall we only rejoice in God and be well apaid [satisfied] both with hiding and shewing. For I saw truly in our lord's meaning, the more we busy ourselves to know his privities in that or in any other thing, the further shall we be from the knowing. (33:27–29.227)

Two *Privities*

Julian pauses to make a distinction between the two kinds of secret Revelations. One is the great *privity* (the Great Deed), which our Lord wishes to keep hidden until such time that he chooses to show it to us. The other *privities* are those *shewings* that Christ has been opening out to Julian in this and in her other Revelations. These are various aspects of the faith he dearly wants all people to know, but which, in our blindness, we often fail to appreciate. Christ has great pity on us because we have not understood or believed these mysteries sufficiently or truthfully, and so "he will make them open to us himself, so that we may know him and love him and cling to him" (34:8–9.227). Julian is convinced that our good Lord wants to show us everything that could possibly be of benefit to our souls, in addition to the usual "preaching and teaching of holy church" (34:10–11.227). By this frank disclosure, Julian is not in any way holding up her private Revelations as being *superior* to the church's preaching and teaching. On the contrary, she remarks that God showed his great pleasure in all "men and women who mightily and meekly and wisely accept the preaching and teaching of holy church" (34:12–13.227). In point of fact, she attests:

> For *he it is*, holy church. He is the ground, he is the substance, he is the teaching, he is the teacher, he is the end, and he is the mede for which every natural soul travails. And this is known and shall be known to each soul to which the holy ghost declares it. And I hope truly that all those who seek thus [through church preaching and teaching] shall prosper, for they seek God. (34:13–17.227, italics added)

Julian is recalling Christ's earlier litany: "I it am." The church *is* the living presence of Christ's Mystical Body, the communion of the faithful. As St. Paul wrote: "Now you are the body of Christ and individually members of it" (1 Cor 12:27). The church is not a building, nor a hierarchy of prelates, nor a collection of canon laws, nor even commonly held doctrines and traditions. Likewise, the ground and substance of Julian's faith are not laws and condemnations. Faith is a personal relationship with Jesus Christ, who is the teacher, the teaching, the goal, and the reward for whom every believer longs. And Julian could not imagine how any new revelation Christ might give her could possibly undermine his own past teachings, as preserved through the sacred traditions of the church.

A Certain Creature

And now Julian records a brief interaction for which she later felt the sharp sting of remorse. She includes it in her text as a cautionary note, but it also reveals something very human about Julian herself: her motherhood. At the very time that "God almighty had shewed so plenteously and fully of his goodness" to her (35:1.229), she thinks of an urgent question she needs to ask before it is too late.

> I desired to know of *a certain creature that I loved if it should continue in good living*, which I hoped by the grace of God was begun. And in this singular desire, it seemed that I letted [hindered] myself, for I was not taught in this time. And then I was answered in my reason, as it were by a friendly intermediary: "Take it generally, and behold the courtesy of thy lord God as he sheweth it to thee. For it is more honor to God to behold him in all than in any specific thing." I assented, and with that advice, I learned that it is more honor to God to know everything in general than to prefer anything specific. (35:2–9.229, italics added)

What a poignant moment this is! After all the Lord's teachings on the two *privities*, and the Great Deed, and other mysteries like it that must be kept hidden (as against those mysteries of the faith the Lord is willing to reveal generally), Julian dares to ask about one special person in her life whom she dearly loves. As we have suggested in Part One, this "creature" was most likely her own daughter, who might have been eleven years old at the time of Julian's Revelations in 1373, prompting this ardent question. In the earlier Short Text,

Julian had originally specified: "I desired of a certain person that I loved, how it should be with *her*" (xvi:13.97, italics added). However, in the Long Text quoted above, written decades later, the female gender of the person has been rendered neuter.

It is very likely that in her great gratitude for God's goodness in revealing so many *privities*, Julian felt inspired to ask Christ for yet one more: a secret glimpse into her daughter's future. *Will she remain virtuous? Will she marry well? Will she survive childbirth? Will she be happy?* These are, understandably, the very questions any mother would wish to ask in a direct encounter with the Lord. However, desiring to know the specifics of an individual's future is a very different request from simply praying for that individual's well-being in the future. Julian immediately realizes she has overstepped her bounds. Her rash inquisitiveness has severely "letted," or hindered, her. By requesting to know more than the Lord has given her to know, she has sabotaged her ability to receive any more Revelations.

Julian is mortified. She knows she has inquired into the very sort of *privity* she has just understood must be kept hidden until such time as the Lord wished to reveal it, the type of *privity* even the Blessed Mother and the saints do not seek to know! Against her own better advice, she has allowed her mind to become "busy to know his privities in that or in any other thing" (33:28–29.227). She has inquired, in essence, if "alle would be wele" with her own daughter. She has asked for a prophecy. An inner voice, which she terms a "friendly intermediary," strictly cautions her that she must accept all the Lord's Revelations "generally," rejoicing in exactly the way the Lord courteously shows them to her, not grasping for more. She understands that she will give greater glory to God by knowing the truth in this all-inclusive way rather than by seeking personal information about her special loved ones, information that must be kept hidden. She hopes that if she can keep to this new teaching all her life she will be neither delighted nor greatly distressed by any new or "secret" knowledge. Rather, she will always be led to trust that, even though she does not know what will happen or when, "alle shalle be wele" (35:11.229).

> For the fullness of joy is to contemplate God in all. For by the same blessed might, wisdom and love that he made all thing, to the same end our good lord leads it continually, and thereto he, himself, shall

> bring it. And when it is time, we shall see it. And the ground of this was shewn in the first revelation, and more openly in the third revelation, where it says: "I saw God in a point." (35:12–16.229)

Tolerating Evil

Needing to make amends, Julian confirms again that all the Lord does is good and just and perfect. And all that he "suffers," or permits, to happen, no matter how incomprehensible it may appear to us at the time, deserves our respect. In this, she gains a more subtle understanding of good and evil.

> For all that is good our lord does, and all that is evil he suffers. I say not that evil is honorable, but I say *the suffrance* of our lord God is honorable, whereby his goodness shall be known without end, and his marvelous meekness and mildness, by this werking of mercy and grace. (35:18–22.229–31, italics added)

In no way does Julian imply that God is *complicit* in any evil that might come to us. Evil arises as the direct result of human sin. But according to theological teaching, the Lord "tolerates" evil in order for us to learn from it, be purified by it, even suffer from it, in the certain hope of seeing it transformed into good. St. Paul wrote: "We know that all things work together for good for those who love God, who are called according to his purpose" (Rom 8:28). And Augustine argued:

> For the great works of the Lord are sought out according to all his purposes in order that even what happens *against* his will should in a wonderful and inexplicable way not be done *despite* his will, since it would not happen if he did not permit it, and he does not permit things unwillingly but willingly; *nor would he in his goodness allow anything evil to happen were he not able in his omnipotence even to bring good out of evil.*[3]

Julian understands that God's "suffrance" of human sin and evil must be seen as a blessing for which we should be supremely grateful (because if God crushed us for every bad deed we commit, who could survive?). On the contrary, by his tolerance of both sin and its negative consquences, God shows "his marvelous meekness and mildness." Instead of wrath, he offers divine mercy; instead of punishment, the grace to endure our sufferings. In this way, God enables human beings to triumph over evil.

For Julian, the rock-solid foundation of her theology is that God is *rightfullehede*, righteousness and goodness, as she has already expounded in the Third Revelation (11:19–48.165). She sees with crystal clarity that righteousness means that the good which God does "may not be better done than it is" (35:23.231). All his works were ordained to be performed perfectly, since the very beginning, "by his high power, his high wisdom, his high goodness" (35:25–26. 231). And just as God ordains all things for the best, so he never stops working to bring all things to perfection. Julian further attests that the contemplation of this accord between what God wills and the way in which God brings it to completion "is very sweet to the soul that sees it by grace" (35:28–29.231). For it is by God's own goodness that all souls destined for heaven will be "endlessly and marvelously kept [protected], above all creatures" (35:31.231).

The Work of Mercy

Julian further defines God's mercy as a divine *werking* that flows directly from the divine goodness:

> ...and it shall last in werking as long as sinne is allowed to pursue rightful souls. And when sinne has no longer permission to pursue them, then shall the werking of mercy cease. And then shall all be reconciled with rightfullehede, and therein remain without end. By his suffrance we fall, and in his blessed love, with his might and his wisdom, we are kept. (35:32–36.231)

Even when we fall into harmful deeds, even when we feel ourselves overcome by the power of spiritual sabotage, we are still held fast by the hand of God. Once we are in heaven, Julian is convinced that "by mercy and grace we are raised to manifold more joys" for having repented, suffered for, and triumphed over our sins, than if we had not sinned in the first place (35:36–37.231).

> And thus in rightfullehede and in mercy he will be known and loved, now and without end. And the soul that wisely beholds this in grace is welle apaid with both [rightfullehede and mercy], and endlessly rejoices. (36.37–39.231)

Another Deed

When the *shewing* resumed, Julian was given to understand that *another* deed will be performed.

> And it shall be honorable and marvelous and plenteous. And it shall be done for my sake and God himself shall do it (and this is the highest joy that the soul understood, that God himself shall do it!), and I shall do nothing at all but sinne. And my sinne shall not hinder the werking of his goodness. And I saw that the beholding of this is a heavenly joy in a fearful soul which evermore naturally by grace desires God's will. (36:2–7.231)

Julian is ecstatic to realize that this other deed will begin here and now, *on earth,* and will be immensely profitable to "all God's lovers on earth" (36:9.231). And it will be entirely God's doing. In fact, because of her afflicted human nature, Julian is only too aware that she will do nothing but sin. *But her sin will not stop Christ working.* This is a sublime joy to anyone who is fearful of committing mortal or venial sin, as was Julian. And this deed will continue to work in us until the end of time. And when we come to heaven, we shall see exactly what this deed was that God has been doing for each one of us all along, and it will give us the greatest joy. "And the honor and the bliss of that deed shall last in heaven before God and all his holy ones without end" (36:10–12.231). With great confidence, Julian writes that she saw and understood the Lord's meaning concerning this second deed and that he revealed it to her precisely so that we would all rejoice "in him and all his werks" (36:14.233).

Julian had fully expected that the Lord would tell her what this particular deed would be, but it was kept secret from her, as was the Great Deed. However, she is certain that God does not want us to worry about what any of his future revelations or deeds might be. For now, Julian is being told only *that* they will happen, not *what* they will be, so that we may all "believe and understand that we shall see them truly in endless bliss" (36:24–25.233). Julian adds that when she had said that the deed should be done "for my sake," by this she understood "the general man," that is, people in general, or "alle that shalle be saved" (36:29.233).

Once again, Julian reminds us that we should rejoice in God both for what he shows and what he hides, which will bring us great peace of mind and an immense sense of gratitude. She understands the Lord's meaning about this second deed as clearly as if he had said to her directly:

> "Behold and see. Here hast thou matter [material] for meekness, here hast thou matter for love, here hast thou matter for noughting thyself, here hast thou matter for enjoying [rejoicing] in me. And for my love, *enjoy in me*, for of alle thing, with this might thou most please me." (36:33–36.233, italics added)

I am enough for thee

> And as long as we are in this life, whenever we by our folly turn ourselves to the beholding of the damned, tenderly our lord touches us and blissfully calls us, saying in our soul: "Leave me alone, my dearworthy child, attend to me, I am enough for thee. And rejoice in thy savior and in thy salvation." (36:37–40.233)

Julian is both chastised and greatly relieved by this realization. She strongly advises that whenever we become obsessed by fears over who might be damned, we should hear Christ speaking gently in our soul: "Stop worrying and turn to me." He will warn us, time and again, not to hinder his work of salvation either in ourselves or in others by becoming preoccupied about it. Instead of indulging in terrifying meditations on hell, so often encouraged in medieval (and other) times, Christ wants us to rejoice in our salvation and *in him*. "And that this is our lord's werking in us I am seker" (36:40–41.233). Julian is absolutely convinced that any soul that is pierced by hearing such words of warning will feel them deeply and cease this folly of useless speculation. Julian mentions that this second deed will be known sooner (that is, when we die and enter heaven), while the Great Deed will not be revealed to anyone in heaven or on earth until it is accomplished at the end of the world.

Miracles

Christ also gave Julian a special understanding and direct teaching on the "werking and shewing of miracles" (36:49–50.233):

> "It is known that I have done miracles here before, many and numerous, high and marvelous, honorable and great. And just as I have done I do now continually, and shall do in coming of time." It

> is known that before miracles, come sorrows and anguish and trouble. And that is so that we should know our own feebleness and mischief that we are fallen into by sinne, to humble us and make us fear God, crying for help and grace. And great miracles come after, because of the high might and wisdom and goodness of God, shewing his virtues and the joys of heaven, as far as it may be possible in this passing life, and that for the strengthening of our faith, and increase of our hope in love. Therefore it pleases him to be known and worshipped in miracles. (36:50–59.233–5)

Julian intimates here that miracles done on earth are a glimpse of God's unsurpassed and everlasting creative delight, a foretaste of both the deed that will be done immediately when we come into heaven, and of the Great Deed to be revealed at the end of time. She cautions, however, that miracles occur only after long periods of "sorrows and anguish and trouble." She understands that this painful process is absolutely necessary. All through the gospels, the pattern is the same: a penitent is in desperate need, paralyzed by illness, sin, and suffering, cries out, seeks forgiveness from Christ, and then is healed of the infirmity, first of soul, then of body.

> For which is easier, to say, "Your sins are forgiven," or to say, "Stand up and walk"? But so that you may know that the Son of Man has authority on earth to forgive sins—he then said to the paralytic—"Stand up, take your bed and go to your home." (Mt 9:5–6, Mk 2:9–11)

Only in true contrition is the suffering soul able to feel the scales fall from its eyes and experience the miracle of regaining its inner sight (Acts 9:18). Julian discloses that Christ does not want us to become overly depressed because of the "sorrows and tempestes that fall to us" (36:60.235). She remarks that it has ever been thus . . . just before miracles happen.

I shuld sinne

At this point, Julian is forced to face a difficult truth: "God brought to my mind that I shuld sinne" (37:1.235). The Middle English *shuld* usually indicates a more imperative future tense, meaning definitely *would*.

> And because of the delight that I had in contemplating him, I attended not readily to that shewing. And our lord full mercifully waited, and gave me grace to attend. (37:1–3.235)

Julian is humble enough to admit that she did not pay attention to the Lord telling her she would continue to fail once the *shewings* ended. She did not want to be distracted from her pleasure in contemplation. Yet, in addition to giving Julian a foretaste of heavenly bliss, the Lord needed to open up the darkest place in her mind, where her deepest afflictions were buried. He did not do this to make her suffer more, but only to direct her focus to those areas that prevented her from fully enjoying him.

We may wonder why, if Julian is still in a trance-like state, far removed from earthly temptations, she needs to be reminded of her tendency to sin. It seems likely that the Lord wants to reassure her that even though he knows she will fall in the future, as she has in the past, it will not affect his love and constant care for her. Julian tells us she experienced this *shewing* as applying "singularly" to herself. She took it very, very personally. Yet, she was also instructed later to apply it to all her *evencristens*, in general, as she had recently been taught to do. "Though our lord shewed me that I shuld sinne, by *me alone* is understood all" (37:6–7.235, italics added).

> And in this, I conceived a soft dread. And to this our lord answered: "I keep thee full sekerly" [I protect thee in complete security]. This word was said with more love and sekernesse of ghostly keeping than I can or may tell. For as it was shewn to me before that I shuld sinne, right so was the comfort shewn; sekernesse of keeping for all mine evencristens. (37:8–11.235)

Julian trembles at the thought of her own ability to sin. She has seen what the effects of evil look like in the plenteous bleeding from the crown of thorns, the gaping wounds from the scourging, the deep drying, and the agonizing thirst, both physical and spiritual, of Christ on the cross. She has seen an imaginative vision of his mother, Mary, weeping in lament at the foot of the cross. She has endured her own anguished compassion for Christ's sufferings and re-experienced all the sorrows and wounds of her whole life. For her to consider that, after being a witness to all this, she would do anything that could wound the Heart of Christ, is abhorrent to her. Yet, Julian knew only too well that the old habits of grasping to her likes and dislikes, wants and needs, her very human tendencies to sloth, depression, even despair (as she will reveal later), were so ingrained that they would indeed return. And there would be future occasions when she would not be able to resist making a hurtful remark, being critical, getting angry, even doubting her Revelations . . . if she lived, that is.

The Lord anticipates this fear and wants to purify Julian at the subconscious level, in the place from which all patterns of selfish thinking and sinful behavior emerge. He directs her to confront these most entangled feelings, to see them arise and let them go in her mind, without giving in to them, while in her current state of deep contemplation. It is only *now*, as Julian experiences Christ's presence, holding and loving and keeping her in total security, that she can dare confront the terrible guilt feelings still festering from her childhood: *Why didn't I die of plague like all the others?* It is precisely *now* that she can face her worst negativity of the past and her most terrifying fears about the future.

Mystic Turmoil

Normally, we do not think of visionary experiences as having such dark aspects. But mystical states are not always blissful and beautiful. Many mystics have experienced the most petrifying confrontations with stark images of evil, battled grave temptations, and wrestled with personal demons. They have had to go deeper within their souls to recognize and beg mercy for sinfulness that was hitherto kept hidden from them. In heightened stages of contemplation, just as the soul can fly to a plane of ecstasy never before experienced, so it can descend into an area of hellish memories, choices, shame, and self-blame that must be unearthed and weeded out if the spirit is to be set free.

Sometimes, these dark *shewings* can be so terrifying that if the mystic did not take refuge again and again in the Lord, as Peter did, crying out "Lord, save me!" (Mt 14:30), the soul would surely implode under the pressure. Julian knew the Lord was present to help her endure whatever darker vision of her sinfulness might arise. Still, she felt fear, a "soft dread," as she called it. But the essential element here is that Julian was *seker* that what the Lord would uncover of her sinfulness he would also forgive and heal. And this he would do, not only for herself, but for all her *evencristens.* In fact,

Julian becomes suddenly jubilant at the thought that nothing could make her love her *evencristens* more than to realize how much God loves them all, "as it were all one soul" (37:12–13.237).

> For in every soul that shall be saved is a *godly will that never assented to sinne, nor never shall.* Just as there is a beastly will in the lower part that may will no good, just so there is a godly will in the higher part, which will is so good that it may never will evil, but only good. And therefore we are those whom he loves, and endlessly we do what he likes. And thus our good lord shewed the holiness of love that we stand in, in his sight: yea, that he loves us now as well while we are here as he shall do when we are there before his blessed face. But because of the failure of love on our part, therefore we have travail. (37:14–21.237, italics added)

In this signature Revelation, Julian anticipates her teaching on the "godly will," a teaching that she will develop at length, later on. It must be made clear that Julian does not imply that our "lower part," our animal nature (having to do with our carnal appetites) is of itself *beast-like*, but that it simply has no will, either good or evil, of its own. (St. Augustine had termed it concupiscence: our non-rational and often unbridled appetites for food, sex, and self-preservation.) Therefore, our lower nature is not able to will higher things. Our mental faculties, on the other hand, which include our reason, memory (with its imagination), and will, being spiritual faculties of the soul, are able to think and remember, imagine and choose. Sometimes, of course, we choose wrongly, or choose a lesser good in place of one that is higher. But what Julian is getting at here is that in the very core of our nature, because we are created by God, we are *good*. And in this ground of our being, we long for the perfect good that alone can satisfy our spiritual hunger and thirst. The labyrinth of our minds and the confusion of our wills, however, often lead us down sinful and dark paths away from the pursuit of that ultimate reality.

What Christ assured Julian in this Revelation on the "godly will" is that the soul that shall be saved is one that *never* fully, completely, willfully assents to serious sin. It may have been sorely tempted in its lower nature; it may even have fallen seriously because of weakness of the flesh, a craving for worldly power, prestige, and wealth. But because such a soul returns again and again in remorse to seek forgiveness from the Lord, it never totally rejects (nor will it ever reject)

God. And such a soul, however circuitous its route to heaven may be, pleases God in its repeated efforts to lead a good life. Julian affirms that our good Lord loves that soul as much *now*, in the midst of the great ordeal, as he will when the soul comes up to heaven and sees God face to face. Christ's love never changes. It is only human love that waxes and wanes. And in this is the root of our suffering.

Sin and Reward

> Also, God shewed that sinne shall be no shame, but honor to humankind. For just as every sinne is answered by a [corresponding] pain according to truth, rightly so for every sinne, the same soul is given a blessing by love. Just as diverse sinnes are punished with diverse pains according to their grievousness, rightly so shall they be rewarded with diverse joys in heaven according to how much the sinne has been painful and sorrowful to the soul on earth. (38:1–6.237)

Is there any traditional support for Julian's conviction that sin bears "no shame" for those who repent? *The Pricke of Conscience*, a Middle English verse poem of 9,624 lines, was widely read during Julian's lifetime.[4] It provided literate clergy and laity with an expansive summary of medieval theology (largely borrowed from the thirteenth-century writings of Bishop Grosseteste and others). It describes in vivid detail the miseries of life on earth and the horrors of death, strongly condemns sin, and affirms church teaching on eternal punishment. However, it also suggests that in heaven the saved, whether Peter, or Magdalene, or any other sinner, will remember their sins *without any shame in them.*[5] So there is some contemporary theological foundation for Julian's understanding of sin as "no shame."

Julian also explains that, for every sort of sin we commit, we will experience a similar type of suffering. For example, expressing anger toward someone else will result in an experience of a similar show of anger toward oneself. An act of betrayal means one will suffer betrayal. Those who inflict violence will inevitably experience violence, "for all who take the sword will perish by the sword" (Mt 26:52). But Julian also intuits, most daringly, that every suffering endured for sin will merit a comparable type of blessing, according to

Christ's love. And the more grievous the sin is, the more extreme the resulting pain and sorrow will be on earth, but the greater the reward shall be in heaven. It is clear that this reward will not be for the sin itself, but for the terrible *effects of sin* that have been patiently endured: mental and emotional anguish, physical suffering, spiritual anxiety, long years of shame, guilt, and penance. And for this, Christ will give honor to the reformed sinner.

> For the soul that shall come to heaven is so precious to God, and the place so worshipful, that the goodness of God will never suffer that soul to sinne that shall come there, unless that sinne shall be rewarded. And it [the sinne] is made known without end and blissfully restored by overpassing honors. (38:6–9.237)

Julian's insight here is quite startling. She herself seems to have had trouble accepting it. And it was only because she was again "lifted up into heaven" in her understanding that she was able to do so (38:10.237). God brought to her mind King David, who committed adultery with Bathsheba and ordered the murder of her husband (2 Sm 11:1–27), as well as numerous others from the Old Law who had sinned grievously and yet were brought up to heaven. And in the New Law, she thought first of Magdalene who, in the Middle Ages, was believed to have been a prostitute (Lk 7:36–50); Peter, who denied even knowing Christ (Mt 26:69–75, Mk 14:66–72, Lk 22:54–62); Paul, who persecuted Christians (Acts 8:1–3, 9:1–9); Thomas, who doubted Christ's Resurrection (Jn 20:24–29); John of Beverley (whose name became linked to a popular legend about a hermit who had committed heinous sins);[6] in addition to so many others.

Julian points out that all these countless saints are allowed to be known on earth both for the gravity of their sins, for which they suffered terrible remorse and often physical pain, and for the honor into which those sins have been transformed, precisely *because* of their suffering. And God continues to show how holy and revered these men and women have become in heaven, by performing miracles associated with the physical remains of their bodies on earth. The courteous Lord reveals this knowledge of their sainthood in part on earth as it will be fully shown in heaven. "For there, the token of sin is turned into honor" (38:16–17.239).

The Scourge of Sin

Julian is still preoccupied with the thought of sin, even the sins of those who eventually become saints:

> Sinne is the sharpest scourge that any chosen soul may be smitten with. Which scourge beats down man and woman, and also breaks him, and disgusts him in his own sight—so much so that sometimes he thinks himself not worthy, except as it were to sink into hell—till contrition takes him by the touching of the holy ghost, and turns the bitterness into hope of God's mercy. And then his wounds begin to heal and the soul to revive, turned into the life of holy church. The holy ghost leads him to confession, willfully to shew his sinnes, nakedly and truly, with great sorrow and with great shame that he hath so defouled the fair image of God. Then he undertakes the penance for every sinne, enjoined by his confessor, that is grounded in holy church by the teaching of the holy ghost. (39:1–10.239–241)

This passage alone would controvert anyone who might suggest that Julian's Thirteenth Revelation is "soft on sin." It is a completely orthodox description of the three conditions the church teaches are necessary for forgiveness: contrition for sin, confession to a priest, performance of a penance. It is also the personal admission of a woman who knew the "scourge of sinne" firsthand, who had suffered the shame, the pain, and the near-despair of having spoiled the image of God within her soul. It is, finally, the testimony of a person who has felt the sweet inspiration of grace to confess her sins, experience forgiveness, and willingly perform a penance. Making confession to a priest was (and is) deemed essential by the church for the absolution of mortal sins and was strongly prescribed for the forgiveness of all lesser, venial sins. As we have discussed, the sacrament of penance was also obligatory once a year, every year, before fulfilling the Easter duty to receive the Eucharist. The Lollards denied the need to confess sins publicly to a priest. They considered personal remorse and the seeking of forgiveness to be a private matter between the soul and God.

But the church held that sin not only damaged the relationship between the individual soul and God, it damaged the whole community, in that every sin affected other *evencristens*. In Julian's time, there were no private confessional boxes; penitents performed a public act of standing in line in a church, waiting to be *shriven* in front of all their neighbors by a priest who was seated near the altar or in the open nave. Penitents knelt down in full view of their fellow Christians and confessed their sins (albeit in a hushed tone of voice) to the priest, who represented Jesus Christ. After being questioned and admonished by the priest, the penitent recited the act of contrition, speaking directly to God: "I am heartily sorry for having offended thee." Thereafter, the person would be required to perform a public (or private) penance, usually selected from a list of penances appropriate to the sins confessed. All these public acts and private attitudes bore witness to the deep need of the whole Christian community for spiritual healing.

Forms of Suffering

Julian identifies penance as one form of meekness "that greatly pleases God," and "bodily sickness of God's sending" as another (39:11–12.241). As we have seen, Julian requested just such an illness out of an ardent desire to become more like Christ. Now she adds that public humiliations such as outward sorrow and shame, condemnations and being despised by the world, are also forms of overt penance. She even considers *temptations* to bodily sins (lechery, gluttony, sloth) and spiritual sins (pride, envy, anger, covetousness) as being types of suffering, as did the customary teachings of her time.[7] Through them all, however, Julian affirms that the good Lord protects the soul, even when we seem to be nearly forsaken and cast out by everyone else because of sin, and even though we recognize that we deserve what we suffer. Affliction fosters humility, which leads, by God's grace, to honor in heaven.

At this point, Julian mentions those whom God visits with his special grace. He bestows on them great remorse for sin, "with compassion and true longing for God" (the "third gift" that Julian had requested in her youth), and then "they are suddenly delivered of sinne and of pain, and taken up to bliss and made even with saints" (39:19–20.241). Julian is, of course, speaking of the likes of St. Paul and, in her own fourteenth century, the testimonies of Richard Rolle, and (if she knew about them) Catherine of Siena and Brigit of Sweden. She also may be indirectly including herself here, in an oblique and cautious reference, lest she seem presumptuous. The fact is, Julian *was* freed from sin by confessing her sins to a priest on her deathbed and receiving the last rites of the church. She *was* cured of her fatal illness and relieved of physical pain during the time of her visions. And, in her periods of total ecstasy, she *was* taken up into heaven in her mind and heart, and for those blissful moments "made even" to the saints. Such is the union in love that mystics enjoy on rare occasions in this life and which they predict will occur at the moment of death.

> By contrition we are made clean, by compassion we are made ready, and by true longing for God we are made worthy. These are three means, as I understand, whereby all souls come to heaven—that is to say, who have been sinners on earth and shall be saved. (39:20–24.241)

Medicines and Honors

Julian reiterates that the three wounds that she had long ago desired (contrition, compassion, and true longing for God) are the spiritual "medicines" by which the illness of sinful souls will be healed. The scourges and lashings of sin will be seen by God not as shameful wounds, but, like Christ's own wounds, *as honors.* Julian makes very clear that when we are "punished" here on earth with sorrow and suffering it is not because of God's "wroth" but as the inevitable result of our personal and collective sinfulness. And God will not allow us to lose one degree of spiritual value from what we must bear, for God sees sin not as a cause for casting us out but "as sorrow and pains to his lovers, in whom he assigns no blame for love" (39:28–30.241).

> The mede [reward] we shall receive shall not be little, but it shall be high, glorious and honorable. And so shall all shame turn to honor and to more joy. For our courteous lord does not want his servants to despair for often falling nor for grievous falling. For our falling does not hinder him from loving us. Peace and love are ever in us, being and werking. But we are not always in peace and in love. (39:31–35.241–43)

The reward for bearing our earthly suffering patiently will not be slight; it will be the vision of God in the company of the saints, all of whom (except Saint Mary, Christ's mother) have undergone the same scourge of personal sin. Julian urges us to consider this, especially when we fall, even through grievous wrongdoing. For she is convinced that Christ does not want us to sink into self-loathing and excessive remorse and debilitating penances (all of which were prescribed medieval practices for those who would combat sin) lest we torture our souls and remain in a state of continual mental and physical anguish. To her great credit, Julian never suggests self-inflicted suffering as the most effective way to purification. Such harsh methods dispel peace and can seriously warp our love. Rather, Julian urges that we give Christ complete freedom to work in us, by keeping our souls in peacefulness and in love.

Our Whole Life in Love

> But he wills we take heed thus: that he is the ground of all our whole life in love, he is our everlasting keeper [protector], and mightily defends us against all our enemies that are extremely dangerous and terribly fierce towards us. And our mede is so much greater if we give him occasion [to love and heal us] by our falling. (39:36–39.243)

This theme of Christ as "the ground of our whole life in love" colors and highlights every aspect of Julian's theology. Christ is not the unapproachable "other," the distant God-man whose anger must be appeased by every extreme means possible. He is, in a very real sense, *what we are*, in our flesh and blood and bones, having taken on the fullness of our human nature, save sin, in order to help us combat the suffering of temptation and guilt, and to show his sublime peace and love. He knows exactly how our minds work, what our failings and compulsions are, and longs to teach us how to reorient our attitudes and desires toward the highest good. And he has endured every possible physical, mental, emotional, and spiritual agony we go through. This is the Christ Julian knows to be at the foundation, the very *ground*, of our being. This is where the "godly will" resides, that never wills sin: in our Christ-redeemed nature.

> And this is the supreme friendship of our courteous lord, that he keeps us so tenderly while we are in our sinne. And furthermore, he touches us most intimately, and shews us our sinne by the sweet light of mercy and grace. (40:1–3.243)

Julian is convinced that even when we are in the midst of harming ourselves or others, and seem to be abandoning God, he does not abandon us. Instead, he whispers in our heart and mind, moves our conscience to feel remorse, and leads us to ask forgiveness, guiding us by his own "sweet light of mercy and grace."

However, Julian is acutely aware that when we sin, "we see ourself so foule," we think (indeed, we assume) that "God is wroth with us for our sinne" (40:4–5.243). Here, Julian is describing her own sense of personal guilt, with a keen understanding that Christians persistently harbor a *wrong* view of God as being wrathful. She explains that though we may remain convinced that God must be angry at us while we are in sin, it is precisely his ever-present mercy and grace which enable us to turn back to him, confess our failure, and ask forgiveness. Christ gathers us up like his prodigal son (or daughter) and encloses us in the royal robe (the restored innocence of our baptism), calls his servants to kill the fatted calf and prepare a banquet (the Eucharist), and invites all the saints to join in the celebration: "because this brother of yours was dead and has come to life; he was lost and has been found" (Lk 15:32). What Julian is describing here is not only the parable of the prodigal son, but also the never-ending story of the exorbitant love of the prodigal *Father*.

My Dear Darling

> And then our courteous lord shews himself to the soul merrily and with the happiest possible expression, with friendly welcoming, as if it had been in pain and in prison, saying thus: "My dear darling, I am glad that thou art come to me. In all thy woe I have ever been with thee, and now see for yourself my love, and let us be oned in bliss." Thus are sins forgiven by grace and mercy, and our soul honorably received in joy, exactly as it shall be when it comes into heaven, as often as it comes back to God by the gracious werking of the holy ghost and the power of Christ's passion. (40:8–15.243)

In contemplating Christ's mercy and grace in never leaving us alone, even in our sin, Julian understands how "all manner of thing" is already being prepared for us in heaven, "by the great goodness of God" (40:16–17.243). This is so true that, whenever we feel ourselves "in peace and in charity, we are truly safe" (40:17–18.243). And we are, by implication, *already saved*.

Julian reports exceptionally intimate terms in this passage, such as "My dear darling" and let us "be oned in bliss," more often employed between earthly lovers than between the sinful soul and God. She remembers the depth of personal feeling Christ showed her as he conveyed this Revelation about sin. He was not only joyous, friendly, welcoming; he was also deeply loving and all-embracing. His ardent desire for unity is that of a lover for the beloved, not in a sexual sense, but in that of complete spiritual oneing. Just hearing words like these spoken by Christ in one's heart would be enough to convince the soul of his unconditional love.

Julian's Warning

Immediately following her reassuring Revelation concerning Christ's compassion on us for sin, and the rewards we will enjoy for our sufferings due to sin, Julian issues a strict caveat.

> But now because of all this ghostly comfort that has been said before, if any man or woman is stirred by folly to say or to think, "If this be truth, then were it good to sinne to have more reward," or else to charge less weight to sinne, *beware of this stirring*. For truly, should it come, it is untrue and of the enemy [Satan]. For the same true love that teaches us all this comfort, the same blessed love teaches us that we should hate sinne only for love. And I am seker by my own feeling, the more that each human soul realizes this in the courteous love of our lord God, the more loath he is to sinne, and the more he is ashamed. (40:22–29.245, italics added)

St. Paul had posed the question himself: "What then are we to say? Should we continue in sin in order that grace may abound? By no means! How can we who died to sin go on living in it?" (Rom 6:1–2). Likewise, Julian warns against anyone thinking that because the Lord is merciful and rewards true repentance, then we should sin all the more to gain more mercy and merit. This way lies madness, as well as grave danger. Any such temptation to presume forgiveness is a deadly sin against the Holy Spirit and greatly to be avoided.

In the Short Text, Julian had even written: "For whichever soul that willfully responds to these stirrings, he may never be safe until he has done penance as for a mortal sin" (xviii:3–4.101). Sin must be abhorred above all other things, because it is done in defiance of God's love. Julian expresses her own feeling that if every soul could experience the love of God, he (or she) would be loath to sin and terribly ashamed if he did. She is certain that if all the pains of hell and purgatory and earth were laid before us, including the pains of death and all other sufferings, we would rather choose all that pain in place of sin.

> For sinne is so vile and so completely hateful that it may be likened to no pain which pain is not sinne. And to me was shewn no harder hell than sinne. For a natural soul hates no hell but sinne, for all is good but sinne, and nought is evil but sinne. And when we give our attention to love and humility by the werking of mercy and grace, we will be made all fair and clean. (40:32–36.245)

Julian adds that as almighty and all-wise as is God, so is he all-willing to save humankind. Christ is the ground of the New Law given to Christians and through it he has taught us how to do good and avoid evil. He is, himself, this law of love, loving us just as he wants us to love one another:

"In everything do to others as you would have them do to you; for this is the law and the prophets" (Mt 7:12). And Christ wills that we become like him in the selfsame holiness toward ourselves and our *evencristens* (and, by extension, toward all of humanity). And just as Christ's love for us will not be broken under the weight of our sins, so he wants our love for ourselves and for everyone else to remain unbroken. We are to "hate sin as God hates it, and love the soul as God loves it" (40:44.247).

How is it possible for us to do this? Julian will reveal the means as she discusses the nature of prayer in the Fourteenth Revelation. Now, at the close of her long exegesis on the Great Deed, the damned, hell and purgatory, two *privities*, "a certain creature," the work of mercy, a second deed, miracles, that she "shuld sinne," the introduction of the "godly will," sin and the rewards of suffering, the danger of presumption, and finally, the depth of Christ's incomparable compassion and unbreakable love, she summarizes the entire Revelation in one sentence:

> For this word that God said is an endless comfort: "I keep thee full sekerly." (40:45.247)

18
On Prayer

The Fourteenth Revelation

> After this, our lord gave a shewing about prayer, in which shewing I saw two conditions [characteristics] in our lord's meaning. One is rightfulle prayer; another is seker trust. (41:1–2.247)

How are we to pray? This same question inspired one of Christ's disciples to ask: "Lord, teach us to pray" (Lk 11:1). In this *shewing*, Julian understands two essential aspects of prayer: having the right attitude and praying with certain trust. In the Short Text, Julian had elaborated what "rightfulle prayer" might be:

> One [condition] is, they will not pray for anything that may be [in the future], except that thing that is God's will and his worship. Another is that they set themselves powerfully and continually to beseech that thing that is his will and his worship. And that is as I have understood by the teaching of holy church. For in this our lord taught me the same: to have of God's gift faith, hope, and charity, and keep us therein to our lives' end. And in this we say Pater noster, Ave, and Credo with devotion, as God will give it. And thus we pray for all our evencristens and for all manner of men, that God's will be done. For we would that all manner of men and women were in the same virtue and grace that we ought to desire for ourselves. (xix:2–11.101–3)

For Julian, to pray "rightly" means to pray *in the right way.* First and foremost, we must pray that "Thy will be done," as is spoken in the Lord's Prayer. To pray rightly also means to pray fervently, continually, and without losing heart. Christ told his disciples to "Be alert at all times, praying that you may have the strength to escape all these things that will take place" (Lk 21:36, cf. Eph 6:18, 1 Thes 5:17). He also urged that we pray with great persistence, like the widow in the parable who was so unrelenting in her pestering of the unscrupulous judge that he finally gave in and granted her request (Lk 18:1–8). These, then, are familiar teachings of the church concerning prayer that Julian would have learned from an early age. She also knew that true prayer meant petitioning God in ardent faith, hope, and charity, not just for oneself and one's family, but for all *evencristens*, as well as for men and women throughout the world. Julian is adamant that Christians should want "the same virtue and grace" for everyone that they desire for themselves. Whether the above passage was deliberately or inadvertently cut by Julian or by a later scribe in its transition from the Short to the Long Text, it is impossible to know. However it does shed some light on Julian's own training in "rightfulle prayer" and her recognition that, in the first part of the Fourteenth Revelation, Christ is reaffirming what she knew from consistent church teaching.

It is in the *second* characteristic of prayer, however, that Julian reveals a deeper dimension, concerning "seker trust." Her use of the Middle English word *seker, sekerly, sekernesse* throughout her text implies not only security but sureness, certainty, and even a sense of joyful relief in being able to let go of all doubt and fear. This is a trust that passes beyond all imagining.

> But yet oftentimes our trust is not full. For we are not seker that God hears us, and we think [it] is because of our unworthiness, and because we feel nothing at all. For we are as barren and as dry oftentimes after our prayers as we were before. And so, in our feeling, our folly is the cause of our weakness. For thus have I felt in myself. (41:3–6.247)

This passage provides a rare insight into Julian's own problems with prayer. Since this passage is in *both* the Short and Long Texts, clearly it was not a difficulty that developed only in her mature years, during the solitude and long hours of prayer while she was confined in the anchorage. Lack of *seker* trust and want of any feeling in prayer may have been repeated obstacles for Julian. Perhaps she was never convinced God heard her prayers, and she attributed that fact to her own sense of being an unworthy sinner who did not deserve to be heard or answered. So she often felt absolutely nothing when she prayed: no comfort, no reassurance, no clarification, no intimacy. By her own account, sometimes she remained as barren and dry *after* she had prayed as when she first knelt down to pray. And again, she thought this was because of her unworthiness. Even though she would have been taught that strength of faith is more important than feelings during prayer, Julian admits her ongoing struggles without any qualification.

I Am the Ground

> And all this our lord brought suddenly to my mind, and shewed these words and said: "I am the ground of thy beseking [beseeching in prayer]. First it is my will that thou have it, and next I make thee to will it, and next I make thee to beseke it—and thou besekest it! How should it then be that thou shouldst not have thy beseking?" (41:7–10.249)

In an astounding moment, the Lord completely inverts the idea that prayer is initiated in any way by Julian with the Revelation that it is entirely his own idea. He identifies *himself* as the instigator and basis of all prayer. First, in his great goodness, Christ wills to give her some grace, then he makes her conscious of the desire for it (as with her requests for "three wounds" in her youth). Next, he inspires her and gives her the desire to enter into prayer in order to beseech it. And then, she actually does beseech it in her prayer. Finally, Christ asks Julian the all-important rhetorical question: "How could it then be that you would not receive what you were beseeching me for?" (since it was Christ himself who conceived the grace he wanted to give Julian in the first place!). Of course, this Revelation assumes that what Julian will be led to pray for will be to her most immediate benefit, as well as her eternal salvation, and will bring the greatest blessings upon those for whom she prays.

Julian became convinced that when we pray it is in response to God's desire to grant what we most urgently need. Our prayers of beseeching do not *cause* graces and gifts to come to us from God. It is God's own goodness, the ground of all that is, that initiates every good thing he ever chooses to give us. He is ready to give before we even ask.

A Mighty Comfort

Julian experienced "a mighty comfort" in receiving this divine illumination, especially in the first instance when Christ said, "I am the ground of thy beseking," and also in the following three (41:11–12.249). And in the fifth reason ("And thou besekest it!"), Julian testifies that Christ showed the greatest delight in the eternal reward that he will give us for our *beseking* in prayer.[1] (Notably, these "five reasons" seem to parallel the Lord's "five words" about making all things well.) As for the sixth reason, in which Christ said, "How should it then be?" (that the soul would not have what it beseeched), Julian realizes that the refusal of the Lord to grant our heartfelt prayer would be "unpossible" (41:15.249).

> For it is the most unpossible [greatest impossibility] that may be that we should seek mercy and grace and not have it. For every thing that our good lord makes us beseke, he himself has ordained it to us from without beginning. (41:15–18.249)

Julian experiences prayer in an entirely new and radically hope-filled way. She is sure that Christ wants all his "lovers on earth" to know how he directs our prayer, because "the more that we know, the more shall we beseech," if we understand this teaching wisely, as our Lord intends (41:22–23.249).

The Treasury of Prayer

> Beseeching is a true, grace-filled, lasting will of the soul, united and fastened into the will of our lord by the sweet, privy werking of the holy ghost. Our lord himself is the first receiver of our prayer, as to my sight, and he takes it most thankfully. And, greatly enjoying, he sends it up above, and sets it in a treasury where it shall never perish. It is there before God with all his holy saints, continually received, ever furthering our needs. And when we shall receive our bliss, it shall be given to us for a degree [specific amount] of joy, with endless, honorable thanking by him. (41:24–30.249–51)

Julian envisions Christ receiving our prayer without the need for any intermediaries, even his Blessed Mother, the angels or saints, and being extremely grateful to us for all our efforts. In this, she goes directly against the trend of medieval devotion that had recourse to

Mary's compassion to intercede with the soul before God. The general idea was that, being human and not of divine origin, Mary could better understand humanity's condition and the extent of our frailty and sinfulness. Therefore, she would more likely be the mediatrix, as we have mentioned, interceding for us with her son (so often considered a harsh judge), who would be persuaded by his mother to show mercy instead of wrath and then, in turn, intercede with the Father. This chain of intercession seriously diminished the sinner's reliance on Christ as the one and only mediator between the human and divine, on Christ as all-compassionate and all-merciful in himself.

Julian's visions refocus the soul's attention on Christ, needing no *meanes*, or intermediaries, as she had mentioned earlier in her Revelations (6:4–7.143). According to Julian's understanding, Christ receives our prayer personally and intimately. He gratefully and joyfully places it in a spiritual "treasury," where it will be a constant source of benefit to us on earth. When we come to heaven, it will be returned to us as an added source of joy, with the Lord's own eternal thanksgiving. Christ told his disciples:

> Do not store up for yourselves treasures on earth, where moth and rust consume and where thieves break in and steal; but store up for yourselves treasures in heaven, where neither moth nor rust consumes and where thieves do not break in and steal. (Mt 6:19–20)

This is the treasure-house of prayer Julian evokes.

Pray Wholeheartedly

Julian also understands that prayer makes us more like Christ through the graces we receive when we pray, as we are already like him in our human nature. Since it is Christ's will that we be fully restored to the image and likeness of God, Julian describes how he urgently exhorts us:

> "Pray interly [wholeheartedly]: though thou think it savour thee not, yet it is profitable enough, though thou feel it nought. Pray interly, though thou feel nought, though thou see nought, yea, though thou think thou might not [have any strength]. For in dryness and barrenness, in sickness and in feebleness, then is thy prayer fully pleasant to me, though thou think it savour thee not but little. And so is all thy living prayer in my sight." (41:33–38.251)

Even when we have no "savour," or taste, for prayer, no sense of enjoyment in it, no palpable feeling during it, no strength to persevere in it, we must still try to turn our hearts to prayer. Julian even suggests that Christ is "covetous" to have us praying often in his sight, because of all the rewards and endless thanks he wishes to give us. Regardless of what prayer feels like to us, "God accepts the good will and the travail of his servants" (41:40.251). He is greatly pleased when we work "in prayer and in good living by his help and his grace" (41:41–42.251). He also cautions Julian that he wants us to be "reasonable with discretion" (41:42.251) and not tire ourselves out with endless repetitions of the same prayers which can become mindless. The main directive is to keep our soul's focus on God's presence within, until such time as "we have him whom we seek in fullness of joy: that is, Jesus" (41:43.251).

Prayer of Thanksgiving

In addition to petitionary prayer, Julian stresses the prayer of thanksgiving. This is "a true, inward knowing, with great reverence and lovely dread," whereby we dedicate all our energies to the good work that the Lord directs us to do, "rejoicing and thanking inwardly" (41:45–47.251). Julian reveals that sometimes this prayer of thanksgiving is so overwhelming that it breaks out in full voice saying: "Good lord, grant mercy, blessed may thou be!" (41:48–49.251). And at other times, when the heart feels dry and empty, or else is undergoing temptations, then prayer "is driven by reason and by grace to cry aloud to our Lord, remembering his blessed passion and his great goodness" (41:50–52.251). Either way, the strength of the Lord's own word will enter into the soul, enliven the heart, begin a new spiritual work by means of grace, and enable the soul to pray more blissfully and to rejoice in him. "This is a very lovely thanking in his sight" (41:54–55.251).

Three Aspects of Prayer

Julian summarizes three aspects that should determine our understanding of prayer. The first, as already mentioned, is to know *from whom* and *how* our prayer originates. Christ made clear that he is the instigator of prayer when he said, "I am the ground." And he revealed how prayer develops because of his goodness when he said,

"First, it is my will that thou have it." The second aspect concerns the *manner* in which we say our prayers. Our will should always be turned entirely toward the will of the Lord, not in fear but in great enjoyment. Christ clarified this for Julian when he said: "I make thee to will it." And the third aspect focuses on the fruit and *goal* of our prayer, which is "to be oned with and like our lord in everything" (42:7–8.251).

> And to this meaning and for this end was all this lovely lesson shewn. And he will help us, and he shall make it so, as he says himself. Blessed might he be! (42:8–10.251–53)

Additionally, Julian suggests that both our prayer and our trust should be equally "large," which in Middle English implies generous and ample, even ambitious (42:11.253).[2]

> For if we do not trust as much as we pray, we do not give the fullest worship to our lord in our prayer, and also we hinder and trouble ourselves. (42:12–13.253)

Julian considers that the reason we become hesitant and lacking in trust is that we think the impetus to pray is coming from ourselves instead of from Christ. If we were *absolutely certain* that Christ is the "ground in whom our prayer springs" and that prayer is itself "given to us by grace of his love," then we would naturally trust that we would have "all that we desire" (42:14–16.253).

Disappointment in Prayer

> But sometimes it comes to our mind that we have prayed a long time, and yet we think that we have not received what we asked for. But therefore we should not become depressed, for I am seker by our lord's meaning that either we must wait for a better time, or more grace, or a better gift. He wills that we have true knowing in himself that *he is being*. And in this knowing, he wills that our understanding be grounded with all our strength, and all our intention, and all our meaning. And in this ground, he wills that we make our [dwelling] place and our wonning [home]. (42:19–25.253, italics added)

Julian knows only too well that even with rightful prayer and persevering trust, sometimes our heartfelt petitions do not seem to receive any answer. Then, we become depressed and perhaps feel rejected by God. It is a too-familiar cycle. Julian is certain that there is a divine reason: a better time, more grace, a better gift. And again, if we rely on our faith that Christ himself is the source of all "being," all that we could possibly long for, we will not lose heart. In fact, if we ground ourselves in this knowledge, holding this awareness in prayer with all our strength of mind and purpose and intention, we will discover a spiritual dwelling place that is immovable: *Christ himself* will become the answer to every prayer.

Julian considers three things that follow upon this realization. First, our creation; second, our precious redemption, which Julian terms *againe-byeing* or "buying back" (42:28.253); and third, everything in creation that Christ, out of love, sustains in order to serve us. It is as if Christ said to us, every time we begin to pray:

> "Behold and see that I have done all this before thy prayer occurred. And now thou art, and prayest to me." (42:30–31.253)

Since Christ has already performed such great deeds in times past, as the church teaches, we should give thanks and pray for the deed that he is doing right now, which is to rule us and guide us to his worship in this life and to bring us to everlasting bliss. Christ wants us both to *see* that he does everything for us and also to *pray* for it to be done. If we only pray and do not see that he does every good deed, we feel depressed and full of doubts, and this does not contribute to his glory. And if we see that the Lord is the cause of all good things and yet do not ask that his will be done, we do not fulfill our responsibility to pray. As a result, we may not be able to "see" God's providence reveal itself in our lives. Julian suggests that, in some mysterious way, our prayer is intimately linked to God's actual working, and God is worshiped best (and we are most benefitted) when we both acknowledge that he does everything that is done, and pray that he may do it.

Julian reiterates this imperative to pray for all that Divine Providence has preordained to do, both in particular instances and in general. This kind of prayer gives such great joy and bliss to Christ and will bring us such thanks and honor that Julian writes: "it passes the understanding of all creatures in this life, as to my sight" (42:44–

45.253). Praying like this shows that we have a right understanding of the fullness of joy that is planned for us, "with true longing and seker trust" (42:45–46.253–55).

Longing and Trust

Julian acknowledges that the inevitable disappointments and failings of this life often make us long for the bliss of heaven, for which we are created. In such difficult times, if we cling to belief in and love of God and continue to be mindful of our Savior, we will be better able to trust, no matter how desperate we may feel. "And thus by nature we long, and by grace we trust" (42:49.255). God continually beholds these two interior activities of longing and trust in us. Yet we should not think that by longing and trusting we have done anything special, because it is our basic human responsibility, our "debt," as Julian calls it, to God. And even when we do pray, we should consider it as nothing.

For Julian, prayer becomes the catalyst that truly *oneth*, or unites, the soul to God. While the soul is made in the image and likeness of God, and therefore is (in its very essence) godlike, it is often most *un*like God because of sin. But prayer bears witness that our soul essentially wills what God wills. Prayer brings great comfort to our conscience and enables us to receive abundant graces. Julian assures her readers that God looks upon us constantly in love and wants to make us "partners" in his good will and holy work (43:6.255). And so he inspires us to pray for exactly what he wants to do in us and then, gratuitously, he will even reward us for our praying. This is what Christ meant in the words: "And thou besekest it!"

> In this word, God shewed such great pleasure and such great delight, as if he were greatly beholden to us for each good deed that we do. *And yet it is he that does it.* And because we beseech him mightily to do that thing that he likes, it is as if he said: "What might please me more than for you to beseech mightily, wisely and willfully to do that thing that I will do?" And thus the soul by prayer is reconciled with God. (43:9–14.255–57, italics added)

Contemplative Prayer

And when, in his great courtesy, the Lord reveals himself to the soul by a special grace, then "we have what we desire" (43:16.257).

Here, Julian moves from an examination of prayers of petition and thanksgiving into the realm of contemplative prayer. In this form of prayer, words fail and the listing of special intentions ceases altogether, since the soul no longer knows what to ask. Instead, the soul yearns to be still and silent, with its powers of reason, memory, and will totally intent on beholding God. "And this is a high, unperceivable prayer, as to my sight" (43:18.257). At times like this, Julian attests that every possible reason for prayer is united in the sight and the beholding of God to whom we pray. Then the soul is filled with the utmost joy, reverent awe, and the sweetest delight. Then the soul only prays as God directs it to pray. "And well I know, the more the soul sees of God, the more it desires him by grace" (43:21–22.257). Contemplative prayer generates an ever greater desire for mystical union with the beloved.

Times of Trouble

Julian admits, however, that when we do *not* experience the joy of beholding God in contemplative prayer, then, because of our frailty, we feel the need to pray in other ways and to prepare the soul to become receptive to contemplation once again.

> For when a soul is tempted, troubled, and left to itself by unrest then is it time to pray to make itself supple [pliable, compliant] and obedient to God. But it [the soul] by no manner of prayer makes God supple to itself. For he is ever unchanging in love. And thus I saw that when we see a need for which we pray, then our lord God follows us, helping our desire. And when we of his special grace plainly behold him, seeing no other needs, then we follow him, and he draws us into him by love. (43:27–30.257)

In times of temptation and trouble, emotional or spiritual stress, it becomes well nigh impossible to let go of our conflicts and fears and to allow ourselves to become fully absorbed in God's goodness, resting quietly in his peace-filled love. But Julian advises that at precisely these times we should strive to pray in order to make our souls more "supple and obedient" to God's good will in all things. We should *never* consider that our prayer could possibly make God more supple and obedient to *our* wills, for God's love is unchanging and cannot be "persuaded" to do anything that is not according to his

Divine Will. Whenever we feel the desire to pray, God follows us (like a protective parent walking behind its child), encouraging and helping us to pray well. And when, at times of special grace, we are able to behold God contemplatively, desiring only him and his will and not thinking of any other thing, then "we follow him" wherever he desires to lead us. And he draws us further into unitive prayer.

By her own testimony, Julian saw and felt that God's great goodness enlarges all the capabilities of the soul. And his constant working in every possible circumstance is done "so well, so wisely and so mightily that it overpasses all our imagining and all that we can imagine or think" (43:31–33.257). Indeed, Christ's own Spirit prays so ardently within us that we become seduced, as it were, into letting go of our most pressing petitions, concerns, and fears as we drop into the arms of the Lord. In such times of contemplative prayer, we realize we can do nothing at all but simply *sit* in God's presence, conceiving an ever greater desire to become *oned* with him, acutely attentive to his dwelling place in the ground of the soul. And there we are graced to rest in rapt silence, rejoicing in the awareness of God loving us and delighting in his great goodness.

Mystical Union

> And thus we shall, with his sweet grace, in our own meek, continual prayer come into him now in this life by many private touchings of sweet, ghostly sights and feelings, measured to us as our simplicity may bear it. And this is wrought and shall be wrought by the grace of the holy ghost, until we shall die in longing for love. And then shall we all come into our lord, knowing ourselves clearly and having God abundantly; and we will endlessly all be had in God, truly seeing and wholly feeling him, and spiritually hearing him, and delectably smelling him, and sweetly swallowing him. And then, we shall see God face to face, intimately and abundantly. (43:36–43.257–59)

In this sensual prophecy, Julian anticipates that, by God's grace and our humble and continual prayer, we may be allowed, now and then, to enter into deep mystical union with God, even in this life. This will be the working of the Holy Spirit and will be given to us only as much as our human limitations allow. And when at last we die in a spirit of great love-longing to be made one with God, we will be gathered into God, truly experiencing him through our spiritualized senses. Then Julian promises we will be able to see God "face to face," which Moses had been told no man could do and live (Ex 33:20).

Julian is poetically erotic in her use of the verb "have," choosing a word that can connote the intimacy of sexual union, as she also wrote in the Second Revelation: "And thus I saw him and sought him, and I had him and wanted him" (10:14.159). Of course, she is speaking of a purely *mystical* union, without going so far as to call it a "spiritual marriage," as did Catherine of Siena. However, Julian suggests that, like the bride in the Song of Songs, the soul shall both "have" God and be "had" by God in a total embrace. All the spiritual senses of the resurrected body will be involved: seeing, feeling (touching), hearing, smelling, tasting. Love-longing will be overtaken by possession, desire by fulfillment. The creature shall be *oned* with the Creator at last, as the bride longs to be with her beloved in the Song of Songs: "Let him kiss me with the kisses of his mouth! For your love is better than wine, your anointing oils are fragrant, your name is perfume poured out; therefore the maidens love you" (Sg 1:2–3). Julian adds that even now, when God wills by a special grace to show himself to the creature, he strengthens the soul above and beyond its own human powers and "measures [moderates] the shewing" to be most profitable for the soul in the moment, according to his will (43:47.259). This is exactly the "measuring" Julian felt the Lord was performing in her soul throughout the Revelations.

The Perfect Soul

Julian declares that God repeatedly showed her that "man werks God's will evermore and his worship, lastingly and without ceasing" (44:1–2.259). This may seem preposterous, given the evil deeds that human beings commit. But Julian is speaking here of the soul as it is continually being created perfectly by God, exemplified by "the werking of the blessed soul of our lady, St. Mary, by truth and wisdom" (44:4–5.259).

> Truth sees God, and wisdom beholds God. And of these two comes the third, and that is a marvelous, holy delight in God, which is love. Where truth and wisdom are, truly there is love, truly

> coming of them both, and all of God's making. For God is endless sovereign truth, endless sovereign wisdom, endless sovereign love uncreated. (44:6–10.259)

Julian exalts the sublime capabilities of the soul as being able to contemplate truth in the Father, wisdom in the Son, and love through delight in the Holy Spirit. She describes the soul "as a creature in God," having the same properties as God (though in a created form), and so "evermore it does that for which it was made: it sees God, and it beholds God, and it loves God" (44:10–12.259). In this, the soul perfectly mirrors the Divine Trinity. Julian testifies that God rejoices in the soul even as the soul rejoices in God, since it is made in his own image and likeness. And yet the Creator is seen as "so high, so great, and so good in comparison with man that is created" that the creature feels itself to be scarcely anything at all (44:14–15.259). However, the clarity and the purity of truth and wisdom allow the soul to see and to realize that it is made "because of love, in which love God endlessly keeps [protects] him" (44:16–17.259). And this recognition gives the created soul immense dignity.

Two *Domes*

How can Julian have such a high estimation of the still-sinful human soul? As if in explanation, Julian introduces a powerful insight that enables her to distinguish between the *dome* (judgment) of God and the *dome* of humankind. God judges the souls of humanity according to our "kindly substance," that is, our purely created *essence*, which is "ever kept one in him, whole and safe without end, and this dome is because of God's rightfullehede" (45:1–2.259). This is sound theology, because God does not create that which is unlike himself: "And God saw that it was good" (Gn 1:18). God does not judge any part of his own creation as being less than perfect.

In the earthly realm, however, humanity passes judgments based on our "changeable sensuality," our highly volatile nature, which now wants one thing, now another (45:3.261). Julian is well aware that this human sensuality is made up of conflicting "parts" or warring impulses, which are sometimes godly, sometimes beastly. This is our soul and our body, considered in its *imperfect* and *fallen* state, having been corrupted by worldly temptations. And this human judgment (that Julian implies is passed on us both by the church and by ourselves) is "mixed, sometimes it is good and easy, and sometimes it is harsh and grievous" (45:4–5.261). Insofar as our human judgment is good, it emanates from Divine Righteousness. Insofar as human judgment is harsh and causes terrible suffering, the Lord himself transforms it "by mercy and grace through the virtue of his blessed passion, and so brings it into rightfullehede" (45:7–8.261). And both these manifestations of God's justice will be harmonized and given due recognition in heaven.

Julian calls "the first dome" that of God's own judgment, connecting it inextricably to Domesday and the Final Judgment. Remarkably, for Julian, God's eternal righteousness is not terrifying but comes from "his own high, endless *love*" (45:11–12.261, italics added). She describes God's *dome* as the "fair, sweet dome that was shewed in all the fair revelations, in which I saw him assign to us no manner of blame" (45:12–13.261). Once again, Julian speaks out boldly and bravely concerning what she saw and heard and understood, not just in one but in all the Revelations: namely, that *there is no wrath nor blame within God.* Yet even though Julian rejoiced in the contemplation of this first, sweet *dome* of God's judgment, she admits she "could not be fully eased," or completely comforted (45:14.261).

> And that was because of the dome of holy church, which I had understood before [9:18–21.157] and which was continually in my sight. And therefore, by this dome, it seemed to me that it was necessary to know myself a sinner. And by the same dome I understood that sinners are sometimes worthy of blame and wrath, and yet these two I could not see in God. And therefore my view and desire were more than I can or may tell. (45:15–20.261)

Julian's propensity to ask questions leads her into a seemingly insoluble dilemma: in her visionary state, she experiences the love of God without any wrath or blame directed at the sinner. Yet the church, drawing on both Old and New Testament scripture, had taught her ever since she was a child that God hates sin, and that his wrath against the sinner demands that sin be punished through suffering on earth and thereafter in purgatory or hell. As we have discussed, the church constantly warned of the dangers of sin and of the grave punishments due to sin so as to keep souls from eternal perdition. And Julian believes the church is right to do so. Christ himself had told Peter, the first head of the church: "Truly I tell you, whatever you bind on earth will be bound in heaven, and whatever you loose on earth will be loosed in heaven" (Mt 18:18, 16:19).

Conflicting Views

The conflict that arises in Julian's soul comes from *two very different viewpoints of sin*: that of her personal Revelation from God, and that of the church's teachings. Julian is desperate for divine clarification.

> For the higher dome God shewed himself at the same time, and therefore it seemed that I must accept it [as revelation]. And the lower dome was taught to me previously in holy church, and therefore I might not in any way abandon the lower dome. Then was this my desire: that I might see in God in what manner the dome that holy church teaches herein is true in his sight, and how it pertains to me to know it truly, whereby they [the two domes] *might both be saved*, so it would be worshipfull to God and the right way for me. (45:20–26.261, italics added)

The intensity of Julian's inner struggle suggests that the Lord wanted her to be bold and face the problem, not to shy away from it. He was leading her in the depths of prayer to ask the difficult questions: How do the lower judgments of the church carry out God's higher judgments? How can the church's teachings on sin and damnation, as well as the Revelation that there is no manner of blame in God, "*both* be saved"? (And this, not only to honor God, but to show "the right way" for Julian to view sin.) Since God had revealed both domes, one through his church and the other in her Revelations, *were they not both true*?

The severity of her mental anguish proves that Julian was no proto-reformer, ready to overthrow the church's age-old teachings on sin and punishment in favor of her own private Revelations. As a faithful daughter of the church, she simply could not leave behind the necessity of making restitution for sin, any more than she could deny the truth she had understood that God "assigns no manner of blame" to the sinner. In her great courage of heart and mind, she refuses to pass over the dichotomy of belief. She confronts it head on. And the Lord rewards her determination.

The *Exemplum*

> And to all this I never had any other answer but a marvelous example of a lord and of a servant, as I shall tell later, and that was very obscurely shewn. (45:26–27.261)

Here, and *only* here in the Long Text, Julian introduces the extraordinary *exemplum*, or parable, which was shown to her at the time of this Revelation, but which she did not understand for almost twenty years. Hence, she did not include any mention of it in her Short Text. The mystery of the parable will clarify much about the inter-relationship of the "two domes," as we shall see. Still, Julian admits that, until the end of her life, she would continually desire to have a greater understanding of these two judgments, especially as they pertained to her.

> For all heavenly things and all earthly things that belong to heaven are comprehended in these two domes. And the more knowing and understanding that we have of these two domes by the gracious leading of the holy ghost, the more we shall see and know our failings. And ever the more that we see them, the more naturally by grace we shall long to be fulfilled with endless joy and bliss, for we are made thereto. (45:29–34.261)

Know Thyself

Whenever Julian attempts to fly upward to the heavenly plane of perception, she is forced to return to the dark fog of mortal human beings on earth. Now she reflects that as long as we try to understand ourselves solely through our sensual nature, we "know not what the self is . . ." (46:1–2.261). Only through the revelations of faith can we truly know what we are and who we are created to be. And only "when we know and see, truly and clearly, what our self is" may we come to know "our lord God" (46:2–4.261–63). Julian affirms that we may acquire knowledge of ourselves in this mortal life through the constant help and nobility of our sublime human nature (reason, memory, and will), through which we may increase and grow by the help of mercy and grace. Still, we long for full disclosure of who we really are:

> But we may never fully know ourself until the last point, in which point this passing life and all manner of woe and pain shall have an

> end. And therefore it belongs properly to us, both by nature and by grace, to long and desire with all our might to know ourself, in which full knowing we shall truly and clearly know our God in the fullness of endless joy. (46:8–12.263)

Noticeably, Julian equates full knowledge of the interior self with true knowledge of God. It is a theme she will revisit and expand on at a later time. For now, Julian identifies two ways of beholding God that she experienced "from the beginning to the end" of this Revelation (46:13.263). One was the absolute certitude of God's endless, constant love with complete *sekernesse* of his protection and joyful salvation. And this first manner of beholding continued throughout the entire *shewing* in that it was precisely what every aspect of the Fourteenth Revelation on prayer was about. The second way of beholding God was "the common teaching of holy church, in which I was previously informed and grounded," the very same teaching that Julian had always tried to live by and to understand (46:16.263). This beholding of the church also came from God and it never left her.

> For by the shewing I was not steered nor led away therefrom [the church] in any manner at all, but I had therein teaching to love it and like it, whereby I might, with the help of our lord and his grace, increase and rise to more heavenly knowing and higher loving. And thus, in all this beholding, it seemed necessary to me to see and to know that we are sinners and do many evil deeds that we ought to leave undone, and leave many good deeds undone that we ought to do, wherefore we deserve pain, blame and wrath. (46:18–23.263)

Here again, Julian freely acknowledges that the church is right to censure sinners for the evils they do and the good they fail to do. As long as human nature is fallen, the church needs to offer strong directives, disciplines, and guidance to help souls turn from sinful ways and walk on the right path, if they are to attain their true destination in heaven. The role of the church is precisely this: to provide instruction, as well as the sacraments of forgiveness and healing (baptism and penance), of strengthening in the Holy Spirit (confirmation), of marital blessing (matrimony), of priestly initiation (holy orders), of the total consecration of all life in unity with the sacrifice of the Lord (Eucharist), and of final anointing (extreme unction). Julian comes to love and appreciate the church *more*, not less, through this paradoxical Revelation of the two domes. In spite of her conflicts, she never questions the *truth* of church teachings, because she knows by faith that the church is the Mystical Body of Christ, protected from serious error and inspired by his Holy Spirit, no matter the unworthiness of many of its members. She evokes the dilemma of St. Paul who wrote: "For I do not do the good I want, but the evil I do not want is what I do" (Rom 7:19). And for this continuing sinfulness, we actually do deserve "pain, blame and wrath."

However, Julian remains equally adamant that these do *not* come to us as divinely inflicted punishments. The mental, emotional, and even physical agonies we endure are our own projections of shame for having fallen into sin. They appear inexorably and in many different forms as direct consequences of our rash or wrong deeds. God does not "send" them. We inflict them upon ourselves.

Never Wroth

> And notwithstanding all this, I saw truthfully that our lord was never wroth nor never shall be. For he is God, he is good, he is truth, he is love, he is peace. And his might, his wisdom, his charity, and his unity do not permit him to be wroth. For I saw truly that it is against the property of his might to be wroth, and against the property of his wisdom, and against the property of his goodness. *God is that goodness that may not be wroth, for God is nothing but goodness.* (46:24–29.263, italics added)

We may wonder if Julian is stepping out on a theological limb here, in spite of her desire to remain a faithful daughter of Holy Church. But she is not. She is only stating, in no uncertain terms, what theology has ever taught and what she, personally, had experienced: that God is unchangeable and loving. He cannot have "mood swings" or exhibit raw emotions as human beings do. He does not wax pleased with the soul one minute and furious the next, like a volatile parent. God is not and can never be angry with us, even though we are sinners. "Every generous act of giving, with every perfect gift, is from above, coming down from the Father of lights, *with whom there is no variation or shadow due to change*" (Jas 1:17, italics added). As we have discussed, the biblical allusions to God's anger flaring out (and they are legion, from the Psalms, to the Book of Job, to the Book of Revelation) are metaphorical devices to drive home to humankind the gravity of its sinful deeds that defy God's unchanging goodness. These depictions of the divine as wrathful are human projections of how we assume God must "feel" towards us (like an angry parent), when we, ourselves, are appalled by our own misdeeds.

Julian may not have known the theology of God's unchangeable existence until she began to ask doctrinal questions of educated clerics in the time period after her Revelations. However, like all true mystics, she knew what she had experienced. And throughout her vision of the sufferings of Christ on the cross, she never saw him angry. He did not suffer in fury against a humanity that made him undergo such a cruel death. He endured his passion in unconditional love, without a single moment of condemnation. If we want to see what God's supposed *wroth* looks like, we have only to contemplate the image of Christ hanging on the cross. It is the true image of God giving everything he is to save humanity from itself.

Unchangeable Goodness

For Julian, it became essential to her sanity to confront the dichotomy between the attitude of Christ toward the sinner she had seen in her Revelations and the harsher, damning attitude she had heard preached from pulpits on so many occasions.

> Our soul is oned to God, unchangeable goodness. *And between God and our soul is neither wrath nor forgiveness in his sight.* For our soul is so abundantly oned to God by his own goodness that between God and our soul may be right nought. And to this understanding was the soul led by love and drawn by might in every shewing. *That* it is thus, our good lord shewed. And *how* it is thus: truly, because of his great goodness. And he wills we desire to know it: that is to say, as far as it belongs to his creature to know it. (46:29–36.263, italics added)

Julian dares to see the soul as being *oned* with God's unchangeable goodness, without possibility of separation. Between God and the soul there is "right nought"; that is, nothing at all. And this is because of God's own goodness in creating the human soul in his own image. Julian might have written, with St. Paul: "For I am convinced that neither death, nor life, nor angels, nor rulers, nor things present, nor things to come, nor powers, nor height, nor depth, nor anything else in all creation, will be able to separate us from the love of God in Christ Jesus our Lord" (Rom 8:38–39).

Then Julian layers in another level of meaning about divine oneness: just as God is not wrathful, so he does not suddenly *relent* his anger and forgive. Like wrath, forgiveness would imply a distinct reversal or "change of heart" on God's part. In the strictest, most literal, sense, Julian is saying that God cannot "forgive" because, ontologically speaking, he cannot be "angry." Again, we are dealing with two planes of reality here, human and divine. On the human plane, we experience guilt and suffering as a result of sinful behaviors and bad habits. Therefore, penitents have a very human need to confess, to hear the words of sacramental absolution, to know through words and actions that they are forgiven, and to accept penances to discipline their natures.

On the divine plane, God is perfect love, unchangeable, unconditional. He sees through the sins and human failings to the sinner's deep hurt and fear, anger and despair within. And he makes unending allowances. He is never *wroth* with us, even though we may feel acutely *wroth* with ourselves. And what we call his forgiveness is but one aspect of his love that we recognize and label as such in our minds. Julian affirms again that all these things that her "simple soul" understood in this Revelation "God wills that it be shewn and known" (46:36–37.263).

In a most personal moment, Julian shares with the reader what she had hitherto been taught to believe: that the mercy of God was to be understood as "forgiveness of his wrath" that was possible only *after* we had repented and received absolution. For a woman like Julian, whose life's desire and purpose was to love, the very thought of God ever being wrathful with her—mad at her—was "harder than any other pain" (47:8.265). And she had always assumed that "forgiveness of his wrath" would be one of the main aspects of God's mercy. But try as she might, and desiring as she did to see this lessening of God's wrath through his mercy, Julian observes: "I could not see this point in all the shewing" (47:10–11.265). Instead, she will try to explain something of how she *did* see and understand the divine work of mercy, "as God will give me grace" (47:12.265).

Human Blindness

> I understood thus: Man is changeable in this life, and by frailty and ignorance falls into sinne. He is powerless and foolish in himself, and also his will is corrupted at this time [by sinne]. He is in turmoil and in sorrow and woe. *And the cause is blindness, for he does not see God.* For if he saw God continually, he would have no mischievous feeling, nor no manner of stirring, nor sorrowing that inclines to sin. (47:13–17.265, italics added)

Julian describes the state of fallen humankind not abstractly but in a palpable and recognizable way. She reveals her own firsthand acquaintance with the moral weakness and spiritual blindness that cause even the devout to fall into sin. She never sets herself apart as someone immune to temptation, but includes herself in the common lot of humanity. Indeed, Julian attests that she experienced this Revelation about human sinfulness very deeply. And while what she "saw and felt" seemed "high and plenteous and gracious" in comparison with our ordinary feeling in this life, she comments that it was "low and small" compared to her great desire to see God and to understand how God sees sin (47:18–21.265). She is constantly aware of her own spiritual blindness, even in a state of high contemplative prayer.

Five States of Soul

> For I felt in myself five manners of werking [in the soul], which are these: enjoying, mourning, desire, dread, and seker hope. *Enjoying*: for God gave me knowing and understanding that it was himself that I saw. *Mourning*: and that was for failing [sinning]. *Desire*: that was that I might see him ever more and more, understanding and knowing that we shall never have full rest until we see him, clearly and truly, in heaven. *Dread* was because it seemed to me, in all that time, that the sight would fail, and I would be left to myself. *Seker hope* was in the endless love that I saw: that I should be kept, by his mercy, and brought to the bliss [of heaven]. And the rejoicing in his sight, with this seker hope of his merciful keeping, made me have feeling and comfort, so that mourning and dread were not greatly painful. (47:21–30.265, italics added)

How honestly Julian describes her changing states of soul throughout this Revelation! She experiences each of these strong emotional responses, one after the other, oscillating between them as she did when she beheld Christ suffering on the cross. She enjoys the intimacy of God's presence, yet is acutely aware of her own inadequacy in that presence. She yearns for ever greater visionary experiences while still in her body, but knows that she can never be satisfied until she sees God, clearly and truly, in everlasting bliss. She feels a painful dread of losing the divine illuminations she is presently enjoying, aware that, at some point, Christ will leave her alone again, and she will have to return to her human state of blindness and doubt. Still, she attests that the pure delight of contemplative "seeing," along with her certain hope that Christ in his mercy would always protect her and bring her to heaven, gave her the greatest spiritual comfort. So it was that delight and hope alleviated her mourning and dread that the visions would inevitably come to an end.

Julian acknowledges that the extraordinary way of "seeing" God she experienced in her *shewings* cannot be maintained in this life. Yet faith in God when we do *not* see him or feel his presence adds to his honor and increases the joy we will have in eternal life. However, it is precisely because we cannot experience God's presence that we often fail to recognize him at work in our lives. And then we fall back into ourselves, relying on our own strengths and tortured by our own weaknesses. In effect, we experience nothing but the *contrariousness* (a Middle English word meaning willfulness, opposition, resistance, even perversity) that is in our nature. Julian remarks that this is because of the "old root of our first sin," with all the sins that have ever followed because of humanity's propensity to go on sinning (47:35–36.267). Therefore, we become "travailed and tempested," that is, belabored and troubled, both spiritually and bodily (47:36–38.267). Such is the conflicted life Julian knew only too well.

The Work of Mercy

> But our good lord the holy ghost, who is endless life wonning [dwelling] in our soul, full sekerly keeps us, and werks therein a peace, and brings it to ease through grace, and makes it obedient, and reconciles it with God. And this is the mercy and the way in which our good lord continually leads us, as long as we are in this life which is changeable. (48:1–5.267)

Julian has just clarified that God's mercy is not a divine "change of heart" from fury, nor even a gracious act of forgiveness after we have recognized our sin, asked pardon, and done penance. Now she defines his work of mercy as the unceasing, gratuitous outpouring of the Holy Ghost, who is "endless life wonning in our souls." This outpouring is like the water that flowed from Christ's Sacred Heart on the cross. It is the cleansing waters of baptism, of sanctifying grace. This abundant mercy protects us even when we are trapped in our mistakenness. It is a mercy that constantly works to draw us out of the war between our mental afflictions, our inner drives, and our sensual needs. Who knows the willful and contrary "stuff" of our fallen human nature better than Christ does? Who wants our salvation more than the Savior who died to set us free from our own perversity? The Spirit of Christ, the Holy Ghost, will never stop trying to lead us out of our self-defeating ways. This is God's sublime work of mercy.

> *For I saw no wrath but on humanity's part, and that God forgives in us.* For wrath is nothing else but a rebelliousness and a contrariousness to peace and to love. And either it comes from failure of strength, or from failure of wisdom, or from failure of goodness, *which failing is not in God but is on our own part.* For we by sin and wretchedness have in us a wrath and a continuing contrariousness to peace and to love, and that he shewed very often in his loving chere [countenance] of compassion and pity. (48:5–8.267, italics added)

Again, Julian bears witness to what she experienced: the Savior does not look on us with anger and a desire to punish, but with divine mercy and a thirst to save. This is the loving face of Christ that Julian saw...and she could not see any wrath therein. She clearly articulates that the experience of wrath is all on *our* side, coming from ourselves, not from God.

> For the ground of mercy is in love, and the werking of mercy is our keeping [protection] in love. And this was shewn in such a manner that I could not perceive the property of mercy otherwise but, as it were, all one in love. (48:10–13.267)

Just as Julian had been taught that God inspires every grace he wishes us to ask for in prayer, precisely so that he can give it to us, likewise the "mercy" we pray for is also offered by God even before we ask. God's mercy, as grounded in his love, is inseparable from the reality of his existence. It is never conditional on us. Our pleading does not earn God's mercy any more than our prayer bends God's will. Still, Julian tells us, we must open ourselves to the *experience* of God's mercy by requesting it repeatedly in prayer. Otherwise, we may not be able to accept the great blessing of being healed, protected, and inspired. Prayer, in effect, enables our minds and hearts to receive what God longs to give.

> That is to say, as to my sight: mercy is a sweet, gracious werking in love, mixed with plentiful pity. For mercy werks, keeping us, and mercy werks, turning all things to good for us. (48:14–16.267)

Freedom to Fail

Julian is also aware that the working of divine mercy respects our freedom, even our freedom to sin.

> Mercy because of love suffers us to fail to a certain degree. And inasmuch as we fail, in so much we fall, and inasmuch as we fall, in so much we die. For it behooves us to die inasmuch as we lose the sight and feeling of God that is our life. Our failing is dreadful, our falling is shameful, and our dying is sorrowful. But yet in all this the sweet eye of pity and of love never depart from us, nor does the werking of mercy cease. (48:16–22.267)

Julian does not gloss over the terrible results of our failure to see and feel the presence of God who is guiding our lives. This elemental failure reinforces our blindness, ignorance, and rebelliousness, and so we fall into greater sin and must suffer the inevitable consequences of spiritual death. Yet Julian is sure that even in all this, Christ's "sweet eye of pity and of love" (which she saw on the cross) never stops looking at us with mercy and love. And his Sacred Heart will never cease pouring out every grace we need to become free from the debilitating habits of sin.

The Activity of Grace

> For I beheld the property of mercy, and I beheld the property of grace, which have two manners of werking in one love. Mercy is a pitiful property, which belongs to motherhood in tender love. And

> grace is a noble property, which belongs to royal lordship in the same love. (48:22–25.267)

Now Julian combines mercy *with grace*, as two complementary aspects of Christ's love, working in unison. She understands mercy as Christ's compassion, which is a motherly tenderness, ever forgiving the wayward child. (This is the first direct mention Julian makes of Christ's Motherhood, a central theme she will develop later on.) And grace comes from Christ's "royal lordship," courteously granting to his subjects the very means they need to escape the ravages of sin and death.

> Mercy werks—keeping, enduring, enlivening, and healing—and all is from the tenderness of love. And grace werks with mercy: raising, rewarding (endlessly overpassing what our loving and our travail deserve), spreading abroad, and shewing the high, plenteous largesse of God's royal lordship in his marvelous courtesy. And this is from the abundance of love. For grace transforms our dreadful failing into plenteous and endless solace, and grace transforms our shameful falling into high, honorable rising, and grace transforms our sorrowful dying into holy, blissful life. (48:26–32.267–269)

Mercy encircles us, even as it endures our sinfulness, inspiring us to mend our ways in order to give us complete healing. And this is exactly what a mother does for her own child, protecting it from all the physical and moral dangers into which it might fall, suffering through its faults and even grave failures, teaching, disciplining, and encouraging it to do better, and employing every possible means to heal its hurt. And "grace werks with mercy" in our souls to raise us up out of our sinful state and reward us, most undeservedly, for having suffered the pains and punishments of our sins. Julian adds that this eternal reward will far surpass all our acts of virtue and labors of love, bearing witness to our royal Lord's generous and noble courtesy to all in heaven. And both mercy and grace come to us gratuitously, because of God's abundant love. It is clear that Julian sees this twofold working as the joint activity of love by which Christ, as both Mother and Lord, will "make alle thing wele."

Therefore, even though our *contrariousness* leads us inevitably into "pain, shame, and sorrow" here on earth, grace will never stop working to bring us into transcendent bliss in heaven (48:34–

35.269). And when we come to heaven and receive the reward that grace has made possible for us, we shall greatly thank and bless Our Lord that we ever had to suffer pain and woe at all.

> And that will be because of an aspect of blessed love that we shall know in God, *which we might never have known without woe preceding it.* And when I saw all this, it behooved me to acknowledge that the mercy of God and the forgiveness of sin is to slake and waste our wrath. (48:37–41.269, italics added)

Mercy even works in us to weaken and wear out our own anger, self-loathing, and shame. And forgiveness becomes something we must learn to do, by grace, toward ourselves and each other.

It Were Unpossible

Julian reiterates her total conviction (which she declares was shown repeatedly in all the Revelations and beheld by her with great care) that God "with respect to himself, may not forgive, for he may not be *wroth.*" She states most emphatically: "It were unpossible" (49:2–3.269).

> For this was shewn: that our life is all grounded and rooted in love, and without love we may not live. And therefore, to the soul that because of his special grace sees so deeply into the high, marvelous goodness of God, and sees that we are endlessly oned to him in love, *it is the most unpossible that may be that God should be wrath.* (49:3–7.269, italics added)

Since love is the foundation of existence itself, it can never be removed from us or we would cease to exist. Further, she who has been gifted with a "special grace" to taste that love directly bears witness that we are fundamentally *oned* (that is, united and even bound) to God. The intimacy of this relationship is so elemental that it can never be broken. God could not possibly "hate" us, since anger and divine friendship are contraries and simply cannot co-exist in God. Julian points out that if God is to lay waste to and destroy our own anger and self-hatred to make us humble and mild-tempered, then he must forever protect and hold us in his gentleness, which is the exact opposite of wrath. How can God, who is perfect peace, make us like himself if he expresses anger and opposition toward us?

> For I saw full sekerly that where our lord appears, peace is established and wrath has no place. For I saw no manner of wrath in God, neither for a short time nor for long. For truly, as to my sight, *if God might be wroth for an instant, we should neither have life, nor place, nor being*. For as truly as we have our being from the endless power of God, and from the endless wisdom, and from the endless goodness, also truly we have our keeping in the endless power of God, in the endless wisdom, and in the endless goodness. For though we feel in ourselves wrath, debate, and strife, yet we are all mercifully enclosed in the gentleness of God and in his meekness, in his benevolence and in his obedience. (49:10–18.269, italics added)

If God were to be even a little bit angry with us, we would be wiped off the face of the earth. Have we ever stopped to consider this? Many of us carry such guilt feelings from childhood, such a deep-seated conviction that our behavior was more often "bad" than "good," that we believe the punishments we received, no matter how harsh, were fully deserved. Even as adults, we have trouble imagining a parent, a friend, a spouse, or a God who does not get angry with us. Yet that is exactly what Julian is challenging us to do, vis-à-vis God. Like the parent who never gives up on the child, God does not turn away from any one of his children. This, in fact, makes God's *unconditional* love much more overwhelming for the soul to accept than his supposed "wrathfulness." Always to be loved, in spite of everything, is a concept so vast and humbling as to defy human comprehension. Yet that is what Christ hangs on a cross to show us: even if we crucify him, he will still love us.

God's Goodness

Julian is convinced that the everlasting goodness that protects us, *even when we sin* (so that we will not perish from sin's consequences), is the exact same goodness that nurtures peace in us to counteract our own wrath. It is God's goodness that enables the soul to recognize its urgent need to seek forgiveness with a true dread of having offended its Maker, and to desire its salvation ever more earnestly. Although Julian has stated that because God's nature is unchangeable, he does not forgive as such, God knows that penitents *need* to turn to him for the human experience of forgiveness and healing. And this is how "free will" opens the door to divine mercy and grace.

> For we may not be blissfully saved until we are truly in peace and in love, for that is our salvation. And though we, because of the wrath and the contrariousness that are in us, are now in tribulation, diseases, and woe, as falls to our blindness and our frailty, yet we are sekerly safe by the merciful keeping [protection] of God, so that we perish not. But we are not blissfully safe in having our endless joy [in heaven] until we are all in peace and in love: that is to say, fully pleased with God and with all his werks and with all his domes, and loving and peaceful with ourselves and with our evencristens and with all that God loves, as love enjoys. And this, God's goodness does in us. (49:24–32.271)

Christ's Peace

Julian sees further that "God is our very peace and he is our seker keeper," even when we ourselves are *not* at peace (49:33.271). How well we know the tumult that crisis, hurt, anger, rejection, sudden accident or injury, the diagnosis of severe illness, the death, or tragic suicide, of a loved one can cause in our souls. But when, through the inspiration of mercy and grace, we seek God in prayer and allow ourselves to be quieted in mind and reassured in soul, then we come to the realization that, no matter what we must bear, we are held completely safe in the love of God. Suddenly, the soul feels itself to be *oned* to God at the same moment that it becomes more peaceful within itself. And then we are better able to cope with life's challenges. Julian assures us that God's goodness will even make those battles we fight to overcome our personal demons accrue to our benefit and become "fully profitable" (49:39.271).

> For contrariousness is the cause of all our tribulation and all our woe. And our lord Jesus takes them and sends them up to heaven, and then they are made more sweet and delectable than heart may think or tongue can tell. And when we come thither, we shall find them ready, all turned into very fairness and endless honor. Thus is God our steadfast ground, and shall be our full bliss, and makes us as unchangeable as he is when we will be there. (49:39–45.271)

Once again, Julian uses the tender metaphor of Christ gathering up our struggles and placing them in a heavenly treasury, where they will be made so appealing (as if they were sweet delicacies!) that her heart cannot conceive it or her tongue speak sufficiently about it. All our inner conflicts and efforts to overcome our negativities will be "saved" by God and transformed into great beauty and honor. And then we will no longer suffer the violent swings between love and anger, joy and depression, certainty and fear, because God will make us as "unchangeable" in our transformed nature as he is in himself. We will realize that our spiritual essence has always been kept safe in God, who is the reliable ground of our entire being. Because of the *dis*grace that we fall into, we are often considered to be dead according to human judgment. "But in the sight of God, the soul that shall be saved was never dead, nor ever shall be" (50:3–4.271).

How May This Be?

> But yet here I wondered and marveled with all the diligence of my soul, meaning thus: "Good lord, I see thee that thou art very truth, and I know truly that we sin grievously all day and are much blameworthy. And I may neither abandon the knowing of this truth, nor can I not see the shewing [Christ has made] to us of no manner of blame. How may this be?" (50:5–9.271)

Even after all the sublime reassurance she has been given, Julian feels caught between the two domes. She knows that, by the common teaching of the church, "the blame of our sins continually hangeth upon us, from the first man [Adam] until the time that we come up into heaven" (50:9–11.271). Given this, she admits she was astounded to see during all her Revelations that God showed us "no more blame than if we were as clean and as holy as angels are in heaven" (50:12–13.273).

> And between these two contraries [opposites], my reason was greatly afflicted by my blindness and could have no rest, for dread that his blessed presence would pass from my sight and I would be left in unknowing *how he beholds us in our sinne*. For either it behooved me to see in God that sinne was completely done away with, or else it behooved me to see in God how he sees it, whereby I might truly know how it is fitting for me to see sin and the manner of our blame. (50:14–19.273, italics added)

Julian freely admits her reason is too weak to understand the complex relationship between the domes of heaven and earth. Nevertheless, she is convinced it would behoove her either "to see in God" that sin was completely eradicated . . . or to see how God "beholds us in our sinne."

> My longing endured, while I was continually beholding him [Christ]. And yet I could have no patience for my great fear and perplexity, thinking: "If I take it thus, that we are *not* sinners nor *not* blameworthy, it seems as if I should err and fail in knowing of this truth. And if it be true that we *are* sinners and *are* blameworthy, good lord, how may it then be that *I can not see this truth in thee*, who art my God, my maker, in whom I desire to see all truth?" (50:19–24.273, italics added)

Her mind was teetering on the precipice between accepting a monumental truth about divine mercy and dropping off the cliff into heresy that denies the grievous nature of sin. She might be misled into disbelieving the full redemption of sin by Christ or belittling the reality of Divine Justice. She was afraid that, in her human blindness, she could not accept *both truths* at once, and therefore she might err either to the right or the left, overstating one or the other, to the detriment of both.

Julian mentions three points that gave her boldness to ask for further clarity. First, she felt her request was "so low a thing; for if it were one high, I should be afraid" (50:25–26.273). She was convinced she was seeking clarification only on how *she* should view sin, for if she believed she was questioning the very fabric of Christian doctrine, she would have felt great terror. Second, she was certain that her question was a general one and applied to all her *evencristens*, and so was not a request for *privy* information about one special person (as her earlier, misguided question about "a certain creature" had been). Third, she states that if she was going to continue to live (and by this time, she seems to have become convinced she would not die after all), she needed to have greater "knowing" of the subtle nature of good and evil, so that "I may, by reason and by grace, better separate them in two, and love goodness and hate evil as holy church teaches" (50:28–29.273). Underlying her need-to-know is the assumption that if her desire is so strong to pray for this deeper understanding, then it must be God's will to grant her some illumination.

Julian's Plea

> I cried inwardly with all my might, seeking into God for help, meaning thus: "Ah, lord Jesus, king of bliss, how shall I be eased? Who

> shall tell me and teach me what I need to know, if I may not at this time see it in thee?" (50:31–33.273)

There could be no more revealing statement about the torment in Julian's soul than this. She has been leading up to this critical moment most of her life. All the sin and blame she has ever experienced, both within herself and all around her, reach a climax. How should human beings consider themselves: as fully saved or justly condemned? It was a question that could not be put aside. This was not a scholastic issue, open to debate. There were *people's eternal lives* involved: Julian's, her family members, both living and deceased (some without benefit of the last rites of the church), friends, servants, all her *evencristens* from the lowliest peasants to the highest overlords, on up the social ladder to kings and queens and two popes, with the whole of Europe being torn apart by the brutalities of war and papal schism. If Julian was to go on living with some measure of divine comfort and reassurance, she had to know the answer to her question: *How does God behold us in our sin?*

19
The Lord and the Servant

> And then our courteous lord answered in shewing, full mistely, by a wonderful example of a lord that hath a servant, and gave me sight to my understanding of both. Which sight was shewn double with respect to the lord, and the sight was shewn double with respect to the servant. That one part was shewn ghostly in bodily likeness. The other part was shewn more ghostly without bodily likeness. (51:1–5.273)

Thus Julian begins her description of the many-layered parable of a lord and a servant. She understood that this *shewing* was a "wonderful example," just like an *exemplum* a preacher might use to illuminate a gospel story. It was also similar to Christ's own parables, yet more visual than oral. Julian recounts that it was revealed "full mistely," which means secretly, mystically, even mysteriously, as "in a mirror, dimly" (1 Cor 13:12). It concerned a lord who had a servant. And Christ gave her insight as to its meaning.

Shewn Double

Right at the outset, Julian makes clear that this *exemplum* was not like the realistic vision of Christ on the cross. This sight was "shewn double," unfolding on two levels at once, with respect to both the lord and the servant. The first level of meaning was shown spiritually but "in bodily likeness," appearing suddenly in her imagination (like her earlier internal visions of the young Virgin Mary). It was as if Julian was watching a mystery play in her mind's eye: seeing the visual circumstances, observing the characters' appearances and actions, discovering their motivations. Much later, Julian came to understand the second level of meaning in an even more spiritual way, "without bodily likeness," through contemplative thought and prayer. The parable would reveal two levels of meaning, one imaginative and one spiritual, about the lord; and two levels of meaning, likewise, about the servant.

> For the first, thus: I saw two persons in bodily likeness, that is to say, a lord and a servant, and with that sight God gave me spiritual understanding. The lord sits solemnly in rest and in peace. The servant stands before his lord reverently, ready to do his lord's will. The lord looks upon his servant very lovingly and sweetly, and meekly he sends him into a certain place to do his will. The servant not only goes, but suddenly he starts and runs in great haste out of love to do his lord's will. (51:6–12.273)

It reads like a play script: the lord sits regally in state, motionless. He is completely "in rest and in peace." Nothing disturbs him. The servant stands before him in an attitude of reverence, but does not bow or kneel. He is attentive to the lord's every wish and ready to do whatever the lord commands. The relationship between lord and servant is a tender one. The lord loves the servant and looks upon him "sweetly." There is no sense of the lord overpowering or frightening his servant. Even when the lord sends him on a mission, he does so "meekly," by which Julian implies the utmost patience and courteous gentleness on the lord's part. Likewise, the servant shows no dread of the lord's authority, only dedication to it. And when the lord bids the servant go off "into a certain place to do his will," the servant not only goes, he "starts," which means he jumps up, bolts, and dashes off "in great haste," because he loves the lord so much he cannot wait to fulfill his command.

> And anon he falls into a slade, and takes very great soreness. And then he groneth and moneth and walloweth and writheth. But he may not rise nor help himself by any manner of way. (51:12–14.273–275)

Suddenly, without warning, the servant falls into a slade (a ditch, or a hollow), the kind that was dug between pasturelands to keep sheep and cattle from roaming, though many a sheep or cow also fell into these ditches. As we have seen, wide ditches were also unearthed both inside and outside the city walls of Norwich to fend off enemy entry into the city. And of course, deep moats were excavated around castles for the same reason. Ditches, moats, and water dikes were a fact of life in Julian's day. While useful, they also symbolized the threat of danger, the possibility of people and animals falling in and getting badly hurt. Indeed, the servant tumbles headlong into just such a ditch. He "takes very great soreness," perhaps injuring his legs, his arms, his back, his head. He groans and moans and wallows in the muddy ditch, writhing in pain. And because he is in such agony, he cannot rise up and get out of the slade. He is incapable of extricating himself from his position.

Seven Great Pains

> And in all this, the most misfortune that I saw him in was his lack of comfort. For he could not turn his face to look up on his loving lord, who was very near to him, in whom is complete comfort. But like a man that was full feeble and unwise at the time, he concentrated on his feelings and enduring in woe. In which woe he suffered seven great pains. (51:15–19.275)

Julian sees that the servant is trapped in the narrow ditch, face down in the muck, in great pain and unable to turn over. He cannot even raise his head to look up and see that the lord is standing over him, ready to give him all the comfort he needs. The servant, thinking he is all alone, becomes weaker from his pains and emotionally distraught over all he has to suffer. He focuses on his negative feelings and on how he is going to last through his agony. Julian identifies seven pains that grieve him most severely. The first was the severe physical bruising he suffered from the actual fall, which caused him great injury all over his body. The second was the sheer heaviness and clumsiness of his body lying in the ditch, as if dead, unable to escape from the mud and stench and offal. The third was the terrible weakness, both physical and emotional, that followed on these two. The fourth was that he became so confused and blind in his reasoning powers and so stunned in his thinking, that he had "almost," writes Julian, "forgotten his own love" for his lord (51:22–23.275). The fifth was that he was unable to rise from his pit of agony. The sixth was the most excruciating pain of all: that he was convinced he lay in this pitiful condition *all alone*, with no one to come to his aid and to comfort him. Julian looks all around the scene as it appears in her imagination and cannot find anyone to help him, neither "far nor near, neither high nor low" (51:25.275).

The seventh pain was that the ditch in which he lay "was a long, hard, and grievous" place in which to be trapped (51:26–27.275). The ditch was so tight and narrow that he could not budge. It was a terrible confinement.

The Servant's Reward

Julian's reaction to this painful drama was to marvel at the servant's "meekness" and patience in suffering so much woe. She looked carefully at the scene, trying to discover if she could detect in the servant "any defect, or if the lord could assign to him any manner of blame" (51:29–30.275). She wanted to know if he was guilty of some dire fault that had precipitated his fall. What could it be? But she could discover none at all.

> For only his good will and his great desire were the cause of his falling. And he was as unloatheful [unhateful] and as good inwardly as he was when he stood before his lord, ready to do his will. And rightly thus continually did his loving lord very tenderly behold him, and now with a double chere [double expression]. (51:31–34.275)

Outwardly, the lord looked at his servant with the greatest compassion and pity. But Julian's understanding was led deeper, into a more spiritual perception of the lord's facial expression. And there she saw the lord "highly enjoy" the honorable and reverential restoring to which "he will and must bring his servant by his plenteous grace" (51:36–38.275). She further understood that she had to hold *both* levels of meaning, the outward and the inward, in her mind at the same time.

> Then said this courteous lord, meaning: "Lo, my beloved servant, what harm and trouble he hath had and taken in my service for my love—yea, and out of his good will! Is it not reasonable that I reward him for his fright and his dread, his hurt and his maiming, and all his woe? And not only this, but is it not my responsibility to give him a gift that is better for him and more honorable than his own health should have been? Otherwise, it seems to me I did him no grace [honor]." (51:40–45.275)

Julian acknowledges that with these words, "an inward ghostly shewing of the lord's meaning" descended into her soul (51:45–46.275). She understood that yes, because of the lord's great goodness and his own high stature, "his dearworthy servant, whom he loved so much, should be highly and blissfully rewarded without end, above that which he should have been if he had *not* fallen" (51:47–49.275, italics added). And his falling and all the woe he suffered would be turned into "high, transcendent honor and endless bliss" (51:50–51.277). It simply had to be so.

Confusion

At this point, the imaginative *shewing* of the example vanished completely; the mystery play ended abruptly. But Julian would be led by the Spirit to contemplate, over a long period of time, its deeper meanings. All the while, she was convinced that the *exemplum* had been shown precisely because it held the answer to her great desire to know how God beholds us in our sin.

> And yet I could not find therein full understanding for my comfort at that time. For in the servant that represented Adam, as I shall say, I saw many diverse properties that might in no manner be attributed to the singular Adam. And thus in that time I remained in great ignorance. For the full understanding of this marvelous example was not given to me at that time, in which misty example the privities of the revelation are yet greatly hidden. And notwithstanding this, I saw and understood that every shewing is full of privities. (51:55–62.277)

While at the time Julian was extremely grateful for the marvelous gift of the parable, she admits she did not understand it. She assumed the servant was supposed to represent Adam, but she could not see how various characteristics that appeared in the servant (his meekness, patience, complete obedience, total lack of fault) could possibly be attributed to the biblical man. Her ignorance of any explanation greatly distressed her. She knew that every Revelation contains its mysterious secrets, but she was especially aware that there were layers of meaning in this parable that she simply could not work through without added illumination.

Writing years later, Julian acknowledges three "properties" or modes of learning which gave her some measure of consolation. The first was "the beginning of the teaching," which she received during the actual time of the *shewing* of the Revelation. The second was the "inward learning" that formed in her understanding thereafter. And the third was "the whole revelation, from the beginning to the end," which God often brought to her mind (51:63–67.277). Eventually, this third mode of learning uncovered deeper layers of meaning not only in the *exemplum* but in all sixteen Revelations. Julian sees this trinity of properties as actually one unified teaching that she neither can nor may pull apart. She must believe and trust that "by these three as one," she was taught directly by God (51:68–69.277). And she is convinced that by the same great goodness and purpose God had in showing it to her, "he shall declare it to us when it is his will" (51:71–72.277).

Take Heed!

> For twenty years after the time of the shewing, save three months, I had teaching inwardly, as I shall say: "It belongeth to thee to *take heed* to all the properties and the conditions that were shewn in the example, though you think that it is misty and indifferent [meaningless or unimportant] to thy sight." I assented willingly with great desire, seeing inwardly, with avisement, all the points and the properties that were shewed at the same time, as far as my intelligence and my understanding would serve: beginning with my beholding of the lord and the servant; at the manner of sitting of the lord and the place he sat on, and the color of his clothing and the manner of shape, and his outward chere and his nobility and his goodness within; at the manner of standing of the servant, and the place, where and how; at his manner of clothing, the color and the shape; at his outward behavior, and at his inward goodness and his unloathefulness. (51:73–84.277, italics added)

Julian gives the reader an important time line to show how long the inner teaching on this parable continued. She also indicates how much spiritual work was needed before she was able to comprehend it with a measure of understanding: "twenty years, save three months." That means that she did not begin writing this section of the Long Text until February 1393 at the very earliest, by which time there is listed from Roger Reed, rector of St. Michael's Coslany, Norwich, a bequest of two shillings for "*Juliane anachorite* at the church of St. Julian in Norwich." So perhaps one of the prime reasons for entering the solitude and quiet of an enclosed hermitage was precisely to set down her newly discovered understanding of the Revelations, in light of the parable that had been maturing within her mind for two decades.

The directive given to Julian to "take heed" and observe very carefully all the characteristics and qualities of the place and its surroundings, as well as the clothing, positioning, behavior, exterior expression, and interior attitude of both the lord and the servant would be instantly recognizable to a playwright, director, or actor as the essential method for interpreting the actions and motivations of the characters in a play. Julian was advised not to overlook any detail on the *literal* level, no matter how innocuous it might appear to be, lest it contain a secret. The parable was a mysterious play of the highest order. And Julian, like any creative artist, had to "dig deeper" to unearth the layers of meaning hidden under the literal representation. She would have to learn to do dramatic exegesis.

The Parable

Julian proceeds to examine "the points and properties" she discovered hidden in the parable:

> The lord who sat solemnly in rest and in peace, I understand that he is God. The servant who stood before him, I understand that he was shewn for Adam: that is to say, one man was shewn at that time, and his falling, thereby to make it understood how God beholds all mankind and his falling. For in the sight of God all men are one man, and one man is all men. (51:85–89.277–279)

Hers is a vision of the story of the fall of Adam, though lacking the presence of Eve, any sign of a forbidden "tree of the knowledge of good and evil" (Gn 2:17), a tempting serpent, the sin of Eve, her seduction of Adam, God's wrath, or an eventual banishment from the garden of Eden. There is only God and there is Adam, his humble servant, who appears to represent all humankind, both male and female, in this dramatic allegory. Adam's fall betokens every human being's fall, in order to clarify "how God beholds all mankind and his falling."

As we have seen, medieval theology, based on the Book of Genesis, taught that all humans derived their ancestry from Adam, the first man, created in the image and likeness of God. What the first man was, all human beings were created to be. When the first man disobeyed God, that original sin was reckoned to all people as their sin. The painful results of Adam's sin would also be passed on to his descendants, from generation to generation. Julian's exegesis follows the story:

> This man was hurt in his powers and made very feeble, and he was stunned in his understanding, for he was turned from the beholding of his lord. *But his will was kept whole in God's sight.* For I saw our lord commend and approve his will, but the man himself was hindered and blinded from knowing his true will. And this is great sorrow and terrible anguish for him, for neither does he see clearly his loving lord, who is to him full meek and mild, nor does he see truly what he himself is in the sight of his loving lord. And well I know, when these two are wisely and truly seen, we shall attain rest and peace; here in part, and the fullness of the bliss in heaven, by God's plenteous grace. (51:89–97.279, italics added)

Because of sin, the servant (and by extension, all humankind) is mortally wounded; his powers of reason and will are greatly enfeebled. His body reflects his inner turmoil, becoming highly susceptible to disease, aging, and death. The servant is stunned by his fall from grace, especially because he can no longer look up and see his lord and master. Still, his highest will, his essential nature, is preserved whole and pure in the sight of God. How could this be?

Julian noticed that the lord, who represents God, honored the good will of the servant, who wanted so much to serve his lord that he had run off in great haste. But the man, the prototype of all humanity, did not know his own true will or appreciate his great value to his lord. Therefore, he was thrown into great remorse, anguish, and doubt. He could see neither his lord, who is "meek and mild" (not judgmental and harsh), nor his own true self. Neither could he truly observe how his loving lord beheld him, even in his fall. Julian is certain that when these two truths are finally seen (God's unconditional love and our own true nature) "we shall attain rest and peace." She adds that we may gain some measure of illumination here on earth, but only in part. The fullness of the sight of God, and of our souls *in* God, will be possible only when we come to heaven, by God's grace.

Julian acknowledges that this insight into the parable was "the beginning of the teaching" that she received at that time, "whereby I might come to understand in what manner he beholds us in our sin" (51:98–99.279). As such, this was Julian's first way of interpreting the *literal* sense of the parable, through examination of its *allegorical* meaning. Even on this level, she saw that only our personal pain blames and punishes us (in effect, we are our own worst enemies), while "our courteous lord comforts and helps us" (51:99–101.279). He is ever present to the soul with a glad countenance, not a condemning look, loving us and longing to bring us to heaven.

The Lord

Now Julian focuses more carefully on the image of the lord. He is not a worldly lord, displaying luxury and splendor. He did not appear in the great hall of a castle, nor was he seated on a high-backed gilded throne raised on a dais, as were all lords in medieval times, looking down upon his lowly servant.

> The place that the lord sat on was simple, on the earth, barren and deserted, alone in the wilderness. His clothing was wide and ample and full seemly, befitting a lord. The color of the clothing was blue as azure, most dignified and fair. His chere [expression] was merciful. The color of his face was fair brown, with a very seemly countenance. His eyes were black, most beautiful and handsome, shewing full of lovely pity, and within him was a high refuge, long and broad, all full of endless heavens. And the lovely looking with which he looked on his servant continually—and especially in his falling—it seemed to me it might melt our hearts for love and break them in two for joy. (51:103–110.279)

The lord, who symbolizes God, is seated on the simple ground of his own creation, the earth, in a vast and deserted space, alone within the great abyss. Julian's attention to the color, quantity, and style of his clothing bears witness to her keen eye for detail and her lifelong experience dealing with fabrics. The lord's robe was not skimpy, but voluminous and "full seemly," perfectly appropriate for such a lord. Extra material, either trailing or ballooning out wide, was much favored in the fourteenth century as a sign of high status. Its blue color signified the azure sky, long associated with the male principle, as well as the spiritual, the distant, the divine. Since the thirteenth century, indigo blue dye for the coloring of fabrics had been fermented from the leaves of the dyer's woad plant and was greatly desired by royalty and the nobility. In respect of clothing, the blue of the lord's clothing delineates the highest estate.

Julian depicts the lord's face as pale brown and very beautiful. His eyes were black, full of loving compassion. Within those eyes, Julian could see a secure and safe haven, stretching into "endless heavens."

All the while, she noticed how tenderly the lord looked upon his servant, even when the servant ran off and fell into the ditch. This look was so full of loving concern, Julian felt it could melt the heart of anyone who saw it, bursting it in two with ecstatic joy. The expression of the lord revealed a mixture of compassion and pity, as well as joy and bliss, which Julian writes "was marvelous to behold" (51:111.279). She adds that the joy and bliss so far surpassed the compassion and pity "as heaven is above the earth" (51:113.279). The pity and compassion were directed toward the falling of the servant (whom Julian now names Adam), "who is his most loved creature" (51:115.279). The joy and bliss will be further illuminated later, as the layers of meaning unfold. The lord's merciful beholding of Adam followed him even into hell, where Adam was believed to have remained until after the crucifixion. The servant, Adam, was "kept from endless death" by the lord's own mercy and pity. Julian attests that "this mercy and pity dwells with mankind until the time that we come up into heaven" (51:118–119.279).

At this point, Julian interjects a caveat about her imaginative "seeing" of God the Father in the guise of a man. She knows full well that the Father is *not* a man, but because of our blindness, she acknowledges that we may not see the Father except as he is depicted (in religious art, mystery plays, and mystical revelation) in a *homely*, familiar manner, "as if" he were a man. Still, Julian maintains that the lord's sitting on the barren and deserted earth was revealed to mean that

> he made man's soul to be his own city and his dwelling place, which is most pleasing to him of all his werks. And at the time man had fallen into sorrow and pain, he was not at all fitted to serve in that noble office. And therefore our kind father would assign himself no other place but to sit upon the earth, waiting for mankind which is mixed with earth, until that time by his grace his dearworthy son had brought again his city into the state of noble beauty by his hard travail. (51:124–29.279–81)

Now Julian goes deeper to explore the *allegorical* levels of the lord's appearance. The blueness of his robes signifies the lord's steadfast loyalty. The brown of his magnificent face, with the deep black of his eyes, bears witness to his majestic seriousness. The expansiveness of his clothing, which was beautiful and billowing, reveals that the lord had enclosed within himself "all heavens and all endless joy and bliss" (51:132–33.281). (Julian uses a medieval word, *flammying*, for the "flaming out" like fire of the lord's robes, which might evoke the tongues of fire that settled on the apostles at Pentecost.) All this was shown to Julian "in a touch," a distinct moment of spiritual insight, during which Julian's understanding "was led into the lord, in which I saw him highly rejoicing for the honorable restoring that he will and shall bring his servant to by his plenteous grace" (51:133–36.281).

The Servant

> And yet I marveled, beholding the lord and the servant before mentioned. I saw the lord sit solemnly, and the servant standing reverently before his lord—in which servant is a double meaning, one without, another within. Outward: he was clad simply, as a laborer who was disposed to travail [ready to do hard labor]. And he stood very near the lord, not exactly in front of him, but slightly to the side, and that on the left side. His clothing was a white kirtel [tunic], single-layered, old, and very deficient, dyed with the sweat of his body, close-fitting on him and short, as it were a hand's width beneath the knee, bare, seeming as if it should soon be worn out, ready to be ragged and rent. And in this I marveled greatly, thinking: "This is now an unseemly clothing for the servant who is so highly loved to stand in before so honorable a lord!" And inward: in him was shewn a ground of love, which love he had for the lord that was even comparable to the love that the lord had for him. (51:137–48.281)

Julian turns her attention to the servant and is astonished at his impoverished appearance, which is like that of the lowliest peasant farm worker. She notices that he stands a little to the left side of the lord, not directly in front of him, but does not bow, kneel, or in any way acknowledge the lord's majesty. The servant's *kirtel*, the tunic worn by every villein, was especially old and thin, dirty, sweaty, stained, tight, short, bare, and ready to be ripped up for the rag heap. As much as Julian was captivated by the lord's appearance, so was she dismayed by the servant's. How dare a servant appear like this before his lord! Yet inwardly, on a deeper level of awareness, Julian recognized that the servant's love for the lord was as boundless as the lord's love for the servant. What was their relationship?

The wise servant realized intuitively that "there was one thing to do which should be worship to the lord" (51:149–50.281). The lord did not tell him specifically what it was; the servant knew. And so, out of his great love, and without thinking about himself or what might happen to him, the servant quickly ran off at the command of his lord "to do that thing which was his will and his worship" (51:152.281). Julian was confused by this, because it appeared to her (by the worn-out clothing) that the servant had been a hard laborer for a very long time. Yet by an inward sight she was given, "it seemed that he was a new-hire," who was just beginning to work and had never been "sent out before" (51:155–56.281).

The Treasure

> There was a treasure in the earth which the lord loved. I marveled and wondered what it might be. And I was answered in my understanding: "It is a mete [food] which is appealing and appetizing to the lord." For I saw the lord sit as a man, and I saw neither mete nor drink wherewith to serve him. This was one marvel. Another marvel was that this stately lord had no servant but one, and him he sent out. I beheld, thinking what manner of labor it may be that the servant should do. (51:157–62.281)

Christ had spoken of the kingdom of heaven as being "like treasure hidden in a field, which someone found and hid; then in his joy he goes and sells all that he has and buys that field" (Mt 13:44). Julian was certainly acquainted with this oft-told parable. Here the concept of "treasure" reappears as the *one thing* the lord personally wanted more than anything else and the singular reason that the servant ran off in such great haste. Yet it was not "one pearl of great value" (Mt 13:46), but "a food" (Julian uses the Old English word, *mete*) hidden in the earth. Julian noticed that the lord, who was so majestic in his demeanor and sumptuously clothed, was not being served any *mete* or drink. Even more surprising, he had only one servant (whereas even merchant householders and anchorites, like Julian, had several). And the servant that the lord sent out to work in his name was such an unappealing, disheveled laborer! She simply could not fathom the meaning of it all. She pondered carefully to discover just what kind of labor this servant might do for the lord.

> And then I understood that he [the servant] should do the greatest labor and the hardest travail that there is: he should be a gardener: delve and dike and swinke and swete [dig and ditch and work and sweat] and turn the earth up and down, and seek the depnesse [depths of the earth] and water the plants in time. And in this he would continue his travail, and make sweet rivers to run, and noble and plenteous fruit to spring forth which he would bring before the lord and serve him therewith to his liking. And he should never return till he had got this mete all ready, as he knew that it was liked by the lord, and then he should take this mete with the drink, and bear it full worshipfully before the lord. And all this time the lord should sit right on the same place, awaiting the servant whom he sent out. (51:162–71.281–83)

It struck Julian that the servant was being sent out to till the earth as Adam had been sent to do: "By the sweat of your face you shall eat bread until you return to the ground, for out of it you were taken; you are dust, and to dust you shall return" (Gn 3:19). The servant was to dig ditches (like the one into which he would fall), toiling and sweating and turning the soil over and over, searching into the "depnesse" to unearth its treasure, sewing seeds and planting crops, and watering the plants in due season. He would never cease his work of making "sweet rivers" run freely and of producing rich and abundant fruit. And the servant would never come back until he had harvested all the foods that he knew the lord liked. Then he would take the foods and drink most reverently to the lord, who would still be sitting patiently in the same place, awaiting his servant.

The Servant's Fall

What was it the servant did wrong? Why did he fall into the ditch? He ran off so hastily, with such eagerness and good will to do exactly what the lord wanted. What failure on his part precipitated his downfall? Was it pride that he thought he knew what the lord wanted, without asking for clarity? Was it over-confidence that he knew where to find it, without seeking direction? Was it over-eagerness to succeed and unwillingness to be guided by the lord? Or was it simply ignorance about the nature of reality itself? Was the servant grasping at a wrong idea of "hidden treasure" in the vast landscape of the universe, as if it were something physical that existed "out there" on its own, waiting to be unearthed, when in fact, it was spiritual? Should he have stayed close to the lord instead, right where he was sitting, and planted in the ground at the lord's feet? Perhaps it was in the very make-up of the servant to be rash, want things too fast, not see clearly where he was going, and then, becoming distracted, trip and fall. Maybe it was none of these.

Julian never specifies what the sin of the servant was. She does not suggest the servant fell prey to the temptation of a serpent and ate a forbidden apple. She leaves the catalyst in the parable a mystery, as is the origin of sin. But she knows that there are clues hidden beneath the surface of the story, clues that she must dig up herself, like the servant. And perhaps the parable was not as much about the original cause of the fall as about *the recovery* that was yet to come. By gradually unfolding layers of meaning, Julian will eventually understand *who* the servant really was, and *why* he had to run off and fall into a ditch in order to retrieve the spiritual "food" the lord wanted. However, at this point in her narrative, re-examining the outward and inward aspects of the servant, Julian has become all the more confused.

> And around the lord, there was nothing at all but wilderness. And I did not understand all that this example meant, and therefore I wondered from whence the servant came. (51:176–78.283)

As potent as this allegory seemed to her mind, Julian simply could not decipher its import. The lord already had within himself "endless life and all manner of goodness, save the treasure that was in the earth" (51:173–74.283). However, as Julian remarks, *even the treasure* had its ultimate source, its true ground, in the lord's boundless love. She understood that the lord would not be completely satisfied and fully honored until his servant had grown the food, prepared the meal, and brought it back to him in person. Julian looked and looked at the images embedded in her mind, much as we might try to reconstruct and make sense of a highly symbolic dream. She searched and searched for the servant's place of origin. But she could see nothing except the vast wilderness of empty space surrounding the lord. She had no idea *who the servant was* until, after twenty years of delving and digging and turning the parable over and over in her mind, "seeking the depnesse," she was finally given divine illumination.

Double Nature

> In the servant is comprehended the second person of the trinity, and in the servant is comprehended Adam: that is to say, all men. And therefore when I say "the son," it means the godhead, which is equal to the father; and when I say "the servant," it means Christ's manhood, *which is the rightful Adam*. By the nearness of the servant is understood the son, and by the standing on the left side is understood Adam. The lord is God the father; the servant is the son Jesus Christ; the holy ghost is the equal love which is in them both. (51:179–85.283, italics added)

At last, Julian received the key that unlocked the mystery of the parable: the servant has the double nature of Jesus Christ. Considered as "the Son" in his divine nature, the servant is the second person of the Trinity, the Son of God, perfectly "equal to the Father." Regarded as "the servant," he is Christ in his human nature, "the rightful Adam," what humankind was meant to be. As equal to God, the Son was worthy to stand very near the Lord, who is God the Father. As the humble servant Adam, Christ was made to stand slightly to the left. The Holy Ghost is the mutual love that exists between Father and Son, one in Trinity.

> When Adam fell, God's son fell. Because of the rightful oneing [perfect union] which was made in heaven, God's son might not be separated from Adam, for by Adam I understand all mankind. Adam fell from life to death: into the slade of this wretched world, and after that into hell. God's son fell with Adam into the slade of the maiden's womb, who was the fairest daughter of Adam—and that was to excuse Adam from blame in heaven and on earth—and mightily he fetched him out of hell. (51:185–91.283)

When "Adam fell" not only did all humanity yet to be born suffer the consequences of his original sin, "God's son fell." And this is because the "perfect union which was made in heaven" of God and man in the person of Jesus Christ could never be separated. Here Julian refers to the hypostatic union of two natures, divine and human, that subsists in the one person, Jesus Christ. Some theologians even held that the human nature of Christ existed from the beginning of time (in the sense that he was the first perfect created being), not just from the moment he took human nature in the virgin's womb by the power of the Holy Spirit (Lk 1:35).

Also, in stating that "by Adam I understand all mankind," Julian is no longer differentiating between "them that shalle be saved" and the rest of humanity, that is, believers from non-believers. She is writing in ***universal terms***, because this is the way in which she was privileged to understand the import of the parable. There can be no essential separation between one man or woman and another. All are included in the appellative "Adam" (even Eve, since for Julian "Adam" includes both sexes), inasmuch as God became man to save *all.* Julian describes the incarnation with poetic originality: God's Son "fell with Adam into the slade of the maiden's womb" (even as Adam fell into the hollow of the ditch). And because of this incarnation of God as perfect humanity, Adam, representing the whole of humanity, was purified in his fundamental nature, excused from blame both in heaven and on earth, and fetched out of his "hell."

Christ and Adam

Now that Julian has been given the key to unlock the symbolism of the parable, new levels of meaning open up to her understanding. She sees that "the wisdom and the goodness that were in the servant" (which had seemed too high and lofty for Adam alone) were the eternal wisdom and goodness of God's Son (51:192–93.283). And the poor, dirty clothing of the servant, appearing as a peasant laborer and standing to the left of the lord, signified the disheveled humanity of Adam, "with all the mischief and feebleness that followed" (51:193–94.283).

> For in all this, our good lord shewed his own son and Adam *but one man*. The virtue and the goodness that we have is of Jesus Christ, the feebleness and blindness that we have is of Adam: which two were shewn in the servant. *And thus has our good lord Jesus taken upon himself all our blame, and therefore our father may not, nor will not, assign any more blame to us than to his own dearworthy son, Jesus Christ.* (51:194–99.283, italics added)

The central Christian doctrine that God became a human being is a mystery that defies comprehension. The implication that by becoming *one* man Christ incarnated *all* humankind is equally sublime. Julian tries to state this idea in simplest terms, as it was shown to her in the parable: God the Father revealed that his Son and Adam were so united, they were, in fact, *one person*. And, by extension, Christ becomes incarnate within all men and women in the same way. Any goodness we possess is Christ's own virtue. Any blindness, ignorance, and degeneration of will that we experience come from our fallen human nature. Both the divine and the human co-exist in the servant, as Julian understood it. And while the servant in the parable did not cease to be weak and blind like Adam, Christ took on himself the blame for the servant's sin. And therefore the Father may not, and will not, "assign blame" to the servant, *because he cannot assign blame to his own Son*. Julian pushes the theological implications of the incarnation to their utmost.

Most perceptively, she also realizes that the servant was seen standing before the lord as Christ himself stands ready "in purpose before the father" from time without beginning, until such time as the Father would send him to earth to accomplish "the worshipful deed by which mankind was brought again into heaven" (51:200–202.283–85). Even though he is God and equal with the Father, Christ in his infinite foreknowledge knew that he would have to become man in order to save humankind by perfectly fulfilling the will of his Father. "So he stood before his father as a servant, willfully taking upon himself all our burdens" (51:204–5.285).

> And then he started very eagerly at the father's will, and anon he fell very low into the maiden's womb, having no regard for himself nor for his hard pains. The white kirtel is his flesh. The thinness of the tunic is that there was nothing at all between the godhead and the manhood. The tightness is poverty. The age is from Adam's long wearing. The deficiency is the sweat of Adam's travail. The shortness shews the servant labourer. (51:205–210.285)

Longing and Waiting

Now Julian references a medieval teaching that the Son of God would have become human *even if Adam had not sinned*. Duns Scotus (1266–1308), a Franciscan theologian, maintained that the fall of Adam was *not* the cause of Christ becoming human, because then mankind would have been able to alter God's original intention for creation as well as God's freedom to act. Such a thought would be irrational. The incarnation could not have been an afterthought, an "adjustment" to human circumstances, because with God there is no time or change in the eternal plan. Therefore, Scotus held that even if neither angel nor man had disobeyed God and fallen from grace, Christ *still* would have become incarnate.[1] Following in this preached tradition, Julian posits that, from all eternity, the Son had stood and waited, ready to do his Father's will, saying, in effect:

> "Lo, my dear father, I stand before thee in Adam's kirtel, always ready to start and to run. I would be on the earth to do thee worship, when it is thy will to send me. How long shall I desire it?" (51:211–14.285)

Julian comments that the Son, being the eternal Wisdom of the Father, knew *exactly* how long he would have to wait and when it would be the Father's will to send him to earth. The pleading question "How long?" comes not from Christ's divinity, but from his *humanity*, in whom is understood "all mankind that shalle be saved by the sweet incarnation and the blissful passion of Christ" (51:217–18.285).

> For he is the head, and we are his members, to which members the day and the time is unknown when every passing woe and sorrow will have an end and the everlasting joy and bliss shall be fulfilled. Which day and time, all the company of heaven longs or desires to see. And for all who are under heaven who shall come there, the way is by longing and desiring; which desiring and longing was shewn in the servant standing before the lord—or else thus, in the son standing before the father in Adam's kirtel. (51:218–24.285)

Julian seems to be paraphrasing St. Paul, who wrote of Christ as the head and the church as members of his body: "For just as the body is one and has many members, and all the members of the body, though many, are one body, so it is with Christ" (1 Cor 12:12). She realizes that those in heaven and on earth continue to ask the same question: when will all this "woe and sorrow" come to an end and salvation be completed? Even though Christ has already died and risen, all creation continues to long and wait to see Christ's second coming in glory. "But about that day or hour no one knows, neither the angels in heaven, nor the Son, but only the Father" (Mk 13:32). So Christ, in his Mystical Body, wearing humanity's *kirtel*, is still full of longing. He is still waiting. He embodies all human longing, desiring, and waiting. "For Jesus is all that will be saved, and all that shall be saved is Jesus" (51:225–26.285). Julian adds that this will be accomplished by the love of God, along with our own obedience, meekness, patience, and other virtues.

A.B.C.

Julian moves from exegesis of the literal and allegorical meanings of the *exemplum* to offer further tropological, or moral, directives that were given to her about the parable's relationship to all the other Revelations. She testifies that the parable was "the beginning of an A.B.C., whereby I may have some understanding of our lord's meaning" (51:229–30.285). She was convinced that the teachings of all the other Revelations were hidden within the *exemplum*. Just as learning to read her A.B.C.s from her *prymer* as a child had provided her with the building blocks of words and the key to unlocking their secrets, now, deciphering the parable afforded her the basic theological structure with which to open up multiple levels of meaning. And this applied not only to the parable itself but to all the other visions and locutions she had received.

Just like the servant who was sent out to "do the greatest labour and the hardest work . . . delving and turning the earth up and down," Julian had to dig into and turn over the soil of the *exemplum* through persistent analysis and prayerful meditation. She had to search out the parable's hidden teachings by using the same stringent methods of exegesis employed by preachers to plumb the depths of the scriptures. In the course of the twenty years of intellectual labor that Julian devoted to this task, she learned how to see and think *double* at all times. She taught herself to hold, balance, and interweave various (and often conflicting) aspects of all the Revelations in her mind simultaneously. She grew more and more confident that she could differentiate between the levels of truth that were being shown. She oscillated between the "two domes," the divine and the human perspectives on existence. She realized that, by glimpsing how God beholds the human soul, she might begin to perceive what the human soul really is.

Then she returned to her original manuscript of the Short Text and began the arduous task of rewriting, inserting these later interpretations into her first account of the Revelations, adding layer upon layer of meaning in order to "make plenteous fruit to spring forth."

Most of the teachings she has already provided up to this point in the Long Text, those not found in the Short Text, *came directly from the insights she received through her work on this parable.* There is a constant cross-referencing within the Long Text. What Julian learned by her exegesis on the *exemplum* deepened her ability to understand and elucidate all the other Revelations, both for herself and the reader. Likewise, what she had seen and heard in the other Revelations directly influenced her comprehension of the *exemplum.*

For example, Julian's realization of the tender love of the lord for the servant and the servant's eagerness to do the lord's will . . . of the seven pains of the servant as potent metaphors for the results of sin . . . of the servant's "godly will" which explained why he could not be cut off from the lord, even when he fell headlong into the ditch . . . these, and many more insights into the intimate relationship between God and humanity resulted from Julian's delving into the multiple layers of the *exemplum.* The parable also helped Julian explain why God rewarded the servant for suffering such pains, giving him a *mede* greater than if he had not fallen into the ditch in the first place. And she recognized from the parable why all woe and suffering would be transformed into eternal bliss.

The *exemplum* also enhanced Julian's understanding of the visual and aural Revelations she had received from Christ on the cross. She began to appreciate *why* God looks upon us without the blame she had been taught to expect, but rather with the utmost pity, compassion, and a constant desire to show us mercy and grace. When God looks at us, he sees his own Son, the Suffering Servant (Is 53:1–12), and will stop at nothing to pull us out of the ditch of our pain in order to bring us into his eternal peace. Julian realized from the parable that, like Adam, we are God's most precious creatures. And, like Christ, we merit eternal bliss. At first, it may have seemed callous to Julian that she saw the lord in the parable *rejoice* in the sufferings of the servant. But then she learned that the rejoicing is because the Father knows the supreme glory to which he will bring his beloved gardener. God eternally anticipates the good ending of our life story. For God, it is only the beginning.

This combination of compassion and rejoicing (even amidst great pain) may be likened to a devoted parent who sees that a beloved child will have to suffer greatly to achieve a goal, or realize a dream, or develop a talent. The parent knows only too well that a life of dedication and hard work involves self-sacrifice, rejection, and times of failure. The normal course of learning anything requires struggle, and every period of growth includes some pain. But the wise parent allows the child to endure these times of suffering (though supporting and encouraging him or her in every possible way), precisely because the parent anticipates the eventual satisfaction and the great joy that will come when the child experiences achievement. To deprive the child of the struggle in order to protect the child from the suffering would be to take away the child's most precious gift: free will. And this no good parent will do, nor will God.

Deeper Meanings

Whenever Julian uses the phrase "to my understanding," or "I understood," or "as I understood it," which she does frequently, we may be fairly sure these intellectual insights arose at a later date than the Revelations themselves and were inserted into her ever-longer version of the original text. As we have seen, Julian had "three properties," or modes of teaching from the Lord: the first was the "beginning of teaching," which she received during the actual time of the Revelations; the second was the "inward learning" she was given for a long time thereafter; and the third was the "whole revelation, from beginning to end, which our lord God of his goodness often brings freely to the sight of my understanding" (51:64–67.277). She considered this teaching as an ongoing expansion of her original Revelations.

Because of the parable's rich layers of soil, Julian returns to it again and again. She realizes anew that the *sitting* of the Father, in total rest and peace, without doing any work, signifies the Godhead, as Isaiah saw "the Lord sitting on a throne, high and lofty; and the hem of his robe filled the temple" (Is 6:1).[2] The *standing* of the servant symbolizes his life of hard labor and his being on the *left* side indicates his unworthiness to take his place directly in front of the Father. In the servant's eternal desire to serve, his divinity was revealed; in his running off in haste, his humanity was seen. And, most surprisingly, in the servant's falling not only Adam's failure but also the Son's incarnation was shown:

> For the godhead started [rushed] from the father into the maiden's womb, falling into the taking of our nature. And in this falling he

> took great hurt. The hurt that he took was our flesh, in which at once he had the feeling of mortal pains. (51:237–39.285)

"Falling" becomes a *double entendre* for the falling of Adam into sin and the falling of the Word of God from heaven into Mary's womb, where it became flesh. This graphic image of the incarnation as "starting" and "falling" brings to mind the words from the Book of Wisdom:

> For while gentle silence enveloped all things, and night in its swift course was now half gone, *your all-powerful word leaped from heaven*, from the royal throne, into the midst of the land that was doomed . . . (Ws 18:14–15, italics added)

Julian explains further that the servant's clothing was so skimpy and threadbare that it was not fitting that he should stand directly in front of the Lord. Therefore, he stood to the side, with some dread. "He might not sit with the lord in rest and peace till he had won his peace rightfully with his hard travail" (51:243–44.287). And the fact the servant stood on the *left* side signifies that the Father "left" his own Son in his manhood to suffer all the pains of humankind, without sparing him anything. The raggedness and tears of the kirtel suggest "the blows and the scourges, the thorns and the nails, the drawing and the dragging, his tender flesh tearing" (51:246–48.287). Julian had seen how Christ's flesh tore away from his skull under the crown of thorns, "falling in pieces until the time the bleeding stopped" (51:248–49.287). And then she had seen the blood dry, clinging to the bone.

> And by the wallowing and writhing, groaning and moaning, is understood that he might never rise all mightily from that time that he had fallen into the maiden's womb, till his body was slain and dead, yielding the soul into the father's hand, with all mankind for whom he was sent. (51:250–53.287)

Long ago, the psalmist had written, presaging the Messiah:

> I am counted among those who go down to the Pit; I am like those who have no help, like those forsaken among the dead, like the slain that lie in the grave, like those whom you remember no more,

> for they are cut off from your hand. You have put me in the depths of the Pit, in the regions dark and deep. (Ps 88:4–6)

Yet after his death, Christ began to show his might by descending into hell, where he plunged into the "depe depnesse" and raised up the great *root* [company] of all mankind "which rightfully was knit to him in high heaven" (51:255–56.287). By so doing, Christ resurrected Adam along with the vast array of men and women who had been kept bound in hell. Meanwhile, Christ's body lay in the tomb, like a hard, narrow ditch, until Easter morning, "and from that time he lay never more" (51:257.287).

> And our foul, mortal flesh, that God's son took upon himself—which was Adam's old kirtel, straight, bare, and short—then by our savior was made fair, new, white, and bright, and of endless cleanness, wide and ample, fair and richer than was the clothing which I saw on the father. For that clothing was blue, and Christ's clothing is now of a fair, seemly mixture which is so marvelous that I can not describe it, for it is all made of very worship. (51:259–64.287)

Christ's mortal body was transformed from a dirty, ragged, torn and tight-fitting kirtel into a new, white, bright, and expansive resurrected body, even more radiant and colorful than the blue clothing of the Father in the parable. Julian describes it in Middle English as a *semely medolour*, a fitting blend of colors (like a fine tapestry of human beings, or a rainbow in the sky), which is so glorious that Julian simply cannot describe it. It signifies that Christ's Mystical Body is composed of all the colors of glory, praise, and thanksgiving of humankind.

The Culmination

> Now the Lord no longer sits on the earth in the wilderness, but he sits on his rich and noble seat which he made in heaven, much to his pleasure. Now the son does not stand before the father as a servant before the lord, fearfully, wretchedly clothed, partly naked, but he stands directly in front of the father, richly clothed in blissful amplitude, with a crown upon his head of precious richness. For it was shewn that "we are his crown"; which crown is the father's joy,

> the son's worship, the holy ghost's liking, and endless, marvelous bliss to all that are in heaven. (51:265–72.287)

Here, Julian begins her *eschatological* interpretation of the parable: Christ, the Son, is welcomed into heaven as co-equal with the Father, magnificent in all the colors of divine light, in his final and most glorious transfiguration. Julian harks back to the Ninth Revelation, when she saw that those who are saved become the crown of jewels worn by Christ (22:17–18.195). And the crown is the Trinity's glory and the joy of all the saints in heaven, evoking the description of Christ from the Book of Revelation:

> His eyes are like a flame of fire, and on his head are many diadems; and he has a name inscribed that no one knows but himself. He is clothed in a robe dipped in blood, and his name is called The Word of God. (Rv 19:11–13)

Now the Son no longer stands at the left side as a peasant laborer, but in front of the Father, and even more, he is invited to sit on the Father's *right* hand, "in endless rest and peace" (51.272–73.287). Here Julian interjects that she does not mean these words literally, "as one man sitting by another in this life," because she knows full well that God the Father, Christ the Lord, and the Holy Spirit do not "sit," literally, side by side in the Trinity (51:273–75.287). She must, of necessity, use words and images allegorically to describe the indescribable. What she is trying to convey is what is spoken in the Apostle's Creed: "He ascended into heaven, and is seated at the right hand of God the Father almighty; from there he will come to judge the living and the dead."

> Now is the spouse, God's son, in peace with his beloved wife, who is the fair maiden of endless joy. Now sits the son, truly God and truly man, in his city in rest and in peace, which his father hath prepared for him in his endless purpose, and the father in the son, and the holy ghost in the father and in the son. (51:276–80.287–89)

Christ, like the lover in the Song of Songs, is reconciled with his beloved bride, the soul of humanity, that is, "the fair maiden." Having come at last into his kingdom, which his Father had long ago prepared for him to inherit, Christ sits in his "holy city, the new

Jerusalem" (Rv 21:2). This is the triumphant culmination of the *exemplum*. The Trinity is eternally one in the glorified Savior, as Julian had understood at the very beginning of her First Revelation: "For where Jesus appears the blessed trinity is understood, as to my sight" (4:11–12.135).

> And thus I saw that God enjoys that he is our father, and God enjoys that he is our mother, and God enjoys that he is our very true spouse, and our soul is his beloved wife. And Christ enjoys that he is our brother, and Jesus enjoys that he is our savior. These are five high joys, as I understand, in which he wants us to rejoice: praising him, thanking him, loving him, endlessly blessing him. (52:1–5.289)

A Marvelous Mixture

Julian knows from her own experience that while we are sojourners on this earth, "we have in us a marvelous mixture both of wele and of woe" (52:6–7.289). We hold the resurrected Christ in our hearts, but we are also marked by the "wretchedness and the harm of Adam's falling" (52:8.289). We are, in a very real way, "double" in our own existence. In our living and dying with Christ, we know we will be everlastingly protected, and by his most gracious inspirations we are encouraged to trust in our salvation. Yet because of Adam's falling, we are so deeply "broken in our feelings" that our minds and hearts have become darkened and "so blind that we can scarcely take any comfort" (52:10–12.289). However, in our purest intention, at the core of our being, we still dwell in God, trusting in his mercy and his grace.

> And this is his own werking in us, and in his goodness he opens the eye of our understanding—by which we have sight, sometimes more and sometimes less, according to which God gives us the ability to receive. And now we are raised into that one [more sight], and now we are allowed to fall into the other [less sight]. (52:13–16.289)

Julian is keenly aware of the constant oscillation of our minds, our moods, our views, from the highest joy to the most wretched despair. And because of this *medolour*, or mixture, she admits we can scarcely know, at any given moment, what state of soul we are in, much less the state of any of our *evencristens.* All we can do is simply assent to God when we feel him, "truly willing to be with him with all our heart, with all our soul, and with all our strength" (52:19–21.289). Acts of love such as these lead us to hate our evil thoughts, our conflicted desires, and anything that could be an occasion of sin, either spiritual or physical. Yet even when we receive spiritual sweetness, it passes, and then "we fall again into blindness and so into woe and tribulation in diverse manners" (52:22–24.289).

> But then is this our comfort: that we know in our faith that by the virtue of Christ, who is our keeper [protector], we never assent thereto [to sin]. But we complain against it and endure it in pain and in woe, praying until the time that he shews himself again to us. And thus we stand in this medolour all the days of our life. (52:24–27.289)

Julian has no illusions that because of her extraordinary visionary experiences, her life is, or could be, any different from the lives of the rest of us. This mixture of "wele and woe" is our common lot as long as we are in this human condition. But Christ wants us to trust that "he is continually with us" (52:28.289). Julian sees this is so in three ways:

> He is with us in heaven, true man in his own person, drawing us up; and that was shewn in the ghostly thirst. And he is with us on earth, leading us; and that was shewn in the third revelation, where I saw God in a point. And he is with us in our soul, endlessly wonning [dwelling at home], ruling and governing us; and that was shewn in the sixteenth revelation, as I shall say." (52:28–32.289–91)

The Parable of Life

Julian then recapitulates the parable, like a good preacher, weaving together the many different threads of meaning she has been exploring. In the servant, she sees both the blindness and the hurt of Adam's wrongdoing (and by extension, our own), and the wisdom and goodness of God's Son. In the lord, she observes the compassion and the pity he had for Adam's suffering (when he sat alone on the earth), as well as the great nobility and honor to which humanity will be brought, "by the virtue of the passion and the death of his dearworthy son" (52:35–38.291). She understands that the servant's eagerness to run off and find the food is Christ's own eagerness to fall to earth and become human. "My food is to do the will of him who sent me and to complete his work" (Jn 4:34). And the one in the ditch is not only Adam, but Christ, moaning and groaning on the cross, constrained in a narrow, hard grave. The incarnation means that there is no separation between God and the soul, not even one as thin as a threadbare *kirtel.* The soul of humanity, since its creation, has always been knitted into God, as close as God's own image. In some inconceivable way, in our essential reality, *we look like God.* We are always being created in God's mind, always flowing forth from his infinite power, wisdom, and love, in spite of our mistakenness.

Julian also reiterates why the lord was able to rejoice, even in the servant's falling, "because of the high raising and fullness of bliss that mankind is come to, overpassing that which we should have had if he had not fallen" (52:38–40.291). Again, it is important to clarify Julian's interpretation here. She does not mean to imply that the servant will be rewarded because of his *sin,* but because of all the *suffering* that he will have to undergo throughout time (the pains, diseases, wars, sorrows, separations, and deaths), as a result of sin.

Why should this be? As we have seen, since its earliest days, the church understood original sin (even in its gravity) as "the happy fault" which merited such a Savior as Jesus Christ. And in Christ, who is sinless and perfectly obedient to his Father's will, humanity is forever changed, as bread and wine are changed in the eucharistic act. We are no longer *merely* sinners. Christ consecrates all of humanity into himself: "This is *my* body. This is *my* blood." Henceforth, everything we experience, of "wele and woe," we may experience "through him, and with him, and in him."[3] We may rejoice and give thanks and love and cherish with him. We may suffer and bleed and die with him. And the rewards for our sufferings in Christ shall be *Christ's own rewards* in heaven, far surpassing anything we might have earned for ourselves. It is indeed a mystery beyond comprehension.

Yes, Julian admits that now we mourn and weep, "for our sin is the cause of Christ's pains" (52:41–42.291). But we also have "continual matter for joy, for endless love made him to suffer" (52:42–43.291). Well might we ask: Why did endless love make him *want* to suffer? We look around at the state of the world, at its deadly cycle of misdeeds. We wonder *why* God loves humanity so much that he wills to become what we are, in all our pain, so that he might transform us into what he is, reflecting his transcendent beauty. We do not lack imagination, yet to imagine God's overwhelming love seems well nigh impossible. The sufferings of hell are almost easier to envision than are the eternal joys of heaven. In our physical, mental, and spiritual agonies, we have already descended into hells of our own making. We know what hell is like. We simply cannot conceive of eternal bliss.

Yet what Julian tells us she saw "in an instant," or felt "in a touch," is that by becoming man, the Son of God took on our human nature *unconditionally*. When Christ was dying on the cross, he was fighting against evil not just for us but for his own dear life. As we have said, God looks upon us and sees Christ, his Son, suffering like this. He "saves" Christ from death through resurrection, and in so doing he saves us. Julian attests repeatedly that no matter how marred and mutilated by sin our souls may have become, no matter how blind and afflicted our minds, no matter how weak and disordered our wills, the truest essence of who we are as human beings is, now and forever, *Christ's own human life*. In spite of our sin, we are lights of Christ that can never go out. We are flames of love that do not have their source in ourselves, but in God's eternal fire. No matter how much we fail or how deeply we fall into the ditches of life, we are still and always infinitely precious to God. As our Creator/Father, he stands over us with pity and compassion for our sufferings as well as great joy in their ultimate value. As our Savior/Mother/Christ, he falls into the ditch of life with us and gives rebirth to our fallen human nature as himself. As our Sanctifier/Lover, he raises himself, and us, out of the grave of death, into everlasting life.

So if we ask: *Why does God love us so much?* the answer is divine in its simplicity. God loves each and every one of us because, by virtue of the incarnation, he sees in us his most beloved Son, Jesus Christ, with whom he is "well pleased" (Mt 3:17, Lk 3:22). From time to time, in deep meditation, we may be privileged, like Julian, to be given "a touch" of this divine view. And then we are overwhelmed by a glimpse into who we truly are: the beloved servant in the parable who is *both* Adam *and* Christ. And with that insight, we have an eternal perspective from which to evaluate our human sufferings and on which to base our hope of heavenly reward.

Hatred of Sin

> And therefore, the creature who sees and feels the werking of love by grace hates nothing but sinne. For of all things, as to my sight, love and hate are the hardest and most immeasurable opposites. And notwithstanding all this, I saw and understood in our lord's meaning that we may not in this life keep ourselves wholly from sinne, in complete purity, as we shall be in heaven. But we may well by grace keep ourselves from the sinnes which would lead us to endless pain, as holy church teaches us, and eschew venial sins reasonably, according to our power. (52:44–50.291)

Julian is sure that one who truly loves God and feels his presence in the soul through "the werking of love by grace" must hate only sin, since love makes it impossible to hate anything but evil. Julian never suggests the sinner should hate himself, only the sin. The medieval church made a strong distinction between mortal sin (which, if unconfessed at the point of death, would send the soul straight to hell) and the less grave venial sins (which could detain the soul in purgatory). As we discussed, anyone in mortal sin was urged to seek out a priest immediately, lest he or she experience sudden death before being shriven, a thought that struck terror in the hearts of Christians. Venial sins did not have to be confessed immediately, as long as the person said an act of contrition as soon as he or she became aware of the misdeed. But at least once a year, venial sins also needed to be confessed and the appropriate penance performed after absolution.

However, the difference between mortal and venial sin was considered only a matter of degree in the seriousness of the deed itself, in the awareness of its sinfulness, and in the willed intentionality to commit the deed. A habit of venial sins could lead to mortal sin. A venial sin of anger at one's neighbor might incite a premeditated act of violence that could result in a mortal sin of murder. A venial sin of desire for a man or woman who was not one's own husband or wife could lead to the mortal sin of adultery. And so on. Venial sins also could have varying degrees of severity. Willful intention dictated the more serious venial sins. Hurtful or deceptive words or actions that arose spontaneously as a result of circumstances beyond one's control were considered less serious venial sins.

Julian acknowledges that no one in this life, no matter how much he or she loves God, is able to keep from committing venial sins. But she is certain that, with the help of grace, we can keep from committing mortal sins. Still, if we fall into serious sin, "by our blindness and our wretchedness," Julian counsels that we rise quickly, with the help of the "sweet touching of grace," and then immediately mend our ways, according to church teaching and the severity of the sin, and "go forth with God in love" (52:50–53.291). She advises that we should neither become too depressed and despairing about our sin nor allow ourselves to grow reckless, as if we did not care about our sin's seriousness. We should simply admit our frailty, knowing full well that we cannot remain sinless for even "a twinkling of an eye but for the keeping [protection] of grace" (52:55–56.291). And then we should cling to God, trusting only in him.

Double Awareness

God sees one way, humankind sees another. Julian considers it right that, as sinners, we humbly *accuse* ourselves of sin (as was the medieval custom in the course of making a good confession). She also affirms it belongs "to the proper goodness of our lord God courteously to *excuse* mankind" (52:59–60.291, italics added). Julian testifies that these two aspects were shown to her through the "double expression in which the lord beheld the falling of his beloved servant" (52:60–62.291). The Lord wants us both to acknowledge our sins (admit the harm they cause ourselves and others, realizing that we cannot make complete restitution for them) and, at the same time, to know God's everlasting love for us and his "plenteous mercy" (52:66–67.291). And through this double awareness we give God "the humble accusing" that he asks of us, which he is always working to effect within our souls (52:68.293).

Julian draws out yet another analogy from the double expression of the lord toward the servant. The lord looked at the servant with an outward expression of great pity for his falling, but also with a countenance of joy in beholding the honorable atonement that Christ has made. And this forms "the lower part of man's life" (52:70.293). She also recognized an even more inward expression of the lord, "that was more elevated, and all one," that is, *not* double (52:72–73.293).

> For the life and the virtue that we have in the lower part comes from the higher. And it comes down to us from the natural love of the self by grace. Between that one and that other is nothing at all—for it is all one love, which one blessed love is now in us a double werking. For in the lower part are pains and passions, compassions and pities, mercies and forgiveness and such other, which are profitable. But in the higher part are none of these, but all one high love and marvelous joy, in which marvelous joy all pains are wholly transformed. (52:73–80.293)

In this difficult passage, Julian begins to set forth her theology of the higher and lower levels of our existence, what she will later refer to as our "substance" (essence), and our "sensuality" (psycho-physical consciousness). She sees that our higher substance works with grace to infuse life and virtue into the lower sensuality. This process enables us to love ourselves, which is absolutely necessary if we are to know how to love our neighbor.

In the First Revelation, Julian referred to the goodness of God coming down to us "to the lowest part of our need," meaning every physical and emotional aspect of our human existence (6:25–26.143). Then, she even included the natural process of digestion. Now, she refers to our lower mixture of "pains and passions, compassions and pities, mercies and forgiveness and such other," all of which she sees God make profitable for human growth. In the higher part, that of our essential nature in God, she recognizes none of these conflicts, needs, and sufferings; only one love and joy. And in this supreme joy all our sufferings are transformed.

At no time does Julian separate these two levels of the person into spiritual form and physical matter, good and bad, pure and sinful, but rather she understands them as a double awareness of God's creative life in us, working in different ways. She sees them as "all one love," flowing from God. And because of this one love informing our whole person, the Lord will forgive us and bring us to the fullness of our highest nature, "turning all our blame into endless honor" (52:81–83.293).

> And thus I saw that he wills that we know he takes no harder the fall of any creature who shall be saved than he took the falling of Adam, who we know was endlessly loved and sekerly kept in the time of all his need, and now is blissfully restored in high, transcen-

dent joys. For our lord God is so good, so gentle, and so courteous that he may never assign fault to someone in whom he shall be ever blessed and praised. (53:1–6.293)

Acceptance

Gradually, Julian must have come to realize that her unanswered question (*How does God behold us in our sin?*) could not be answered. It was the wrong question. What she was really asking God was: *Do you still love us in spite of our sin?* Yet this, too, was the wrong question. It assumed God could "see" sin in humankind and could choose to forgive or not to forgive, depending on individual circumstances, like a soul's level of contrition. She understood that not only is God's merciful love for us unchanging, but when God "looks" at humanity, God sees only Christ on the cross and all those who sin and suffer as bleeding in the wounds of his dearworthy Son. And God can only love.

The Father wishes to raise us up as he did his only Son because each one of us is as precious to him as Jesus Christ. It is *we* who have such monumental trouble believing this, and for good reason. We view only the catastrophic results of our failures within ourselves, our relationships, and throughout the world. Like the servant lying face down in the ditch, we feel mired forever in our own mess. We do not see *Christ* in ourselves, or in the "other." Until we do, we will not begin to fathom the incomprehensible breadth and length and height and depth of the love of God which is in Christ Jesus. And in us.

After an intense period of crying out for light and confirmation, praying for an answer, Julian's questions began to fall away. There was nothing for her to do but drop into the vast abyss of unknowing: *I can not know, I may not know, I do not know, I shall not know.* But by then, Julian was living so deeply embedded in the depth of Divine Love, in the ground of God's being within her soul, that she did not *need* to know or understand anymore. She knew only that *God knows.*

20
The Godly Will

> And in this [*exemplum*] that I have now said was my desire in part answered, and my great fear somewhat eased, by the lovely gracious shewing of our lord God. *In which shewing I saw and understood full sekerly that in each soul that shall be saved is a godly will that never assented to sin, nor never shall.* Which will is so good that it may never will evil, but evermore continually it wills good and werks good in the sight of God. Therefore our lord wills we know it in the faith and in the belief, and specifically and truly that we have all this blessed will whole and safe in our lord Jesus Christ. (53:7–14.293, italics added)

Julian admits that the answer to her question (How does God "behold us in our sinne?") was only a partial one. But her gradual understanding of the parable alleviated "somewhat" her desperation and her great fear. The *shewing* revealed that in every soul that will be saved there is a "godly will," flooded with sanctifying grace, that never completely assents to sin. It desires only the good and does only good works in the sight of God. It prays the great petition in the Lord's prayer: "Thy will be done, on earth as it is in heaven." Julian is certain that God wants us to believe, as an actual tenet of faith, that by this "godly will," souls are kept "whole and safe" in Jesus Christ (53.12–14.293). She declares that every soul that reaches heaven has been necessarily "knit and oned" into God, as a result of God's own *rightfullehede* (53.14–17.293). The soul's essential substance could never have been separated from God at any time. And this is according to God's "own good will in his endless foreseeing purpose" (53:17.293).

Existential Union

At creation, human beings are intertwined into an existential union with God which is beyond the will of any man or woman to deny or destroy. It is a union between Creator and creature that takes place in the very core of the person, initiating and sustaining life. It is a union that no amount of human sinfulness can break. It is the very fact that *we exist.*

Orthodox theology teaches that the *image* of God in the soul can never be erased, even though the *likeness* to God has been deeply tarnished by original and personal sin. In her intuition of the "godly will," Julian is using an original term to describe just this: that the spiritual powers of the soul (reason, memory, and will) are holy, given to us by God, and therefore, *godly.* We may use our reason to think negative thoughts, our memory to harbor jealousy, anger, and revenge, our will to make wrong choices. Even so, our sinful thoughts and actions do not make the soul's powers, in and of themselves, evil. (Most theologians consider that no human person ever deliberately chooses evil, since even the most hardened criminal thinks he or she is choosing something good that will satisfy his desire, even though that "good" is a harmful lie masquerading as something desirable. Our worst sin is therefore our "blindness" to the true good. In addition, human beings cannot fully *assent* to sin because we are not pure intelligences, like angels.) Yet because of our strong tendency to misuse our soul's powers, Julian understands that Christ's redemption of mankind was necessary to liberate us from the distorting influence of evil.

God's Eternal Love

> For I saw that God never began to love mankind. For just as mankind will be in endless bliss, fulfilling the joy of God (with respect to his werks), just so has that same mankind, in the foresight of God, been known and loved from without beginning in his righteous intent. And by the endless intent and assent and the full accord of all the trinity, the mid-person [Christ] would become the ground and head of this fair nature out of whom we are all come, in whom we are all enclosed, into whom we shall go, finding in him our full heaven in everlasting joy, by the foreseeing purpose of all the blessed trinity from without beginning. (53:21–29.295)

Julian's ecstatic summary of salvation history echoes through the ages. God is Love. He never "began" to love us. He has always loved all human beings, "from without beginning," for they are his own creation. And love is the only answer to *why* anything exists at all. And so, by the will of the Father, the assent of the Son, and the full agreement of the Holy Spirit, the "mid-person" (Julian's particular name for Jesus Christ) was ordained to become the ground of human nature "from without beginning." In due course, he would be born as a human being in every respect except sin. And it would be out of Christ that we, in turn, would be born anew, in whom we would be enclosed, and into whom we would go. Likewise, St. Paul had written of Christ:

> He is the image of the invisible God, the firstborn of all creation; for in him all things in heaven and on earth were created, things visible and invisible, whether thrones or dominions or rulers or powers—all things have been created through him and for him. He himself is before all things, and in him all things hold together. (Col 1:15–17)

It would be in Christ that we would find our heaven (as Julian herself chose him to be, during her vision of his passion). And by rebirth through Christ, all humankind would arise out of the "foreseeing purpose" of the Blessed Trinity. Julian does not issue any caveats here about who shall or shall not be saved. On the contrary, she cites God's prescient love that came to earth in the form of the Savior as the most compelling reason to believe that "mankind will be in endless bliss."

> For before he made us he loved us, and when we were made we loved him. And this is a love made of the natural and essential goodness of the holy ghost, mighty by reason of the might of the father, wise in mind by the wisdom of the son. And thus is man's soul made of God, and in the same point knit to God. (53:30–33.295)

Jeremiah wrote: "I have loved you with an everlasting love; therefore I have continued my faithfulness to you" (Jer 31:3). Love creates us to be trinitarian, in its own image and likeness, filled with the potential to be strong in the Father's might, wise in the Son's wisdom, good in the love of the Holy Spirit. Even more daringly, Julian states that our souls are "made of God," who is unmade. In this sense, we are truly made of love, and at the moment the soul is created, in that same moment Divine Love "knits it to God" forever.

The Soul

> And thus I understood that man's soul is made of nothing. That is to say, it is created, but of nothing that is made, as thus: when God would make man's body, he took the slime of the earth, which is a matter mixed and gathered from all bodily things, and thereof he made man's body. But to the making of man's soul he would take nothing at all, but made it. And thus is the [created] nature rightfully made united to the maker who is essential nature uncreated, that is God. And therefore it is that there may nor shall be truly nothing at all between God and man's soul. (53:34–40.295)

What *is* the soul that God creates? According to the Genesis story of creation, God said, "Let us make humankind in our image, according to our likeness" (Gn 1:26). Since God has no body, the image and the likeness must be a *spiritual reality* created out of nothing. The idea of a soul connects the human inseparably to the divine, since it is precisely *the soul* that is made in the image and likeness of God. Since nothing at all can exist between God and the soul, Julian sees that, in the boundless love of God, the human soul is led and protected, from the moment of its creation, "and never shall be lost" (53:40–43.295). And this is the essential meaning of the extended Fourteenth Revelation.

> For he wills that we know that our soul is a life; which life, of his goodness and his grace, shall last in heaven without end, loving him, thanking him, praising him. (53:44–45.295)

And just as the soul will live forever, so "we were treasured in God and hidden, known and loved from without beginning" (53:46–47.295). The scriptural parable of the treasure hidden in a field for which a man will sell everything he owns in order to buy that field is suddenly reversed. *We* are the "treasure" hidden in the ground of God's love from all eternity. *We* are the food the Lord desires above all things. *We* are the reason God will sacrifice his only begotten Son to "buy back" our souls from the grip of evil.

Substance

> Wherefore, he wills that we know that the noblest thing that he ever made is mankind, and the fullest substance and the highest virtue is the blessed soul of Christ. And furthermore, he wills we know that this dearworthy soul was preciously knit to him in its making. Which knot is so subtle and so mighty that it is oned into God, in which oneing it is made endlessly holy. Furthermore, he wills we know that all the souls that shall be saved in heaven without end are knit in this knot, and oned in this oneing, and made holy in this holiness. (53:47–54.295)

Julian, like every theologian, struggled to find words worthy of characterizing the nature of Christ's human soul. She chose the word, "substance," to describe that aspect of Christ's soul that was most closely knit to God "in its making." Substance, as adopted from Aristotelian metaphysics by St. Thomas Aquinas, defines "what a thing is" in its own right, that is, its *nature*, such as a man, a dog, a tree, a rock. Substance is distinguished from the *accidents* of nature that can only exist *in* something else, such as quantity, quality, relation, time, place, and so forth. Julian was not a trained philosopher, but that does not mean she did not learn from university clerics who were. While we may think of substance as being something solid and "substantial," the word in medieval times carried no intrinsic connection with physical mass having matter, weight, dimension, extension, mobility. It was a metaphysical concept. Julian uses substance to mean non-material *essence*: that which makes something to be what it is. Since Christ, as Man, is the most perfect of all human beings, Julian extols his human soul as the "fullest substance and the highest virtue." Moreover, Christ's human substance was knit so intricately and so firmly into Divine Essence that it was made eternally holy.

Then Julian makes a stunning leap: *she extends this understanding of Christ's substance to include all of sanctified humanity.* "All the souls that shall be saved in heaven without end are knitted in this knot, and oned in this oneing and made holy in this holiness." We are partakers in Christ's holy human substance. It is *our* essential nature as well. It is the primal definition of our being. The divine act of creation makes every one of us exist and sustains us in existence. Without this unceasing creativity, we simply would not *be* at all. And because our human substance is designed on the pattern of Divine Reality, it is unstained by sin. "Substance" is Julian's term for what we are created to be: the perfect image and likeness of God, according to the prototype of Jesus Christ.

Julian goes even further. She dares to suggest that because of God's endless love for humanity, God does not make *any distinction* between "the blessed soul of Christ and the least soul that shall be saved" (54:1–3.297).

> For it is very easy to believe and trust that the wonning [home] of the blessed soul of Christ is very high in the glorious godhead. And truly, as I understood in our lord's meaning, *where the blessed soul of Christ is, there is the substance of all the souls that shall be saved by Christ.* Highly ought we to enjoy that God wonneth [lives] in our soul, and much more highly ought we to enjoy that our soul wonneth in God. (54:3–7.297, italics added)

Julian is certain that just as Christ's soul dwells high in the eternal Godhead, so every soul that is saved dwells there within him. (She uses the lovely Middle English word, *wonneth*, which implies the intimacy of dwelling in a home.) She attests that it is an exalted understanding to see and know mystically that the Creator lives in the soul. But it is an even more exalted understanding to see and know that the created soul, in its very essence, lives in God, its true home. By this substantial union with Christ in God, "we are what we are" (54:12.297). And in this lies the unfathomable dignity of human personhood. Julian attempts to describe this indwelling of God and the soul:

> And I saw *no difference* between God and our substance, but as it were all God. And yet my understanding accepted that our substance is *in* God; that is to say, that God is God and our substance is a creature in God. (54:13–15.297, italics added)

Nondualism?

While Julian is stretching the identity of God and the soul to the *nth* degree, she is extremely careful not to fall into a nondualist notion that God and the soul are the *same* substance without any distinction; that is, all one soul. Julian clearly distinguishes between God's *uncreated* substance (Divine Essence) and the human soul's *created* substance (human essence). She is mindful never to gloss over this crucial theological distinction, even in a mystical sense. Nonetheless, Julian admits that in her deep state of contemplation it was difficult for her to differentiate between God and the human soul.

> For the almighty truth of the trinity is our father, for he made us and keeps us in himself. And the deep wisdom of the trinity is our mother, in whom we are all enclosed. And the high goodness of the trinity is our lord, and in him we are enclosed and he in us. We are enclosed in the father, and we are enclosed in the son, and we are enclosed in the holy ghost. And the father is enclosed in us, the son is enclosed in us, and the holy ghost is enclosed in us: all might, all wisdom, and all goodness; one God, one lord. (54:15–21.297)

The sheer majesty of Julian's rhythmic phrases conveys her conviction that this sublime mutual indwelling is real. She became so absorbed in God that she experienced the truth of the Trinity as our own Father; the wisdom of the Trinity as our own Mother (an extraordinary statement which presages what is soon to come); and the goodness of the Trinity as the Lord himself, in whom "we are enclosed and he in us." She stresses again and again how intimately "enclosed" we are within Trinity: Father, Son, and Holy Ghost. This echoes her earlier experience of Christ as "our clothing, that for love wraps us and winds about us, embraces us and wholly encloses us, hanging about us for tender love, that he may never leave us" (5:3–5.139). And, at the same time, she bears witness that Trinity is "enclosed" within us. We carry the divine imprint of Trinity within our souls. Christ himself said to his disciples: "Abide in me as I abide in you. Just as the branch cannot bear fruit by itself unless it abides in the vine, neither can you unless you abide in me" (Jn 15:4). For Julian, this *oneing* of God and the soul is never indistinguishable identification. She is not the type of mystic who seeks to *dissolve* differences between Creator and created. Nevertheless, for Julian, this union of God and the soul is a mystical intimacy beyond description.

Faith

Still, the question arises: How is one to know that the soul's human substance is indeed grounded in God? In answer, Julian turns to examine faith. And for Julian, it is faith, and faith alone, that enables us to know our true origin, our true substance: who we are. She understands faith as flowing from our created substance into our sensual soul by the power of the Holy Spirit. She realizes that not only faith but all virtues come from the Spirit, and that without the Spirit's gifts no one receives any virtue. Faith, in fact, is the most exalted kind of understanding.

> For it [faith] is nothing else but a right understanding with true belief and seker trust within our being, that we are in God and he is in us, which we cannot see. (54:24–26.297)

Julian does not lay out doctrines (though she never denies that faith involves believing what the church teaches). Her concentration here is different. For her, faith is the secure trust that, within the ground of our being, the soul is in God and God is in the soul. It is an inspired understanding of all she has been discussing about our creation and redemption which, because of the blindness caused by sin, we are obviously unable to experience directly. Faith is precisely the *spiritual insight* that enables us to "know" what we cannot comprehend by human reasoning alone. Faith is essential to our self-awareness, lest we remain like the servant in the ditch, lying face down, moaning and groaning about our sufferings because we cannot turn our heads and behold the Lord's pity and compassion.

Sin has deprived humanity of the ability to "see" God, but faith appears as inner vision. As St. Paul has written: "Now faith is the assurance of things hoped for, the conviction of things *not* seen" (Heb 11:1, italics added). If we dare to believe, faith (along with all the other virtues that God grants the soul) "werks great things in us" (54:26–27.297). It is actually Christ who does the monumental work of mercy in the soul at all times, constantly reconciling us to himself. By his divine activity we are made able to see and understand more and more, through the gifts and virtues of the Holy Spirit. Julian identifies this inner working of the Lord as that which enables us to become "Christ's children and christian in living" (54:29.297). It is always and ever *Christ's* work in our souls, not our own.

Julian affirms that Christ is our way, continually leading us and teaching us by his laws. He delights in this work, as does his Father. She recalls the Ninth Revelation, in which she saw Christ bear all who are members of his Mystical Body into heaven, where he presents them to his Father, who receives these souls thankfully and then graciously returns them to his Son. "Which gift and werking is joy to the father, and bliss to the son, and liking to the holy ghost" (55:5–6.299). Of all the things that we are obliged to do in this life, we must give God the greatest pleasure by rejoicing in this joy.

> And notwithstanding all our feeling, woe or wele, God wills we understand and believe that we are more truly in heaven than on earth. (55:10–11.299)

What an astounding statement! Julian is certain that, because Christ has already saved us and incorporated us into his Mystical Body, our true lives are not here, in our mortal bodies, but in the joyful embrace of the Trinity. For Julian, we are more spiritual than fleshly, more at home in heaven than on earth.

She further describes faith as arising from "the natural love of our soul" for what is good, and from "the clear light of our reason," which enables us to think and inform the will in order to make good decisions, as well as from the "steadfast memory" that we have of God in our creation (55.11–13.299). We might consider faith as a sacred remembrance that never forgets where we have come from: God. It is a spiritual homesickness that longs to return where it belongs. Finally, Julian states that at the precise moment that "our soul is breathed into our body in which we are made sensual," immediately mercy and grace begin to work, "taking care of us and keeping us with pity and love" (55:13–15.299). By means of this work, the Holy Spirit nurtures in us the hope that our sensuality will "come again up above [and be united] to our substance" within the virtue of Jesus Christ and be brought to complete fulfillment (55:15–17.299).

Sensuality

Now we must examine what Julian means by the soul's *sensuality*. Again, careful definition is of the utmost importance. By sensuality, Julian does not mean our physical bodies, or human sexuality. Sensuality, for Julian, pertains to the sensual powers *of the soul*, what we might call our embodied mind, with its ability to experience a psycho-physical self in a world, along with our individual capacities to function in that world.[1]

As we have seen, Julian defines our soul's substance as made *ex nihilo*, that is, out of "nothing that is made" (53:35.295). Our physical body, on the other hand, is created from matter, as described in the Book of Genesis: "then the Lord God formed man from the dust of the ground, and breathed into his nostrils the breath of life; and the man became a living being" (Gn 2:7). Once the soul is "breathed" by God into flesh, it directs every aspect of the growth, functioning, and maintenance of our bodies. Sensuality is the soul's ability not only to be aware but to be aware of *something*; to perceive colors, shapes, sounds, smells, tastes, textures, pleasure, pain, and so forth and to label these sensations with words. Sensuality includes our mental consciousness of having flesh, blood, bone, muscle; of being a certain height and weight, using our limbs, being mobile, having certain physical characteristics and capabilities and the like. All these various sensations derive from the sensual (though still spiritual) powers of the soul. For Julian, our flesh-and-blood physicality in all its complex manifestations is the natural and inevitable extension of the sensuality of our soul.

The City of God

Julian explains that everything we experience as our individual selves flows from the soul's sensuality that is "grounded in nature, in mercy, and in grace" (55:18–19.299). And this ground of the soul enables us to receive all the divine gifts and graces that lead to everlasting life.

> For I saw full sekerly that our substance is in God. And also I saw that God is in our sensuality. For in the same moment that our soul is made sensual, *at the same moment exists the city of God*, ordained for him from without beginning; into which city he comes and never shall leave it. For God is never out of the soul, in which he shall dwell blissfully without end. (55:19–24.299, italics added)

Notably, Julian does not confine God's graced presence to the higher part of the soul, the substance. She finds God's presence within the totality of our sensuality as well. In fact, at the moment of our creation, when our soul is "given" its physical body, Julian understands that God enters the human person as into a holy city, in which he reigns, and from which he will never depart. She might well have been recalling the psalmist's image: "There is a river whose streams make glad the city of God, the holy habitation of the Most High. God is in the midst of the city; it shall not be moved; God will help it when the morning dawns" (Ps 46:4–5). Christ, dwelling in our souls as in his holy city, is the responsible caretaker of our lives. He holds within himself everything we require to reach both physical and spiritual maturity. Like a good parent, he waits to teach us until we are ready to learn. If we respond, he teaches us more. If we resist, he teaches us in another way. When the body is cast down, the powers of the soul help to lift it up. When the soul is heavy, the body finds means to reinvigorate the spirit. Both energies, of soul and body, emanate from the ground of the soul, its pure substance. And all activities of the soul are guided by Christ's working of mercy. This process of rising and falling and rising again is repeated over and over throughout our lives. And the tender love of Christ is as solicitous toward our ups and downs as is that of a loving mother. Christ's own Spirit, the Holy Ghost, gives us whatever we need to grow, as the boy Jesus grew, "in wisdom and in years, and in divine and human favor" (Lk 2:52). And the Spirit gives it exactly when, where, and in what way we most need it.

> And all the gifts that God may give to the creature he has given to his son Jesus for us. Which gifts he, wonning [dwelling] in us, has enclosed in himself until the time that we are waxen and grown, our soul with our body and our body with our soul, either of them taking help from the other until we are brought up into maturity, according to nature. And then, in the ground of being, with the werking of mercy, the holy ghost graciously breathes into us gifts leading to endless life. (55:26–31.299)

Original Sin?

As illuminating as is Julian's description of the soul as the city of God, conceivably one might question her lack of attention here to original sin. Julian never refers to Adam's sin as a stain on the soul which baptism must cleanse before God will "enter" it. Neither does she speak of God "quitting" the soul because of mortal sin. We must understand that Julian is writing here in *existential* terms. She is talking about the essential *ground* of our being. God does not create the substance or the sensuality of the soul in sin. What God creates is a perfect reflection of himself. And this is humanity's fundamental truth. The doctrine of original sin seeks to "explain" the ignorance and alienation of our current human condition. Experientially, we can confirm what sin feels like because we recognize our wrong choices and we suffer the results of personal and collective sinful behavior. But sin is *not* an essential component of our human nature. It can be and will be transformed by the sufferings of Christ on the cross into divine rewards, as Julian has already discussed.

But how can sin be transformed into something else? Isn't sin really "out there"? We have seen that, following the teachings of St. Augustine, sin was not considered to have any form of *real* existence. It was understood, theologically, as an "absence of good." Julian herself became aware that sin was "no deed" (11:17–18.163). In fact, if sin were self-existently "real" and able to exist on its own, *it could never be changed into something else.* If original sin or actual (personal) sins were an essential part of our nature, they could never be forgiven, never be purified, either by the sacrament of baptism or the sacrament of penance, and sinners could never be transformed into saints and *oned* into the Mystical Body of Christ.

According to Julian's ontology, sin does not arise from the soul's pure being, the substance. Sin arises from the soul's interactive *sensuality*, produced by deep conflicts within the human mind and will. Since it is produced in the mind, a sinful thought, image, or emotion can also be erased by deliberate virtuous thoughts of contrition, remorse, and a heartfelt desire to make amends. Where does the sin go? In God's mind, it never *really* was. On the other hand, twisted thoughts and emotions do produce harmful actions. And the consequences of these actions multiply and cause untold suffering in human lives. Yet even this suffering can be "turned into honors," as Christ revealed to Julian (39:32–33.241).

A Created Trinity

Julian affirms that she was led by God to see that the human soul is a created trinity (of reason, memory, and will) like the uncreated Blessed Trinity, "known and loved from without beginning, and in the creation, united to the maker, as it was said before" (55:33–35.299).[2] Julian remarks that this insight gave her much sweetness, peace, rest, security, and delight. And she realized further that, because the human soul is so intimately united to God, reflecting his own trinitarian powers, it was, indeed, absolutely necessary that humankind be redeemed from the "double death" of both body and soul. In a certain sense, God's own honor demanded it. But this restoring had to wait until the Son of God took on our sensuality in a physical body. As we have seen, according to medieval theology, Christ's perfect human substance had already been united to God in the "first creation," that is, at the very beginning of time (55:40.299). Then at the incarnation, Christ's human sensuality became enfleshed in the womb of Mary: "And the Word became flesh, and lived among us" (Jn 1:14). The Son of God became fully incarnate in both human substance *and* human sensuality.

> And these two parts were in Christ, the higher and the lower, who is but one soul. The higher part was ever in peace with God, in full joy and bliss. The lower part, which is sensuality, suffered for the salvation of mankind. (55:40–43.299–301)

Julian recalls that these two parts were seen and felt deeply by her in the Eighth Revelation, when she experienced the sufferings and the "mind of Christ's passion and his dying" (55:43–45.301). She ascribes her ability to remain focused on Christ's sufferings (rather than follow the temptation to raise her eyes toward heaven) to "a subtle feeling and secret inward sight" she was given of Christ's higher substance (55:45–46.301). In that timeless moment, she realized that the higher aspect of Christ's human soul (the substance) was "ever in peace with God" and could blissfully enjoy the fact of his own sufferings because of the glorious salvation they would effect. Meanwhile, "the lower part, which is sensuality," was suffering every conceivable pain for that same salvation. She understood that both aspects of Christ's human soul were, in fact, "one soul," as in every human person. And it was precisely from this powerful *double vision* of Christ's substance (which forever rejoices in the Trinity) and his sensuality (that suffered on the cross), that she derived her understanding of the two aspects of *every* human soul. As always, Julian's mystical theology pours forth from her Revelations, clarifying and elaborating what she had first seen "in a touch."

God and The Soul

> And thus I saw full sekerly that it is quicker for us and easier to come to the knowing of God than to know our own soul. For our soul is

> so deeply grounded in God, and so endlessly treasured, that we may not come to the knowing thereof until we first have knowing of God, who is the maker to whom it is oned. But notwithstanding, I saw that we have naturally, out of a desire for completion, to desire wisely and truly to know our own soul, whereby we may be taught to seek it where it is, and that is within God. And thus, by the gracious leading of the holy ghost, we shall know them both in one. (56:1–8.301)

Julian's words fly in the face of ancient and medieval wisdom that insisted we must know the human soul first before we can come to a knowledge of the divine. "Know thyself," Plato wrote. "Know God," Julian insists. She suggests that we will make more progress in the spiritual life by keeping our focus *on God* rather than on trying to understand the depths of our own souls. She writes that "God is nearer to us than our own soul" (56:9.301). Perhaps she was paraphrasing St. Augustine, who had written of God in his *Confessions*: "Thou wast more inward to me than the most inward part of me; and higher than my highest reach."[3]

At the same time, Julian is well aware that the human mind hungers and searches for knowledge of its own soul. She anticipates that eventually, in the same moment, we shall know God and the soul in one transcendent leap onto another plane of understanding. And whether we sink deeply into God or into our own soul, "it is both good and true" (56:8–9.301).

> For he [God] is the ground in whom our soul stands, and he is the intermediary who keeps the substance and the sensuality together, so that it shall never separate. For our soul sits in God in true rest, and our soul stands in God in seker strength, and our soul is naturally rooted in God in endless love. (56:9–13.301)

After considering both approaches, Julian concludes that since God is the very ground of our being, it stands to reason that we should seek knowledge of our soul not in ourselves but in God. Only in the contemplation of God can our soul find its rest, its strength, and become deeply rooted "in endless love." Therefore, we must seek our soul in God, "in whom it is enclosed" (56:14.301).

How are we to *experience* God in our soul? Julian asserts that there is no other method of union with Christ but by cultivating a great desire for God and enduring the slow process of purification. We must remain "in longing and in penance, until the time that we are led so deep into God that we verily and truly know our own soul" (56:22–24.301). She assures us that the Lord himself will lead us into this "hye depnesse," that is, the high ecstasy of deep contemplation (56:24–25.301). And he will do it "in the same love with which he made us, and in the same love with which he bought us, by mercy and grace, through the virtue of his blessed passion" (56:25–27.301).

Nature, Mercy, and Grace

Then, as if arguing with herself on parchment, Julian reverses her previous statement and writes that "we may never come to the full knowing of God until we first clearly know our own soul" (56:28–29.303). And this is because, until we achieve our full powers (when "our sensuality, by virtue of Christ's passion, is brought up into our substance"), our souls will not be "fully holy," and therefore not *capable* of perceiving God (56:29–32.303). Julian attributes her insight on this point to a "partial touching," or a direct inspiration of the Holy Ghost, that she received concerning the soul's nature; namely, that our reason is grounded in God "who is substantial kindhede [Ultimate Being]" (56:33–34.303).

> From this substantial kindhede, mercy and grace spring and spread into us, werking all things in the fulfilling of our joy. These are our ground, in which we have our being, our increase, and our fulfilling. For in nature we have our life and our being, and in mercy and grace we have our increase and our fulfilling. These are three properties in one goodness. And where one werks, all werk in the things which are now appropriate for us. (56:34–40.303)

Within the pure ground of our rational nature, mercy heals and grace flows, like divine waters, enabling our sensuality to increase and come to joy. We might think of our reason, along with mercy and grace, as a holy synergy that functions to bring us to completion. And all is from God's magnanimity. Would mercy and grace have been necessary to heal and guide our sensuality had we not fallen into sin? Julian does not consider this possibility. She deals only with what is: our broken nature that is in constant need of God's healing mercy and sanctifying grace. However, it is conceivable that the soul would always have had need of divine mercy and grace, even if there had been no sin, in order to bring it from an earthly paradise into the fullness of the beatific vision.

Julian stresses that God wants us to understand as much as we possibly can about these three properties (reason, mercy, and grace) because such clarity of understanding is the beginning of our eternal joy and bliss. We should develop knowledge of the depths of our souls while we are here on earth. Yet she warns that by using our reasoning powers alone we cannot come to this knowledge; only reason combined with memory and love can enable us to do so. Julian is clear that we cannot consider ourselves to be saved simply because our substance is grounded in God by our creation. We also need the constant outpouring of mercy and grace into our sensual souls to attain salvation.

Yet again, Julian extols the essential goodness with which God fills us in the initial creation of our substance. But he wills that we be made sensual as well, and so it is that these two "parts" of the soul must be united by the working of God's mercy and grace. Our being fashioned "double" was not an accident, a mistake, or an afterthought. Our dual human nature is exactly what God intended to create: "his foreseeing purpose in his endless wisdom willed that we were made double" (56.50–51.303). Indeed, Julian's perception that the powers of the soul are double (substance and sensuality) might well have developed from her insight into the parable: that the nature of the lord in the *exemplum* was double, and the nature of the servant was double, too.[4] And Christ is double, having both divine and human natures united in one Person.

At this point, Julian's hope-filled view of human nature bursts out. She declares that in the creation of our pure substance, God made us "so noble and so rich that always we werk his will and his worship" (57:1–2.303). She specifies here that she is referring to "man[kind] that shall be saved" (57:2–3.303). She is simply unable to consider any souls except those who *will* be saved.

> For truly I saw that we are those whom he loves, and we do what he likes constantly without any ceasing. And from this great richness and this high nobility [of our substance], proportionate virtues come into our soul, at the time that it is knit to our body, in which

> knitting we are made sensual. And thus in our substance we are full and in our sensuality we fail; which failing God will restore and fulfill by the werking of mercy and grace, plenteously flowing into us because of his own natural goodness. (57:3–8.303)

Our Lady, Our Mother

If Christ is the perfect man, enclosing all of humanity within himself, then Mary, his mother, is also our mother as well, enclosing all of us as her children. It is by her that we are "born in Christ. For she who is mother of our savior is mother of all who are saved in our savior" (57:40–42.305). This maternal thought leads Julian to yet another, more startling, truth, one that will seriously affect the direction of her text:

> And *our savior is our very mother*, in whom we are endlessly born and never shall come out of him. Plenteously, fully, and sweetly was this shewn; and it is spoken of in the first revelation, where it said: "We be all in him beclosed." (57:42–44.305, italics added)

Julian realized that, even more than Mary, *Christ* is our true Mother, who ceaselessly gives birth to us and yet never allows us to "come out of him." This mystical awareness was part of the very first *shewing* Julian received, when she understood how intimately and tenderly we are protected in the maternal "womb" of God. It is only now that she will attempt to elaborate its import. The Motherhood of God will become one of Julian's most profound teachings. Aspects of it appear in all of Julian's Revelations, in the tenderness and solicitousness, pity and compassion that Christ shows towards souls. However, as with the parable of the lord and the servant, not until Julian had contemplated the Revelation of God's Motherhood for a long time could she dare to elaborate on its significance.

Julian's Method

At this point, we may feel inclined to ask the question: *How did Julian know what she knew?* How did she then manage to develop a mystical theology unlike any other in the medieval world? The answer can only be: first, from the life-altering experience of the Revelations themselves; and second, from the continuing teachings she received both at the time of the *shewings* and through the years following, as she herself has stated. In other words, *through the art of contemplation*. Being alone in silence with God must have been, for Julian, as essential to her life as breathing.

Every day, she left the myriad thoughts, activities, emotional upheavals, family and business responsibilities that were hers for a period of time alone in silence and in stillness. She followed the Lord's own prescription: "But whenever you pray, go into your room and shut the door and pray to your Father who is in secret; and your Father who sees in secret will reward you" (Mt 6:6). Perhaps she took refuge in the bedchamber of her house, during the 1370s, 1380s, and early 1390s. (After that, she chose the complete privacy of the anchorage.) She would withdraw from the bustling, noisy world around her, the rattle of wagons of commerce on the street, the press of daily duties. She would sit with her eyes closed, body unmoving. She would meditate on a phrase she had memorized from one of the gospels or the psalms, or on a thought that had arisen, or on one aspect of her visions and locutions, turning it over and over in her mind, like the Blessed Mother herself: "Mary treasured all these words and pondered them in her heart" (Lk 2:19). In the course of these prayerful meditations, Julian would reach a point beyond which analysis could not go. Then the thoughts, as well as the images, words, and feelings attached to those thoughts, would drop away. Her awareness of sensory stimuli would become distant and faint, like a cacophony of voices disappearing beneath a vast and open field of pure consciousness.

As her powers of single-pointed focus developed, she was able to expand this inner field of her mind almost to infinity. And when she saw "in a point," it was a sudden moment of boundless joy and "hye depnesse," so pure and unalloyed by sensory distraction that she knew it came directly from God. For a long time, she would rest in the still, empty space of her mind, where the Lord "sat" on the ground of her being, as in his "holy city," in perfect peace. She would remain perfectly silent, enjoying the presence of her hidden God. Such stillness taught her to see interiorly, to hear spiritually, to understand with her heart. And when she emerged from such contemplation, she knew what she must write.

21
The Motherhood of God

It seems inevitable that Julian's desire to fathom the unconditional love and compassion of Christ on the cross, as well as of the lord and the suffering servant in the parable, would lead her to ask the question: *Do I know what such love is like?* She would discover the answer within the most elemental experience of her life: her own motherhood.

Christian tradition has consistently viewed God as the eternal Father, the all-powerful Creator, as well as the Divine Judge. Christ spoke repeatedly of "my Father in heaven" (Mt 12:50, 18:35). As we saw in Part One, the first estate (the hierarchy of the Catholic Church, from the pope down to the poorest deacon) was, and always had been, exclusively male. The second estate of emperors, kings, aristocracy, lords, and knights at all levels bequeathed their estates to the eldest male heirs, lest they be forfeit or ruled over by a surviving female who would not be able to defend them effectively. The entire feudal structure of the Middle Ages was built upon the undisputed foundation of the male as superior to the female in every way. Any publicly preached theology that presented God as *maternal*, or taught that there could be "feminine" qualities manifested by Divine Nature, might challenge this concept of human male dominance and cause great confusion in the minds of *evencristens.*

The Wisdom Tradition

It was not always so. The Greek word for wisdom is *sophia*, a feminine noun. And in the Old Testament, the Hebrew word for Divine Wisdom (*Hochma*) is also feminine. In the Book of Proverbs, the female principle of Wisdom was created before anything else (Prv 8:22–23), and it was by Wisdom that the earth was formed (Prv 3:19). In the Book of Wisdom the qualities of *Sophia* are countless and sublime: "For she is a breath of the power of God, and a pure emanation of the glory of the Almighty; therefore nothing defiled gains entrance into her. For she is a reflection of eternal light, a spotless mirror of the working of God, and an image of his goodness" (Ws 7:25–26). *Sophia/Hochma* is the nurturing Mother figure: "All good things came to me along with her, and in her hands uncounted wealth" (Ws 7:11). Isaiah also suggests that Jehovah is Divine Mother: "Can a woman forget her nursing child, or show no compassion for the child of her womb? Even these may forget, yet I will not forget you" (Is 49:15).

Following in the Wisdom tradition, St. Paul wrote of Christ as "the wisdom of God" (1 Cor 1:24). The letter to the Ephesians spoke of the church as the allegorical "bride of Christ," for which he sacrificed himself (Eph 5:21–33). The church was also understood to act like a mother to Christ's children, rearing them in the teachings and dispensing the abundant graces he earned from his sacrifice on the cross. In the eleventh century, St. Anselm's "Prayer to St. Paul," considered Christ as a mother who, during his passion, suffered an agonized labor to bring forth his children:

> And you, Jesus, are you not also a mother?
> Are you not the mother who, like a hen,
> Gathers her chickens under her wings?
> Truly, Lord, you are a mother;
> For both they who are in labour
> And they who are brought forth
> Are accepted by you.
> You have died more than they, that they may labour to bear.
> It is by your death that they have been born,
> For if you had not been in labour,
> You could not have borne death;
> And if you had not died, you would not have brought forth.[1]

In the twelfth century, Cistercian monks like Bernard of Clairvaux, William of St. Thierry, and Aelred of Rievaulx used maternal analogies to suggest Christ's compassion and spiritual nourishing as well as the intimate bond between the human soul and God. The scholastic writers of the twelfth and thirteenth centuries, from Peter Lombard and Abelard to St. Albert the Great, St. Thomas Aquinas, and St. Bonaventure employed maternal imagery to describe the

Creator, the Wisdom of Christ, or the Holy Spirit.[2] Meanwhile, the early thirteenth-century *Ancrene Riwle*, composed for anchoresses following a solitary life of prayer, portrayed Jesus as the kindly Mother who plays hide-and-seek games with his children, testing them that they might not become proud, but know their own infirmity and weakness.[3] In the late thirteenth century, the visionary nuns of Helfta (Mechthild of Hackeborn, Mechthild of Magdeburg, and St. Gertrude the Great) described divine motherhood as being expressive of authority, glory, justice, even stern disciplinary action, as well as merciful love.[4] In the early fourteenth century, Richard Rolle, in his lengthy Latin commentary on the first verse of the Song of Songs, depicted Christ's breasts as full of the spiritual milk of maternal love.[5] And Julian's contemporaries, Brigit of Sweden (1303–1373) and Catherine of Siena (1347–1380), both used tender and protective maternal images for God. Therefore, by Julian's time there already existed a long and varied tradition of monks, scholastics, nuns, and visionary laywomen who referred to Wisdom, God, and Christ as generative and self-sacrificing, unconditionally loving, and spiritually nourishing.[6] And this was described in maternal, though clearly *metaphorical*, terms.

God, Our Mother

However, to define Jesus Christ as being *truly* our Mother, as fully as God is our Father; to make God's Motherhood an indispensable cornerstone of her trinitarian theology; and to convey this theology directly to uneducated *evencristens* in the vernacular... these were Julian's unique contributions to the tradition. We do not know whether Julian ever read or heard sermons preached on the Wisdom literature, or if she even knew about the Latin tradition of monastic, scholastic, and continental writings that imaged God as a Mother. It seems highly unlikely. We do know that, in the course of writing her Revelations, she came to realize that since the Second Person of the Trinity *gives birth* to the entire creation ("for in him all things in heaven and on earth were created, things visible and invisible, whether thrones or dominions or rulers or powers—all things have been created through him and for him" Col 1:16), *then Christ must be our essential and truest Mother.* Julian centers her maternal theology entirely within the Trinity, in the ongoing act of creation, and in the divine process of *oneing.*

> God, the blessed trinity, who is everlasting being, truly as he is endless from without beginning, so truly was it his endless purpose to make mankind; which fair human nature was first assigned to his own son, the second person. And when he wished, by full accord of all the trinity, he made us all at once. And in our making he knit us and oned us to himself, by which oneing we are kept as clean and as noble as we were made. (58:1–6.307)

Julian proclaims again that it was God's purpose from all eternity to create humanity, with Christ, the God-man, as its prototype. In Christ, God-in-Trinity created everyone and everything "all at once," in an instant. This is because God acts in eternity, beyond time, space, or sequence. (It is we mortals, bound by our limited knowledge, who see everything occurring in time, space, and causal progression.) In our individual creations we are knitted and *oned* to Christ, by which our "godly will" is kept forever pure. Julian adds that by the virtue of this precious *oneing*, "we love our maker and like him, praise him and thank him and endlessly take great joy in him" (58:6–8.307).

> And thus in our creation God almighty is our natural father, and *God all wisdom is our natural mother*, with the love and the goodness of the holy ghost, who is all one God, one lord. And in the knitting and in the oneing he is our very true spouse, and we are his beloved wife and his fair maiden, with which wife he was never displeased. For he says: "I love thee and thou lovest me, and our love shall never be separated in two." (58:9–14.307, italics added)

Unlike her predecessors, Julian does not treat God's Motherhood merely as a *metaphor* for divine wisdom, kindness, compassion, authority, or justice. Neither does she speak of God's maternity as an apt *simile*, inferring that Christ is "like" an earthly mother. She considers the Motherhood of the Son of God as perfectly equal to the Fatherhood: *existentially*, God *is* our Mother as truly as God *is* our Father. In fact, God's Motherhood is not a metaphor at all. For Julian, it is divine Revelation.

Theological Risk

One cannot underestimate the theological risk that Julian took, as an uneducated layperson, in developing a theology of the Motherhood of God. She stretched the maternal analogy far beyond the earlier monastic and devotional traditions. To her way of thinking, there is absolutely no reason why God is not *equally* Father and Mother. By the knitting and *oneing* to humanity that is effected through the incarnation, Christ becomes our true Spouse, and we, his beloved wife (not to mention his dearest children, as we shall see). In the course of her exposition, Julian will have no qualms about interchanging gender references for Christ, referring to him repeatedly as "our mother" and then, in the same sentence, using the pronoun, "he." Julian's creative use of language enables her to consider Christ "double," just as she learned to see the lord and the servant "double." Christ is *both* our Mother and our Spouse (although Julian never mentions experiencing a mystical "espousal," as do Catherine of Siena and Margery Kempe). Likewise, all of humanity is his "beloved wife" and "fair maiden." And the human wife is assured that this Spouse is "never displeased." This is an especially revealing comment, given the strong possibility that Julian may have felt her own husband's displeasure. (We must never forget that Julian is writing as a flesh-and-blood woman with a personal history. In this implied contrast of Christ-as-Spouse with an earthly husband, she may be hinting at painful memories.) Whether considering Christ as Mother or Christ as Spouse, Julian attests that the words said to the human soul at its creation are the same: "I love you. And you love me. And nothing can break that love." She strongly implies: *not even sin.*

Three Aspects of Trinity

As Julian contemplates the glorious working of the Blessed Trinity, she distinguishes three "properties" or aspects:

> . . . the property of the fatherhood, and the property of the motherhood, and the property of the lordhead in one God. In our father almighty we have our keeping [protecting] and our blessing, as regards our natural substance, which is given to us by our creation from without beginning. And in the second person, in knowledge and wisdom, we have our keeping, as regards our sensuality, our restoration, and our salvation. *For he is our mother, brother and savior.* And in our good lord the holy ghost we have our rewarding and our payment for our living and our travail, and endlessly overpassing [transcending] all that we desire in his marvelous courtesy from his high, plenteous grace. (58:16–24.307, italics added)

Of course, there is no "division of labor" in the Trinity; God is One and acts as One. But Julian realizes that the only way she (and her readers) can possibly appreciate the Three Persons of the Trinity is by attributing a different work to each of them (creation, redemption, and sanctification), according to the classic theological division. But Julian goes even further. She ascribes the creation, protecting, and blessing of our *substance* to the Father; the protecting, restoration and the salvation of our *sensuality* to the Son; and the abundant rewarding and eternal payment for our faithful *living and laboring* to the Holy Ghost. She incorporates her theology of the substance and sensuality of the soul, as well as the recompense for our earthly labors (which she saw distinctly in her Revelations), into the three Divine Persons.

Julian summarizes what she has previously explicated. She sees that "all our life is in three" (58:25.307). First, we exist because of our substantial nature; then we increase and grow through the working of mercy; and finally, we experience our fulfillment as a result of grace. Then she introduces another, even more fundamental, reality: "the high might of the trinity is our father, the deep wisdom of the trinity is our mother, and the great love of the trinity is our lord" (58:28–29.307). Julian is certain that we receive this might, wisdom, and love in the creation of our substantial nature. Additionally, she states that the Second Person of the Trinity, "who is our mother substantially," has become, by virtue of the incarnation, "our mother *sensually*" (58:30–32.307, italics added). Christ, as God, created our soul's essence; Christ, as man, gave birth to our soul's sensuality. Therefore, our Divine Mother is our truest, most physical, *human* mother as well.

> For we are double from God's creation: that is to say, substantial and sensual. Our substance is the higher part, which we have in our father God almighty. And the second person of the trinity is our mother in nature in our substantial making, in whom we are grounded and rooted, and he is our mother of mercy by taking our sensuality. (58:32–36.307–9)

Christ our Mother works in many ways in our souls, yet keeping the different aspects (nature, mercy, and grace) undivided. By his creative motherhood, we gain great profit and achieve every aspect of human growth. In his mercy, he reforms and restores us. And through his passion, death and resurrection, he "oneth us to our substance," that is, he raises our fallen sensuality to the level of our higher nature (58.39–40.309). This is the sanctifying work Christ does for "all his beloved children who are compliant and obedient to him" (58.40–41.309). And the grace of the Holy Spirit works in tandem with Christ's mercy in two ways: rewarding us with truth for having travailed and giving us gifts of grace out of his courtesy, gifts that far exceed anything we could possibly deserve.

Julian further clarifies that "our substance is in our father, God almighty, and our substance is in our mother, God all wisdom, and our substance is in our lord God the holy ghost, all goodness" (58:50–52.309). But our *sensuality* is only in the Second Person, Jesus Christ, who became man, within whom is also the Father and the Holy Ghost.

> And in him and by him we are mightily taken out of hell and out of the wretchedness on earth, and honorably brought up into heaven, and blissfully united to our substance, increased in riches and nobility by all the virtue of Christ, and by the grace and werking of the holy ghost. (58:54–57.309)

The Catalyst

Having established the Motherhood of the Second Person of the Blessed Trinity, Julian now examines the astonishing fact that sin, for all the suffering it brings, was the catalyst for our salvation, without which we might never have had "all this bliss we have by mercy and grace" (59:1.309). She cannot explain *why* evil entered the world (any more than she can explain why the servant fell into the ditch). She can only suggest that it was "suffered" (that is, permitted) to rise in opposition to goodness, even as Christ's mercy and grace fought against wickedness, "and turned all to goodness and honor for all that shall be saved" (59:3–6.309).

> Thus Jesus Christ, who does good against evil, *is our very mother*: we have our being from him, where the ground of motherhood begins, with all the sweet keeping of love that endlessly follows. (59:6–9.309, italics added)

For Julian, Christ is the only *true* mother who fights against evil and turns it to good for his children's sake. Divine Motherhood is the prototype for the highest characteristics of human motherhood, not the other way around. As the best of all mothers, Christ's sweet protection follows us all our lives.

I It Am: Mother

> As truly as God is our father, as truly is God our mother. And that he shewed in all the revelations, and namely in these sweet words where he said: "I it am." That is to say: "I it am, the might and the goodness of the fatherhood. I it am, the wisdom and the kindness of motherhood. I it am, the light and the grace that is all blessed love. I it am, the trinity. I it am, the unity. I it am, the high sovereign goodness of all manner of thing. I it am that maketh thee to love. I it am that maketh thee to long. I it am, the endless fulfilling of all true desires." (59:10–16.309–11)

Julian declares that all the Revelations bore witness to God's Motherhood being equal to the Fatherhood, most especially, when Christ said: "I it am" in the Twelfth Revelation. Now Julian adds to the previous litany of meanings that she intuited from Christ's words. She writes an outpouring song of the Divine "I AM." Whatever is good, Christ is that. And because Christ is all that is good, he *is* Motherhood itself, in its myriad aspects of wisdom, kindness, light, and love. Where Christ is, there is Trinity, unity, the highest good in everything. Most personally, Christ's Motherhood teaches Julian herself to love and to long, and then fulfills all her truest desires. (It also enabled her to become a mother.) Julian adds that the soul's substantial being, which is so high and noble and honorable when considered on its own, is extremely low, meek, and mild before the majesty of Christ's united divine and human natures.

The Father, "who is being," knew and loved us from before time began (59:20–21.311). And out of this wisdom and love, in union with the whole Trinity, the Father ordained that the second person should become "our mother, our brother, and our savior" (59:21–23.311).

> Our father wills, our mother werks, our good lord the holy ghost strengthens. And therefore it belongs to us to love our God in whom we have our being, reverently thanking and praising him for our creation, mightily praying to our mother for mercy and pity, and to our lord the holy ghost for help and grace. (59:24–28.311)

Julian sees that in these three, Father, Mother, and Holy Spirit, "is all our life: nature, mercy, and grace..." (59:29.311). And from these three, we receive the virtues of meekness, mildness, patience, and pity, all conducive to living a holy life. We also learn to hate sin and wickedness, which we need to do if we would be virtuous. Julian clarifies that Jesus is the true Mother of our *original* human nature through the creation. Jesus is also the true Mother of our *restored* human nature through the incarnation, when he took on our humanity and suffered his passion and death.

> All the fair werking and all the sweet natural function of dearworthy motherhood is appropriated to the second person. For in him we have this godly will, whole and safe without end, both in nature and in grace, from his own proper goodness. (59:33–36.311)

Julian understands three ways of beholding Motherhood in God: first, in the ground of our human creation when God gave us birth; second, in the assuming of our sensual human nature when Christ begins his "motherhood of grace"; and third, in the "motherhood of werking," by which grace spreads itself abroad "in length and breadth, in height and in depnesse," covering everything that is, without end (59:39–41.311). And these various manifestations of God's motherly love are *all one love.*

A Mother's Love

Julian feels compelled to explain how we are brought back "by the motherhood of mercy and grace" into our pristine natural state, in which we were first created "by the motherhood of essential love," a love that never leaves us (60:3–4.311). Christ, Mother of our nature and Mother of grace, wanted to become our Mother in all things. He chose as the ground of his divine work the humble and gentle womb of the maiden. Julian comments that she saw this in the First Revelation, when Mary was revealed to the eye of her mind "in the simple stature that she had when she conceived" (60:7–9.313). Stunningly, Julian interprets the fact of the incarnation as the maternal desire of the most exalted Wisdom of God *to become our Mother in physical form.* Christ arrayed and prepared himself in our poor flesh in the maiden's womb precisely so that he could "do the service and the office of motherhood in all thing" (60:10–11.313).

One is reminded of Christ's words: "Let the little children come to me, and do not stop them; for it is to such as these that the kingdom of heaven belongs" (Mt 19:14, Mk 10:14, Lk 18:16–17). And again, at the Last Supper, Christ took a towel, wrapped it around his waist, knelt down and washed the feet of his disciples, as a slave, a servant, or *a mother* might do (Jn 13:3–5). Time and again, we see Christ acting as a mother to his disciples, to the sick, the sinner, the outcast, the dying. And when he wept over the city of Jerusalem, he ached with a mother's heart: "Jerusalem, Jerusalem . . . How often have I desired to gather your children together as a hen gathers her brood under her wings, and you were not willing!" (Mt 23:37). Julian understood this maternal aspect in Christ because she recognized it within herself.

> The mother's service is nearest, rediest, and sekerest: nearest, for it is most natural; rediest, for it is most loving; and sekerest, for it is truest. This office might not nor could ever be performed to the fullest except by him [Christ] alone. (60:12–14.313)

Here, Julian shows her easy familiarity with the role of mothering, and how Christ's own maternal care is the paradigm for all earthly mothers, nurturers, and caregivers. In trinitarian fashion, she considers a mother's service as most *natural* because it begins at the moment of conception and continues on long after birth; most *accessible*, for it is the continual presence of loving care and devotion; and (using one of her favorite words) *sekerest* because it is the most reliable, stable, and unconditional.

Yet, after this paean of praise to an earthly mother's love, Julian issues a caveat: "All our mothers here bear us into pain and into dying. Ah, what is that?" (60:15–16.313). It seems a harsh reflection on human motherhood and a sudden turnaround. But is it not true? We are born in pain, and we suffer and die in pain. No earthly mother, not even the Blessed Mother herself, no matter how boundless the love in her heart for her offspring, can prevent her child from suffering and dying. That is the greatest cause of Julian's own sadness. Having labored painfully to bring her own children into the world, and then having endured the agony of losing at least one, and perhaps two, of them during separate cycles of the plague, she was well aware of her total helplessness to save them.

> But our true mother Jesus, he alone bears us to joy and to endless living—blessed may he be! Thus he sustains us within himself in love, and travailed until the full time that he would suffer the sharpest birth pangs and the most grievous pains that ever were or ever shall be, and died at the last. (60:17–19.313)

Julian envisions Christ as a mother, large with child, carrying us in his womb during his life on earth. And then, at the time of his passion and death on the cross, he goes into excruciating physical labor and suffers birth pangs more terrible than any woman could ever undergo. And then he dies in childbirth. Yet how many women whom Julian had known had *also* died in childbirth, while giving life to their children? It is an analogy that tears at her heart. Then she adds that even when Christ had completed the labor of the crucifixion, he wanted to do still more for his children.

> And when he had died and so born us to bliss, yet all this still could not make enough satisfaction for his marvelous love. And that he shewed in these high, overpassing words of love: "If I might suffer more, I would suffer more." He might not die any more, but he would not stop werking. Wherefore it behooves him to feed us, for the dearworthy love of motherhood has made him our debtor. (60:19–24.313)

Julian recalls the words Christ spoke in the Ninth Revelation and relates them now to what a mother is willing to do for her child, not only at birth, but all through its lifetime. "If only" she could do more. "If only" she had done something differently. "If only" she could keep on working for her child's benefit, forever and ever. Julian so identifies with Christ's feeling of never being able to do *enough* for his children that she is absolutely certain that Christ our Mother could never stop working to help us. In fact, even after he has died to give us birth, he must continue to feed us, as a mother feeds her child in countless ways throughout the years. And this is because, once Christ has birthed us on the cross, he is fully responsible for us forever.

Nurturing

> A mother may give her child her milk to suck. But our precious mother Jesus, he may feed us with himself, and does so most cour-

> teously and most tenderly with the blessed sacrament that is the precious food of true life. And with all the sweet sacraments he sustains us most mercifully and graciously. And so he meant in these blessed words where he said: "I it am that holy church preacheth [to] thee and teacheth thee." That is to say: "All the health and life of the sacraments, all the virtue and grace of my word, all the goodness that is ordained by holy church to thee, I it am." (60:25–32.313)

Most revealingly, Julian considers Christ as a *nursing* Mother. As we saw in Part One, according to medieval medicine, the mother's blood that had nurtured the child in utero was transformed into milk by the very act of nursing. Julian comments that while an earthly mother gives her child milk to drink, our Mother Christ gives her children his own body and blood in the precious food of the sacrament of Eucharist, and nurtures them through all the other sacraments as well. The entire work of the church is actually the work of Mother Christ. Preaching, teaching, and blessing, Christ tends to his children, sustaining and increasing their health, life, virtue, and grace.

The medieval church was greatly criticized for its excessive power, wealth, ecclesiastical crimes and excesses as well as the apparent lack of holiness in many of its members. But for Julian, regardless of its egregious failures, the church was still and always the Mystical Body of Christ; the teacher of faith, doctrines, and traditions since apostolic times; the liturgical life of the seven sacraments; the hierarchy of pope, bishops, priests, and the entire community of believers; the sacred repository of graces that Christ gained for all humankind on the cross, watched over and protected by the power of the Holy Spirit. Julian loved the church "just as Christ loved the church, and gave himself up for her" (Eph 5:25). If Christ is our Mother, then the Church is none other than his personal family, for which he must continually provide.

> The mother may lay her child tenderly to her breast. But our tender mother Jesus, he may homely [intimately] lead us *into* his blessed breast by his sweet, open side, and show us therein part of the godhead and the joys of heaven, with ghostly certainty of endless bliss. And that he shewed in the tenth revelation, giving the same understanding in this sweet word where he said: "Lo, how I loved thee," looking into his own blessed side, enjoying. (60:33–38.313, italics added)

Julian continues her intimate comparison between an earthly mother and Christ, the heavenly Mother, with the classic image of a woman holding her child on her breast to comfort it or rock it to sleep. As we discussed, medieval paintings and sculpture extolled the mother-and-child image, depicting Mary with the infant Jesus nursing or sleeping on her breast. But Julian sees that our Mother Christ does not simply hold the child on his breast; he leads it, with the greatest intimacy, *into* his breast through the open wound in his side. There he reveals secrets of the Godhead to the soul and assures the child of its salvation. Julian implies that Christ whispers "Lo, how I loved thee" to every soul who wishes to enter into the safety of his Sacred Heart.

Properties of Motherhood

Such comparisons lead Julian to conclude, yet again, that the word "mother" can only truly be used for Christ, "who is true mother of life and of all" (60:39–41.313). Then she lists the three main properties of motherhood: love, wisdom, and knowing. And of course, these evoke the defining attributes of the Trinity, though ascribed in reverse order. Yet Julian does not confine Christ's maternity to the plane of spiritual qualities. She dares to say that there is no aspect of *physical* motherhood that Christ does not feel.

> For though it be so that our bodily delivery is but little, low and simple as compared with our spiritual delivery, yet it is he that does it in the creatures by whom it is done. (60:42–44.313–15)

This is a remarkable statement: even though the process of giving birth physically is such a small thing (humble and commonplace in comparison with our high spiritual rebirth), Julian claims that it is still *Christ who labors to deliver a child* in every woman who undergoes childbirth. She imagines Christ as a flesh-and-blood mother experiencing birth pangs, with all the attendant fears, cries, and pouring out of blood and water during childbirth, similar to the agony he suffered on the cross. And then he continues to nurture his newborn to bring it to maturity.

> A natural, loving mother who knows and understands the need of her child, keeps [protects] it very tenderly, as the nature and condi-

> tion of motherhood will. And even as it waxes in age and in stature, she changes her werking, but not her love. And when it is more fully grown, she allows it to be chastised to break down its vices, to make the child able to receive virtues and grace. This werking, with all that is beautiful and good, our lord does in them by whom it is done. (60:45–50.315)

As with giving physical birth, Julian knows well the day-to-day work of attending to the constant needs of a child, protecting it from the many dangers that could harm it (in fourteenth-century Norwich) and teaching it everything it needs to learn. Julian understands that as the child matures, the mother has to adjust her way of dealing with her offspring so that she does not become over-protective, preventing the child from taking risks, making its own decisions, learning from its mistakes, and reaching adult independence. This was crucial in the Middle Ages when a boy was often sent away to school or to court to become a page at the age of seven, and could be legally married at fourteen. Likewise, as we have seen, girls needed to become fully accomplished in household chores, weaving, sewing, cooking, and caring for servants, so they could be married as young as twelve years old. There was little time for an extended childhood, since marriage and the production of offspring were both a social and familial responsibility.

And if a child becomes rebellious, disobedient, or lax in the accomplishment of its duties, the good mother will have to speak firmly and punish the child so that its vices may be broken down and it may grow in virtue and grace. Yet no matter how the mother must alter her way of teaching her child, now being tender, now becoming more strict, Julian knows from experience that *she never alters her love.* (On the contrary, the chastising of the child costs the mother as much, if not more, than it does the child. And Christ our Mother suffered infinitely more during his passion and death than did any of his children.) In short, the mother is continually "giving birth" to her child, in countless different ways. And Julian is sure that this daily nurturing is really being done by our Mother Christ "in those by whom it is done," that is, through the efforts of all earthly mothers.

Julian reiterates that Christ is truly our Mother in our most basic physical and emotional needs, in our growing and our learning process, in our disciplining and our chastising, in leading us away from vices and toward the virtues, in the working of grace. And she adds that Christ wants us to know how intimately he is involved in every aspect of our daily lives, so that all our love becomes fastened to him in everything we think and feel and do. Like an earthly mother, he may change his method of teaching and directing us as we grow older, *but he will never change his love.* Julian sees that the biggest debt we owe to our earthly fathers and mothers is fulfilled by our own "true loving of God" (60:53–54.315). And even this blessed loving of God is Christ's own work in us.

It should be noted here that the maternal role of nurturing children in medieval times was sharply distinguished from the paternal role of disciplining and punishing them (and, in the case of sons, training them for governance and the waging of war, or for a life of commerce or hard manual labor). In our post-modern era, the roles of mothering and fathering often overlap, collaborate, intertwine, and sometimes reverse. "Mothering" may be the work of either a mother or father or both. And, by extension, maternal care may be given by those who are not immediate biological mothers at all: grandparents, step-parents, foster parents, sisters, brothers, teachers, friends, mentors, counsellors, spiritual directors . . . the list goes on. Therefore, when we hear Julian speak of motherhood, we should assume she is referring to all the noblest qualities and aspects of nurturing, teaching, guiding, healing, and inspiring (regardless of who provides them) that are necessary to raise a healthy, happy, productive, and responsible human being. And according to Julian, whoever is such a caregiver is doing the work of Christ.

Spiritual Birthing

After having described Christ's birthing and nourishing of our physical selves like a human mother, Julian turns to the way in which he brings us forth *spiritually.* She calls it our "ghostly forthbringing" (61:1.315). And just as our immortal soul is of greater value in God's sight than our mortal body, so in this work of spiritual bringing-to-birth, Christ uses even more tenderness and care.

> He kindles our understanding, he prepares our ways, he eases our conscience, he comforts our soul, he enlightens our heart, and gives us partial knowing and loving of his blissful godhead—with gracious mind [understanding] of his sweet manhood and his blessed pas-

> sion, with courteous marveling over his high, surpassing goodness—and makes us love all that he loves for the sake of his love, and to be well satisfied with him and with all his werks. (61:3–8.315)

All this spiritual nourishment Julian has experienced in the course of her life, and most especially during her Revelations. She feels Christ at work in every aspect of her coming-to-understand the meaning hidden within the visions, the locutions, and the parable. She adds that when we fall into sin, Christ hastily "raises us by his lovely embracing and his gracious touching" (61:8–9.315). And when he strengthens us, by the working of grace, we are able to choose to become "his servants and his lovers, everlastingly without end" (61:9–11.315). The entire process of spiritual growth is seen in terms of Christ's maternal care for the human soul. Our work is one of cooperation and responsiveness.

But what of those who sin grievously, even though they believe and want to follow Christ? Julian admits that sometimes, for reasons not able to be understood, "he [Christ] suffers some of us to fall harder and more grievously than ever we did before, as we think" (61:12–13.315). Notice that Julian includes *herself* among those who fall harder and more seriously than they ever could have thought possible. Later in her text, we shall discover what she is alluding to here. For now, she is simply stating what she knows to be true: no one is safe from serious sin.

> And then we, who are not at all wise, think that all we have begun is nothing. But it is not so. Because it is necessary for us to fall, and it is necessary for us to see it. (61:13–15.315)

Julian tells us here what *she* felt when she fell so low in her own estimation. She was convinced that all her love and life of devotion and desire to be Christ's faithful servant had been a complete failure. How else could she have fallen into sin? But she was told (and she reassures her readers) that this is a wrong view. We are ignorant both about the value of our good intentions and efforts and about the damage done by our sinful deeds. Julian attests that it is necessary for us to sin, recalling Christ's earlier words to her, "Sinne is behovely" (27:9–10.209), in order that, like any child, we may learn from our mistakes, even from our grievous wrongdoings.

Unconditional Love

> For if we did not fall, we should not know how feeble and how wretched we are in ourselves, nor also we should not so completely know the marvelous love of our creator. For we shall truly see in heaven without end that we have grievously sinned in this life. And notwithstanding this, we shall truly see that we were never hurt in his love, nor were we ever of less value in his sight. And by the trial of this falling we shall have a high and marvelous knowing of love in God without end. *For strong and marvelous is that love which may not, nor will not, be broken for trespass.* (61:16–23.315–17, italics added)

Julian considers the first "profit" of sin, as well as she can fathom it. Not only does sin teach us valuable life-lessons, but by the shame and sorrow, remorse and contrition associated with sin, we may come to rely ever more completely on the love of God as our only salvation. Nothing makes us more aware of our human frailty, what Julian terms our "wretchedness," than our fall from grace. In our minds, we punish ourselves mightily. Eventually, in desperation, we turn to God. Even so, Julian tells us that we shall see the true enormity of sin only when we come to heaven, in comparison with the goodness of God. But by then we shall also understand that we were never "hurt" in God's love for us. Divine, unconditional love has never loved or valued us less, even for a moment, while we were in our sinful state.

On the contrary, God knows that grievous sin demands that human beings must suffer terrible consequences for their actions. Nonetheless, God will reward us for our heartfelt contrition and desire to amend our lives. Julian is absolutely certain, from all that has been personally revealed to her in her vision of Christ on the cross, dying for love, that God's love for us will never be "broken for trespass," that is, for sin.[7] We human beings may be "conditional" in our response to this love. At various times and in various circumstances we may choose to accept it, ignore it, avoid it, or refuse to consider it altogether. Nevertheless, God's love is strong and enduring enough to overcome every evil in the universe, even our own blind and ignorant resistance: "Herewith is the fiend overcome" (13:4–5.169).

Another "profit" of sin is that we are humbled and made meek and docile by the painful recognition of having fallen. And Julian asserts that we will be raised up high in heaven, to a height we could not have attained without that hard-earned humility. However, she is firm that we need to "see" our failure for what it is; otherwise, we cannot profit from it.

> And commonly, first we fall and then we see it, and both are by the mercy of God. The mother may suffer [permit] the child to fall sometimes and be distressed in diverse ways for its own profit, but she may never suffer that any manner of peril might come to her child, for love. And even if our earthly mother might suffer her child to perish, our heavenly mother Jesus may never suffer we who are his children to perish. For he is almighty, all wisdom, and all love, and so is none but he. Blessed may he be! (61:28–33.317)

How can our falling occur "by the mercy of God"? It seems a contradiction. But Julian is alluding to God's mercy that "allows" our free will to fall into error, even grave sin; that will is, in itself, God's gift. And when we feel remorse and repentance, these too are "by the mercy of God." Julian knows from her own experience that a human mother has to allow her child to make mistakes in order to learn about life and people and love. And in the process she knows the child will be distressed, hurt, rejected, perhaps even badly injured, either physically or morally. The loving mother will also do everything in her power to prevent her child from making a bad decision or falling into the wrong company that could destroy its happiness or imperil its immortal soul. Sometimes, a mother will even risk her child's anger and rejection in order to expose the harmful relationship or sinful behavior in which the child is involved, out of concern for the child's best interests. Julian is sure that when mothers do this, it is Christ our Mother risking human anger in order to save his children from their blindness and willfulness. Yet Julian recognizes that even the best of human mothers often fail to save their children from tragedy. And, as she has already observed, no mortal mother can save her child from suffering and death. What would Julian not have done to rescue her baby from the peril of the Great Pestilence? Only "our heavenly mother Jesus" may never suffer his children to perish . . . ultimately. "For God so loved the world that he gave his only Son, so that everyone who believes in him may not perish but may have eternal life" (Jn 3:16).

None of these observations about the sinfulness and frailty of the human condition and the unconditional love of God is a mere abstraction. For Julian, they are all intensely *personal* realizations. It is apparent that she first learned a great deal about mothering from her own mother. Their relationship must have been a very close one. As we have seen, in the Short Text Julian mentions that her mother was among those standing at her bedside during her long illness (x:26–28.83). And Julian herself must have been a devoted mother. Her knowledge of how a mother nurtures, teaches, and disciplines her child for its own good does not come from a *prymer* on child rearing. It could only proceed from her own life experience.

Contrition and Confession

Now Julian addresses the very deep suffering that is caused by sin. She recounts how, after we have fallen into disgrace and the wretchedness of what we have done is revealed to us, we become so terribly afraid of God and so ashamed of ourselves, that "we scarcely know where to put ourselves" (61:34–36.317). But she is adamant that, at times like these, our courteous Mother does not want us to flee from his sight, for that would be the most loathesome thing we could do. Instead, Christ wants us to turn and run to him, throw ourselves on his mercy, confess our sin, and ask for all the help and grace we need to amend our ways.

> For when it [the child] is distressed and adread, it runs hastily to the mother. And if it may do no more, it cries on the mother for help with all its might. So he [Christ] wills that we do as the humble child, saying thus: "My kind mother, my gracious mother, my dearworthy mother, have mercy on me. I have made myself foul and unlike to thee, and I may not nor can not amend it but with thy help and grace." And if we feel ourselves not then eased swiftly, we should be seker that he is using the method of a wise mother. For if he sees that it is more profitable to us to mourn and to weep, he suffers it with compassion and pity until the best time, for love. And he wills then that we use the quality of a child, who evermore naturally trusts in the love of the mother in wele and in woe. (61:36–46.317)

Julian knows that even the most sincere contrition and confession will not always result in immediate relief from feelings of guilt and remorse. The memory continues to relive the sinful thought or act, causing an ever-deepening sorrow and shame for the wrong we have done. Julian attributes even this penitential syndrome to the work of our Mother Christ. He sometimes "suffers" us to weep and mourn over our sins long after they have been forgiven in order to purify our souls and prevent us from ever committing those sins again. Julian admits that Christ may seem to be withholding his presence from us for a while, but that does not mean he is not full of pity and compassion for what we are suffering. Like a mother who must discipline her child by sending him out of her sight for a period of time, the pain of separation is shared by *both* mother and child. No matter how we feel about ourselves, Christ wants us to trust "in wele and in woe" that nothing we ever do can alter his motherly love.

The Church as Mother

Perhaps we should mention here that even though there was the tradition of sin as the "happy fault" that brought humanity such a Savior as Jesus Christ, the church would not have dared teach publicly that sin can become "behovely" or beneficial in any way, lest the faithful take it as license to commit evil. Julian herself would never advocate sinning in order to learn a lesson or to test the limits of God's love. But she is strongly urging those (like herself) who suffer from the painful recognition of having fallen, *not to despair*; God never stops loving his fallen people. Christ came, not for the ninety-nine sheep of the flock who do not sin, but for the one stray lamb that is most in need of forgiveness and healing (Mt 18:12–14, Lk 15:4–7). That one is always oneself.

> And he wills that we take ourselves mightily to the faith of holy church, and find there our dearworthy mother in solace and true understanding with the whole blessed community. For one single person may oftentimes be broken, as it seems to the self, but *the whole body of holy church was never broken, nor never shall be without end.* And therefore it is a seker thing, a good and a gracious thing, to will humbly and vehemently to be fastened and united to our mother holy church, who is Christ Jesus. For the flood of mercy that is his dearworthy blood and precious water is plenteous enough to make

> us fair and clean. The blessed wounds of our savior are open and rejoice to heal us. The sweet, gracious hands of our mother are ready and diligent about us. (61:47–55.317, italics added)

Julian refers to Christ's "dearworthy blood and precious water" that flowed from the wound in his side on the cross as the veritable "flood of mercy." She had seen that endless flow of blood in her vision, thinking "if it had been so [plenteous] in nature and in substance during that time, it would have covered the bed completely in blood, and have passed over all about," that is, it would have covered everything in her bedroom (12:7–8.167). Christ's wounds are always open wide to receive and heal the penitent. And his mercy is always greater than the greatest sin. His hands are ready to enfold and heal our brokenness, as a mother embraces her wayward children and attends to their injuries. Christ is the consummate prodigal *mother*, always standing at the top of the hill, looking afar off, waiting for her children to come home (Lk 15:20).

> For he, in all this werking, takes on the same office as an actual nurse, who has nothing else to do but to attend to the salvation of her child. It is his office to save us, it is his honor to do it, and it is his will that we know it. For he wills we love him sweetly and trust in him meekly and mightily. And this he shewed in these gracious words: "I keep thee full sekerly." (61:56–60.317)

Switching from the mother image to that of a nurse in the mother's household, Julian sees that Christ is willing to be the servant, as in the parable, to all his children. His only thought is their salvation. This is his responsibility and his glory. He wants us to know that he will go to any lengths to take care of us, which he proved on the cross. All Christ asks in return for his great love and sacrifice is that we love him gently and trust him greatly. Julian reads this meaning into the indelible words she had heard her Divine Mother and gentle Nurse speak to her: "I keep thee full sekerly" (37:8–9.235).

Julian recalls that, at the time of the Thirteenth Revelation, which dealt largely with the problem of sin, Christ had shown her a glimpse of our human frailties and failures, our brokenness and humiliations, our being despised and rejected and all our woe, as much as it seemed possible to experience in this lifetime. And she saw that this *shewing* was not for herself alone. The teachings about sin were intended to apply to all humankind. What Julian understood during that earlier Revelation was that, even in our weakness, ignorance, and sin, we are kept safe by Christ's power, wisdom, and love. Now she realizes *why*.

Christ is our *Mother* who takes the same tender care of us when we feel broken and battered, like the servant in the ditch, as at those times when we are in the most blissful state of grace and consolation. We may be cast out by others—our families, friends, even the hierarchy of the church—but Christ never turns away. On the contrary, he lifts our degraded spirits out of the predicament into which we have fallen, restores us to our original purity, and transforms everything we suffer into his glory and our everlasting joy.

Divine Goodness

Julian adds: "And all this is of the natural goodness of God, by the werking of grace" (62.8–9.319). Why is it we are so valuable that God goes to such great lengths to save us? Julian would answer that it is because of God's own nature: Divine Goodness produces and protects all natural goodness. "And all natures that he has made to flow out of him to werk his will, shall be restored and brought again into him" through the action of grace (62:12–14.319). God does not create and then leave creatures to sink or swim, to grow or wither, on their own. He is intimately involved with every aspect of created beings, since "he is the true father and true mother" of our natures. He cannot ever let us go.

According to medieval thinking, God has placed "mirrors" of Divine Being in a wide variety of natures: namely, "existence" in inanimate objects, "life" in animate objects, and "sensation" in animals. But only in humankind are all these natures found in one, the greatest virtue, beauty, goodness, and nobility; in short, human nature is the most precious of all natures to God. And so Julian asserts that we are "bound to God by nature, and we are bound to God by grace" (62:18–19.319). Julian concludes from this observation that we do not need to seek far afield to learn about other natures in order to understand our own, but only into "holy church, into our mother's breast" (62:19–20.319). And there we will discover "our own soul where our lord dwells," and we shall also find all other natures contained within our own soul (62:20–21.319).

This we may perceive to a certain extent now on earth, through faith and understanding; and afterward, we will see it most clearly in heaven. She cautions, however, that no man or woman should think that the totality of all created natures lies in him or in her *alone*. (That would be the worst pride and self-glorification.) She states adamantly that this is a general teaching about the perfect humanity *of Christ*:

> For it is our precious mother Christ, and for him was this fair [human] nature prepared, for the honor and the nobility of man's creation, and for the joy and the bliss of man's salvation, just as he [Christ] saw, knew, and recognized from without beginning. (62:24–26.319)

Sin as Perverse

Since our human nature comes from God's goodness, Julian reiterates that we should hate sin because it is both *against* our nature and against grace. "For nature is all good and fair in itself, and grace was sent out to save nature, and keep nature, and destroy sin," and to bring our beautiful nature back from its self-corruption into the "blessed point from whence it came—that is, God . . ." (63:2–4.319). And the virtuous working of grace will do this with even more nobility and honor than if we had not sinned. This continues to be Julian's strong contention.

> For it shall be seen before God by all his holy saints, in joy without end, that nature has been tried in the fire of tribulation and therein was found no lack nor any fault. Thus are nature and grace of one accord; for grace is God, as uncreated nature is God. He is two in manner of werking, and one in love, and neither of them werks without the other, nor can either be separated. (63:5–9.319–21)

St. Peter wrote of faith "being more precious than gold that, though perishable, is tested by fire" (1 Pt 1:7). This is the tribulation of hellfire-on-earth that Julian envisions human nature having to undergo, as did the body of Christ. But human nature will be restored to its original goodness by the purification process of suffering and the work of grace flowing directly from God, operating in one magnificent work of love to fashion a "new creation" out of the ashes of the old.

Julian maintains that when we live in accordance with our true nature and grace, we see ever more clearly that "sinne is much worse, more vile, and more painful than hell without any comparison, for it is contrary to our fair nature" (63:10–12.321). Sin alienates our substance from our sensuality, our "godly will" from our misguided will, our true mind from our deceptive mind.

> For as truly as sin is unclean, as truly is sin unnatural, and thus a horrible thing to see for the loving soul that would wish to be all fair and shining in the sight of God, as nature and grace teach. But we must not be fearful of this (except inasmuch as dread may be useful), but humbly make our moaning to our dearworthy mother. And he shall all sprinkle us in his precious blood, and make our soul very soft and very humble, and heal us very beautifully by the process of time, exactly as it is most honor to him and joy to us without end. (63:12–18.321)

The strong undertow of these words comes from a personal experience of sin that Julian will describe after the Fifteenth Revelation, yet to come. It tore at her soul all her life and allowed her to identify completely with others who, like her, had fallen headlong into the ditch of betrayal. She knows firsthand the horror of sin that sets the loving soul against itself. Yet she has learned, and bids her readers take heed, that we must not allow ourselves to fall even further into despair over sin. Remorse and sorrow are prerequisites for healing; but despair is a further sin, the lack of trust in God's mercy and love, a living hell.

Christ our Mother is ever ready, as Julian has described previously, to gather us into his arms when we run to him like a child, still moaning and groaning from our woundedness.

> And from this sweet, beautiful werking he shall never cease nor stop, until all his dearworthy children are born and brought forth. And that he shewed when he gave the understanding of the ghostly thirst: that is, the love-longing that shall last till domesday. (63:19–22.321)

Julian concludes that our life is grounded in the foreseeing wisdom of "our true mother Jesus," with the power of the Father, and the most high goodness of the Holy Ghost (63:23–25.321). By becoming human, Christ himself gave birth to us as does a mother, and by his passion and death "he bore us to endless life" (63:25–26.321). What more could Christ our Mother do for us? He will never stop nursing, feeding, and fostering us, as his Motherhood demands and as every child needs. And this is the most beautiful of relationships:

> Beautiful and sweet is our heavenly mother in the sight of our soul. Precious and lovely are the gracious children in the sight of our heavenly mother, with mildness and meekness and all the fair virtues that belong to children by nature. For naturally the child does not despair of the mother's love, naturally the child does not presume of itself, naturally the child loves the mother and each one of them loves the other. These are beautiful virtues, with all others that are like them, whereby our heavenly mother is served and pleased. (63:29–35.321)

As Julian writes for the last time of the Motherhood of Christ, her own great love of children shines through her words. She must have asked herself many a time what a good mother would do for her child. And she knows that if a human mother would spare nothing to nourish her children and help them grow, heal their wounds, and bless their efforts . . . then our heavenly Mother would not, either.

> And I understood no higher stature in this life than childhood, in feebleness and failing of might and of intellect, until the time that our gracious mother has brought us up to our father's bliss. And there shall it truly be made known to us, his meaning in the sweet words where he says: "Alle shalle be wele, and thou shalt see it thyself that alle manner of thing shalle be wele." (63:36–40.321)

For Julian, the highest human achievement is to be able to come to Christ as trustingly as a little child. It is the very helplessness of the child that makes it so appealing. And the ignorance of the child will make Christ responsible for explaining everything in heaven: how exactly "alle shalle be wele." Julian returns to the great theme of the Revelations and realizes that its mystery will be revealed, not to self-reliant and wise adults, but only to the little ones. As Christ himself prayed on earth: "I thank you, Father, Lord of heaven and earth, because you have hidden these things from the wise and the intelligent and have revealed them to infants" (Mt 11:25).

Julian's Motherhood

> And then shall the bliss of *our motherhood in Christ* begin anew in the joys of our father God; which new beginning shall last without end, ever newly beginning. Thus I understood that all his blessed children who have come out of him by nature shall be brought again into him by grace. (63:40–44, italics added)

Perhaps by deliberate intention, perhaps by accident, Julian emerges from her author's anonymity for a brief moment. *She identifies herself as a mother* along with all human mothers by affirming that, in heaven, "*our* motherhood in Christ" will "begin anew in the joys of our father God." There, she will be privileged to become the spiritual "mother" of countless souls confided to her care. And this "new beginning" will be an everlasting nurturing process, part of Christ's "new creation." And all the children to whom Christ has given birth through his death on the cross will be new-born into eternal life, through the grace of Christ's own Motherhood.

22
Close of the Day

During the previous fifty-three divisions of her Long Text (chapters 10 to 63),[1] Julian has provided the reader with a much more expansive account of her Revelations and her understanding of their meaning than she had in the Short Text. She has written about the goodness of God coming down to the "lowest part of our need," of being led into the "sea ground," of the shaking of the church like "a cloth in the wind," and has added poignant details about Christ's sufferings on the cross. She has also introduced completely new insights like the Great Deed, the second deed, the two *privities*, and she has developed her teachings on the forms of prayer. Additionally, she has explored the dual nature of the soul's substance and sensuality; the "two domes" or judgments; the lack of *wroth* or blame in God (as against human *contrariousness*), and extolled God's marvelous *rightfullehede*. She has examined the properties of mercy and grace that work to diffuse our own wrath, and described her desperate plea to know how God sees us in our sinfulness. She has revealed the *exemplum* of the lord and the servant and, by masterly exegesis, uncovered its rich theological implications. The parable has deepened her understanding of the "godly will" through the knitting of humanity to Christ in an endless process of *oneing* and allowed her to explore the possibility of knowing both the soul and God. She has delved into the nature of being, reason, and faith. And finally, she has revealed her groundbreaking theology of the Motherhood of God, including the human mother's devotion to her child as a reflection of Christ's own tender care of the soul, and the *werking* of the Blessed Trinity as being truly our Father, Mother, and Spouse. *None of these mystical teachings appeared in the Short Text.* Now, in the sixty-fourth chapter, the Long Text resumes a more exact correspondence with the Short Text, although there will be further additions and elaborations to come.

Fifteenth Revelation

After the astounding insights of the exceptionally long Fourteenth Revelation, which developed over a period of more than twenty years, Julian returns to her personal story and arrives at the Fifteenth Revelation. Immediately, the reader is reminded of the *earlier* state of Julian's soul. Here again is the anguished thirty-year-old woman, rather than the mature theologian and mystic of fifty or sixty we have been encountering. Once again, Julian takes us back into her mental and physical crisis, describing her desire to be liberated from suffering.

> Before this time [of the Revelations] I had a great longing and desire by God's gift to be delivered from this world and from this life. For oftentimes I beheld the woe that is here and the wele and the blessed being that are there. And if there had been no pain in this life but the absence of our lord, it seemed to me sometimes that it was more than I might bear. And this made me mourn and earnestly long, and also because of my own wretchedness, sloth and weariness, I did not like to live and to travail [labor] as it was my duty to do. (64:1–7.323)

These sorrowful words recall Julian's deathbed desire "to be soon with my God and maker" (2:27.129). They are the words of many a devout medieval Christian who, like St. Paul, felt torn between living and dying: "my desire is to depart and be with Christ, for that is far better; but to remain in the flesh is more necessary for you" (Phil 1:23–24). But they are also the words of a young woman who had seen too much violence and brutality, too much sadness and mourning, and much too much death. She had pain-filled questions burdening her mind and bitter memories filling her soul. She had not yet learned how God beholds humanity in its sinfulness. She had not yet become an anchoress, nor had she written the mystical theology she would develop from her Revelations.

At this point in her life, in 1373, Julian was thoroughly ashamed of her wretchedness, sloth, and weariness, classic signs of *melancholia* (believed to be produced by an excess of black bile and often warned against by spiritual writers). Her candid confession of major faults was not an affectation; it seems she felt that her misery, lack of will power, and physical exhaustion were keeping her from fulfilling her responsibilities to her family, her friends, her servants, and most of all, to God. She did not find any pleasure in living. She did not like working to support all those in her charge. And perhaps she did not even like praying, because she had lost a sense of God's presence in her soul. She wanted to escape to heaven and be liberated from all her demons, doubts, and pains. Yet even if it were possible to be pain-free in her outer life, the spiritual agony of dragging herself through every day without the sense of Christ's presence, she admits, was sometimes more than she could bear. As we have discussed, it is highly possible that her mental and emotional trials contributed to her debilitating physical illness at the age of thirty and a half.

Patience

> And to all this our courteous lord answered to give me comfort and patience, and said these words: "Suddenly thou shalt be taken from all thy pain, from all thy disease, from all thy distress, and from all thy woe. And thou shalt come up above, and thou shalt have me for thy reward, and thou shalt be filled with joy and bliss. And thou shalt never more have any manner of pain, nor any manner of sickness, nor any manner of displeasure, nor wanting of will, but ever joy and bliss without end. Why should it then aggrieve thee to suffer [be patient] awhile, since it is my will and for my honor?" (64:8–15.323)

In this startling Revelation, the Lord responds to Julian's longing for release with the assurance that the moment of her "being taken" will be sudden, "like a thief in the night" (1 Thes 5:2). She will immediately "come up above" and be forever free of sickness, displeasure, lack of will, in short, all the aspects of her life that she found so hard to bear. The Lord questions her heart as if to say, "Are you not willing to wait a little while until I come for you?"

This Revelation alters Julian's attitude toward enduring life's hardships. She realizes the great value of *patience* in waiting for God's will to be performed. As Christ himself had warned the disciples: "Keep awake therefore, for you know neither the day nor the hour" (Mt 25:13). Julian understands that every soul must learn to practice immense patience in the course of life. And this is greatly profitable, because if we knew the moment of death, we would not have to exercise any patience. As long as the soul is in the body, "it seems to itself that it is ever at the point of being taken" (64:21.325). And so it should be. Julian sees that our life (with all the suffering that we experience here on earth) is, in reality, no more than a "point," an instant of time, that will change forever when we are taken to heaven and "pain shall be nothing" (64:23.325).

A Body on the Earth

Julian connects this realization to an inner vision she had at the time of the Fifteenth Revelation. It is reminiscent of the servant lying face down in the ditch:

> And in this time I saw a body lying on the earth, which body appeared gross and fearful and without shape and form, as if it were a bog of stinking mud. And suddenly, out of this body sprang a very beautiful creature, a little child, fully shaped and formed, swift and lively and whiter than the lily, who swiftly glided up into heaven. (64:24–28.325)

Who is this child? Is it every human being ever born to die? Is it merely a symbolic child to impress upon Julian how quickly suffering will be turned into joy when the pure soul leaves the body of stinking mud? Or is it, as we have suggested, *a recollection of Julian's own child, at the moment of its pitiful death*? Black and swollen and marked with oozing pustules from the plague, there was nothing beautiful to be found in her baby's agonized body. It evoked only dreadful fear and horror. Yet Julian trusted, by faith, that at the moment of death, her baptized child's soul would have risen straight up to heaven. Now, after all these years, in this Revelation she may have been granted an inner vision of its flight to God that gave her mother's heart an abundance of consolation.

As with the *exemplum* of the lord and the servant, Julian did not record this vision in the Short Text. It only appeared in the Long Text once she had learned how to do exegesis and find the hidden meanings in parables, voices, and visions. Employing the same method she used for the lord and the servant, Julian examines this appearance more closely:

> The bog of the body betokens great wretchedness of our mortal flesh, and the littleness of the child signifies the cleanness and the

> pureness of our soul. And I thought: "Within this body lives no beauty of this child, nor in this child dwells no foulness of the body. It is very blissful for man to be taken from pain, more than pain to be taken from man. For if pain is taken from us, it may come again. Therefore this is a sovereign comfort and a blissful beholding in a longing soul, that we shall be taken from pain. For in this promise I saw a marvelous compassion that our lord has on us for our woe, and a courteous promising of pure deliverance. (64:28–36.325)

Julian had felt the terrible distress of her illness disappear in an instant when her Revelations began. However, she expects that they will return once the *shewings* cease. She becomes acutely aware that by dying we are taken from all pain, as was her beloved child. She admits that, for her child, it was far better for its soul to be released from terrible pains and fly to heaven than to have been miraculously cured, only to suffer pain and the threat of another plague thereafter. Still, it is a hard interpretation to accept.

The most important teaching Julian takes from this Revelation is that Christ wants us to find comfort in the transcendent joy he is preparing for the soul. She understood this from his words: "And thou shalt come up above, and thou shalt have me for thy reward, and thou shalt be filled with joy and bliss." Julian tells us that we must focus "the point of our thought" on this beholding as often as possible, and for as long as the Lord will lead us into such exalted contemplation, by his grace (64:39–41.325). In other words, Julian urges us to learn to meditate *not* on our sufferings but on the glorious love and compassion of Christ who will release us from them forever. Here she goes directly counter to the usual medieval recommendations for meditations on death that detailed the excruciating torments awaiting the soul in hell, should it die in mortal sin. Urging a totally different approach, Julian suggests that we concentrate less on our wretchedness and fear of damnation and more on the future joy of our salvation. If we do, she says it will be greatly to God's honor and our own reward.

Spiritual Darkness

> And when we fall back again into ourselves, through sadness and spiritual blindness, and with feelings of pains, both spiritual and

> bodily, through our frailty, it is God's will that we know that he has not forgotten us. (64:43–45.325)

Julian knows we will not be able to keep our mind single-pointedly focused on the ultimate release of our sufferings, any more than she was able to do it. Sometimes, bodily pain overwhelms us (as it did Julian). Then we fall back onto our own resources, like the servant in the ditch who was weighed down by both physical misery and spiritual depression, unable to feel his lord's compassion and pity. We forget the glimpse of heavenly bliss we may have enjoyed before. We succumb to self-destructive thoughts and feelings, thinking God has abandoned us. We neglect our duties, we become dull in spirit, unable to pray.

Yet Julian reassures us (as she often had to reassure herself) that even in the midst of agony and doubt, God never forgets us. This is what Christ meant when he said that we would be released "suddenly" from our pains and realize that he had been with us during the time of our suffering. We must believe in his promise and his abiding comfort as completely and confidently as we possibly can. And we must try to endure the long years of waiting amid the diseases and emotional distresses of our lives as "lightly" as possible, even counting them as nothing.

> For the more lightly that we take them, and the less price that we set on them for love, the less pain shall we have in the feeling of them, and the more thanks and reward shall we have for them. (64:52–54.327)

Julian never suggests that this way of living will be easy (as it was not easy for her), but it must have become her graced way of alleviating her own *melancholia*. Her approach was the very opposite of the cultivation of sadness and self-loathing that many medieval mystics espoused. As we have discussed, these anorexic and often depressed women inflicted bodily pain on themselves in order to achieve an altered state of mind. On the contrary, Julian never encourages ascetic disciplines or increased suffering for its own sake. She recommends *the cultivation of joy*. She encourages us to set less importance on how much we undergo and to trust in the Lord who is continually working through what we suffer to prepare our eternal reward.

Chosen by Love

> And thus I understood that any man or woman who willingly chooses God in this lifetime for love, he may be seker that he is loved without end, with endless love that werks in him that grace [of choosing God]. For he [God] wills we recollect this trustfully, that we are as seker in hope of the bliss of heaven while we are here as we shall be in sekernesse [certainty] when we are there. And ever the more pleasure and joy that we take in this sekernesse, with reverence and humility, the more it delights him. (65:1–6.327)

Here, Julian maintains that we are offered "endless love" by God, and if we choose to accept it by living a life of love, then we may be sure that we have been "chosen." This, at last, seems to indicate Julian's personal interpretation of the doctrine of predestination: it is none other than human love responding to Divine Love. We may recall Christ's words: "You did not choose me but I chose you. And I appointed you to go and bear fruit, fruit that will last, so that the Father will give you whatever you ask him in my name" (Jn 15:16). According to Julian, the *fact* that we choose to love God, and try to express that love through our love of each other, is itself proof that the love of God dwells within us. How could it be otherwise? St. John writes: "Whoever does not love does not know God, for God is love" (1 Jn 4:8). And again: "So we have known and believe the love that God has for us. God is love, and those who abide in love abide in God, and God abides in them" (1 Jn 4:16). The natural expression of this love of God is love of neighbor: "The commandment we have from him is this: those who love God must love their brothers and sisters also" (1 Jn 4:21). Julian advises that we reflect on God's love often and gain confidence from it, even to the extent of being as certain of the hope of heaven *now* as we will be when we are in heaven.

Julian's leap of *sekernesse* echoes her earlier belief that she "would be saved by the mercy of God" (2:14–15.127). She is convinced that God wants us to believe firmly in our own salvation, for it pleases him that we do so. This is not presumption on Julian's part. Medieval devotion promised that the blessed ones would receive their eternal "dowry" from God: "For they shall be there seker and certain / To have endless joy, and nevermore pain."[2]

Courteous Dread

However, Julian does not suggest her readers take this expectation of salvation lightly. She stresses that our attitude toward God should always be one of reverence, "a holy, courteous dread of our lord, to which humility is knit" (65:7–8.327). This awe-filled fear shows the appropriate respect for his great majesty. We should see the Lord as "marvelously great and the self as marvelously little" (65:8–9.327). The virtues of reverence and humility are even experienced by the saints in heaven and can be known by his beloved on earth who are given a partial sight of God's presence, as was Julian herself. And in every situation, this presence is most desirable because it creates in the soul a wonderful sense of security in true faith, certain hope, and reverent love, that is most "sweet and delectable" (65:13.327).

> It is God's will that I see myself as greatly bound to him in love *as if he had done for me alone* all that he has done. And thus should every soul think in relation to his lover. That is to say, the love of God makes such unity in us that when it is truly seen, no man can separate himself from another. *And thus ought each soul to think that God has done for him all that he has done.* (65:13–17.327–29, italics added)

Julian becomes extremely personal in her interpretation of this Revelation. She understands that Christ's passion was undergone for her *as if she were the only person alive.* And far from apologizing for this attitude, she maintains that *every* soul should think the same way. We are one common humanity. Christ took on that humanity. Therefore, if he dies for one, he dies for all, and vice versa. As Julian wrote previously: "For in the sight of God, all men are one man, and one man is all men" (51:88–89.279). No one "can separate himself from another." And if it helps us to consider that all Christ said, did, taught, and suffered was to save our individual soul, then it is to our profit to do so. Julian is convinced that Christ showed her this practice "to make us love him, and delight in him, and dread nothing but him" (65:19–20.329).

> For it is his will we know that all the might of our enemy is locked in our friend's hand. And therefore the soul that sekerly knows this,

> he shall not dread anything but him whom he loves. All other dreads, he counts them among the passions and bodily sicknesses and imaginations. And therefore, though we are in so much pain, woe, and disease that it seems we can think of nothing at all but that pain we are in or that we feel, as soon as we may, we should pass lightly over it, and count it as nothing. (65:19–24.329)

The only thing we have to fear is our own ability to conceive evil. Yet Christ has assured Julian that by his sacrifice, "Herewith is the fiend overcome" (13:4–5.169). Satan is bound and locked tightly in Christ's hand, a powerful metaphor. Then indeed, what have we to fear except offending God? All our unruly passions, our physical illnesses, our overwrought imaginings arise from our afflicted minds. And even though we may be so consumed by our unhappiness that we can think of nothing else, as was Julian herself at times, she reminds us again and again that we should pass over the pain as lightly as we are able to do so and, as much as possible, refuse to dwell on it. This, in itself, is the greatest "self-noughting."

Then she asks rhetorically: "And why [should we do this]?" (65:25.329). She answers that God wants us to know him, in the sense of really *understanding* him. And if we do come to know and love and fear to offend him, our souls will grow in patience and be given a spiritual rest, and we shall even come to appreciate the mysterious work he is doing within us. We shall develop the ability to bear our sufferings with greater equanimity, for the sake of love. This, Julian says, was the meaning of Christ's earlier words: "Why should it then aggrieve thee to suffer a while, since it is my will and for my honor?" (65:27–28.329).

The Final Scene

Immediately after this, Julian writes:

> Now have I told you of fifteen shewings, as God vouchsafed to minister them to my mind, renewed by lightenings and touchings [illuminations and inspirations], I hope from the same spirit who shewed them all. Of which fifteen shewings the first began early in the morning, about the hour of four, and it lasted—shewing by procession, very beautifully and seriously, each following the other—till it was *none* of the day or past. (65:29–33.329)

With these simple words, Julian concludes the account of the Fifteen Revelations she received on that one extraordinary day, the eighth or the thirteenth day of May, 1373 (depending on which scribal version one prefers).[3] She clearly states they were shown *to her mind* and that they were renewed by further illuminations and inspirations over the decades to come, all proceeding from the Holy Ghost, who she hopes was the same Spirit who "shewed them all." Julian remembers that the first vision began early in the morning, "about the hour of four," when she must have heard the bells of Norwich Cathedral chime for the monastic office of *Lauds.* Thereafter, each Revelation appeared in procession, much like the pageant wagons following one after the other, starting at the break of dawn, for the performance of the mystery plays. Julian attests that the Revelations were extremely beautiful and full of profound meaning. The Fifteenth Revelation occurred at *none*, which is the ninth hour of the day, at about three o'clock in the afternoon, at which the Divine Office was also sung.[4] Julian must have remembered that Christ hung on the cross from noon to three: "From noon on, darkness came over the whole land until three in the afternoon" (Mt 27:45).

23
Betrayal and Affirmation

The Sixteenth Revelation took place during the night that followed, and it was the "conclusion and confirmation to all the fifteen" (66:2–3.331). However, before Julian speaks of it, she feels obliged to make a confession.

> But first it behooves me to tell you about my feebleness, wretchedness, and blindness. I have said at the beginning, where it says, "And in this suddenly all my pain was taken from me," of which pain I had no grief nor any discomfort as long as the fifteen shewings lasted in shewing. And at the end all was closed, and I saw no more, and soon I felt that I should live longer. And anon my sickness came again; first in my head, with a sound and a din; and suddenly all my body was filled with sickness just as it was before, and I was as barren and as dry as if I had never had but a little comfort, and like a wretch I mourned and heaved for feeling of my bodily pains and for the failing of comfort, ghostly and bodily. (66:3–11.331)

After what Julian has told us about the need to pass "lightly" over our pains, this description stands as a testimony to her humble admission that it is sometimes beyond human ability to do so. Following the Fifteenth Revelation, the curtain on the living passion play closed completely. She "saw no more." Now she is like the poor servant, just fallen into the ditch because of the "feebleness and blindness that we have" from Adam (51:196–97.283). After being relieved of all her previous symptoms during the Revelations, she experiences the same excruciating bodily pains she had suffered ten or eleven hours earlier, when she thought she was dying. Just as the Lord had told her she would be taken "suddenly" *out* of her pain, now she watches her mind plunge her body "suddenly" back *into* pain. First, the throbbing returns to her head with a cacophony of noise, perhaps a pounding migraine. It moves from her head swiftly into her body, like a reverse projection of the pure soul arising out of the body of the child. And her soul immediately feels barren of any sweetness of love and devotion, as dry as if she had never received any visions or locutions.

She becomes overwhelmed. She begins groaning and moaning, wallowing and writhing, and cannot rise from her bed or help herself in any way. As terrible as her physical pain may be, she is in even deeper emotional torment. Like the fallen servant, she has no source of comfort because she cannot turn her head to see her Lord, who is her only heaven. He is no longer "present" to her on the cross. She is utterly bereft. And she admits she complained bitterly, letting everyone around her know just how miserable she was, because all her comfort, spiritual and bodily, had been taken from her. For her self-absorbed behavior, she calls herself a "wretch." Julian makes no excuses for her reversal. None at all. And there is more to come.

Betrayal

> Then a religious person came to me and asked me how I fared, and I said I had raved today. And he laughed loud and heartily. And I said: "The cross that stood before my face, it seemed to me that it bled heavily." And with this word, the person that I spoke to grew all serious and marveled, and anon I was sorely ashamed and stunned because of my recklessness. And I thought: "This man takes seriously the least word that I might say, who saw no more thereof [but what I told him]." (66:12–17.331)

A local friar, a member of a religious order (a Franciscan, Dominican, or perhaps an Austin canon), stopped in to visit Julian. It seems she did not know his name; she may never have seen him before. Her mother or one of her friends may have called him in from the street to comfort Julian, now that she was again writhing in such pain and distress. In answer to the friar's question about how she was doing, Julian blurts out that she had "raved today." This was not said frivolously. In her physical agony, Julian was so disconcerted that she mischaracterized everything she had seen and felt and understood from the Lord. *Rave*, the Middle English word Julian chose to describe her mental state, implies mental derangement, producing hallucinations, delusionary apparitions, wild speech, complete delirium. This is how Julian represented herself to the friar in that moment: *as stark, raving mad.*

To his great credit, the friar did not believe her. He laughed heartily at such nonsense, brushing it off. He saw a woman before him who, in spite of her physical discomfort, seemed utterly sane. And if by chance he knew of Julian's life of devotion and service in the Norwich community, he certainly would not have believed her to be a lunatic. And then, when Julian told him that the cross standing before her had bled profusely, the friar's whole demeanor suddenly changed. He became serious and reverent, as in the presence of a miraculous event. This time, he *believed* what Julian said was true, though he knew no more about it than the little she had just told him. When Julian saw in his face that he took what she had said seriously, and with total reverence, she "grew very greatly ashamed" (66:18–19.331). She knew she had committed a great sin; she had *doubted* the Revelations God had so graciously shown her. By telling the friar that she had "raved," she implied that the bleeding of the crucifix had been part of her *dementia*. No sooner had she realized the import of what she had said than she wanted to "be shriven," to have the friar hear her confession.

> But I could not tell it to any priest. For I thought: "How can a priest believe me? I did not believe our lord God." This I believed truthfully for that time that I saw him [Christ], and so it was then my will and my meaning forever to believe without end. But like a fool I let it pass from my mind. Ah, lo I, wretch! This was a great sin and a great unkindness, that I, because of the folly of feeling a little bodily pain, so unwisely abandoned for the time the comfort of all this blessed shewing of our lord God. (66:19–25.331–33)

Here is Julian who will, decades later, counsel her *evencristens* not to hide from God's love if they feel ashamed because of sin (but to run like a child to the mother's breast and say, "I have made myself dirty" and then trust to be cleansed immediately), unable to confess her sin to a priest because she does not think he will believe her since *she* had not believed what came from God! Her self-recrimination cannot be understated. It seared her soul. Added to her physical pain, she must have suffered terribly. In Julian's mind, this betrayal of her Lord was every bit as serious as that of Peter who, having spent three years as a close personal disciple of Christ, in a moment of fear, denied to a mere servant girl that he even *knew* the Man.[1] Likewise, Julian had spent an entire day seeing Christ suffer and then appear transformed in radiance on the cross, hearing him speak to her in the depths of her soul, being raised up to the "third heaven" and seeing God "in a point"; yet because of the return of her physical pain, she had described her Revelations as delusionary "ravings" to a friar she may never have seen before.

Did she really doubt? She clearly states that "for that time that I saw him [Christ]" she totally believed the apparition was a real presence, not the product of delirium. Then why did she feel the need to portray her Revelations as "ravings" in that fateful moment? Was she momentarily angry with God for allowing her physical pain to return? She suggests that because she felt "a little bodily pain" she "unwisely abandoned for the time the comfort of all this blessed shewing of our lord God." We may certainly identify with the experience of forgetting or doubting the deepest convictions of our lives in moments of personal tragedy and unbearable pain. For the duration of that time, we are literally "out of our minds" with grief and suffering. The fact that Julian knew in her heart that her Revelations were most certainly *not* ravings made her sense of betrayal all the more devastating. She had lied to a friar/priest about the most transcendent experience of her life. And this lie threw her soul into incalculable torment. If she had really "raved that day," she could not possibly have felt such guilt over her betrayal.

> Here you may see what I am of myself. But herein would our courteous lord not leave me. And I lay still till night, trusting in his mercy, and then I began to sleep. (66:26–28.333)

Yet, even in her shame and confusion, she held on to her trust in God's mercy and his grace, both of which she needed desperately that night. And because her soul took refuge in the very God whom she had betrayed, she felt forgiven. Perhaps this is why, when she wrote down her Revelations, she made sincere contrition and *seker* trust absolutely essential to her theology.

Nightmare

> And in my sleep, at the beginning, it seemed to me that the fiend set himself at my throat, putting forth his face very near my face like that of a young man, and it was long and amazingly thin. I

> never saw any such. The color was red, like the tilestone when it is newly burnt, with black spots therein like freckles, fouler than the tilestone. His hair was red as rust, not shorn in front, with side locks hanging on the temples. He grinned upon me with a shrewd look; shewed me white teeth and so large, it seemed to me very ugly. Neither his body nor hands were shapely, but with his paws he held me by the throat, and would have strangled me, but he might not. (67:1–8.333)

Julian's guilt works its way deep into her subconscious and produces a nightmare of extreme intensity. She is being choked by an elongated devil whose face glows burning red as if he had just emerged from hell, with black freckles all over it, like soot on hot tiles in front of a fireplace. His hair is also red, not cut in bangs as was the style of medieval males, but hanging down in long curls on either side of his face. He grins at her, cunningly, as if in triumph of his power over her. His teeth are too big, too white, too many. His body and extremities are disfigured; rather than human hands, he has paws like an animal. She can feel this apparition holding her in a death grip.

Julian had seen many a devil painted on the walls of churches, tempting Eve, lurking in the background of scriptural depictions, emerging from the hell-mouth. Devils appeared in illuminated devotional books, grimaced in wood carvings at the ends of church pews, sat sculpted in stone on the inside and outside of Norwich Cathedral. Devils came alive in the mystery plays, dressed in red from head to toe, with tails, horns, spears, and chains, evoking both laughter and fear in the audience, the one to exorcise the other. But Julian had obviously never seen a monster like this. There may have been a strong suggestion of sexual aggression in this long, lean, leering man with his face, body and paws so close to her *in bed*. Did she think he would brutally rape her? The possibility cannot be discounted. It would have been a fate worse than death.

Julian's ability to describe the color, shape, and physical qualities of this fiend is reminiscent of her extraordinary visual recall of every aspect of Christ's face during the bleeding, drying, and hanging of his torn flesh on the cross. She would also remember every smallest detail of the parable of the lord and the servant. In fact, it is her acute *sensory perception* that makes the nightmare so terrifyingly real for Julian.

> This ugly shewing was made while sleeping, and so was none other. And in all this time I trusted to be saved and kept by the mercy of God. And our courteous lord gave me grace to wake, and I barely had my life. The people who were with me beheld me and wet my temples, and my heart began to be comforted. And anon a little smoke came in at the door with a great heat and a foul stench. And then I said: "Benedicite dominus! Is it all on fire that is here?" And I supposed it had been a bodily fire that should have burned us all to death. I asked those who were with me if they noticed any stench. They said, "nay," they noticed none. I said: "Blessed be God!" For then I knew well it was the fiend that had come to torment me. (67:9–17.333–35)

Julian makes very clear the difference between this ghoulish vision and her *shewings*; this nightmare descended on her while she slept, the Revelations appeared while she was wide awake. As horrifying as the experience was, Julian testifies that she never stopped trusting that God would protect her. She attributes to God the fact that she actually woke up rather than dying in her sleep in the devil's grip. All those around her must have been shocked to see her sweating profusely and gasping for breath, not knowing she was being strangled by an hallucinatory devil. The women wiped her face and head with wet towels, murmuring prayers. As Julian gradually regained consciousness and came back to her senses, her heart stopped pounding.

Then there was the stench, the apparition of smoke under the door, all "classic signs" of the presence of Satan. Were they all going to burn up and die? As at the beginning of her Revelations, she misquoted "Benedicite dominus" (it should be *domino*), a prayer for the Lord's blessing in the presence of evil. But though she questioned the women desperately, no one smelled or saw any smoke. This was a great relief. She said in English: "Blessed be God!" Now she knew the smoke and stench were indeed further projections of the presence of a devil, but because of God's protection they could have no real power over her or anyone else.

As the onslaught of imaginative and sensory stimuli subsided, Julian recollected what the Lord had shown her "on the same day with all the faith of holy church," because she saw the Revelations and her faith as being one in truth (67:18–20.335). And she took refuge in them and found great comfort.

> And anon, all vanished away, and I was brought to great rest and peace, without sickness of body or dread of conscience. (67:20–21.335)

Her nightmare images disappear, the stench in her nostrils abates, the fear of burning to death ceases. She realizes these were all illusory fabrications of her mind that expressed her soul's deep-seated fear of damnation for her sin of doubt. The Lord did not punish her; she punished herself. And now, her soul has come through the trial of fire and fear, and is once again at peace. Her physical pains decrease, she can breathe more easily. She must have looked around at the faces of those still keeping watch at her bedside and felt as if she had returned from a distant universe. How was she ever to convey to them what she had seen and heard?

The Sixteenth Revelation

> And then our good lord opened my ghostly eye and shewed me my soul in the middle of my heart. I saw the soul as large as if it were an endless citadel, and also as if it were a blissful kingdom, and by the conditions that I saw therein I understood that it is a worshipful city. In the middle of that city sits our lord Jesus, true God and true man: a fair person and of large stature, highest bishop, most solemn king, most honorable lord. And I saw him solemnly clothed in honors. (68:1–7.335)

Following her nightmare, Julian writes in the Short Text that she was "left still awake" (xxii:1.111). In both the Short and Long texts, she records that at this point, her spiritual eye was opened and she was given a vision of Christ Triumphant, sitting in her soul enclosed "in the middle of her heart." *Heart* was a term often used in the Middle Ages to indicate the secret and most interior part of the individual, where the record of the person is carried and where the conscience either accuses or defends him. There, the "Book of the Heart" was constantly being written, the core (from the Latin, *cor*, meaning heart) of a person's spiritual life. Julian's soul-within-her-heart expands outward to become a vast citadel, a Holy See (the bishop's seat), a sacred city, a heavenly Norwich. Christ is seated at the center, magnificent in face and in stature, "clothed in honors" as the highest bishop, greater than the pope himself, and also highest king and lord of all kingdoms. This image evokes the one Julian was shown at the end of the *exemplum* of the lord and the servant, when the Son/Servant is seated with the Father/Lord in peace and rest in the holy city (51:278–80.289). However, there is a difference. Here, Julian understands that the holy city is not only a figure in the parable or a symbol of Christ reigning in heaven; it is Divine Reality radiating from the center of her human soul.

> He sits exactly in the middle of the soul in peace and rest, and he rules and governs heaven and earth and all that is. The manhood [of Christ] sits in rest with the godhead; the godhead rules and governs, without any instrument or business; and the soul is all occupied by the blessed godhead: that is, sovereign might, sovereign wisdom, and sovereign goodness. (68:7–11.335–37)

Julian extends the vision of Christ in her own soul to include the souls of all humanity who will be saved. All are called to become Christ's holy city, set high on a hill, shining in glory. In this heavenly city, Christ's human nature is forever united with his divine nature, needing no intermediary between the divine and the human, since he is both God and Man. Nor does he expend himself in any more activity or working, since all has been accomplished, all is fulfilled, all is perfected. It is a spiritual city so vast, a landscape so incomprehensibly large and noble, the entire universe could not contain it. Here Christ's human soul manifests the might, wisdom, and goodness of the Trinity, arising eternally on the ground of pure awareness. Here Christ draws all suffering creation into his perfect human nature. Here he heals all human woundedness through his now-radiant wounds. Here he comforts all those who mourn and weep. Here he transforms all that is broken and destroyed by sin into his own pristine beauty. Here he is the reward and the eternal blessedness of all those who strive to love. Here he brings back all his lost sons and daughters into the home of his Sacred Heart. This blessed indwelling of the Trinity in Christ Jesus at the center of the soul is the core of the Sixteenth Revelation.

Holy Prophecy

What Julian sees evokes the holy city of the Book of Revelation:

> And I saw the holy city, the new Jerusalem, coming down out of heaven from God, prepared as a bride adorned for her husband. And I heard a loud voice from the throne saying, "See, the home of God is among mortals. He will dwell with them; they will be his peoples, and God himself will be with them; he will wipe every tear from their eyes. Death will be no more; mourning and crying and pain will be no more, for the first things have passed away." And the one who was seated on the throne said, "See, I am making all things new." Also he said, "Write this, for these words are trustworthy and true." Then he said to me, "It is done! I am the Alpha and the Omega, the beginning and the end. To the thirsty I will give water as a gift from the spring of the water of life. Those who conquer will inherit these things, and I will be their God and they will be my children." (Rv 21:2–7)

We must not think that the literal images of this eschatological prophecy, or of Julian's descriptions of the heavenly city, are their true import, any more than the initial figures of the lord and the servant revealed the *exemplum's* deepest meaning. As we have seen, it is the multiple layers of inexplicable mystery, the *privities*, hidden within the images that Julian is trying to uncover. Images and metaphors only point to Divine Reality; they are not the Reality itself.

Endless Dwelling

> The place that Jesus takes in our soul he shall never leave it without end, as to my sight, for in us is his homeliest home and his endless wonning [dwelling, home]. And in this he shewed the delight that he has in the making of man's soul. For as well as the father might make a creature, and as well as the son knew how to make a creature, so well would the holy ghost ordain that man's soul be made. And so it was done. And therefore the blessed trinity rejoices without end in the making of man's soul, for he saw without beginning what should please him without end. (68:12–18.337)

Julian is convinced that "alle shalle be wele" in the end because all was well in the beginning, when the Trinity fashioned the human soul in the image and likeness of itself. The making of the soul is so perfect, that, *through Christ, with Christ, and in Christ* it will be brought up into a perfection greater even than its first creation. This perfection will not be human perfection alone, as it was in the garden of Eden. It will be the divine perfection of the God/Man, Jesus Christ. This theme has reverberated throughout the Revelations.

Now Julian receives the last *exemplum.* It concerns a creature (Julian, herself) who is allowed to see great nobility and all the kingdoms belonging to a lord on earth. After observing this nobility, the creature is directed "to seek up above to that high place where the lord himself wonneth [dwells], knowing by reason that his dwelling is in the worthiest place" (68:22–23.337). Through this parable, Julian understands that "our soul may never have rest in any thing that is beneath itself" (68:24–25.337). And when the soul rises above all creatures in a state of contemplative prayer, it cannot even rest in beholding itself. It must set its concentration on the vastness of God's presence *within* the soul. "For in man's soul is his [God's] true wonning," and "the highest light and the brightest shining of the city" within that soul is God's glorious love (68:27–29.337). And what could make the soul happier than to know that God "delights in us, the highest of all his werks" (68:29–30.337)?

> For I saw in the same shewing that if the blessed trinity might have made man's soul any better, any fairer, any nobler than it was, he [God] should not have been fully pleased with the making of man's soul. But because the trinity made man's soul as beautiful, as good, as precious a creature as it might make it, therefore the blessed trinity is fully pleased without end in the making of man's soul. And he [God] wills that our hearts be mightily raised above the depnesse of the earth and all vain sorrows, and rejoice in him. (68:30–36.337)

Beholding

> This was a delectable sight and a restful shewing that is without end. And the beholding of this while we are here, it is very pleasant to God, and a very great benefit to us. And the soul that thus beholds, makes itself like to him that is beheld, and oneth it in rest and in peace by his grace. And this was a singular joy and bliss to me that I saw him sit, for the sekernesse of sitting shewed endless dwelling. (68:37–41.337–39)

Julian takes great comfort in this final Revelation that God dwells in her soul. And she is certain that God wants us all to take the same comfort through the practice of "beholding." This type of contemplative prayer (waiting on God, in stillness, without asking for anything) gives God great pleasure and the soul great profit. Such silent prayer forms the soul into a truer image and likeness of the very One who is being contemplated. Julian is especially delighted that she saw the Lord *seated* in her soul (rather than standing or moving), because sitting symbolizes the familiar rest one takes at home, in complete contentment, peace, and love. God is not going anywhere. It is *we* who rush about, too busy with our lives and too distracted by our sufferings to take time to experience his inward presence. He thirsts for us to "Be still, and know that I am God!" (Ps 46:10). And if we come to him with our labors and our heavy burdens, he promises to give us true rest (Mt 11:28). Julian rejoices that God's true dwelling is forever in the soul. As Christ said to his disciples: "the kingdom of God is among you" (Lk 17:21).

Affirmation

> And he [Christ] gave me knowing truthfully that it was he who shewed me all before. And when I had beheld this with avisement, then our good lord revealed words very humbly, without voice and without opening of lips, just as he had done before, and said very sweetly: "Know it now well, it was no raving that thou saw today. But take it and believe it, and keep thee therein, and comfort thee therewith, and trust thee thereto, *and thou shalt not be overcome.*" (68:42–47.339, italics added)

Julian is given confirmation, not through audible sound but in the depths of contemplative silence, that what she had experienced all day long was no raving, no hallucination, no aberration of mind, no temporary madness. Julian receives this tender reassurance with immense gratitude. She declares that these last words Christ spoke in her heart were said to teach her *absolute certainty* that all the Revelations had come directly from himself, and that she should accept, believe, and hold onto them with her life. She was also instructed to take comfort in them during times of temptation and suffering, and in moments of darkness to trust all that she had seen in the light.

> And just as in the first word that our good lord revealed, meaning his blessed passion—"Herewith is the fiend overcome"—just so he

> said in the last word with very true sekernesse, meaning us all: "Thou shalt not be overcome." And all this learning and this true comfort, it is general for all my evencristens, as it is before said, and such is God's will. (68:49–53.339)

These words of reassurance are not for Julian only; they are to be applied generally for all who read and take her Revelations to heart. If we reflect on them, trust in them, and learn to take comfort in them, *we* will not be overcome by temptations to doubt, or to despair. Julian is very insistent about this. She reiterates that these words, "Thou shalt not be overcome," were said by Christ most fiercely and passionately, to give us "sekernesse and comfort against all tribulation that may come" (68:54–55.339).

> He did not say, "Thou shalt not be tempested [tormented], thou shalt not be travailed [wearied], thou shalt not be diseased [distressed]," but he said, "Thou shalt not be overcome." God wills that we take heed of this word, and that we be ever mighty in seker trust, in wele and woe. For he loves us and likes [delights in] us, and so he wills that we love him and like him and mightily trust in him, and alle shalle be wele. (68:55–60.339–41)

Julian clarifies that the Revelations of God's love, mercy, grace, and protection will not prevent us from suffering what we must endure as a result of our personal and communal sin, and because of our imperfections. The *shewings* will not stop disappointment, betrayal, failure, illness, aging, tragic accidents, untimely deaths. These are the common lot of humanity. Nor do the Revelations ever guarantee that our spiritual lives will proceed smoothly, that our relationships will be without conflict, that everything we strive for will be accomplished. Nor are these words of Christ meant to belittle the depths of our private agonies. But they *are* meant to reassure us that, no matter how tormented or desperate we may become, we will not be overcome by the darkness of evil. God wants us to rely on his care in good times and bad, in success and in failure, in joy and sorrow. He is our Mother who loves us simply because he loves us, not because of what we do or fail to do. God *likes* being in our lives. He *enjoys* dwelling within our souls as in his homeliest home. He wants nothing more than that we love him, and really, really *like* him, and always trust in him. If we do, "alle shalle be wele," even though we cannot imagine how.

Darkness

> And soon after all was closed, and I saw no more. (68:60.341)

This comes as a shock. Immediately following this reassurance that she (and we) will never be overcome, the Revelations end abruptly. Everything is finished. There will be no more visions, no more locutions, no new parables to decipher. There will be the work of decades to interpret and write and rewrite endlessly, but the long, miraculous day and night of Julian's *shewings* has finally come to a close. As if to test her resolve not to be overcome, Julian writes that the fiend returned "with his heat and with his stench, and made me very busy" with new temptations (69:1–2.341). The bodily heat she feels becomes dreadful and physically exhausting; the smell is vile. And her mind erupts into a cacophony of arguing and chatter.

> Also I heard a bodily jangeling [arguing, squabbling], as if it had been between two bodies, and both to my thinking jangled at one time, as if they [the devils] had held a parliament with great business. And all was soft muttering, and I understood not what they said. And all this was to make me despair, so I thought; it seemed to me that they scorned the bidding of beads which are said loudly with the mouth, lacking devout intention and wise diligence, which we owe to God in our prayer. And our good lord God gave me grace mightily to trust in him, and to comfort my soul with bodily speech, as I should have done to another person who had been travailed. (69:3–10.341)

In spite of the taunts causing havoc in her mind, Julian prays earnestly, reassuring her soul as the Lord has just shown her how to do. She tells herself exactly what she would tell someone else in her condition: to trust in Christ's protection, no matter how insistent the inner voices and temptations of devils become.

> I set my bodily eye on the same cross where I had seen comfort before that time, my tongue with words of Christ's passion and

> rehearsing the faith of holy church, and my heart on fastening on God with all the trust and the might that was in me. And I thought to myself, meaning: "Thou hast now great business to keep thyself in the faith, so that thou should not be captured by thine enemies. Wouldst thou now from this time evermore be so busy to keep thyself from sinne, this would be a good and sovereign occupation." For I thought truly: "Were I safe from sinne, I would be fully safe from all the fiends in hell and enemies of my soul." (69:12–19.341–43)

Focusing her eyes on the same crucifix that had "come alive" during her Revelations, Julian recounts aloud the passion of Christ and his words from the cross, even as she recites the truths of her faith over and over in the *Credo*. Notably, she hears blasphemous words of mockery arise within her head, even as she had mocked her own visions as "raving." She tries to drown out argumentation and heresy, even as she had doubted Christ truly spoke to her. She knows she must work hard not to be tempted to doubt again . . . or to despair. She recognizes that the best thing she could do would be to work this hard for the rest of her life not to fall into sin, because if she were free of sin, she would be safe from all the fiends that could possibly seduce her soul. But she knows it cannot be. She will always have to do battle with her mental demons in this life.

The fiend (now singular, not double) tortures her mind all night long and into the next morning until the monastic hour of *Prime* (6 AM). Then, suddenly, all the fiends are gone and only their terrible stench remains to haunt Julian, perhaps induced by an aspect of her bodily illness. She was probably suffering from hypoglycemia (low blood sugar) and severe dehydration by this time, having been unable to eat or drink for days. This deprivation in itself could have produced severe fluctuations in bodily temperature, sweating, an extremely bad taste in her mouth, and a foul smell in her nostrils. Now, however, even amidst these mental and physical onslaughts, Julian scorns the fiend, as Christ himself had scorned him, "and thus was I delivered from him by the virtue of Christ's passion. For 'therewith is the fiend overcome,' as our lord Jesus Christ said before" (69:22–24.343).

Julian lay in bed, exhausted, but victorious. No doubt she heard the women gathered around her, reciting the familiar words of the opening psalm of *Prime*:

> God, in thy name, make thou me safe; and in thy power redeem
> me!
> God, hear my prayer; with thine ears listen to the words of my
> mouth.
> For aliens have risen against me, and strong men sought my life;
> And they set not God before their sight.
> But lo, God helpeth me; and the lord is the supporter of my soul.
> Turn their evils back on themselves; and banish them in thy truth!
> Willfully I shall make sacrifice to thee;
> And, lord, I shall acknowledge thy name, for it is good;
> For thou deliverest me from all tribulations;
> And my eyes look scornfully on my enemies.[2]

No Sign

Julian was given to understand from the very beginning that her Revelations would end (unlike those of other mystics like Catherine of Siena and Brigit of Sweden, who enjoyed visions and locutions throughout their lives). But she was also assured that her faith would enable her to recall everything she had seen and heard, according to God's will and grace.

> For he left with me neither sign nor token whereby I might know it. But he left with me his own blessed word in true understanding, bidding me full mightily that I should believe it, and so I do. Blessed may he be! I believe that he is our savior who shewed it, and that it is within the faith that he shewed it. And therefore I believe it, forever rejoicing. And thereto I am bound by all his own meaning, with the next words that followed: "Keep thee therein, and comfort thee therewith, and trust thereto." Thus I am bound to keep it in my faith. (70:3–9.343)

She has no visible sign on her body, like the stigmata of St. Francis, to prove her mystical experience of Christ on the cross. Nor has she been left any personal token of the visions that would work future signs and cures: no holy hazelnut, no relic from the crown of thorns, no stains of the "dearworthy blood" on her sheets (as might have been expected by those looking for visible signs). Even the crucifix that had shown Julian the suffering and glorified images of Christ no longer appeared as it had during her Revelations. It was simply a crucifix. There is no indication it was ever deemed to be miraculous, like so many dubious relics of Julian's time. Presumably, the crucifix had to be returned to the curate at the local parish, once Julian fully recovered from her illness. One can only imagine what it meant to Julian every time she laid eyes on it in church!

Without any proof of the truth of her Revelations, the only true relic Julian can rely on is the solemn word of Christ within her heart that it was indeed he who had shown everything to her, and his command that she should cling to that certainty forever. She is convinced that everything she was shown is orthodox, and true, and "within the faith." Once more, Julian confesses that she forsook the Revelation briefly and denied it, on the very same day that it had been revealed to her, when she said openly that she had "raved." But now she realizes that this failure in some sense "obliged" the Lord to affirm the truth of the Revelation, so that it (and she) should not be lost to the forces of hell. She will never again doubt or deny a single aspect of what she has been shown.

> Then our lord Jesus in his mercy would not let it perish, but he shewed it all again within my soul, with more fullness, with the blessed light of his precious love, saying these words very mightily and very humbly: "Know it now well, it was no raving that thou saw this day"—as if he had said: "Because the sight was passed from thee, thou lost it and could or might not keep it. But know it now: that is to say, now thou seest it." (70:12–17.343)

On the one hand, because her Revelations have ended, Julian has lost the sight of the Lord. On the other hand, *her faith* in the visions she has seen and the words she has heard becomes stronger than ever because for one fateful moment, in the crisis of extreme pain, she doubted and almost lost everything that was so precious to her. Now she is committed as by a sacred vow to believe that she was not raving, but was privileged to "see" into the depths of divine mysteries, a seeing granted to very few. In a real sense, *she* must become the sign of the truth of the Revelations—and some day, her book.

She has been told to "take it, and believe it, and keep thee therein, and comfort thee therewith, and trust thereto, and thou shalt not be overcome" (70:18–20.345). Henceforth, her faith in the Revelations must be as full and true as her faith in the reality of Eucharist: "Take, eat; This is my body" (Mt 26:26). In these six words (*take, believe, keep, comfort, trust*, and *overcome*), Julian is firm that the Lord wishes not only her but all her readers to fasten the Revelation "faithfully in our heart," so that it may dwell there until the end of our lives and thereafter, in the fullness of heaven (70:21–23.345). She wants us to have *seker* trust in his promises, because we know his absolute goodness.

Julian understands that our faith is constantly being tested and challenged in many different ways by our human blindness (because, like the servant fallen in the ditch, we cannot see the Lord's face looking at us with compassion), and by the many spiritual enemies that tempt us, both within and without. But Christ, our precious lover, helps us continually, "through spiritual light and true teaching in diverse manners within and without, whereby we may know him" (70:26–27.345). And in whatever way he chooses to teach us, he wills that "we perceive him wisely, receive him sweetly," and preserve ourselves faithfully in his grace (70:28–29.345).

> For above the faith is no goodness preserved in this life, as to my sight, and beneath the faith there is no health of soul. But in the faith, there our lord wills we keep ourselves. For we must by his goodness and his own werking keep ourselves in the faith, and by his suffrance of ghostly enemies [spiritual adversaries or demons], we are tested in the faith and made strong. For if our faith had no enemies it should deserve no reward, by the understanding that I have of our lord's meaning. (70:29–35.345)

Julian is finally able to express her complete joy in the Sixteen Revelations, after the temptation to doubt their validity has been overcome. She testifies that the Lord's face is ever "glad and merry and sweet" in our souls because he beholds our living in great "love-longing" (71:1–2.345). And, as she has understood many times before, Christ wants us to have a joyous expression when we pray to him, not a dour one, for our happiness is his reward for all he has done and is doing for us. Of course, we cannot see this clearly, by sight, but only by faith. And yet, Julian trusts that if we try to maintain a joyous outer expression, Christ will draw that outer countenance inward "and make us all at one with him, and each of us with the other in true lasting joy that is Jesus" (71:4–5.345).

The Face of Christ

Julian recalls the strongest images she saw during her Revelations and defines three aspects of Christ's *chere*, or facial expression. The first is his face in the passion, "as he shewed while he was with us in this life, dying" (71:6–7.345). And even though the beholding of this suffering countenance is a cause for mourning and sorrowing, yet it is also the source of great gladness and joy for all humanity, "for he is God," the Savior of all (71:7–8.345). The second expression is Christ's face of pity, sympathy, and compassion that he shows to all who love him and have need of his mercy, offering *sekernesse* of constant protection. And the third is his blissful visage, "as it shall be without end, and this was most often shewn and the longest continued" (71:10–12.345).

She comments that in life's woes, Christ shows us his *suffering* face on the cross and helps us to bear our own crosses through the strength of his virtue. And when we fall into sin, he shows us his *compassionate* face, defending us against all our enemies. These are the most common faces Christ reveals to us in this life. But occasionally Julian attests that Christ allows the third expression to mingle with the other two, that is, his *blissful* face, as she was privileged to see it in her Revelations and as we shall see it in heaven. And this will happen by a "gracious touching of sweet illumination in our spiritual life," through which we feel totally protected in secure faith, hope, and love, contrition and devotion, with every kind of truest solace and comfort (71:18–21.347). This, the blissful face of the glorified Christ, works in us by grace.

Mortal Sin

Julian's piercing question in the Third Revelation had been: "What is sinne?" (11:4.163). As we have seen, the fact of human sinfulness played a major role in her Revelations, most especially in her recognition of the inconceivable sufferings that sin cost Christ on the cross. Now Julian wants to clarify how she came to understand *mortal sin* in the souls of those "who will not die because of sin, but live in the joy of God without end" (72:1–2.347). This is especially personal and pertinent, because Julian considers her own sin of momentary disbelief so grave that it might well have been mortal and condemned her soul to hell had it been left unconfessed. (We may assume that Julian did eventually confess her sin to a priest.)

Julian alludes to the fact that, according to medieval physics and common understanding, two opposites cannot exist in the same place, and the two most extreme polar contraries are the "highest bliss" and the "deepest pain" (72:3–4.347). Julian knew that the highest bliss is to behold God in the clarity of endless light, truly seeing and feeling him, possessing him in peace and complete joy. And Julian had experienced this bliss in mystical contemplation. At the same time, she saw that the state of sin was the most extreme opposite of perfect happiness. Therefore, "as long as we are mixed with any part of sinne we shall never see clearly the blissful chere of God" (72:7–8.347).

> And the more horrible and the more grievous that our sinnes are, the further are we for that time from this blissful sight. And therefore it seems to us oftentimes that we were in peril of death and in a part of hell, for the sorrow and the pain that sinne is to us. And thus we are dead for that time to the very sight of our blissful life. (72:9–12.347)

Julian has agonized through her own experience of serious sin, falling into the abyss of mental and spiritual torment, being oppressed by demons, perhaps feeling for a time that she might be damned. She has also suffered the horror of being cut off from the bliss of God's presence and peace. Thus she is able to identify mortal sin as being "in a part of hell." She is way ahead of her time in her psychological understanding of hell as being (at least at one level) a tortured state of mind, an intense anguish of soul, a dying of hope. Yet she knows that for the souls who love God, Christ "descended into hell," according to the *Credo*. He does not abandon the sinner to his or her sin.

> But in all this I saw truthfully that *we are not dead in the sight of God*, nor does he ever pass from us. But he shall never have his full bliss in us until we have our full bliss in him, truly seeing his beautiful, blissful chere. For we are ordained thereto by nature and brought thereto by grace. Thus I saw how sinne is deadly *for a short time* to the blessed creatures of endless life. (72:13–17.347, italics added)

Even though the soul is plunged into darkness by mortal sin, in God's eyes, the soul is not completely dead. Here again, Julian alludes to the two *domes*, or realms of judgment: that of the church on earth that must condemn the sin and punish the sinner in order to bring him or her to full repentance and purification, and that of God who shows pity and compassion for all the sinner must inevitably suffer because of mortal sin. Even though the sinner cannot rest in the peace and joy of God's presence in the soul when it is mired in sin, God never leaves the soul's ground of being. If God did, the sinner would cease to be. On the contrary, God waits, like the lord in the parable, sitting on the vast wasteland of the soul until the fallen servant is restored to grace by the work of his divine Son. And as soon as the sinner recognizes the sin, feels contrition, confesses guilt, and receives absolution, the free gift of God's grace once again flows upon the ground of the soul. Then "there will be more joy in heaven over one sinner who repents than over ninety-nine righteous persons who need no repentance" (Lk 15:7). Sin is deadly "for a short time" for those who seek to love God, but it is not damnation for eternity. And Julian attests that the more the soul sees Christ's countenance through the eyes of faith and love, the more it will long to see his face in all its glory.

> For notwithstanding that our lord God dwells now in us, and is here with us, and embraces us and encloses us because of tender love so that he may never leave us, and is nearer to us than tongue may tell or heart may think, yet we may never tire of mourning nor of weeping, nor of seeking nor of longing till the time when we see him clearly in his blissful countenance. For in that precious sight there may no woe abide, nor wele [well-being] fail. (72:19–24.347)

Only in the full vision of God's blessed face will we finally be free of all our tendency to sin, of all our suffering as a result of wrong choices, and be able to contemplate the Ultimate Good that can never fail to fulfill us. Julian understands in this observation both a reason to rejoice and a reason to mourn. We rejoice that our Lord and Creator "is so near to us and in us, and we in him by sekernesse of keeping because of his great goodness" (72:25–27.347). At the same time, we mourn

> for our ghostly eye is so blind, and we are so weighed down with the weight of our mortal flesh and darkness of sin, that we cannot see our lord God clearly in his beautiful, blissful chere. No, *and*

> *because of this darkness, we can scarcely believe or trust his great love and our sekernesse of keeping.* And therefore it is that I say, we may never stop mourning nor weeping. (72:27–31.347, italics added)

Julian poignantly identifies the perennial difficulty sinners have in believing they are loved and protected by God, even in their sin. The servant in the ditch is in such darkness that he cannot imagine the Lord could be standing so close, his face full of pity and compassion. Because of shame, the soul is thrust down into the depths of despair. And so it weeps. However, Julian advocates that the sinner should not only shed *bodily tears* but seek a more spiritual type of repentance, one that includes a deep, internal *love-longing.* Julian explains that this is because the natural desire of our soul for God is so immeasurable that if all the noblest comforts of heaven and earth were offered to us, yet we could not have the sight of God, we would continue to mourn and weep in painful yearning until we could see our Creator. Alternately, if we were thrust into the greatest pain that the mind could conceive or the tongue describe, and we could still see God's beautiful, blissful Face, all the pain in the world could not make us grieve.

> Thus is that blissful sight the end of all manner of pain to loving souls, and the fulfillment of all manner of joy and bliss. And he shewed this in the high, marvelous words where he says: "I it am that is highest, I it am that thou loveth, I it am that is all." (72:40–42.349)

In summary, Julian stresses that we must have three forms of "knowing" in our lifetime: first, of our Lord, God; second, of our self as we are created by God in our nature and as redeemed by grace; and third, of our self "as regards our sin and as regards our feebleness" (72:45–46.349). Julian is convinced that it was to reveal the depths of these three forms of knowing that "all this shewing was made, as to my understanding" (72:46–47.349).

24
At Her Window

All this blessed teaching of our lord God was shewn in three parts: that is to say, by bodily sight, and by words formed in my understanding, and by ghostly sight. For the bodily sight, I have said as I saw, as truly as I can. And for the words, I have said them exactly as our lord revealed them to me. And for the ghostly sight, I have said somewhat, but I may never fully tell it. And therefore about this ghostly sight I am directed to say more, as God will give me grace. (73:1–6.351)

Julian has come full circle. At the end of the First Revelation she told us that it was shown "by bodily sight, and by words formed in my understanding, and by ghostly sight" (9:24–25.157). She also mentioned at that time that she could not disclose the spiritual insights as fully as she would like to do. Now, after she has recounted all her *shewings*, the situation has not changed. She still acknowledges that the fullness of divine revelation cannot be put into words or images. Nevertheless, in these final chapters of her book (73–86), Julian feels compelled to record what she has learned from the "ghostly sight," the further inspiration that came to her over the years, if God will help her do it. She wants to disclose additional aspects of the divine and human love-longing, and to warn against the impediments to perfect union that she, herself, has suffered. She speaks to the reader as directly and intimately as she must have counseled the men and women who came to the window of her anchorage during the last two decades of her life. She gives spiritual direction and "lessons of love" based on personal experience. However, unlike her modern readers, those who visited Julian at her window *may never have known the source of her wisdom.*

Sloth and Despair

For those devout souls seeking God, she warns of two forms of spiritual sickness. One is impatience or sloth, "for we bear our travail and our pain heavily"; the other is "despair or doubtful dread," which she will treat later on (73:8–9.351). While God had only shown her "sinne" in a general manner, these two deadly sins were shown specifically. Julian confesses that sloth and despair are what we must amend most diligently, if we truly hate sin and wish to do God's will.

Sloth implies a heaviness of body and laziness of soul, perhaps even a permanent state of *melancholia* and mental depression, which in medieval times was usually ascribed more to women than to men. As we have seen, it suggests *acedia*, a state of indifference to the spiritual life. It was a torpor of body and mind much dreaded by those in monastic life and one that Julian herself must have had to combat during her long years enclosed as an anchoress. St. Bernard of Clairvaux had warned against the "nighttime dread" (during Divine Office), the arrow of temptation by day, and the "noontide devil" of torpor that wishes to snatch the soul from contemplation: "For we cannot defend ourselves from the attack of the noontide devil except with the aid of noontide light [Christ]."[1] The *Ancrene Riwle* also railed against the deadly sin of sloth as being a bear whose "whelps" eat away at the soul: the whelps of torpor (a lukewarm heart), pusillanimity (a faint heart), dullness of heart, idleness, a grudging heart, deadly sorrow (for loss of a friend or a possession), negligence (in saying, doing, remembering, or providing protection), and finally, despair. "This last bear's whelp is the fiercest of all, for it gnaws and wastes the benignant kindness, and great mercy, and unlimited grace of God."[2]

When the spirit feels tired and dry, holy words seem lifeless, the mind is unable to focus, and prayer itself becomes a chore. Especially when one has been granted a glimpse of heavenly bliss, as Julian had, contemplative life without inspiration can become a veritable purgatory on earth. Even more, sloth (and the accompanying impatience with the burdens of life) can lead to the complete abandonment of the practice of prayer as being pointless. And this debilitating attitude, in turn, may sink the soul into dark despair, convincing the mind that God is not at all present and active in one's life. In short, Julian knows from personal experience that sloth and despair can make us doubt all that is most precious to us and deprive us of the very *love-longing* that first inclined us to pray. She is adamant that we must battle these two deadly sins as much as (if not more than) all other sins. She firmly counsels that we take refuge in Christ's own patience in suffering his passion, and also in his continuing joy in being able to endure so much pain out of his great love for us. Therefore, we should be strengthened to bear our own trials and tribulations, "for that is greatly pleasing to him and endless profit to us" (73:19.351). She suggests that the reason we are so troubled and belabored by our pains is that we simply do not know what love really is.

Previously, Julian has spoken of the three persons of the Trinity as divine might, wisdom, and love. Here she declares that even though all the powers of the Trinity are equal, "the soul learned the most about love."

> Yea, and he wills in all things that we have our beholding and our enjoying in love. And of this knowing we are most blind. For some of us believe that God is almighty and *may* do all, and that he is all wisdom and *can* do all. But that he is all love and *will* do all, there we stinte [balk]. (73:22–25.353, italics added)

Julian pinpoints the source of sloth and impatience, doubt and despair: we are not fully convinced of the love God has for each and every one of us, or of the lengths to which he will go to express it. We believe God is all-powerful and *may* do anything he wishes, and that he is all-wise and *can* do the best thing for us, but we are not yet absolutely certain in our hearts that he is "all love" and that he *will* help us in the most perfect way possible. Something in us balks at believing that God cares about us *that much.* To drive home her point, Julian chooses the same strong auxiliary verbs she heard Christ speak: "I *may* make alle thing wele, and I *can* make alle thing wele, and I *will* make alle thing wele." She wants to impress upon the reader that God is always willing to come to our aid, if only we will trust in his love. Yet it is up to us to make the blind leap of faith that, no matter how overwhelming our sorrow or suffering, God is still and always caring for us, holding us, enveloping us. Unless we practice believing this, we may lose our capacity to hope. And we may forfeit our ability to love.

False Humility

> And this ignorance [of God's love] is what most impedes God's lovers, as to my sight. For when we begin to hate sinne, and amend ourselves according to the ordinances of holy church, yet there dwells a dread that hinders us because of the beholding of ourselves and of our sinnes done before, and with some of us, for our everyday sinnes.

> For we do not keep our promises nor maintain the purity that the Lord places us in [through the sacraments], but fall oftentimes into so much wretchedness that it is a shame to say it. And the beholding of this makes us so anxious and depressed that we can scarcely see any comfort. And this dread we sometimes mistake for meekness, but it is a foul blindness and a weakness. And we fail to despise it like other sinnes that we know, for it comes from the enemy and it is against truth. (73:26–35.353)

Next, Julian speaks out against the lie of "false humility" with a conviction that is no less than fierce. When we doubt God's love for us under the guise of our *unworthiness* to be loved, it is a terrible temptation from "the enemy," Satan, even though it may not be numbered among the better-known seven deadly sins. Julian admits that self-doubt arises because, no matter how much we try to amend our lives, "some of us" look into our souls and see only our failings. How many people must have come to Julian's window who had previously confessed their sins with true contrition, done penance, but still lived in the debilitating fear that they had forgotten to mention something from their past? How many brooded over their "everyday (venial) sins" as if they were mortal? And how many privately confessed to Julian that they had made promises to themselves and to God that they had failed to keep: to reform their lives, to live in greater purity of body and soul, to pray more often and more earnestly, to enter more deeply into the sacramental life of the church, to show compassion and care for their neighbors? Julian includes herself among those who feel such sorrow and shame that the soul is left barren of any spiritual consolation. And the worst thing of all is that such souls *think* this self-inflicted misery is the virtue of humility, whereas it is a state of wretchedness that alienates good people from God and leads souls into despair. Julian counters this negativity with the greatest hope:

> For of all the properties of the blissful trinity, it is God's will that we have the most sekernesse and delight in love. For love makes might and wisdom very humble to us. For just as by the courtesy of God he forgets our sinne from the moment that we repent, exactly so he wills that *we* forget our sin, as regards our unskillful heaviness and our doubtful dreads. (73:36–40.355, italics added)

Four Kinds of Dread

For those who are full of fears (and they must have been legion), Julian identifies four common types of "dread." The first is dread of "afray," that is, fear of sudden attack or the sound of alarm, "that comes to man suddenly through frailty [vulnerability]" (74:1–2.355). This fear arises in an instant at the all-too-common "hue and cry" for help, the smell of smoke, the frantic ringing of church bells. As we now know, this elemental and instinctive fear triggers the fight, flight, or freeze mechanism. Julian sees that this fear can sometimes be of benefit, for it helps to purge human beings of their self-reliant arrogance, as does the experience of bodily sickness or any other pain that is not sinful. "For all such pains help man, if they be patiently received" (74:3–4.355).

The second most common fear is that of pain "whereby man is stirred and awakened from the sleep of sinne" (74:5–6.355). While Julian acknowledges that human beings may indeed be shaken out of their sinful habits by meditating on the imminence of death, the pains of purgatory, and the fires of hell, she also knows from her own experience what tortures these thoughts can inflict upon sensitive souls. Still, she admits that, in some cases, the fear of damnation could lead the soul to throw itself on the mercy and consolation of God. "And thus this dread helps us as an approach [to God], and enables us to have contrition by the blissful touching of the holy ghost" (74:9–10.355).

The third fear is "doubtful dread," or doubting fear as to the completeness of God's forgiveness, which, as Julian has described, can seduce the soul into despair. God wants to transform this dread "into love by true knowing of love" and by the working of grace: "For it may never please our lord that his servants doubt his goodness" (74:12–14.357).

Finally, Julian comes to the fourth fear, which is very different from all other fears. It is "reverent dread," what we might term, "holy awe." She insists that this is the *only* fear the Lord wants us to have, because it is very gentle and lacks any hint of terror. It is inextricably linked to love.

> Love and [reverent] dread are brothers, and they are rooted in us by the goodness of our maker, and they shall never be taken from us without end. (74:17–18.357)

In our essential human nature, the soul remains in eternal reverence of its Creator, and by grace, the soul remains in awe at the gift of its salvation. We are made to love and we are made to fear God in a most holy way. Julian affirms that it belongs to God's Lordship and Fatherhood to be thus feared, as it belongs to his Goodness (the Holy Spirit) to be totally loved. And so it is proper to his servants both to fear and love him. And though reverent fear and love are two separate properties in us, neither one may be present without the other. "And therefore, I am seker, that he who loves, he dreads, though he feels it but little" (74:25–26.357).

Julian concludes that any *other* fears, worries, terrors, or doubts that the mind presents to itself, even though they might appear disguised as "holy" fears, are definitely not so. These impostors can be differentiated in a very simple way:

> That dread that makes us hastily flee from all that is not good and fall into our lord's breast, as the child in the mother's bosom, with all our intention and with all our mind—knowing our feebleness and our great need, knowing his everlasting goodness and his blissful love, only seeking into him for salvation, clinging to him with seker trust—that dread that induces this werking in us, it is natural and gracious and good and true. *And all that is contrarious to this, either it is wrong, or it is mixed with wrong.* (74:29–35.357, italics added)

Julian advises her readers (as she must have advised those who came to her for spiritual guidance) to know all the types of dread so as to be able to separate them in their minds, choose "reverent dread," and refuse all other fears. In the Short Text, she was very explicit as to how to discern holy fear from its enemy, like differentiating a good angel from the devil appearing as an angel of light. She testifies that the more often that reverent dread is felt, the more it softens and comforts the soul and gives it immeasurable rest and peace, whereas false fear "travails and tempestes and troubles" (xxv: 21–23.119). Christ himself taught: "You will know them by their fruits" (Mt 7:16). Julian's remedy is "to know them both, and refuse the wrong [kind of dread]" (74:36.357). The reverent fear of God that we have in this life "by the gracious werking of the holy ghost" is the same reverence we will experience in heaven: "gentle, courteous, fully delectable" (74:36–38.357).

> And thus we shall in love be homely and near to God, and we shall in reverent dread be gentle and courteous towards God, and both in one manner, the same. We should desire then of our lord God to dread him reverently and to love him humbly and to trust in him mightily. For when we dread him reverently and love him humbly, our trust is never in vain. For the more that we trust and the mightier, the more we please and worship our lord in whom we trust. And if we fail in this reverent dread and humble love, as God forbid we should, our trust will soon be misruled for that time. And therefore we need greatly to pray to our lord of grace, that we may have this reverent dread and humble love by his gift, in heart and in werk, for without this no man may please God. (74:39–48.359)

It is worth noting that it is precisely at this point that *Julian ends her Short Text* with the words:

> For God wills ever that we be seker in love, and as peaceful and restful as he is to us. And in exactly the same relationship as he is to us, so he wills that we be to ourself, and to our evencristens. Amen. Explicit [the final words of] Juliane de Norwich. (xxv:32–35.119)

Love, Longing, and Pity

In the Long Text, Julian continues with further reflections on what God does for us:

> I saw that God may do all that we need. And these three that I shall say are what we need: love, longing, and pity. Pity in love keeps us in the time of our need, and longing in the same love draws us into heaven. For the thirst of God is to have the general man [humanity] into himself, in which thirst he has drawn his holy souls that are now in bliss. And so in getting his living members, ever he draws and drinks, and still he thirsts and longs. (75:1–6.359)

The love, longing, and pity of God for souls has been a theme of the Revelations since Julian witnessed Christ's great thirst on the cross. "Therefore, this is his thirst: a love-longing to have us all together, wholly in himself to his endless bliss" (31:14–15.219). This is the divine longing of the lover to be united with the beloved in the Song of Songs: "For I am faint with love" (Sg 2:5). Julian returns to this theme and recognizes three forms of God's own love-longing (in which human beings also share). First, God longs for us to know him and love him more and more, and if we do, it will be greatly to our profit. Second, God longs to bring us to heaven, removed from all the pains and sufferings of this life. Third, God longs to fill us with bliss on the Day of Judgment.

> And not only shall we receive the same bliss that souls before us have had in heaven, but also we shall receive a new bliss, which plenteously shall flow out of God into us and fulfill us. And these are the good things which he has ordained to give us from without beginning. (75:15–18.361)

We shall be given resurrected bodies, reunited with our perfected souls, and we shall finally see the fulfillment of all Christ's promises. These sublime gifts are still hidden in God because, until the end of time, the human creature is not empowered or worthy to know the *privities* of salvation.

> In this we shall see truly the cause of all the deeds that God has done. And, furthermore, we shall see *the cause of all things that he hath suffered* [permitted to happen]. And the bliss and the fulfillment will be so deep and so high that, by wondering and marveling, all creatures shall have so great a reverent dread for God—overpassing that which has been seen and felt before—that the pillars of heaven shall tremble and quake. (75:20–25.361, italics added)

Julian becomes apocalyptic in her certainty of receiving a complete answer to all her persistent questions about sin, the value of suffering, and the Great Deed that will "make alle thing wele." She believes firmly that everything good will be accomplished in the Parousia, when, in the words of the Book of Revelation, there will be "a new heaven and a new earth; for the first heaven and the first earth had passed away, and the sea was no more" (Rv 21:1). She has been granted a glimpse of this exquisite glory in her visions. In a true and mystical way, she has experienced not only the "mind" of the passion but also the "mind" of the resurrection. Now she seeks to make this reality an ardent hope for her readers, against all present sorrow.

Julian assures us that the trembling and reverent dread of seeing the Face of God in heaven will not involve any terror; it will be a "trembling and quaking for greatness of joy, endlessly marveling at the greatness of God the creator, and at the littleness of all that is created" (75:26–29.361). This is the same wonder Julian had experienced at the littleness of the hazelnut that appeared in her hand at the very beginning of her Revelations.

She stresses to the reader, as she must have stressed to those who came to seek her counsel, that God wills that we know, and our own natures need to know, that this ultimate fulfillment *will truly happen*. And we should ardently desire the sight of it and the completion of it. Thus we must cultivate reverent dread that is "the beautiful courtesy that is in heaven before God's face" (75:35–36.361). For just as God will be eternally known and loved in heaven, far surpassing the way we know and love him on earth, so much more will he be reverenced, high above the still-imperfect reverence we give him now. For Julian, "reverent dread" is the complete and intimate contemplation of divine power, wisdom, and love; the satisfaction of the heart's desire to *behold* the Face of God.

Avoiding Sin

At this point, Julian admits that, throughout the Revelations, the Lord never showed her any souls who did not fear God (which does not imply that she ever *excluded* such souls from her considerations). And she is sure that those who truly listen to the teachings of the Holy Spirit will naturally hate and fear sin for its vileness, more than they do the pains of hell.

> For the soul that beholds the kindness of our lord Jesus hates no hell but sinne, as to my sight. And therefore it is God's will that we know sinne, and pray busily and travail willfully and seek teaching humbly, so that we do not fall blindly therein [to sinne]; and if we fall, that we rise quickly. For it is the most pain that the soul may have, to turn from God any time by sinne. (76:5–9.361)

As she must have done on a regular basis, Julian counsels those who long to love God to avoid all contact with sin. She also advises that when the sins of other people come to mind, we should not reflect on them, or talk about them, but flee them like hellfire itself, lest we fall into similar temptations. In the Middle Ages, it was considered a spiritual work of mercy to admonish others for their sins. Julian disagrees. Judging or accusing others, even in one's mind, forms "a thick mist before the eye of the soul, and we can not for that time see the fairness of God" (76:12–13.363). We should only consider sinners in order to hope for their full contrition, to have compassion on them, and to pray with great desire for their salvation. For, unless we do this, our own souls will be disgusted, and tortured, and even hindered in love by the thought of others' sins.

We live in the mix (what Julian calls "two contrarious" or opposites) between "the most wisdom" and "the most folly" (76:18–20.363). The greatest wisdom is to do the will of God and to follow all the counsels of our dearest friend, Jesus Christ, and to fasten ourselves to him in a most familiar manner, no matter what state of soul we may be in. "For whether we be foul or clean, we are ever one in his loving. For wele nor for woe, he never wills we flee him" (76:23–24.363). Yet because we are so changeable, so unreliable, we often fall into the greatest folly of sin, both through temptation from our enemy and through our own faults and mental blindness. Again she warns that, at such times, our personal demons will try to convince us that we are the most wretched of mortal creatures, we are sinners and liars who fail to keep our sacred covenant with God; that we keep promising to do better, but we are slothful and waste precious time. Julian reiterates, strongly and bluntly, that attending to such inner accusations is "the beginning of sin" (76:30.363). It is *especially* dangerous for those who serve the Lord through lives of contemplative prayer. Julian is speaking in very personal terms here, fully aware that dreadful doubts and self-accusations can make even the most dedicated religious person, like herself, "afraid to appear before our courteous lord" (76:32–33.363). And if a personal demon can prevent her, or any one else, from praying, it will have achieved a great victory.

> Then it is that our enemy will set us back with his false dread of our wretchedness, because of the pain that he threatens us with. For it is his intention to make us so heavy and so sorry in this state that we should forget the beautiful blissful beholding of our everlasting friend. (76:34–37.363)

Spiritual Guidance

Here is the voice of the mature Julian, speaking from her own lifelong battle with depression, having been plagued by demons who convicted her repeatedly of sloth, doubt, and betrayal. It is also the voice of Julian as spiritual guide, a woman who has listened for decades to the cries of shame and the pent-up anguish of her *evencristens* who came to her home, and later to her anchorage, needing to unburden themselves of their pain. By the time Julian wrote these passages, she knew more than enough about spiritual demons that bombard the mind with scruples, with self-destructive blame, with the *wrong* kind of fear of the Lord. She knew what a futile temptation "guilt" really is. She viewed her culture's preoccupation with God's avenging wrath and her *evencristens'* inordinate fear of death and damnation as a spiritual plague weighing down souls, destroying their capacity for love and hope and joy in the Lord.

There were no psychiatrists or psychologists in Julian's time, no family counselors or social workers, and very few wise spiritual directors available to those in crisis. In his *Scale of Perfection,* Walter Hilton actually warned *against* spiritual guides who might do more harm than good: "For they [souls] should not show themselves unadvisedly or lightly to any unskillful or worldly man, who never felt such temptations, for such may easily by their unskillfulness bring a simple soul to despair."[3] To whom did people go for help? We can only imagine that a woman like Julian must have been much in demand as a trustworthy spiritual guide for those wrestling with problems of the spirit (like Margery Kempe, by her own testimony). We know that some of these souls then expressed appreciation for Julian's wise counsel with financial bequests.

Arguing forcefully against the accusatory tone of much medieval preaching and spiritual writing, Julian is adamant that "all that is contrary to love and to peace, it is of the fiend and his party" (77:1–3.363). While admitting that, because of our feebleness and passions, we fall into sin, she insists that because of the mercy and grace flowing from the Holy Spirit, we are able to rise to even greater joy. *This is Julian's unwavering viewpoint.* And if our "inner demon" now and then wins us over to his side by our falling, Julian is certain that when at last we rise from our sin, through love and humility, the fiend loses many times more than he has gained. Julian sees our contrition and absolution as such great pain and sorrow for the fiend (who, because of his hatred, wishes to destroy us) that he literally "burns in envy" (77:6–7.363). All the suffering the fiend wants to place on our shoulders turns back onto himself instead. And for his hatred and evil works, "our lord scorned him, and shewed that he should be scorned, and this made me mightily to laugh" (77:8–10.365). Julian sees the remedy for sin as simply recognizing our wretchedness and always fleeing to our Lord.

> And thus we say in our intention: "I know well I have deserved pain, that our lord is almighty, and may punish me mightily; and he is all wisdom, and can punish me skillfully; and he is all goodness, and loves me tenderly." And in this contemplation it is helpful for us to abide. (77:13–16.365)

Penitential Practices

As for voluntary ascetical disciplines and extreme penances that people take upon themselves, Julian writes that these were never shown to her, specifically. Only this fact was revealed: that we should humbly and patiently bear the suffering that God allows to come to us and be mindful of his own blessed passion. "For when we have mind of his blessed passion, with pity and love, then we suffer with him, as did his friends who saw it," namely the three Marys and the disciple John (77:25–26.365).

> For he says: "Accuse not thyself much too much, thinking that thy tribulation and thy woe are all thy fault; for I do not will that thou become heavy nor sorrowful indiscretely. *For I tell thee, no matter what you do, thou shalt have woe.* And therefore I will that thou wisely know thy penance, which thou art in continually, and that thou meekly take it as thy penance. And then shalt thou truly see that all this living is profitable penance." (77:27–32.365, italics added)

Christ's words to Julian indicate that each life will have its measure of suffering; however, he does not want us to fault ourselves for everything that is wrong in our world, or our families. Neither does Christ want us to be inordinately depressed by the extent of human suffering. It is inevitable, given the perils and risks of the journey, that evil will come; human beings will commit sin. It is far beyond our powers of mind or heart to comprehend. Instead of being tortured by it, Julian tells us we should try to accept our "penance" for sin in whatever form it comes (mental, emotional, spiritual, physical, social) and understand that it can be made useful for our purification and our growth in likeness to Christ on the cross. At no point, however, does Julian ever imply that we should *welcome* or *perpetuate* suffering in a masochistic fashion, or cultivate suffering for its own sake. Nor does she imply we should ever refuse to combat those human sufferings, illnesses, and social evils that are in our power to alleviate or change. This would be a totally wrong view of Christian "acceptance" of suffering. Only when we have done all that we can do to resist the evil that is coming upon us and have "fought the good fight" (2 Tm 4:7) may we submit, as Christ did, to accepting the cross.[4]

A Prison

Now, writing in her old age, Julian confesses quite openly that, "This place is prison, this life is penance, and as the remedy, *he wills that we rejoice*" (77:33.365, italics added). What a privileged glimpse this is into the hidden Julian! The "prison" she refers to may be her own self-chosen imprisonment in the anchorage. It may be the sufferings of her aging body, or the imprisonment of her soul within her body, when it longs to flee to God. The "prison" metaphor might also allude to life on earth in general, with all its fears and woes. What she means to stress, however, is not the fact of human suffering as being like confinement in a prison, but the sure "remedy" for discouragement about our suffering. And this remedy is to know beyond a doubt that the Lord is always with us, "keeping us and leading us into fullness of joy" (77:34.365). In this remedy we are to take constant comfort.

> For this is an endless joy to us in our lord's intention: that he who shall be our bliss when we are there [in heaven], he is our keeper while we are here, our way and our heaven, in true love and seker trust. And of this he gave me understanding in all the revelations, and namely in the shewing of his passion, where he made me mightily choose him for my heaven. (77:35–39.365)

Julian is vigorously affirming the promise of eternal glory that Christ has prepared for those who love him. She wants her *even-cristens* who bear pain and heartache, and who come to her for advice, *to believe in heaven more than in hell.* She is sure that if people take refuge in the Lord, they will be forgiven, healed, taught, and sanctified beyond their wildest hopes. As St. Paul wrote: "What no eye has seen, nor ear heard, nor the human heart conceived, what God has prepared for those who love him..." (1 Cor 2:9).

In her constant focusing on heaven, Julian is not advocating "escape" from the world, nor is she distancing herself from the nobility of the human effort and the everyday concerns of mortal beings (as might be assumed of a hermit shut up in a cell). Even in the anchorage, Julian was *involved* in the human effort, perhaps at a deeper, more truly transformative level than those in the bustling marketplace. And because she was so attuned to the minds and hearts of her *evencristens*, Julian was acutely aware that those who had lived through the same torturous times she had were much more tempted to fearful doubts and lack of hope than to any presumption about being saved. At her anchorage window, as throughout her text, she sought to overcome the all-pervasive terror and mistrust of God by stressing his utmost *approachability*.

Familiarity and Courtesy

Julian advises those seeking her help that if we flee to our Lord he will comfort us; if we touch him "we shall be made clean," if we "cleave to him" we shall be *seker* from whatever peril could harm us (77:40–42.365). This reassurance brings to mind the nameless woman in the gospel who had suffered for twelve years from a hemorrhage. Trembling, she drew near to Christ in a large crowd, saying to herself: "If I but touch his clothes, I will be made well." Christ rewarded her for her great faith: "Daughter, your faith has made you well; go in peace, and be healed of your disease" (Mk 5:25–34; cf. Lk 8:43–48; Mt 9:20–22). Likewise, Julian assures us that "our courteous lord wills that we be as homely with him as heart may think or soul may desire" (77:42–43.365).

However, while Julian extols familiarity with the Lord, she also cautions against disrespect:

> But beware that we do not take this homelyhed [familiarity] so recklessly as to forget courtesy. For our lord himself is sovereign homelyhed, and as homely as he is, so he is courteous. For he is true courtesy. (77:43–45.365)

The combination of intimacy and courtesy mirrors the divine intimacy of the Blessed Trinity and the great courtesy of Christ who "emptied himself," not clinging to his Godhead as he stooped to save humanity (Phil 2:7). Julian is sure that all the saints in heaven who have become like Christ imitate both this intimacy and this courtesy. If we do not know how to behave in this way, we must ask the Lord to teach us how, and he will gladly do so.

Julian summarizes *four things* that the Lord, in his graciousness, wants us to know. First, he is our ground, from whom and through whom "we have all our very life and our very being" (78:4–5.367). Second, he protects us powerfully and with the greatest mercy, even when we are mired in our confusion, beset by all our enemies from within and without, as in the midst of a great battle. (She adds that when we give our enemies an opening to take advantage of us, we are in such dire peril that we do not even realize how great is our need.) The third is how courteously "he keeps us and makes us know that we go amiss" (78:10.367). He is, after all, our watchful Mother. And the fourth is how faithfully he waits for us, and does not alter his expression or attitude toward us, "for he wills that we be turned and oned to him in love as he is to us" (78:11–12.367).

This beautiful depiction of God's infinite courtesy toward the sinner would strain the bounds of human belief had it not arisen from Julian's personal experience of Christ on the cross. There she watched him suffering his agony without ever once changing his expression from love to anger. She knows for certain that this is the *true countenance* of God. And she is sure that if we commit these four realities to our hearts, we will be able to see even our sin as potentially profitable, and not fall into despair. As always, this does not mean we overlook the scourge of sin. We need to acknowledge it, and at the sight of its horror become truly ashamed of ourselves, admit our pride and our presumption, and admit that we are, in truth, "nothing but sinne and wretchedness" (78:16–17.367). Yet Julian asserts that we see only a small part of the real ugliness of sin; our Lord will not show us its full evil because we could not bear it. Out of his courtesy, he dispels the terrible weight of our transgressions.

> Also our courteous lord, in that same time, he shewed full sekerly and full mightily the endlessness and the unchangeability of his love. And also, by his great goodness and his grace inwardly keeping us, he shewed that the love between him and our souls shall never be separated in two without end. And thus in the dread [of

sinne], I have matter for humility, that saves me from presumption. And in the blessed shewing of love, I have matter of true comfort and joy, that saves me from despair. (79:12–18.369)

Yet again, Julian wants to impress upon the reader that Christ's love is eternal and *can* not, *will* not, change. He continually protects us and remains with us so that his love and our love will never be parted. And in this "blessed shewing of love" (which is in all the Revelations), Julian discovers a source of exquisite consolation and deepest joy that keeps her from ever despairing over her own sinfulness (79:16–18.369).

All this homely shewing of our courteous lord, it is *a lovely lesson* and a sweet gracious teaching by himself for the comforting of our soul. For he wills that we know, by the sweetness of his homely love, that all that we see or feel, within or without, which is contrarious to this [lesson], that it is of the enemy, and not of God. (79:19–23.369, italics added)

Julian conceives of Christ still standing all alone, as piteously and mournfully as when he was on earth, in anticipation of our homecoming. He is most impatient to "have us for himself, for we are his joy and his delight, and he is our salvation and our life" (79:32–33.371).

Another A.B.C.

Nearing the end of her teaching, Julian reminds her readers that God has given us *three noble gifts* to sustain and guide us throughout life. By using them well, "God is worshipped and we are profited, kept, and saved" (80:1–2.371). The first is our natural reason that enables us to come to know ourselves and to know God. The second is the common teaching of the church, through which we grow in our faith and are made holy. And the third is the "inward gracious werking of the holy ghost," by which we are rescued from our sins and brought into eternal life (80:3–4.371). We might call this "gracious werking" our conscience and inspiration.

And these three are all from one God. God is the ground of our natural reason, and God is the teaching of holy church, and God is the holy ghost. And all are different gifts, for which he wills we have great regard, and conform ourselves thereto. For these werk in us

> continually, all together. And these are great things, of which greatness he wills we have knowing here, as if it were an A.B.C. That is to say, that we may have a little knowing, of which we shall have fullness in heaven. And that is in order to profit us. (80:4–10.371)

While our reason may be able to establish the existence of God, it is ignorant in its understanding of sin, suffering, and salvation. For this, we must rely on the faith of the holy church that Christ, the God-man, took pity on our human condition, suffered, died, and rose again to save us from eternal death. Yet our faith, like our reason, is also imperfect, our hope full of doubt, our love often lacking. Therefore, we must count on the working of the Holy Spirit to lift us out of our shortcomings, and lead us into the light and bliss of heaven. At all times, these three realities are operative in us: reason, faith, and the grace-filled working of the Holy Spirit.

Once again Julian compares our earthly way of knowing to that of a child learning the A.B.C.s in order to read simple sentences. We may be able to decipher the words of scripture, but we will never know their entire meaning until we see them fulfilled in eternal life. We may begin to see a pattern to the highs and lows of our lives, but we cannot possibly comprehend the deeper message hidden in every circumstance, every personal encounter, every loving relationship, every success or failure. But Julian assures us we are always offered the three gifts of knowledge, faith, and merciful grace that we need to direct us on life's uncertain paths.

God's Holy City

> Our good lord shewed himself to his creature in diverse manners, both in heaven and on earth. But I saw him take no place but in man's soul... He has taken there his resting place and his worshipfull city, out of which worshipfull see [bishop's throne] he shall never rise nor remove himself without end. Marvelous and solemn is the place where the lord dwells, and therefore he wills that we readily attend to his gracious touching, rejoicing more in his holy love than sorrowing in our frequent fallings. (81:1–2, 8–12.373)

Julian returns to the Sixteenth Revelation when she saw her soul expand to become God's holy city. She suggests that if we pay attention to God's gracious presence in the very ground of our being, where he delights in resting, we will not be able to entertain thoughts of our sins. We will desire only more of God's goodness, God's infinite compassion, God's overwhelming tenderness and courtesy. And this is what God wants for us, not eternal self-recrimination, but eternal loving and joy. Julian adds that the greatest honor we can give to God is that "we live gladly and merrily for his love," even while undergoing our earthly penance (81:13–14.373). God in his infinite tenderness sees that our lives are full of suffering and pain. In fact, our natural longing for God is itself a form of penance and he knows this is a great trial for our souls, not yet to be united with him. We must believe that God's love continues to long for us, while his wisdom and truth, along with his *rightfullehede*, permit us to endure here a while longer. This is how God wants us to view our lives. For we will never be free of penance until we are finally made perfect in heaven, "when we shall have him as our reward" (81:19–21.373).

> And therefore he wills that we set our hearts on the overpassing [transcending]: that is to say, from the pain that we feel into the bliss that we trust. (81:21–22.373)

A Lesson of Love

Because of the humility that the sight of our sin gives us, and the faithful trust we have in God's eternal love, thanking and praising him for his mercy, *we actually do please him.* All this is what Christ meant when he told Julian:

> "I love thee and thou lovest me, and our love shall never be separated into two, and for thy profit I suffer": and all this was shewn in ghostly understanding, saying this blessed word: "I kepe thee full sekerly." (82:15–17.375)

This is the incomparable "lesson of love" Christ desires to teach us: that we should live in "longing and enjoying" of God (82:18–20.375). And all that is contrary to this teaching, Julian declares "is not of him, but it is of the enemy" (82:20–21.375). Julian frankly remarks that if there is anyone alive "who is continually kept from falling," such a soul was never shown to her (82:22–23.375). What *was* shown was "that in falling and in rising we are ever preciously kept in one love" (82:23–24.375).

Three Properties of God

> I had a partial touching, sight, and feeling of three properties of God, in which the strength and effect of all the revelations stand. And it was seen in every shewing, and most properly in the twelfth, where it says oftentimes: "I it am." The properties are these: life, love, and light. In life is marvelous homelyhed, in love is gentle courtesy, and in light is endless being. (83:1–5.377)

The "I it am" litany came to Julian as an internal locution, expressing *who God is* in an outpouring of psalmic words. Now, nearing the end of her book, she sums it up using just three: "life, love, and light." By God's life, she means his familiarity, intimacy, and enduring closeness to us in the ground of our being, out of which he will never come.[5] By God's love, she understands his all-embracing and courteous care for our souls.[6] And by God's light, she sees his everlasting Being that will never change or alter its expression toward us.[7] She recognizes this trinity of properties as the one goodness of God, to which her mind wants to be united and her heart wants to cleave "with all its powers" (83:5–7.377). She marveled at the sweet feeling of unity she gained from realizing that our human reason exists *in* God. She appreciated, with much greater depth after many years of contemplation, that this reason "is the highest gift that we have received, and it is grounded in nature" (83:7–10.377). In addition to our reason:

> Our faith is a light, naturally coming from our endless day that is our father, God; in which light our mother, Christ, and our good lord, the holy ghost, lead us in this mortal life . . . And at the end of woe, suddenly our eye shall be opened, and in clearness of sight our light shall be full, which light is God our maker, father and holy ghost in Christ Jesus our savior. Thus I saw and understood that our faith is our light in our night, which light is God, our endless day. (83:11–13, 17–20.377)

Julian further identifies the source of our light as none other than "charity" or spiritual love, which is measured out as is most profitable to us, according to the wisdom of God. The light of divine love is never allowed to be quite bright enough for us to be able to see our salvation clearly, nor is the heavenly light kept completely hidden from us, but it is enough light in which to live and work productively, thereby earning "the honorable thanks of God" (84:2–4.377).

> Thus charity keeps us in faith and in hope, and faith and hope lead us in charity. And at the end alle shalle be charity. (84:6–7.377)[8]

Julian was also shown three ways of understanding this light of charity: uncreated charity (which is God's love), created charity (which is the soul *within* God's love), and charity given (which is the virtue of love). This gift of love that is bequeathed to us through the working of grace enables us to "love God for himself, and ourself in God, and all that God loves, for [the sake of] God" (84:10–12.377). She marveled greatly at this virtue of love because she realized that even though we live foolishly and blindly here on earth, yet God always beholds our efforts to lead lives of love. And he takes great joy in our good deeds. Julian reiterates that the best way we can please God is by wisely and truly *believing* that we please him, and "to rejoice with him and in him" (85:3–4.379).

> For as truly as we shall be in the bliss of God without end, praising and thanking him, as truly have we been in the foresight of God, loved and known in his endless purpose from without beginning, in which unbegun love he created us. In the same love he keeps us, and never suffers us to be hurt by which our bliss might be lessened. And therefore when the dome [final judgment] is given, and we are all brought up above, then shall we clearly see in God the privities which now are hidden from us. (85:4–10.379)

We will not understand how it is that each soul is given plenteous grace to rise again after every fall, or how even the most hardened sinners are converted into saints, until at last we come up to heaven and see in God's eyes the hidden mystery of the magnificent process of salvation. But we can be sure of one thing: we will see that all has been done by God to perfection. This will be the Great Deed.

> And then shall none of us be moved to say in any thing: "Lord, *if* it had been thus, it would have been well." But we shall all say with one voice: "Lord, blessed may thou be, because it *is* thus, it is well. And now we see truly that every thing is done as it was thine ordinance to do, before any thing was made." (85:10–13.379, italics added)

25
A Gospel of Love

> This book is begun by God's gift and his grace, *but it is not yet performed*, as to my sight. For charity, pray we all together, with God's werking: thanking, trusting, enjoying. For thus will our good lord be prayed to, according to the understanding that I took in all his own meaning, and in the sweet words where he says full merrily: "I am the ground of thy beseeching." (86:1–5.379, italics added)

Writing as an elderly woman, alone in her anchorage, increasingly frail and infirm, perhaps going blind and deaf, Julian has far outlived medieval life expectancies (and her own near-death at thirty). Yet she acknowledges that her life's work on the text of her *Revelations* is not yet finished. Like a mystery play that has not been produced, her *shewings* have not yet been "performed" in public. Julian may be alluding to the fact that the Long Text could not yet be freely copied and published, given the climate of censorship and fear in the early fifteenth century. She may be lamenting that her book cannot even be read by most of her illiterate *evencristens*, for whom she has labored so long and so hard to write it. In any case, her Revelations have not yet been "acted out" by men and women, taking them to heart and living them to the fullest possible extent. Certainly Julian is aware that until every soul is brought up to heaven, her *shewings* will not have been truly "seen" by all those for whom Christ intended them.

Her greatest concern is that *God's* work through the Revelations might be left incomplete. She begs her future readers, whom she will never know, to "pray together" out of love, as Christ himself taught us, ever thanking, trusting, and fully rejoicing in him. Recalling that God is the very foundation of our beseeching, Julian knows that if we pray earnestly for God's work to be done in us, it will be. The fulfillment is already embedded in the initial desire to pray. She writes that "our lord's" intention in showing her the Revelation from beginning to end was that "he will have it known more than it is" (86:6–7.379). Christ's love and compassion for humankind need to be affirmed in times of cynicism, condemnation, and overwhelming pain. In our post-modern world, no less than in Julian's medieval one, many seek a God who loves us in spite of ourselves, and who can be counted on never to leave us alone in our wretchedness and despair. We long for Someone we can trust to be true to his Word.

Through "knowing" of the Revelations, which implies an ongoing process of contemplation, Julian is confident that Christ will give us the "grace to love him and cling to him," both in times of joy and in times of suffering (86:7.379). She reminds us that we are Christ's treasure, for whom he sacrificed his earthly life, living and dying for our salvation, and for whom he thirsts even in heaven. He beholds us "with such great love on earth that he will give us more light and solace in heavenly joy, by drawing our hearts from the sorrow and darkness which we are in" (86:8–10.379). These Revelations are meant to increase the light, hope, and joy by which we walk in faith.

Our Lord's Meaning

> And from the time that it was shewn, I desired oftentimes to know what was our lord's meaning. And fifteen years after and more, I was answered in ghostly understanding, saying thus: "What, wouldest thou know thy lord's meaning in this thing [the whole revelation]? Know it well, love was his meaning. Who shewed it to thee? Love. What shewed he to thee? Love. Wherefore shewed he it to thee? For love. Hold thee therein, thou shalt know more of the same. But thou shalt never know therein other without end." Thus was I taught that love is our lord's meaning. (86:11–17.379)

In this one word, Julian learned what she most needed to know: love is the beginning and the end of all true Revelation. God is love and all that God does is because of love, to show his love, and to increase our ability to respond in love. If we hold and cherish Julian's Revelations, pondering them in our hearts, we shall discover more and more of the ways in which Divine Love expresses itself to us. We shall discover that there is nothing else that is "real" but love, and that for all eternity. We shall begin to glimpse, as Julian did, that everything lasts, and ever shall, from a hazelnut to a universe, "because God loveth it. And so hath all things being by the love of God" (5:12–13.139). The very fact that anything exists at all is simply because Love *loves.*

> And I saw full sekerly in this and in all [the Revelations], that before God made us he loved us, which love was never satiated, nor ever shall be. And in this love he has done all his werks, and in this love he has made all things profitable to us. And in this love our life is everlasting. In our creation, we had a beginning, but the love wherein he made us was in him from without beginning, in which love we have our beginning. And all this shall we see in God without end. *Deo Gracias* [Thanks be to God]. (86:17–23.379–381)

With these last words, Julian sums up all that the Lord has shown her, all that she has heard and understood, all that she has tried to set down in her gospel account. She has spared herself nothing to share with us the depths of her spiritual pilgrimage on this earth. She has revealed her *shewings* and, in so doing, revealed herself. She has disclosed her own doubt and depression, impatience and sloth, and also affirmed her overarching confidence that the Lord lifts her up out of the ditch after every fall, as he does for each one who turns to him. She has shown us how we should walk: in faith, in *seker* trust, in hope, and most of all in joyful love, no matter what obstacles and pains we may suffer, even serious sins we may commit. For the soul in love, fear and despair have no place. Indeed, they are temptations away from the truth.

Julian's Revelations are, finally, a gospel of love. They testify that we are created out of love, by love, and for love. *Love* is the ground and the meaning of our creation, our redemption, our ultimate enclosure in God's glory. And just as we have been loved since "without beginning," so Julian bears witness that the Revelations were shown to her for the sake of love, that all might be brought to everlasting fruition. Christ our Mother will never leave us, never stop waiting and working in us until he has brought us up to be with him.

He sits within our substance and our sensuality as in his own home. He has become what we are in his incarnation. He cannot shed his humanity; it has become his glory. He is one of us . . . forever. And he has no greater thirst than to transform us into his own Mystical Body, intimately enclosed in Trinity.

Indeed, Julian has borne witness that the Heart of Christ thirsts for every soul as if it were the *only* soul ever created. She assures us that, as we contemplate this marvelous wonder of God's everlasting and intimate love, dwelling and working within our souls, we shall become transformed human beings. We shall experience our lives as a whole new creation, by the power of the Holy Spirit. When this salvific work is finally completed, within us and within every soul, then indeed: "Alle shalle be wele, and thou shalt see it thyself that alle manner of thing shalle be wele" (63:39–40.321). This is Christ's promise. And Julian's.

> Here unfolds [ends] the book of the revelations of Julian, anchorite of Norwich, in whose soul may God be pleased. (86:24–25.380)[1]

Waiting

Julian began her Long Text in the 1390s and quite possibly, did not finish the final version until she neared her death, sometime after 1416.[2] As we have seen in Part One, by 1401, Archbishop Arundel, along with King Henry IV and Parliament, had sanctioned the statute *De Haeretico Comburendo*, directed against those heretics of the faith who usurp "the office of preaching," who presume to teach new doctrines both openly and privately, and who "make and write books." If those convicted of these offenses did not abjure such heresy, or if, after confessing, relapsed, then they were to be handed over to the sheriff, mayor, or bailiff of the secular court who would pronounce sentence, and "before the people in an high place cause [them] to be burnt, that such punishment may strike fear into the minds of others."[3] (Julian was an "unlettered" laywoman who could have been accused of usurping "the office of preaching" by teaching what might be misinterpreted as "new doctrines," both openly and privately; and this, by the very act of making and writing a vernacular book of mystical theology.)

Then, in 1409, Arundel's Oxford *Constitutions* were published, prohibiting any secular priest or regular monk from preaching God's word "either in Latin or in the vulgar tongue" unless examined and found to be fit to preach, and then duly licensed to do so. If any *un*licensed preacher presumed to preach after he had been silenced, and "do the second time, take upon him[self] to preach," he could be lawfully convicted and "incur *ipso facto* the penalties of heresy and schismacy, expressed in the law."[4] (Julian was not even an ordained preacher; she was *an unlicensed lay woman who wrote about God in the vulgar tongue.* Her provocative exegesis on the parable of the lord and the servant, and her theological insights on the lack of wrath in God, the Motherhood of God, the "godly will," etc., if taught to her *evencristens*, could have been considered suspiciously heterodox, if not outright heretical.)

In 1414, Sir John Oldcastle, an avowed Lollard, headed a conspiracy to kidnap the new King Henry V and form a commonwealth. Oldcastle was eventually caught, condemned, hanged, and burned. Meanwhile, Parliament passed a statute that made Lollard or other heretical views not only a religious offense, but also a *civil* offense, an outright act of treachery against the kingdom. All secular justices were henceforth empowered to examine anyone even faintly suspected of heresy and then to refer such persons to the bishops' courts for trial. If heretics did not recant their wrong views, they would be executed. Eventually, seventy Lollards were burned. (Despite her repeated protestations of orthodoxy, *Julian's writings could easily have been quoted out of context, and Julian herself mistaken for a Lollard.*)

During this same time, Julian would have heard a report of King Henry V's overwhelming victory against the superior French forces at the Battle of Agincourt on St. Crispin's Day, 1415, even though the English were outnumbered at least two to one. (Five years later, the English King Henry would marry the French king's daughter, Catherine, and be named "Heir of France" by the Treaty of Troyes. His son, Henry VI, would finally become the king of France exactly eighty years after Edward III's claim to the title had initiated the wars in 1340, before Julian was born. *The war, its atrocities, and its countless casualties had informed her entire life.*)

Yet, even amidst the political and religious repression at home that must have prevented the publication and distribution of Julian's Long Text, it is intriguing to note that in 1413, the Short Text was *still being copied* (presumably by a Carthusian monk in the northeast of England), as part of a much larger collection of fourteenth-century works of contemplative spirituality.[5] We know this from the colophon that appears at its beginning:

> Here is a vision, shewed by the goodness of God to a devout woman. And her name is Julian, that is a recluse at Norwich and yet is on life, anno domini 1413. (colophon, i.63)

Is it possible that, since Julian's 1370s Short Text *predated* the proliferation of Lollard preachers and Archbishop Arundel's condemnations against them, it was considered to be "old-established," and therefore safely orthodox? And does the copying of the Short Text in 1413 further suggest that it was assumed by the monastic scribe to be the one-and-only account of Julian's *Revelations*? Was this because Julian had *deliberately kept the existence of the Long Text secret*, precisely in an attempt to forestall repercussions from the church and civil authorities?

Whatever the situation, it seems extremely doubtful that Julian's Long Text enjoyed much circulation either during, or immediately after, her lifetime. Given the Norwich heresy trials (1428–1431) and the subsequent burning of unrecanted heretics in the Lollards' Pit in Thorpe Wood, just half a mile from Julian's anchorage, the Long Text simply could not have been copied and published freely in such a repressive climate. And we may assume that only heavily edited and quite brief excerpts were published thereafter, such as those found in the Westminster collection, c.1500. By the sixteenth century, in the wake of the dissolution and the destruction of hundreds of monasteries and priories, along with their vast libraries, the surviving manuscripts had to be carefully hidden or smuggled out of England. Since no original versions of the Short or Long Texts have been discovered, it is indeed fortunate that *copies* of both were well preserved.

As she lay dying, some time after 1416, Julian may have considered that her great labor in giving birth to her Long Text would come to "nought." Even more, she may have feared that the full extent of Christ's Revelations might never be read or known. She may have breathed her last with the manuscript still hidden under her bed, or placed on her little anchorage altar, as her love offering, thinking it would never see the light of day. It may only have been found after her death. Even then, there is no evidence at all that her *Revelations of Divine Love* were ever widely copied and circulated, or that a posthumous cult of devotion to Julian of Norwich ever developed.[6]

As we saw in the introduction, it was not until the early twentieth century that Julian's Short and Long Texts were rediscovered and began to receive the appreciation, examination, and dissemination that they deserved. Perhaps Julian realized that her Revelations were not meant solely for the *evencristens* of her time, many of whom might not have been able to understand her theological subtleties. Perhaps she was aware that her work would not find its audience until a different world arose. Whatever her thoughts on this, she must have been *seker* that he who gave her the Revelations and inspired her to write them down would eventually reveal them to a people who needed them most. We may be thankful that we are that people.

Notes

Introduction

1. *The Writings of Julian of Norwich: A Vision Showed to a Devout Woman and A Revelation of Love*, edited by Nicholas Watson and Jacqueline Jenkins, henceforth W&J (University Park, PA: Pennsylvania State University Press, 2006). Note: Julian begins this sentence with the Middle English word, "methought," which I have translated throughout as "it seemed to me."

2. There exists an incomplete fifth-century Coptic papyrus *Gospel of Mary*, dating back, perhaps, to the second century. However, this gnostic gospel was most certainly *not* written by Mary Magdalene, but by a scribe in an early Christian community who gives no account of the passion, death, and resurrection of Jesus Christ. See Karen L. King, *The Gospel of Mary of Magdala: Jesus and the First Woman Apostle* (Santa Rosa, CA: Polebridge Press, 2003), 3–12.

3. *Julian of Norwich: Showings*, edited by Edmund Colledge, OSA and James Walsh, SJ (New York: Paulist Press, 1978), Introduction, 21.

4. *The Shewings of Julian of Norwich*, edited by Georgia Ronan Crampton, TEAMS Middle English Texts series (Kalamazoo, MI: Western Michigan University, Medieval Institute Publications, 1994), Introduction, 20.

5. W&J, Introduction, 11.

6. *The Shewings*, Crampton, 21.

7. Ibid.

8. Bequests of religious books in contemporary wills during this time period do not include manuscripts of Julian's *Revelations of Divine Love*. See Norman P. Tanner, *The Church in Late Medieval Norwich, 1370–1532*, (Toronto: Pontifical Institute of Mediaeval Studies, 1984), Appendix 6, 193–97.

9. *The Cambridge Medieval History*, edited by John B. Bury (Cambridge: Cambridge University Press, 1932), 7:807.

10. T. S. Eliot, *Four Quartets (Little Gidding, V)* (New York: Harcourt, 1968).

11. Francis Blomefield, *The History of the City and County of Norwich, Part II*, vol. 4 of *An Essay Towards a Topographical History of the County of Norfolk* (London: 1806), ch. 42, #22. Available at http://www. british-history.ac.uk/. My translation.

12. Thomas Merton, *Seeds of Destruction* (New York: Farrar, Straus & Giroux, 1964), 275.

PART ONE

Chapter 1: *Norwich*

1. Ian Mortimer, *The Time Traveler's Guide to Medieval England* (New York: Simon & Schuster, 2008), 36–37.

2. By 1325, a clock on Norwich Abbey Cathedral struck the hours. See Kenneth Leech and Sr. Benedicta Ward, SLG, *Julian Reconsidered* (Oxford: SLG Press, 2001), 30.

3. Map © 1984 by Pontifical Institute of Mediaeval Studies, in Norman P. Tanner, *The Church in Late Medieval Norwich, 1370–1532* (Toronto: PIMS, 1984). See the Appendix in this book for numerical correlations.

4. Photo © Norfolk Museums & Archaeology Service (Norwich Castle Museum & Art Gallery). The etching was made by Henry Ninham in 1864 from a drawing by John Kirkpatrick. Used with permission.

5. *The Complete Julian of Norwich*, edited with translations by Fr. John-Julian, OJN (Brewster, MA: Paraclete Press, 2009), 381–84.

6. Brian Fagan, *The Little Ice Age: How Climate Made History, 1300–1850* (New York: Basic Books, 2002), 62–63.

7. George Gordon Coulton, *The Medieval Village* (1925; repr., New York: Dover Publications, 1989), 115.

8. http://www.medieval-life-and-times.info/medieval-life/medieval-health.htm.

9. Erasmus (1466–1536), in a letter to a friend. Online at http://www. middle-ages.org.uk/middle-ages-hygiene.htm.

10. Photo © S. E. Poulton Collection: A. D. White Architectural Photographs. Division of Rare and Manuscript Collections. Cornell University Library. Used with permission.

11. Two more gates were added in the fifteenth century: Erpingham Gate, built c.1411 by Sir Thomas Erpingham (who fought at the Battle of Agincourt), directly opposite the cathedral's western façade; and the Bishop's Gate, c.1435, situated in the northern section of the cathedral wall near the bishop's palace.

12. Photo © by George Plunkett, www.georgeplunkett.co.uk. Used with permission. The Church of St. Julian was almost completely destroyed by high-explosive bombs during an air raid in the early hours of June 27, 1942. The Norman tower was reduced to rubble, and only the north and east walls of the church were left standing. It was rebuilt in 1953 and became the Shrine Church for Julian of Norwich.

13. King Henry II (1133–1189), the great-grandson of William the Conqueror, had been born and baptized in Le Mans, and so Bishop Julian of Le Mans became much revered in England, especially in Benedictine monasteries in the south.

14. Philip Ziegler, *The Black Death* (New York: Harper Perennial, 2009), 119.

Chapter 2: *Ancestry*

1. David Knowles and Dimitri Obolensky, *The Middle Ages* (London: Darton, Longman & Todd, 1969), 120.

2. Ian Mortimer, *The Time Traveler's Guide to Medieval England* (New York: Simon & Schuster, 2008), 47.

3. Ibid., 47–48.

4. Indulgences are either plenary or partial remissions of the punishments due to sins already repented, confessed, forgiven, and absolved. The church held that indulgences drew from the superabundant treasure of merit of Christ's passion and death on the cross, as well as the virtuous deeds and penances of the saints, in order to alleviate the length of time a soul would have to spend in purgatory before going to heaven. Notoriously, in the Middle Ages such indulgences were *sold* by unscrupulous "pardoners" and friars to all ranks of Christians. This abuse of spiritual gifts for profit would become a major bone of contention during the Reformation.

5. "The God of Love," in *Roman de la Rose*, lines 2149–53, quoted in Barbara W. Tuchman, *A Distant Mirror: The Calamitous 14th Century* (New York: Random House, 1978), 193.

6. *The Complete Julian of Norwich*, edited with translations by Fr. John-Julian, OJN (Brewster, MA: Paraclete Press, 2009), 23–25.

7. *Wastours* were spendthrifts, or destroyers. A *wastour* was also a wooden sword used by peasants to practice warfare.

8. William Langland, *The Vision of Piers Plowman*, edited by A. V. C. Schmidt (1978; repr., London: J. M. Dent, Orion Publishing, 1995), Passus VI, lines 25–28. My translation.

9. George Gordon Coulton, *The Medieval Village* (1925; repr., New York: Dover Publications, 1989), 10–11.

10. See also Lv 27:30; Nm 18:26; Dt 26:1–11; 2 Chr 31:5.

11. Coulton, *Medieval Village*, 294n1.

12. Ibid., 291.

13. Ibid., 293.

14. Ibid., 291–92.

15. Ibid., 79.

16. Ibid., 80.

17. Ibid., 17.

18. Ibid., 289.

19. Ibid., 296, 293.

20. The Emperor Constantine had issued legislation tying the *coloni,* formerly Roman freemen, to the land, effectively making them serfs in 332 CE.

21. Nicholas Orme, *English Schools in the Middle Ages* (London: Methuen and Co. Ltd/Routledge, 1973), 60ff.

22. Even as far back as the twelfth century, a poor boy from the town of Stradbroke in Suffolk attended a monastic school, was ordained a priest, and rose to become Archbishop Grosseteste of Lincoln Cathedral, one of the most influential prelates, preachers, writers, and scholars of the High Middle Ages. And in the sixteenth century, the son of a butcher became the highest prelate in the land and chief advisor to Henry VIII: Cardinal Wolsey.

Chapter 3: *Childhood*

1. Conisford was also known in the Middle Ages as Southgate, and was later renamed King Street.

2. Photo © English Heritage. Used with permission.

3. Nicholas Orme, *Medieval Children* (New Haven: Yale University Press, 2001), 6–8.

4. Ibid., 8.

5. Aquitaine had belonged to England since Henry II of England had gained the French fiefdom through his marriage to Eleanor of Aquitaine in 1152.

6. Jean Froissart, *Chronicles*, translated and edited by Geoffrey Brereton (London and New York: Penguin Books, 1968), 69.

7. May McKisack, *The Fourteenth Century, 1307–1339* (New York: Oxford University Press, 1991), 134.

8. Ibid., 135.

9. Thomas Walsingham, chronicler of St. Albans, as quoted in Maurice Keen, *English Society in the Later Middle Ages*, 1348–1500 (New York: Penguin Books, 1990), 138.

Chapter 4: *The Great Pestilence*

1. Nicholas Wade, "Europe's Plagues Came from China, Study Finds," *The New York Times*, Health Section (October 31, 2010).

2. *Encyclopedia of Plague and Pestilence: From Ancient Times to the Present*, edited by George C. Kohn (New York: Infobase Publishing, 2008), 31.

3. *The Grey Friars Chronicle*, quoted at http://www.visitweymouth.co.uk.

4. Wade, "Europe's Plagues."

5. Barbara W. Tuchman, *A Distant Mirror: The Calamitous 14th Century* (New York: Random House, 1978), 94.

6. Giovanni Boccaccio, "The Decameron," in *Stories of Boccaccio,* translated by John Payne (London: Bibliophilist Library, 1903), Introduction, 2–6.

7. Letter of Ralph of Shrewsbury, Bishop of Bath and Wells, quoted in Philip Ziegler, *The Black Death* (New York: Harper Perennial, 2009), 124–25, italics added.

8. Ibid., 125.

9. Agnolo di Tura del Grasso, "The Plague in Siena: An Italian Chronicle," from *Cronica Maggiore,* quoted in William M. Bowsky, *The Black Death: A Turning Point in History?* (New York: Holt, Rinehart and Winston, 1971), 13–14.

10. Jean Froissart, *Chronicles*, translated and edited by Geoffrey Brereton (London and New York: Penguin Books, 1968), 111.

11. See Y. Renouard, *Conséquences et intérêt démographique de la peste noire de 1348* (1948), referred to in R. S. Bray, *Armies of Pestilence: The Effects of Pandemics on History* (England: Lutterworth Press, 1997), 60.

12. Philip Daileader, *The Late Middle Ages* (audio/video course produced by The Teaching Company, 2007).

13. Bray, *Armies of Pestilence*, 61.

14. Ibid., 60.

15. Ziegler, *The Black Death*, 227, 230.

16. Ibid., 119.

17. Francis Blomefield, *The History of the City and County of Norwich, Part I*, vol. 3 of *An Essay Towards a Topographical History of the County of Norfolk* (London: 1806), ch. 15. Available at http://www.british-history.ac.uk/.

18. Rev. Augustus Jessopp, *The Coming of the Friars and Other Historic Essays, including "The Black Death in East Anglia"* (London: T. Fisher Unwin, 1894), 200–1, quoted in Ziegler, *The Black Death*, 167.

19. J. C. Russell, *British Mediaeval Population* (Albuquerque, NM: University of New Mexico Press, 1948), 293, quoted in Ziegler, *The Black Death*, 170.

20. Ziegler, 170–71.

21. Ibid., 170.

22. Ibid., 228.

23. Friar John Clyn, *Annals of Ireland*, edited by R. Butler (Dublin: Irish Archeological Society, 1849), 37, quoted in Ziegler, *The Black Death*, 194–95.

24. Ziegler, *The Black Death*, 228.

25. Ibid., 172.

26. Nicholas Orme, *Medieval Children* (New Haven: Yale University Press, 2001), 53.

27. Ibid., 55.

28. Shulamith Shahar, *Childhood in the Middle Ages* (London and New York: Routledge, 1992), 25.

29. Ziegler, *The Black Death*, 163.

30. They based their theories on the second-century physician, Galen of Pergamos (129–c.200/216 CE), whose theories were based on those of Hippocrates (460–c.370 BCE).

31. Ziegler, *The Black Death*, 73.

32. Ibid., 76.

33. Ibid., 74–75.

34. Guy de Chauliac, *La Grande Chirurgie*, edited by E. Nicaise (Paris: 1890), 171, quoted in Ziegler, *The Back Death*, 71.

35. Henry Knighton, Augustinian canon of Leicester, quoted in *The Black Death*, edited by Rosemary Horrox (Manchester: Manchester University Press, 1994), 78.

Chapter 5: *Education*

1. Carding or brushing the wool is done with two paddles containing metal pins that align the fibers. This makes spinning proceed more smoothly.

2. *Women's Lives in Medieval Europe: A Sourcebook,* edited by Emilie Amt (New York: Routledge, 1993), 196.

3. Photo © the British Library Board, from Giovanni Boccaccio, *De mulieribus claris* [On Famous Women]. First published 1374. MS Royal 16G. V, f.56, Shelfmark: Royal 16 C.V. Used with permission.

4. Shulamith Shahar, *The Fourth Estate: A History of Women in the Middle Ages* (London and New York: Routledge, 2007), 216–17.

5. Ibid., 176.

6. Ibid., 175.

7. *Prymer* was the English name most often used for vernacular versions of the *Horae* or Hours, psalms and prayers recited throughout the day by

layfolk in imitation of the monks' Divine Office. See James A. Devereux, SJ, "The Primers and the Prayer Book Collects," *Huntington Library Quarterly* 32, no.1 (November 1968): 29–44.

8. *The Prymer or Lay Folks' Prayer Book*, edited by Henry Littlehales (London: E.E.T.S., 1895), historical notes, xxxix.

9. Ibid., xlvii.

10. Ibid.

11. *The Lay Folks' Mass Book or Manner of Hearing Mass*, edited by Thomas Frederick Simmons, MA (London: E.E.T.S., N. Trübner & Co., 1879), 2–4. My translation.

12. Ibid., 28.

13. Ibid., 58–59.

14. Such as the Auchinleck manuscript, which contains forty-four individual texts compiled during the 1330s. Referred to in Ian Mortimer, *The Time Traveler's Guide to Medieval England* (New York: Simon & Schuster, 2008), 273.

15. "Bidding of beads" meant the saying of the scriptural psalms and praises of Mary by fingering beads on a string, which, in the fifteenth century, was formalized into the recitation of the rosary as it is practiced today.

16. Grace M. Jantzen, *Julian of Norwich: Mystic and Theologian* (New York: Paulist Press, 1988; repr., Eugene, OR: Wipf and Stock, 2005), 18.

17. *Julian of Norwich: Showings*, edited by Edmund Colledge, OSA, and James Walsh, SJ (New York: Paulist Press, 1978), Introduction, 19–20.

18. Ibid., 26.

19. Kenneth Leech and Sr. Benedicta Ward, SLG, *Julian Reconsidered* (Oxford: SLG Press, 2001), 19–21.

20. See Eileen Power, *Medieval English Nunneries, c.1275–1535* (Cambridge: Cambridge University Press, 1922), 237–81; see also Leech and Ward, *Julian Reconsidered*, 26.

21. Shahar, *The Fourth Estate*, 52.

22. Ibid., 47–48.

23. *Julian of Norwich: Showing of Love,* edited and translated by Julia Bolton Holloway (Collegeville, MN: Liturgical Press, 2003), viii, xii. See also *Julian of Norwich: Showings*, Colledge and Walsh, Introduction, 20–21.

24. Although the church strictly forbade this practice as a form of simony (financial payment to purchase holy offices or positions), it persisted because it was so necessary to the upkeep of the monasteries, both male and female.

25. Jennifer C. Ward, *Women in England in the Middle Ages* (London and New York: Hambledon Continuum, 2006), 157.

26. Leech and Ward, *Julian Reconsidered*, 21. Note: I had also reached the conclusion that Julian was not a nun (through textual analysis done several years prior to reading Sr. Benedicta).

27. Leech and Ward, *Julian Reconsidered*, 21.

28. Ibid.

29. Ibid., 22.

Chapter 6: *Marriage and Sexuality*

1. Shulamith Shahar, *The Fourth Estate: A History of Women in the Middle Ages* (London and New York: Routledge, 2007), 178.

2. Ibid., 81.

3. *The Sarum Missal in English,* translated by Frederick E. Warren (London: De La More Press, 1906), quoted in *Women's Lives in Medieval Europe: A Sourcebook*, edited by Emilie Amt (New York: Routledge, 1993), 84, italics added.

4. Ibid., 85.

5. Ibid.

6. Ibid., 86.

7. Ibid.

8. Ibid., 88.

9. Ibid.

10. *The Good Wife's Guide: A Medieval Household Book (Le Ménagier de Paris)*, translated by Gina L. Greco and Christine M. Rose (Ithaca, NY, and London: Cornell University Press, 2009).

11. Ibid., Art. 1.6.2, 104.

12. Ibid., Art. 1.6.24, 123.

13. Ibid., Art. 1.7.1, 138.

14. Ibid.

15. Ibid., Art. 1.7.6, 140.

16. Ibid., Art. 1.7.2, 138.

17. Ibid., Art. 1.7.3, 139.

18. Shahar, *The Fourth Estate*, 183.

19. Philippe de Beaumanoir, *Coutumes de Beauvais*, edited by A. Salmon (Paris: A. Picard et fils, 1899), vol. 2, par. 1631, as referred to in Shahar, *Fourth Estate*, 89.

20. Shahar, *The Fourth Estate*, 183.

21. Ibid., 86.

22. Ibid., 82.

23. Ibid., 92.

24. Ibid., 91.

25. de Beaumanoir, *Coutumes*, vol. 2, par. 1054, par. 1796.

26. *Recueil général des Anciennes Lois françaises*, vol. 1, 546. See Shahar, *Fourth Estate*, 93.

27. *Liber Augustalis*, 100. See Shahar, *Fourth Estate*, 92.

28. Tertullian, *On the Apparel of Women* (Whitefish, MT: Kessinger Publishing, repr. 2004), ch. 1.1, 3.

29. St. Jerome, *Lettres*, 8 vols., *Collection Budé*, edited by J. Labourt (Paris: 1949–1963), *Epistola XXII, Ad Eustochium*, 128.

30. Quoted in Grace M. Jantzen, *Power, Gender and Christian Mysticism* (Cambridge: Cambridge University Press, 1995), 54.

31. Quoted in Joyce E. Salisbury, *Church Fathers, Independent Virgins* (London and New York: Verso, 1991), 26.

32. St. Augustine, *The Trinity*, translated by Edmund Hill, OP (Hyde Park, NY: New City Press, 1991), bk. XII.3.10, 329. See also *Augustine in His Own Words*, edited by William Harmless, SJ (Washington, DC: Catholic University of America Press, 2010), 302–5.

33. *The Confessions of St. Augustine*, translated and edited by Albert Cook Outler (New York: Dover Publications, 2002), bk. 13, ch. XXXII, 300.

34. St. Augustine, *The Trinity*, bk. XII.3.12, 332.

35. Ibid., XII.3.10, 329, italics added.

36. Ibid., 330, italics added.

37. Ibid.

38. Ibid.

39. Ibid., XII.3.12, 332.

40. Ibid.

41. St. Augustine, "On the Good of Marriage," in *St. Augustine on Marriage and Sexuality*, edited by Elizabeth Clark (Washington, DC: The Catholic University of America Press, 1996), sec. 3, ch. 1, 43.

42. Ibid.

43. Ibid., ch. 3, 45.

44. Ibid., ch. 6, 48.

45. Ibid., 47–48, italics added.

46. Ibid., 48.

47. Ibid., ch. 7, 49.

48. Ibid., ch. 8, 50.

49. Ibid., ch. 11, 55.

50. Ibid., ch. 10, 52–53.

51. St. Augustine, "On the Words of the Gospel, Mk 8:34," in *The Works of St. Augustine: A Translation for the 21st Century, Sermons III/4 (94A–147A)*, translated by Edmund Hill, OP, edited by John E. Rotelle, OSA (Brooklyn, NY: New City Press, 1992), ser. 96.10, 34.

52. St. Augustine, "Against Julianum," bk. III.25:53, in Harmless, *Augustine in His Own Words*, 423.

53. St. Augustine, "Against Julianum," bk. V.15.54, in Clark, *St. Augustine on Marriage and Sexuality*, 96.

54. St. Augustine, "On Marriage and Desire," in *The Works of St. Augustine: Answer to the Pelagians II* (Hyde Park, NY: New City Press, 1999), bk. I.5, 30.

55. St. Augustine, *The Works: Revisions*, edited by Roland Teske, SJ (New York: New City Press, 2010) I.9.2, 52 and I.11.8, 63. See also Mary T. Clark, RSCJ, *Augustine* (London and New York: Continuum, 1994), 124.

56. Henri Marrou, *Saint Augustine and His Influence through the Ages* (New York: Harper and Brothers, London: Longmans, Green and Co., 1957), 162.

57. *Corpus Iuris Canonici*, vol. 1, col. 1128–1129.

58. John T. Noonan, Jr., *Contraception: A History of Its Treatment by the Catholic Theologians and Canonists* (Cambridge: Belknap Press of Harvard University, 1965), see ch. 3.

59. Shahar, *The Fourth Estate*, 68.

60. Thomas Aquinas, *Summa Theologica,* vol. 4, 546; vol. 5, 249–58; and *In Decemi Libros Ethicorum Aristotelis ad Nicomachum*, edited by P. F. Raymundi and M. Spiazzi, OP (Turin-Rome, 1949), 452, as cited in Shahar, *The Fourth Estate*, 68.

61. Aquinas, *Summa Theologica*, I.Q.92, Art. 1, Reply to Objection 2, quoted in Bede Jarrett, *Social Theories of the Middle Ages, 1200–1500* (London: Earnest Benn, Ltd., 1926), 72.

62. Aquinas, *Summa Theologica*, II.ii.Q.26. Art. 10, referred to in Jarrett, *Social Theories,* 74.

63. Ibid., II.ii.Q.154, Art. 2, quoted in Jarrett, *Social Theories,* 74.

64. Ian Mortimer, *The Time Traveler's Guide to Medieval England* (New York: Simon & Schuster, 2008), 55.

65. Joan Cadden, *Meanings of Sex Difference in the Middle Ages* (Cambridge: Cambridge University Press, 1995) 94–95, 143. Also, Mortimer, *Time Traveler's Guide*, 56.

66. See also Mt 22:30.

67. Caroline Walker Bynum, *Holy Feast and Holy Fast* (Berkeley and Los Angeles: University of California Press, 1987), 215.

68. Ibid.

Chapter 7: *War and Childbirth*

1. Barbara W. Tuchman, *A Distant Mirror: The Calamitous 14th Century* (New York: Random House, 1978), 136.

2. Ibid., 139.

3. Ibid., 138.

4. Ibid., 144.

5. Ibid., 151.

6. Maurice Keen, *English Society in the Later Middle Ages, 1348–1500* (New York: Penguin Books, 1990), 139.

7. May McKisack, *The Fourteenth Century, 1307–1399* (New York: Oxford University Press, 1991), 140.

8. Tuchman, *A Distant Mirror*, 188.

9. Ibid., 216.

10. Geoffrey Chaucer reworked several of these stories in his *Canterbury Tales.*

11. Shulamith Shahar, *The Fourth Estate: A History of Women in the Middle Ages* (1983; London and New York: Routledge, 2003), 102.

12. Ibid., 98.

13. Ibid., 99.

14. Humbert de Romans, *De Eruditione Praedicatorum*, 274. See Shahar, *The Fourth Estate*, 103.

15. Ruth Mohl, *The Three Estates in Medieval and Renaissance Literature* (1933; New York: Frederick Ungar, 1962), 347. See Shahar, *The Fourth Estate*, 103.

16. Eustache Deschamps, *Le Miroir de Mariage*, quoted in Shahar, *The Fourth Estate*, 104.

17. T. H. Hollingsworth, "A Demographic Study of the British Ducal Families," *Population Studies* 11, no. 1 (1957): 4–26. See also Ralph A. Houlbrooke, *The English Family, 1450–1700* (London: Longman, 1984), 129, as referred to in Shulamith Shahar, *Childhood in the Middle Ages* (London and New York: Routledge, 1992), 35.

18. Even as late as the sixteenth and seventeenth centuries, for which demographic data are more accurate, the estimate is that 25 out of every 1,000 women in England died in childbirth, and 200 to 300 out of every 1,000 infants died before reaching their fifth birthday. Shahar, *Childhood*, 35.

19. E. A. Wrigley and R. Schofield, *The Population History of England, 1541-1871* (London: Edward Arnold, 1981), 248–49; Dorothy McLaren, "Fertility, Infant Mortality, and Breast Feeding in the Seventeenth Century," *Medical History* 22 (1978): 380–81; Z. Razi, *Life, Marriage and Death in a Medieval Parish: Economy, Society and Democracy in Halesowen 1270–1400* (Cambridge: Cambridge University Press, 1980), 129, 151. As referred to in Shahar, *Childhood*, 35.

20. Shahar, *Childhood*, 43.

21. According to the *Legenda Aurea* (*Golden Legend*), the popular medieval book of the lives of the saints, St. Margaret of Antioch was a late third-century virgin who was tortured and put to death in 304 CE because she would not renounce Christianity to marry a Roman pagan. She became one of the most popular saints in the Middle Ages, especially for pregnant women and women in labor who might die suddenly. More than 250 English churches were dedicated to her.

22. Shahar, *Childhood*, 43. During the reign of Emperor Antoninus (fourth century), St. Felicitas and her seven sons were all imprisoned by pagan priests for holding to their Christian faith, and delivered to four separate judges who condemned them to different modes of martyrdom. They are buried in four different catacombs in Rome.

23. Shahar, *Childhood*, 32.

24. Ibid., 36.

25. In the *Legenda Aurea*, St. Anne was said to have been married three times and to have borne a daughter each time: first, Mary, the mother of Jesus; then, the "two Maries" of Jn 19:25 and Mk 16:1, from whose subsequent marriages came the six "brothers" (actually cousins) of Jesus, mentioned in the gospels. By 1300, English monasteries claimed to have relics of St. Anne from the crusades and a multitude of chapels, shrines, and altars were dedicated to her *cultus* throughout England and on the Continent.

26. Shahar, *Childhood*, 41.

27. Frances and Joseph Gies, *Marriage and the Family in the Middle Ages* (New York: Harper & Row, 1987), 198.

28. Shahar, *Childhood*, 49.

29. Ibid., 47.

30. *Select English Works of John Wycliffe*, edited by Thomas Arnold (Oxford: Clarendon Press, 1871), 3:199–200. Online at: www.archive.org.

31. A. J. Schulte, "Churching of Women," *The Catholic Encyclopedia*, vol. 3 (New York: Robert Appleton Company, 1908), 761.

32. Shahar, *Childhood*, 69.

33. Ibid., 54.

34. Quoted in Tuchman, *A Distant Mirror*, 285.

35. Ibid.

36. Ibid., 223–24.

37. Ibid., 224.

38. Ibid., 196.

39. Ranulf Higden, *Polychronicon*, translated by John of Trevisa (London: Longman, Green, Longman, Roberts, and Green, 1865), 411, quoted in Tuchman, *A Distant Mirror*, 196.

40. The association of this passage with the death of Julian's child was arrived at by this author independently many years ago, and later supported by reading *Julian Reconsidered* (Oxford: SLG Press, 2001), 24–25, in which Sr. Benedicta also suggests that the baby Julian remembers in her text might have been her own.

41. Jennifer C. Ward, *Women in England in the Middle Ages* (London and New York: Hambledon Continuum, 2006), 93–94.

42. *Anonimalle Chronicle*, 77, quoted in *The Black Death*, edited by Rosemary Horrox (Manchester: Manchester University Press, 1994), 88.

43. Note that the most deadly form of cattle disease, known as Rinderpest, was completely eradicated only in 2010–2011. James Mackenzie, "Scientists Poised to Wipe Out Deadly Cattle Disease" (Reuters, October 14, 2010).

44. William Ralph Inge, *Studies of English Mystics, St. Margaret's Lectures, 1905* (London: John Murray, 1906), 53, 61.

45. J. Willis Hurst, MD, MACP, *The Heart Book*, 11th ed. (Google Books.com), bk. 2, ch. 99, 2333.

Chapter 8: *Schism, Heresy, and Revolt*

1. Margaret Deanesly, *A History of the Medieval Church 590–1500* (1925; repr., London: Methuen, 1972), 176.

2. Using the comparative retail price index, it would take approximately £39,200,000 (approximately $61,490,000) in today's currency to have the purchasing power of £100,000 in 1370.

3. Herbert B. Workman, *John Wyclif: A Study of the English Medieval Church* (1926; repr., Hamden, CT: Archon Books, 1966), vol. 2, bk. III, ch. iii, 87.

4. Ibid., vol. 2, bk. III, ch. ii, 60.

5. Ludolf of Sagan, *Tractatus de Longevo Schismate*, edited by J. Loserth, in Archiv für Österreichische Geschichte (Vienna: 1880), 60:345–561. Quoted in Workman, *John Wyclif*, vol. 2, bk. III, ch. ii, 62–63.

6. Workman, *John Wyclif*, vol. 2, bk. III, ch. ii, 63–64.

7. This theory of "unworthy lordship" was borrowed in part from Richard FitzRalph, Archbishop of Armagh from 1346 to 1360. See Workman, *John Wyclif*, vol. 2, bk. II, ch. ii, 260–66.

8. Ibid., 263.

9. Ibid., vol. 2, bk. III, ch. iii, 98.

10. Ibid., 95.

11. Ibid., vol. 2, bk. III, ch. ii, 80.

12. Ibid., 80–81.

13. Ibid., 74.

14. John Wyclif, *The Select English Works of John Wyclif*, edited by T. Arnold (Oxford: Clarendon Press, 1871), 3:345. Online at www.archive.org.

15. In 1302, Pope Boniface VIII had issued a bull entitled *Unam Sanctam,* which declared that there is One Holy Church, symbolized by the seamless garment of Christ himself, and that outside of this church there is no salvation.

16. May McKisack, *The Fourteenth Century, 1307–1399* (New York: Oxford University Press, 1991), 513.

17. Workman, *John Wyclif*, vol. 2, bk. III, ch. iii, 97.

18. Transubstantiation was initially referred to by Pope Innocent III in 1215; however, the *belief* in the real presence of Jesus Christ in the sacrament of the Eucharist dates from the earliest Christian practice of coming together to re-enact the Last Supper of the Lord.

19. Workman, *John Wyclif*, vol. 2, bk. III, ch. i, 36. See also 33–41.

20. Ibid., 38.

21. Wyclif, *De Eucharistia*, 15.29. Cited in Workman, *John Wyclif*, vol. 2, bk. III, ch. i, 37.

22. Ibid., vol. 2, bk. III, ch. i, 38.

23. Scholars of the Talmud would have argued that ancient Orthodox Hebraic tradition would never countenance leaving the formal interpretation of sacred scripture to non-educated laypeople.

24. Workman, *John Wyclif*, vol. 2, bk. III, ch. i, 41–42.

25. Wyclif, *De Ecclesia,* 74.11.140. Cited in Workman, *Wyclif*, vol. 2, bk. III, ch. i, 8.

26. H. Leith Spencer, *English Preaching in the Late Middle Ages* (Oxford: Clarendon Press, 1993), 293.

27. McKisack, *The Fourteenth Century*, 406–7.

28. Tuchman, *A Distant Mirror*, 375.

29. Thomas Walsingham, *Historia Anglicana*, quoted in Richard B. Dobson, *The Peasants' Revolt of 1381* (Bath: Pitman, 1970), 375. See also Paul H. Freedman, *Images of the Medieval Peasant* (Stanford, CA: Stanford University Press, 1999), 60.

30. Tuchman, *A Distant Mirror*, 373.

31. McKisack, *The Fourteenth Century*, 410.

32. Walsingham, *Historia*, quoted in Tuchman, *A Distant Mirror*, 376.

33. McKisack, *The Fourteenth Century*, 411.

34. Tuchman, *A Distant Mirror*, 376.

35. McKisack, *The Fourteenth Century*, 412.

36. Ibid., 413.

37. Ibid.

38. Ibid., 414–15.

39. Ibid., 416–17.

40. Ibid.

41. Walsingham, *Historia*, quoted in McKisack, *The Fourteenth Century*, 417.

42. McKisack, 418.

43. Ibid.

44. Ibid., 419.

45. Quoted in Tuchman, *A Distant Mirror*, 403.

46. Walsingham, *Historia*, quoted in Richard Allington-Smith, *Henry Despenser: The Fighting Bishop* (Norfolk: Larks Press, 2003), 107, italics added.

47. McKisack, *The Fourteenth Century*, 513–14.

48. Ibid., 514.

49. Ibid. 514–15.

50. Margaret Deanesly, *The Lollard Bible* (Cambridge: Cambridge University Press, 1920), 241.

51. Ibid., 242.

52. Ibid., 242–43.

53. Ibid., 245.

54. Ibid., 242.

55. John Wyclif, *De Veritate Sacrae Scripturae*, 3 vols., edited by R. Buddensieg (London: Trübner & Co. for the Wyclif Society, 1905–1907), 1.158.

56. *Patrologia Latina* (Migne, 1844), 148, c.555, printed in Deanesly, *The Lollard Bible*, 24.

57. Giovanni Domenico Mansi, *Sacrorum Conciliorum nova et amplissima collectio* (Florence and Venice, 1758–1798), vol. 23, 197, quoted in Deanesly, *The Lollard Bible*, 36–37.

58. Deanesly, *The Lollard Bible*, 262.

59. Ibid., 254ff.

60. Ibid., 245.

61. Ibid., 70n1.

62. Ibid., 283.

63. *De Haeretico Comburendo*. Online at http://www.ric.edu/faculty/rpotter/heretico.html.

64. Ibid.

65. Frederick Sanders Pulling, *The Dictionary of English History* (London and New York: Cassel & Company, Ltd., 1884), 362.

66. Wilkins, *Concilia Magnae Britanniae,* 1737, III.317; Lyndwood, Provinciale, Appendix, 66. Quoted in Deanesly, *The Lollard Bible*, 296, italics added.

67. Deanesly, *The Lollard Bible*, 296.

68. Pulling, *Dictionary*, 562.

69. Deanesly, *The Lollard Bible*, 334.

70. Ibid. 335.

Chapter 9: *Preaching and Poetry*

1. *Latin Sermon Collections from Later Medieval England,* translated and edited by Siegfried Wenzel (Cambridge: Cambridge University Press, 2005), Preface, xv.

2. Ibid., 230.

3. John Gower, *Confessio Amantis*, bk. V, quoted in G. R. Owst, *Preaching in Medieval England, An Introduction to Sermon Manuscripts of the Period c. 1350–1450* (New York: Russell & Russell, 1965), 173.

4. *Encyclopedia of the Middle Ages*, edited by André Vauchez (London and New York: Routledge, 2001), 1:1179.

5. H. Leith Spencer, *English Preaching in the Late Middle Ages* (Oxford: Clarendon Press, 1993), 236.

6. Owst, *Preaching*, 195–96.

7. Wilkins, *Concilia Magnae Britanniae,* 1737, III. 282, quoted in Owst, *Preaching*, 148.

8. MS Harley 3839, fol. 79b, quoted in Owst, *Preaching*, 221.

9. Ranulf Higden, quoted in Spencer, *English Preaching*, 236.

10. Jacques de Fusignano, quoted in Spencer, *English Preaching*, 240.

11. Wenzel, *Latin Sermon Collections,* 16.

12. Ibid., 14.

13. Owst, *Preaching*, 305.

14. Dr. Bromyard, *Summa Predicantium, Advocatus*, quoted in Owst, *Preaching*, 33.

15. Ibid., *SP, Mercator*, quoted in Owst, *Preaching*, 124.

16. Ibid., *SP, Oratio*, quoted in Owst, *Preaching*, 218.

17. Ibid., *SP, Predicatio*, quoted in Owst, *Preaching*, 212.

18. Ibid., *SP, Predicantium*, quoted in Owst, *Preaching*, 334. My translation.

19. Dr. Bromyard, quoted in Owst, *Preaching*, 335, italics added.

20. From *The Boke of the Craft of Dying* (MS Rawl. C. 894, etc.), cap. ii, printed in Horstmann, *Yorkshire Writers, Richard Rolle of Hampole, An English Father of the Church, and His Followers*, edited by Carl Horstmann (New York: Macmillan, 1895), 2:406ff., quoted in Owst, *Preaching*, 342. My translation.

21. MS Harley 2398, fol. 181, etc. Cf. also Add. MS 21253, fol. 134, quoted in Owst, *Preaching*, 343.

22. Owst, *Preaching*, 338–39.

23. MS Roy 18. B. xxiii, fol. 60b, quoted in Owst, *Preaching*, 340. My translation.

24. Julian is referring here to the last day of her life and her *particular* judgment, not the final judgment of the world.

25. John of Mirfield, *Florarium Bartholomei*, MS Cambridge University Library, Mm.ii.10 (Cat. No. 2305), *De Indumentis*, quoted in Owst, *Preaching*, 218.

26. *Chasteyz thow children, wyl thei be yownge*
Of werk, of dede, of speche, of townge.
Ffor if ye lete them to be bolde
Thei wole you greveyn wan they ben hold.

Sermo de Primo Mandato 2nd Tabule, MS Lincoln Cathedral Library A.6.19, fol.164, quoted in Owst, *Preaching*, n272. My translation.

27. MS Harley 3760, fol. 191, quoted in Owst, *Preaching*, 206, italics added.

28. Ibid., fols. 191b–192b, quoted in Owst, *Preaching*, 207.

29. Thomas Brinton, *Sermons*, edited by Mary Aquinas Devlin, OP, Camden Third Series 85–86, quoted by Siegfried Wenzel, *Preaching in the Age of Chaucer* (Washington, DC: Catholic University of America Press, 2008), 130.

30. Margaret Deanesly, *The Lollard Bible* (Cambridge: Cambridge University Press, 1920), 146–52.

31. Spencer, *English Preaching*, 259, 276.

32. MS Worcester F, 10, dating from c.1400, as mentioned in Spencer, *English Preaching*, 277.

33. Wenzel, *Latin Sermon Collections*, 10.

34. Deanesly, *The Lollard Bible*, 153.

35. The "A" text can be dated between 1367 and 1370; the "B" text between 1377 and 1379; and the "C" text c.1385–1386. It was widely copied during the 1380s and 1390s. See William Langland, *The Vision of Piers Plowman,* edited by A. V. C. Schmidt (1978; repr., London: J. M. Dent, Orion Publishing, 1995), Introduction, xxiv–xxxv.

36. G. G. Coulton, *From St. Francis to Dante* (London: David Knutt, 1906), 302.

37. Thomas Walsingham, *Historia Anglicana 1272–1422*, 1:319, 409–11, quoted in *The Black Death*, edited by Rosemary Horrox (Manchester: Manchester University Press, 1994), 88.

38. Ibid., 89.

39. Walsingham, *Historia*, vol. 2, 197, 203, quoted in Horrox, *The Black Death*, 91–92.

40. Norman P. Tanner, *The Church in Late Medieval Norwich, 1370–1532* (Toronto: Pontifical Institute of Mediaeval Studies, 1984), 58.

41. During the rebuilding of the Church of St. Julian and Julian's cell in 1953, it became possible to measure the original foundation of the anchorage. See *The Complete Julian of Norwich,* edited with translations by Fr. John-Julian, OJN (Brewster, MA: Paraclete Press, 2009), 38; cf. 420n70.

42. Francis Darwin Swift, *The English Medieval Recluse* (London: Society for Promoting Christian Knowledge, 1944), 10.

43. *The Ancrene Riwle*, edited and translated by James Morton (London: Camden Society, 1853; digitalized as a Google eBook from Oxford University), Part II, 51.

44. Ibid., Part II, 69.

45. *The Complete Julian*, 30–31. Note that two shillings would be worth approximately £45 in modern English currency (approximately $70) using the retail price index, or approximately £542 (approximately $848) using average earnings.

46. 8d = 8 pence or pennies; 12d = 12 pence, or 1 shilling, which in modern English currency would be worth approximately £22 (approximately $35) using the retail price index, or approximately £271 (approximately $424) using average earnings.

47. See also *The Writings of Julian of Norwich: A Vision Showed to a Devout Woman and A Revelation of Love*, edited by Nicholas Watson and

Jacqueline Jenkins (University Park, PA: Pennsylvania State University Press, 2006), Appendix, 431–35. Note that 20s = 20 shillings, which equals 1£ in modern English currency, would be worth approximately £447 ($699) using the retail price index, or approximately £5,420 ($8,475) using average earnings.

48. Tanner, *The Church in Late Medieval Norwich, 1370–1532*, 60.

49. See Joan M. Nuth, *Wisdom's Daughter: The Theology of Julian of Norwich* (New York: Crossroad, 1991), 179n88. See also Margaret Aston, *Lollards and Reformers: Images and Literacy in Late Medieval Religion* (London: Hambledon Press, 1984), 13.

50. Margery Kempe, *The Book of Margery Kempe*, edited by Lynn Staley (Kalamazoo, MI: Medieval Institute Publications, 1996), Book I, Part I, lines 959– 962. Online at: TEAMS Middle English Texts Series: www.teamsmedieval. org/texts/index.html. My translation.

51. Ibid., lines 962–66.

52. Ibid., lines 966–68.

53. Ibid., lines 968–70. See 2 Cor 6:16: "We are the temple of the living God."

54. Ibid., lines 971–72.

55. Ibid., lines 974–76.

56. Ibid., lines 982–83.

57. Ibid., lines 984-86.

58. Ibid., lines 987–89.

Chapter 10: *Corpus Christi Plays*

1. Glynne Wickham, *Introduction: Trends in International Drama Research* (Cambridge: Cambridge University Press, 1991), 5.

2. *The Corpus Christi Play of the English Middle Ages*, edited by R. T. Davies (Metuchen, NJ: Rowman and Littlefield, 1972), 39.

3. Richard Beadle, Pamela M. King, *York Mystery Plays: A Selection in Modern Spelling* (Oxford: Oxford University Press, 1999), xxii.

4. *Corpus Christi Play*, Davies, 23.

5. Ibid., 83.

6. Ibid., 68.

7. Ibid., 29.

8. E. K. Chambers, *The Medieval Stage* (New York: Dover Publications, 1996), vol. 2, Appendix W, 354.

9. *Staged Properties in Early Modern English Drama,* edited by Jonathan Gil Harris and Natasha Korda (Cambridge: Cambridge University Press, 2006), 41.

10. It was believed that the River Jordan *stood still* at the moment of Christ's baptism. Hence, in pursuit of good coagulation after drawing blood, the Guild of Barbers (surgeons) had a special devotion to St. John the Baptist and performed this scene in the Corpus Christi plays. Often, the Barbers' urine jar was used, humorously, to pour the baptismal water over Christ's head; thus, its popular name, *jordan*. Carole Rawcliffe, *Medicine and Society in Later Medieval England* (London: Sandpiper Books, 1999), 134–35.

11. *Staged Properties*, Harris and Korda, 41.

12. *Corpus Christi Play*, "Council of the Jews," Davies, 279.

13. Chambers, *Medieval Stage*, 2:141.

14. Note: All play quotations are my own translation of the Middle English in *The N-Town Plays*, edited by Douglas Sugano, TEAMS Middle English Texts Series in association with the University of Rochester (Kalamazoo, MI: Medieval Institute Publications, 2007). Online at www.lib.rochester.edu/camelot/teams/sdnttoc.htm.

15. Chambers, *Medieval Stage*, Appendix W, 354.

16. R. B. Dobson, "Craft Guilds and City: The Historical Origins of the York Mystery Plays Reassessed," in *The Stage as Mirror: Civic Theatre in Late Medieval Europe*, edited by Alan E. Knight (Cambridge: D. S. Brewer, 1997), 91–105.

17. Margaret Rogerson, *Playing a Part in History: The York Mysteries, 1951–2000* (Toronto: University of Toronto Press, 2009), 21.

18. Chambers, *Medieval Stage*, 2:138.

19. Ibid.

20. Some scholars date the N-Town Plays to the second half of the fifteenth century, based on a 1468 date attached to *one play only*, the Purification Play, that was added to the collection at a later time. However, Douglas Sugano suggests that: "The [N-Town] manuscript's status as a compilation makes its date and purpose problematic, for such manuscripts could often be assembled over a period of time, using material and texts drawn from different places, and by their very nature these texts often comprehend many different intentions . . . In actuality, *no one can be sure what the date [1468] means*. It could be the date when the compiler incorporated the play into the manuscript; it could be a date that was on the exemplar from which the compiler copied; it could be a commemorative date of the last or of a future performance of the Purification Play." See *The N-Town Plays*, Sugano, Introduction, 7–8, italics added.

21. Ibid., 17–18.

22. Chambers, *Medieval Stage*, 2:421.

23. Rosemary Woolf, *The English Mystery Plays* (Berkeley and Los Angeles: University of California Press, 1980), 55.

24. Ibid., 73.

25. Geoffrey Chaucer, *The Canterbury Tales,* 1.3384 (The Miller's Tale).

26. *Corpus Christi Play*, Davies, 272.

27. Chambers, *Medieval Stage*, 2:137, 142.

28. Walter Hilton, *The Scale (or Ladder) of Perfection* (Scotts Valley, CA: CreateSpace, 2010), 20, 31, 79.

29. Forks are also used to force the crown down in the *Holkham Bible Picture-Book*, commentary by Michelle P. Brown (London: British Library, 2007), fol. 29v.

30. The word "harrow" comes from the Old English *hergian* (to harry or despoil). The term, "harrowing of hell," refers not only to the fact that Christ *descended* into hell, as in the Apostles' Creed, but to the tradition that he *triumphed* over hellfire itself and the power of Satan by releasing righteous souls who had died in Old Testament times.

PART TWO

Chapter 11: *Three Gifts*

1. *The Writings of Julian of Norwich: A Vision Showed to a Devout Woman and A Revelation of Love*, edited by Nicholas Watson and Jacqueline Jenkins, henceforth W&J (University Park, PA: Pennsylvania State University Press, 2006), sidenote on 1:1.122.

2. The Sloane manuscript, quoted here, gives "the viiith [8th] day of May" as the date of the Revelations, and since this manuscript was the more popular text during the twentieth century, it became the accepted date on which Julian is honored in the Anglican Church of England and in the Episcopal Church of the United States. The "May xiii [13th]" date given in the Paris manuscript may be due to a misreading or misrecording by a copyist of the Roman numerals viii.

3. *The Shewings of Julian of Norwich*, edited by Georgia Ronan Crampton, TEAMS Middle English Texts Series (Kalamazoo, MI: Western Michigan University, Medieval Institute Publications, 1994), Sloane (SI) Text, II:41–45.39. My translation.

4. The colophon to the Short Text, however, describes the writer in more detail: "Here is a vision, shewn by the goodness of God to a devout

woman. And her name is Julian, that is a recluse at Norwich and yet is in life [alive], *anno domini* 1413." W&J, colophon, 63.

5. W&J, sidenote on 2:1.124.

6. St. Bernard of Clairvaux, *On the Song of Songs*, translated by Kilian Walsh, OCSO, Cistercian Fathers Series, no. 4 (Kalamazoo, MI: Cistercian Publications, 1971), vol. 1, ser. 20, section V.6, 152.

7. William of St. Thierry, *Epistola Aurea (The Golden Epistle)*, *A Letter to the Brethren at Mont Dieu*, translated by Theodore Berkeley, OCSO (Kalamazoo, MI: Cistercian Publications, 1971), 69.

8. Aelred of Rievaulx, *De Institutione Inclusarum* (*Rule of Life for a Recluse*), as referred to in Nicholas Love, *Mirror of the Blessed Life of Jesus Christ*, edited by Michael G. Sargent (Exeter: University of Exeter Press, 2004; New York: Garland, 1992), Introduction, xii.

9. St. Bonaventure, *On the Perfection of Life, Addressed to Sisters,* as quoted in Sargent, *Mirror*, Introduction, xiii.

10. Pseudo-Bonaventure, *Meditations on the Life of Christ: An Illustrated Manuscript of the Fourteenth Century*, edited by Isa Ragusa and Rosalie B. Green, translated by Isa Ragusa (Princeton, NJ: Princeton University Press, 1961), 178.

11. See Richard Rolle, *The English Writings*, translated and edited by Rosamund S. Allen (New York: Paulist Press, 1998), 44–45.

12. Caroline Walker Bynum, *Holy Feast and Holy Fast* (Berkeley and Los Angeles: University of California Press, 1987), 203–6.

13. Ibid., 214.

14. Ibid., 203.

15. Julian uses the Middle English word, *kind* or *kinde*, repeatedly in her text. *Kinde* derives from the Old English *cynd*, akin to Old English *cynn* or kin. As a noun, it can mean "being," "nature," "creation," "race," "family," "lineage." As an adjective, it implies "natural," "according to human nature"; thus, in this case, "natural compassion."

16. Jacobus de Voragine, *The Golden Legend: Readings on Saints (Legenda aurea)*, translated by William Granger Ryan (Princeton, NJ: Princeton University Press, 2012), 704–9.

17. Carole Rawcliffe, *Medicine and Society in Later Medieval England* (London: Sandpiper Books, 1999), 49.

18. Between 1359 and 1399, fourteen *barbers* (the medieval term for those who cut hair, as well as for surgeons) and four *leeches* (experts at applying leeches and drawing blood) were licensed to practice and duly registered as freemen in the city of Norwich.

19. After the Fourth Lateran Council of 1215, no subdeacons, deacons, or priests were allowed to engage in any activity that could possibly shed blood (to prevent them from engaging in battle). Therefore, they were forbidden to perform surgery or to draw blood, even for diagnostic purposes. Since most university-trained physicians were clerks in higher ecclesiastical orders, this left the actual diagnostic and surgical procedures to members of the guild of *non*-clerical barber-surgeons. See Rawcliffe, *Medicine*, 112, 126.

20. Ibid., 47.

21. Ibid., 50.

22. Ibid., 51.

23. *Cupping* was the application of intensely heated glass, brass, or bone cups to the infected area of the body (after scratching or gashing the skin surface) to initiate a slow flow of blood. *Cauterization* involved heating metal instruments in a brazier and then using them to sear individual areas of the body deemed responsible for the production of excessive wet and cold humors. See Rawcliffe, *Medicine*, 68–69.

24. Ibid., 87.

25. G. R. Owst, *Literature and Pulpit in Medieval England* (Cambridge: Cambridge University Press, 1933), 30, 36.

26. Rawcliffe, *Medicine*, 60.

27. The English physician, John of Gaddesden (d.1361) diagnosed pleurisy as an apostume (or swelling filled with infected matter) of the ribs or midriff; pneumonia as an apostume of the lungs; and excited frenzy or depressed lethargy as apostumes of the brain. *Rosa Angelica* from *Medicinae Johannis Anglici*, edited by W. Wulff, 163–99, 227, quoted in Rawcliffe, *Medicine*, 36.

28. Rawcliffe, *Medicine*, 98–99.

29. *The Prymer or Lay Folks' Prayer Book*, edited by Henry Littlehales (London: E.E.T.S., 1895), *Matins*, 1. My translation.

30. Ibid., *Lauds*, Ps 63:8–9, italics added.

31. The sun rises in London on May 8 at approximately 5:20 AM and on May 13 at approximately 5:12 AM, but that is calculated according to modern daylight saving time which was not in effect, of course, during the Middle Ages. Hence, actual sunrise in Norwich, which is 115 miles east of London, might be as early as 4:00 AM, with dawn's approaching light as much as half an hour before.

32. In the Long Text account, Julian excised the female appellation, "Daughter" (3:19.131).

Chapter 12: *The Vision*

1. See a similar effect described in Fr. Pierre Teilhard de Chardin, SJ, *Hymn of the Universe* (New York: Harper & Row, 1965), 47–50. The priest/mystic recounts his own visionary experience arising from his contemplation of the eucharistic host displayed in a gilded monstrance upon an altar.

2. Based on those of St. Teresa of Avila. See *The Life of Saint Teresa of Avila by Herself*, translated by J. M. Cohen (New York: Viking Penguin, 1957), ch. 25, 174ff.

3. Ibid., 176.

4. St. Augustine, *The Trinity*, translated by Edmund Hill, OP (Hyde Park, NY: New City Press, 1991), bk. I.2.7, 70.

5. Ibid., I.2.7, 70–71, italics added.

6. Ibid., I.3.19, 83.

7. Ibid., I.4.25, 88, italics added.

8. Ibid., I.4.28, 91.

9. Ibid., italics added.

10. See: http://www.usccb.org/beliefs-and-teachings/what-we-believe/.

11. *The Writings of Julian of Norwich: A Vision Showed to a Devout Woman and A Revelation of Love*, edited by Nicholas Watson and Jacqueline Jenkins, henceforth W&J (University Park, PA: Pennsylvania State University Press, 2006), Introduction, 4. W&J based this section on the Paris Codex (P), collated with the Short Text (A) and Sloane (S). In the British Library, Sloane Manuscript No. 2499 (S1), the phrase appears as *Benedicite Domine*. In the Paris Bibliothèque Nationale Fonds Anglais No. 40 version, the spelling has been corrected to *Domino*.

12. W&J, sidenote on 4:15.136.

13. *Yorkshire Writers, Richard Rolle of Hampole, An English Father of the Church, and His Followers*, edited by Carl Horstmann (New York: Macmillan, 1895), 2:130–31, italics added.

14. Walter Hilton, *The Scale (or Ladder) of Perfection* (Scotts Valley, CA: CreateSpace, 2010), bk. 2, II.6., 143–44, italics added.

15. *The Confessions of St. Augustine,* translated and edited by Albert Cook Outler (New York: Dover Publications, 2002), bk. 1, ch. I, 1.

16. "Nought" can also suggest the mathematical signatory for nothing, the number zero, in colloquial use by the English until recently. See American Heritage Dictionaries, editors, *Word Histories and Mysteries: From Abracadabra to Zeus* (New York: Houghton, Mifflin, Harcourt, 2004), 188–89.

17. In the writings of the German mystics, especially Meister Eckhart, and in Marguerite Porete's *Mirror of Simple Souls,* "noughting" (in its most

extreme sense) refers to the total *self-annihilation* of reason and will, so that the soul is completely absorbed into the Divine Will. At this point, Porete maintained, the soul attains to perfect goodness and can no longer sin, since it is united with God who is All-Good. As a result, the soul is above conventional morality, has no need of virtues (since in God it attains to complete perfection), and is no longer subject to the authority or control of the church. For these extreme and possibly heretical beliefs, Porete underwent a lengthy trial, refused to recant, and was burned at the stake in Paris in 1310.

18. See John Hick, *Evil and the God of Love*, revised ed. (San Francisco: Harper and Row, 1978), 382–83.

19. The late Middle English word *soule*, from the French *saulee*, meant a food or meal. Alternate English medieval spellings are *saule/sawlee*. See W&J, sidenote on 6:29–31.142.

20. The Middle English *bowke* is from the Old English *buc*, which means a body or carcass of a dead man or animal on a battlefield. Julian chose the most carnal word she could think of. See W&J, sidenote on 6:36.144.

21. W&J, sidenote on 6:33.142.

22. The Middle English phrase, *reverent dread*, implies deep reverence, fear that is awe-inspiring, or great wonder. It does not necessarily mean shrinking in terror at the power of God. On the contrary, Julian uses the term as a virtue to be cultivated through contemplative prayer.

23. The scales of herring are numerous, glistening, closely aligned in tight rows, and perfectly round. Herring from fisheries in the North Sea was a very common food in medieval Norwich, highly valued because of its salt content.

24. Julian refers here to the iconography of the Middle Ages that depicted the "tokens," or symbols, of the passion (the crown of thorns, the nails, the pillar at which Christ was scourged, the whips, the spear that lanced his side, and the cross) as worthy of reverence in themselves, since each represented an aspect of Christ's sufferings. We have also seen this worship of the passion enacted in the Corpus Christi plays.

25. W&J, sidenote on 9:16–21.154.

26. St. Augustine, "Against Two Letters of the Pelagians," in *The Works of Saint Augustine: Answer to the Pelagians*, vol. 2, edited by John E. Rotelle, OSA (Hyde Park, NY: New City Press, 1999), I.2.5, 117.

27. Ibid., I.3.6, 119.

28. Ibid., I.3.7, 119.

29. St. Augustine, "On the Grace of Christ and Original Sin," in *The Works of St. Augustine: Answer to the Pelagians*, vol. 1, edited by John E. Rotelle, OSA (Hyde Park, NY: New City Press, 1997), 416–17, italics added.

30. St. Augustine, "On Nature and Grace," in *The Works of St. Augustine: Answer to the Pelagians,* vol. 1, 3.3 and 5.5, 226, 227.

31. See Mary T. Clark, RSCJ, *Augustine* (London and New York: Continuum, 1994), 45–50.

32. Ibid., 51.

33. St. Augustine, "The Preaching of Predestination," in *Four Anti-Pelagian Writings,* translated by John A. Mourant, *Fathers of the Church,* vol. 86 (1992; repr., Washington, DC: Catholic University of America Press, 2002), 14.35, 302–3.

34. St. Thomas Aquinas, *Summa Theologica,* translated by the Fathers of the English Dominican Province, revised by Daniel J. Sullivan, OP (Chicago: Encyclopaedia Britannica, 1952), Q.23, A.1, 133.

35. St. Augustine, *The Augustine Catechism, The Enchiridion on Faith, Hope, and Love,* translated by Bruce Harbert (Hyde Park, NY: New City Press, 1999), #98, 113.

36. St. Augustine, "The Predestination of the Saints," in *The Works of St. Augustine: Answer to the Pelagians,* vol. 4, edited by John E. Rotelle, OSA (Hyde Park, NY: New City Press, 1999), #16, 163.

37. St. Augustine, "On Rebuke and Grace," ix, 20, as quoted in Peter Brown, *Augustine of Hippo* (London: Faber and Faber, 2000), 408.

38. Jan van Ruusbroec, *The Chastising of God's Children and The Treatise of Perfection of the Sons of God,* edited by Joyce Bazire and Eric Colledge (Oxford: Oxford University Press, 1957), 176. W&J, sidenote on 9:17–18, 156.

Chapter 13: *The Passion*

1. Ewa Kuryluk, *Veronica and Her Cloth: History, Symbolism, and Structure of a "True" Image* (Cambridge, UK: Basil Blackwell, 1991), 118.

2. See Millard J. Erickson, *Christian Theology,* second ed. (Grand Rapids, MI: Baker Book House, 1998), 522.

3. St. Anselm, *Cur Deus Homo?* (*Why God Became Man*) ii.14.7. Cited in George C. Foley, *Anselm's Theory of the Atonement* (New York, London: Longmans, Green, and Co., 1909), 130.

4. St. Anselm, *Cur Deus Homo?* ii.17.40.

5. In the Latin Rite, the words of absolution are as follows: "God the Father of mercies, through the death and resurrection of his Son, has reconciled the world to Himself and sent the Holy Spirit among us for the forgiveness of sins; through the ministry of the Church may God give you pardon and peace, and *I absolve you from your sins* in the name of the Father, and of the Son, and of the Holy Spirit." Italics added.

6. See Sarah Beckwith, *Signifying God* (Chicago: University of Chicago Press, 2001), 93–94.

7. See Evelyn Underhill, *Mysticism: A Study in Nature and Development of Spiritual Consciousness* (London: Methuen, 1911; repr., Stilwell, KS: A Digi-reads.com Book, 2005), 186.

8. St. Augustine, *The Augustine Catechism, The Enchiridion on Faith, Hope, and Love,* translated by Bruce Harbert (Hyde Park, NY: New City Press, 1999), #11, 41, italics added.

9. St. Augustine, "Against the Letter of the Manichees," translated by Richard Stothert, in *Nicene and Post-Nicene Fathers of the Christian Church* (Grand Rapids, MI: Eerdmans, 1979) First Series, vol. 4, 147, italics added.

10. Gillian R. Evans, *Augustine on Evil* (Cambridge: Cambridge University Press, 1982), 36.

11. St. Augustine, "On Free Will," bk. 2:19.53 in *Augustine in His Own Words,* edited by William Harmless, SJ (Washington, DC: Catholic University of America Press, 2010), 222.

12. St. Augustine, *The City of God*, edited by Vernon J. Bourke (New York: Image Books, 1958), bk. XII, ch. 6, 252.

13. St. Augustine, "On Marriage and Desire," in *The Works of St. Augustine: Answer to the Pelagians,* vol. 2, edited by John E. Rotelle, OSA (Hyde Park NY: New City Press, 1998), bk. I.21, 42.

14. Evans, *Augustine on Evil,* 76. See also *The Confessions of St. Augustine,* translated and edited by Albert Cook Outler (New York: Dover Publications, 2002), bk. 2, ch. VIII, 28–29.

15. See Mt 11:29–30.

16. St. Teresa of Avila, *The Life of Saint Teresa of Avila by Herself,* translated by J. M. Cohen (New York: Viking Penguin, 1957), 175.

17. The origin of *seming* is from Middle English *semen,* "to appear to be," or "be fitting," which is of Scandinavian origin. It was first used in the thirteenth century.

18. *The Shewings of Julian of Norwich,* edited by Georgia Ronan Crampton, TEAMS Middle English Texts series (Kalamazoo, MI: Western Michigan University, Medieval Institute Publications, 1994), note on 166.

19. *The Writings of Julian of Norwich: A Vision Showed to a Devout Woman and A Revelation of Love,* edited by Nicholas Watson and Jacqueline Jenkins (University Park, PA: Pennsylvania State University Press, 2006), sidenote on 12:1–2.166. Also, Mt 27:26.

20. St. Augustine, *The Augustine Catechism,* #29, 59–60.

21. St. Irenaeus, *Adversus Haereses* (Against Heresies), *The Catholic Encyclopedia*, vol. 2, William Kent: "Doctrine of the Atonement" (New York: Robert Appleton, 1907), bk. V.1.b, italics added. Online at http://www.newadvent.org.

22. St. Augustine, "Expositions of the Psalms," in *The Works of Saint Augustine* (Hyde Park, NY: New City Press, 2002), Ps 95:4.5, 428.

23. St. Thomas Aquinas, *Summa Theologica*, III.Q.48, Art. 2 (*Editio Leonina*, vol. 11, 1903), 464.

24. See Gn 19:24–25, where God destroys Sodom and Gomorrah in a rain of fire and brimstone (sulphur) and Dt 29:22–24, where the Israelites are threatened with the same punishment if they break their covenant with God. Similarly, in Rv 19:20, the devil and the damned are cast into a "lake of fire" burning with sulfur.

25. St. Augustine, *The City of God*, in *Basic Writings of St. Augustine,* edited by Whitney J. Oates, vol. 2 (New York: Random House, 1948), XXI.24, 595.

26. Ibid.

27. St. Augustine, *The Trinity*, translated by Edmund Hill, OP (Hyde Park, NY: New City Press, 1991), bk. II.4.17, 112.

28. St. Augustine, *On Christian Teaching*, translated by R. P. H. Green (Oxford and New York: Oxford University Press, 1997), bk. 2, chs. VI–VII, 13–14, 33.

29. St. Augustine, *The Trinity*, bk. II.7.34, 125.

30. The Middle English word, *travelle*, was first used in the fourteenth century. It derives from *travailen, travelen,* and from Anglo-French *travailler,* meaning to torment, labor, strive, journey, or work. It might also be Julian's way of suggesting the painful work of labor in childbirth.

31. Jan van Ruusbroec, *The Chastising of God's Children,* line 99. Cited by W&J, sidenote on 15:5.174.

Chapter 14: *The Dying*

1. *The Complete Julian of Norwich*, edited with translations by Fr. John-Julian, OJN (Brewster, MA: Paraclete Press, 2009), sidenote #8, 120.

2. Pierre Barbet, MD, *A Doctor at Calvary* (Fort Collins, CO: Roman Catholic Books, 1953), 47–48.

3. C. Truman Davis, MD, "A Physician Testifies about the Crucifixion" (The Review of the NEWS, April 14, 1976). Available online at http://www.konnections.com/Kcundick/crucifix.html.

4. It has been shown that blows to the chest in animals resulted in rupture

of the air spaces in the lung (*alveoli*) and spasms of the air tubes (*bronchi*). See R. A. Daniel Jr. and W. R. Cate Jr., "Wet Lung—An Experimental Study," *Annals of Surgery* 172 (1948): 836–57. The term "traumatic wet lung" (pleural effusion) indicates the build-up of blood, fluid, and mucus from any severe injury to the chest. See Frederick T. Zugibe, MD, PhD, "Pierre Barbet Revisited," *Sindon*, n.s., Quad. no. 8 (December 1995).

5. The Syrian Christ-thorn plant. Barbet, *A Doctor*, 85.

6. Ibid., 49.

7. See Zugibe, "Barbet Revisited."

8. Barbet, *A Doctor*, 60.

9. See Zugibe, "Experimental Studies in Crucifixion," online at: www.crucifixion-shroud.com/experimental_studies_in_crucifix.htm..

10. Ibid., Zugibe, "The Man of the Shroud Was Washed," *Sindon*, n.s., Quad. no. 1 (June 1989).

11. Vernon J. Geberth, MS, MPS, P.H.I. Investigative Consultants, Inc., "State Sponsored Torture in Rome: A Forensic Inquiry and Medicolegal Analysis of the Crucifixion of Jesus Christ" (AAFS Proceedings Annual Scientific Meeting Washington, DC, Feb. 18–23, 2008), 176–77.

12. Barbet, *A Doctor*, 108.

13. Ibid., 66, 113.

14. Ibid., 121–23.

15. Davis, "A Physician Testifies." It was previously held by Dr. Pierre Barbet that the cause of death by crucifixion was asphyxiation, from the eventual inability of the crucified to raise himself to draw breath. This theory has been thoroughly disproven through scientific simulations of crucifixion by Dr. Zugibe.

16. "And it is by God's will that we have been sanctified through the offering of the body of Jesus Christ once for all."

17. *The Writings of Julian of Norwich: A Vision Showed to a Devout Woman and A Revelation of Love*, edited by Nicholas Watson and Jacqueline Jenkins (University Park, PA: Pennsylvania State University Press, 2006), sidenote on 2:7.124 and 4:1.134.

Chapter 15: *Transformation*

1. *The Writings of Julian of Norwich: A Vision Showed to a Devout Woman and A Revelation of Love*, edited by Nicholas Watson and Jacqueline Jenkins (University Park, PA: Pennsylvania State University Press, 2006), sidenote on 22:4–5.194.

2. Richard Rolle, *The Fire of Love*, bk. 2, vii, cited in Evelyn Underhill,

Mysticism: A Study in Nature and Development of Spiritual Consciousness (London: Methuen, 1911; repr., Stilwell, KS: A Digi-reads.com Book, 2005), II.8.249.

3. St. Teresa of Avila. See *The Life of Saint Teresa of Avila by Herself,* translated by J. M. Cohen (New York: Viking Penguin, 1957), 20.136.

4. Ibid., 20.142, italics added.

5. Mother Margaret Williams, RSCJ, *The Sacred Heart in the Life of the Church* (New York: Sheed & Ward, 1957), 35.

6. *The Ancrene Riwle*, edited and translated by James Morton (London: Camden Society, 1853; digitalized as a Google eBook from Oxford University), Part 4, 293, italics added.

7. *History of Devotion to the Sacred Heart of Jesus*, by Brother Craig. Online at http://www.leonce.com/shrine/devotion.htm.

8. Ibid.

9. There are no surviving medieval roods in England, since they were removed or completely destroyed during the Reformation and the later English Civil War. Some rood stairs that once led to rood lofts do survive, however, and bear witness to the former presence of rood screens.

10. *Julian of Norwich: Showings*, edited by Edmund Colledge, OSA, and James Walsh, SJ (New York: Paulist Press, 1978), Long Text, 223.

11. *The Complete Julian of Norwich*, edited with translations by Fr. John-Julian, OJN (Brewster, MA: Paraclete Press, 2009), 145.

Chapter 16: *Making All Things Well*

1. St. Augustine, *On the Literal Interpretation of Genesis*, 6.36; 11.42; *The City of God*, 13.20; 14.11; 14.17; *Admonition and Grace*, 34. Referred to in J. N. D. Kelly, *Early Christian Doctrines* (San Francisco: Harper Collins, 1978), 362.

2. St. Augustine, *The Augustine Catechism: The Enchiridion on Faith, Hope, and Love,* translated by Bruce Harbert (Hyde Park, NY: New City Press, 1999), #11, 41.

3. *The Writings of Julian of Norwich: A Vision Showed to a Devout Woman and A Revelation of Love*, edited by Nicholas Watson and Jacqueline Jenkins (University Park, PA: Pennsylvania State University Press, 2006), sidenote on 27:10.208.

4. St. Augustine, "Against Julianum," in *The Fathers of the Church Series* (Washington, DC: The Catholic University of America Press, 2004), vol. 35, 6.22; 3.57.

5. Ibid. See also St. Augustine, *Catechism*, #27, 58.

Chapter 17: *The Great Deed*

1. From a television broadcast which included questions and answers, April, 2011. Italics added. Available online at http://ncronline.org/blogs/bulletins-human-side/which-man-pope-today.

2. See Fr. Pierre Teilhard de Chardin, SJ, *The Divine Milieu* (New York: Harper & Brothers, 1960), 129: "*You have told me, O God, to believe in hell, But You have forbidden me to hold with absolute certainty that a single man has been damned. I shall therefore make no attempt to consider the damned here, nor ever to discover—by whatsoever means—whether there are any.*"

3. St. Augustine, *The Augustine Catechism: The Enchiridion on Faith, Hope, and Love,* translated by Bruce Harbert (Hyde Park, NY: New City Press, 1999) #100, 116–17, italics added.

4. *The Pricke of Conscience, A Northumbrian Poem (Stimulus Conscientiae)*, edited by Richard Morris (Berlin: A. Asher, 1863; repr., New York: AMS, 1973.) This manuscript has survived in 117 copies, considerably more than the 84 copies of Chaucer's *The Canterbury Tales.* It was once thought to have been written by Richard Rolle, but is now considered to be the work of an anonymous fourteenth-century author.

5. See *The Writings of Julian of Norwich: A Vision Showed to a Devout Woman and A Revelation of Love*, edited by Nicholas Watson and Jacqueline Jenkins (University Park, PA: Pennsylvania State University Press, 2006), sidenote on 38:1.236.

6. John of Beverley became a local bishop, died in the year 721, and was canonized in 1037. Notably, his feast day in the English calendar fell on May 7, the day before Julian's Revelations began on May 8. Julian may well have heard prayers to St. John of Beverley being recited at her bedside throughout her illness. He was an extremely popular saint throughout the fourteenth and early fifteenth centuries. See *Historie van Jan van Beverley*, first printed by Thomas van der Noot in Brussels in 1543.

7. See *The Ancrene Riwle*, edited and translated by James Morton (London: Camden Society,1853; digitalized as a Google eBook from Oxford University), part 4, 197–99; 231–41.

Chapter 18: *On Prayer*

1. The five reasons seem to scan as follows: (1) "I am the ground of thy beseking," (2) "it is my will that thou have it," (3) "and next I make thee to will it," and (4) "and next I make thee to beseke it," (5) "and thou besekest it!"

2. *The Writings of Julian of Norwich: A Vision Showed to a Devout Woman and A Revelation of Love*, edited by Nicholas Watson and Jacqueline Jenkins

(University Park, PA: Pennsylvania State University Press, 2006), sidenote on 42:11.252.

Chapter 19: ***The Lord and The Servant***

1. *Reportata Parisiensa*, III Sen., d.7, 4, Comment during the pope's general audience on July 7, 2010, Copyright 2010—Libreria Editrice Vaticana. It is interesting to note that Pope Benedict XVI concurs that: "Duns Scotus, though aware that because of original sin Christ redeemed us with his passion, death and resurrection, makes it clear that the Incarnation is the greatest and most sublime work in the history of salvation—and that it is *not conditioned by any contingent circumstance* but is God's original idea for ultimately uniting all of creation with himself in the person and in the flesh of his son." Italics added.

2. See *The Writings of Julian of Norwich: A Vision Showed to a Devout Woman and A Revelation of Love*, edited by Nicholas Watson and Jacqueline Jenkins (University Park, PA: Pennsylvania State University Press, 2006), sidenote on 51:232.284.

3. The Doxology is said after the consecration of the bread and wine: "Through him, and with him, and in him, O God, almighty Father, in the unity of the Holy Spirit, all glory and honor is yours, for ever and ever."

Chapter 20: ***The Godly Will***

1. See Grace M. Jantzen, *Julian of Norwich: Mystic and Theologian* (New York: Paulist Press, 2000; repr., Eugene, OR: Wipf and Stock, 2005), 142.

2. See St. Augustine, *The Trinity*, translated by Edmund Hill, OP (Hyde Park, NY: New City Press, 1991), XV.6.43, 433. See also Walter Hilton, *The Scale (or Ladder) of Perfection* (Scotts Valley, CA: CreateSpace, 2010), bk. 1, III, 41–42: "Whereby you may see that man's soul (which may be called a created Trinity) was, in its natural estate, replenished in its three powers with the remembrance, sight and love of the most blessed uncreated Trinity which is God."

3. *The Confessions of St. Augustine*, translated and edited by Albert Cook Outler (New York: Dover Publications, 2002), bk. 3, ch. VI, 11, 38.

4. *The Writings of Julian of Norwich: A Vision Showed to a Devout Woman and A Revelation of Love*, edited by Nicholas Watson and Jacqueline Jenkins (University Park, PA: Pennsylvania State University Press, 2006), sidenote on 56:33.302.

Chapter 21: ***The Motherhood of God***

1. St. Anselm, *Prayer to St. Paul*, from *The Prayers and Meditations of St. Anselm, with the Proslogion*, translated by Benedicta Ward, SLG (New York: Penguin, 1973), 153–56.

2. Caroline Walker Bynum, *Jesus as Mother: Studies in the Spirituality of the High Middle Ages* (Berkeley: University of California Press, 1982), 151.

3. *The Ancrene Riwle*, edited and translated by James Morton (London: Camden Society, 1853; digitalized as a Google eBook from Oxford University), part 4, 231–33.

4. Bynum, *Jesus as Mother*, 187, 190.

5. Robert Boenig, "The God-as-Mother Theme in Richard Rolle's Biblical Commentaries," *Mystics Quarterly* 10, no. 4 (December 1984): 171–74.

6. Bynum, *Jesus as Mother*, 131.

7. The *Pater Noster* petitions: "Forgive us our trespasses as we forgive those who trespass against us."

Chapter 22: ***Close of the Day***

1. Watson and Jenkins suggest that the chapter headings were added in the early seventeenth-century copy from which the Sloane 2499 (S1) manuscript was made. See *The Writings of Julian of Norwich: A Vision Showed to a Devout Woman and A Revelation of Love*, edited by Nicholas Watson and Jacqueline Jenkins, henceforth W&J (University Park, PA: Pennsylvania State University Press, 2006), Introduction, 11.

2. *The Pricke of Conscience*, lines 8559–60, cited in W&J, sidenote on 65:4–5.326. My translation.

3. See Part Two of this book, chapter 11, note 2.

4. In medieval times, the day was divided up into two halves of twelve hours each, beginning with sunset, which changed, of course, from season to season. Time was never exact. If sunset was at 6 PM, then dawn was set at 6 AM, and *none*, the ninth hour, would be at 3 PM. If dawn in England in May (as previously suggested) arrived as early as 5 AM, then the ninth hour would be at 2 PM. Since there were no timepieces except sundials and extremely rare water clocks, Julian cannot be sure. Thus she writes that her visions ended at "*none* of the day or past." Italics added.

Chapter 23: ***Betrayal and Affirmation***

1. Mt 26:69–75, Mk 14:66–72, Lk 22:54–62, Jn 18:15–18 and 25–27.

2. *The Prymer or Lay Folks' Prayer Book*, edited by Henry Littlehales (London: E.E.T.S., 1895), *Prime*: Ps 54:1–7, 16. My translation.

Chapter 24: ***At Her Window***

1. See St. Bernard of Clairvaux, *On the Song of Songs*, translated by Kilian Walsh, OCSO, Cistercian Fathers Series, no. 4 (Kalamazoo, MI: Cistercian Publications, 1983), vol. 2, ser. 33, sec. V.9, 152.

2. *The Ancrene Riwle*, edited and translated by James Morton (London: Camden Society, 1853; digitalized as a Google eBook from Oxford University), part 4, 203.

3. Walter Hilton, *The Scale (or Ladder) of Perfection* (Scotts Valley, CA: CreateSpace, 2010), bk. 1, II.2, 36.

4. For a beautiful elucidation of this point, see Pierre Teilhard de Chardin, SJ, *The Divine Milieu* (New York: Harper & Brothers, 1960), 65–66.

5. See Jn 1:4: "In him was life, and the life was the light of all people."

6. See 1 Jn 4:16: "God is love, and those who abide in love abide in God, and God abides in them."

7. See 1 Jn 1:5: "God is light, and in him there is no darkness at all." Cf. 1 Jn 1:7: "but if we walk in the light as he himself is in the light, we have fellowship with one another, and the blood of Jesus his Son cleanses us from all sin."

8. See 1 Cor 13:13.

Chapter 25: ***A Gospel of Love***

1. This ending, from the Paris Codex, is in Latin: *Explicit liber revelationum Juliane anacorite Norwiche, cuius anime propicietur Deus.* It was probably added much later by a scribe.

2. *The Writings of Julian of Norwich: A Vision Showed to a Devout Woman and A Revelation of Love*, edited by Nicholas Watson and Jacqueline Jenkins (University Park, PA: Pennsylvania State University Press, 2006), Introduction, 2.

3. *De Haeretico Comburendo.* Online at http://www.ric.edu/faculty/rpotter/heretico.html.

4. Online at http://www.thereformation.info/Arcbp%20Thomas%20Arundel.htm.

5. W&J, Introduction, 13. Note: The collection in which the Short Text is found (Amherst MS Additional 37790) includes translations of Richard Rolle's *Incendium amoris* (*Fire of Love*) and *Emendatio vitae* (*Amending of Life*), as well as Jan van Ruusbroec's *Sparkling Stone* and Marguerite Porete's *Mirror of Simple Souls.* Notably, Julian's text is the only one in the collection originally written in Middle English, and the only visionary work.

6. Norman P. Tanner, *The Church in Late Medieval Norwich, 1370–1532* (Toronto: Pontifical Institute of Mediaeval Studies, 1984), 90.

Appendix

Numerical Chart for Map of Norwich*

T Cathedral
+ Parish Churches

Northern Ward
1 St. Augustine
2 St. Martin of Coslany
3 St. Botolph
4 St. Mary of Coslany
5 St. Michael of Coslany
6 St. George of Colegate
7 St. Olave of Colegate
8 St. Clement at Fye Bridge
9 St. Edmund
10 St. James
11 St. Saviour
12 All Saints at Fye Bridge
13 St. Margaret at Fye Bridige
14 St. Mary Unbrent

Wimer Ward
15 Sts. Simon and Jude
16 St. Swithin
17 St. George at Tombland
18 St. Michael at Plea
20 St. Andrew
21 Holy Cross or St. Crowche
22 St. John's Maddermarket
23 St. Gregory
24 St. Laurence
25 St. Margaret of Westwick
26 St. Benedict

Mancroft Ward
27 St. Giles
28 St. Peter Mancroft (previously known as St. Peter and St. Paul, or St. Peter of Gloucester)
29 St. Stephen

Conisford Ward
30 St. John of Timberhill
31 All Saints of Berstreet
32 St. Catherine or St. Winewaloy
33 St. John and the Holy Sepulchre
34 St. Bartholomew
35 St. Peter Southgate
36 St. Etheldreda
37 St. Edward
38 **St. Julian**
39 St. Clement of Conisford
40 St. Peter Permentergate
41 St. Vedast
42 St. Cuthbert
43 St. Mary the Less
44 St. Michael of Berstreet
45 St. Martin in the Bailey

Liberties of the Cathedral Priory
46 St. Martin at the Palace Gates
47 St. Matthew
48 St. Paul
49 St. Helen
50 St. Mary in the Marsh

*Norman P. Tanner, *The Church in Late Medieval Norwich, 1370–1532*. Studies and Texts 66. Toronto: Pontifical Institute of Mediaeval Studies, 1984, xii.

Religious Houses and Hospitals

- a Benedictine Cathedral Priory
- b Dominican Priory
- c Franciscan Priory
- d Carmelite Friary
- e Augustine Friary
- f Benedictine Nunnery of Carrow
- g College of St. Mary in the Fields
- h Carnary College
- i College of Chantry Priests in the Bishop's Palace
- j St. Gile's Hospital
- k St. Paul's Hospital
- l Hildebrond's Hospital
- m Daniel's Alms-Houses
- n Sick-House outside St. Stephen's Gate
- o Sick-House outside St. Giles Gate
- p Sick-House outside St. Benedict's Gate
- q Sick-House outside St. Augustine's Gate
- r Sick-House outside Magdalen Gate

- A Anchorage or Hermitage
- B Community resembling a Beguinage

Bibliography

Selected Primary Sources

Julian of Norwich:

The Writings of Julian of Norwich: A Vision Showed to a Devout Woman and A Revelation of Love. Edited by Nicholas Watson and Jacqueline Jenkins. University Park, PA: Pennsylvania State University Press, 2006.

The Complete Julian of Norwich. Edited with translations by Fr. John-Julian, OJN. Brewster, MA: Paraclete Press, 2009.

The Shewings of Julian of Norwich. Edited by Georgia Ronan Crampton. TEAMS Middle English Texts Series. Kalamazoo, MI: Western Michigan University, Medieval Institute Publications, 1994.

Julian of Norwich, A Revelation of Divine Love. The Long Text, British Library, Sloane MS 2499 (S1). Rev. ed. Edited by Marian Glasscoe. Exeter Medieval English Texts. Exeter: University of Exeter Press, 1986.

Julian of Norwich's Revelations of Divine Love: The Shorter Version Edited from BL Add. MS 37790. Edited by Frances Beer. Middle English Texts 8. Heidelberg, Germany: Carl Winter Universitätsverlag, 1978.

A Book of Showings to the Anchoress Julian of Norwich. Edited by Edmund Colledge, OSA, and James Walsh, SJ. Vols. 1–2. Studies and Texts 35. Toronto: Pontifical Institute of Mediaeval Studies, 1978.

Julian of Norwich: Showings. Translated by Edmund Colledge, OSA, and James Walsh, SJ. Classics of Western Spirituality. New York: Paulist Press, 1978.

Revelations of Divine Love: Recorded by Julian, Anchoress at Norwich, Anno Domini, 1373. Edited by Grace Warrack. London: Methuen, 1901 etc., 1958.

Saint Augustine:

The Works of Saint Augustine: A Translation for the 21st Century. Hyde Park, NY: New City Press, 1990–2012.

Augustine in His Own Words. Edited by William Harmless, SJ. Washington, DC: The Catholic University of America Press, 2010.

The Confessions of St. Augustine. Translated and edited by Albert Cook Outler. New York: Dover Publications, 2002.

The Augustine Catechism, The Enchiridion on Faith, Hope, and Love. Translation and notes by Bruce Harbert. Hyde Park, NY: New City Press, 1999.

On Christian Teaching. Translated by R. P. H. Green. Oxford and NY: Oxford University Press, 1997.

St. Augustine on Marriage and Sexuality. Edited by Elizabeth A. Clark. Washington, DC: The Catholic University of America Press, 1996.

The Trinity. Introduction, translation and notes by Edmund Hill, OP. Hyde Park, NY: New City Press, 1991.

The City of God. Edited by Vernon J. Bourke. New York: Image Books, 1958.

Other Primary Sources:

The Ancrene Riwle. Edited and translated by James Morton. London: Camden Society, 1853.

An Anthology of Christian Mysticism. Edited by Harvey D. Egan, SJ. Collegeville, MN: The Liturgical Press, 1991, 1996.

An Essay Towards a Topographical History of the County of Norfolk. Vols. 3 and 4: *The History of the City and County of Norwich*, Parts I and II. Francis Blomefield. London: 1806.

The Apocryphal New Testament. Edited by William Wake and Rev. Nathaniel Lardner. London: Simpkin, Marshall, Hamilton, Kent, & Co.; Glasgow: Thomas D. Morison, 1880.

Babees Book, Medieval Manners for the Young: Done into Modern English from Dr. Furnivall's Texts. Edited by Edith Rickert. London: Chatto and Windus; New York: Duffield & Co., 1908.

The Book of Margery Kempe. Edited by Barry Windeatt. New York: Longman, 2000.

The Canterbury Tales. Geoffrey Chaucer. Vol. 4 of *Chaucer's Works.* Edited by Joseph Skeat. Oxford: Clarendon Press, 1900.

The Cathedral Church of Norwich: A Description of Its Fabric and a Brief History of the Episcopal See. C. H. B. Quennell. London: George Bell & Sons, 1898.

The Chastising of God's Children and The Treatise of Perfection of the Sons of God. Jan van Ruusbroec. Edited by Joyce Bazire and Eric Colledge. Oxford: Oxford University Press, 1957.

Chronicles. Jean Froissart. Edited by Geoffrey Brereton. London and New York: Penguin, 1968.

The Cloud of Unknowing and the Book of Privy Counseling. Anonymous. Edited by William Johnston. New York: Image Books, Doubleday, 1973.

The Corpus Christi Play of the English Middle Ages. Edited by R. T. Davies. Metuchen, NJ: Rowman and Littlefield, 1972.

The English Writings. Richard Rolle. Translated and edited by Rosamund S. Allen. New York: Paulist Press, 1988.

The Essential Sermons, Commentaries, Treatises and Defenses. Meister Eckhart. Translated by Edmund Colledge, OSA, and Bernard McGinn. New York: Paulist Press, 1981.

Everyman with Other Interludes, including Eight Miracle Plays. Edited by Ernest Rhys. London and Toronto: J. M. Dent & Sons, Ltd.; New York: E. P. Dutton & Co., 1930.

The Golden Legend: Readings on the Saints (Legenda aurea). Jacobus de Voragine. 2 vols. Translated by William Granger Ryan. Princeton, NJ: Princeton University Press, 2012.

The Goodman of Paris. Translated by Eileen Power. London: Routledge, 1928.

The Good Wife's Guide: A Medieval Household Book (*Le Ménagier de Paris*). Translated by Gina L. Greco and Christine M. Rose. Ithaca, NY: Cornell University Press, 2009.

Historia Anglicana. Thomas Walsingham. Edited by H. T. Riley. London: Longman, Green, etc., 1864.

Holkham Bible Picture-Book, A Facsimile with Accompanying Commentary, Transcription and Translation. Michelle P. Brown. London: Folio Society and British Library, 2007.

The Holy Bible (*in the Earliest English Versions Made from the Latin Vulgate by John Wycliffe and His Followers*). 4 vols. Edited by Rev. Josiah Forshall and Sir Frederic Madden. London: British Museum. Oxford: Oxford University Press, 1850. Reprint, New York: AMS Press, 1982.

Latin Sermon Collections from Later Medieval England; Orthodox Preaching in the Age of Wyclif. Translated and edited by Siegfried Wenzel. Cambridge: Cambridge University Press, 2005.

The Lay Folks' Mass Book or Manner of Hearing Mass. Edited by Thomas Frederick Simmons, MA. London: E.E.T.S., N. Trübner & Co., 1879.

The Luttrell Psalter: A Facsimile with Accompanying Commentary. Edited by Michelle P. Brown. London: Folio Society and British Library, 2006.

Medieval Drama, An Anthology. Edited by Greg Walker. Oxford: Blackwell Publishing, 2000.

A Medieval Garner: Human Documents from the Four Centuries Preceding the Reformation. Selected, translated, and annotated by G. G. Coulton. London: Archibald Constable & Co., Ltd. 1910.

The Mediaeval Mystics of England. Edited by Edmund Colledge, OSA. New York: Scribner, 1961.

Medieval Woman's Guide to Health: The First Gynaecological Handbook. Edited by Beryl Rowland. Kent, OH: Kent State University Press, 1981.

Meditations on the Life of Christ: An Illustrated Manuscript of the Fourteenth Century. Pseudo-Bonaventure. Edited by Isa Ragusa and Rosalie B. Green. Translated by Isa Ragusa. Princeton, NJ: Princeton University Press, 1961.

The Mirror of Life of Blessed Jesus Christ. Nicholas Love. Edited with Introduction, Notes and Glossary by Michael G. Sargent. Exeter: University of Exeter Press, 2004; New York and London: Garland Publishing, 1992.

The N-Town Plays. Edited by Douglas Sugano. Published for TEAMS, in association with the University of Rochester. Middle English Texts Series. Kalamazoo, MI: Medieval Institute Publications, 2007.

On the Song of Songs. St. Bernard of Clairvaux. Translated by Kilian Walsh, OCSO. 4 vols. Cistercian Fathers Series. Kalamazoo, MI: Cistercian Publications, 1971–2005.

The Prayers and Meditations of Saint Anselm, with the Proslogion. Translated by Benedicta Ward, SLG. New York: Penguin Books, 1973.

Preaching in the Age of Chaucer, Selected Sermons in Translation. Edited and translated by Siegfried Wenzel. Washington, DC: The Catholic University of America Press, 2008.

The Pricke of Conscience (Stimulus Conscientiae), A Northumbrian Poem. Edited by Richard Morris. Berlin: A. Asher, 1863. Reprint, New York: AMS, 1973.

The Prickynge of Love. Edited by Harold Kane. 2 vols. Elizabethan and Renaissance Studies 92:10. Salzburg: Institut für Anglistik und Amerikanistik, Universität Salzburg, 1983.

The Prymer or Lay Folks' Prayer Book. Edited by Henry Littlehales. London: E.E.T.S., 1895.

The Psalter: Or Psalms of David and Certain Canticles. Richard Rolle. Translated and edited by Henry Ramsden Bramley. Oxford: Clarendon Press, 1884.

The Records of the City of Norwich. Edited by William Hudson and John Cottingham Tingey. Norwich: Jarrold, 1910.

Revelations. Birgitta of Sweden. Edited by Bridget Morris, translated by Denis Searby. New York: Oxford University Press, 2006.

The Sarum Missal in English. Translated by Frederick E. Warren. London: The De La More Press, 1906.

The Scale (or Ladder) of Perfection. Walter Hilton. Scotts Valley, CA: CreateSpace, 2010.

The Select English Works of John Wycliffe. Vol. 3. Edited by T. Arnold. Oxford: Clarendon Press, 1871.

The Soul's Journey into God, The Tree of Life, The Life of Saint Francis. Saint Bonaventure. Translated and edited by Ewert Cousins. New York: Paulist Press, 1978.

The Spiritual Espousals and Other Works. John Ruusbroec. Translated by James A. Wiseman, OSB. New York: Paulist Press, 1985.

The Vision of Piers Plowman. William Langland. Edited by A. V. C. Schmidt. 1978. Reprint, London: J. M. Dent, Orion Publishing, 1995.

Women's Lives in Medieval Europe, A Sourcebook. Edited by Emilie Amt. New York: Routledge, 1993.

The York Cycle of Mystery Plays: A Complete Version. Edited by J. S. Purvis. London: SPCK, 1957.

Yorkshire Writers, Richard Rolle of Hampole, An English Father of the Church, and His Followers. Edited by Carl Horstmann. 2 vols. New York: Macmillan, 1895.

Selected Secondary Sources

Aers, David, and Lynn Staley. *Powers of the Holy: Religion, Politics, and Gender in Late Medieval English Culture.* University Park, PA: Pennsylvania State University Press, 1996.

Addy, Sidney Oldall. *Church and Manor: A Study in English Economic History.* New York: A. M. Kelley, 1970.

Allchin, A. M., et al. *Julian of Norwich: Four Studies to Commemorate the Sixth Centenary of the Revelations of Divine Love.* 1973. Reprint, Oxford: Fairacres, SLG Press, 2001.

Aston, Margaret. *Lollards and Reformers: Images and Literacy in Late Medieval Religion.* London: Hambledon Press, 1984.

Baker, Denise Nowakowski. *Julian of Norwich's Showings: From Vision to Book.* Princeton, NJ: Princeton University Press, 1997.

Barbet, Pierre, MD. *A Doctor at Calvary.* Fort Collins, CO: Roman Catholic Books, 1953.

Brown, Peter. *Augustine of Hippo.* Rev. ed. London: Faber and Faber, 2000.

Brown-Grant, Rosalen. *Christine de Pizan and the Moral Defense of Women: Reading Beyond Gender.* Cambridge: Cambridge University Press, 1999.

Bynum, Caroline Walker. *Holy Feast and Holy Fast.* Berkeley: University of California Press, 1987.

———. *Jesus as Mother: Studies in the Spirituality of the High Middle Ages.* Berkeley: University of California Press, 1982.

Cammack, M. M. *John Wyclif and the English Bible.* New York: American Tract Society, 1938.

Chambers, E. R. *The Mediaeval Stage.* 2 vols. New York: Dover Publications, 1996.

Clark, Mary T., RSCJ. *Augustine.* London and New York: Continuum, 1994.

Coleman, T. W. *English Mystics of the Fourteenth Century.* Westport, CT: Greenwood, 1971.

Corbett, Tony. *The Laity, the Church and the Mystery Plays: A Drama of Belonging.* Ann Arbor, MI: University of Michigan Four Courts Press, 2009.

Coulton, George Gordon. *The Medieval Village.* 1925. Reprint, New York: Dover Publications, 1989.

———. *Studies in Medieval Thought*. London, New York: T. Nelson and Sons, 1940.

Daly, Robert J., SJ, editor. *Apocalyptic Thought in Early Christianity*. Grand Rapids, MI: Holy Cross Orthodox Press, 2009.

Davidson, Clifford. *Festivals and Plays in Late Medieval Britain*. Farnham, Surrey: Ashgate Publishing, 2007.

Deanesly, Margaret. *A History of the Medieval Church 590–1500*. 1925. Reprint, London: Methuen, 1972.

———. *The Lollard Bible*. Cambridge: Cambridge University Press, 1920.

Devereux, James A., SJ. "The Primers and The Prayer Book Collects." *Huntington Library Quarterly* 32, no.1 (November 1968).

Duffy, Eamon. *The Stripping of the Altars*. 1992. Reprint, New Haven and London: Yale University Press, 2005.

Eliot, T. S. *Four Quartets*. 1935–42. Reprint, New York: Harcourt, 1968.

Emmerson, Richard Kenneth, and Bernard McGinn, eds. *The Apocalypse in the Middle Ages*. Ithaca, NY: Cornell University Press, 1992.

Erickson, Millard J. *Christian Theology*. 2nd ed. Grand Rapids, MI: Baker Book House, 1998.

Evans, Gillian R. *Augustine on Evil*. Cambridge: Cambridge University Press, 1982.

Finucane, Ronald C. *Miracles and Pilgrims: Popular Beliefs in Medieval England*. London: Dent, 1977.

Foley, George C. *Anselm's Theory of the Atonement*. New York, London: Longmans, Green, and Co., 1909.

Ford, Judy Ann. *John Mirk's Festial: Orthodoxy, Lollardy and the Common People in Fourteenth-Century England*. Cambridge: D. S. Brewer, 2006.

French, Katherine L. *The People of the Parish: Community Life in a Late Medieval English Diocese*. Philadelphia, PA: University of Pennsylvania Press, 2000.

———. *The Good Women of the Parish: Gender and Religion after the Black Death*. Philadelphia, PA: University of Pennsylvania Press, 2008.

Gibson, Gail McMurray. *The Theater of Devotion*. Chicago: University of Chicago Press, 1989.

Gies, Frances, and Joseph Gies. *Marriage and the Family in the Middle Ages*. New York: Harper & Row, 1987.

———. *Life in a Medieval City*. 1969. Reprint, New York: Harper Perennial, 1981.

Glasscoe, Marion. *English Medieval Mystics: Games of Faith*. Edited by C. Brewer and N. H. Keeble. London and New York: Longman Medieval and Renaissance Library, 1993.

Harris, Jonathan Gil, and Natasha Korda, eds. *Staged Properties in Early Modern English Drama*. Cambridge: Cambridge University Press, 2006.

Hide, Kerrie. *Gifted Origins to Graced Fulfillment: The Soteriology of Julian of Norwich*. Collegeville, MN: Liturgical Press, 2001.

Hill-Vasquez, Heather. *The Politics of Response in the Middle English Religious Drama*. Washington, DC: The Catholic University of America Press, 2007.

Hodgson, Geraldine Emma. *English Mystics*. London: A. R. Mowbray, 1923; reissued, Nabu Press: 2010.

Horrox, Rosemary. *The Black Death*. Manchester: Manchester University Press, 1994.

Huizinga, Johan. *The Waning of the Middle Ages*. New York: Dover Publications, 1999.

Inge, William Ralph. *Studies of English Mystics: St. Margaret's Lectures*, 1905. London: John Murray, 1906.

Jantzen, Grace M. *Julian of Norwich: Mystic and Theologian*. New York: Paulist Press, 1988. Reprint, Eugene, OR: Wipf and Stock, 2005.

———. *Power, Gender and Christian Mysticism*. Cambridge: Cambridge University Press, 1995.

Jessopp, Rev. Augustus. *The Coming of the Friars and Other Historic Essays, including "The Black Death in East Anglia."* London: T. F. Unwin, 1884.

Jones, Edward Alexander, editor. *The Medieval Mystical Tradition in England: Exeter Symposium VII: Papers Read at Charney Manor, July 2004*. Cambridge: D. S. Brewer, 2004.

Keen, Maurice. *English Society in the Later Middle Ages, 1348–1500*. New York: Penguin Books, 1990.

King, David. *The Medieval Stained Glass of St Peter Mancroft Norwich*. Oxford: Oxford University Press for the British Academy, 2006.

Knowles, David, with Dimitri Obolensky. *The Middle Ages*. London: Darton, Longman & Todd, 1969.

———. *The English Mystical Tradition*. New York: Harper, 1965.

———. *The English Mystics*. London: Burns, Oates, and Washbourne, 1927.

Kroll, Jerome, and Bernard Bachrach. *The Mystic Mind*. New York: Routledge, 2006.

Lasko, P., and N. J. Morgan, eds. *Medieval Art in East Anglia 1300–1520*. Norwich: Jarrold & Sons, 1973.

LaVerdiere, Eugene. *The Eucharist in the New Testament and the Early Church*. Collegeville, MN: Liturgical Press, 1996.

Leech, Kenneth, and Sr. Benedicta Ward, SLG. *Julian Reconsidered*. Fairacres Publications 106. 1988. Reprint, Oxford: SLG Press, 2001.

Llewelyn, Robert, ed. *Julian: Woman of Our Day*. London: Darton, Longman & Todd, 1985.

Lossky, Vladimir. *In the Image and Likeness of God*. Crestwood, NY: St. Vladimir's Seminary Press, 1997.

MacLeish, Andrew, ed. *The Medieval Monastery*. Minneapolis, MN: University of Minnesota Press; Minnesota Archive Editions, Northstar Press of St. Cloud, 1991.

Malone, Mary T. *Women and Christianity*. Vol. 3. New York: Orbis Books, 2003.

McAvoy, Liz Herbert. *Authority and the Female Body*. Cambridge and New York: D. S. Brewer, 2004.

McEntire, Sandra J., and Joyce E. Salisbury, eds. *Julian of Norwich: A Book of Essays*. Garland Medieval Casebook 21. New York: Garland Reference Library of the Humanities, Taylor and Francis, 1998.

McGinn, Bernard. *The Mystical Thought of Meister Eckhart*. New York: Crossroad, 2001.

———. *The Presence of God: A History of Western Christian Mysticism*. 5 vols. New York: Crossroad, 1991–2012.

McKisack, May. *The Fourteenth Century, 1307–1399*. New York: Oxford University Press, 1991.

Merton, Thomas. *Conjectures of a Guilty Bystander*. New York: Image, Doubleday, 1965, 1966.

———. *Seeds of Destruction*. New York: Farrar, Straus and Giroux, 1964.

Mohl, Ruth. *The Three Estates in Medieval and Renaissance Literature*. 1933. Reprint, New York: Frederick Ungar Publishing Co., 1962.

Molinari, Paolo. *Julian of Norwich: The Teaching of a Fourteenth-Century English Mystic.* London: Longmans, Green, 1958. New York: Arden Library, 1979.

Mortimer, Ian. *The Time Traveler's Guide to Medieval England.* New York: Simon & Schuster, 2008.

Nuth, Joan M. *Wisdom's Daughter: The Theology of Julian of Norwich.* New York: Crossroad, 1991.

Oliva, Marilyn. *The Convent and the Community in Late Medieval England: Female Monasteries in the Diocese of Norwich, 1350–1540.* Rochester, NY, and Suffolk, England: Boydell Press, 1998.

Olson, Linda, and Kathryn Kerby-Fulton, eds. *Voices in Dialogue: Reading Women in the Middle Ages.* Notre Dame, IN: University of Notre Dame Press, 2005.

Orme, Nicholas. *English Schools in the Middle Ages.* London: Methuen and Co. Ltd./ Routledge, 1973.

———. *Medieval Children.* New Haven: Yale University Press, 2001.

Owst, G. R. *Preaching in Medieval England, An Introduction to Sermon Manuscripts of the Period c. 1350–1450.* New York: Russell & Russell, 1965.

———. *Literature and Pulpit in Medieval England.* Cambridge: Cambridge University Press, 1933.

Palliser, Margaret Ann, OP. *Christ, Our Mother of Mercy: Divine Mercy and Compassion in the Theology of the Shewings of Julian of Norwich.* Berlin and New York: Walter de Gruyter, 1992.

Pantin, W. A. *The English Church in the Fourteenth Century.* Cambridge: Cambridge University Press, 1955.

Pelikan, Jaroslav. *The Growth of Medieval Theology 600–1300* in *The Christian Tradition: A History of the Development of Doctrine,* Vol. 3. Chicago: University of Chicago Press, 1978.

Pelphrey, Brant. *Christ Our Mother: Julian of Norwich.* Wilmington, DE: M. Glazier, 1989.

———. *Love was His Meaning: The Theology and Mysticism of Julian of Norwich.* Salzburg: Institut für Anglistik und Amerikanistik, Universität Salzburg, 1982, Prometheus Books, 1983.

Peters, Edward, ed. *Heresy and Authority in Medieval Europe.* Philadelphia, PA: University of Pennsylvania Press, 1980.

Phillips, Brian D., trans. *European Art of the Fourteenth Century.* Los Angeles: J. Paul Getty Museum, 2007.

Power, Eileen. *Medieval English Nunneries, c.1275–1535*. Cambridge: Cambridge University Press, 1922.

Prosser, Eleanor. *Drama and Religion in the English Mystery Plays.* Palo Alto, CA: Stanford University Press, 1961.

Rawcliffe, Carole. *Medicine and Society in Later Medieval England.* London: Sandpiper Books, 1999.

Renevey, Denis, and Christiania Whitehead, eds. *Writing Religious Women: Female Spiritual and Textual Practices in Late Medieval England.* Toronto: University of Toronto Press, 2000.

Rickert, Edith, comp., and Clair C. Olsen and Martin M. Crow, eds. *Chaucer's World.* New York: Columbia University Press, 1948.

Riehle, Wolfgang. *The Middle English Mystics.* Translated by Bernard Standring. London: Routledge & Kegan Paul, 1981.

Rogerson, Margaret. *Playing a Part in History: The York Mysteries, 1951–2000.* Toronto: University of Toronto Press, 2009.

Salter, F. M. *Medieval Drama in Chester.* Toronto: University of Toronto Press, 1955.

Schell, Edgar T., and J. D. Shuchter. *English Morality Plays and Moral Interludes.* New York: Holt, Rinehart & Winston, 1969.

Shahar, Shulamith. *Childhood in the Middle Ages.* London: Routledge, 1992.

———. *The Fourth Estate: A History of Women in the Middle Ages.* London: Routledge, 2007.

Spencer, H. Leith. *English Preaching in the Late Middle Ages.* Oxford: Clarendon Press, 1993.

Sullivan, Edward, OP. *The Image of God: The Doctrine of St. Augustine and Its Influence.* Dubuque, IA: Priory Press, 1963.

Tanner, Norman P. *The Church in Late Medieval Norwich, 1370–1532.* Studies and Texts 66. Toronto: Pontifical Institute of Mediaeval Studies, 1984.

Teilhard de Chardin, Fr. Pierre, SJ. *The Divine Milieu.* New York: Harper & Brothers, 1960.

———. *Hymn of the Universe.* New York: Harper & Row, 1965.

Thouless, Robert Henry. *The Lady Julian: A Psychological Study.* London: Society for Promoting Christian Knowledge, Sheldon Press, 1924.

Tuchman, Barbara W. *A Distant Mirror: The Calamitous 14th Century.* New York: Random House, 1978.

Ullmann, Walter. *A Short History of the Papacy in the Middle Ages.* 2nd ed. London: Routledge, 2003.

Underhill, Evelyn. *Mysticism: A Study in Nature and Development of Spiritual Consciousness.* London: Methuen, 1911. Reprint, Stilwell, KS: A Digi-reads.com Book, 2005.

———. *The Essentials of Mysticism and Other Essays.* London: Dent, 1920.

Vinogradoff, Paul. *Villainage in England.* Oxford: Clarendon Press, 1892.

Ward, Jennifer C. *Women in England in the Middle Ages.* London: Hambledon Continuum, 2006.

Webster, Alan. *Suffering: The Jews of Norwich and Julian of Norwich.* 1981 St. Paul's Lecture, delivered at St. Botolph's Church, Aldgate.

Williams, George Hunston. *Anselm: Communion and Atonement.* Saint Louis, MO: Concordia, 1960.

Williams, Mother Margaret, RSCJ. *The Sacred Heart in the Life of the Church.* New York: Sheed & Ward, 1957.

Wood, Diana. *Women and Religion in Medieval England.* Oxford: Oxbow Books, 2003.

Woolf, Rosemary. *The English Mystery Plays.* Berkeley: University of California Press, 1980.

Workman, Herbert Brook. *John Wyclif: A Study of the English Medieval Church.* 2 vols. Oxford: Clarendon Press, 1926. Reprint, Eugene, OR: Wipf and Stock Publishers, 2001.

Young, Karl. *The Drama of the Medieval Church.* Vol 1. 1933. Reprint, Oxford: Clarendon Press, 1962.

Ziegler, Philip. *The Black Death.* New York: Harper Perennial, 2009.

Index

Numbers in italics indicate images.

Abbey of the Holy Ghost, 180
abbeys, 40–41
Abelard, Peter, 513–14
absolution, 579–80
acedia, 141–42, 232, 570
Achler, Elsbet, 232–33
Act of Contrition, 239
Adam: role of, in parable of the lord and the servant, 466, 468–69, 471, 474–77. *See also* original sin; sin of, 392–95
adoption, theology of, 360–61
Aelred of Rievaulx, 228, 513
affective devotion, 227–29
Albert the Great, Saint, 513–14
Albigensians, 42
allegorical poems, 179–80
"alle shalle be wele," 211, 383–84, 387, 388, 396–97, 399–402, 405, 408, 409, 413, 536, 556, 559–60, 592
Amherst MS, 6, 9
anchorages, 187–88
anchoresses, suspicions about, 190
Ancrene Riwle ("Anchorite's Rule"), 180, 188, 284, 374, 514, 570
Angela of Foligno, 123, 232
Anglia, 22. *See also* East Anglia
Anglo-Saxons, 22
Anne, Saint, 131
annulments, 111
anorexia mirabilis (marvelous fasting), 232
Anselm, Saint, 304–5, 323, 513
antipope, 145
apocalypse, anticipation of, in the fourteenth century, 389
Apostles' Creed, 407, 485
apprentices, 56
Aquinas, Thomas. *See* Thomas Aquinas, Saint
Aristotle, 119
art: depicting Old and New Testament scenes, 18–19; graphic depictions in, of Christ's passion, 217
artistic mind, creative imagination of, 262–63
Arundel, Thomas, 163–65, 179, 190, 592
asceticism, 100, 123, 239, 543, 580
astrological signs, analysis of, 246–47
atonement, 348, 362, 392–93
atonement theory, 304–5, 323
Augustine, Saint, 99, 115–19, 160, 168, 169, 321, 323, 384, 421, 507; on evil, 311–13, 386; on God's purpose, 414; on grace, 291–93; homiletic style of, 170; on images and signs in scripture, 326–27; on predestination, 291–94; on sin, 393, 505; on the Trinity, 268–69; on the wrath of God, 325
Augustinians (Austin canons), 43, 177, 270
Aurelius, Marcus, 238
Austin Friars. *See* Augustinians
Avignon, popes in, 143–44
avisement, 308
awareness, heightened level of, 263

Badby, William, 170
Ball, John, 151, 152–53, 155
baptism, 133
barber-surgeons, 88, 244, 245, 246

Battle of Agincourt, 593
Battle of Crécy, 64–65
Battle of Poitiers, 126–27
beastly will, 421
Beatrice of Nazareth, 6, 232
Beaumanoir, Philippe de, 111–12
Beauvais, Vincent de, 96–97
Beer, Frances, 10
beholding, 307–8; Christ, 298, 318, 460; church, 447; as a form of contemplative prayer, 557–58; God, 157, 272, 284–85, 399, 440, 447, 571; the passion, 356, 367–68, 385
behovely, 383–84, 386
Benedict XIII, 145
Benedict XVI, 407
Benedicte, 270–71
Benedictines, 21, 39–40, 176–77, 270–71, 374
Benedict of Nursia, 39
benefices, 143
bequests, 188–89
Berkeley, William, 127
Bernard of Clairvaux, Saint, 99, 227–28, 374, 513, 570
Bible: authority of, 160; English translations of, 162–63, 165–66; vernacular translation of, 160–62. *See also* scripture
Bibliothèque Nationale MS Fonds Anglais 40, 6
birth girdle, 131
bishops, naming of, 41
Black Death. *See* plague
Blackfriars synod, 159
blame, for sin, 387, 388
blessings, linked to suffering, 422–23
blindness, human, 451, 460, 495
bliss, 576; degrees of, 329–30; sin and, 566
Blomefield, Francis, 9
blood, analysis of, 246
bloodletting, 246
blue, associated with royalty, 470
Boccaccio, Giovanni, 70
bodily sickness, Julian's desire for, 230–31, 233–38
bodily sights, 5, 227, 230, 256–57, 260, 261, 265, 285, 295
body, holistic approach to, 283–84
Bonaventure, Saint, 99, 228, 513–14
Book of Margery Kempe, The (Kempe), 192–93
Book of Privy Counseling, The, 179
Book of Showings to the Anchoress Julian of Norwich (Julian), 10
breast feeding, 133–34, 136
Brigit of Sweden, Saint 6, 425, 514, 562
British Library MS Additional 37790, 6
brode water. See Norfolk Broads
Bromyard, John. *See* John of Bromyard
bubonic plague, 69

Caesarius of Arles, 168
Canterbury Tales, The (Chaucer), 181
Carnary College, 93
Carrow Priory. *See* St. Mary of Carrow Priory
Carthusians, 39, 375
Catherine of Aragon, 129
Catherine of Genoa, Saint, 123, 232
Catherine of Siena, Saint, 6, 144, 232, 233, 425, 442, 514, 516, 562
causalgia, 341
Cavendish, John, 152
Cecilia, Saint, martyrdom of, 238–39
chantry priests, 19
charity, 587–88
charity given, 588
Charlemagne, 168
Chasteau d'Amour (Castle of Love), 179
Chastising of God's Children, The, 179, 331
chastity, 40, 96, 107, 108, 113
Chaucer, Geoffrey, 8, 11, 180, 181, 183, 204
Chauliac, Guy de, 68, 81
chevauchée, 64
childbirth, 131–32
child rearing, directives about, 176
children: growth stages of, 62–63; illegitimate, 128; joy from, 130;

mortality rate of, 130, 136; sermons on, 129; troubles from, 129–30
chivalry, code of, 45–46
chrism, holy, 19
Christ: as answer to prayer, 438; appearing to Mary Magdalene, 261; baptism of, 368; as basis of all prayer, 433–34, 436–37; bearing members of his Mystical Body into heaven, 501–2; bleeding, Julian's vision of, 272–73, 285–87; bliss in, fullness of, 367–69; blood of, 319–23; bodily wounds of, 318–22; bride of, 513; choosing to suffer and die, 367, 368–69; church as living presence of, 412; as clothing, 272–74; compassion of, 140, 388–91, 455; converting suffering to joy, 356, 360; counting on, to make things well, 400–401; courtesy of, 582–83; death of, 349; descending into hell, 407, 484; dual nature of, 509; dying of, Julian's vision of, 296–97, 301–4, 334–39, 344–46; eradicating death, 359, 361–62; explaining how "alle shalle be wele," 397; facial expression of, Julian's reflection on, 565; five wounds of, 228, 232, 239, 373, 375; gender references for, Julian changing, 516; giving birth to humankind, 132; as God and man, 398; as ground of human nature, 496; holy names for, 379–81; "*homely*" appearance of, 286–87; hosting the heavenly banquet, 329; humankind reborn through, 496; human salvation as gift to, 365–66; human substance of, 498; humility of, 362–63; incarnating all humankind, 477–78; laboring to deliver every child, 524–25; lesson of love, 586; love of, for Mary, 378–79; lowering himself, 271; Motherhood of, 47, 105, 361, 391, 455, 510, 513, 518–27, 529, 530–37; Mystical Body of, 17, 398, 404, 412, 448, 484; nourishing us spiritually, 526–27; obedience of, 313; offering Julian insight into Divine Love, 373–75; peace of, 458–59; perfect humanity of, 534; personal relationship with, 412; physical sufferings of, modern medical view of, 339–44; presence of, continual, 487; as prototype of God's perfect image and likeness, 498–99; reconciled with humanity, 485–86; re-creating creation, 394; royal lordship of, 396, 455; Sacred Heart of, 374–75; salvation through, 134, 148; soul of, 498–99; speaking in familiar language, 384; suffering with, 228–29, 231; taking on all pain, 348; telling followers to be watchful, 140; thirst of, 336–37, 397–98, 575; transformation of, 357–59; two natures in, 476, 478; unchanging love of, 422, 584; unconditional love of, 428–29, 457; union with, 507–8; victory of, over Satan, 323–24; as wisdom of God, 513; working in our souls, 501; wounds of, as refuge against temptation, 374. *See also* Jesus
church: authority of, Wyclif's view, 147–50; as bride of Christ, 513; increased attendance at, 80; as Mystical Body of Christ, 448, 523; plague causing personnel shortages for, 71, 74–75; reform of, 41, 42, 144, 147; role of, 447–48; teachings of, as gift from God, 584–85; teachings on marriage, 114–15; teachings on sickness, 248; teachings on women, 112–17
churching ritual, 19, 133
Church of St. Julian (Norwich), *37*, 38, 59
Church of St. Peter and St. Paul (Church of St. Peter of Gloucester; Church of St. Peter Mancroft), 36–37, 204
Cistercians, 39, 374
city, heavenly. *See* holy city
City of God, The (Augustine), 325
Clement VI, 67, 68, 71

Clement VII, 145, 184
clergy, 39–41, 71, 147
cloth industry, 56–57, 82, 136
clothing, 273–74, 283
Cloud of Unknowing, The, 8, 11, 179–80
Clyn, John, 74
clyster, 248
Cogit Nos (Urban V), 135
Colledge, Edmund, 10
Collins, Henry, 7
Columba of Rieti, 233
commendations, 89
compassion, 238, 239, 256–57, 345–46; Christ's, 390–91; rejoicing and, 481–82
concupiscence, 117, 118, 421
Confessio (Wyclif), 159
confession, 149, 177, 424–25, 531
Confessions (Augustine), 119, 507
Conisford (Norwich), 59
Conisford Gate (King Street Gate), *27*
conscience, 584–85
consent, mutual, for marriage, 105
Constitutions of 1409, 164, 165, 166, 190, 592–93
consubstantiation, 149
contemplative prayer, 439–40, 441, 557, 558
contrariousness, 452, 455
contrition, 238, 239, 418, 424, 425, 531, 579–80
coral, healing power of, 131
Corpus Christi plays, 194–95, 205–6, 364, 552; actors for, 198–99; authorship of, 198; craft guilds resulting from, 201; crowd control during, 202; influence of, on Julian, 221–22; laicization of, 197–99; pageant wagons for, 195–97; performance of, 202, 206–9; production of, 199–201; sponsorship of, 197; staging of, 195–96
corruption, 312
Council of Constance, 159–60
Council of Rome, 159–60
Council of Vienne, 196
Courtenay, William, 159
courtesie, 46–47
courtly love, 45–46
craft guilds, 55–56, 86, 88, 138; chapels of, 38; sponsoring Corpus Christi plays, 197, 198–200
created charity, 588
creation, 438; Christ re-creating, 394; expressing Divine Love, 276; fate of, linked with humankind, 349; from God's point of view, 314–15; Great Deed and, 404; Creator, maternal imagery for, 513–14
Credo, 270
Cressy, Serenus, 7
Cressy Long Text, 8
cross, paradox of, 390
crown of thorns, 338, 340
crucifixion, 341–44; compared with labor, 522; medieval paintings of, 377
Crump, Henry, 163
Cursor Mundi, 179

damned, the, 405–8
death: as beginning, 359; by crucifixion, 339–44; Christ eradicating, 359, 361–62
death tax, 51
De Civili Dominio (Wyclif), 146
De Domino Divino (Wyclif), 146
De Ecclesia (Wyclif), 148
De Eucharistia (Wyclif), 148–49
De Haeretico Comburendo, 163–64, 592
De Potestate Papae (Wyclif), 148
depression, 141–42, 232, 307
Deschamps, Eustache, 129–30
desire, as a state of the soul, 451, 452
despair, 535, 570, 571
Despenser, Henry, 154–57, 184, 186, 187
De Trinitate (Augustine), 115–17, 268–69
De Veritate Sacrae Scripturae (Wyclif), 160
devils: bondage to, 322; depictions of, 552
devotional practices, 281–83

disappointment, in prayer, 437–39
Divine Being, mirrors of, 533
divine-human contact, 263
Divine Love, 47, 497, 587–88, 591; expressed in the creation, 276; human love responding to, 544
Divine Motherhood, 518–19
Divine Names, 379–81
Divine Office, 21, 151
Divine Providence, praying for, 438–39
Divine Reality, 404–5
Divine visitations, 232
Divine Will, 440–41
divorce, 111
dogma, mysticism and, 407, 409
domes, 443–44, 445, 446–48, 459, 480, 567
Domesday, 139, 175, 219, 288, 398, 444
Dominicans, 35, 41, 42, 43, 161, 169, 173, 177, 375
Dominic of Osma, 41, 42
donum superadditum, 303
Doomsday Book of 1086, 24
Dorothy of Montau, 123
doubt, 571, 572
dowry, 105
dread, 570; as a state of the soul, 451, 452; types of, 573–74
drowning, fear of, 299
drying, types of, 338–39
duality, of body and soul, 354

East Anglia: deaths of clergy in, from the plague, 74; marketplace in, 28–30; nuns in, 99; settlement of, 22; spirituality in, 213; weather in, 30–31; weavers invited to, 57
Eastern Orthodox Church, 151
Easton, Adam, 35, 176
Eckhart, Meister, 95
ecstasy, 371, 373
education, 53–54, 85, 87–89, 92–97, 128
Edward, the Black Prince, 65, 125–27, 150
Edward II, 44
Edward III, 28–29, 44, 57, 64, 65, 125, 126, 150, 593
Eliot, T.S., 8
Elizabeth of Hungary, Saint, 123
Emund, Thomas, 188
England: attack in, fear of, 135; cloth-making industry in, 56–57; coastal raids on, 127; deaths in, from the plague, 72–73; in the Hundred Years' War, 63–66, 125; knights returning to, 134–35; monasteries in, 7, 40; optimism in, after the Hundred Years' War, 66; during the Papal Schism, 145; peasants' revolt in, 151–57; plague in, 68–69, 136, 139, 185–86; preaching in, golden age of, 168; religious life in, 15–21; social upheaval in, during the plague, 82–84; soldiers returning to, 134–35; survival in, 31–32; taxes in, increasing, 150–51; troubles in, linked to sin, 177; women's economic dealings in, 88
enjoying, as a state of the soul, 451, 452
Erpingham, Julian, 46
Erpingham, Thomas, 46
essence, 498, 500
estates, 39, 44, 47–48
Eucharist, 19, 148–49, 319, 366, 523
Europe: deaths in, from the plague, 67–69, 72–73; division of, during the papal schism, 145–46; extremes in, after the plague, 80; friar revolution in, 169; Hundred Years' War in, 63–66, 125; Turks invading, 125
evencristens, 5, 46, 100, 582; Julian's love for, 421; Lollards appealing to, 184; love toward, 287–90
evil, 311–13; all-pervasiveness of, 400; choice of, 495; conceiving of, 546; effects of, 399–400; experience of, 313; God's tolerance of, 414–15; God working through, 317; human beings triumphing over, 414–15
exemplum, 370, 446
existence, higher and lower levels of, 492
Exsultet, 383

fabliaux, 128
faith, 300, 412, 500–501, 502; leading to self-awareness, 446–47; strength of, 433; testing of, 564
fall, the, 112, 120, 207–8, 221, 303, 304–5, 486. *See also* original sin
fasting, 231, 232–33
fasting women, 231–32, 233, 284
Faverches, Richeldis de, 129
fear, 545–46, 573–74
feast of Corpus Christi, 196–97, 202
feast day processions, 196–97
Felicitas, Saint, 131
femme sole, 138
Festial (Mirk), 178
feudal system, 39, 44–45, 47–55, 512
fidelity, 117
fiefdoms, 44
Final Judgment, 444
first estate, 39, 40, 512
First Lateran Council, 41
Flete, William, 94
folly, greatest, 578
food, obsession about, 231. *See also* fasting
foremariage, 50
forgiveness, 239, 429, 450; human experience of, 457; learning to practice, 456; three conditions for, 424–25
Fourth Lateran Council, 41, 50–51
Francis of Assisi, Saint, 41, 143, 228, 231, 562
Franciscans, 35, 41–42, 43, 119, 143, 161, 169, 177, 228–30, 375
freedom: failure and, 454; for villeins, 53–55, 58
free will, 291–93, 303, 457–58, 529
friars, 41–43, 169–71
Friars Minor, 41–42, 74
Friary de Domina (Friars of Our Lady), 74
Froissart, Jean, 64, 72

Galen of Pergamon, 120–21, 245
garland, 338
Gertrude the Great, Saint (Gertrude of Helfta), 6, 374–75, 514
ghostly forthbringing, 526
ghostly sights, 261–62, 265, 285, 295, 569
girls, education of, 87, 96–97
glad giver, 370
Glasscoe, Marion, 9–10
God: anger of, 448–49; approachability of, 582–83; beholding, 307, 447; creating the soul perfectly, 442–43; defiance of, 393–94; depiction of, 471; disrespect of, 582; eternal love of, 495–96; existential union of, with human beings, 494–95, 499; experiencing, in our soul, 507–8; fear of, 19–20; forgiveness of, 450; goodness of, 283–84, 433, 438, 448–50, 457–58, 492, 533–34, 587; as ground of our being, 507, 508; grumbling against, 307; "*homely*" aspect of 328–29; immanence of, 308–11, 315–17; incomprehensibility of, 400; judgment of, 443–44; mercy of, 174, 415; Motherhood of, 105, 120, 134, 510, 512, 515–16, 520; mystical union with, 441–42; presence of, 330–32, 452; properties of, 587; protection of, 551; reverence for, 545; *rightfullehede* of, 314, 318, 327, 415, 443; seeing Christ in all humans, 489; seeking of, 306–8; service to, 330; trusting in, 571; unchangeable nature of, 449–50; unchanging love of, 440–41, 493; understanding, 546; will of, 300, 415; willingness of, to save humankind, 430; working through evil, 317; wrath of, 173–77, 325–26, 428, 444–45, 456–57
godly will, 421, 427, 494, 495, 515, 535
Golden Epistle (William of St. Thierry), 228
Golden Legend, The (Voragine), 238, 351
goodwife, 108–10
gospel, women's, 2
gospel harmonies, 178, 182

Gospel of Nicodemus, 218
gospel stories, related to people's own situations, 18
grace, 239, 260, 261, 267, 287, 354, 428, 508–9; activity of, 454–58; fall from, 528; humility leading to, 425; leading to salvation, 395; predestination and, 291–92; prevenient, 297–98; reception of, grace enabling, 439
Gratian, 119
Great Deed, 403–4, 409–11, 417, 418, 588
Great Mortality. *See* plague
Great Pestilence. *See* plague
Great Terror. *See* plague
Gregory VII, 161
Gregory XI, 144, 147, 163
Gregory the Great, Saint, 168, 169
Grosseteste, Robert, 422

Hadewijch of Antwerp, 6
Hailes, Robert, 153
Handlyng Synne, 179
Harford, Dundas, 9
Hauteyn, Roger, 46
hazelnut, Julian's vision of, 274–77, 278, 280, 285
healing: human experience of, 457; prayers for, 251
heart, 554–55. *See also* Christ, Sacred Heart of
heaven, 359; as banquet, 329; foretaste of, 372; Julian's focus on, 582; reward in, 423; sinners brought to, 423; three aspects of, 364–68
heavenly treasuries, 434, 435, 458–59
Helfta, visionary nuns of, 514
hell, 21, 149; Christ's descent into, 407, 484; church teaching on, 407–8, 410; harrowing of, 218, 407
hematidrosis, 339
Henry, Duke of Lancaster, 125, 127
Henry III, 129
Henry IV (Henry of Bolingbroke), 46, 163, 164, 166, 592
Henry V, 166, 593
Henry VI, 166, 593
Henry VII, 166
Henry VIII, 7, 129
Henry of Knighton, 82
herbal remedies, 249–50
Hereford, Nicholas, 162
heresy, 146, 162; as civil offense, 165; laws regarding, 190
heriot, 51
Hildegard of Bingen, Saint, 6
Hilton, Walter, 8, 11, 180, 193, 211, 276
Hochma, 512–13
holiness, chastity and, 113
holy city, 28, 503–4, 554–56, 585–86
Holy Ghost. *See* Holy Spirit
holy orders, sacrament of, 19
Holy Spirit: indwelling of, 291; love of, 504; maternal imagery for, 513–14; outpouring of, in mercy, 453; visitation of, 309
Holy Trinity Cathedral (Norwich), 21
Holy Vernicle, 302
Holy Week, 16, 17, 19
homely, Julian's use of, 271
home schooling, 92–93
homilies, 168
homilists, requirements of, for preaching, 18
honor, sin as, 426
Huguccio, 119
human beings: blindness of, 451, 460, 495; dignity of, 499; dual nature of, 509; existential union of, with God, 494–95, 499; judgment of, 443–44; as lights of Christ, 489; nature of, broken, 508–9; saved or condemned, 461
human condition, 487, 505
humankind: bliss of, endlessness of, 496; reborn through Christ, 496; trinitarian nature of, 496
human nature: goodness of, 421; preciousness of, to God, 533; purification of, 534; restored, 520; volatility of, 443
humility, 425, 529, 545, 572, 586
humoral medicine, 81, 132, 244, 245–46, 247, 249–50

Hundred Years' War, 63–66, 125
hypovolemic shock, 343, 344

Ida of Louvain, 232
idolus Northfolkorum, 156
"I it am," 379–81, 411–12, 519–20, 587
illness, social aspect of, 251
imagination, inspired, 180
imago Dei, 115, 303
imitatio Christi, 231
impatience, 569–71
in-breeding, 50–51
incarnation, 506; God's maternal desire for, 520; Julian's description of, 477; necessity of, 362; Scotus's view on, 478–79
indulgences, 148; plenary, 135; sale of, 43
infants: baptism of, 133; death rates of, 130; health of, 132
Inge, Dean W.R., 8
inner will, 354
Innocent III, 42
Innocent VI, 125
inspiration, 584–85
instant gratification, 313
Instruction for the People: The Book of Vices and Virtues, 179
intercession, 435
intermediaries, 281–82
Irenaeus, Saint, 303, 322
Italy, plague's effect on, 68

Jean II, 126–27
Jehovah, as Divine Mother, 513
Jerome, Saint, 115, 117
Jesus: blessing marriage, 121; *courtesie* of, 46–47; incarnate in human substance and sensuality, 506; Julian choosing, for her heaven, 352–55; as Mother, 514, 520; resurrection of, 2; teachings of, on poverty and humility, 147; women around, 1–2, 12, 217, 347. *See also* Christ
John of Bromyard, 104, 171–76
John of the Cross, Saint, 179
John of Gaunt, 150, 152, 163
jongleurs, 128
journeymen, 56
joy: Christ preparing, for the soul, 541; cultivating, 543
judgment, 288, 443–44, 459. See also *domes*
Julian, Saint (bishop of Le Mans, France), 38
Julian the Hospitaller, 38
Julian of Norwich: acting against contemporary church standards, 5–6; adoption theology of, 360–61; anchorage of, 187–88; as anchoress, 188–93; attending church as a youth, 35–36; becoming an anchoress, 184–88; bequests for, 188–89; on childbirth, 132; childhood of, 59, 62–64, 67, 69, 75–80, 102–3; clarity of mind of, 250; compared to Chaucer, 181; compassion of, 345–46; contemplative practice of, 510–11; context for life and writings of, 2–4; desiring liberation from suffering, 539; doubt of, 406, 549–51; education of, 85–89, 92–97, 99; euphoria of, 330–32; on evil, 157; exegetical skills of, 182; expecting to die, 251, 260, 280, 288, 299; on faith, 500–2; faithfulness of, to the church, 445; family of, 75–77, 79–80; family home of, 59–62, 94–95, 99; first woman author of book in Middle English, 2; gratitude of, 297; growing up in walled city, 28; humility of, 146, 235, 254, 289; illness of, 101–2, 252–55; keeping her Revelations a secret, 187, 193; Kempe and, 191–93; language of, 350–51, 428–29, 442, 516; life status of, 11; longing for union with God, 277–78; love for books, 63; love for children, 536; marital duties of, 108–10; marriage of, 104–7, 111; meditations of, 511; memorizing scripture passages, 182–83;

metaphors of, 274–75; on miracles, 417–18; on motherhood, 100–101, 105, 120, 134; motherhood of, 412–13, 537; near-death illness of, 241–42; as nun, unlikelihood of, 98–102; observational skills of, 86; optimism of, 140–41; oratorical speech patterns of, 183; paralyzed by her vision, 298; parenthood of, 135–36; personal guilt of, 428; potential for, as suspect for heresy, 184, 189–91; on prayer, 281–83, 376, 431–32, 435–40; prayers of, 281, 460–61; on predestination, 294; pregnancy of, 128; prophecies about the church, 150; psychic experience of, 258–61; rationality of, 10–11; refusing to blame God for evil, 400; religious formation of, 97–98; sadness of, 521; on salvation, 290; seeing no wrath in God, 325–26; seeing transformation of Christ, 357–58, 360; seeking compassion, 256–57; self-noughting of, 280–81; self-recrimination of, 549–51; on sensuality, 123; on sin bearing no shame, 422; sloth and, 141–42; spiritual direction of, 569, 579; suffering and, 76, 79–80, 139–41, 227, 235; temptations of, 351–52, 560–61; testing of, 316–17; theological riskiness of, 515–16; theology of, 105, 134, 179, 180, 234–35, 266, 325, 360–61, 427, 492, 506, 510–11, 514; under threat of persecution, 267; three gifts desired by, 226–27, 229–31, 233–40; on the Trinity, 267–68, 269, 270, 277; understanding human suffering, 140; on universal suffering, 385–86; unknowing of, 493; unlettered, 5, 46, 95, 97, 226; unself-consciousness of, 260; visited by local friar, 549–51; wanting to share in Christ's passion, 222, 226–27, 229, 257, 258; warning against sin, 429; wholesome mystical approach of, 234; on women lacking the right to preach, 189–90; writing in secret, 183–84; writings about, 10; writing skills of, 181–83. *See also* Long Text; *Revelations of Divine Love*; Short Text

Kempe, Margery, 123, 191–93, 516, 579
kingdom of God, 316
kingdom of heaven, 473
knights, 44, 45–46, 65, 125–26, 134–35
knowing, forms of, 568

La Beata Umiltà, 123
laboring class, rise of, 82–84
labors, earthly, recompense for, 517
lamb, sacrifice of, 348–49
Langland, William, 8, 11, 47–48, 180–81, 183
Last Supper, 319
Lateran Councils, 41, 50–51
Latin, 17, 97
Latin Breviary and Manual, 89
Latin Church, 161
Lay Folks' Catechism, The, 179
Lay Folks' Mass Book, 89–92
lectio divina, 182
leeches, 244, 246
Le Ménagier de Paris [The Goodman of Paris], 108–10, 128
Le Miroir de Mariage (Deschamps), 129–30
leywrite penalty, 51
life expectancies, 20
Litster, Geoffrey, 154–55, 156–57
Little Gidding (Eliot), 8
liturgical calendar, 16, 17
locutions, 263, 264
Lollard Bible, 162–63, 164–66
Lollards, 163–67, 171, 178, 183–84, 190, 424, 593
Lombard, Peter, 105, 513–14
Long Text (*Revelations* [Julian]), 6–8, 9–10, 225, 538, 541, 592; circulation of, 594–95; Julian's production of, 189; motivation for writing, 180; passages removed from, 191; preface

of, 225; rediscovery of, 595; removing references to Julian's gender, 191; on the shaking of the church, 388–89; writing of, 225–26
longing, 439. *See also* love-longing
lords, 44, 48–51
lordship, theory of, 146–47
Losinga, Herbert de, 33
Louis II, 184
love: Christ's lesson of, 586; as God's meaning, 590–91
Love, Nicholas, 178–79
love-longing, 568, 569, 570, 575–76
lower nature, 421

Maille, Jean Marie de, 232
male dominance, in the Middle Ages, 512
Mancroft marketplace, 28–29, 59
mankind, redemption of, necessity of, 495
manumission, 49
Margaret of Ypres, Saint, 232
marital duties, 108–10
marketplace, women engaging in, 88
marriage, 104–22, 525
marriage debt, 108, 120
marriage-fine, 50
Mary, Mother of God: appearing to Julian, in a ghostly sight, 272, 378–79; calling on, for intercession, 281–83; carvings of, 377; depictions of, 129, 217; holy house of, in Walsingham, 129; humility of, 285; interceding before God, 435; Julian's devotion to, 377; as mother of all, 510; prayer to, 131; purification of, 133; reverence for, 129; suffering of, 346–47
Mary of Oignies, 123
Mass, 89–92, 324, 366
masters, 56
maturatives, 249
meanes, 281–82
Mechthild of Hackeborn, Saint, 514
Mechthild of Magdeburg, 6, 514
medical treatments, 243, 245–49
medicine, spiritual, 426
meditation, 300, 511, 542
Meditationes Vitae Christi, 178
meditation manuals, 178–79, 228, 229–30
Meditations on the Life of Christ, 228–29
Meditations on the Passion (Rolle), 178, 229, 233–34, 274
meditative prayer, 227
meekness, 425
melancholia, 539–40, 543, 570
merchant guilds, 55–56, 86, 138
merchant middle class, 53, 95
merchants, wives of, 86–88, 94, 131, 138
merchet, 50
mercy, 174, 415, 428, 452–54, 501, 508–9; allowing free will and sin, 529; grace and, 454–58; seeking, 387; seven corporal works of, 219
Merton, Thomas, 11
Michael, Saint, 45
middle class, 53; emergence of, 48; hungry for intellectual stimulation, 168
Middle English, increasing preference for, over Latin, 181
miracles, 417–18
Mirror, the, 178
Mirrour of the Blessed Lyfe of Jesu, The (Love), 178–79
Miserabilis Nonullorum (Urban V), 135
misogyny, 97, 120, 124
monasteries, 39–40, 73–74
monastic clergy, 147
monastic houses, 38
monastic life, 570
monastic rule, 100
monks, 39–41, 71
moon, influence of, on human body, 247–48
morality poems, 178
moral virtues, 303
mortality rate: children's, 130, 136; women's, 128
mortal sins, 19–20, 490, 491, 565–68

mortification, 231–33
mortuary tax, 51
mother-and-child image, 524
motherhood, 521; holiness of, 129; Julian's, 537; Julian's writings on, 100–101; properties of, 524–26, 529, 530–31, 536; prototype for, 518–19; sermons on, 129; Trinity and, 524
Motherhood of God. *See* Christ, Motherhood of; God, Motherhood of; Jesus, as mother
mourning, as a state of the soul, 451, 452
mousetrap theory of atonement, 323
MS Sloane 2499, 7, 8
MS Sloane 3705, 7
mystery plays. *See* Corpus Christi plays
mystical experience, purity of, 309
mystical seeing, 307. *See also* beholding
mystical theology, suspicion regarding, 189
mystical union, 441–42
mysticism, 98, 179; dark aspects of, 420–21; dogma and, 407, 409; women and, 113–14
mystic mind, 263
mystics, predictions of, about death, 426

neighbor, love of, 544
Newman, John Henry, Cardinal, 11
nondualism, 499–500
Norfolk, Earl of, 36
Norfolk Broads, 30–32, 35
Norwich, 9, 15; bells ringing in, 21–22; building boom in, 25; churches in, 36–38; colleges in, for secular priests, 93; craft guild chapels in, 38; defense of, 127; fields around, 26; fishing in, 25–26; flooding in, 35, 30–31; fortification of, 26; gates of, *23*, 26–28; growth of, as import/export route, 23–24, 26; heresy trials in, 594; history of, 22, 24; independence of, 24; industry in, 25–26; marketplace in, 28–30; marshlands around, 30; monastic houses in, 38; peasants' revolt in, 154–58; plague in, *73–77*; population of, 38; religious institutions in, *23*; sanitation in, 32–33; towers in, 27–28; walls around, *23*, 26, 28; weather in, 30; weavers moving into, 57
Norwich Barbers' Guild, 244
Norwich Castle, 24, 154
Norwich Cathedral, preaching at, 176–77. *See also* Priory Cathedral of the Holy Trinity
Norwich cycle of plays, 203, 205
Norwich Priory, 39, 176, 244
noughting, 278–81, 285, 327
Novare, Philippe de, 96, 130
N-Town Collection, 203, 204, 209; passion plays, 209–220, 336–37; *Play of the Creation and Fall*, 207–8
nuns, 40–41, 97–99, 114
nursing, 133–34

Oldcastle, John, 593
Order of Preachers, 42
Ordinance of Labourers (1349), 83
original sin, 97, 112, 118, 123, 208, 291, 305, 489, 505; Christ's atonement and, 392–95; inherited, 312
Ottoman Empire, 125

pageant wagons, 195–97, 204
pain, reaction to, 543
pamphlets, Wycliffites disseminating, 163
papal schism (1378–1417), 144–46
parable of the lord and the servant, 86, 120, 182, 208, 221, 286, 446, 541; analysis of, related to other Revelations, 480–81; deeper meanings of, 482–84, 491–93 ; eschatological interpretation of, 484–86; two meanings in, 462–63, 465
parchment compendiums, 94
parenthood, 128–29
Paris Codex, 6, 7, 10
Parousia, 576–77

passion of Christ: evoking sin for Julian, 385; helping us endure sin's effects, 386–87; beholding, manners of, 356, 367, 368; mind of, 373–74
passion plays, 204–5, 209–20, 222, 288, 325, 336–37, 347, 407
Passover, 348–49
Pasteurella pestis, 77
patibulum, 341–42
patience, 540–41
Paul, Saint: on celibacy, 118; on predestination, 290; on sin transformed into glory, 386
pax-brede (peace board), 91
peasants: education for, 53–54; life of, 48–49; revolt of, 151–58; rising standards for, 83–84; taxation of, 49–53. *See also* villeins
penance, 149, 239, 305–6, 424–25; accepting, 580–81; penitential syndrome, 531
Pestis Secunda, 136
Philip IV, 64
Philip VI, 64
phlebotomists, 246, 247
physicians, 244, 245, 246
Pieta, 217
pilgrimages, 19–20, 306
plague: aftermath of, 79–80, 103, 125; cause of, 69, 77; church's response to, 71, 74–75, 76–77; explanations for, 81; heavenly causes of, 248; in Norwich, 73–77; protection from, 81–82; return of, 136, 139, 185–86; social upheaval during, 82–84; spread of, 67–69, 70; symptoms of, 69–71; toll of, 72–73, 78; types of, 69–70
platea-and-scaffold staging, 204–5
Play of Judgment Day, 219–20
plays. *See* Corpus Christi plays; passion plays; Play of Judgment Day
Plumpton, John, 188
pneumonic plague, 69–70
poor priests, 163, 166
popes: allegiance to, questioned, 146; in Avignon, 143–44
post-traumatic stress disorder (PTSD), 141
prayer, 251; Christ as answer to, 438; Christ as basis of, 433–34, 436–37; Christ's love and, 376; contemplative, 440, 441; disappointment in, 437–39; essential aspects of, 431–32; goal of, 437; God's response to, 434, 438; manner for, 437; placed in a spiritual treasury, 434, 435; requesting mercy in, 454; of thanksgiving, 436; turning our hearts to, 435–36; uniting soul to God, 439; unitive, 441
"Prayer to St. Paul" (Anselm), 513
preaching: ancient form of, 168–69, 171; England's golden age of, 168; friars', 169–71; John of Bromyard, 171–76; at Norwich Cathedral, 176–77; regulation of, 164–65; requirements for, 18; women lacking right to engage in, 189–90; about women, 175–76
preaching crosses, 169
precious plenty, of Christ's blood, 319–21
predestination, 290–94, 544
pregnancy, 128, 130–31
preparatyffe, 248
prevenient grace, 297–98
Pricke of Conscience, The, 179, 422
priests, 40, 41, 71
priories, 40–41
Priory Cathedral of the Holy Trinity (Norwich Cathedral), 33–36
privities, 411, 413
procreation: marriage and, 117–19; women's desperation for, 136
proper sanatyff, 248
prose treatises, 179–80
Prymer or Lay Folks' Prayer Book, The, 89
Psalter (Rolle), 179
psychic fatigue, 392
public humiliations, 425
pulse, measuring, 245
purgation, 279, 410
purgatory, 21, 36, 149, 410

purgatyfe, 248
purification, 21, 133, 508, 534
Purvey, John, 162–63

Ralph of Shrewsbury, 71
rapture, 371–73
ravishment, 371
reading groups, 94–95
reality, Divine, 404–5
reason, 508–9, 584–85
redemption, 438
Reed, Roger, 188, 467
Reformation, the, 150
regular clergy, 39–40
rejoicing, 481–82
religious authority, evil in, 146–47
religious debates, 95
religious formation, 97–98
religious guilds, 19, 199
religious literature, 177–80
religious persecution, 165
religious theatre, 195–96, 197–98
remarriage, 111
Remedies Against Temptation (Flete), 94
remorse, 531
repercussives, 249
revelation, 258–59
Revelations of Divine Love (Revelations; Julian of Norwich), 4, 594–95; analysis in, related to parable of a lord and a servant, 480–81; appearance of, 5; biographical information in, 226; counteracting misogyny, 124; development of, 350; faith in, 563–64; as gospel of love, 591; introduction to, 225–26; lessons of love in, 284; orthodox context for, 294–95; parable in, of a lord and a servant, 462–93; progression of, 350, 546–47; rediscovery of, 8–10; secret, two types of, 411–12; time in, language for, 350; timelessness of, 12; two versions of, 6–8; written from women's viewpoint, 120. *See also* Long Text; Short Text
Revelations, Julian's, by number: first, 259–95, 379–80, 486, 492, 519: second, 296–308, 442; third, 308–18, 382, 386, 414, 415, 565: fourth, 318–21; fifth, 321–28; sixth, 328–30; seventh, 330–33; eighth, 334–62, 506; ninth, 362–73, 398, 485, 501–2, 522; tenth, 373–76; eleventh, 377–79; twelfth, 379–81, 398, 519; thirteenth, 382–430, 532–33; fourteenth, 430, 431–537; fifteenth, 535, 539–47; sixteenth, 548, 554–60, 585
reverence, 545
reverent dread, 573, 574–75, 577
Revisions (Augustine), 118–19
rhymed gospels, 178
Richard II, 44, 150, 152–53, 155, 158, 163, 184
Richard of St. Victor, 374
righteousness, 314, 415
rightfullehede, 314, 327, 415
rights, legal, 111–12
Rita of Cascia, Saint, 123, 232
Rite of Enclosure, 187
River Wensum, 23, 25–26, 32, 64
Robert of Geneva (Butcher of Cesena), 144–45
Rolle, Richard, 8, 11, 178, 179, 229, 274, 371, 373, 425, 514
Royal Order of the Garter, 125–26
royalty, authority from, 147
Rule of Life for a Recluse (Aelred of Rievaulx), 228
Ruusbroec, Jan van, 179

sacrament, communal, 306
sacraments, 19
Sacred Heart: devotion to, 374–75; entering, 523–24
saints, 19–20; calling on, for intercession, 281–83; relics of, 131; reverence of, 423; scorning Satan, 328; sins of, 423, 425, 426–27
salvation, 21, 114, 121, 134, 290, 320–21, 323, 401, 428, 509; belief in, 544–45; Christ and, 148; depiction of, 195–96, 198, 218; divine perspective on, 387; as gift to Christ,

365–66; grace leading to, 395; gratitude for, 388; history of, 495–96; medieval view of, 215; rejoicing in, 417; sin as catalyst for, 518
sanctity, supra-normal manifestations of, 233
Sarum Missal, 106, 253
Satan: Christ's victory over, 324; impotence of, 327; power of, 322–23; scorning of, 327–28
Sawtre, William, 164, 190
scaffolding, in staging, 204–5
Scale of Perfection (Hilton), 180, 276, 579
schools, public secular, 54
scorning, 327–28
Scotus, Duns, 478–79
scourging, 340
scripture: fourfold levels of interpreting, 160; memorizing, 182–83; using images and signs, 326–27. *See also* Bible
sea ground, 298–300
second coming, 479–80
second estate, 44–45, 512
Second Lateran Council, 41
secular clergy, 40–41, 74, 147
seeking, aspects of, 307–8
seker, 15, 307–8, 432
seker hope, as a state of the soul, 451, 452
self-awareness, faith and, 446–47, 501
self-doubt, 572
self-indulgence, 307
self-love, 492
sensuality, 492, 502–4; changeability of, 443; increasing, 508; sin and, 505, 535; Trinity and, 517
septicemic plague, 69, 70
sermo modernus (modern sermon), 169, 170–71, 177
sermons: ancient form of, 168–69, 171; Latin, translation of, 178; modern form of, 169, 170–71, 177
Sermons on the Song of Songs (Bernard of Clairvaux), 227–28
seven deadly sins, 141, 174, 220, 318
Severus, Alexander, 238
sexuality, 115, 117–23
Shewings (Julian), 7
Short Text (*Revelations* [Julian]), 6, 8, 9–10, 157–58, 554; on Christ dying often, 366; containing revelations, 225; copying of, 593–94; end of, 575; Julian's mother in, 530; on prayer, 431; rediscovery of, 595; rewriting of, 480–81; on sin, 429; story in, of St. Cecilia, 238; on women lacking the right to preach, 189–90; writing of, 225
shrines, 19–20
sickness, as form of meekness, 425
sin, 112–13, 501: abhorrence of, 429–30; acknowledging, 491; bearing no shame for, 422; bliss and, 566; as bondage, 322–23; as catalyst for salvation, 518; causing suffering, 530; confession of, 149; conflicting viewpoints on, 445; damaging the community, 424–25; evil of, 385–86; existence of, 382–83; freedom and, 454; God's tolerance of, 414–15; hating, 490, 534; Julian preoccupied with, 122, 384; Julian's vision of, 314; lacking existence, 311, 382–83, 505; lacking substance, 386; linked to England's troubles, 177; mortal, 239, 490, 491, 565–68; nature of, 382; pain caused by, 385–86; presence of God and, 310, 311; profit of, 528–29; punishment for, 305–6; remedy for, 580; scourge of, 424, 426; suffering linked to, 422; tendency to, freedom from, 567; transformation of, in Christ, 384, 386–87; usefulness of, 383–84, 386–87; venial, 117, 239, 305, 424, 490–91; warning against, 429; wellness in spite of, 383–84; women and, 121, 175–76. *See also* original sin; seven deadly sins
sin-as-debt, 304–5
Sloane manuscripts, 6, 7
sloth, 141–42, 232, 307, 569–71
Sophia, 512–13

sorrow, 307
soul: as the city of God, 503–4; created perfectly by God, 442–43; as created Trinity, 505–6; dignity of, 443; essential substance of, 498; experiencing God in, 507–8; guided by Christ's mercy, 504; knowledge of, 507–9; living forever, 497; living in God, 499–500; made in image and likeness of God, 497; mirroring the Trinity, 443; rejoicing in God, 443; sensuality of, 502–4; spiritual powers of, 495; substance of, made *ex nihilo*, 497, 503; Trinity indwelling in, 555–58
spiritual autobiography, 11
spiritual endowment, 303
spiritual extremes, necessity of, 332–33
Spiritual Franciscans, 143
squint window, 188
Statute of Labourers (1351), 83–84, 156
Statute of the Staple, 57
Stephen, King, 97
stigmata, 228, 232
stipes, 341–42
St. Jerome's Vulgate, 162
St. Mary of Carrow Priory, 41, 97–98, 99, 102
Story of a Soul (Thérèse of Lisieux), 100
Stratford, John, 74
stress, effects of, 141
Studies of English Mystics (Inge), 8
stupefactives, 249
substance, 492, 498–99, 499–500; sin and, 535; Trinity and, 517
Sudbury, Simon, 153
suffering: blessing linked to, 422–23; discouragement about, remedy for, 581–82; forms of, 425–26; God enjoying, 389–90; inevitability of, 580; reward for, 489; root of, 422; sin linked to, 422, 530; universal, 385–86
Summa Predicantium (Compendium of Preaching; John of Bromyard), 171–72
Suso, Heinrich, 95
Synod of Toulouse, 162
Tauler, Johannes, 95
taxes, 49–53; increased rate of, 150–51; for peasants, 49–53; poll, 51, 156; wool and, 57
Teilhard de Chardin, Pierre, SJ, 179
temptations, 425
Teresa of Avila, Saint, 100, 264, 315, 371–72, 373
Tertullian, 114
thanksgiving, prayer of, 436
theology: maternal, 514, 515–16; medieval, 422, 468; trinitarian, 514–20. *See also* Julian, theology of
Thérèse of Lisieux, Saint, 100
third estate, 47–50
thirst, 336–37, 397–98
Thomas Aquinas, Saint, 99, 513–14; on begetting children, good of, 128; on marriage, 119–20; on predestination, 292–93; on sin, forgiveness of, 323; on substance, 498
Thomas of Brinton (Brunton), 176, 177
three wounds, Julian's desire for, 238–40
tithing, 50, 52
trance, 371
transcendence, 234
transubstantiation, 148–49
trauma, effects of, 78–79, 80, 141
Treaty of Calais, 134
Treaty of Troyes, 593
Trinity: doctrine of, 268–70; humanity enclosed in, 500; indwelling of, at the soul's center, 555–58; intimacy of, 582–83; in Julian's parable of the lord and the servant, 476; Julian's writings on, 267–68, 270, 277; motherhood and, 524; soul mirroring, 443; transcendence of, 400; wisdom of, as Mother, 500; working in Christ's passion, 369
Trinity-in-Christ, 268
trust, 437, 439
Tura, Agnolo di, 71–72
Tyler, Wat, 151, 152–53
Tyrrell, George, 8

Ufford, Isabel, 189
unconditional love, 375, 409, 429, 457, 512, 528–30, 531
uncreated charity, 588
Underhill, Evelyn, 8
unitive prayer, 441
universal salvation, 320–21
University of Oxford, 165
Upholland Anthology, 7
Urban V, 135
Urban VI, 144, 145, 159, 184

venial sins, 117, 239, 305, 424, 490–91
Venta Icenorum, 22
vernacular teaching, 17–19
Veronica, veil of, 212–13, 302
verse plenaries, 178
Via Dolorosa, 341
villeins: freedom for, 53–55, 58; life of, 48–52; scarcity of, during the plague, 82; seeking freedom after the plague, 82–84
Vision of Piers Plowman, The (Langland), 47–48, 180–81
visions: authenticity of, 263–65, 266–67; suspicion of, 230; types of, for Julian, 261–62
Voragine, Jacobus de, 238

Walsh, James, 10
Walsingham, Thomas, 66, 157, 159, 190
Walsingham (village), 76, 129, 130, 131
Ward, Benedicta, 100, 102
warfare, changes in, 65
Warrack, Grace, 8
Westminster Cathedral Treasury MS 4, 7
wet nurses, 133–34
will: beastly, 421; godly, 421, 427, 494, 495, 515
William the Conqueror, 24, 36
William of St. Thierry, 228, 374, 513
Wisdom, of God, 520
wisdom, greatest, 578
Wisdom of Christ, maternal imagery for, 513–14
wisdom tradition, 512–14
womanly arts, 96–97
women: beating of, 110–11; denied right to speak up in church, 5; economic rights of, 138–39; forbidden to write on spiritual issues, 5–6; as images of God, 115–16; around Jesus, 217, 347; knowledge of husbands' financial affairs, 88; lacking the right to preach, 189–90; lay, few books addressed to, 180; learning crafts, 88; legal rights of, 111–12; mortification and, 231–33; mysticism and, 113–14; preaching about, 175–76; punishment of, 97; purification of, after childbirth, 133; salvation and, 114; shame of, 114–15; teachings about, from the church, 112–17; viewed as cause of everyman's sin, 121
wool, women working with, *87*
wool industry, 25, 26, 56–57, 82
woolsack, 25
wrath, 325–26, 453; absence of, in God, 325–26, 407, 414–15, 428, 444, 449, 450, 453, 456–57; as literary device, 326–27
Wyclif, John, 144, 145, 151, 282; on the Bible's authority, 160; death of, 159; denunciations of, 158–60, 161; opinions of, 146–50, 159, 160; producing an English Bible, 162
Wyclif Bible, 165, 166–67
Wycliffites, 163

Yarmouth, designated as staple port, 57
Yersinia pestis, 77

zodiac man, 247